Computer and Cyber Security

Computer and Cyber Security
Principles, Algorithm, Applications, and Perspectives

Edited by
Dr. Brij B. Gupta
National Institute of Technology Kurukshetra, Haryana, India

Dr. Dharma P. Agrawal
University of Cincinnati, USA

Dr. Haoxiang Wang
GoPerception Laboratory & Cornell University, USA

CRC Press
Taylor & Francis Group
Boca Raton London New York

CRC Press is an imprint of the
Taylor & Francis Group, an **informa** business

AN AUERBACH BOOK

CRC Press
Taylor & Francis Group
6000 Broken Sound Parkway NW, Suite 300
Boca Raton, FL 33487-2742

First issued in paperback 2020

© 2019 by Taylor & Francis Group, LLC
CRC Press is an imprint of Taylor & Francis Group, an Informa business

No claim to original U.S. Government works

ISBN 13: 978-0-367-65691-1 (pbk)
ISBN 13: 978-0-8153-7133-5 (hbk)

Visit the Taylor & Francis Web site at
http://www.taylorandfrancis.com

and the CRC Press Web site at
http://www.crcpress.com

Dedicated to my wife **Varsha Gupta** for her constant support during the course of this book

Brij B. Gupta

Dedicated to my wife **Purnima Agrawal** for her constant support during the course of this book

Dharma P. Agrawal

Dedicated to my wife **Angelia Yao** for her constant support during the course of this book

Haoxiang Wang

Contents

Preface

Nowadays, computers have become essential and are increasingly being used for storing and retrieving information. It has almost become impossible to imagine a world where people can live without these electronic machines. With the rapid development in the electronics business, a number of inventions have come into picture including laptops, tablets, palmtops, and so forth. These are being used by individuals of different age groups and in almost all business processes because of the significant rise in productivity of the work done and overall efficiency.

Vast amounts of data and information in private or public sectors along with the personal information of the individuals are stored over these computers, most of which are highly sensitive. High dependency on the information systems, applications, and services is a clear sign that organizations are becoming more and more susceptible to security issues. Cyber attacks and computer safety have become an important concern as high-end vulnerabilities can endanger economies across the globe. It has become essential to provide adequate security measures to safeguard sensitive information. Thus, awareness about the tools and techniques for securing information has become unavoidable.

This book contains chapters dealing with different aspects of computer and cyber security. These include fundamentals, overviews, and trends of computer and cyber security, security and privacy in ad hoc networks, security and privacy in e-services, security and privacy in mobile systems, security and privacy in wireless sensor networks, cyber risk and vulnerability assessment cybercrime, cybercrime and warfare, cyber threat analysis and modeling, human factors in security and privacy, cyber forensic tools, techniques, and analysis, visual analytics for cyber security, cyber security testbeds, tools, and methodologies, security and privacy in smart grid and distributed generation systems, security and privacy in social applications and networks, active and passive cyber defense techniques, critical infrastructure protection, security and privacy in industrial systems, security and privacy in pervasive/ubiquitous computing, intrusion detection and prevention, botnet detection and mitigation, security and privacy of robotic systems, security and privacy in ambient intelligence, biometric security and privacy, security and privacy of web service, security and privacy in cloud computing, human factors in security and privacy, security and privacy in e-services, cybercrime and warfare, cryptography and stenography, security and privacy in cloud computing, honeypots and security, security policies and access control, cryptography and cryptosystems, network security and management, wireless security, bluetooth, WiFi, WiMax security, cyber threats, implications, and their defense, security standards and law, and security modeling.

Specifically, this book contains discussion on the following topics:

- Context-aware systems and how to protect sensitive information and control the network behavior in these systems.
- Cyber ports and how they are acting as a challenge in networks across the globe.

- Forecasting problems in cyber security along with how econometric techniques can be used to measure risk in information technology (IT).
- How cyberspace and cyber security are becoming an important and evolving concern in the digital security world.
- A review of the attack graph generation and analysis techniques.
- Biometrics-based authentication in cloud computing.
- Analysis of various trust computation methods to secure Flying Ad hoc Networks (FANETs).
- Security in wireless LAN (WLAN) and WiMAX systems.
- Botnet behavior and detection techniques.
- Attacks and defense techniques in smartphone security.
- Cryptography for addressing cloud computing security along with privacy and trust issues.
- Medical image enhancement techniques.
- Extraction of indicators of compromises (IOCs) and tactic techniques and procedures (TTPs)-mapping with course of actions (CoAs).
- Implementing a secure web-based application using Microsoft Security Development Lifecycle (SDL).
- Preserving privacy for trust-based unwanted traffic control with homomorphic encryption.
- Document Object Model (DOM)-guard: defeating DOM-based injection XSS worms in mobile-based HTML5 web applications on cloud platforms.
- Secure and fault tolerant computing in mobile ad hoc networks.
- Applications of digital signatures in cryptography.
- Credit scoring using birds swarm optimization.
- 4-, 8-, 32-, 64-bit substitution box generation using irreducible or reducible polynomials over Galois Field GF(p^q).
- Role of software-defined networking (SDN) in internet of things (IoT) security along with the possible attack types and their countermeasures.
- Security issues and challenges in online social networks (OSNs) on the basis of user's perspective.
- Security issues in wireless sensor networks.
- Identity theft, malware, and social engineering in dealing with cybercrime.

Acknowledgements

Many people have contributed greatly to this book on *Computer and Cyber Security: Principles, Algorithm, Applications and Perspectives*. We, the editors, would like to acknowledge all of them for their valuable help and generous ideas in improving the quality of this book. With our feelings of gratitude, we would like to introduce them in turn. The first mention is the authors and reviewers of each chapter of this book. Without their outstanding expertise, constructive reviews and devoted effort, this comprehensive book would become something without contents. The second mention is the CRC Press/Taylor & Francis Group staff, especially Richard O'Hanley and his team for their constant encouragement, continuous assistance, and untiring support. Without their technical support, this book would not be completed. The third mention is the editor's family for being the source of continuous love, unconditional support and prayers not only for this work but also throughout our life. Last but far from least, we express our heartfelt thanks to the almighty for bestowing over us the courage to face the complexities of life and complete this work.

August 2018

Brij B. Gupta

Dharma P. Agrawal

Haoxiang Wang

Editors

Dr. Brij B. Gupta received his PhD from the Indian Institute of Technology, Roorkee, Uttarakhand, India, in the field of Information and Cyber Security. In 2009, Dr. Gupta was selected for Canadian Commonwealth Scholarship Award by the Government of Canada. He has published and presented more than 150 research papers (including 4 books and 18 book chapters) in international journals and conferences of high repute, including IEEE, Elsevier, ACM, Springer, Wiley, Taylor & Francis Group, and Inderscience. He has visited several countries, including Canada, Japan, Australia, China, Spain, Hong Kong, Italy, Malaysia, and Macau, to present his research work. His biography was selected and published in the 30th edition of *Marquis Who's Who in the World,* 2012. In addition, he has been selected to receive "2017 Albert Nelson Marquis Lifetime Achievement Award" by *Marquis Who's Who in the World,* USA. Dr. Gupta also received Sir Visvesvaraya Young Faculty Research Fellowship Award in 2017 from Ministry of Electronics and Information Technology, Government of India. Recently, he has been awarded with "2018 Best Faculty Award for research activities" and "2018 Best Faculty Award for Project and Laboratory Development" from the National Institute of Technology, Kurukshetra, Haryana, India.

Dr. Gupta is also working as a principal investigator of various R&D projects sponsored by various Government of India funding agencies. He is serving as an associate editor of IEEE Transactions on Industrial Informatics, IEEE Access, and the executive editor of IJITCA and Inderscience. Moreover, Dr. Gupta is also leading the *International Journal of Cloud Applications and Computing (IJCAC),* IGI Global, as an editor in chief. He is also serving as a reviewer for various journals of IEEE, Springer, Wiley, Taylor & Francis Group, etc. He also served as the TPC chair of 2018 IEEE INFOCOM: CCSNA. Moreover, he served as a publicity chair of 10th NSS 2016 and 17th IFSA-SCIS 2017, which were held in Taiwan and Japan, respectively. He is also the founder chair of FISP and ISCW workshops that are organized by different countries every year. Dr. Gupta has served as the organizing chair of Special Session on Recent Advancements in Cyber Security (SS-CBS) in IEEE Global Conference on Consumer Electronics (GCCE), Japan, every year since 2014. He received outstanding paper awards in both regular and student categories in 5th IEEE Global Conference on Consumer Electronics (GCCE) in Kyoto, Japan, on October 7–10, 2016. Dr. Gupta is a senior member of IEEE, Member ACM, SIGCOMM, SDIWC, Internet Society, Institute of Nanotechnology, Life Member, International Association of Engineers (IAENG), Life Member, and International Association of Computer Science and Information Technology (IACSIT). He was also a visiting researcher in Yamaguchi University, Japan; in Deakin University, Victoria, Australia; and in Swinburne University of Technology, Melbourne, Victoria, Australia, during 2015 and 2018, 2017, and 2018, respectively. At present, Dr. Gupta is working as an assistant professor in the Department of Computer Engineering, the National Institute of Technology, Kurukshetra, Haryana, India. His research interests include information security, cyber security, mobile/smartphone, cloud computing, web security, intrusion detection, and computer networks and phishing.

Dr. Dharma P. Agrawal is a distinguished professor of the Ohio Board of Regents and the founding director for the Center for Distributed and Mobile Computing in the Department of Electrical Engineering and Computing Systems. He has been a faculty member in the ECE Department, Carnegie Mellon University, Pittsburgh, Pennsylvania (on sabbatical leave); NC State University, Raleigh, North Carolina; and the Wayne State University, Detroit, Michigan. His current research interests include applications of sensor networks in monitoring patients with Parkinson's disease and neurosis, applications of sensor networks in monitoring fitness of athletes' personal wellness, applications of sensor networks in monitoring firefighters' physical condition in action, efficient secured communication in sensor networks, secured group communication in vehicular networks, use of femto cells in LTE technology and interference issues, heterogeneous wireless networks, and resource allocation and security in mesh networks for 4G technology. His recent contribution in the form of a co-authored introductory text book on *Introduction to Wireless and Mobile Computing*, 4th edition, has been widely accepted throughout the world. The book has been reprinted both in China and India and translated into Korean and Chinese languages. His co-authored book on *Ad Hoc and Sensor Networks*, 2nd edition, has been published in the Spring of 2011. A co-edited book entitled *Encyclopedia on Ad Hoc and Ubiquitous Computing* has been published by the World Scientific, and co-authored books entitled *Wireless Sensor Networks: Deployment Alternatives and Analytical Modeling, Innovative Approaches to Spectrum Selection, Sensing, On-Demand Medium Access in Heterogeneous Multihop Networks*, and *Sharing in Cognitive Radio Networks* have been published by Lambert Academic. He is a founding editorial board member of *International Journal on Distributed Sensor Networks, International Journal of Ad Hoc and Ubiquitous Computing (IJAHUC), International Journal of Ad Hoc & Sensor Wireless Networks*, and *the Journal of Information Assurance and Security (JIAS)*. He has served as the editor of the *IEEE Computer Magazine*, the *IEEE Transactions on Computers, the Journal of Parallel and Distributed Systems,* and *the International Journal of High Speed Computing*. He has been the program chair and general chair for numerous international conferences and meetings. He has received numerous certificates from the IEEE Computer Society. He was awarded a *Third Millennium Medal* by the IEEE for his outstanding contributions. He has delivered keynote speeches at 34 different international conferences. He has published more than 655 papers and given 52 different tutorials and extensive training courses in various conferences in the United States and numerous institutions in Taiwan, Korea, Jordan, UAE, Malaysia, and India in the areas of ad hoc and sensor networks and mesh networks, including security issues. He has graduated 72 PhDs and 58 MS students. He has been named as an ISI highly cited researcher, is a fellow of the IEEE, the ACM, the AAAS, and the World Innovation Foundation, and is a recent recipient of 2008 IEEE CS Harry Goode Award. Recently, in June 2011, he was selected as the best mentor for doctoral students at the University of Cincinnati, Cincinnati, Ohio. Recently, he has been inducted as a charter fellow of the National Academy of Inventers. He has also been elected as a fellow of the International Association of Computer Science and Information Technology (IACSIT), since 2013.

Dr. Haoxiang Wang is currently the director and lead executive faculty member of GoPerception Laboratory, New York, and has been a Cornell University Alumni since 2014. His research interests include multimedia information processing, pattern recognition and machine learning, remote sensing image processing, and data-driven business intelligence. He has co-authored more than 30 journals and conference papers in these areas, including IEEE SMC, ICPR, and ICTAI. He severed as the guest editor for *Multimedia Tools and Applications, International Journal of Information Technology and Web Engineering*, and *International Journal of Computer Science & Applications*. He has been serving as a technical program committee member or the session chair for dozens of international conferences and the reviewer for more than 20 prestigious international journals.

List of Contributors

Palvi Aggarwal is a research scholar at the Applied Cognitive Science Laboratory, School of Computing and Electrical Engineering, Indian Institute of Technology Mandi, India. She received her master's degree in information security from Thapar University, Patiala, India. Her current research areas include cyber security, cognitive modeling, machine learning, and deep learning.

Mohammed Al-Refai received his undergraduate studies in computer science from Mutah University, Jordan, and MSc degree in computer science from Al al-Bayt University, Al-Mafraq, Jordan. He received his PhD in computer science from Amman Arab University for Graduate Studies, Amman, Jordan. He currently works as an associate professor in the faculty of science and information technology. His main research interests include many aspects in parallel and distributed systems, simulation, and data mining.

Masoom Alam received his PhD degree in computer sciences from the University of Innsbruck, Innsbruck, Tyrol, Austria. He is currently an associate professor in the Department of Computer Sciences, COMSATS Institute of Information Technology, Islamabad, Pakistan. His interests include access control systems, model-driven architecture, and workflow management systems.

Mohammad Alauthman received his PhD degree from Northumbria University Newcastle, England, in 2016. He received his BSc degree in computer science from Hashemite University, Az-Zarqa, Jordan, in 2002 and MSc degree in computer science from Amman Arab University, Amman, Jordan, in 2004. Currently, he is an assistant professor and a senior lecturer in the Department of Computer Science, Zarqa University, Zarqa, Jordan. His main research areas are cyber security, cyber forensics, advanced machine learning, and data science applications.

Ammar Almomani received his PhD degree from Universiti Sains Malaysia (USM), Penang, Malaysia, in 2013. He has published and presented more than 45 research papers in international journals and conferences of high repute. Currently, he is an assistant professor and a senior lecturer at the Department of Information Technology, Al-Huson University College, Al-Balqa Applied University, As-Salt, Jordan. His research interest includes advanced Internet security and monitoring.

Nauman Aslam is a reader (associate professor) in the Department of Computer and Information Science, Northumbria University Newcastle, England. Prior to joining Northumbria University as a senior lecturer in 2011, he has worked as an assistant professor at Dalhousie University, Nova Scotia, Canada. He received his PhD in engineering mathematics from Dalhousie University in

2008. Dr. Nauman's research interests include network security, wireless ad hoc sensor and body area networks, energy-efficient protocols, and application of artificial intelligence (AI) in communication protocols. Dr. Nauman is a member of IEEE and IAENG.

Lalit K. Awasthi is a director at NIT Jalandhar, Punjab, India. He has completed his MTech in computer science and engineering (CSE) from IIT Delhi, Hauz Khas, India, in 1993, and PhD in CSE from IIT Roorkee, Uttarakhand, India, in 2002. He was the first faculty member to join CSE Department at Regional Engineering College (now the National Institute of Engineering and Technology) Hamirpur, Himachal Pradesh, India. He has been an active faculty member at CSE Department, NIT Hamirpur, and has contributed in various positions for 25 years. He had planned, designed, and implemented the BTech CSE program at NIT, Hamirpur, along with laboratories and buildings of CSE Department and Computer Centre. He had worked as the head of CSE Department and Computer Centre and dean (Students and Alumni) for quite a good number of years, and the experience of interacting with students, faculty members, and the various academic and administrative heads of the institution has been wonderful. He is responsible for overall planning, organizing, and execution of all functions related to the establishment of a new Government Engineering College, Atal Bihari Vajpayee Government Institute of Engineering and Technology, Pragtinagar, Himachal pradesh, India. This includes recruitment of faculty and staff, planning of construction work and its execution, planning and establishment of laboratories, and mentoring of new faculty. Also, he has engaged in designing and setting up workshops, play facilities, hostels, auditoriums, etc., for students. He is the founder faculty of CSE, NIT Hamirpur Himachal Pradesh, India.

Baidyanath Biswas completed his bachelor's degree in engineering (electronics and telecommunications) in the Indian Institute of Engineering Science and Technology, Kolkata, India. He is currently a doctoral scholar at the Indian Institute of Management, Lucknow, Uttar Pradesh, India. His research interests are information security, information systems risk, software vulnerability analysis, and economics of information security. Previously, he has worked for 9 years with top software firms—Infosys Technologies, IBM India, and Cognizant Technologies. Baidyanath has regularly presented papers at top international conferences including the HICSS 2018, AMCIS 2016, and AMCIS 2017. He has been a reviewer for top international conferences HICSS 2018, AMCIS 2016 and AMCIS 2017, PACIS 2016, and ICIS 2017. Baidyanath has recently published an article in the *Journal of Enterprise Information Management*.

Alberto Huertas Celdrán is a research associate in the Department of Information and Communication engineering at the University of Murcia, Murcia, Spain. Huertas Celdrán received MSc and PhD degrees in computer science from the University of Murcia. His scientific interests include medical cyber-physical systems (MCPS), brain–computer interfaces (BCI), cybersecurity, data privacy, software-defined networking (SDN), semantic technology, and policy-based context-aware systems. His teaching includes courses in network security and programming languages. He is the co-author of more than 15 scientific publications (including journal and conference papers) and an active member in different national and international research projects. Furthermore, he has performed several international internships during his doctoral research.

Ramalingaswamy Cheruku is currently working as an assistant professor at Mahindra Ecole Centrale, Hyderabad, India. Prior to this, he was a full-time PhD scholar in CSE Department at the National Institute of Technology Goa, India. He received BTech degree in CSE from

Jawaharlal Nehru Technological University (JNTU), Kakinada campus, in 2008, and MTech degree in CSE from Atal Bihari Vajpayee (ABV)-Indian Institute of Information Technology, Gwalior, in 2011. He has served as a developer in Tata Consultancy Services for 2 years. He has also published several papers in reputed journals and conferences.

Andrea Chiappetta has graduated in international economics, received his PhD in economy and institution at the University of Rome Tor Vergata, Rome, Italy—faculty of economics, is a professor in geopolitics economy at Marconi International University, and is also the director of the Cyber Security Observatory on Critical Infrastructure Protection of the Marconi International University (CSOCIP). Currently, he is the executive director of ASPISEC, a company specialized in cyber security, in particular on firmware security and critical infrastructure protection. He is a speaker in several international conferences, and he has published papers and articles. His research interests include ICT in transport, energy, and cybersecurity. He has participated in more than 10 research projects at EU level in various fields related to the transport; he participated in several workshops and published in international journals of high repute including IEEE. He is the member of the editorial board and reviewer for various journals and international conferences. He is the author of one textbook in fundamentals of transport and co-author of one book on critical infrastructure protection published in the framework of Nato AWR.

Sushma Devi is a PhD research scholar at the Centre for Security Studies, School of International Studies, Central University of Gujarat (CUG), Gandhinagar, India. She holds MPhil with a focus on "National Security in the Digital Age: A Study of Cyber Security Challenges in India" and master's degree in information technology from Central University of Himachal Pradesh, Shahpur, India. She pursued a bachelor's degree in computer applications from Himachal Pradesh University, Shimla, India. She has written on various cybersecurity issues, and her current area of research is "Understanding India's Cybersecurity Challenges." Her research interests include information and communications technology, digital India, e-governance, environmental security, and national security.

Sankhanil Dey has been a registered PhD student of A. K. Choudhury School of Information Technology, University of Calcutta, Kolkata, West Bengal, India. He did MTech from the Department of Radio Physics and Electronics, University of Calcutta, and was a senior research fellow in Institute of Radio Physics and Electronics, University of Calcutta, up to November 30, 2016. He was a teaching assistant as well as a guest teacher in A. K. Choudhury School of Information Technology, Kolkata, West Bengal, India.

His research interests include cryptography and cryptology, Boolean functions, applications of finite fields or Galois fields in cryptography, elliptic curve cryptography, lightweight cryptography, and application of cryptographic algorithms in field programmable gate array (FPGA) technology.

He authored and presented many research articles in several archives, international journals, books, and conferences.

Osama M. Dorgham received his BSc degree in computer science from Princess Sumaya University for Technology, Amman, Jordan; MSc degree in computer science from Al-Balqa Applied University, Al Salt, Jordan; and PhD degree from the University of East Anglia, Norwich, England. He is currently an assistant professor in the Department of Computer Information Systems, Al-Balqa Applied University, As-Salt, Jordan. His research interests include medical imaging and computer graphics.

Damodar Reddy Edla is an assistant professor and the head of the Computer Science and Engineering Department in the National Institute of Technology (NIT) Goa, India. He received MSc degree from the University of Hyderabad in 2006, and MTech and PhD degrees in computer science and engineering from the Indian School of Mines, Dhanbad, in 2009 and 2013, respectively. His research interests include data mining and wireless sensor networks. He has published more than 20 research papers in reputed journal and international conferences. He is a senior member of the International Association of Computer Science and Information Technology (IACSIT). He is also a member of the Editorial Board of several international journals.

Pedunayak G has studied BTech in computer science and engineering from NIT Goa, India.

Félix J. García Clemente received MSc and PhD degrees in computer science from the University of Murcia, Murcia, Spain. He is an associate professor in the Department of Computer Engineering at the same university. His teaching includes courses in computer networks, network management, ubiquitous computing, and mobile device programming. Felix's major research interests focus on distributed management of networks and services and interaction systems. He is the co-author of more than 80 scientific publications (including journal and conference papers) and an active member in different national and international research projects. He has also been a supervisor on different projects of technology transfer in areas related to advanced services such as location-based services, distributed management, and industrial automation. Currently, he is a co-author of EjsS, a member of UNEDLabs, and a collaborator in the Open Source Physics project at Singapore. He was a visiting professor at UNED, EPFL, and NTU-NIE.

Urvashi Garg is a research scholar in NIT Jalandhar, Punjab, India. She received her BTech degree in CSE from the Kurukshetra University, Haryana, India in 2010. After completing her bachelor's degree, she had completed MTech in CSE from NIT Jaipur, Rajasthan, India, in 2012, and is currently pursuing a PhD degree in CSE from NIT Jalandhar, Punjab, India from 2015 onwards. In 2012, she joined the Department of CSE, Lovely Professional University, Jalandhar, Punjab, India, as an assistant professor. Her current research interests include cyber security, parallel computing, information security, and machine learning. She is a member of IEEE society and Computer Society of India (CSI). She is the recipient of two copyrights on software. She has also filed one more patent in 2017.

Ranjan Ghosh, born on November 1947, is now associated with Dumkal Institute of Engineering and Technology, Murshidabad, West Bengal, India, after complete retirement at the age of 65 from the Department of Radio Physics and Electronics of the Calcutta University, Kolkata, West Bengal, India, as an associate professor after rendering continuous services since March 1980. Professor Ghosh received his BTech, MTech, and PhD (Tech) degrees from the same department in Calcutta University between 1967 and 1980. Between 1982 and 1984, he had a brief stay at the Ioffe Physico-Technical Institute, Leningrad (now St. Petersburg) for postdoctoral research. The area of his predoctoral and postdoctoral research interests was the simulation studies of IMPATT devices and its applications in microwave and optical engineering. Subsequently, he shifted to simulation studies of ion implantations undertaken in silicon process technology. His latest interest is involved with security issues of data, text as well as video, covered by the field of cryptography.

Satya Prakash Ghrera completed 34 years of service in Corps of Electronics and Mechanical Engineers of the Indian Army, and then he joined Jaypee Institute of Engineering and Technology,

Waknaghat, Himachal Pradesh, India, in January 2006 as an associate professor in the Department of Computer Science and Engineering. Since September 2006, he has taken over the responsibilities of HOD (computer science and engineering and IT) at Jaypee University of Information Technology, Waknaghat, Himachal Pradesh, India. His research interests include information security and cryptography.

Diksha Goel has received her bachelor of technology in computer science and engineering from the University Institute of Engineering and Technology, Kurukshetra, Haryana, India. Currently, she is pursuing master of technology in computer engineering (specialization in cyber security) from the National Institute of Technology, Kurukshetra, Haryana, India. Her research interests include mobile security, web security, machine learning, and smishing detection.

Dr. Brij B. Gupta received his PhD from the Indian Institute of Technology Roorkee, Uttarakhand, India, in the field of information and cyber security. In 2009, Dr. Gupta was selected for Canadian Commonwealth Scholarship Award by the Government of Canada. He has published and presented more than 150 research papers (including 4 books and 18 book chapters) in international journals and conferences of high repute, including IEEE, Elsevier, ACM, Springer, Wiley, Taylor & Francis Group, and Inderscience. He has visited several countries, including Canada, Japan, Australia, China, Spain, Hong Kong, Italy, Malaysia, and Macau, to present his research work. His biography was selected and published in the 30th edition of *Marquis Who's Who in the World,* 2012. In addition, he has been selected to receive "2017 Albert Nelson Marquis Lifetime Achievement Award" by *Marquis Who's Who in the World,* USA. Dr. Gupta also received Sir Visvesvaraya Young Faculty Research Fellowship Award in 2017 from Ministry of Electronics and Information Technology, Government of India. Recently, he has been awarded with "2018 Best Faculty Award for research activities" and "2018 Best Faculty Award for Project and Laboratory Development" from the National Institute of Technology, Kurukshetra, Haryana, India.

Dr. Gupta is also working as a principal investigator of various R&D projects sponsored by various Government of India funding agencies. He is serving as an associate editor of IEEE Transactions on Industrial Informatics, IEEE Access, and the executive editor of IJITCA and Inderscience. Moreover, Dr. Gupta is also leading the *International Journal of Cloud Applications and Computing (IJCAC),* IGI Global, as an editor in chief. He is also serving as a reviewer for various journals of IEEE, Springer, Wiley, Taylor & Francis Group, etc. He also served as the TPC chair of 2018 IEEE INFOCOM: CCSNA. Moreover, he served as a publicity chair of 10th NSS 2016 and 17th IFSA-SCIS 2017, which were held in Taiwan and Japan, respectively. He is also the founder chair of FISP and ISCW workshops that are organized by different countries every year. Dr. Gupta has served as the organizing chair of Special Session on Recent Advancements in Cyber Security (SS-CBS) in IEEE Global Conference on Consumer Electronics (GCCE), Japan, every year since 2014. He received outstanding paper awards in both regular and student categories in 5th IEEE Global Conference on Consumer Electronics (GCCE) in Kyoto, Japan, on October 7–10, 2016. Dr. Gupta is a senior member of IEEE, Member ACM, SIGCOMM, SDIWC, Internet Society, Institute of Nanotechnology, Life Member, International Association of Engineers (IAENG), Life Member, and International Association of Computer Science and Information Technology (IACSIT). He was also a visiting researcher in Yamaguchi University, Japan; in Deakin University, Victoria, Australia; and in Swinburne University of Technology, Melbourne, Victoria, Australia, during 2015 and 2018, 2017, and 2018, respectively. At present, Dr. Gupta is working as an assistant professor in the Department of Computer Engineering, the

National Institute of Technology, Kurukshetra, Haryana, India. His research interests include information security, cyber security, mobile/smartphone, cloud computing, web security, intrusion detection, and computer networks and phishing.

Deepak Gupta received his master of science degree from Illinois Institute of Technology, Chicago, in the area of computer forensics and cyber security with a specialization in voice over Internet protocol (VOIP). As an undergraduate student, he became certified on the major networking platforms, first as a Cisco Certified Network Administrator (CCNA) and then as a Microsoft Certified Professional (MCP), which would come to serve him well in his professional life. As a graduate student, he continued to challenge himself by working on a number of research papers and projects related to computer network security and forensics research, including the topics of multiboot computer systems with change of boot loader and MP3 steganography. He also developed and furthered his interest in VOIP technology by working on and leading research projects with Bell Labs, a prominent VOIP research laboratory based in Chicago. He also wrote research papers in this field on the topics of P2P communication and SIP protocols, which won him the best student VOIP project award in 2007.

Over the last ten years of professional experience, Gupta has gained a broad range of experience in computer security and technology that spans multiple fields and industries. After graduating with distinction with a MS in computer science, he went on to work for Sageworks, a financial software company based in Raleigh, North Carolina. There, among other things, he developed a centralized integration process for core banking platforms that would allow customers to easily port and map their data to the central banking database. He is a product visionary who founded a web agency and two other start-ups as a software entrepreneur to help businesses to simplify their user communication. It was during this time that Gupta's passion for innovation and entrepreneurship led him to found LoginRadius, a cloud identity and access management (cIAM) SaaS platform that helps businesses improve and optimize their customer experience by creating unified digital identities across multiple touch points, where he remains today as co-founder and CTO. At LoginRadius, he makes use of his expertise in security and forensics to innovate and improve how identity services are delivered and secured in the cloud identity space and helps businesses deliver social media integrations by a simplified REST API. Currently, LoginRadius is a leading provider of cloud-based CIAM solutions for mid-to-large sized companies, and the platform serves more than 3,000 businesses with a monthly reach of 850 million users worldwide. The company has been named as an industry leader in the cIAM space by Gartner, Forrester, Kuppingercole, and Computer Weekly. Gupta is also passionate about helping businesses improve and optimize their customer experience. He lives and breathes this topic with customers everyday by helping them think through questions such as how users interact with their website, how to simplify the customer's experience (via single sign-on, one touch login, etc.), and how to keep the customer's data secure. Gupta is an active member of IEEE, ACM, OpenID Foundation, Cloud Security Alliance (CSA), etc., tech communities. Gupta is doing his current research in machine learning, artificial intelligence, and blockchain technologies.

Shashank Gupta is currently working as an assistant professor in computer science and information systems division at Birla Institute of Technology and Science, Pilani, Rajasthan, India. He has done his PhD under the supervision of Dr. Brij B. Gupta in the Department of Computer Engineering specialization in web security at the National Institute of Technology, Kurukshetra, Haryana, India. Recently, he was working as an assistant professor in the Department of Computer Science and Engineering at Jaypee Institute of Information Technology (JIIT), Noida, Uttar Pradesh, India, Sec-128. Prior to this, he has also served his duties as an assistant professor in the Department of IT at

Model Institute of Engineering and Technology (MIET), Jammu, Jammu and Kashmir, India. He has completed MTech in the Department of Computer Science and Engineering specialization in information security from Central University of Rajasthan, Ajmer, India. He has also done his graduation in bachelor of engineering (BE) in the Department of Information Technology from Padmashree Dr. D.Y. Patil Institute of Engineering and Technology Affiliated to Pune University, Pune, Maharashtra, India. He has also spent two months in the Department of Computer Science and IT, University of Jammu, Jammu and Kashmir, India, for completing a portion of postgraduation thesis work. He bagged the first cash prize in poster presentation at national level in the category of ICT applications in Techspardha 2015 and 2016 event organized by the National Institute of Technology, Kurukshetra, Haryana, India. He has numerous online publications in international journals and conferences including IEEE, Elsevier, ACM, Springer, Wiley, Elsevier, Inderscience, and IGI-Global, along with several book chapters. He is also serving as a reviewer for numerous peer-reviewed journals and conferences of high repute. He is also a professional member of IEEE and ACM. His research areas of interest include privacy, web security, cross-site scripting (XSS) attacks, online social network security, cloud security, fog computing, and theory of computation.

Shiza Hasan received the master's degree in information security from COMSATS Institute of Information Technology Islamabad, Pakistan. She is currently working as a lecturer in higher education department. Her research interests include malware analysis, threat intelligence, and security.

Mustapha Hedabou received his MSc degree in mathematics from the University of Paul Sabatier, Toulouse, France. In 2006, he received his PhD degree in computer science from INSA de Toulouse, France. He is currently an associate professor at ENSA de Safi, University of Marrakech in Morroco. His areas of interest cover information security, public key cryptography based on elliptic curves, identity-based cryptography, and cloud computing.

Ankit Kumar Jain is presently working as an assistant professor in the National Institute of Technology, Kurukshetra, Haryana, India. He received his master of technology from Indian Institute of Information Technology Allahabad (IIIT), Uttar Pradesh, India. Currently, he is pursuing PhD in cyber security from the National Institute of Technology, Kurukshetra, Haryana, India. His general research interests are the area of information and cyber security, phishing website detection, web security, mobile security, online social network, and machine learning. He has published and presented many papers in reputed journals and conferences.

Nadeem Javaid received his master's degree in electronics from Quid-I-Azam University, Islamabad, Pakistan, and PhD degree from the University of Paris-Est, France, in 2010. He is currently an associate professor and the founding head of the ComSens (Communications over Sensors) Research Group, Department of Computer Science, COMSATS Institute of Information Technology, Islamabad, Pakistan. He has supervised more than 70 MS and 6 PhD theses. He has authored more than 400 papers in peer-reviewed technical journals and international conferences. His research interests include wireless ad hoc networks, wireless sensor networks, and energy optimization in smart grids.

Tejaswini K has studied BTech in computer science and engineering from NIT Goa, India.

Hareesh K has studied BTech in computer science and engineering from NIT Goa, India.

Raimo Kantola is a professor of networking technology at Aalto University, Espoo and Helsinki, Finland. He received his MSc degree in computer science in Leningrad Electrotechnical Institute in 1981 and the doctor of technology degree from Teknillinen Korkeakoulu in 1995. Dr. Kantola worked for Nokia for more than 15 years on switching R&D, product marketing, and research and joined Aalto University as a professor of telecommunications technology in 1996. Professor Kantola is the Finnish national representative to TC6 of IFIP.

Parmeet Kaur received her PhD in computer engineering from NIT, Kurukshetra, Haryana, India, in 2016; MTech in computer science from Kurukshetra University, India, in 2008; and BE in computer science and engineering from Punjab Engineering College, Chandigarh, India, in 1998. She is currently working in Jaypee Institute of Information Technology, Noida, India. Her research interests include fault tolerance in mobile systems and scheduling in cloud computing.

Abid Khan is working as an assistant professor of computer science at COMSATS Institute of Information Technology, Islamabad, Pakistan. His research interests include security and privacy of cloud computing (outsourced storage and computation), security protocols, digital watermarking, and secure provenance. Before joining CIIT, he was a postdoctoral fellow at e-Security Laboratory of Politecnico De Torino, Italy. He was awarded the prestigious fellowship for young researcher by Politecnico De Torino for his postdoctoral studies (December 2009 to December 2011). He did his PhD in Harbin Institute of Technology, China, under the supervision of Professor Xiamu Niu. His PhD dissertation was "Secure Mobile Agent Computation" (2004–2008). He received his master's degree in computer science (MSc) from Quaid-i-Azam University Islamabad, Pakistan, in 2002.

Tanveer Khan received his master's degree in information security from COMSATS University, Islamabad, Pakistan. He is currently a research assistant in the Department of Computer Sciences, COMSATS Institute of Information Technology, Islamabad, Pakistan. His interests include cryptography and security.

Sonali Maharajan received his BTech (CSE) from the Beant College of Engineering and Technology, Gurdaspur, Punjab, India, in 2015. Presently, she is pursuing MTech in the Department of Computer Science and Engineering, Jaypee University of Information Technology, Waknaghat, Himachal Pradesh, India. Her key research area is digital image processing, particularly in the application area of medical images.

Anupama Mishra has received an MTech degree in the area of computer science and engineering in 2010. She has published and presented many of her research works in international journals and conferences of high repute including IEEE, Elsevier, ACM, Springer, and Wiley Inderscience. She is also serving as a reviewer for journals of IEEE, Springer, Inderscience, and many other reputed journals. She is a lifetime member of ISTE and also certified with IBM RAD. Her special interest lies in network security, cloud computing, cyber security, information security, and cluster computing.

Pavan S. Mudundi is a master's student at the School of Computing, University of North Florida, Jacksonville, Florida. He is currently working as an associate IT developer at Florida Blue. His research interest is in the area of cybersecurity. He is currently working on his MS thesis on secure software development.

Sukanya Patra has completed her bachelor of technology (information technology) in the Government College of Engineering and Leather Technology, Kolkata, West Bengal, India. Her research interests are Android programming, applications of data analytics in cyber security, marketing, and social media. Patra has worked as a research assistant at the International Management Institute (IMI), Kolkata, West Bengal, India. She spent 4 months at the Hewlett Packard Institute for developing POS System for merchant store and Indian Railway PNR App. Patra has recently presented a research paper at the International Marketing Conference MARCON 2017.

Manuel Gil Pérez is a research associate in the Department of Information and Communication Engineering at the University of Murcia, Spain. His scientific activity is mainly devoted to cyber security, including intrusion detection systems, trust management, privacy-preserving computer, and cyber security: principles, algorithm, applications and perspectives data sharing, and security operations in highly dynamic scenarios. Gil Pérez received his MSc and PhD degrees (latter with distinction) in computer science from the University of Murcia. He is the co-author of 50 scientific publications in journals and conference papers, as well as an active member in different national and international research projects.

Gregorio Martínez Pérez is a full-time professor in the Department of Information and Communication Engineering at the University of Murcia, Spain. Martínez Pérez received his PhD degree in computer science from the University of Murcia. His research interests include cybersecurity including attack modeling, and management and security in cyberphysical scenarios; distributed management of networks and services including policy-based networking and semantic-aware management; 5G networking including security considerations, management models, network slicing, and communication architectures; and advanced computational models and paradigms including network machine learning, swarm computation, cloud computing, and autonomic computing. He is the co-author of more than 150 scientific publications (including journal and conference papers) and an active member in different national and international research projects. Martínez Pérez has more than 20 intellectual property rights. Furthermore, Martínez Pérez has chaired different international conferences and workshops and is working as an associate editor in 16 journals.

Megha Quamara received her bachelor degree in computer science and engineering from the University Institute of Engineering and Technology (UIET), Kurukshetra University, Haryana, India, in 2015. Currently, she is pursuing master's degree specialized in cyber security from the National Institute of Technology (NIT), Kurukshetra, Haryana, India. Her research interests include security in internet of things (IoT) and cloud computing, authentication in smart card technology, and data privacy.

Prashant Singh Rana is currently a faculty in the Department of Computer Science and Engineering at Thapar University, Patiala, Punjab, India. He earned his PhD from ABV-Indian Institute of Information Technology and Management, Gwalior, India. He has 7 years of teaching experience. He has published and presented approximately ten research papers in various international/national journals and conferences. He has guided seven MTech dissertations. His areas of research are machine learning, soft computing, and combinatorial problems.

Mohd Aarif Rather is a senior doctorate fellow at the School of International Studies, Central University of Gujarat, Gujarat, India. He pursued his master's degree in political sciences from the University of Kashmir, Srinagar, Jammu and Kashmir, India, and MPhil from the Centre of Security Studies with a focus on human security challenges in the Kashmir valley. He has recently submitted PhD thesis with the area of study as "Understanding the Strategic Dimension of India-Pakistan-China Triangle: A Study of Post-Cold War Period." He has written on various issues including human security, cybersecurity, bilateral and multilateral relations in international politics, security sector reform in Afghanistan, United Nations and US hegemony, etc.

Swapnoneel Roy is an assistant professor at the School of Computing, University of North Florida, Jacksonville, Florida. Dr. Roy teaches primarily upper-level undergraduate courses in the broad field of cybersecurity. He earned his PhD in computer science and engineering from the University of Buffalo, New York, SUNY, in 2013. Prior to relocating the United States in pursuit of higher education, Dr. Roy spent 2 years with IBM as a software developer and 2 years at IIT Madras, Chennai, Tamil Nadu, India, for his master's degree in computer science and engineering. His research interests are in the areas of cybersecurity, green computing, and algorithms. He serves as a faculty advisor of the AITP Club, UNF's only hacking club.

Somya Ranjan Sahoo is a PhD scholar in the Department of Computer Engineering at the National Institute of Technology (NIT), Kurukshetra, Haryana, India, under the supervision of Dr. Brij B. Gupta. His research areas include data mining, online social networking security, and Big data security. Prior to joining PhD at NIT, Kurukshetra, he has worked as a lecturer in NIT, Hamirpur, Himachal Pradesh, India, and Vivekananda Institute of Technology, Bhubaneswar, India. He received his MTech (computer science and engineering) from Biju Patnaik University of Technology, Odisha, India, prior to BTech (information technology) from Silicon Institute of Technology, Bhubaneswar, India. He has actively participated in different faculty development programs and workshops. His areas of interest include information and cyber security, social networking security, and Big data security.

Sima Sahu received the BE degree (ECE) from the Institution of Engineers, Kolkata, India, in 2008. She obtained her MTech degree in digital electronics and systems from Kamla Nehru Institute of Technology, Sultanpur (U.P.), India, in 2011. She has more than 6 years of teaching experience. Currently, she is pursuing her PhD in image processing in Dr. A.P.J. Abdul Kalam Technical University, Lucknow, Uttar Pradesh, India. Her research interests include digital image processing with application to medical images, signal processing, and computer-aided detection/diagnosis.

Poonam Saini is currently an assistant professor in Computer Science and Engineering Department, Punjab Engineering College, Chandigarh, India [2013 to date]; assistant professor in Computer Science and Engineering Department, National Institute of Technical Teachers' Training and Research, Chandigarh, India [2011–2013]; and research scholar in Computer Engineering Department, National Institute of Technology, Kurukshetra, Haryana, India [2008-2011]. Her research interests include fault-tolerant distributed computing systems, mobile computing, ad hoc networks, wireless sensors networks, cloud computing and security, and Big data analytics. She has a teaching and research experience of more than 11 years. She has taught more than ten courses at both UG and PG levels. She has published and presented more than 30 publications in reputed journals and conferences and has traveled national institutions and internationally to present papers in conferences and participate in academic and research activities. She has attended more than 15 faculty development courses of 1–2 weeks at National Universities, IITs, NITs, Industry, and other institutions. She has supervised more than 20 dissertations at MTech level and has three ongoing PhD research scholars under her supervision. She has initiated interdisciplinary research in the area of data analytics for solar panels and internet of things (IoT)-based smart manufacturing applications. Under this research, she has applied for DST projects and has awarded one project from DST Chandigarh to design a data analysis framework for solar panels deployed in PEC and around.

Jasminder Kaur Sandhu obtained her MTech (CSE) in 2014, majoring computer science and engineering from Punjabi University, Patiala, India. Presently, she is working toward her PhD in dependability evaluation of wireless sensor networks from Computer Engineering Department at Thapar University, Patiala, Punjab, India. She is having approximately 3 years of teaching experience. Her research interests include dependability evaluation, wireless sensor networks, ad hoc networks, and machine learning.

Geeta Sikka is an associate professor and the head in the Department of CSE in NIT Jalandhar, Punjab, India. She has completed her MTech in CSE from Punjab Agriculture University Ludhiana, Punjab, India, in 2004, and PhD in CSE from NIT Jalandhar in 2013. She has more than 20 years of experience in teaching. She started working in NIT Jalandhar in 1996 as an assistant professor. She has attended various courses and conferences and given expert talks on various fields. She is the recipient of one copyright on a software. She is the member of various societies and activities in NIT Jalandhar. She has attended various STC and workshop as the session chair. She has organized various courses and workshops in the Department of Computer Science and Engineering at NIT Jalandhar.

Amit Kumar Singh is currently working as an assistant professor (senior grade) in the Department of Computer Science and Engineering at Jaypee University of Information Technology (JUIT) Waknaghat, Himachal Pradesh, India, since April 2008. He has completed his PhD degree from the Department of Computer Engineering, NIT Kurukshetra, Haryana, India, in 2015. He has presented and published more than 60 research papers in reputed journals and various national and international conferences. His important research contributions include developing watermarking methods that offer a good trade-off between major parameters, i.e., perceptual quality, robustness, embedding capacity, and the security of the watermark embedding into the cover digital images. His research interests include data hiding, biometrics, and cryptography.

Awadhesh Kumar Singh received his BE degree in computer science and engineering from Gorakhpur University, Uttar Pradesh, India, in 1988. He received his ME and PhD (engineering) degrees in the same area from Jadavpur University, Kolkata, West Bengal, India. He is a professor in Computer Engineering Department, the National Institute of Technology, Kurukshetra, Haryana, India. His current research interests include distributed algorithms, fault tolerance, and mobile computing.

Awadhesh Kumar Singh is currently a professor in Computer Engineering Department, the National Institute of Technology, Kurukshetra, Haryana, India (2013 to date). His research interest includes fault-tolerant distributed computing systems, mobile computing, ad hoc networks, cloud computing, and security. He has a teaching and research experience of more than 25 years. He has taught more than ten courses at both UG and PG levels. He has published and presented more than 150 publications in reputed journals and conferences and has traveled national institutions and internationally to present papers in conferences and participate in academic and research activities. He has attended more than 70 faculty development courses of 1–2 weeks at national universities, IITs, NITs, industry, and other institutions. He has supervised more than 30 dissertations at MTech and PhD levels.

Kuldeep Singh has done his masters in engineering in information security from Thapar University. Prior to that, he has completed master's degree in computer applications. Now, he is currently working in the area of ad hoc network security as a full-time PhD research scholar at Thapar University, Patiala. He has cracked national level exams such as GATE and CSIR-UGC NET in India. He has commendable and a growing list of publications. He has authored a book under the banner of Wiley publication. He is a member of reputed computer societies like IEEE.

Pankaj Siwan is pursuing his bachelor degree from the Department of Computer Engineering, National Institute of Technology, Kurukshetra, India. His research interests include information security, privacy, and mobile security.

Himanshu Soni is pursuing his bachelor degree in the Department of Computer Engineering, National Institute of Technology, Kurukshetra, Haryana, India. His research interests include mobile security, privacy, and intrusion detection systems.

Dr. Sarvesh Tanwar has completed his PhD in computer science and engineering from Mody University of Science and Technology, Lakshmangarh (Rajasthan), India, having 12 years of teaching and research experience. She is working as an assistant professor (Research) in Chitkara University Institute of Engineering and Technology, Chitkara University, Punjab. Her areas of research include public key infrastructure, cryptography, and information security. She has published more than 30 research papers in international journals and conferences. She is currently guiding two PhD scholars and has guided five MTech research students. She is a reviewer of *Journal of Cases on Information Technology (JCIT)*, member of editorial reviewer board of IJISP, IGI Global, USA. She is a member of editorial board in *International Journal of Research in Science & Technology (IJRST)*, Ghaziabad, Uttar Pradesh, India; *Advances in Science, Technology and Engineering Systems Journal (ASTESJ)*, USA; and *International Association of Engineers (IAENG)*.

Anil Kumar Verma is currently a faculty in the Department of Computer Science and Engineering at Thapar University, Patiala, Punjab, India. He received his BS, MS, and PhD degrees in 1991, 2001, and 2008, respectively, majoring in computer science and engineering. He has worked as a lecturer at Madan Mohan Malaviya Engineering College, Gorakhpur, Uttar Pradesh, India, from 1991 to 1996. He joined Thapar University in 1996 and is presently associated with the same institute. He has been a visiting faculty to many institutions. He has published and presented around 250 papers in reputed journals and conferences (India and abroad including the United States, South Korea, Japan, and Ireland). He has chaired various sessions in the international and national conferences. He is an active member of MIEEE, MACM, MISCI, LMCSI, MIETE, and GMAIMA. He is a certified software quality auditor by MoCIT, Government of India. His research interests include wireless networks, routing algorithms, and mobile clouds.

Zheng Yan is a computer scientist with interests in trust, security, and privacy. She is currently a professor in Xidian University, Xi'an, China, and a visiting professor in Aalto University, Greater Helsinki, Finland. Before joining academia in 2011, she has worked as a senior researcher at Nokia Research Center, Helsinki, Finland, since 2000. She received her PhD in electrical engineering from Helsinki University of Technology, Espoo, Finland. She authored more than 180 publications and 2 books. She is the inventor of 18 patents and 36 patent applications. She serves as an associate editor or a guest editor for many reputable journals and an organization committee member for numerous international conferences. She is a senior member of IEEE.

Lifang Zhang received her BSc degree in electrical engineering from Beijing Forestry University, China. She is currently a master's degree student in the Department of Communications and Networking, Aalto University, Espoo, Finland. Her research interests include network security and privacy.

Chapter 1

Context-Aware Systems: Protecting Sensitive Information and Controlling Network Behavior

Alberto Huertas Celdrán, Manuel Gil Pérez,
Félix J. García Clemente, and Gregorio Martínez Pérez
University of Murcia

Contents

1

1.1 Introduction to Information Management Systems

The first proposal in charge of categorizing the different areas that should be considered by information management systems (IMSs) to reduce the complexity of the management process was called FCAPS (Fault, Configuration, Accounting, Performance, and Security). This solution was proposed by ISO (International Organization for Standardization) in the OSI Systems Management (OSI-SM) [1]. Among the five proposed areas, this chapter is focused on security and configuration, although the management of these areas also affects important aspects of others like, for example, the systems' performance or the fault tolerance.

The security management area is oriented to emphasize security considerations like the protection of the information handled by IMSs. The increment of the information managed by these systems during the past decades has influenced the necessity of protecting some sensitive pieces of information. For example, in Spain, depending on the nature of the information, the legislation [2] categorizes it into three levels of security. The basic level contains personal information like, for example, the name, age, sex, address, telephone, or bank account number. The medium level contains the information related to financial operations and personalities, for example, patrimonial assets, habits of consumers, criminal records, or curriculum. Finally, the last category has the highest level of security and is composed of information such as the ideology, political affiliations, religion, or health. The protection of these pieces of information is known in the literature with the terms of privacy. Privacy refers to the rights of persons and organizations to determine for themselves when, where, how, and what information about them can be revealed [3]. In that sense, the consideration of the information's privacy also increases the complexity of the management process performed by IMSs. These systems should allow their users to control what pieces of information they want to reveal, the place where these pieces of information can be revealed, the moment or period of time, the situation in which the information should be revealed, and the person(s) or organization(s) to whom the information can be revealed.

On the other hand, another area proposed by FCAPS, in which this chapter is focused on, is the management of the systems' configuration and behavior to control the deployment of hardware and software components. In this sense, the networking paradigm is one of the topics in which industry and academic sectors are making more efforts to manage at real time the resources composing the network infrastructure. Networks are dynamic systems composed of distributed and heterogeneous resources managed by different administrators. When the network status varies depending on different aspects like, for example, the number of connected users or the availability of resources, it is needed to reconfigure the network resources in order to continue providing services. The Software-Defined Networking (SDN) paradigm arose with the goal of reducing the complexity during the network management process by separating the control and data planes, and "softwarizing" the configuration of the network resources. However, performing reconfiguration and management of distributed resources is still a difficult task that needs new mechanisms to ease it. These new mechanisms should allow network administrators to control at real time the network resources according to the current status of the network. The behavior of network resources should be adapted automatically, taking into account the network status and the decisions of administrators oriented to guarantee network requirements like the Quality of Service (QoS), energy efficiency, or fault tolerance.

Several proposals have been made during the past decades to reduce the complexity in the management processes performed by IMSs, as commented at the beginning of this section. One of the most relevant ones was made by the Internet Engineering Task Force (IETF) with the definition of a new paradigm called policy-based management (PBM) [4]. This paradigm arose with the aim of separating the behavior of systems from their functionality. This separation allowed the flexible, automatic, and dynamic management of the systems behavior and their information while reducing maintenance costs. One of the main goals of PBM consists in managing systems, information, and resources at a high abstraction level. Using this paradigm, systems administrators define policies, or rules, indicating the actions that should be applied when certain events are triggered. These rules are composed of conditions and decisions, where conditions are representations of the prerequisites that must be accomplished in order to enforce the actions established by the decisions. According to the Policy Core Information Model [5] developed jointly by IETF and Distributed Management Task Force (DMTF), policies are stored in a repository called Policy Repository, and the entities in charge of checking if conditions are accomplished and making the policy decisions are called Policy Decision Point. Finally, entities enforcing decisions of the policies are called Policy Enforcement Point.

In order to express the intention of administrators and information's owners, several technologies and policy-based languages have been proposed during the past decades. eXtensible Access Control Markup Language [6] is one of the most well-known languages. It is accepted in industry and academia as de facto standard, and it is mainly focused on access control management in distributed systems. KAoS (Knowledge Acquisition in automated Specification) [7] is another well-known language designed for goal-directed software requirements analysis. KAoS provides the capability of assigning system-level and organizational objectives rather than lower-level processor action-oriented descriptions. Among the proposed technologies, semantic web techniques [8] are a promising way to manage the information and the behavior of systems. Administrators of systems or users can manage the behavior of the systems' resources and the handled information by using semantic rules, also called policies. These policies let control the system's behavior at run-time and dynamically taking into account the preferences of the administrators or the owners of the information. Furthermore, ontologies [9] allow the formal representation of the information in a way that together with certain governing rules, it is possible to infer new knowledge by using semantic reasoners. Ontologies also allow sharing knowledge between independent systems and using semantic reasoning about the context to offer advanced services to customers.

The remainder of this chapter is organized as follows. Section 1.2 presents the main objectives and contributions of this chapter. In Section 1.3, we discuss the related work regarding policy-based IMS solutions. Section 1.4 reviews the current status of context-aware solutions and some of their most common scenarios. Current challenges of context-aware systems about privacy and other important aspects are highlighted in Section 1.5. Finally, the conclusions and future work are drawn in Section 1.6.

1.2 Objectives and Contribution

The goal of this chapter consists in showing how the evolution of technology has increased the complexity of the IMSs and how new paradigms and solutions are needed to face their increasing complexity. In particular, the increasing of heterogeneous information provided by new technologies and paradigms, the evaluation processes to make decisions and protect the privacy of sensitive pieces of information, and the diversity of components distributed along different organizations are few of the most important aspects that have increased the complexity in IMSs, thus creating the need to design new mechanisms to address them.

The intention of this chapter is also to provide a clear vision of the current state-of-the-art context-aware and privacy-preserving solutions as well as how the contextual information can be used to manage efficiently distributed systems like, for example, computer networks. To reach it, this chapter focuses the efforts on knowing how the advances made by new paradigms, scenarios, and technologies have influenced the management of the information and protection of the privacy of sensitive pieces of information, as well as their influence in the management and control of the behavior of the IMSs. Specifically, this chapter is focused on:

■ Context-aware solutions in charge of controlling automatically the information of users and contexts as well as the systems behavior. Architectures based on semantic web techniques to gather and handle large volumes of heterogeneous information, evaluate and protect the privacy of sensitive pieces of information, consider independent administrators distributed along different organizations, and manage diverse components with different requirements and locations.

■ Policy-based solutions to protect dynamically the privacy of sensitive information considered by the context-aware paradigm. Solutions that allows users to decide when, where, how, and to whom they want to disclose private pieces of information handled by the context like, for example, locations, activities, and identities, among others. Privacy-preserving and context-aware policies in charge of allowing users to protect their information at real time and dynamically.

■ Privacy-preserving mechanisms to exchange personal and contextual information between independent and different contexts. Current IMSs require solutions that exchange sensitive information in multi-context scenarios in a secure way. In this sense, this chapter will focus on solutions oriented to semantic web that model the information in a formal way and allow the secure exchange of information, taking into account the privacy preferences of the information's owners.

■ Autonomic management of the network resources by considering location-based and context-aware information. This chapter is also focused on the analysis of mechanisms that control dynamically and at real time the network infrastructure, taking into account the information about the context of both where the network provides services and where end users are receiving these services.

This analysis has detected some of the main challenges of this domain which are explained in the next section.

1.3 Policy-Based IMS Solutions

In the current literature, several works can be found that trace the history and evolution of the PBM paradigm [10,11]. The early works oriented to this paradigm were focused on emphasizing security considerations. In this sense, security policies were the first policies in charge of defining rules according to which access control systems were regulated [12]. Access control mechanisms [13] manage if the access to given resources should be granted or denied according to the security policies defined by the system administrator. Security policies can be grouped into different access security levels with diverse criteria for defining what should and should not be allowed. The access control matrix [14] was introduced to protect different objects in shared computers. Different access rights protected objects such as files, memory, and terminals which were shared between different domains. Each entry of the matrix contained a list of access attributes that define the access rights of that domain to the objects. Attributes could be of different forms, such as read, write, owner, call, and control. Access Control Lists (ACLs) [15] were another solution proposed as an alternative approach of the access control matrix presenting the matrix information in a column fashion.

Confidentiality and integrity are two important aspects belonging to the security topic which are considered by IMSs. The confidentiality policy model was the earliest formal model designed to prevent any unauthorized disclosure of information [16]. This model was proposed to formalize the security of the U.S. Department of Defense. It followed the state machine concept, where there are a defined set of access control policies grouped by states, and the transition functions between them. Security states ranged from the most sensitive (*Top Secret*) to the least sensitive (*Public*). Users of this model could access and create content only at or above their own security level. Finally, although role-based access control (RBAC) [17] is not directly concerned with policy specification, it was accepted as a security model that permits the specification and enforcement of organizational access control policies. Specifically, RBAC is a security mechanism that allows the authorization management by separating user assignment to roles. On the other hand, information integrity is the assurance that the data have not been altered or damaged by malicious users or system errors [18]. In this sense, integrity policies describe how the validity of the information in the system should be maintained. The first model for integrity policy established the required considerations for secure computer systems [19].

Privacy is another key aspect of the security domain. Privacy is the ability of individuals or organizations to control the terms under which their private information is acquired and used [20]. During the past years have been proposed many works based on privacy policies and oriented to protect the sensitive information. Privacy policies represent long-term promises made by an enterprise to its end users and are determined by business practice and legal concerns [21]. In this sense, a system that facilitates privacy policy authoring, implementation, and compliance monitoring was proposed in [22]. Another solution was proposed in [23], where a framework was able to express and enforce privacy policies by giving a formal definition of purpose, and proposing a modal-logic language for formally expressing purpose constraints. In [24], a platform was described for Enterprise Privacy Practices (E-P3P) that defines technology for privacy-enabled management and exchange of customer data. This solution separates the enterprise-specific deployment policy from the privacy policy that covers the complete life cycle of collected data. Regarding the evaluation of the privacy policies' effectiveness, several tests were performed in [25] to determine if apps with privacy policies were more likely to protect personal information than apps without privacy policies. In [26], an empirical study of online privacy policies as well as tools for users with privacy concerns was presented. Related to the e-commerce domain, in [27] was investigated the relationship between privacy policies and users' reactions, showing that privacy risks transfer the effects of a privacy policy's contents on user behavior. In [28], different security models and techniques that are being utilized during the past years to ensure computer security are studied. The authors of this study also discuss numerous security principles and present the models that ensure these security principles. Security models (such as access control models and protection ring) form the basis of various higher-level and complex models. In [29], an authentication and confidentiality scheme oriented to Mobile Cloud Computing (MCC) and based on homomorphic encryption was presented. This work also provides a recovery mechanism to secure access for mobile users to the remote multi-cloud servers. The authors of this work also provided a prototype of the proposed framework to demonstrate its robustness, efficiency, and security. The Internet of Things (IoT) paradigm is also a topic where privacy and security are critical. In this sense, the security issues of IoT and MCC technologies are analyzed and surveyed in [30]. The authors of this work state that Cloud Computing technology improves the function of the IoT.

Among the wide spectrum of active research topics where policies can be applied to simplify management tasks [31], the networking paradigm has received attention both from industry and the academic research community in recent years. In the literature, we can find several proposals oriented to the policy-based network management (PBNM) with different purposes [32]. Regarding the security and privacy of networks, a framework to refine policies in PBM systems was proposed in [33]. The refining process was carried out following a list of steps to convert high-level goals into low-level policies. Another proposal was defined in [34], where a policy-based access control framework overcame harmful interference created by malfunctioning devices or malicious users. In this solution was designed a set of policy-based components integrated with the algorithms employed by software-defined radios to detect interference caused by malfunctioning devices. The proposed policy-based components ensured that a radio did not violate the requirements established by policies. This work also proposed secure policy management and distribution mechanisms to avoid malicious users from being added or modifying the existing policies. FRESCO [35] was an OpenFlow security application development framework designed to facilitate the rapid design and modular composition of detection and mitigation modules. Regarding the anonymity of network communications, in [36] was studied the compatibility of the Destination Addressing Control System (DACS) scheme for the cloud environment with virtualization technology. Specifically, they proposed the consideration of the DACS into the PBNM to manage network resources through policies. Ethane [37] was another solution that allowed network administrator to define access control policies using the Flow-based Security Language (FSL). During the past years, with the advent of SDN, the network management has evolved to become more dynamic [38]. In this sense, OpenSec [39] was a framework based on OpenFlow that allowed network administrators to create and implement security policies. These policies defined which security services must be applied and specified the security levels that define how OpenSec reacts to a malicious traffic.

Energy-efficient network approaches are also focused on the efforts of industry and academics during the past years. In this sense, in the current literature can be found a deep survey with a deep comparison of a number of energy-efficient network approaches [40]. The solution presented in [41] quantified the power consumption of mobile communication systems. It established that there is a high potential to reduce the energy consumption when improving the energy efficiency of the Base Stations (BSs) at low traffic load. Another proposal to enhance the efficiency of power amplifier for wireless BSs was made in [42]. The variation in the traffic patterns over time, in order to decide when BSs should sleep or not, was considered in [43]. Another solution was proposed in [44], where a control mechanism enabled small cells to switch off all components while not serving active connections. In order to speed up the decision process of switching on/off the BSs, a transfer actor-critic algorithm (TACT) was proposed in [45], making use of the historical data from neighboring regions. In [46], the use of software routers for emulating network equipment functionality was proposed, and the benefits of the emulation environment were also discussed. Finally, another solution oriented to energy efficiency was proposed in [47]. Specifically, it was defined as a policy-based platform oriented to the management of resources in fog computing. This solution expanded the fog computing concept to support secure collaboration and interoperability between different user-requested resources. Several scenarios were proposed to show the necessity of policy management as a core security management module in a fog ecosystem.

The QoS is another important topic belonging to networks in which several policy-based solutions have been proposed. Procera [48] was an event-driven network control framework that used high-level policies to manage and configure the network state. This solution enabled dynamic policies, which were translated into a set of forwarding rules to manage the network state by the controller. Oriented to overcome the limitations of the standardized objective functions, a new objective function for IPv6 Routing Protocol for Low Power and Lossy Networks (RPL) was proposed based on Fuzzy Logic that allows selecting the best paths to the destination [49]. A proposal about a novel solution to transfer learning applied to spectrum management in cognitive radio networks to improve the QoS was made in [50]. In this proposal, it was demonstrated that transfer learning achieves a significantly higher QoS and throughput than distributed reinforcement learning. When several policies coexist, conflict resolution is a crucial aspect to managing a system using policies. Indeed, in [51], the problem of conflict resolution when using policies to provide QoS is addressed. Following the SDN approach, PolicyCop [52] was a QoS policy management framework oriented toward OpenFlow and based on SDN. PolicyCop allowed to define QoS service level agreements (SLAs) and control the policy enforcement. This solution also monitored the network status to reconfigure the network parameters through policies.

1.4 Context-Aware IMS Solutions

1.4.1 Location and Context-Awareness

Users' location is a concept that IMSs started to consider with the rise in the number of mobile devices and the mobile paradigms [53]. Systems that provide information considering the location of persons or devices are called *Location-Based Services* (LBSs) [54]. Some of LBSs go a step further providing useful services by taking into account the users' location to infer other aspects about the place where they are. To reach it, current IMSs monitor the users' location in order to consider it during the management processes. Depending on the focus of services, an LBS can be either person-oriented or device-oriented. In the person-oriented approach, the focus on applications uses the position of a person to enhance the service. One example of an LBS belonging to this approach could be a friend-finder application. On the other hand, device-oriented LBSs may also focus on the position of a person, but they do not need it. In this approach, objects like cars in navigation systems could also be located. In addition to this classification, there are two different application designs: push and pull services. In push services, users receive information without having to actively request it. Pull services, in contrast, mean that users actively request the information. Most of the early location services have been pull services, although during the past years push services have gained popularity in certain domains.

Helped by the location information provided by the mobile paradigm, the *pervasive computing* paradigm arose at the beginning of the 1990s. The pervasive concept was introduced by Weiser [55] as the seamless integration of devices into the users' everyday life. The main goals of pervasive computing were the effective and efficient use of the elements that compose the smart spaces where users were, the invisibility or complete disappearance of computing technology from the user's perspective, the number of users and computing resources that compose the environment and the scalability of the system, and the context-awareness. The pervasive paradigm made people the central focus rather than computing devices and technical issues. The users' mobility records were an essential piece of information for this paradigm, and they were provided by LBSs. In this sense, IMSs considered not only the users' location but also information about the users' life. As pervasive computing is still a very active and evolving field, the rate of penetration into the everyday life varies considerably depending on technical and nontechnical factors such as the infrastructure, computation resources, security, or economics.

The *context-awareness* concept [56] is the core of the *pervasive computing* paradigm [55]. Context-awareness is a mobile paradigm where services discover the information of the context or environment in which users are located, and adapt their behavior taking into account that information without users' interaction. It is important to notice that users do not interact with context-aware systems, but they consent the acquisition and management of their information. Context-aware solutions use location-based systems so as to obtain the users' location with which to gather information about the people, objects, and elements that compose the context or environment in which the users are located. In the literature, we can find several definitions of context. The first one appeared in 1994 was made by Schilit et al. [57]. They described context as location, identities of nearby people, objects, and changes to those objects. After that, several authors included new aspects like, for example, identity and time (Ryan et al. [58]), emotional states and focus of attention (Dey [59]), context dimensions (Prekop and Burnett [60], and Gustavsen [61]), and any environmental data (Tajd and Ngantchaha [62]).

The progresses obtained by previous solutions also increase the complexity of the information management process. This fact implies the increment of the information considered during the management processes and therefore the increment of their complexity. Furthermore, the protection of the location information is another important aspect to consider. In other case, users' locations could be tracked without the users' consent, and this information could be used in a potential malicious way. One example of this situation could be the possibility of knowing the current location of a given user to know when he/she is at home or not. At this point, it is required not only preserving the privacy of the location information like in location-based services but also controlling other sensitive pieces of information of the users' life. In other case and following the previous example, it would be possible to know not only if a given user is at home but also the identity of that user, if he/she is married, his/her emails, and other pieces of information about his/her personal life.

As it is stated by the previous definitions of context, the number of heterogeneous pieces of information managed by the context-aware paradigm is really high. The evolution experienced from traditional paradigms to the new ones has influenced this fact. First, the mobile paradigm incorporated the location of users and elements into the management processes of IMSs. Later, pervasive systems added other important pieces of information of the users' life like the users' identities, emails, notifications, and information related to smart spaces. Finally, the information about the context in which users are located, together with the information considered by the previous paradigms, has increased the complexity of the management processes. Figure 1.1 shows the evolution of IMSs considering the influence of new emerging paradigms and the most representative pieces of information usually managed by them. By considering that an important number of these pieces of information are sensitive or private, current IMSs need to consider the privacy of this information. In this sense, additional research on automatic mechanisms in charge of protecting the privacy of the sensitive information handled during the management processes of IMSs is needed. Otherwise, malicious users could get to know more information about the life of a given user himself/herself.

The context-awareness is a paradigm that can be helpful in many different scenarios like, for example, the network management. Network administrators can incorporate contextual information to manage dynamically the network resources by adapting their behavior according to the network status. The location of connected devices and network resources, the kind of devices connected to the network infrastructure, or the status and statistics of the network have been found as much appreciated pieces of contextual information that can be considered by network administrators before taking management decisions. These decisions could go from the reconfiguration of a

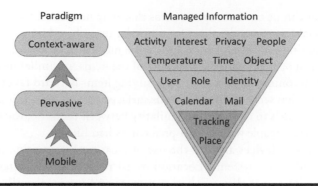

Paradigm

Managed Information

Context-aware

Pervasive

Mobile

Activity Interest Privacy People
Temperature Time Object
User Role Identity
Calendar Mail
Tracking
Place

Figure 1.1 Evolution of management systems.

given network component, which is not being used in an energy-efficient way, to the deployment of new resources located in a given place to ensure the QoS of certain users.

1.4.2 Context-Aware Application Scenarios

This section shows different scenarios where the PBM paradigm helps IMSs in the processes of handling and protecting the information, as well as in the management of the systems' configuration and behavior.

1.4.2.1 Management of Location Privacy

Protecting the privacy of the users' information in location-based services being part of users' everyday life represents a novel challenge [63]. Nowadays, location-based services run on computers, smartphones, tablets, and smart watches, providing users with value-added services. Examples of these services could be social networks, car navigation systems, and recommender systems. The protection of large volumes of heterogeneous information related to the users' location is a complex task that requires an automatic mechanism to address it accordingly. Location policies are a promising way to accomplish this protection at real time and dynamically. In this sense, location policies should allow users to:

- Mask their location by generating one or more fictitious positions for a particular user. In this way, other users cannot distinguish the real position of the target.
- Hide their location when they do not want to release it to others. This will avoid requester(s) to know the position of the target.
- Indicate the maximum accuracy at which users want to be located. Depending on the environment in which users are located, several levels of granularity can be defined such as country, city, building, and floor, among others.
- Define the minimum level of nearness at which users want to be located. Nearness levels correspond to the same values defined for the granularity policies.

1.4.2.2 Hybrid Recommender Systems

The increasing volume of information received by people in their daily lives usually presents the challenge of deciding what information is useful for them, and which does not. Recommender systems are tools that can be used to suggest items that may not have been found by users themselves [64]. Traditional recommenders like, for example, those based on content-based (CB) [65] and collaborative filtering (CF) [66] tend to use simple models in order to provide recommendations. The CB approach operates with the similarity of the items, so similar items to the ones liked by the target user are recommended. However, classifying items is a hard task that usually requires human knowledge. In that sense, the CF methods surfaced to overcome this drawback, considering stereotype-based models to establish the similarity between users. So, the CF models targeted to recommend items that people with similar preferences had liked.

The advent of mobile devices allowed the use of location information to improve the recommendations of traditional systems. Location-based recommender systems provide recommendations by considering the distance between users and items, as well as their subsequent movements. The ability to combine users' location and movements, together with other aspects like users' preferences, items' properties, or users' ratings, provides more valuable information that can help to suggest more accurate items of potential interest to users. The apparition of the context-aware paradigm provoked the consideration of contextual information to recommend items located close to the users. An example of contextual information could be the time, companion, or weather conditions found in the environment in which users are located. Usually, these context-aware recommenders not only consider pieces of contextual information but also information related to other approaches like locations, preferences, or properties. The combination of the previous information during the recommendation process lets a better adaptation of the recommendations to the context status. An example of this fact could be that context-aware recommender systems are able to recommend umbrellas or raincoats when it starts raining close to a shopping center. The combination of contextual information, together with information belonging to other approaches, also presents certain privacy challenges that have to be addressed adequately. Users should be able to dynamically control what pieces of their information they want to reveal to recommender systems. In this sense, users should define their privacy preferences by using policies related to their location, identity, and personal information.

1.4.2.3 Protecting Information in eHealth Scenarios

The evolution of traditional health systems has been influenced by the progress experienced by technologies, communications, and medical services. During the past years, there has been a lot of research in the healthcare topic with the goal of evolving from traditional paper-based systems toward electronic-based systems that manage digital records. Personal health records (PHRs) and electronic health records (EHRs) are the electronic versions of patient health information. The former is controlled by patients themselves, while the latter is managed by healthcare systems. The provision of health services using digital technology is known in the literature as eHealth [67].

Despite the profits presented by this evolution, some open challenges have also appeared like the necessity of a common infrastructure and standard information models to guarantee the interoperability of systems. Furthermore, the large volume of data related to EHR and PHR, along with the contextual information provided by the proliferation of context-aware services ubiquitously accessible, means that managing and protecting the privacy of the patients' information are even a greater challenge. In order to partially address this challenge, context-aware applications can be useful and helpful in managing the patients' information, with concern for patients' privacy and how personal information, location, and context information are revealed. In this sense, users of context-aware eHealth systems should be able to manage dynamically the privacy of their medical records, personal information, locations, and information related to the environment or context in which they are located. In order to cover these requirements, the PBM paradigm can help with the definition of policies that allow both users and administrators to manage and control sensitive information.

1.4.2.4 Networking Paradigm

Computer networks are dynamic and complex systems, and therefore their configuration and management continue to be challenging. Networks are composed of a large number of resources such as switches, routers, firewalls, and middleboxes in charge of forwarding packages between them. Network administrators are responsible for configuring and managing these resources, representing a really difficult task due to the number of different events occurring simultaneously and the heterogeneity of the network resources. To automatize this management, the PBNM paradigm [68] allows network administrators to define policies to control the behavior of the network resources as well as the packages traveling along the network. Using policies, network administrators are able to specify, for example, which kind of services has more priority to guarantee the QoS, or what network resources should be switched off because they are consuming energy in an inefficient way.

Despite the progress carried out by the PBNM paradigm, the recent technology advancements in mobile devices and networks have encouraged users' mobility, thus being location one of the most important aspects for knowing where devices, resources, or people are. Combining location and mobility information, together with other important contextual information like the status of the network resources, or the statistics of the packages traveling along the network, has made the network management an actual difficult task. Nowadays, network administrators must define increasingly sophisticated policies and complex tasks, which requires considering the previous context-aware information. Furthermore, the rigidity of the infrastructure provides few possibilities for on-demand innovation or improvement, since network devices have generally been closed, proprietary, and vertically integrated.

Context-aware systems management aims to take the availability of dynamically changing resources and services during a particular period of system operation into account. Management policies and automated mechanisms need to be able to adapt to dynamic changes such that they offer the best possible level of service to the user in the given situation. Self-management capabilities include automated configuration of components, automated recognition of opportunities for performance improvement (self-optimization), automatic detection, diagnosis and repair of local hardware and software problems, and automatic defense against attacks. The objective is to minimize the degree of external intervention, e.g., by human system managers, and, at the same time, to preserve the architectural properties imposed by its specification. The concept of self-configuration refers to a process in which an application's internal structure changes depending on its environment.

Networks are large-scale distributed systems that require management solutions that dynamically change the behavior of the managed resources. This network management is a hard task that bears a great complexity. Enforcing network QoS and selecting different routes to reach given network resources in certain situations became a necessity in the use of the PBM oriented to the network management. The PBNM paradigm arose to perform network management based on policies. This paradigm enables an administrator to specify what he/she wants to do, the end results, without having to know how to accomplish it for the specific devices.

1.4.3 Context-Awareness Proposals

During the past years, many context-aware services have been proposed in order to make life easier. Despite that the context term was proposed in 1994, it is commonly agreed that the first context-aware solution found in the literature was proposed in 1991 [69]. They introduced a novel system for the location of people in an office environment called Active Badge. This system was able to know the location of users in order to forward phone calls to the phones close to the user. The users' location was known because users wore badges transmitting signals to a centralized location system. After that, many different solutions have been proposed in different topics, as the one presented by Wood et al. in [70], for example. They described a *teleporting* solution that was able to make the user' environment available to any computer running a web browser with Java. By using this solution, users did not have to carry any computing platform, and they were able to execute their applications on any nearby machine. These context-aware systems opened new possibilities to users in terms of acquiring custom services by gathering context information, especially in applications where the high mobility of users increased their usability. Car navigation systems, emergency services, and recommender systems are well-known examples of context-aware solutions where the mobility of users increases their usability.

Nowadays, a depth survey on context-aware systems analyzes a large number of solutions considering different topics [71]. Systems such as Feel@Home [72], Hydra [73], CroCo [74], SOCAM [75], and CoBrA [76] provide support to "security and privacy" features. Feel@Home was a context-aware framework that supported communications between contexts or domains, considering intra- and inter-domain interactions. Hydra was an ambient intelligence middleware oriented to the IoT, which integrated the device, semantic, and application contexts to offer context-aware information. On the other hand, CroCo was a cross-application context management service for heterogeneous environments, while SOCAM used a collection of ontologies to shape the quality, dependence, and classification of the context information. This collection was built on a common upper ontology for all contexts, as well as for domain-specific ontologies that defined concepts of each one. Another related work in this context, which is not included in the survey presented in [71], is CoCA [77]. This proposal presented a collaborative context-aware service platform, where a neighborhood-based mechanism to share resources was introduced. CoCA inferred users' location by considering information about the context and the location of the elements. SHERLOCK [78] was a framework with functionalities for location-based services that used semantic technologies to help users to choose the service that best fits their needs in the given context. Hydra [73] was another solution oriented to IoT. It was a middleware in charge of delivering solutions to wireless devices and sensor used in ambient awareness. It considered a powerful reasoning procedure toward various context sources including physical device based, semantic, and abstract layer based. PerDe [79] was a development environment focused on pervasive computing applications oriented toward the user's needs. It provided a domain-specific design language and a set of graphical tools to cover some development stages of pervasive applications. DiaSuite [80] was another development methodology that used a software design approach to develop applications in the domain of Sense/Compute/Control (SCC) applications. In addition, DiaSuite had a compiler that produced a dedicated Java programming framework, guiding the programmer to implement the various parts of the software system.

Some of the solutions described above made use of semantic rules for different purposes. Hydra, CroCo, SHERLOCK, and SOCAM used semantic rules to infer new information about a given context, taking into account information from others. Instead, CoCA made use of semantic rules to manage the ontologies, e.g., a property is the inverse of another property, as well as additional information about the domain. Yet, none of these four solutions used semantic rules to define policies oriented to protect users' privacy preferences. Users' privacy should be supported by any context-aware framework, with which the users are capable of dynamically restricting or disclosing information to others depending on their location and their preferences in terms of privacy. Consequently, the current trend in context-aware systems focuses on controlling the disclosure of users' location by using policies.

There are a number of systems based on semantic web that manage policies to preserve users' privacy. For example, CoBrA presented a context-aware architecture that allowed distributed agents to share information with each other. CoBrA defined an ontology that shaped spaces composed of smart agents, devices, and sensors and protected the privacy of its users by using rules that deduce whether they have the right permissions to share and/or receive information. Another example was the Preserving Privacy in Context-aware Systems (PPCS) solution presented in [81], where a semantically rich, policy-based framework with different levels of privacy to protect users' information in environments with mobile devices was presented. Dynamic information observed or inferred from the context, along with static information about the owner, was taken into account to make access control decisions. Location and context information of the users were shared (or not) depending on their privacy policies. Another proposal supporting privacy policies without using semantic web technologies was CoPS [82]. In CoPS, users could control who access their context data, when, and at what level of granularity. In Table 1.1 is illustrated a comparison between the previous solutions taking into account the contextual information managed by them and their privacy support.

In addition to the previous solutions and oriented to protect the users' privacy in context-aware scenarios, SeCoMan [83] is a solution in charge of obtaining the information from the context or environment in which users are located, modeling and protecting their information, and providing context-aware applications. SeCoMan proposes an architecture oriented to the semantic web. On the one hand, the information about users and contexts is modeled by using a collection of ontologies defined in OWL 2. On the other hand, the users' information is protected using policies defined in the Semantic Web Rule Language (SWRL). These policies allow users to share their location to the selected users, at the desired granularity, at the right place, and at the right time. This work also includes the analysis and comparison of the different context-aware systems. On the other hand, the Prophet framework [84] provides an effective security scheme for allowing users to share their location information. The authors of this proposal define a Fingerprint identification based on Markov chain and state classification to describe the users' behavior patterns. In addition, they also propose a location-based anonymization mechanism that considers a strategy based on indistinguishability to protect the sensitive information of users. Several experiments demonstrate a good performance and effectiveness of the proposed solution.

PRECISE [85] is another privacy-preserving and context-aware system that provides context-aware recommendations by considering the information that users want to reveal to given services. By using this solution, users can release their locations to specific services, hide their positions to specific users, mask their locations to other users by generating fictitious (fake) positions, establish the granularity and closeness at which they want to be located by services or users, and preserve their anonymity to specific services. To this end, an architecture oriented to the MCC paradigm has been designed. This architecture is composed of services, allocated at the Software as a Service (SaaS) layer of the MCC paradigm, providing users with recommendations about context-aware information. The main element of the solution is a middleware allocated at the Platform as a Service (PaaS) layer, which preserves the users' information and manages the information about the context and space that can be provided by independent systems. ProtectMyPrivacy (PmP) [86] is a solution designed and implemented to protect the users' privacy in Android. This proposal

Table 1.1 Comparative of Context-Aware Systems

Solutions	Managed Contextual Information	Privacy-Preserving Support		
		Identity	Location	Context
SHERLOCK	Place, people, object, identity, tracking	X	X	X
CoCA	Place, people, object, identity, tracking, calendar	X	X	X
PerDe	Place, people, object, identity, tracking, time, activity	X	X	X
DiaSuite	Place, people, object, identity, tracking, temperature, role	X	X	X
SOCAM	Place, people, object, identity, tracking, activity, time	X	X	X
CroCo	Place, people, object, identity, tracking, activity, time	Partially supported by ACL		
Hydra	Place, people, object, identity, tracking, time	Partially supported by ACL		
Feel@Home	Place, people, object, identity, tracking, calendar	Partially supported by ACL		
CoBrA	Place, people, object, identity, tracking, activity, role	V	X	X
CoPS	Place, people, object, identity, tracking, time, role, notification	V	V	V
PPCS	Place, people, object, identity, tracking, time, role, notification, interest, mail	V	V	V

is able to detect critical contextual information at run-time when privacy-sensitive data accesses occur. PmP infers the purpose of the data access based on crowd-sourced data. The authors demonstrate that the control of sensitive data accessed by these libraries can be an effective mechanism for managing the users' privacy.

The next block of solutions is focused on protecting the users' information when they move between independent contexts or environments (intra- and inter-context scenarios). In that sense, CAPRIS [87] is a solution in charge of protecting the users' information in the context of where they are. Using CAPRIS, users were able to decide at real time what, where, when, how, to whom, and at which level of precision they want to release their information. This information can be the *space* in which they are located with different levels of granularity, the users' *personal information* with different levels of precision, the users' *activity*, and the information oriented to the *context* in which they are located. Using CAPRIS, users did not have to manage their privacy, but they just have to choose the most appropriate group of policies suggested by the system. As evolution of CAPRIS, covering the same goals, MASTERY [88] suggests to the users several sets of privacy-preserving and context-aware policies, called *profiles*. In order to protect their information, users just have to choose the most suitable profile according to their interests in the context where they are, being able to modify these profiles by adding, deleting, or modifying some of the policies shaping them. Finally, when the information is going to be shared the owner receives a notification at real time and he/she decides if to grant or deny the exchange of information. Finally, h-MAS [89] is a privacy-preserving and context-aware solution for health scenarios with the aim of managing the privacy of the users' information in both intra- and inter-context scenarios. In a health scenario, h-MAS suggests a pool of privacy policies to users, who are aware of the health context in which they are located. Users can update the policies according to their interests. These policies protect the privacy of the users' health records, locations, as well as context-aware information being accessed by third parties without their consent. The information on patients and the health context is managed through semantic web techniques, which provide a common infrastructure that makes it possible to represent, process, and share information between independent systems more easily. Regarding network management, important improvements in terms of automatic management, energy saving, and security can be achieved by managing the network resources at run-time and considering contextual information. In this sense, in [90], a mobility-aware, policy-based system in charge of reducing the energy consumption in networks oriented to the SDN paradigm is proposed. The policies defined in this solution allow the SDN paradigm to switch on/off network resources when they are consuming energy in an inefficient way, as well as to create virtualized network resources like proxies to reduce the network traffic generated by users consuming services close to the network infrastructure. Network administrators define policies that will decide the list of potential actions to be taken by the SDN components, in accordance with the energy consumption, the users' mobility, and the network statistics. This solution also proposes an architecture in charge of managing the resources of mobile networks considering the previous policies and the ontology that models the concepts that belong to the mobile network topic. With the ontology, a set of primitives are provided with which to describe a collection of the resources managed by the SDN paradigm and the relationships among them. Finally, in [91], a proposal was designed oriented to ensure the QoS and end-user experience in dynamic scenarios of mobile networks by considering contextual information. This solution proposes an architecture in charge of managing the SDN resources at run-time by using high-level policies. Among the different sets of policies, the authors emphasize the use of mobility-aware, management-oriented policies, defined by the service provider network administrator to decide the actions made by the SDN according the network infrastructure statistics and location, and the mobility of users and services. These policies are oriented to guarantee end-users experience in very crowded places (e.g., stadiums, shopping malls, or unexpected traffic jams). To this end, the policies decide when the SDN should balance the network traffic between the infrastructure located close to the congested one, when the SDN should create or dismantle physical or virtual infrastructure in case of the congested one is not enough to accomplish the end-user demand, and when the SDN should restrict or limit specific services or network traffic in critical situations produced by large crowds using services at specific areas.

1.5 Challenges of IMS

The early days of IMSs were focused on the management and storage of business information in companies and public organisms, such as administrations or universities. The evolution experienced by software and hardware technologies changed the focus and functionality of IMSs.

Nowadays, these systems provide services that are consumed not only by companies or administrations but also by people at anyplace and anytime. In order to provide these services to this wide variety of users, IMSs should now evolve to:

- Gather and handle large volumes of heterogeneous information.
- Evaluate and protect the privacy of sensitive pieces of information.
- Consider independent administrators distributed along different organizations.
- Manage diverse components with different requirements and locations.

These facts have increased the complexity of information management processes, thus requiring additional research efforts on new management mechanisms that consider the previous requirements. These mechanisms should be as automatic as possible in order to allow dynamic detections of events that imply the reconfiguration of the management processes. Furthermore, automatic mechanisms avoid delays during the management processes due to possible human fails or misconfigurations, and help to reduce the complexity of the management of distributed heterogeneous components.

1.6 Conclusions and Future Work

The evolution of technology has increased the complexity of the information management processes performed by IMSs. Current IMSs handle large volumes of heterogeneous information, protect the privacy of sensitive pieces of information, allow different administrators to manage the resources, and consider distributed scenarios. The majority of IMSs are nowadays consumed by users, companies, or public administrations at anytime and anyplace. This fact has influenced that the location of users has become a very valuable piece of information in order to provide services located close to the users. With the consideration of the location, the pervasive and context-awareness paradigms have also included new pieces of information about the environment or context where users are like, for example, locations, activities, identities, time, emotional states, or any environmental data. This new heterogeneous information has increased the complexity of the previous management processes influencing the emergence of new automatic management mechanisms.

Controlling the behavior of the system resources and also managing and protecting the users' information in IMSs that consider contextual information are open issues that still require efforts to be addressed. Administrators of IMSs systems should be able to consider the contextual information during the management processes in order to make decisions about the behavior of the system resources. Furthermore, users of IMSs should decide and control what information they want to reveal, where and when the information will be exchanged, and to whom. Semantic web techniques are a promising way to accomplish the management and protection of contextual and personal information in context-aware systems. This technology allows modeling the information in a formal way, exchanging information between independent systems, defining privacy policies to protect the information, and inferring new knowledge by considering the information and the policies. In this sense, this chapter has reviewed the state-of-the-art context-aware solutions that allow protecting sensitive information as well as controlling the behavior of the system resources. Subsequently, we have analyzed location-based and context-aware systems in charge of exchanging and protecting the users' information in intra- and inter-context scenarios by considering semantic web techniques. Finally, we also have considered location-based and context-aware systems to securely manage network resources by considering aspects such as QoS, energy efficiency, or performance.

As future work, it is needed to consider the privacy of the users' information and contexts when administrators manage the system resources. An example of this fact consists in allowing users to define the granularity at which they want to reveal their location to network administrators when they are managing the network infrastructure taking into account the distance and location of devices. Regarding the network management topic, the combination of concepts like SDN and Network Functions Virtualization (NFV) could ease the management of the network infrastructure and its services. In this sense, the Network Slicing technique can combine the previous technologies to manage the network resources and services depending on the current networks' requirements. These slices and their resources should be managed automatically considering the contextual information.

References

1. OSI. *Information Processing Systems-Open System Inteconnection-Systems Management Overview.* ISO 10040, 1991.
2. Jefatura del Estado. Ley Orgánica de Protección de Datos de Carácter Personal. www.boe.es/boe/dias/1999/12/14/pdfs/A43088-43099.pdf.
3. D. W. Samuel, and D. B. Louis. The right to privacy. *Harvard Law Review,* 4(5): 193–220, 1890.
4. A. Westerinen, J. Schnizlein, J. Strassner, M. Scherling, B. Quinn, S. Herzog, A. Huynh, M. Carlson, J. Perry, and S. Waldbusser. *Terminology for Policy-Based Management.* IETF Request for Comments 3198, November 2001.
5. B. Moore. *Policy Core Information Model (PCIM) Extensions.* IETF Request for Comments 3460, January 2003.
6. S. Godik, and T. Moses. *OASIS EXtensible Access Control Markup Language (XACML).* OASIS Committee Specification, 2002.
7. A. Dardenne, A. Van Lamsweerde and S. Fickas. Goal-directed requirements acquisition. *Science of Computer Programming,* 20(1–2): 3–50, 1993.
8. F. L. Gandon, and N. M. Sadeh. Semantic web technologies to reconcile privacy and context awareness. *Web Semantics: Science, Services and Agents on the World Wide Web,* 1(3): 241–260, April 2004.
9. I. Horrocks. Ontologies and the semantic web. *Communications ACM,* 51(12): 58–67, December 2008.
10. R. Boutaba and I. Aib. Policy-based management: A historical perspective. *Journal of Network and Systems Management,* 15(4): 447–480, 2007.
11. P. A. Carter. *Policy-Based Management,* In *Pro SQL Server Administration,* pages 859–886. Apress, Berkeley, CA, 2015.
12. D. Florencio, and C. Herley. Where do security policies come from? In *Proceedings of the 6th Symposium on Usable Privacy and Security,* pages 10:1–10:14, 2010.
13. K. Yang, and X. Jia. DAC-MACS: Effective data access control for multi-authority Cloud storage systems, *IEEE Transactions on Information Forensics and Security,* 8(11): 1790–1801, 2014.
14. B. W. Lampson. Dynamic protection structures. In *Proceedings of the Fall Joint Computer Conference,* pages 27–38, 1969.
15. B. W. Lampson. Protection. *ACM SIGOPS Operating Systems Review,* 8(1): 18–24, January 1974.
16. D. E. Bell and L. J. LaPadula. *Secure Computer Systems: Mathematical Foundations.* Technical report, DTIC Document, 1973.
17. D. F. Ferraiolo, and D. R. Kuhn. Role-based access controls. In *Proceedings of the 15th NIST-NCSC National Computer Security Conference,* pages 554–563, 1992.
18. V. P. Astakhov. Surface integrity: Definition and importance in functional performance, In *Surface Integrity in Machining,* pages 1–35. Springer, London, 2010.
19. K. J. Biba. *Integrity Considerations for Secure Computer Systems.* Technical report, DTIC Document, 1977.

20. M. J. Culnan, and P. K. Armstrong. Information privacy concerns, procedural fairness, and impersonal trust: An empirical investigation. *Organization Science*, 10(1): 104–115, 1999.
21. A. I. Antón, E. Bertino, N. Li, and T. Yu. A roadmap for comprehensive online privacy policy management. *Communications ACM*, 50(7): 109–116, July 2007.
22. J. Karat, C. M. Karat, C. Brodie, and J. Feng. Privacy in information technology: Designing to enable privacy policy management in organizations. *International Journal of Human Computer Studies*, 63(1–2): 153–174, 2005.
23. M. Jafari, R. Safavi-Naini, P. W. L. Fong, and K. Barker. A framework for expressing and enforcing purpose-based privacy policies. *ACM Transaction Information Systesms Security*, 17(1): 3:1–3:31, August 2014.
24. G. Karjoth, M. Schunter, and M. Waidner. Platform for enterprise privacy practices: Privacy-enabled management of customer data, In *Proceedings of the International Workshop on Privacy Enhancing Technologies*, pages 69–84, 2003.
25. S. R. Blenner, M. Kollmer, A. J. Rouse, N. Daneshvar, C. Williams, and L. B. Andrews. Privacy policies of android diabetes apps and sharing of health information. *JAMA*, 315(10): 1051–1052, 2016.
26. R. Ramanath, F. Liu, N. Sadeh, and N. A. Smith. Unsupervised alignment of privacy policies using hidden Markov models. In *Proceedings of the Annual Meeting of the Association of Computational Linguistics*, pages 605–610, June 2014.
27. J. Gerlach, T. Widjaja, and P. Buxmann. Handle with care: How online social network providers' privacy policies impact users' information sharing behavior. *The Journal of Strategic Information Systems*, 24(1): 33–43, 2015.
28. O. Badve, B. B. Gupta, and S. Gupta. Reviewing the Security Features in Contemporary Security Policies and Models for Multiple Platforms. In *Handbook of Research on Modern Cryptographic Solutions for Computer and Cyber Security*, pages 479–504. IGI Global, Hershey, PA, 2016.
29. K. Zkik, G. Orhanou, and S. El Hajji. Secure mobile multi cloud architecture for authentication and data storage. *International Journal of Cloud Applications and Computing* 7(2): 62–76, 2017.
30. C. Stergiou, K. E. Psannis, B. Kim, and B. Gupta. Secure integration of IoT and cloud computing. *In Future Generation Computer Systems*, 78(3): 964–975, 2018.
31. D. C. Verma. Simplifying network administration using policy-based management. *IEEE Network*, 16(2): 20–26, March 2002.
32. D. C. Verma. *Policy-Based Networking: Architecture and Algorithms*. New Riders Publishing, Thousand Oaks, CA, 2000.
33. J. Rubio-Loyola, J. Serrat, M. Charalambides, P. Flegkas, and G. Pavlou. A methodological approach toward the refinement problem in policy-based management systems. *IEEE Communications Magazine*, 44(10): 60–68, October 2006.
34. F. Perich. Policy-based network management for next generation spectrum access control. In *Proceedings of International Symposium on New Frontiers in Dynamic Spectrum Access Networks*, pages 496–506, April 2007.
35. S. Shin, P. A. Porras, V. Yegneswaran, M. W. Fong, G. Gu, and M. Tyson. FRESCO: Modular composable security services for Software-Defined Networks. In *Proceedings of the 20th Annual Network and Distributed System Security Symposium*, pages 1–16, 2013.
36. K. Odagiri, S. Shimizu, N. Ishii, and M. Takizawa. Functional experiment of virtual policy based network management scheme in Cloud environment. In *International Conference on Network-Based Information Systems*, pages 208–214, September 2014.
37. M. Casado, M. J. Freedman, J. Pettit, J. Luo, N. McKeown, and S. Shenker. Ethane: Taking control of the enterprise. In *Proceedings of Conference on Applications, Technologies, Architectures, and Protocols for Computer Communications*, pages 1–12, August 2007.
38. M. Wichtlhuber, R. Reinecke, and D. Hausheer. An SDN-based CDN/ISP collaboration architecture for managing high-volume flows. *IEEE Transactions on Network and Service Management*, 12(1): 48–60, March 2015.
39. A. Lara, and B. Ramamurthy. OpenSec: Policy-based security using Software-Defined Networking. *IEEE Transactions on Network and Service Management*, 13(1): 30–42, March 2016.

40. W. Jingjin, Z. Yujing, M. Zukerman, and E. K. N. Yung. Energy-efficient base stations sleep-mode techniques in green cellular networks: A survey. *IEEE Communications Surveys Tutorials*, 17(2): 803–826, 2015.

41. G. Auer, V. Giannini, C. Desset, I. Godor, P. Skillermark, M. Olsson, M. A. Imran, D. Sabella, M. J. Gonzalez, O. Blume, and A. Fehske. How much energy is needed to run a wireless network? *IEEE Wireless Communications*, 18(5): 40–49, 2011.

42. W. Yun, J. Staudinger, and M. Miller. High efficiency linear GaAs MMIC amplifier for wireless base station and Femto cell applications. In *IEEE Topical Conference on Power Amplifiers for Wireless and Radio Applications*, pages 49–52, January 2012.

43. M. A. Marsan, L. Chiaraviglio, D. Ciullo, and M. Meo. Optimal energy savings in cellular access networks. In *IEEE International Conference on Communications Workshops*, pages 1–5, June 2009.

44. H. Claussen, I. Ashraf, and L. T. W. Ho. Dynamic idle mode procedures for femtocells. *Bell Labs Technical Journal*, 15(2): 95–116, 2010.

45. L. Rongpeng, Z. Zhifeng, C. Xianfu, J. Palicot, and Z. Honggang. TACT: A transfer actor-critic learning framework for energy saving in cellular radio access networks. *IEEE Transactions on Wireless Communications*, 13(4): 2000–2011, 2014.

46. G. C. Januario, C. H. A. Costa, M. C. Amarai, A. C. Riekstin, T. C. M. B. Carvalho, and C. Meirosu. Evaluation of a policy-based network management system for energy-efficiency. In *IFIP/IEEE International Symposium on Integrated Network Management*, pages 596–602, May 2013.

47. C. Dsouza, G. J. Ahn, and M. Taguinod. Policy-driven security management for fog computing: Preliminary framework and a case study. In *Conference on Information Reuse and Integration*, pages 16–23, August 2014.

48. H. Kim and N. Feamster. Improving network management with Software Defined Networking. *IEEE Communications Magazine*, 51(2): 114–119, February 2013.

49. O. Gaddour, A. Koubaa, and M. Abid. Quality-of-service aware routing for static and mobile IPv6-based low-power and loss sensor networks using RPL. *Ad Hoc Networks*, 33: 233–256, 2015.

50. Q. Zhao, D. Grace, and T. Clarke. Transfer learning and cooperation management: Balancing the quality of service and information exchange overhead in cognitive radio networks. *Transactions on Emerging Telecommunications Technologies*, 26(2): 290–301, 2015.

51. M. Charalambides, P. Flegkas, G. Pavlou, A. K. Bandara, E. C. Lupu, A. Russo, N. Dulav, M. Sloman, and J. Rubio-Loyola. Policy conflict analysis for quality of service management. In *Proceedings of the 6th IEEE International Workshop on Policies for Distributed Systems and Networks*, pages 99–108, June 2005.

52. M. F. Bari, S. R. Chowdhury, R. Ahmed, and R. Boutaba. PolicyCop: An autonomic QoS policy enforcement framework for software defined networks. In *2013 IEEE SDN for Future Networks and Services*, pages 1–7, November 2013.

53. C. Bennewith and R. Wickers. The mobile paradigm for content development, In *Multimedia and E-Content Trends*, pages 101–109. Vieweg+Teubner Verlag, 2009.

54. I. A. Junglas, and R. T. Watson. Location-based services. *Communications ACM*, 51(3): 65–69, March 2008.

55. M. Weiser. The computer for the 21st century. *Scientific American*, 265(3): 94–104, 1991.

56. G. D. Abowd, A. K. Dey, P. J. Brown, N. Davies, M. Smith, and P. Steggles. Towards a better understanding of context and context-awareness. In *Handheld and Ubiquitous Computing*, pages 304–307, September 1999.

57. B. Schilit, N. Adams, and R. Want. Context-aware computing applications. In *Proceeding of the 1st Workshop Mobile Computing Systems and Applications*, pages 85–90, December 1994.

58. N. Ryan, J. Pascoe, and D. Morse. Enhanced reality fieldwork: The context aware archaeological assistant. In *Proceedings of the 25th Anniversary Computer Applications in Archaeology*, pages 85–90, December 1997.

59. A. K. Dey. Context-aware computing: The CyberDesk project. In *Proceedings of the AAAI 1998 Spring Symposium on Intelligent Environments*, pages 51–54, 1998.

60. P. Prekop and M. Burnett. Activities, context and ubiquitous computing. *Computer Communications*, 26(11): 1168–1176, July 2003.

61. R. M. Gustavsen. Condor-an application framework for mobility-based context-aware applications. In *Proceedings of the Workshop on Concepts and Models for Ubiquitous Computing*, volume 39, September 2002.

62. C. Tadj and G. Ngantchaha. Context handling in a pervasive computing system framework. In *Proceedings of the 3rd International Conference on Mobile Technology, Applications and Systems*, pages 1–6, October 2006.

63. S. Dhar and U. Varshney. Challenges and business models for mobile location-based services and advertising. *Communications ACM*, 54(5): 121–128, May 2011.

64. F. Ricci, L. Rokach, and B. Shapira. *Recommender Systems: Introduction and Challenges*, pages In *Recommender Systems Handbook*, pages 1–34. Springer, Boston, MA, 2015.

65. J. B. Schafer, D. Frankowski, J. Herlocker, and S. Sen. *Collaborative Filtering Recommender Systems*, In *The Adaptive Web*, pages 291–324. Springer, Berlin, Heidelberg, 2007.

66. P. Lops, M. de Gemmis, and G. Semeraro. *Content-Based Recommender Systems: State of the Art and Trends*, In *Recommender Systems Handbook*, pages 73–105. Springer, Boston, MA, 2011.

67. D. Slamanig and C. Stingl. Privacy aspects of eHealth. In *Proceedings of Conference on Availability, Reliability and Security*, pages 1226–1233, March 2008.

68. C. Wang. Policy-based network management. In *Proceedings of the International Conference on Communication Technology*, volume 1, pages 101–105, 2000.

69. R. Want, A. Hopper, V. Falcao, and J. Gibbons. The active badge location system. *ACM Transactions on Information Systems*, 10(1): 91–102, January 1992.

70. K. R. Wood, T. Richardson, F. Bennett, A. Harter, and A. Hopper. Global teleporting with Java: Toward ubiquitous personalized computing. *Computer*, 30(2): 53–59, February 1997.

71. C. Perera, A. Zaslavsky, P. Christen, and D. Georgakopoulos. Context aware computing for the Internet of Things: A survey. *IEEE Communications Surveys Tutorials*, 16(1): 414–454, 2014.

72. B. Guo, L. Sun, and D. Zhang. The architecture design of a cross-domain context management system. In *Proceedings of Conference Pervasive Computing and Communications Workshops*, pages 499–504, April 2010.

73. A. Badii, M. Crouch, and C. Lallah. A context-awareness framework for intelligent networked embedded systems. In *Proceedings of Conference on Advances in Human-Oriented and Personalized Mechanisms, Technologies and Services*, pages 105–110, August 2010.

74. S. Pietschmann, A. Mitschick, R. Winkler, and K. Meissner. CroCo: Ontology-based, cross-application context management. In *Proceedings of Workshop on Semantic Media Adaptation and Personalization*, pages 88–93, December 2008.

75. T. Gu, X. H. Wang, H. K. Pung, and D. Q. Zhang. An ontology-based context model in intelligent environments. In *Proceedings of Communication Networks and Distributed Systems Modeling and Simulation Conference*, pages 270–275, January 2004.

76. H. Chen, T. Finin, and A. Joshi. An ontology for context-aware pervasive computing environments. *The Knowledge Engineering Review*, 18(03): 197–207, September 2003.

77. D. Ejigu, M. Scuturici, and L. Brunie. CoCA: A collaborative context-aware service platform for pervasive computing. In *Proceedings of Conference Information Technologies*, pages 297–302, April 2007.

78. R. Yus, E. Mena, S. Ilarri, and A. Illarramendi. SHERLOCK: Semantic management of location-based services in wireless environments. *Pervasive and Mobile Computing*, 15: 87–99, 2014.

79. L. Tang, Z. Yu, H. Wang, X. Zhou, and Z. Duan. Methodology and tools for pervasive application development. *International Journal of Distributed Sensor Networks*, 10(4): 1–16, 2014.

80. B. Bertran, J. Bruneau, D. Cassou, N. Loriant, E. Balland, and C. Consel. DiaSuite: A tool suite to develop sense/compute/control applications. *Science of Computer Programming*, 79: 39–51, 2014.

81. P. Jagtap, A. Joshi, T. Finin, and L. Zavala. Preserving privacy in context-aware systems. In *Proceedings of Conference on Semantic Computing*, pages 149–153, September 2011.

82. V. Sacramento, M. Endler, and F. N. Nascimento. A privacy service for context-aware mobile computing. In *Proceedings of Conference on Security and Privacy for Emergency Areas in Communication Networks*, pages 182–193, September 2005.

83. A. Huertas Celdrán, F. J. García Clemente, M. Gil Pérez, and G. Martínez Pérez. SeCoMan: A semantic-aware policy framework for developing privacy-preserving and context-aware smart applications. *IEEE Systems Journal*, 10(3): 1111–1124, September 2016.

84. J. Qu, G. Zhang, and Z. Fang. Prophet: A context-aware location privacy-preserving scheme in location sharing service. *Discrete Dynamics in Nature and Society*, 2017, 1–11, Article ID 6814832, 2017.

85. A. Huertas Celdrán, M. Gil Pérez, F. J. García Clemente, and G. Martínez Pérez. PRECISE: Privacy-aware recommender based on context information for Cloud service environments. *IEEE Communications Magazine*, 52(8): 90–96, August 2014.

86. S. Chitkara, N. Gothoskar, S. Harish, J.I. Hong, and Y. Agarwal. Does this app really need my location? Context-aware privacy management for smartphones. In *Proceedings of the ACM Interactive Mobile, Wearable and Ubiquitous Technologies*, 1(3): 42:1–42:22, September 2017.

87. A. Huertas Celdrán, M. Gil Pérez, F. J. García Clemente, and G. Martínez Pérez. What private information are you disclosing? A privacy-preserving system supervised by yourself. In *Proceedings of the 6th International Symposium on Cyberspace Safety and Security*, pages 1221–1228, August 2014.

88. A. Huertas Celdrán, M. Gil Pérez, F. J. García Clemente, and G. Martínez Pérez. MASTERY: A multicontext-aware system that preserves the users' privacy. In *IEEE/IFIP Network Operations and Management Symposium*, pages 523–528, April 2016.

89. A. Huertas Celdrán, M. Gil Pérez, F. J. García Clemente, and G. Martínez Pérez. Preserving patients' privacy in health scenarios through a multicontext-aware system. *Annals of Telecommunications*, 72(9–10): 577–587, October 2017.

90. A. Huertas Celdrán, M. Gil Pérez, F. J. García Clemente, and G. Martínez Pérez. Policy-based management for green mobile networks through software-defined networking. *Mobile Networks and Applications*, In Press, 2016.

91. A. Huertas Celdrán, M. Gil Pérez, F. J. García Clemente, and G. Martínez Pérez. Enabling highly dynamic mobile scenarios with software defined networking. *IEEE Communications Magazine, Feature Topics Issue on SDN Use Cases for Service Provider Networks*, 55(4): 108–113, April 2017.

Chapter 2

Critical Infrastructure Protection: Port Cybersecurity, Toward a Hybrid Port

Andrea Chiappetta
Marconi International University

Contents

2.1 Introduction

Today, 2.9 billion people, or 40% of the world's population are online. By 2020, it is predicted that over 40 billion more devices will become "smart" via embedded processors and intelligence. Internet of Things (IoTs) has already grown beyond niche industrial and medical applications into every market and industry, and growth is anticipated to be exponential.

Future developments will inevitably rely on state of the art platforms and systems that enable advanced semi-autonomous IoT applications. Such applications are anticipated to integrate smart objects, embedded intelligence, and smart networks across different systems of systems. Figure 2.1 shows that the data created and consumed by IoT devices is an ever-growing challenge. IoT devices are the foundational layer, where data is created. The IoT industry assumes you can trust the data

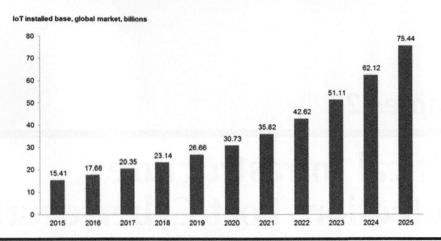

Figure 2.1   IoT installed base, global market, billions.

Source: IHS—Markit, as reported in Forbes.

from device, but in most cases, this is not true. The mobile devices of today are essential to decentralized data processing, but that processing can be easily corrupted.

Current changes in Intelligent Transport System and the adoption of a collaborative paradigm in information systems generate a new and evolving cybernetic space of processes, operations, and connections associated to new vulnerabilities and defense requirements. Innovative social abilities and functions in cognitive/artificial intelligence systems technologies and a cooperative approach to information gathering and processing. Ports and Maritime Transports play a key role in the world trade and are part of economic and strategic interests. Threats to ports and ships can impact on the trade flows between nations, and it can cause damage to corporations. All maritime stakeholders are possible targets and need to consider this threat as concrete. While there is no standard definition of cyberspace, it refers to the domain of information flow and communication between computer systems and networks, and includes physical as well as purely virtual elements. Cybersecurity refers to the domain of systems playing a key role in the prevention or response to threats to critical operations and indicates prevention of or reaction to deliberate malicious acts undertaken via cyberspace to compromise a system directly or indirectly. In this field, models accepted by a unified community are expected to evolve as expression and regulation of changing necessities and priorities to represent a stable and flexible basis for communication in terms of functional, technical, organizational, or service provision specifications and procedures. Ports have a crucial role in the economy of nations and are considered as a critical infrastructure that still need a common standard at global level: some ports started to define their cybersecurity strategies but without a "common framework," and some other ports can already be considered as victims of the cyber threat. Ports and their stakeholders are becoming increasingly complex and dependent on the digitalization of the process related to the IT and platform solutions that interest the entire supply chain. Nowadays, few countries launched a maritime cybersecurity strategy or programs, for example, United States launched in 2014 the port security grant program, allowing funds to provide cyber vulnerability assessments, a second approach was launched by the United Kingdom, where the Department for Transport, Maritime Sector issued a guidance on ship security: cybersecurity code of practice that provides a guidance to assist ship operators to develop a cybersecurity assessment and plan, devices the most appropriate mitigation measures and ensures to establish a correct structure with roles and responsibilities. Last but not the least is the work done by the IMO (International Maritime Organization) that issued guidelines on maritime cyber risk management that provide high-level recommendations on maritime cyber risk management to safeguard shipping from current and emerging cyber threats and vulnerabilities. The guidelines also included functional elements that support effective cyber risk management.

2.2 Critical Infrastructure Protection in the Maritime Sector

The critical infrastructure means assets and systems that are essential for the maintenance of vital social functions, health, safety, security, and economics or social well-being of people. This definition covers a wide range of sectors and key government services including energy, utilities, emergency services, banking and finance, transport, health, food supply, and communication systems. At global level, all nations defined a list of Critical Infrastructures (and related services) that must be considered strategic and need to respect determinates rules. The first approach was issued by the U.S. level during the Clinton Administration in the 1990s, then followed by Canada (in February 2001, Canada started its Office of Critical Infrastructure Protection and Emergency Preparedness [OCIPEP] within the Department of National Defense organizational structure) and Europe (the European Commission adopted a Green Paper on a European Programme for Critical Infrastructure Protection and in 2008, the European Council issued the Directive 2008/114/EC). The main characteristics important for evaluating Critical Infrastructure are resilience, absorbability, adaptability, robustness, structural robustness, precautionary robustness, susceptibility, preparedness, recoverability, responsiveness, reparability, redundancy, overload capacity, safety, and security. These characteristics are generally applicable to each type of Critical Infrastructures (e.g., transport) and for any level of detail selected for the Critical Infrastructure analysis (system, subsystem, component). In order to exactly describe Critical Infrastructure characteristics and assess them through parameters, the set of characteristics must be internally consistent.

The Critical Infrastructure characteristics tree shows the relationship between the Critical Infrastructure characteristics by the logic gates AND. Resilience is an umbrella attribute, which is formed by partial characteristics (Figure 2.2). Resilience so can be divided down to the basic indivisible characteristics. These basic characteristics can be evaluated through one or several

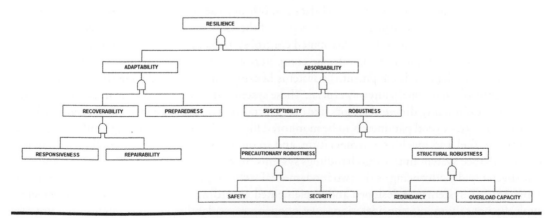

Figure 2.2   Critical Infrastructure characteristic tree.

parameters. Furthermore, the characteristics at the higher level can be evaluated through appropriate parameters. Based on the Critical Infrastructure characteristic tree, we can identify two types of interrelations among the Critical Infrastructure: additive and nonadditive. The additive interrelation is valid for the Critical Infrastructure characteristics. The resilience can be fully described as the sum of the individual characteristics. However, it is not possible to obtain the value of the resilience parameter as a sum of values of parameters of partial Critical Infrastructure characteristics. This nonadditivity must be respected when tools and methods of Critical Infrastructure assessment are selected.

Another important aspect is related to the Critical Infrastructure interdependencies that usually fall into four principle classes:

■ Physical: The operation of one infrastructure depends on the material output of the other.
■ Cyber: Dependency on information transmitted through the information infrastructure.
■ Geographic: Dependency on local environmental effects that simultaneously affects multiple infrastructures.
■ Logical: Any kind of dependency not characterized as Physical, Cyber, or Geographic. A comprehensive analysis of all types of interdependencies is challenging and requires extensive modeling efforts to provide better understanding of CI systems.

In this framework ports are considered as Critical Infrastructure, it is truly affirming that while no two ports are exactly alike, many share certain characteristics such as their size, proximity to a metropolitan area, the volume of cargo they process, and connections to complex transportation networks. These NO characteristics/standards can make them vulnerable to physical security threats because a common procedure is not yet developed. Ports mean physical and virtual infrastructure that move goods, data, persons, etc. Ports are a fundamental player of the economy and growth of nations, during the years several steps ahead were taken to improve and increase the perimeter security, less in term of cybersecurity and this is the topic that we will try to explain as a need to define standard and provide common criteria to be adopted.

2.3 From SCADA to Cloud Computing and IoT in the Supply Chains

SCADA means supervisory control and data acquisition, the first use is started in the 1960s to monitor and control remote gear grew that is part of the Control Systems family, that include ICS (Industrial control system), DCS (Distributed control systems), PCS (process control system), etc. Early systems were built from mainframe computers and required human oversight to operate. With the technological development the systems became automated reducing the involvement of human control, that remain anyway crucial. These systems are used to monitor and control a plant on industries in many different sectors like energy, transport, waste control, etc. In the Maritime Sector, there are several parameters to be monitored like the GPS. Hull opening, hull stress, radar, ship speed, fuel and machinery temperature, and so on, from landside SCADA allow the control of Surveillance system until cargo handlings systems. In recent years, Cloud Computing and IoTs have been rapidly advancing as the two fundamental technologies of the "Future Internet" concept. Different IoT systems are designed and implemented according to the IoT domain requirements, typically not taking into consideration issues of openness, scalability, interoperability, and use case independence. This leads to a variety of new potential risks concerning information security and privacy, data protection, and especially safety, all of which need to be considered in unison. Clearly, the risk assessment model is influenced by the circumstances in which each IoT application and system is configured, deployed, and used. Large-scale connectivity of intelligent objects coupled with complex constraints inevitably leads to many security challenges, which are not included into the classical formulation of security problems and solutions. Consequently, securing data, objects, networks, infrastructure, systems, and people in IoT will have a prominent role in the research and standardization activities over the next several years. This imperative is the need to pay close attention to increasing amounts of data, with the associated concerns for security, privacy, and protection of personal, proprietary, business, and confidential information of all kinds. The costs of cyberattacks in such settings is estimated to reach over 2 trillion USD by 2020, and today IoT is just beginning to emerge with exploits reported at a steady pace and suggesting that information security and operational security are already major challenges. Such security threats are broad, and have the potential to incapacitate IoT systems and/or significantly alter their intended operation. Since the IoT ecosystem can oftentimes have Critical Infrastructure components, it will inevitably be a target for attack and espionage, as well as vulnerable to denial-of-service and many other types of cyberattacks. Likewise, the heterogeneous functional and operational nature of interconnected and cooperating IoT systems of systems will evolve to a point where the security threat canvas is of a size and scale that will be difficult (if not impossible) to accurately represent in formalized security threat models, implying a need for compensatory techniques to help guarantee security imperatives are met. IoT, Industry 4.0, and interconnected devices and infrastructures are likely to be a standard in the near future, bringing disruptive changes as we move from the era of personal devices to an era that is promoting large-scale interconnected and highly integrated devices and platforms that support real-time monitoring, autonomous adaption, instrumentation, peer-peer/master-slave communications, actuation, control logic, and more. The European Bratislava agenda acknowledges that even "modest innovators" need to "adopt the latest smart technologies" in Europe, and to a large extent this is already happening. Early threats and risks identification from a physical and cybersecurity in port operations is a vital aspect in the overall security concerns of Europe and its Member States, not only in terms of homeland security but also in terms of economic and legal interests. However, with ever-increasing potential threats and decreasing budgets in the Member States physical and cybersecurity in Critical Infrastructures need to become efficient and cost-effective. In this framework though infrastructure protection and infrastructure resilience represent complementary elements of a comprehensive risk management strategy, the two concepts are distinct but both need to be considered. Infrastructure protection is the ability to prevent or reduce the effect of an adverse event. Infrastructure resilience is the ability to reduce the magnitude, impact, or duration of a disruption. The spread in the continuous discovery of new threats that target Critical Infrastructures, stress the importance of a whole re-thinking around the concept of protection. That's where resilience emerges from and becomes important part of the playing field. A resilient approach is a holistic set of procedures and measures that encompasses the entire structure of an institution, from physical parts to the management, to ensure the ability to prevent, absorb, adapt, and recover to an attack, either physical or cyber. We need to have in mind without confusing the concepts of resilience, security, business continuity and risk management, crisis and emergency. Research efforts about intrusion detection have been conducted since the beginning of the 1980s, when Anderson published his seminal work about network security monitoring, here below (Figure 2.3) are listed the main cybersecurity breach that show how these are constantly growing in all sectors.

There are several motivations behind a cyberattack that could be interested in a port. The impact of a cyberattacks could have on society has become clear in recent years and is going to

Sector											
Defence	Drone video feed interception in Iraq (2009)										
Transport	Worcester Airport (1997)	Port oh Houston DoS (2001)	CSX, Washington (2003)	Railcorp, Sydney (2004)	L.A. Traffic engineers' Strike (2007)	Lodz Trams (2008)	Port Of Antwerp (2011 and 2013)	Tesla Hijacking competition (2014)	San Francisco Public Transport (2015) Sweden Airports (2015) Port of LA (2015)	Uber (2016) Port of Rotterdam (2016)	Maersk (2017) JNPT (2017)
Health	Epilepsy website(2007)	Arlington clinic (Hvac)	UK (2017)								
Water	Salt River Project (1994)	Ariichy (2000)	Harrisburg Water filtering plant (2006)	Sacramento River (2007)	South Huston Water Treatment Facility (2011)						
Energy	Hatch Nuclear Plant (2008)	Stuxnet (2009)	Aramco (2011)	Texas Energy Grid (2011)	Ukraine – Black Energy (2015)						

Figure 2.3 Historical cyberattacks until 2017.

increase in terms of damage and frequency. The unlimited scalability of these attacks shows how cyber criminals, states and corporations are "investing" on the cybersecurity in offensive and defensive side. In terms of actors, we can identify, in a simplified way, the following categories: Cyber Criminal, States, Terrorist, and Hacktivist.

The Cyber criminals. The development of new methods by criminals is manifesting itself in, among other things, exploring the lucrative revenue models of ransomware. In addition to un-targeted attacks, criminals are employing ransomware more frequently to target organizations where the impact is significant and who will be more inclined to pay a higher amount of ransom. This year the trend of these targeted attacks manifested itself worldwide, particularly at schools, hospitals, and other health institutions. Attacks by criminals are also having an even greater impact on everyday life because processes or services can be (unintentionally) disrupted. Examples include the ransomware attack that affected the payment system on San Francisco's public transport and the attack on the systems in an Austrian hotel which prevented the key passes from working.

States. In recent years, more and more countries have acquired the capability to gather intelligence from the digital domain. It is a relatively inexpensive method; it is quick and has fewer risks than traditional espionage because its use can be denied. Over the last year, Dutch government agencies were repeatedly the victim of large-scale and persistent digital espionage attacks by other countries, including the countries not previously identified as a threat to Dutch government networks. More than 100 countries currently have the capacity for digital espionage and their professionalism is growing, as is the threat it poses. This growing digital espionage threat is aimed at both public and private parties and comes from

(Continued)

countries that want to position themselves more favorably in the world both politically and economically. It is primarily used by intelligence and security services.

Terrorists Jihadists. They are primarily responsible for the present-day terrorist threat. In the reporting period, manifestations on the digital front were mainly by ISIS and ISIS sympathizers. According to experts' estimates, jihadists—and terrorists in a broader sense—are not yet capable of mounting sophisticated, complex attacks. Their power to strike and recruiting potential may increase now that a number of hackers and hacker groups have united in the United Cyber Caliphate. They are calling for hackers to join them. In addition, jihadists are gaining experience with simple cyberattacks. It is a matter of concern that many products and services for cyberattacks are being sold through various forums. This could reduce the threshold for cyberattacks by jihadists. In any case, ISIS certainly has less money compared to previous years, which makes the financial opportunities to purchase the most sophisticated products and services less credible.

Hacktivists. Cyber vandals and script kiddies Hacktivists carry out digital attacks for ideological or activism reasons. Cyber vandals and script kiddies carry out cyberattacks as pranks, as a challenge, or to demonstrate their own capabilities. Both their motives and their skill levels can vary widely. For example, in March 2017, the rising diplomatic tension with Turkey was the reason various people mounted (small-scale) digital attacks for activism or nationalist reasons.

The costs and benefits of cybersecurity do not always lie with the same party: exploitation of vulnerabilities can lead to damage to parties other than the users of device. In this framework, the next global issue will be to provide safe and secure IoTs that show how things can go wrong if do not considered correctly. Many devices contain vulnerabilities since their entrance in the market for which security updates are not published. Recently, millions of devices were exploited to conduct large-scale distributed denial of service (DDoS) (MIRAI Botnet) attacks a number of times using botnets, which resulted in major disruptions showing how criminals or states can carry out attacks. The outbreak of Mirai and find the botnet infected nearly 65,000 IoT devices in its first 20 h before reaching a steady-state population of 200,000–300,000 infections. These bots fell into a narrow band of geographic regions and autonomous systems, with Brazil, Columbia, and Vietnam disproportionately accounting for 41.5% of infections. The table below provides insight into the threats that various actors have posed over the period from May 2016 to April 2017 to the target governments, private organizations, and citizens elaborated by the Netherlands government (Figure 2.4).

Within the DDoS attack another growing threat is related to the RANSOMWARE, that unlike the traditional malware, an IoT attack could be more extreme than others. From 2005 to March 2016, approximately 7,600 ransomware attacks were reported by Internet Crime Compliant Center (IC3). The literature review shows that early attacks were not immensely dangerous because of less connectivity of computers and difficulties in collection of ransom money from users. However, current technology trends such as gigantic growth of IoT devices, connectivity of devices and users, exposure of user's personal data through social media, and the prevalence of cryptocurrencies have enabled hackers to easily infiltrate devices and collect ransom money from device owners (Table 2.1).

In Figure 2.5, it is described the taxonomy of IoT security based in various parameters providing the threats, requirements, IEEE Standards, deployment levels and technologies. From this taxonomy, it is clearly shown how the IoT and cyber threats are something that cannot be considered as an issue solved.

Source of threat	Gov	Private Org	Citizens
Professional Criminals	Disruption of IT	Disruption of IT	Disruption of IT
	Manipulation of Information	Manipulation of Information	Manipulation of Information
	Theft and publication or selling of information	Theft and publication or selling of information	Theft and publication or selling of information
	It takeover	It takeover	It takeover
State Actors	Digital espionage	Digital espionage	Digital espionage
	Offensive cyber capabilities	Offensive cyber capabilities	Offensive cyber capabilities
	Theft and publication of information	Theft and publication of information	Theft and publication of information
Terrorist	Disruption/Takeover of IT	Disruption/Takeover of IT	
Cyber vandals and script kiddies	Theft of information	Theft of information	
	Disruption of IT	Disruption of IT	
Hacktivists	Theft and publication of obtained information		
	Defacement	Defacement	
	Disruption of IT	Disruption of IT	
Internal Actors	Theft and publication or selling of obtained information	Theft and publication or selling of obtained information	
	Disruption of IT	Disruption of IT	
Private Organizations		Information theft (industrial espionage)	Commercial use/abuse or 'resale' of information
No Actor	IT Failure	IT Failure	IT Failure

Figure 2.4 Threat Matrix.

Source: Ministry of Security and Justice, Netherlands 2017.

Table 2.1 Popular Ransomware Attacks

Ransomware	Year	Type	Target Devices and Systems
AIDS Trojan	1989	Locker	Floppy Disk
Archievus	2005	Crypto	Computers
Gpcode.AK	2008	Crypto	Computers, OS
Unnamed Trojan	2011	Locker	Computers, Mobile Devices
Reveton	2012	Social Engineering	Computers, Mobile Devices

(Continued)

Table 2.1 (*Continued*)   Popular Ransomware Attacks

Ransomware	Year	Type	Target Devices and Systems
CryptoLocker	2013	Crypto	Computers
CryptoDefence	2014	Crypto	Android Mobile Devices, Wearable Devices
CryptoWall	2014	Crypto	Computers
Sypeng	2014	Social Engineering	Android Mobile Devices
Koler	2014	Locker	Android Mobile Devices
CTB-Locker	2014	Hybrid	Computers
SimplLocker	2014	Crypto	Mobile Devices
LockerPin	2015	Locker	Mobile Devices
TeslaCrypt	2015	Crypto	Data Encryption on Disk
Chimera	2015	Malvertsement	Data Encryption on Disk
LowLevel04	2015	Crypto	Remote Desktop Computers
7ev3n	2016	Crypto	Data Encryption on Disk
Ransomware32	2016	Locker	Computers
SamSam (SAMAS)	2016	Crypto	Computers
Locky	2016	Downloader	Computers
Petya	2016	Locker	Windows computers
KeRanger	2016	Crypto	Mac computers
Jigsaw	2016	Crypto	Data Encryption on Disk
Maktub	2016	Crypto	Data Encryption on Disk
Cryptxxx	2016	Crypto	Windows OS
PowerWare	2016	Locker	Windows OS
ZCryptor	2016	Crypto	Data Encryption on Disk
GoldenEye	2016	Locker	Windows OS
zCrypt	2016	Crypto	Data Encryption on Disk
WannaCry/ WannaDecryptor	2017	Criptoware	Data Encryption on Disk

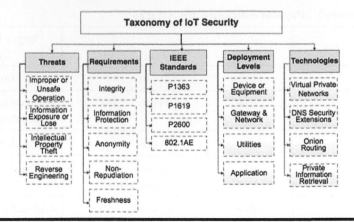

Figure 2.5   Taxonomy of IoT Security.

Source: The rise of ransomware and emerging security challenges in the IoTs—Sep 2017—Computer Networks.

2.4 Cyber Risks within the Ports

Incidents such as the recent increase in illegal migrants entering Europe through the Mediterranean coastal areas as well as smuggling of illicit goods requires increased protection of the Critical Infrastructure such as port operations. Software systems that support Critical Infrastructure operations are becoming more and more attractive to outside cyberattacks from cyber-criminal interested in wreaking havoc in cyber environments. Not only sensitive data needs to be protected from any malicious intentions, but if the overall control that these software systems have on the operational aspects in Critical Infrastructure is harmed then negative results with high risk, impact and visibility can arise. Innovative physical and cybersecurity mechanisms have to be created in order to be able to prevent and respond to all potential threats in these Critical Infrastructures. Transportation is a key economic sector, facilitating the movement of people, food, water, medicines, fuel, etc. Port Authorities play an important role in the international trade and economy environment. Transportation infrastructures face multiple threats, ranging from physical disasters, sabotage, insider threats, terrorist attacks, etc. The increasing need for protecting transport infrastructures is recognized by most countries; the transportation sector is among the sectors recognized as critical. Ports and the maritime industry compete as part of entire supply chains. After 2009 crisis, to strengthen their position, a great number of top container shipping companies are integrating vertically with port terminals, hinterland logistic operators, and shipping agencies. More concentrated volumes of cargo, as well as the need to remain competitive versus other modes of transport, also necessitate speedier execution of formalities and better coordination of logistic operations. Digitalization is considered to be crucial in simplifying administrative processes, enabling efficient management of freight flows through exchange of information on cargo, infrastructure, and equipment. Increased pressure on environmental resources has already required corrective action to contribute to the "greening" of shipping. Though infrastructure protection and infrastructure resilience represent complementary elements of a comprehensive risk management strategy, the two concepts are distinct but need to be considered both. The spread in the continuous discovery of new threats that target Critical Infrastructures, stress the importance of a whole rethinking around the concept of protection. That's where resilience emerges from and becomes important part of the playing field. A resilient approach is a holistic set of procedures and measures that encompasses the entire structure of an institution, from physical parts to the management, to ensure the ability to prevent, absorb, adapt, and recover from an attack, either physical or cyber. We need to have in mind without confusing the concepts of resilience, security, business continuity and risk management, crisis and emergency. Concerning the maritime cyberattacks, they are not too much, at least declared due to reputational damage or because they still do not know to be attacked. The known cyberattacks are the following: the Port of Antwerp where drugs were hidden in containers and these containers were misled without early recognition; the Port of Rotterdam in 2016 where the customs systems were shut down, stopping operations for hours, probably to extort ransom; disruption of the GPS signal stopped operations of vessels as well as of terminal cranes that store and locate containers basing on GPS for the same reason; piracy attacks use Artificial Immune System (AIS) signals to identify vessels and hack into the shipping companies' systems to identify their loaded goods. Global ransomware campaign known as "WannaCry" and detected on May 12, 2017, affected various organizations with tens of thousands of infections in over 150 countries after the "WannaCry" attack, on June 27, 2017, further threats were launched, using among other attack vectors the same exploit as "WannaCry." It exploited vulnerability in a Ukrainian tax preparation software update mechanism to propagate and attack entire networks. Besides several Ukrainian ministries, banks, and metro systems, large companies became also victims of the attack. Merck Sharp & Dohme and India's largest container terminal JNPT were affected and, as a consequence, had to deal with business interruptions. The malware's attack path leading from a Ukrainian software update to several international company networks shows how malware can propagate among the connected systems in supply chains.

2.4.1 Cyber Ports: Risk and Opportunities

Since 2009, initiatives were undertaken to establish a true "European maritime transport space without barriers," removing unnecessary administrative obstacles to maritime transport, developing into the Union a Maritime Information and Exchange system (Safe Sea Net), simplifying formalities for regular shipping services (Blue Belt), investing in the port sector and in the connection between ports and hinterland (Trans-European Network Transport projects), last but not least a revisited concept of (Hybrid) Port could improve the economic process of the Mediterranean Area, with the support of Digital Tools, that is, a target of UE Strategy (ports 2030). The ocean and short shipping ports constitute part of the European Critical Infrastructure, as indicated in the Directive 114/2008, and concurrently critical part of the supply chains and transport routes, transferring goods and passengers (Figure 2.6).

The Maritime Sector sustains the society and the economy through the movement of people and vital goods, such as energy, food, etc. The ports have a direct impact on connectivity across Europe, enabling the connection of islands and isolated areas, while significant proportion of economic activities are occurred in the ports, mainly through the transfer of goods. Currently, the European ports serve around 3,733 million tons of freight flows and 397,506,000 passengers per year (data for year 2012, available by Eurostat). Moreover, 74% of goods entering or leaving Europe go by sea, and Europe boasts some of the finest port facilities in the world while around 90% of European Union (EU) external trade and more than 43% of the internal trade takes place via maritime routes while the gross weight of sea-borne goods handled in EU reached in 2014. A part from the above, the ports are significant for the economy in terms of employment, as 1.5 million workers employed in European ports, while the number of indirect employed work is almost equal. According to Review of Maritime Transport 2015 during the past decades, world

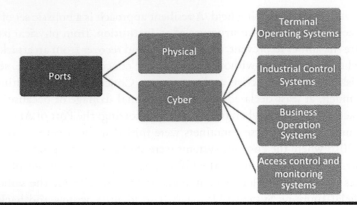

Figure 2.6 Port cyber needs.

container traffic grew substantially, reflecting the expansion of world trade and rapid economic growth in the developing world and further increase in wealth worldwide. Accordingly, preliminary UNCTAD estimates indicate that global seaborne shipments have increased by 3.4% in 2014, which is equal to the same rate as in 2013. This performance unfolded in the context of a number of developments, including a slowdown in large emerging developing economies, lower oil price levels and new refinery capacity developments, and a slow-moving and uneven recovery in the advanced economies. Finally, the maritime transport has a positive impact on the environment, owing to the reduced amount of GHG emissions per ton or passenger transferred.

Figure 2.7 underlines the critical and vital role of maritime transport and consequently ports in the society and economy of EU showing how and why a port is a complex cyber environment that encompasses both land, waterside, and economic activities and interdependencies. The enhancement of security, both physical and cyber, at ports is essential in order to ensure the smooth operation, serving the passenger and freight flows. On the other side, the ports are considered as vulnerable infrastructure mainly due to their proximity to the sea and the problems faced in controlling the threats coming through it, the number of operations taking place in the ports and their

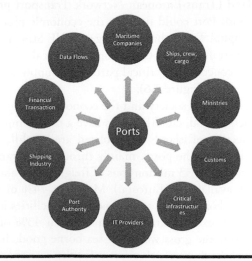

Figure 2.7 Ports interdependencies.

different nature and the considerable number of people working or involved in several operations in the ports. Internationally, the relevant legislation on port security is the ISPS Code (International Ship and Port Facility Security Code), implemented at EU level by the EU/725/2004 and the EU/65/2005, which requires the identification of authority, acts skills, and objectives to establish and maintain security measures. In this context, it takes the definition of a Port Security Plan, drawn up by the Port Security Officer (PSO), which takes into account the analysis of the risks of ships and the port facility. Also, it identifies the port facility responsibilities and tasks of the Port Facility Security Officer (PFSO). It is also important to note that many European ports are to all parts of the city and therefore the effects of splitting the areas under Security checks presents greater complexity. A port's role in EU policy and strategy has been defined by several regulations, from the white book to new TEN-T and CEF papers, which integrate 2020 European Strategy, to promote a smarter, sustainable, inclusive growth. In all these views, ports are the center of economic development of a country. In fact, port activities affect all the following steps in supply chain, industrial activity, and manufacturing. The TEN-T programme and corridor WorkPlan (art.47), UE 1316/2013, Connection European Facilities,—Mediterranean Transport Action Plan (2014–2020). Nowadays, implemented security solutions within the port areas aim to achieve the desired security levels through the implementation of a network of active sensors (high-resolution cameras, IR barriers, biometric fingerprint reader, microphone cable, etc.), functional subsystems (vehicular video, license plate reading and container codes units, video over IP, turnstiles, automatic barriers, metal detectors, baggage scanners, radar, etc.), and passive protection systems (metal fences, etc.) for control and protection of the different port area (perimeter) gates of vehicular/pedestrian access, cruise terminals, parking lots, docks, electrical substations, etc. Although the above security network seems well structured, the use of modern technology is not enough.

With regard to the ENISA report on cybersecurity challenges in the Maritime Sector seems evident that cyber threats are a growing menace, spreading to all industry sectors that are relying on ICT systems. Such incidents could be prevented by policies that neutralize the various market failures acting as a barrier to optimize private investment in cybersecurity from public and private institutions. The cost of breach may not entirely be on the immediate victim. Many computer systems store valuable information about entities other than the system's owner. From a legislation point of view in starting from 2018, payments service provider will have to comply with the new payments services directive (PSD2) which mandates very high standards of cybersecurity for all digital payments where central banks or other regulators can also impose obligations. Something similar will be done in the framework of the NIS Directive that will cover also the Critical Infrastructure (Table 2.2). Cyberattack to maritime transports are an issue already consolidated: infiltrating a port's computers, or transmitting fake GPS signals to alter ship's route, altering a ship's automatic identification system signal to misreport it location, accessing electronic chart display and information systems software to modify maps, as well as pirates listening into AIS transmissions to locate potential victims. Recent deliberate disruptions of critical automation systems, such as Stuxnet, prove that cyberattacks have a significant impact on Critical Infrastructures. Disruption of these ICT capabilities may have disastrous consequences for the EU Member States' governments and social well-being. The need to ensure ICT robustness against cyberattacks is thus a key challenge at national and pan-European level. Some key findings of the report emphasized that Maritime cybersecurity awareness is currently low and a holistic, risk-based approach coupled with an assessment of maritime specific cyber risks, as well as identification of all critical assets within this sector is highly necessary. An answer is represented by the holistic security: physical and cybersecurity of the network to guarantee Privacy Integration Protocols of the users. There are so many initiatives that

Table 2.2   Regulations Overview

EU Regulations	International Regulations	US Regulations
CIIP directive (2012)	ISO 27001	USA H.R. 3878(2015)
The cybersecurity strategy for the EU (2013)	ISO 27005:2008	NIST 800-30
EIDAS Regulations (2014)	ISO 27005:2005	Port security grant program (2014)
European Agenda on security (2015)	IMO — ISPS and Circular 1526 (2016)	Maritime & Port Security Information Sharing and Analysis Organization (MPS-ISAO, 2017)
CPPP Initiative (2015)		Presidential policy directive 21 (PPD-21)
NIS Directive (2016)		
EU Cybersecurity Strategy		

come in response to recent computer hacks that enabled containers to be abstracted from the port in an apparently legal manner. For instance, MSC introduced a new Container Release System that enables containers to be collected from the port in a more secure manner. Users have to log into a secure portal site where they must identify themselves in order to gain access to the container release data. This technology has now been made available port wide, thanks to APCS. Furthermore, the Port of LA took a significant step toward reducing its cyber risks with the implementation of a state-of-the-art CyberSecurity Operations Center (CSOC). The CSOC includes advanced hardware and software that is used to proactively monitor the computer environment to prevent a breach and be able to quickly detect and respond if a breach does occur. The CSOC is also the technical nerve center, which collects cybersecurity data that can be analyzed and shared with other agencies.

2.4.2 An Hybrid Port Proposal

Ports are known as physical space where trades meet the market needs. Ships are a visible and touchable instrument to transfer goods from an origin to a destination. All these actions now are managed by a system and/or OS. Nowadays, it is fundamental to take into account the next challenges, related to the connectivity and to capacity to provide solutions and (cyber)security to guarantee the economic flows and development. Ports and ships now require a multilevel intelligence and surveillance system, aimed at creating a comprehensive Port Hybrid Security System providing real-time, accurate physical and cyber situational awareness and early warning to port stakeholders, as well as decision-making in terms of threat and impact assessment and suggested response or mitigation actions. The HYBRID PORT concept is based upon a fusion of inputs from different types of front end (physical) sensory systems and cyber detection systems—legacy and new innovative—from different security sectors. Such threat events are detected through "bottom-up" integration of different types of real-time sensors and sub-systems for data collection in a variety of modes, including physical and cyber, and correlate each other to generate (1) hybrid threat prioritized alarm/s, (2) decisions sequence for the security operators. This "fusion" is based upon predefined threat scenarios as determined by the Port Security Operation Center (P-SOC), as a "top-down" approach. The hybrid port idea aims to ensure that the technological solution is composed of set of loosely coupled elements and things linked by a functional cohesion. Furthermore, together with the appropriate use of standards, hybrid port will facilitate the implementation in the industry and will provide a reference model for research activity within IoT paradigm and cybersecurity issues. In order to meet these aims the hybrid port idea adopts the architecture (Figure 2.8).

The Hybrid Port Common framework aims at providing a means (in terms of standards and system architecture) for interoperable service provisioning among cargo carries and ports across. In Europe two proposals for a relevant EU port services directive (PSD) failed to produce a new

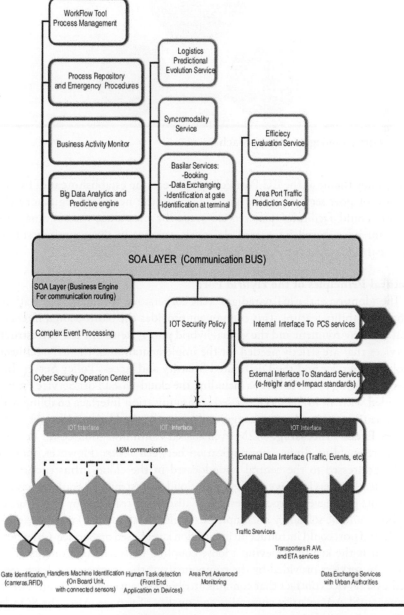

Figure 2.8 Hybrid port proposed structure.

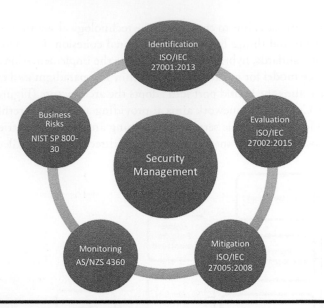

Figure 2.9 **Security management approach.**

policy regime, a key theme of the EU Port Policy has been the establishment of free market access to the provision of port services in EU ports. Leaving the necessary regulatory changes aside, the hybrid port could facilitate open service access by providing the roadmap and necessary infrastructure for ports-based integrated electronic services in the container supply chain and passengers, in particular, concerning the motorways of the sea (Figure 2.9).

Architectural Principles of the Hybrid Port
■ **IoTs:** The adoption of the IoT paradigm is the cornerstone of the communication architecture and interoperability feature. This component provides the bidirectional interaction between the real port environment and the virtual hybrid port system. The IoT infrastructure provides the services that are strictly needed for the implementation of the IoT architecture, namely a Resolution Service and the Distributed Security and Access Policy Server. In addition, all devices pertaining to the IoT, thus including the cloud-based Port Service Framework, could be provided with an IoT: a service-based communication interface enabling real-time M2M communication, secure data exchange, and remote-embedded service subscription support.
■ **Complex Event Processing:** M2M event-based communication could be implemented in hybrid port enabling direct communication between *things*. However, most of the events could be addressed to the central node located in the cloud infrastructure through "IoT Communication Service Layer." Then, the cloud infrastructure could receive a huge quantity of events that have to process, resend, or discard in real time by applying complex rules. This labor could be solved by a Complex Event Processing (CEP) component.
■ **SOA:** Hybrid port could introduce an integration layer based on Service-Oriented Architecture (SOA) that is the key to achieving a loose coupling between components. This layer could expose SOA services provided by the components of the architecture. Each service could be defined by a service contract that contains attributes as a well-defined interface, Service Level Agreements (SLAs), security constrains and quality of service. Also, the SOA layer provides common services to Things.

- **Cloud Computing:** Rather deploying the solution in a traditional data center, hybrid port could use cloud computing. During the project progress could be considered the cloud computing model more appropriately taking into consideration cost, security, and quality of service. It could also explore the possibility of mixing different models of cloud computing.
- Cloud computing and SOA are complementary. Cloud computing provides services related to computing while, in a reciprocal manner, service-oriented computing consists of the computing techniques that operate on software-as-a-service.

Business-Oriented Applications

- **Business Intelligence (BI):** In order to understand the behavior of port operations, it is needed to provide historical, current, and predictive view. The operations could be stored for later analysis. It could generate reports and dashboards to identify trends and relationships that could be useful in view of the decision-making.
- **Business Activity Monitoring (BAM):** Beyond BI, hybrid port could provide dashboards to present and analyze in real time the operations among the port by integration of a BAM solution. Furthermore, BAM enables to establish SLAs on real-time measurements and is focused to improve the speed and effectiveness of port operations.

Infrastructures

- **Cloud infrastructure:** The platform should consider a context where multiple port system instances are allowed. This means that the architecture infrastructure needs to provide the right support in terms of port system instance lifecycle management. In other words, use cases like adding new port system instance, managing scalability issues, managing data provisioning, addressing privacy and security issues, system efficiency, and SLA compliancy will be considered in the definition of Multi-Tenant versus Multi-Instance Cloud architecture.

Identity and access management: The number of Virtual Identities, which represent real objects belonging to a port system, is going to increase tremendously. This factor should be systematically managed by well-defined infrastructure. Also, because of the IoT's distributed nature, this theme needs an in-deep solution approach. Each port system instance will leverage a common infrastructure where security issues like "who am I" and "how am I allowed to do" are well-governed and where actor's intercommunication and interoperability are allowed in trusted security context. The hybrid port idea has incorporated the latest technologies, is scalable and empowered with the flexibility to expand and enrich the system by adding new sensors and applications according to specific requirements and future needs. In addition, each sensor can be activated independently and/or fused with other specific sensors to achieve the necessary output. The hybrid port should integrate with ease into the existing Port Front End (F/E) sensors and information systems. Under previous Port Security conditions (security plan schemes), the end user is overwhelmed with the magnitude of data needed to be filtered individually, step by step. The hybrid port, through its automatic selection and fusion of the input data, transforms the process into a user-friendly interface and presents only relevant alert information to the end user in a straightforward and clear manner. This enables an advanced, more accurate decision-making process in the face of the growing multitude of threats and dangers each port is faced with on a daily basis. The hybrid port divides the port security into "security control" sectors (Port Facilities & People, Land Borders & Gates, Last Mile Surface & Underwater, AIS & GNSS and Cyberspace). Each segment is monitored by tailored technologies, which are incorporated into the system creating a multisource labyrinth fusion logic, which enables situational and security awareness of the port anytime, anywhere. This mode is less effective in creating a comprehensive intelligence system compared to the "fused mode." The hybrid port approach brings the capability to integrate solutions already available in ports, yet stand-alone mode with further implementations these in-place technologies (mobile and fixed) and the new detection technologies and to merge their collected data into a central point where it will be analyzed together with data from other sources. Most physical processes within the port community (e.g., vehicles and cargo loading/unloading, LNG distribution, and storage) are executed with autonomous or semi-autonomous mechanical physical systems and machineries (e.g., ships, trucks, cranes, electronic gates/fences) under the control of sophisticated logistic software systems (e.g., Industrial Cyber-Physical Systems, SCADA, surveillance systems). Utility network categorization, threats taxonomy in industrial and utility communication infrastructures, comprises a diverse set of technologies and network topologies that cannot be effectively secured without having categorized the utility network components and technologies in respect of cyber threats and their impact in terms of service availability. A typical solution for the detection of attacks in a network environment consists of leveraging signature-based NIDS (Network Intrusion Detection System) technologies that aim at detecting attacks by recognizing specific patterns in network data streams. However, current signature-based technologies are not effective in Critical Infrastructure systems because there is often little information about system internals (let alone attack vectors). Hence, developing effective signatures is a difficult task. On the other hand, behavior-based NIDS technologies are not based on needing complete knowledge of all possible attack vectors. During a training phase, these techniques build a statistical model of the input that is then used in the detection phase to raise an alert when the input does not match the expected statistical profile. Using more than one technical or procedural protection measure could be recommended (Figure 2.10).

It is essential to protect critical systems and data with layers of protection measures which take into account the role of personnel, procedures, and technology to: increase the probability that a cyber-incident is detected; increase the effort and resources required to protect information, data or the availability of IT and OT systems. This defense in-depth approach encourages a combination of: physical security of the ship in accordance with the ship security plan; protection of networks, including effective segmentation; intrusion detection; software white listing; access and user controls; appropriate procedures regarding the use of the removable media and password policies; personnel's awareness of the risk and familiarity with appropriate procedures. The first step is start with a third-party risk assessments, targets to be considered are as follows: the communication systems; integrated communication systems; satellite communication equipment; VOIP equipment; WLANs, public address, and general alarm

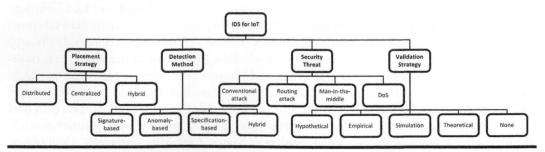

Figure 2.10 Taxonomy of IDSs for IoT.

systems; with reference to the bridge systems: the integrated navigation system; GPS; electronic chart display information system, dynamic positioning systems; global maritime distress and safety system, radar equipment; and voyage data recorders. Concerning the propulsory and machinery management and power control systems: engine governor; power management; integrated control system; alarm system; emergency response system; for the access control systems: surveillance system; bridge navigational each alarm system, shipboard security alarm systems; electronic personnel on board systems; Cargo management systems: cargo control room; level indication system; valve remote control system; ballast water; passenger servicing and management systems; ship passenger boarding access systems; infrastructure support systems like domain-naming system and user authentication/authorization systems. Passenger facing networks; passenger Wi-Fi, WLAN; guest entertainment systems; passenger Wi-Fi, core infrastructure systems; security gateways; routers; switches; firewalls, VPN, intrusion, or prevention systems; security event logging systems; administrative and crew welfare systems administrative systems; review of the onboard networks. It is important to clarify that a critical role is played by the SCADA systems that are part of several processes and operations (seaside and landside), when the vessel arrives at the port the vehicle that unload cargos from the ship is performed by a yard tractors and forklifts with their auxiliary equipment that are monitored by a SCADA system. This system as described at the beginning are the predecessor of IoT and works as automation system that is used to gather data from sensors and instruments located at remote points and to transmit them at the central unit for either control or monitoring purposes. These systems work following these approaches: Human-Machine Interface (HMI), Programming Logic Controllers (PLC), Remote Terminal Unit (RTU) (acting as microprocessors that connect physical equipment with the supervisory stations via WLAN and receive messages from the master station to control the interconnected objects), SCADA Master Terminal Unit (MTU), supervisory stations that are responsible for communicating between SCADA equipment such as RTUs, or PLCs and HMI that are controlled via sensors (wired or wireless). Different behavior-based NIDS technologies have been devised by researchers, mostly focusing on the modeling of network interactions. However, behavior-based detection systems have been rarely successfully applied to business solutions for a variety of reasons. First, such systems usually raise too many false positives to be of practical use. Second, most recent engines have been mainly tailored for and tested against the HTTP protocol. Thus, the effectiveness of current detection engines, when deployed in Critical Infrastructure networks, could be biased by the fact that a large part of protocols is binary-based, and it might be hard (or infeasible) to adapt the detection algorithm to a different lower layer protocol. AIS is a relatively new bio-inspired model, which is applied for solving various problems in the field of information security. The unique features of AIS encourage the researchers to employ these techniques in variety of applications and especially in Intrusion Detection Systems (IDSs). Originally created for applications in immune networks, the application of its ideas is mainly focused on anomaly detection in computer networks connected to Internet, exposed to many kinds of cyber-crimes. Over the years, it has become a fertile and wider research field. In particular, it is of great interest its application in isolated networks as those of Critical Infrastructures (communication and control systems), promoting active research on efficient IDSs. Some of the research is oriented to a specific kind of infrastructure, for example, modern and future electrical grid. The security management processes are fundamental to provide common criteria to be used as references. In order to provide a useful approach, we can follow five security levels in a port (Table 2.3).

Table 2.3   Security Level

Security Level	Description
ZERO	Port services with low business impact. Disruption of such services has neither impact on security or privacy or business, while there are no critical dependencies to other services.
ONE	Port services with low to medium business impact oriented to facilitate users from the maritime environment with their transactions. Disruption of such services has no impact on security or privacy, while there are no critical dependencies to other services.
TWO	Port-services with low to medium businesses impact oriented to facilitate users from the maritime environment with their transactions. Disruption of such services has a mere impact on security or privacy, while critical dependencies to other services are possible.
THREE	Port services with medium business impact provided to maritime entities by automating traditional business process, rendering them as the main transaction channel with government for a service whose disruption would have a crucial impact on either security or privacy or with critical dependencies to other services.
FOUR	Port services provided to maritime entities with medium to high business impact by automating traditional maritime processes, rendering them as the main transaction channel for a service whose disruption would have a crucial impact on security and/or privacy issues and/or with critical dependencies to other services and maritime entities.
FIVE	Port services with high business impact provided to maritime entities, by automating traditional maritime, business, and governmental processes, rendering them as the main transaction channel for a particular service whose disruption would have a crucial impact on security and/or privacy issues and/or with critical dependencies to other maritime entities and especially other Cis.

2.5 Conclusion

Cybersecurity is becoming a vital concern for the functioning of a modern economy and as a fundamental shift in the relations between physical and cyber it is inevitable. The rising cost of cybersecurity damages reflects a failure of the security field to offer a solution that is both simple enough to warrant adoption by industry and government, and secure enough to protect our most valuable assets and data. Merely increasing spending without changing the way we think about modern security is insufficient. The existing tools: firewall, virtual private networks, and passwords all assume that the edge of the network is the network perimeter. This makes it too easy for non-authenticated user to probe and hack systems. Cybersecurity is now one of the most complex threats faced by the maritime industry and its Critical Infrastructure. Ports and terminals are under attack from cyber criminals, organized crime and terrorist groups looking to disrupt national infrastructure and hostile governments. There is an urgent need for improvement understanding of microeconomic mechanism in the cybersecurity market and for reliable data upon which policy design can be based: this with particular reference to transportation sector, where the goal of securitization can only be reached by a strong and continuous cooperation between public and private sector. Ports are continuously improving their security aspects and approaching the cyber programs. Working in cyberspace requires immediate actions and capacity to be able to adapt and respond quickly to cyber threats. Every single day, cybersecurity software proves unsuccessful in stopping attacks. Malware, malicious users, and targeted attacks create massive risk. For industry, government, and consumers to realize cybersecurity success, they must begin with a foundation built on trusted hardware execution.

Key Terminology and Definitions

Critical Infrastructure: Critical Infrastructure is an asset or system which is essential for the maintenance of vital societal functions. The damage to a Critical Infrastructure, its destruction or disruption by natural disasters, terrorism, criminal activity, or malicious behavior, may have a significant negative impact for the security and the well-being of its citizens.

Cybersecurity: The state of being protected against the criminal or unauthorized use of electronic data, or the measures taken to achieve this.

IOT: The IoTs enable objects sharing information with other objects/members in the network, recognizing events and changes so to react autonomously in an appropriate manner. The IoT, therefore, builds on communication between things (machines, buildings, cars, animals, etc.) that leads to action and value creation.

Phygital: Nowadays physical and digital are always more linked and connected. In near future, these two conditions will be merged in one concept becoming Phygital.

SCADA: SCADA Supervisory Control and data Acquisition systems are a set of Software and hardware used generally in the control and monitoring of geographically dispersed assets and process (Ex: Gas Distribution) where the centralization of data acquisition and control are critical to System Operation.

Bibliography

Alomari E., Manickam S., Gupta B.B., Karuppayah S., Alfaris R. (2012) Botnet-based distributed denial of service (DDoS) attacks on web servers: Classification and art. *International Journal of Computer Applications.* 49(7), 10.5120/7640-0724.

Alsmirat M.A., Jararweh Y., Obaidat I., Gupta B.B. (2017) Internet of surveillance: A cloud supported large-scale wireless surveillance system. *The Journal of Supercomputing* 73(3): 973–992.

Anderson J.P. (1980) *Computer Security Threat Monitoring and Surveillance*, Tech. rep., Technical report, James P. Anderson Company, Fort Washington, PA.

Bou-Harb E., Kaisar E., Austin M. (2017) *On the Impact of Empirical Attack Models Targeting Marine Transportation.* Conference Paper July 2017, doi:10.1109/MTITS.2017.8005665, *5th IEEE International Conference on MODELS AND TECHNOLOGIES FOR INTELLIGENT TRANSPORTATION SYSTEMS.*

Brunner E.M., Suter M. (2008) *International CIIP handbook 2008/2009.* Center for Security Studies, ETH Zurich, Zurich, Switzerland.

Brunner E.M., Suter M. (2008) Australia. Eds. A. Wenger, V. Mauer and M. D. Cavelty. *In International CIIP Handbook.* Center for Security Studies, ETH Zurich, Zurich, Switzerland.

Chiappetta A., Cuozzo G. (2017) Critical infrastructure protection: Beyond the hybrid port and airport firmware; security; cybersecurity applications on transport. *IEEE 2017-5th IEEE International Conference on MODELS AND TECHNOLOGIES FOR INTELLIGENT TRANSPORTATION SYSTEMS* doi:10.1109/MTITS.2017.8005666.

Directive (EU) 2016/1148 of the European parliament and of the council of 6 July 2016 concerning measures for a high common level of security of network and information systems across the Union ["NIS Directive"], Brussels, July 2016.

Ducruet C, Notteboom T. (2012) The worldwide maritime network of container shipping: Spatial structure and regional dynamics. *Journal Global Networks* 12(3): 395–423.

European Commission (2005) COM 576 final, Green paper on a European Programme for critical infrastructure protection, Brussels, 17 Nov 2005.

European Council (2008) Council Directive 2008/114/EC of 8 December 2008 on the identification and designation of European critical infrastructures and the assessment of the need to improve their protection (Text with EEA relevance), Brussels, Dec 2008.

European Commission (2013) Staff Working Document on a new approach to the European Programme for Critical Infrastructure Protection Making European Critical Infrastructures more secure, Brussels, 28 Aug 2013, SWD (2013) 318 final.

Fuchs P., Kraus J. (2016) Resilience parameters for critical infrastructure protection. *Proceedings of 20th International Scientific Conference*. Transport Means.

Giannopoulos G., Filippini R., Schimmer M. (2012) *Risk Assessment Methodologies for Critical Infrastructure Protection. Part I: State of the Art*. Office of the European Union, Luxembourg.

Gupta B., Agrawal D.P., Yamaguchi S. (2016) *Handbook of Research on Modern Cryptographic Solutions for Computer and Cyber Security*. IGI Global, Hershey, PA.

Hosseinpour F., Bakar K.A., Hardoroudi A.H., Dareshur A.F. (2010) Design of a new distributed model for intrusion detection system based on artificial immune system. *Advanced Information Management and Service (IMS), 2010 6th International Conference on*. pp. 378–383.

Ibtihal M., Driss E.O., Hassan N. (2017) Homomorphic encryption as a service for outsourced images in mobile cloud computing environment. *International Journal of Cloud Applications and Computing (IJCAC)* 7(2): 27–40.

Michel D. (2017) United States Coast Guard—Dep. Of Homeland Security—2017-Cyber Risks in the Marine Transportation System The U.S. Coast Guard Approach, U.S. Coast Guard Rear Admiral Paul F. Thomas, U.S. Coast Guard Captain Andrew E. Tucci, U.S. Coast Guard.

Moteff J.D. (2014) *Critical Infrastructures: Background, Policy, and Implementation*. Congressional research report for congress, RL30153. Congressional Research Service, Washington, DC.

Pishva, D. (2017) "Internet of Things: Security and privacy issues and possible solution" *Advanced Communication Technology (ICACT), 2017 19th International Conference on*. IEEE.

Rinaldi S.M., Peerenboom J.P., Kelly T.K. (2001). Identifying, understanding, and analyzing critical infrastructure interdependencies. *IEEE Control Systems Magazine*, pp. 11–25.

Schauer S., Stamer M., Bosse C., Pavlidis M., Mouratidis H., König S., Papastergiou S. (2017) An adaptive supply chain cyber risk management methodology, *In Digitalization in Supply Chain Management and Logistics. Proceedings of the Hamburg International Conference of Logistics (HICL); Hamburg International Conference of Logistics (HICL)*, 2017 ISBN 9783745043280.

Stergiou C., Psannis K.E., Kim B.G., Gupta B. (2018) Secure integration of IoT and cloud computing. *Future Generation Computer Systems* 78: 964–975.

Svendsen N.K., Wolthusen S.D. (2012) Modelling approaches. Eds. J. Lopez, R. Setola, and S.D. Wolthusen, *Critical Infrastructure Protection, Information Infrastructure Models, Analysis, and Defense*, pp. 68–97. Berlin: Springer.

Tsamboulas D., Chiappetta A., Moraiti P., Karousos I. (2015) Could subsidies for maritime freight transportation achieve social and environmental benefits? *The Case of Ecobonus*, 2015 TRB doi:10.3141/2479-10.

White House (1998) The Clinton's administration's policy on critical infrastructure protection: Presidential decision directive 63/PDD-63, White paper, 22 May 1998.

Yaqoob, I., Ahmed, E., ur Rehman, M. H., Ahmed, A. I. A., Al-Garadi, M. A., Imran, M., and Guizani, M. (2017) The rise of ransomware and emerging security challenges in the Internet of Things. *Computer Networks* 129(P2), 444–458.

Zhang, Z., Sun, R., Zhao, C., Wang, J., Chang C.K., Gupta B.B. (2017) CyVOD: A novel trinity multimedia social network scheme. *Multimedia Tools and Applications* 76(18): 18513–18529.

Chapter 3

Forecasting Problems in Cybersecurity: Applying Econometric Techniques to Measure IT Risk

Baidyanath Biswas
International Management Institute Kolkata

Sukanya Patra
Government College of Engineering and Leather Technology Kolkata

Contents

3.1 Introduction

Every software product created by an IT vendor is prone to vulnerabilities that reside in its software codes and programs. Attackers can exploit these weaknesses and inflict severe financial, reputation, and social damage to the users of the concerned software products. Telang and Wattal (2007) show that firms suffer billions of dollars in losses due to computer security breaches arising from vulnerabilities. One can imagine how destructive breaches can be if these software vulnerabilities are announced in public. Organizations frequently report that C-I-A (confidentiality, integrity, and availability) in their IT systems were compromised through cyber-attacks (Alomari et al. 2012, Arora et al. 2010, Dickey and Fuller1981, Ljung and Box 1978, Makridakis et al. 2008, Osanaiye et al. 2016, Patrikakis et al. 2004, Rahman et al. 2017, Sen and Borle 2015, Yu et al. 2017). According to the IBM-Ponemon 2017 study, average cost of breach amounted to $3.62 million per firm among 419 companies surveyed from 13 countries.[1] So, assessment of the criticality of vulnerabilities and planning mitigation strategies are crucial practices in an organization.

 As technology is advancing every day, physical inputs are being replaced by virtual ones, and entire IT applications are being virtualized. Cloud-based office productivity suites based on Software-as-a-Service (S-a-a-S) design are enabling faster business for organizations.[2] They include Google Docs, Google Sheets, Dropbox, Microsoft 365, and Adobe Online Office. Mobile apps are replacing daily activities such as shopping with Amazon, Flipkart; ticket booking in railways,

---

[1] Ponemon Institute 2017 Cost of Data Breach Study: Global Overview: https://www-01.ibm.com/common/ssi/cgi-bin/ssialias?htmlfid=SEL03130WWEN (accessed January 20, 2018).

[2] Laurence Goasduff "Widespread Adoption of Cloud Office Is Now Well Underway": https://www.gartner.com/smarterwithgartner/widespread-adoption-of-cloud-office-is-now-well-underway/ (accessed January 20, 2018).

airlines, and buses with IRCTC, MakeMyTrip; cab-booking with Uber, Ola; news; weather updates, reading books with Amazon Kindle; and controlling Internet-of-Things (IoT) with Amazon Alexa. However, mobile apps need a steady connection to the cloud via the Internet, to authenticate via usernames and passwords, and exchange sensitive information. Such environmental conditions give rise to tremendous dependency over the network availability and the Internet, thereby making the application layer of a Transmission Control Protocol/Internet Protocol (TCP/IP) configured network susceptible to vulnerabilities.[3] Based on their risk-rating metric, the Open Web Application Security Project (OWASP) reports the ten recent dangerous application threats—injection defects, broken authentication, exposure of sensitive information, XML error entities, improper access mechanisms, misconfiguration of security, XSS flaws, deserialization flaws, continuous use of software libraries, frameworks, and other modules with known vulnerabilities, and insufficient user monitoring and asynchronicity with the existing incident recording system.[4]

Security researchers propose different disclosure mechanisms based on the reward structure and concern for responsible disclosure (Ransbotham et al. 2012). For example, the HP Tipping Point Zero Day Initiative (ZDI)[5] promotes responsible reporting of software vulnerabilities. Further, the existing studies prove that publicly disclosed vulnerabilities are responsible for increased software attacks (Arora et al. 2006, Arora et al. 2008). The National Vulnerability Database (NVD) maintained by the U.S. Department of Homeland Security acts as a data store for publicly reported software vulnerabilities. Having said so, publicly reported vulnerabilities in NVD had increased radically from a cumulative 900 till 1999, to more than 90,000 at the time of this study.[6] Figure 3.1 illustrates the consolidated number of security vulnerabilities disclosed between 1999 and 2017 annually (source: www.cvedetails.com).

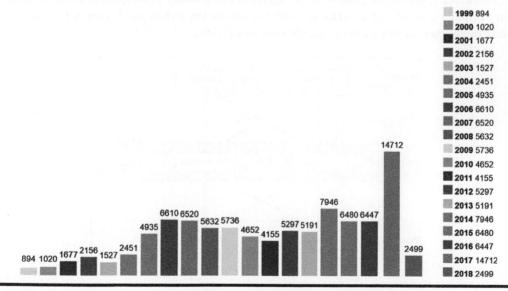

Figure 3.1 Overall disclosure of software vulnerabilities between 1999 and 2017.

---

[3] Andrew Hickey "Application layer DDoS attacks rising": https://www.csoonline.com/article/3222824/network-security/application-layer-ddos-attacks-rising.html (accessed January 20, 2018).
[4] The Ten Most Critical Web Application Security Risks: https://www.owasp.org/images/7/72/OWASP_Top_10–2017_%28en%29.pdf.pdf (accessed January 20, 2018).
[5] Tipping Point Zero Day Initiative: http://www.zerodayinitiative.com/
[6] National Vulnerability Database, Retrieved from: https://nvd.nist.gov/ (accessed January 20, 2018).

3.1.1 Importance of Vulnerability Disclosures to Businesses

According to Gartner Research, over 70% of attacks against a company's network come at the "Application Layer," not at the network or system layer. In other words, accurate prediction of the vulnerabilities of recognized categories becomes the most crucial aspect through timely access to information and news regarding the vulnerability discovery and announcement. Apart from incumbent software products such as Operating Systems (OSs), application software, and network software, cyber-attacks can impact a multitude of other systems. Igure et al. (2006) showed that industrial control systems are affected by supervisory control and data acquisition (SCADA) vulnerabilities. Again, due to increased usage of mobile devices and high adoption of Android mobile OSs, users face a higher number of privacy breaches and cyber-attacks. NVD reports that the number of Android vulnerabilities in the years 2015, 2016, and 2017 were 125, 523, and 842, respectively.[7] These figures show that top software vendors are severely affected in cyber-attacks due to the overall increased adoption of their products among both *white* and *black* users (Alhazmi et al. 2007, Ruohonen et al. 2015). So businesses need a robust and precise machine learning-based system to calculate predictions for publicly announced vulnerability exposures in future. Research in Information Security (InfoSec) has come a long way from simply installing security technologies to thwart perpetrators to systems. Figure 3.2 presents the classification of threats to information system threat, which consists of four distinct dimensions *internal*, *external*, *human*, and *nonhuman* sources. Recent industry surveys from IBM-Ponemon and Checkpoint advice that bots and DDoS attacks remain among the most challenging external threats to computer systems and networks. As a part of this study, we classify the extant literature into separate methodological dimensions. These reasons establish the relevance of our study in forecasting software vulnerability through a novel and accurate econometric estimation technique. Figure 3.2 presents the various dimensions of threats to information systems (Loch et al. 1992).

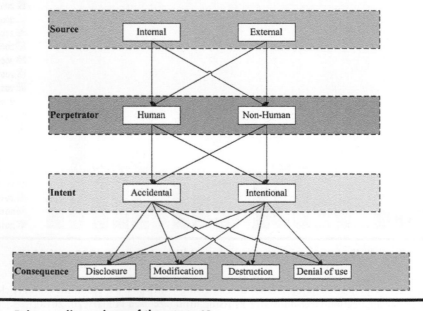

Figure 3.2   Primary dimensions of threats to IS.

---

[7] Symantec 2017 Internet Security Threat Report, Retrieved from: https://www.symantec.com/security-center/threat-report (accessed on January 20, 2018).

3.1.2 Importance of Econometric Analysis of Vulnerabilities

Econometric forecasting has long been used in financial and economic planning, to enable the organization with enough information to manage unexpected business changes and events. Econometric modeling is a quantitative forecasting technique and contributes to production planning, inventory stocking, control and optimization of inventory processes. Box and Jenkins (1970) defined time-series data as *a series of observations taken sequentially in time*. Econometric techniques can examine a time-series phenomenon with the primary objective of forecasting in the future period and so most econometric models are exploratory. In this study, we assume an ordered sequence of values at equally spaced time intervals. This underlying assumption enables us to consider econometric time-series models as a tool for vulnerability analysis.

3.1.3 Research Motivation: Vulnerability Discovery Models

Most of the current research in cybersecurity considers software vulnerabilities as a random variable and performs fitting and estimation exercises with the help of distributions. As a result, there is lack of clear understanding of the particular vulnerability discovery process, and it has led to specific forms of stochastic models only which can partially explain software vulnerability discovery (Amin et al. 2013). In a way, Vulnerability Discovery Models (VDMs) attempt to estimate and predict the count of future vulnerabilities that have been historically affecting a software application. Significant among them, Alhazmi and associates (Alhazmi and Malaiya 2005, Alhazmi et al. 2007, Alhazmi and Malaiya 2008) present several studies on VDMs. Alhazmi and Malaiya (2008) proposed VDMs for Microsoft and Red Hat Linux OS, Woo et al. (2006) analyze VDMs for Apache and IIS Web Servers. Models with time-dependent functionality with linear and nonlinear behavior are *thermodynamic* (Anderson 2002), *quadratic* (Rescorla 2005), *logistic* (Alhazmi et al. 2007), *Weibull* (Joh et al. 2008) and *sigmoidal* (Ruohonen et al. 2015). Another stream of contemporary studies in cybersecurity attempts to analyze the growth of data breach and attacks through statistical distributions—*Negative Binomial* (Sen and Borle 2015), *Gamma* (Johnson et al. 2016), *logistic* (Guo et al. 2016, Mitra and Ransbotham 2015). Often, a popular software product or platform is more alluring to attackers than other contemporary products in the market. Ruohonen et al. (2015) show the existence of distinct lifecycle phases of a software product deriving from the product lifecycle theory proposed by Bass (1969).

3.1.4 Contributions of This Chapter

In this study, we apply time-series modeling to vulnerability data obtained from operating systems, application software, and Internet browsers. Following are the contributions of this chapter:

i. Business enterprises will be able to successfully estimate and predict the count of vulnerabilities for the future period.
ii. Accurate implementation of the estimation measure will help to reduce reactive IT security spending of the firm significantly.
iii. A business organization always needs to minimize the risk of future software breaches and exploits of its IT systems. A proactive way of performing this activity involves the selection and use of software with standard functionality but the lowest vulnerability count among a set of available software products in the market.

    iv. We consider time-based approaches where time across which the vulnerabilities are recorded, is the independent variable.

    v. We also consider the contribution of the patched vulnerabilities which are closed and to continue with them throughout the entire empirical modeling is ineffective,

In the next section, we discuss and compare security issues in social networks, cloud computing, IoT, and web-based attacks. Next, we present the existing techniques of vulnerability estimation and discuss their limitations and shortcomings. In the subsequent section, we explore the vulnerability data and describe the Box–Jenkins Methodology for this study. In the next section, we apply different time-series techniques with Box–Jenkins methodology with Microsoft vulnerability data. In the subsequent section, we apply different exponential techniques to Microsoft vulnerability data. We take a real-life business scenario and apply econometric techniques to forecast software vulnerabilities. In the final section, we conclude the chapter with future research directions.

3.2 Literature Review

3.2.1 The Open System Interconnection (OSI) and Transmission Control Protocol/Internet Protocol (TCP/IP) Model

The Open System Interconnection (OSI) is a theoretical framework proposed in the ISO/IEC 7498-1 manual to define network components into seven distinct layers. Recently, the TCP/IP protocol has replaced OSI protocol in most networks and the Internet. Figure 3.3 compares the various layers in

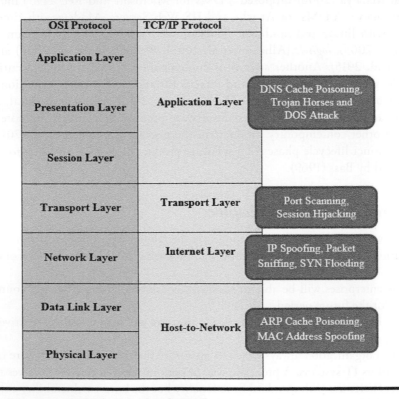

Figure 3.3 OSI versus TCP/IP and related attacks.

each of these frameworks and maps them layer by layer. Learning these models in depth can help IT managers to cope with attacks and subsequent defense of each layer after specific attacks.

3.2.1.1 Types of Attacks in the Application Layer

Most programs use application layer for network communication. For communication, the data is encapsulated in the application layer and then passed to the transport layer. Some common security attacks in application layer are Trojan Horses, DNS Cache Poisoning, and DoS Attack.

Trojan Horses: A Trojan horse is a malicious computer program which can hide its extension and appear as a regular file. It is then used to access the target computer illegally. Unlike worms or viruses, it cannot spread itself.

DNS Cache Poisoning: When browsing the Internet, a domain name system (DNS) server converts the given URL address to the corresponding IP address. In DNS Cache Poisoning or Spoofing, the cache information on the DNS server is compromised. It corrupts the data of the cache, and as a result, the DNS server returns incorrect IP addresses. In this way, attacker can divert legitimate traffic to its computer and acquire sensitive information.

DoS Attack: In Denial of Service (DoS) attack, the application layer is compromised. It is achieved by flooding targeted machine or resource with unnecessary traffic which makes impossible for the computer or resource to serve legitimate requests and so affects the availability metric of the server. Distributed DoS (DDoS) attack is a category of DoS outbreak where the malicious agent typically sends requests from thousands of IP addresses thus making it impossible to stop these type of attacks (Badve et al. 2016). According to Ginovsky (2014), DDoS attacks on application layer constitutes about 20% of all DDoS attacks.[8]

3.2.1.2 Types of Attacks in the Transport Layer

The Transport layer performs end-to-end data transmission along with error control, flow control, and fragmentation. Some alarming attacks on transport layer are Port Scanning and Session Hijacking.

Port Scanning: In this attack, the attacker transmits access requests to a particular series of IP addresses on the target machine to find active ports based on which he can get an idea of what services are running and also about the operating system installed on the device.

Session Hijacking: Session Hijacking, also known as Cookie Hijacking takes advantage of an established session to access the information or services of a computer illegally. Mostly, source-routed IP packets are used for session hijacking. The attacker intercepts the conversation between the client and server by influencing them to send the relevant IP packets through the attacker's machine.

3.2.1.3 Types of Attacks in the Internet Layer

The Internet layer determines the best path through the network. Most common attacks on the Internet layer are IP Spoofing, Packet Sniffing, and SYN Flooding.

---

[8] John Ginovsky (2014). "What you should know about worsening DDoS attacks". ABA Banking Journal (last accessed 28 January 2018)

IP Spoofing: In this attack, the attacker creates IP data packets marked with spurious origin IP addresses to hide his own identity. Sometimes the intruder can use an authorized IP address to break the IP address-based authentication to access information. It is used in executing DoS attacks.

Packet Sniffing: Packet Sniffing is a process of abducting packets which flow through the network. The attacker then analyzes the packets to get sensitive information. It is an attack on confidentiality service.

SYN Flooding: Packet sniffing is another category of DoS where the malicious agent transmits source IP address to flood the network with SYNs.

3.2.1.4 Types of Attacks in the Host-to-Network Layer

The Host-to-Network layer is responsible for transferring data between several network entities. Common security attacks on this layer are ARP Cache Poisoning and MAC Address Spoofing.

ARP Cache Poisoning: In this attack, the attacker sends ARP messages on the LAN to associate its MAC address with a legitimate user's IP address. An Address Resolution Protocol (ARP) is used to find the media access-control address corresponding to an IP. Through this attack, the attacker can abduct data, modify data or prevent regular data flow on the network. With the help of this DoS, Man-in-the-Middle attack or Session Hijacking can be done.

MAC Address Spoofing: MAC address is burnt on every Network Interface Card (NIC) to identify them uniquely in a network. In this attack, the attacker masks the MAC address of a NIC to change its identity. In this way, one machine can receive the data of another computer in a LAN.

3.2.1.5 C-I-A Triad and Related Vulnerabilities

The basic goal of network security is to maintain the C-I-A triad.

■ *Confidentiality:* When an attacker attempts to learn some information from a system, then it is an attack on confidentiality.

■ *Integrity:* When an attacker attempts to modify the system resources, then it is an attack on Integrity.

■ *Availability:* When it affects the operation of resources, then it is an attack on Availability such as DoS.

Security attacks are of four types as follows. In each of these types of attacks, there is a possibility that the attacker shall exploit vulnerability.

■ *Interruption:* In this attack, the attacker cuts the communication channel between the sender and receiver. Figure 3.4 illustrates the procedure of Interruption Attack.

■ *Interception:* It is an attack on confidentiality of an organization and attacker only learns information in this type of attack. Figure 3.5 illustrates the procedure of Interception Attack.

■ *Modification:* In this attack, the intruder accesses and modifies the data. It is an attack on the data integrity of an organization. Figure 3.6 illustrates the procedure of Modification Attack.

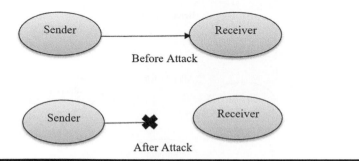

Figure 3.4   Illustration of interruption attack.

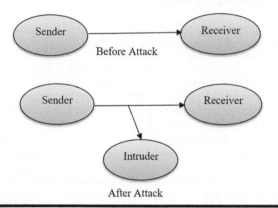

Figure 3.5   Illustration of interception attack.

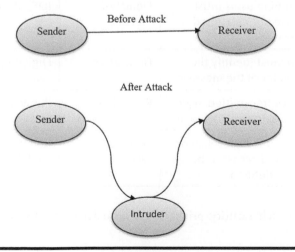

Figure 3.6   Illustration of modification attack.

- *Fabrication:* In this attack, the intruder sends fabricated personal information of the sender to receiver. It is an attack on the authentication level of an organization. Figure 3.7 illustrates the procedure of Fabrication Attack.

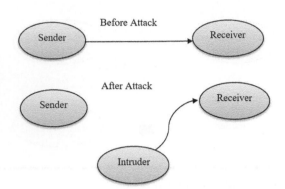

Figure 3.7   Illustration of fabrication attack.

Table 3.1   Major Principles of Cybersecurity and Their Details

Security Principle	Description	Concerned Attack	Resolution
Confidentiality	Apart from the intended recipient, no one else can access the secret message.	Interception	Apply symmetric key techniques—Data encryption standards, advanced encryption standards
Integrity	Alteration of the message contents is not allowed	Modification	Message digest techniques—secure hash, cryptographic hash.
Availability	Genuine users must have uninterrupted services	Denial-of-service	IDS, IPS for DoS
Authentication	On must identify the sender of the message.	Fabrication	Digital signatures, public key encryption
Non-repudiation	Once transmitted, user refusal cannot happen.	Refusal of transmission	Public key encryption
Access control	Role of the user(s) and related access to be well-defined.	Unauthorized access	Role based access • RACI

Table 3.1 summarizes each security principle and associated attacks and recovery techniques (Gupta et al. 2016).

3.2.2 Security Issues in Social Networks

Online social networks (OSNs) and associated social media are built upon the linkage between its active users by up-to-date Internet technology and mobile platforms. With exponential and explosive increase of social users, current (mobile) social media management tools and services, the

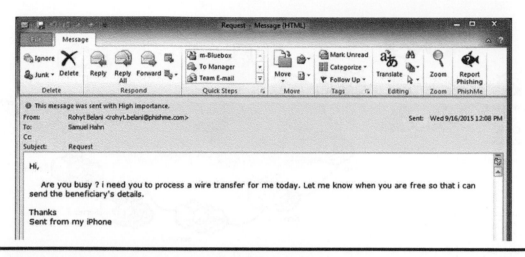

Figure 3.8　A typical CEO spam circulated through email.

Source: https://krebsonsecurity.com/2016/04/fbi-2-3-billion-lost-to-ceo-email-scams/.

OSNs are in an endeavor to uphold the count of regular users and platform-based service providers. Gradually, OSN users are developing an addiction to the habit of sharing status in daily life, personal thoughts, sentiments to a relatively broader spectrum of direct connections, as well as indirect relationships. Unfortunately, such OSN-based ecosystem can be disastrous—data may be intercepted by malicious users, fraudulent information transmission, privacy snooping. Social engineering, spam, Sybil, and CEO scams are some the common security issues. Figure 3.8 illustrates a CEO spam email.[9]

In a seminal study on information security issues in social media and trustworthiness, Zhang and Gupta (2016) propose a crowd computing framework to attain the following (i) expression of social media platform signaling, (ii) trustworthiness of an OSN platform through evaluation of crowd, and (iii) security evaluation and optimization of an OSN platform. Various attacks are identity theft, spam attack, malware attack, Sybil attacks, social phishing, impersonation, hijacking, fake requests, financial gains, revenge, emotional attacks, hacktivism, and job offers. Muhammad Al-Qurishi et al. (2017) propose an efficient key management protocol among OSN users to maintain secure communication services. The protocol recognizes botnet accounts and blocks them by assigning a manually intervening task which is possible only for every human user who joins the OSN group.

3.2.3　Security Issues in Cloud Computing

Cloud computing in mobile networks can handle on-demand tasks such as storing personal information, accessing them, and running complex computations with the data dynamically. For example, human activity data for running, cycling, swimming, and winter sports recorded on Garmin bio-tracking devices are available on Strava Cloud Heat Map.[10] Such facilities allow more advantages and possibilities to the users and offer additional storage resources and calculation power. However, the heat map sparked privacy and security challenges, when the daily exercise regimens

---

[9] FBI: Extortion, CEO Fraud among Top Online Fraud Complaints in 2016: https://krebsonsecurity.com/tag/ceo-fraud/ (accessed January 20, 2018).

[10] https://labs.strava.com/heatmap/#7.00/-120.90000/38.36000/hot/all (accessed January 20, 2018).

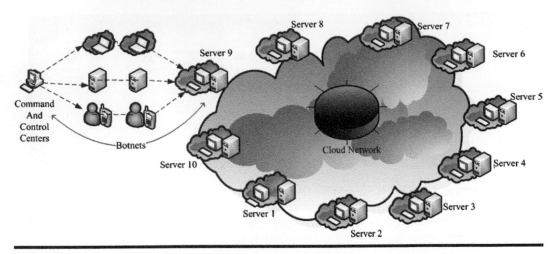

Figure 3.9 Cloud infrastructure under DDoS attack.

of U.S. soldiers posted in Afghanistan began to emanate. So the primary challenge in fully utilizing the capabilities of mobile cloud computing lies in its security issues security (Fernando et al. 2013). Ab Rahman and Choo (2015) present a comprehensive literature review on incident handling in clouds using 139 publications for five years from 2009 to 2014. They also propose a conceptual model to handle cloud incidents that combine concepts from cyber-incident management, forensics of digital information and Service-based Capability Maturity Model. Their survey finds significant literature gap in cloud incident handling and proposes more effective cloud incident management for organizations. Figure 3.9 illustrates a typical cloud infrastructure under DDoS attack (Somani et al. 2017).

Security problems are increasing every day due to the growing data circulation that has ignited the interest of attackers who try to exploit the vulnerabilities in cloud networks to access the data stored. To mitigate such security issues, multi-cloud computing proposed by Ardagna (2015) is highly efficient regarding security and data management. Further to reduce the possibility of insecure connections through any connected cloud network, Zkik et al. (2017) propose a homomorphic encryption-based authentication and confidentiality scheme for genuine mobile users connected to the remote cloud servers. In their algorithm, they also generate a new password for every fresh cloud connection while categorizing the user-data according to their degree of sensitivity. These mechanisms help cloud users to remain connected to the mobile cloud without the fear of persistent attacks. Additionally, mobile cloud networks are frequently used by millions of users, in addition to automated data backups so that they can act as vast repositories of digital evidence and personal data. To mitigate such advanced persistent threats (APTs), D'Orazio and Choo (2018) present a risk assessment taxonomy to analyze iOS apps that can inadvertently bypass SSL (Secure Sockets Layer) and TLS (Transport Layer Security). They further demonstrate the applicability of the taxonomy on 18 existing iOS apps and present a unique secure iOS cloud-based app to investigate mobile cloud-based attacks.

With the increasing reliance on cloud-based Internet services, these facilities are at the risk of being vulnerable to security incidents, data breach attacks, and other malicious activities. These incidents may hold the risk of compromising the C-I-A of IT assets, as well as to minimize financial loss incurred by the service providers and organizational users. Thus, we need to acknowledge, categorize, measure, and rank the associated cloud-risk elements.

Zhou et al. (2018) propose a novel encryption method by generating random dense matrices to improve the security level of outsourced data. Such encryption technique can be used by a client company who wants to efficiently perform large-scale data and application migration to the public cloud. Additionally, the client can run large-scale statistical techniques such as linear regression for a customer while preserving the privacy of input and output results. Often cloud computing supports additional features such as Mobile Edge Computing (MEC) to provide seamless wireless-based video surveillance similar to the IoT networks.

In a novel approach, Alsmirat et al. (2017) design and evaluate a reliable IoT-based wireless video surveillance system to minimize the overall distortion during the surveillance. Additionally, the proposed framework is capable of full utilization of the available bandwidth to reach significant scalability. The system also accounts for an optimal bandwidth distribution and allocation. The performance evaluation of the surveillance system is done with NS-3 simulation.

To implement security in image storing over public cloud storage, Ibtihal et al. (2017) propose a secure architecture that includes—(i) implementation of a private cloud using OpenStack, (ii) encryption and decryption of images by Paillier homomorphic cryptosystem, and (iii) discrete wavelet transform to test homomorphicity of the scheme. A drawback of the system is the necessity of a calculator and handler of an enormous key generated from the secure algorithm.

Recent advances in Cloud of Things devices (CoTs) need rethinking regarding mobile phones that are also mostly CoT devices. The extent to which data can be extracted from a mobile phone in the case of a terrorist attack,[11] privacy issue, or a cybersecurity incident is a matter of grave concern and national security. Cahyani et al. (2017) study the details of mobile forensics with Windows Lumia smartphone, and the chances of data modification after settings modification steps such as screen lock and device reset. The study also examines an alternative data acquisition methodology based on single or combined user activity. The study uses three Windows Nokia phones—Lumia 900, Lumia 735, and Lumia 625 for experiments. Findings show that the technical support and forensic extraction tools for Windows devices were limited. Additionally, the study finds that forensic support during logical acquisition works more comprehensively than physical acquisition.

AlertLogic Report 2015[12] provides evidence about the fact that attacks on cyber-physical cloud systems (CPCS) are increasing significantly including three major types—brute force attacks, application attacks, and suspicious activity. In spite of the associated risks, organizations are flocking to adopt cloud services in their IT systems due to related advantages. In this context, Ab Rahman et al. (2016) propose a forensic-by-design integrated model to handle cloud-based security incidents. The model considers six major principles and practices—risk management, incident management, preparedness in forensics, compliance with cyber-laws and regulation, CPCS, and industry-specific needs.

Cloud forensics help to analyze essential sources of criminal evidence that may arise from regular IT system activities—such as user login, file upload, file download, directory upload and directory download, file and directory deletion, file and directory sharing. Based on timestamps of file modification, Daryabar et al. (2017) show that all of these activities could be significant forensic evidence if adequately recovered. To establish the findings, they analyze MEGA which is a cloud-based file-sharing app serving as a competitor to Google Drive, Dropbox, and OneDrive on iOS and Android platforms.

---

[11] FBI–Apple encryption dispute: https://en.wikipedia.org/wiki/FBI%E2%80%93Apple_encryption_dispute (accessed January 20, 2018).

[12] https://www.alertlogic.com/resources/cloud-security-report-2015/ (accessed January 20, 2018).

Organizations are migrating from physical systems to CPCS, and attackers are busily trying to exploit the cloud vulnerabilities. An ideal digital forensic investigation method should be able to answer *what, how, why, who, when,* and *where* of a cyber-incident. Ab Rahman et al. (2016) present a forensic-by-design incident handling and forensic investigation model for the integrated cloud environment. Further, they apply the six major principles and practices of CPCS especially forensic-by-design in the development phase of the model following the ISO/IEC 27043:2015 processes groups.

Cloud-enabled IoT devices allow storage of big-data streams, high-end data processing for end-nodes with IoT devices. They are also known as CoT and are prone to cyber-attacks, information theft, DDoS attacks, and malicious software usage. Using peer-to-peer cloud storage services such as BitTorrent sync with iOS and Android apps can often act as evidence left over for attackers to sniff and target users. In this context, Teing et al. (2017) seek to identify and mark the data remnants including logs, history, cache, as well as physical memories. Their study also enables users with devices running on Windows, Mac OS, iOS, and Android OS to find data files and pieces related to software/app installation, removal, and file synchronization.

Attribute-based encryption (ABE) is an essential technique needed to ensure highly granular access-control services for cloud-based storage (such as Amazon S3, Google Drive, and Microsoft Azure) and maintain the scalability and flexibility of real-time data sharing over cloud at the same time. In a recent study with Pairing-Based Cryptography (PBC), Yang et al. (2015) introduce a revocable security policy for cloud data encryption assisted by proxy/mediator to weaken the cloud trust. The study also draws from the *all-or-nothing principle*, ciphertext-policy attribute-based encryption (CP-ABE). Additionally, a web-based proof-of-concept as follows: the cloud server executes *PxDec*, user application executes *UDec,* and data owner application executes *Setup*, *PxKGen*, and *Encrypt* algorithms. Finally, the method ensures that user revocability and the trust of not disclosing users' keys with additional applicability on smartphones and mobile devices.

A recent focus on security protocols associated with application areas that have limited battery consumption includes lightweight mobile devices such as laptops and smartphones. The existing cipher-text-based security policies use bilinear maps and are costly to implement. In this context, Vanga Odelu et al. (2017) propose a new RSA-based CP using cipher-texts and secret keys of constant size. They also prove that the new scheme is secure against an attacker who attempts to crack the cipher-text and deployable on lightweight mobile devices.

Fog computing is a new research area in the extended cloud computing discipline designed to decrease network congestion and latency. A comprehensive survey by Osanaiye et al. (2017) reviews 96 scientific articles on DDoS attacks and ensuing protection services in cloud computing environment between 2009 and 2015. They also discuss fog computing architecture, an emergent technology that has emerged from cloud computing and summarize the salient features of cloud, fog, and IoT. They propose a taxonomy of fog computing and classify it into real-time and near-real-time applications. Future research trends from Osanaiye et al. (2017) suggest that live migration for virtual machines (VMs) can enable more scalability and reduced security risks in both cloud and fog computing platforms.

In fog computing, elastic resources are extended to the edge of the network where devices such as IoTs, sensors, and smart devices are installed. Both fog and cloud computing environments can support (VMs) technology that can share resources to coexist in a host. Such coexistence could lead attackers to target VMs as well as the physical server leading to system failures, and unavailability of essential services. In this context, Osanaiye et al. (2017) present a smart pre-copy approach for migration of VMs and ensure uninterrupted availability of resource and service to the end users. Such techniques can be widely used in real-time applications—video streaming, healthcare, online gaming, and smart traffic signaling, as well as near-real-time applications such as—intelligent meters for utilities, smart city projects, and smart vehicle management.

3.2.4 Security Issues in IoTs

IoTs is a contemporary technological sensation interested in linking daily physical objects to the World Wide Web, thereby transforming commonplace things into talkable devices. IoT will enable information sharing amongst each other through seamless integration of the wireless sensor networks (WSN) with the Internet. With the introduction of IoTs, the concept of smart cities and smart homes are enabling massive transformation in the society.

A smart city can integrate information inputs from millions of IoTs in traffic, healthcare, supply chain, retail and thus make a successful intermix of information and communication technology (ICT) and IoTs. Sometimes, the integration of cloud technology and IoTs can render faster and more secure wireless communications in a real-time environment. In a comprehensive literature review, Stergiou et al. (2018) present the persistent security issues in IoT and cloud computing. They point out that the idea of security has not been the initial focus while designing these devices and making them interact with each other. Such multi-platform communication has led to privacy issues, and often with low (or no) level of security in the communication channel.

Figure 3.10 illustrates the IoT devices that a hacker can use to generate cyber-attacks.[13]

Figure 3.11 illustrates the different types of security threats in IoT (Hwang 2015).

IoTs can bring significant changes to the operational issues of a city, and hence a new terminology emerges—"Smart City." With the increase in the use of smart surveillance cameras and video recorders, it is essential that these devices are integrated adequately with the entire WSN. In this

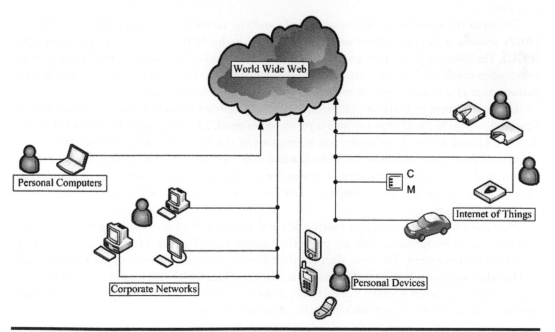

Figure 3.10   How hackers can target IoT to attack.

---

[13]'World's First Solution' to Mirai-like Botnets: http://www.newsweek.com/mirai-botnet-ddos-cybersecurity-iot-hackers-securifi-538473 (accessed January 20, 2018).

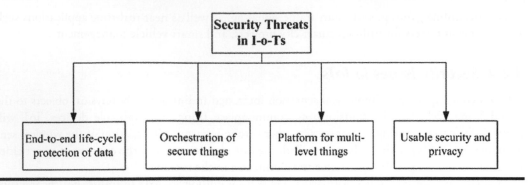

Figure 3.11   Different security threats in IoT.

context, Memos et al. (2018) apply High Efficiency Video Coding (HEVC) method to propose EAMSuS, a unique Efficient Algorithm for Media-based Surveillance. Further, the scheme adapts into a future smart city project with significant accuracy and efficiency. Experimental results also support the reduced memory consumption of the lightweight EAMSuS scheme in comparison to other incumbent algorithms.

In multimedia social networks, the need for security is often unique. The content being delivered needs to be maintained securely, and saved from piracy while maintaining ease of distribution among users. In this context, Zhang et al. (2017) propose CyVOD—a novel framework designed to perform the following tasks—(i) prevent piracy of copyrighted multimedia contents by digital rights management (DRM) and (ii) provide practical recommendations to the users of the social network.

To make the communication between IoTs and the server more secure, Tewari and Gupta (2017) propose a unique authentication structure with the help of elliptic curve cryptography (ECC). The lightweight security protocol performs more efficiently and works with reduced communication overhead. It is also better than the existing schemes in preventing attacks. Further, the performance of scheme is verified and tested against incumbent methods.

Extant literature in CoTs device technology reveals that an efficient three-factor user authentication protocol in multi-cloud servers is yet to be designed. In this context, Kumari et al. (2017) devise a biometric-based authentication scheme using the bio-hashing technique. The scheme consists of four major phases—*user initialization, user registration, login, authentication with key consent,* and *modification of password*. The security scheme is verified against various attack types such as *privileged-insider, user anonymity, user impersonation,* and *cloud-server impersonation* to ensure its efficiency.

Preservation of data privacy in smart grids and metering data has led Jiang et al. (2018) to propose a high-performance privacy-preserving query (P2Q) using MapReduce in Hadoop-distributed environment. The input data has the following features: encrypted, multidimensional, and big-data and the security model focusses on data confidentiality and user privacy over distributed and heterogeneous systems. Further, they employ a Locality Sensitive Hashing (LSH)-based similarity search for the query tasks in the big-data environment.

3.2.5 Security in Web-Based and Distributed Denial-of-Service Attacks

In recent times, organizations of any size—small, medium, and big—are being riddled with DoS and DDoS attacks. According to IBM-Ponemon 2017 study, DoS and DDoS attacks can lead

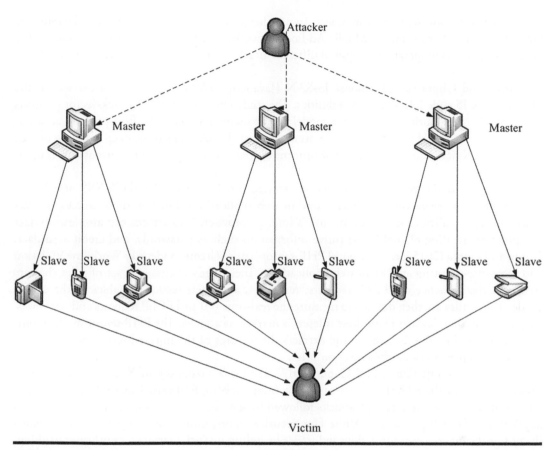

Figure 3.12   How attackers execute a typical DDoS attack.

to financial losses on an average of US $1.5 million, datacenter downtimes in 48% of cases, followed by loss of reputation in the business. In a DDoS attack, the malignant user tries to disrupt a target by flooding it with prohibited packets. These attacks concern a web server in most of the cases, whose predefined bandwidth is hence jeopardized and genuine web inquiries cannot pass. The incumbent anomaly-based DDoS detection services build a regular network-traffic profile and attempts to mark the anomalies whenever those regular traffic profiles deviate from normal maintained within a threshold. Figure 3.12 illustrates a typical DDoS attack with master and slaves—which can be any device according to Mirai botnets that include laptops, smartphones, printers, and video cameras.

Gupta et al. (2012) employ artificial neural network (ANN) technique to estimate the number of zombies involved in a DDoS attack. The proposed method can quickly solve the prevalent issue of low precision in the detection stability of the ANN for low-frequency attacks. Additionally, the network can forecast a number of zombies trying to create a DDoS attack with minimal error.

In a novel study, Almori et al. (2012) explain the risks of botnet-based DDoS attacks on the application layer and the web server. Botnet-based DDoS attacks are highly severe and can cause severe financial losses of business firms as well as governmental web pages. Tripathi et al. (2013) propose a novel technique based on MapReduce to detect DDoS attacks. The model derives from the features of the existing DDoS attacks, previous other technical models involved, and proposes a timeline of defense with improvements. In another study, Chhabra et al. (2013) demonstrate how DDoS attacks can impact Mobile Ad-hoc Networks and how these attacks can block. The paper also offers a comparative analysis of different attack mechanisms and problems due to DDoS attacks.

Gupta and Gupta (2016) propose JS-SAN (JavaScript SANitizer) framework based on the mitigation of JS code injection vulnerabilities. The study clusters extracted attack-vector payloads based on their similarity and create a model attack-vector template. To find possible attacker-injection points and HTML5-based XSS attack vectors, JS-SAN performs deep crawling of web pages. JS-SAN has improved novelty and runtime overhead in comparison to current sanitization-based studies.

According to the researchers at security service provider SecureWorks,[14] XSS attacks are among the most severe vulnerabilities found in web applications. Further, these attacks are executed through malicious scripts on the user's Internet browser. XSS attacks can also lead to data compromise, stealing of cookies, sensitive information such as passwords, and credit card data. Gupta and Gupta (2015) present a novel PHP-sensor-based scheme to identify Workflow Violation and cross-site-scripting attacks in web applications. Their study deciphers a set of rules that are based on the sequence of HTTP requests, responses, and their session variables in the offline mode. These rules are then devised to measure the real-time online HTTP requests and responses. Any anomaly that deviates from these rulesets is marked as attacks. The PHP-sensor model monitors outgoing HTTP web requests and extracts the features of the injected scripts of the HTTP response web page to build the detection rules.

In a recent study, Gupta and Gupta (2017) develop a taxonomy of XSS vulnerabilities to highlight severe vulnerabilities that occasionally infect web applications. This study also discusses a taxonomy of cross-site-scripting attacks followed by specific incidences of these attacks on web applications. Drawing from the White Hat Security report, Gupta and Gupta (2017) provide a list of significant concerns for various industries including financial services, healthcare, banking, and retail.

3.2.6 Vulnerabilities Discovery Models

VDMs are essentially software reliability growth models (SRGMs) that use publicly disclosed software exposure data (Amin et al. 2013, Nguyen and Massacci 2012). SRGMs help to identify the statistical distribution that best describes the vulnerability behavior of a particular software product. This information can be further used to measure reliability, current state, and predict the future. In another study, Alhazmi and Malaiya (2006) apply vulnerability density metric to predict the vulnerability discovery rate of new software developed within an existing product family. Other studies also consider the cumulative growth of vulnerabilities across time for multiple software products to analyze vulnerabilities (Alhazmi et al. 2007, Younis et al. 2011). The existing studies discuss vulnerability growth with the help of probability distributions—logistic (Alhazmi and Malaiya 2006, Alhazmi et al. 2007, Woo et al. 2011), sigmoidal (Ruohonen et al. 2015), quadratic, exponential, (Rescorla 2005), and thermodynamic (Anderson 2002) models. In a study performed on Red Hat Linux and Microsoft OS versions, Ruohonen et al. (2015) find that known vulnerabilities and patches follow a sigmoid curve. Mitra and Ransbotham (2015) also confirm that exploits trail public disclosures while attacks diffuse into a network by exploiting

---

[14] Web App Attacks like SQL Injection, Cross Site Scripting on the Rise: http://www.firstpost.com/biztech/web-app-attacks-like-sql-injection-cross-site-scripting-on-the-rise-1869573.html (accessed January 20, 2018).

Table 3.2   Statistical Vulnerability Estimation Models

Study	Statistical Technique	Objective
Alhazmi & Malaiya (2006)	Logistic	Vulnerability discovery
Alhazmi et al. (2007)	Linear, Log, Sigmoid	Vulnerability density
Alhazmi & Malaiya (2008)	Linear, Log, Sigmoid	Model comparison
Joh et al. (2008)	Weibull	Vulnerability discovery
Woo et al. (2011)	Logistic	Vulnerability discovery
Ransbotham et al. (2012)	Sigmoid	Diffusion/Risk/Volume of attack
Younis et al. (2011)	Folded normal	Vulnerability Discovery Rate
Mitra & Ransbotham (2015)	Sigmoid	Diffusion of attacks
Ruohonen et al. (2015)	Linear, Log, Sigmoid	Vulnerability discovery, patches
Johnson et al. (2016)	Gamma	Time between disclosures

vulnerabilities in a sigmoidal pattern. Table 3.2 illustrates the extant literature on vulnerability estimation using statistical models. From Table 3.2, we observe that vulnerability estimation models based on statistical distributions have the following shortcomings:

i. They consider vulnerability as a random variable and not as a time-dependent stochastic process.
ii. They fail to associate specific attack/breach events and their importance to observations.
iii. They are not able to anticipate changes in the vulnerability trend across time.
iv. They cannot impart higher weights in estimation models for more recent observations.

Another stream of literature analyzes vulnerability estimation applying the techniques of text-mining and examination of actual software codes. However, such analysis rests on the firm underlying assumption that lines of codes are *static*. Shin and Williams (2013) propose vulnerability prediction models through the development of security metrics. Rahimi and Zargham (2013) apply *scrying technique* to predict vulnerable codes. Extant studies use state-of-the-art text-mining algorithms such as decision trees, Random Forest, Support Vector Machines (Scandariato et al. 2014), and N-gram analysis (Pang et al. 2015) to Java source codes to identify relevant vulnerability metrics. Stuckman et al. (2017) applied dimensionality reduction techniques along with text mining identify software metrics to improve the performance of vulnerability prediction models. Table 3.3 illustrates the extant literature on vulnerability estimation models with software code analysis. From Table 3.3, we observe that vulnerability estimation models based on software code analysis have several shortcomings:

i. They inherently assume that software codes are written in the same manner throughout time.
ii. They consider static codes to analyze and identify relevant metrics in different applications.
iii. Do not use real vulnerability database to develop the prediction models.

Table 3.3 Vulnerability Estimation Techniques for Softare Codes

Study	Analysis Technique	Objective
Rahimi and Zargham (2013)	Logistic regression	Vulnerability discovery
Scandariato et al. (2014)	Static code analysis	Vulnerability metric
Pang et al. (2015)	N-Gram and text mining	Predict vulnerable Java classes
Jimenez et al. (2016)	Machine learning	Software metrics
Younis et al. (2016)	Machine learning	Vulnerability metric in code
Stuckman et al. (2017)	Dimensionality reduction	Vulnerability features in codes

Based on these shortcomings of the existing literature on vulnerability analysis, we intend to develop econometric modeling of vulnerability analysis. In the next section, we briefly present these time-series methods.

3.3 Data Exploration and Preparation

Data exploration is an essential activity before proceeding with the econometric analysis of the vulnerability data. We have performed the analysis for the entire chapter using NVD data for *Microsoft*. We downloaded the data into a text file and extracted it into R environment. Next, we converted the text data into time-series. Figure 3.13 displays the time plot of the Microsoft vulnerabilities disclosed per month.

3.3.1 Diagnostic Tests and Stationarity

Before applying the econometric technique, we need to check stationarity condition with the vulnerability data. A time-series is stationary if it has the following properties:

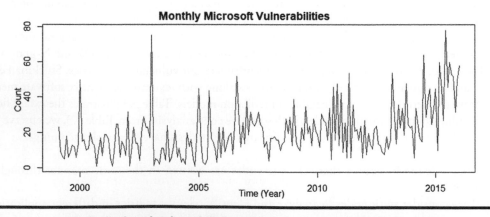

Figure 3.13 Publicly disclosed vulnerabilities of Microsoft per month: 1999–2016.

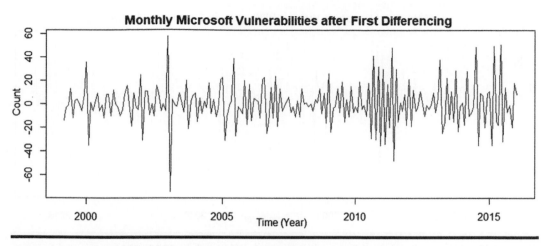

Figure 3.14   Microsoft vulnerabilities after first differencing: 1999–2016.

    i. a finite mean,

    ii. autocorrelations remain constant over time,

    iii. the error terms are as close as "white noise" after fitting a model.

Based on the augmented Dickey–Fuller (ADF) test, we derive that security vulnerability time-series are nonstationary. So, we need to apply suitable transformation techniques to make it stationary. Popular methods in econometric include *differencing of consecutive terms* and *log-transformation*. For example, if our original time-series was represented by $x_1, x_2, x_3, \ldots x_n$, then our modified time-series becomes

$$(x_1 - x_2),(x_2 - x_3),(x_3 - x_4), \ldots,(x_{n-1} - x_n)$$

after first-order differencing. We note that the number of terms reduces from n to $(n-1)$ due to first-order differencing. Figure 3.14 shows the first-order differenced time-series for Microsoft vulnerabilities derived from the original series in Figure 3.13. With further differencing to second degree, the time-series becomes

$$(x_1 - 2x_2 - x_3),(x_2 - 2x_3 - x_4),(x_3 - 2x_4 - x_5), \ldots,(x_{n-2} - 2x_{n-1} - x_n)$$

We note that the number of terms reduces from n to $(n-2)$ due to second-order differencing. Figure 3.15 represents the time-series of second-order differenced Microsoft vulnerabilities. Another transformation mechanism involves subsequent differencing after performing natural log of the terms of a time-series. So after log differencing, our series will become

$$\left[\ln(x_1) - \ln(x_2)\right],\left[\ln(x_2) - \ln(x_3)\right],\ldots,\left[\ln(x_{n-1}) - \ln(x_n)\right]$$

We note that log-differenced time-series is a growth series of vulnerabilities. Figure 3.16 represents the time-series for Microsoft vulnerabilities after log differencing.

After necessary differencing, we checked with the ADF test again on the NVD data and confirmed stationarity. Often, the degree of differencing needed to perform for a given time-series can be integrated into Autoregressive moving average (ARMA) to achieve an autoregressive

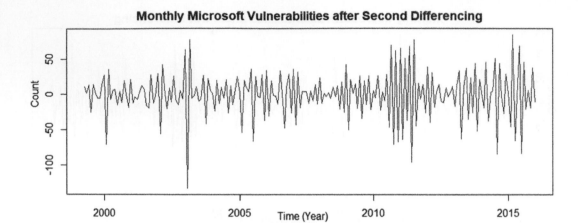

Figure 3.15 Microsoft vulnerabilities after [second differencing: 1999–2016].

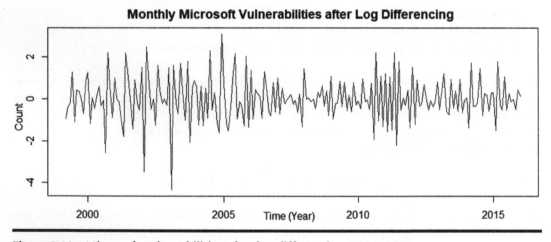

Figure 3.16 Microsoft vulnerabilities after log differencing: 1999–2016.

integrated moving average (ARIMA). Doing so produces an ARIMA model, with the "I" standing for "Integrated." Hence, the necessary stationarity transformation can be executed before ARMA model fitting, or as a part of ARIMA modeling.

3.3.2 Box–Jenkins Methodology

We adopt the widely accepted Box–Jenkins methodology to analyze our time-series data. Regarding the length of the period of analysis, a moderately extensive series is a good fit for applying Box–Jenkins method. Studies propose that at least 50 observations are required for a good fit (Chatfield 1996). Our research consists of monthly data for 17 years with $12 \times 17 = 204$ data points for Microsoft, and so Box–Jenkins is applicable. Figure 3.17 demonstrates the three steps—*identification of order*, *estimation of parameters*, and *validation* in details.

Identification: The first step in developing a Box–Jenkins model involves checking any existing seasonality and stationarity. In the previous section, we have discussed the steps to achieve stationarity and associated diagnostic tests. Often a slow decaying Autocorrelation Function (ACF)

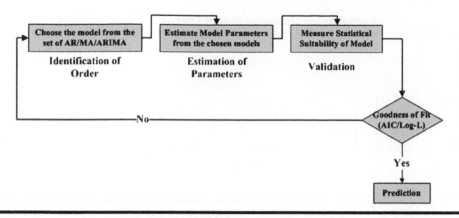

Figure 3.17   Box-Jenkins Methodology adopted for our analysis.

may indicate series non-stationarity. The Partial Autocorrelation Function (PACF) plot for a stationary series is a function of its Autocorrelation Function plot. Figure 3.18 shows the ACF plot for Microsoft vulnerabilities across time. Figure 3.19 shows the PACF plot for Microsoft vulnerability exposures.

From the shape and nature of the ACF and PACF plots, we can identify the order of the ARIMA series (Brockwell and Davis 1987, 2002). Following rules help us to determine the order of the time-series based on the shape of ACF plot.

a. If ACF plot is exponential and gradually decays to zero, or,
b. If ACF plot takes positive and negative values alternatively and finally declines to zero, then we choose a pure autoregressive (AR) model.

Otherwise, if the shape of ACF plot:

c. shows high fixed values at constant intervals, then we choose a seasonal model.
d. decays start after a few lags; then it is a mixture of AR and moving average (MA).
e. does not decay to zero at all, then the series is non-stationary.

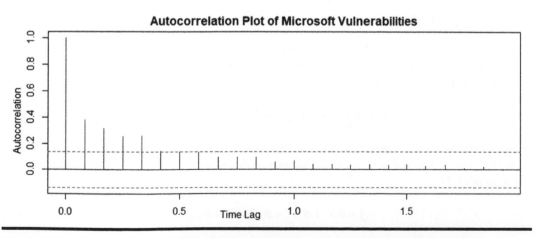

Figure 3.18   Autocorrelation (ACF) plot for Microsoft security exposures 1999: 2015.

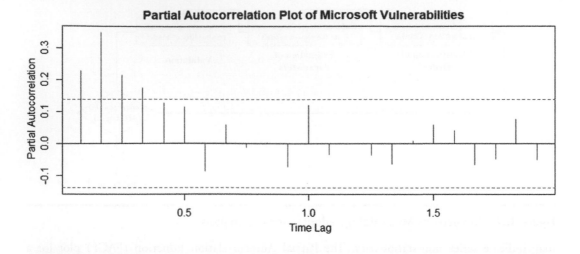

Figure 3.19   Partial autocorrelation (PACF) plot for Microsoft security exposures 1999: 2015.

For our case, Figure 3.18 shows that the ACF plot starts decaying after a few lags. Figure 3.19 shows that the PACF plot decays rapidly and becomes insignificant beyond lag 4. These symptoms indicate that our final model may include a combination of both AR and MA terms *not beyond the 4th order* (Box et al. 1994).

Estimation: We conduct the parameter estimation with the help of maximum-likelihood estimation and nonlinear least-squares method that are frequently used techniques employed in such parametric estimates.

Validation: Given that the Box–Jenkins methodology generates sufficiently good fit for the data, the residuals must satisfy the i.i.d (independent and identically distributed when their distributions are normal) conditions. The Akaike Information Criteria (AIC), log-likelihood, and standard deviation (σ^2) values should be lower for a better-fitted model.

3.4 Econometric Techniques

3.4.1 AR Technique

An AR model is fundamentally stochastic which considers that the present value of a process y_t is some combination of the values from the previous time periods. With Equation (3.1), we represent y_t as an AR series of order "p."

$$\hat{y}_t = \phi_1 \hat{y}_{t-1} + \phi_2 \hat{y}_{t-2} + \phi_3 \hat{y}_{t-3} + \cdots + \phi_p \hat{y}_{t-p} + e_t \tag{3.1}$$

where ϕ_i denotes the coefficient of the ith previous observation from mean represented by $\hat{y}_{t-1}$ such that $\hat{y}_t = y_t - \mu$ and e_t is the error. So we can describe y_t in a model form of order (p) with the help of (3.2).

$$\hat{y} = \phi_1 x_1 + \phi_2 x_2 + \phi_3 x_3 + \cdots + \phi_p x_p + e \tag{3.2}$$

In essence, we are conducting a linear regression of the present observation as dependent variable on its previous observations as predictors, hence the name *AR*. When the process is purely AR, we can take the help of the PACF plot to identify the order. Table 3.4 shows the results from fitting the Microsoft vulnerability data with AR(1) and AR(2) models and derives the coefficients. Table 3.5 reports forecasts using these AR models as well as Seasonal AR (SAR) models. From Table 3.6, we understand that the model needs to incorporate at least AR(2). Also, the data is monthly, so there is a visible indication of seasonality. Results in Table 3.6 show a significant reduction in the AIC, Log-L, and σ^2 values with a seasonal model than with a regular one. Comparing different model runs from Table 3.6 shows that choosing AR(2) over AR(1) resulted in a significant reduction of these performance values. Additionally, when we choose SAR (2,0,0)–(2,0,0) over SAR (1,0,0)–(1,0,0), there is significant improvement in the model performance. This finding supports the use of SAR models instead of simple AR.

Table 3.4   AR Models and Their Prediction Equations

Autoregressive Model	Prediction Equation
AR(1)	$y_t = 20.623 + 0.2335\,y_{t-1} + e_t$
AR(2)	$y_t = 20.841 + 0.1559\,y_{t-1} + 0.3684\,y_{t-2} + e_t$

Table 3.5   Microsoft Vulnerability Predictions Estimated by AR Models

2016	Actual	Predicted				
		AR(1)	AR(2)	SAR(1,0,0)–(1,0,0)	SAR(2,0,0)–(2,0,0)	SAR(3,0,0)–(3,0,0)
January	25	29.35	37.38	22.70	27.64	28.69
February	36	22.66	37.11	36.58	44.84	51.24
March	40	21.10	29.47	30.20	33.20	38.65
April	29	20.73	28.18	23.42	26.13	28.85
May	58	20.65	25.16	42.09	34.93	39.11
June	37	20.63	24.22	30.35	39.98	41.46
July	41	20.62	22.96	35.48	33.21	36.07
August	28	20.62	22.42	32.91	33.69	34.18
September	54	20.62	21.87	32.55	35.03	38.59
October	36	20.62	21.58	25.21	25.23	26.84
November	67	20.62	21.34	31.81	31.46	31.59
December	41	20.62	21.19	34.74	36.05	35.45

Table 3.6   Comparison of Autoregressive Model Performance Metrics

Metric	AR(1)	AR(2)	SAR(1,0,0)–(1,0,0)	SAR(2,0,0)–(2,0,0)	SAR(3,0,0)–(3,0,0)
AIC	1670.55	1643.93	1650.26	1623.9	1620.52
σ^2	204.70	177.60	181.90	155.80	149.80
Log-L	−832.27	−817.97	−821.13	−805.95	−802.26

3.4.2 MA Technique

MA models consider the current observation with a finite number of past errors. Equation (3.3) represents a typical MA model with order "q."

$$\hat{y}_t = c + a_t + \theta_1 a_{t-1} + \theta_2 a_{t-2} + \theta_3 a_{t-3} + \cdots + \theta_q a_{t-q} \tag{3.3}$$

Here a_t is the white noise such that the value of y_t is derived from a set of the weighted MA of the past errors from each period until the order of the series "q." Table 3.7 shows the results from fitting the Microsoft vulnerability data with MA(1) and MA(3) models and derives the coefficients. Table 3.8 reports forecasts using these MA models as well as seasonal MA (SMA) models.

Results in Table 3.9 show a significant reduction in the AIC, log-likelihood, and standard deviation (σ^2) values with a seasonal model than with a regular one. This finding supports the use of SAR models instead of simple AR.

3.4.3 Disadvantages of AR and MA Techniques

The AR technique assumes that the estimated process depends only on the linear combinations of its time-lagged values. Further, AR models may remain nonstationary with the presence of unit-roots (Box et al. 1994). AR methods require least-square estimation approach while estimating the model coefficients.

On the other hand, MA technique requires the mean of the series and combine with the weighted average of the past forecast errors only. MA methods work well with stationary time-series data. So the inherent assumption is that the series is always stationary (Tsay 2005). MA models require maximum-likelihood estimation and are more cumbersome.

3.4.4 Autoregressive Integrated Moving Average

Statistics has combined the existing AR and MA models to achieve greater flexibility and offers a new family of techniques—autoregressive integrated moving average, also known as ARIMA. Combining (3.2) and (3.3), we get (3.4).

Table 3.7   MA Models and Their Prediction Equations

Moving Average Model	Prediction Equation
MA(1)	$y_t = 20.58 + a_t + 0.139 a_{t-1}$
MA(3)	$y_t = 20.681 a_t + 0.1249 a_{t-1} + 0.2763 a_{t-2} + 0.0985 a_{t-3}$

Table 3.8 Microsoft Vulnerability Predictions by MA Models

2016	Actual	MA(1)	MA(3)	SMA(0,0,2)–(0,0,1)	SMA(0,0,3)–(0,0,2)	SMA(0,0,4)–(0,0,2)
				Predicted		
January	25	25.24	31.36	28.29	23.65	22.56
February	36	20.59	30.49	36.96	37.40	36.90
March	40	20.59	20.67	26.22	28.59	32.03
April	29	20.59	20.67	22.44	23.84	28.15
May	58	20.59	20.67	34.06	30.59	29.08
June	37	20.59	20.67	24.39	35.95	37.24
July	41	20.59	20.67	29.38	30.42	30.00
August	28	20.59	20.67	27.21	32.43	32.79
September	54	20.59	20.67	26.97	30.58	30.98
October	36	20.59	20.67	23.26	24.49	24.79
November	67	25.24	20.67	26.77	29.74	29.58
December	41	20.59	20.67	28.04	34.79	35.35

Table 3.9 Comparison of Moving Average Model Performance Metrics

Metric	MA(1)	MA(3)	SMA(0,0,2)–(0,0,1)	SMA(0,0,3)–(0,0,2)	SMA(0,0,4)–(0,0,2)
AIC	1657.14	1656.55	1647.71	1638.64	1634.00
σ^2	189.70	187.30	178.80	166.50	160.8
Log-L	−824.57	−821.28	−818.85	−812.32	−809.00

$$y'_t = c + \phi_1 y'_{t-1} + \phi_2 y'_{t-2} + \cdots + \phi_p y'_{t-p} + \theta_1 e_{t-1} + \theta_2 e_{t-2} + \cdots + \theta_q e_{t-q} + e_t \qquad (3.4)$$

Here, the differenced series y'_t is regressed against the lagged y'_{t-1}, y'_{t-2} and errors e_{t-1}, $e_t \ldots$

So, we combine AR and MA into ARIMA to remove the disadvantages of both techniques.

- ARIMA methods use a combination of both past observations (AR) as well as historical forecasting errors (MA).
- ARIMA technique offers a huge research potential for fitting models that remained inadequate by an AR or an MA alone.
- Automatic differencing removes any nonstationarity in the time-series.

Table 3.10 reports the forecasts using ARIMA models.

Results in Table 3.11 show a significant reduction in the AIC, log-likelihood, and standard deviation (σ^2) values with higher-order model than with a lower-order one. This finding supports the use of seasonal ARIMA (SARIMA) models instead of simple ARIMA.

Table 3.10 Microsoft Vulnerability Predictions by ARIMA Models

2016	Actual	Predicted			
		ARIMA (1,1,1)	ARIMA (1,1,2)	ARIMA (2,1,2)	ARIMA (2,1,3)
January	25	46.41	31.36	28.29	23.65
February	36	48.67	30.49	36.96	37.40
March	40	48.23	20.67	26.22	28.59
April	29	48.32	20.67	22.44	23.84
May	58	48.30	20.67	34.06	30.59
June	37	48.30	20.67	24.39	35.95
July	41	48.30	20.67	29.38	30.42
August	28	48.30	20.67	27.21	32.43
September	54	48.30	20.67	26.97	30.58
October	36	48.30	20.67	23.26	24.49
November	67	48.30	20.67	26.77	29.74
December	41	48.30	20.67	28.04	34.79

Table 3.11 Comparison of ARIMA Model Performance Metrics

Metric	ARIMA (1,1,1)	ARIMA (1,1,2)	ARIMA (2,1,2)	ARIMA (2,1,3)
AIC	1613.70	1608.71	1609.7	1611.61
σ^2	159.90	154.30	153.60	153.5
Log-L	−803.85	−800.35	−799.85	−799.81

3.4.5 BackShift Notation

The backshift notation (B) is an alternate way of mathematically representing an ARIMA. Equation (3.5) illustrates a single- and double-order ARIMA with backshift notation.

$$By_t = y_{t-1}; B^2\, y_t = y_{t-2}, \text{and so on.} \tag{3.5}$$

So ARIMA (1,1,1) model can be represented as

$$\left(1 - \phi_1 B\right)\left(1 - B\right) y_t = \left(1 + \theta_1 B\right) e_t \tag{3.6}$$

Generalizing the form in (3.4), we can write it as (3.7)

$$\left(1 - \phi_1 B - \phi_2 B^2 \cdots - \phi_p B^p\right)\left(1 - B\right)^d \, y_t = c + \left(1 + \theta_1 B + \cdots + \theta_q B^q\right) e_t \tag{3.7}$$

3.4.6 SARIMA Models

The ACF and PACF plots for Microsoft vulnerability time-series in Figures 3.18 and 3.19 indicate the presence of a seasonal component. Additionally, there is a significant reduction in the AIC, log-likelihood, and standard deviation (σ^2) with SARIMA models. So we apply seasonal ARIMA (or SARIMA) technique which includes additional seasonal components apart from the regular ARIMA. SARIMA (p,d,q) (P,D,Q) notation represents SARIMA where "P," "D," and "Q" indicate the orders of seasonality. Table 3.12 reports the vulnerability forecasts using SARIMA models. Table 3.13 shows that **SARIMA(1,0,2) (2,1,0)[12]** is the best-fit model with the lowest AIC, Log-L, and σ^2.

Table 3.12 Microsoft Vulnerability Predictions Estimated by SARIMA Models

		Predicted		
2016	Actual	SARIMA (1,0,0) (2,1,0)[12]	SARIMA (1,0,2) (2,1,0)[12]	SARIMA (1,1,2) (1,0,1)[12]
January	25	15.46	27.22	40.70
February	36	50.05	45.79	54.56
March	40	33.82	49.14	49.90
April	29	20.43	35.57	44.84
May	58	45.13	56.15	54.86
June	37	47.69	46.58	55.40
July	41	42.65	51.05	53.59
August	28	39.89	39.64	52.16
September	54	48.49	60.50	54.21
October	36	27.83	39.03	47.76
November	67	38.05	47.24	50.39
December	41	45.64	53.95	55.20

Table 3.13 Comparison of SARIMA Model Performance Metrics

Metric	SARIMA (1,0,0) (2,1,0)[12]	SARIMA (1,0,2) (2,1,0)[12]	SARIMA (1,1,2) (1,0,1)[12]
AIC	1559.00	1535.22	1597.07
σ^2	184.30	158.30	140.90
Log-L	−775.50	−761.61	−792.54

3.5 Exponential Smoothing

Exponential smoothing-based forecasts are a family of robust and straightforward forecasting techniques. ARIMA models are a particular case of exponential models with linear trend. A particular feature is common to all types of exponential models—observations are assigned exponentially decreasing weights such that recent ones are more significant than older ones. We apply the simple exponential smoothing technique, Holt's linear trend models (Holt 1957), and Holt–Winters seasonal models (Winters 1960) to analyze the growth of software vulnerabilities.

3.5.1 Simple Exponential Smoothing

Simple exponential smoothing models can forecast without any trend or seasonality. Equation (3.9) represents the simple exponential forecasting model:

$$\hat{y}_{t+1} = \alpha y_t + \alpha (1-\alpha) y_{t-1} + \cdots + \alpha (1-\alpha)^k y_{t-k} + \cdots \tag{3.8}$$

where $0 \leq \alpha \leq 1$ is the smoothing parameter. Table 3.14 reports Microsoft vulnerability forecasts using simple exponential models with varying smoothing parameter α.

3.5.2 Holt's Linear Trend

Holt's linear trend model considers level as well as a linear trend of the previous observations across time. Exponential model with Holt's linear trend is given by (3.9–3.11):

Table 3.14 Microsoft Vulnerability Estimations by Simple Exponential Models

2016	Actual	Predicted			
		$\alpha = 0.2$	$\alpha = 0.4$	$\alpha = 0.6$	$\alpha = 0.8$
January	25	48.96	51.25	28.29	23.65
February	36	48.96	51.25	36.96	37.40
March	40	48.96	51.25	26.22	28.59
April	29	48.96	51.25	22.44	23.84
May	58	48.96	51.25	34.06	30.59
June	37	48.96	51.25	24.39	35.95
July	41	48.96	51.25	29.38	30.42
August	28	48.96	51.25	27.21	32.43
September	54	48.96	51.25	26.97	30.58
October	36	48.96	51.25	23.26	24.49
November	67	48.96	51.25	26.77	29.74
December	41	48.96	51.25	28.04	34.79

$$\text{Level:} \quad l_t = \alpha y_t + (1-\alpha)(l_{t-1} + b_{t-1}) \tag{3.9}$$

$$\text{Trend:} \quad b_t = \beta(l_t - l_{t-1}) + (1-\beta)b_{t-1} \tag{3.10}$$

$$\text{Forecast:} \quad \hat{y}_{t+h} = l_t + hb_t \tag{3.11}$$

where $0 \le \alpha \le 1$ is the smoothing parameter for the level and β is the smoothing parameter for the trend with $0 \le \beta \le 1$. The estimate of the level and trend are given by l_t and b_t, respectively. Equation (3.9) shows that the level l_t is a weighted average of current observation and the combination of previous level l_{t-1} and trend b_{t-1}. Equation (3.10) shows that the trend b_t is a weighted average of the previous trend b_{t-1} and the change of the previous level values l_t and l_{t-1}. Table 3.15 reports Microsoft vulnerability forecasts using Holt's linear models with varying smoothing parameter α and β (Figure 3.20).

3.5.3 *Holt–Winters Seasonal Models*

Additionally, the extended Holt–Winters seasonal model proposed by Holt and Winters (Winters 1960) can record the seasonality in the data. Apart from the smoothing parameters for level and trend, it consists of an additional smoothing parameter γ for seasonality. The Holt–Winters seasonal model has two variations: (i) *additive*: for fixed seasonal components and (ii) *multiplicative*: for varying seasonal components. Table 3.16 reports Microsoft vulnerability forecasts using Holt–Winter's seasonal models for both additive and multiplicative versions (Figure 3.21):

Table 3.15   Microsoft Vulnerability Prediction by Holt's Linear Models

		Predicted	
2016	*Actual*	*α = 0.15, β = 0.01* *(Linear)*	*α = 0.8, β = 0.2* *(Exp.)*
January	25	38.28	63.62
February	36	48.31	64.74
March	40	42.14	65.88
April	29	41.99	67.04
May	58	45.83	68.22
June	37	52.55	69.42
July	41	47.96	70.64
August	28	48.70	71.89
September	54	42.35	73.15
October	36	46.21	74.44
November	67	40.35	75.75
December	41	59.15	77.08

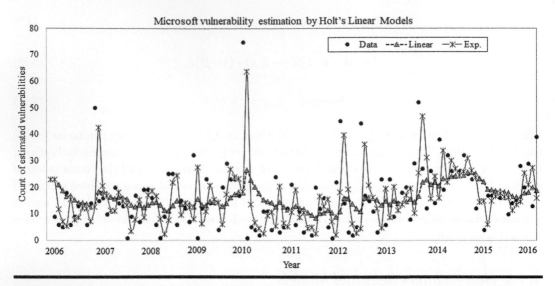

Figure 3.20 Microsoft vulnerability estimation with Holt's linear and exponential models.

Table 3.16 Microsoft Vulnerability Prediction by the Holt–Winters Seasonal Models

| 2016 | Actual | Forecasted | |
		Additive	Multiplicative
January	25	37.98	25.48
February	36	49.25	51.40
March	40	41.20	36.34
April	29	43.35	40.60
May	58	47.56	51.86
June	37	53.47	58.63
July	41	48.71	56.09
August	28	50.36	51.54
September	54	45.25	40.15
October	36	48.45	37.47
November	67	42.96	37.60
December	41	61.32	72.52

$$\text{Level:} \quad l_t = \alpha\left(y_t - s_{t-k}\right) + (1-\alpha)\left(l_{t-1} + b_{t-1}\right) \tag{3.12}$$

$$\text{Trend:} \quad b_t = \beta\left(l_t - l_{t-1}\right) + (1-\beta)\, b_{t-1} \tag{3.13}$$

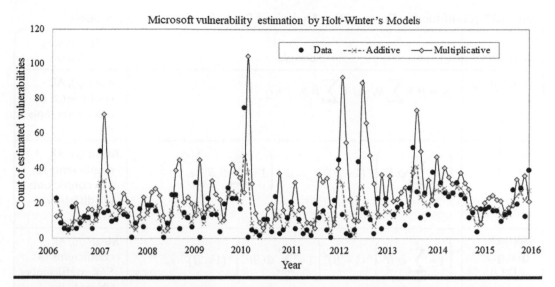

Figure 3.21 Microsoft vulnerability estimation with the Holt–Winters Seasonal (linear and multiplicative) models.

$$\text{Seasonality:} \quad s_t = \gamma\left(y_t - l_{t-1} - b_{t-1}\right) + \left(1 - \gamma\right)s_{t-k} \tag{3.14}$$

$$\text{Forecast:} \quad \hat{y}_{t+h} = l_t + hb_t + s_{t-k} \tag{3.15}$$

3.5.4 Comparative Analysis of Various Econometric Models

In this chapter, we use the AIC-based selection techniques to choose between multiple econometric models based on their performance. Based on all the econometric time-series models discussed in this chapter so far, we present a comparative analysis of each method, parameters used. Table 3.17 presents the comparative analysis of econometric models discussed in this chapter.

Table 3.17 Comparative Analysis of Predictive Econometric Models

Model	Formula	Parameters Used
AR(p)	$y_t = \mu + \sum\limits_{i=1}^{p} \phi_i y_{t-i} + e_t$	Mean (μ), AR coefficients (ϕ)
MA (q)	$y_t = \mu + \sum\limits_{i=1}^{q} \theta_i a_{t-i}$	Mean (μ), MA coefficients (θ)

(Continued)

Table 3.17 (*Continued*)   Comparative Analysis of Predictive Econometric Models

Model	Formula	Parameters Used
ARMA (p,q)	$y_t = \mu + \sum_i \varphi_i y_{t-i} + \sum_j \theta_j a_{t-j} + e_t$	Mean (μ), AR coefficients (θ), MA coefficients (θ)
ARIMA (p,d,q)	$\left(1 - \sum_{i=1}^{p} \varphi_i B^i\right) * (1-B)^d \, y_t = \mu + \left(1 + \sum_{i=1}^{q} \theta_i B^i\right) e_t$	Mean (μ), AR coefficients (ϕ), MA coefficients (θ), difference (d)
SARIMA (p,d,q) (P,D,Q)	$\left(1 - \sum_{i=1}^{p} \varphi_i B^i\right) * (1-B)^d \left(1 - \sum_{j=1}^{P} \Phi_j B^j\right) * (1-B)^D \, y_t$ $= \mu + \left(1 + \sum_{k=1}^{q} \theta_k B^k\right)\left(1 + \sum_{l=1}^{Q} \Theta_l B^l\right) e_t$	Mean (μ), AR coefficients (ϕ), SAR coefficients (Φ), MA coefficients (θ), SMA coefficients (Θ), difference (d), Seasonal difference (D)
Exponential smoothing	$y_{t+1} = \alpha \sum_i (1-\alpha)^i \, y_{t-i}$	Smoothing parameter α
Holt's linear trend	$y_{t+h} = l_t + h b_t,\ l_t = \alpha y_t + (1-\alpha)(l_{t-1} + b_{t-1}),$ $b_t = \beta(l_t - l_{t-1}) + (1-\beta) b_{t-1}$	Smoothing parameter for level α, Smoothing parameter for trend β
Holt–Winters seasonal	$y_{t+h} = l_t + h b_t + s_{t-k},$ $l_t = \alpha\left(y_t - s_{t-k}\right) + (1-\alpha)(l_{t-1} + b_{t-1})$ $b_t = \beta(l_t - l_{t-1}) + (1-\beta) b_{t-1}$ $s_t = \gamma\left(y_t - l_{t-1} - b_{t-1}\right) + (1-\gamma)s_{t-k}$	Smoothing parameter for level α, Smoothing parameter for trend β Smoothing parameter for seasonality γ

3.6 Application of Econometric Modeling With a Case Study

We show that sound forecasting with econometric methods is essential for top management in business firms for future planning and mitigating IT-related risks. When security vulnerabilities are announced for a particular software, few users will invest in it. By applying our proposed forecasting methods(s), we aim to reduce the associated IT risk through a case study.

Indian Community Co-operative Investments, a co-operative bank plans to buy Office Software Suite for its new offices at New Delhi, Mumbai, and Kolkata. The dominant players in the market are Microsoft, Apple, IBM, and Google. The Chief Information Security Officer (CISO) at Community Co-operative Investments is worried about the recent Wannacry cyber-attacks. He expects his team to come up with a safe and flawless explanation to support the purchase of an Office Software suite from the four available players. In the meantime, analysts have gathered the disclosure data for Microsoft, Apple, IBM, and Google from NVD for the last ten years. Table 3.18 lists the planned distribution of computers with these software installations. The CISO believes that planning for future IT risk will save lots of spending at Community Co-operative. Assuming that each employee of Indian Community Co-operative bank will generate a revenue of US$20 per hour, how much will the bank lose when there is an exploit for (i) Microsoft, (ii) Apple, (iii) IBM, and (iv) Google. Throughout the analysis, we ignore correlated vulnerability condition across software platforms (Tables 3.18–3.22).

Table 3.18   Planned Distribution of Computers for Community Bank

Location	Software				Total
	Microsoft	*Apple Mac*	*IBM Lotus*	*Google Office*	
New Delhi	119	41	67	43	270
Mumbai	33	98	85	75	291
Kolkata	121	34	55	80	290

Table 3.19   Monthly Vulnerabilities Recorded for Microsoft Office

Month	Count of Vulnerabilities in Each Year									
	2006	*2007*	*2008*	*2009*	*2010*	*2011*	*2012*	*2013*	*2014*	*2015*
January	14	20	30	28	21	16	18	22	17	15
February	16	21	30	29	23	26	20	27	17	12
March	18	20	21	24	14	20	25	21	22	10
April	17	16	28	18	18	26	24	17	25	14
May	19	12	25	9	14	19	24	19	21	10
June	13	8	20	20	15	19	23	23	17	28
July	13	25	20	17	20	16	18	30	19	24
August	23	22	19	14	20	20	15	24	26	28
September	20	18	12	15	25	21	13	31	25	17
October	16	22	16	26	19	20	15	22	19	14
November	14	24	22	30	13	24	11	13	18	17
December	17	35	18	30	12	18	20	8	15	13

Table 3.20   Monthly Vulnerabilities Recorded for Apple Office

Month	Count of Vulnerabilities in Each Year									
	2006	*2007*	*2008*	*2009*	*2010*	*2011*	*2012*	*2013*	*2014*	*2015*
January	19	18	17	18	19	19	16	21	15	8
February	16	18	15	20	17	14	17	24	14	11
March	18	13	20	22	11	17	29	22	13	21
April	18	10	18	9	14	15	29	18	25	25
May	17	7	23	14	16	15	27	10	26	28
June	14	17	23	15	19	13	22	21	19	22
July	17	22	25	16	23	12	21	22	13	21
August	22	18	23	21	17	15	18	23	16	21
September	29	18	20	14	11	23	16	18	21	20
October	27	22	19	12	14	25	20	18	23	24
November	24	21	23	17	13	18	19	20	25	25
December	19	20	17	18	15	19	22	18	19	22

Table 3.21   Monthly Vulnerabilities Recorded for IBM Office

Month	Count of Vulnerabilities in Each Year									
	2006	*2007*	*2008*	*2009*	*2010*	*2011*	*2012*	*2013*	*2014*	*2015*
January	20	19	19	21	23	23	25	29	27	23
February	17	19	17	23	21	19	22	33	26	27
March	19	15	21	25	14	22	23	31	24	37
April	19	12	20	11	18	20	35	27	37	42
May	18	9	25	17	20	20	36	19	39	45
June	16	19	25	18	23	19	34	31	32	40
July	18	24	28	19	27	17	29	32	26	38
August	24	20	25	24	21	20	29	33	30	40
September	30	20	22	17	16	28	25	29	34	39
October	28	24	21	15	18	31	24	29	37	43
November	25	23	25	20	17	24	28	31	39	44
December	20	22	19	21	20	23	27	29	34	42

Table 3.22   Monthly Vulnerabilities Recorded for Google Office

Month	Count of Vulnerabilities in Each Year									
	2006	2007	2008	2009	2010	2011	2012	2013	2014	2015
January	14	15	13	14	15	14	15	16	16	15
February	14	15	13	14	14	13	16	16	16	13
March	14	15	14	16	15	16	15	15	14	15
April	15	15	16	16	15	15	14	15	14	16
May	15	15	15	16	16	16	15	14	16	17
June	16	15	14	16	17	15	15	14	15	15
July	13	15	17	14	14	16	15	16	15	15
August	13	15	15	14	15	16	16	15	16	16
September	16	16	14	14	16	15	15	16	16	16
October	17	15	15	16	15	14	13	14	15	16
November	16	16	17	15	14	14	14	13	15	14
December	17	17	16	16	15	15	15	17	15	13

3.6.1 Case Solution

We adopt the Box–Jenkins methodology described earlier in this chapter. We execute the ADF test to confirm stationarity for the software vulnerability data. Apart from *IBM*, all of the software products demonstrate stationarity. Time-series plots for *Microsoft* (Figure 3.22), *Apple* (Figure 3.23), and *Google* (Figure 3.24) also confirm that there is stationarity around 20, 18, and 15, respectively, while *IBM* (Figure 3.25) is nonstationarity. Inevitably *IBM* needs an ARIMA (or SARIMA) model which can restore stationarity.

Next, we choose the final model for each software based on the minimum AIC value. Table 3.23 illustrates that MA (2) reports a lower AIC value than AR (1). So we choose MA (2) as the final model for estimating Microsoft vulnerabilities. Similarly, AR (2) is a best-fit model for Apple (Table 3.24), SARIMA for IBM (Table 3.25), and Holt–Winters for Google (Table 3.26). Table 3.27 aggregates these results for each model for the final decision-making of *Indian Community Co-operative Investments*. Table 3.28 illustrates the forecasts made with these finalized models for each software—Microsoft, Apple, IBM, and Google. Next, we calculate the monthly likelihood of exploit for a vulnerability in each type of software. Table 3.29 reports the month probability for each software during our prediction year 2016. Tables 3.30–3.32 report expected loss suffered per hour of system downtime for each type of software at the three proposed locations of *Indian Community Co-operative Investments*.

We define the expression for the monthly probability of exploit for a software product as (3.16):

$$\text{Monthly Probability of exploit of ith software product } P_i = \frac{n_i}{\sum_{j=1}^{4} n_j} \qquad (3.16)$$

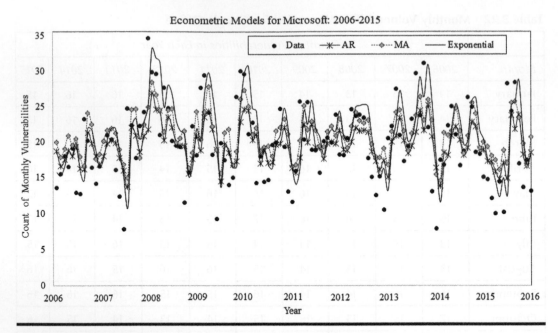

Figure 3.22   Econometric model for Microsoft from 2006 to 2015.

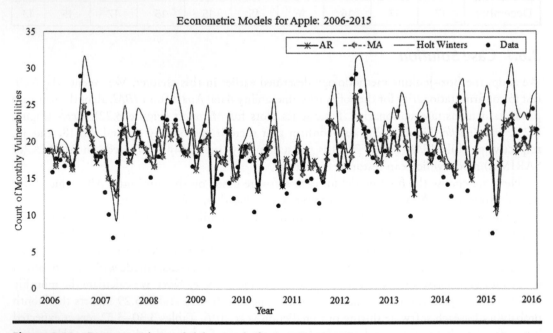

Figure 3.23   Econometric model for Apple from 2006 to 2015.

And the expressions for expected loss per hour after an exploit are given by (3.17):

Expected Loss per hour (EL) for ith software product at location $k = P_i * N_{i,k} * l$ (3.17)

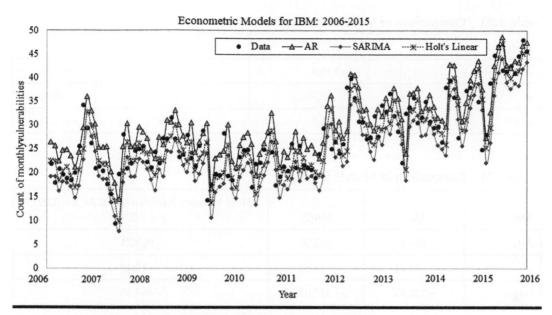

Figure 3.24   Econometric model for Google from 2006 to 2015.

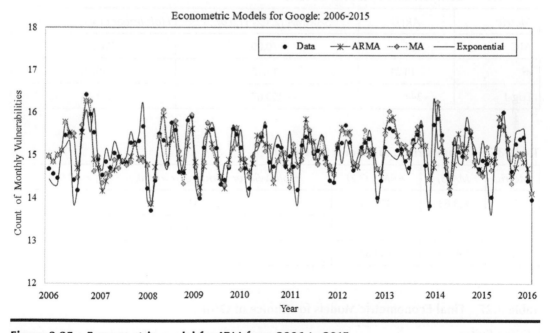

Figure 3.25   Econometric model for IBM from 2006 to 2015.

where l is the hourly loss per employee when his/her system is down, $N_{i,k}$ is the number of systems with ith software product at location k;

$$i, j = 1, 2, 3, 4 \ for \ \{ Microsoft, Apple, IBM, Google \},$$

Table 3.23 Comparison of Models for Microsoft

Metric	AR(1)	MA(2)	EXP (α = 0.73)
AIC	719.8	715.34	982.36
σ^2	22.76	21.72	28.46
Log-L	−356.9	−353.67	−488.16

Table 3.24 Comparison of Models for Apple

Metric	AR(2)	MA(2)	Holt–Winters additive (α = 0.24, β = 0.001, γ = 0.001)
AIC	660.3	692.06	962.71
σ^2	13.72	13.93	19.14
Log-L	−326.45	−327.03	−464.35

Table 3.25 Comparison of Models for IBM

Metric	AR(1)	SARIMA (2,1,2) (1,0,0)[12]	Holt linear (α = 0.91, β = 0.11)
AIC	694	670.09	734.71
σ^2	18.21	15.15	19.16
Log-L	−344	−353.67	−384.43

Table 3.26 Comparison of Models for Google

Metric	MA(5)	ARMA (3,2)	Holt–Winter additive (α = 0.08, β = 0.2, γ = 0.001)
AIC	323.83	319.74	316.5
σ^2	0.88	0.78	0.76
Log-L	−159.33	−152.87	−151.25

Table 3.27 Final Econometric Models for Choice of Office

Office Suite	Selected Model with lowest AIC
Microsoft	MA(2)
Apple	AR(2)
IBM	SARIMA(2,1,2)(1,0,0)
Google	Holt–Winter additive

Table 3.28 Forecasts with Chosen Models

| Month | Software | | | |
	Microsoft	Apple	IBM	Google
January	16.96	19.06	37.21	13.11
February	17.35	18.08	35.25	12.80
March	17.89	18.18	33.72	12.49
April	18.33	18.78	32.44	11.90
May	18.88	18.93	31.36	12.88
June	19.05	19.25	30.46	14.10
July	19.43	19.84	29.05	13.89
August	19.91	18.23	29.87	13.56
September	20.10	18.56	28.19	11.88
October	19.67	18.23	27.45	10.54
November	19.45	18.55	28.13	9.74
December	18.67	18.75	28.51	10.88

Table 3.29 Monthly Exploit Prob. for Each Software

| Month | Software | | | |
	Microsoft	Apple	IBM	Google
January	0.196	0.221	0.431	0.152
February	0.208	0.217	0.422	0.153
March	0.217	0.221	0.410	0.152
April	0.225	0.231	0.398	0.146
May	0.230	0.231	0.382	0.157
June	0.230	0.232	0.368	0.170
July	0.236	0.241	0.353	0.169
August	0.244	0.223	0.366	0.166
September	0.255	0.236	0.358	0.151
October	0.259	0.240	0.362	0.139
November	0.256	0.244	0.371	0.128
December	0.243	0.244	0.371	0.142

Table 3.30 Expected Loss (US$) per Hour at New Delhi

Month	Software				
	Microsoft	Apple	IBM	Google	Total
January	530	181	578	131	1419
February	561	178	566	132	1436
March	587	181	549	131	1448
April	608	189	534	126	1456
May	621	189	512	135	1458
June	621	191	493	146	1450
July	638	198	474	145	1455
August	659	183	491	143	1476
September	689	193	480	130	1492
October	700	197	485	119	1501
November	692	200	497	110	1500
December	656	200	497	122	1476

Table 3.31 Expected Loss (US$) per Hour at Mumbai

Month	Software				
	Microsoft	Apple	IBM	Google	Total
January	1623	433	560	531	3147
February	1717	424	566	537	3244
March	1796	433	549	531	3309
April	1859	452	534	511	3356
May	1901	452	512	549	3414
June	1899	455	493	596	3443
July	1952	473	474	591	3490
August	2016	438	491	582	3527
September	2109	462	480	528	3579
October	2141	471	485	486	3583
November	2118	479	497	449	3543
December	2008	478	497	496	3479

Table 3.32 Expected Loss (US$) per Hour at Kolkata

| Month | Software | | | | |
	Microsoft	Apple	IBM	Google	Total
January	475	150	474	264	1364
February	503	147	464	267	1382
March	526	150	451	264	1391
April	545	157	438	254	1394
May	557	157	420	273	1407
June	556	158	404	296	1415
July	572	164	389	294	1419
August	591	152	403	289	1435
September	618	160	394	263	1435
October	627	163	398	242	1430
November	620	166	408	223	1418
December	588	166	408	246	1409

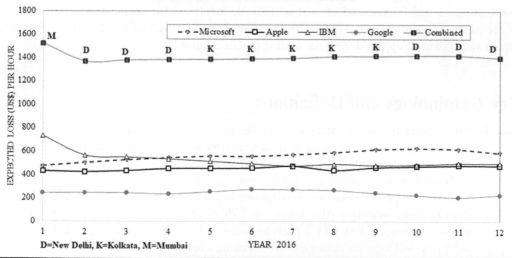

Figure 3.26 Projected loss due to exploits at each location every month.

$$k = 1, 2, 3 \ for \ \{New \ Delhi, Mumbai, Kolkata\}$$

We define the expression for critical level loss for Community Investments as (3.18) (Figure 3.26):

$$\text{Critical Level Loss of Community Investments} = maximize\{P_i * N_{i,k} * l\} \qquad (3.18)$$

3.7 Conclusion and Future Scope

In this chapter, we discuss and compare the existing security issues in social networks, cloud computing, IoT, and web-based attacks. Many software applications are installed on handheld devices, smartphones, IoT, which were not designed with stringent security principles in mind. As a result, ordinary users are becoming victims of software vulnerabilities exploits and increased IT risks. An important way to reduce the IT risk is through exact and evocative prediction of software vulnerabilities for future time-period. In this chapter, we propose novel econometric methods to estimate and predict security vulnerabilities and reduce the likelihood of cyber-attacks arising from them. These techniques will help both cybersecurity researchers and practitioners to analyze security vulnerabilities in software products and make accurate predictions for future. A good forecasting model, such as the proposed time-series techniques can assist a business firm to foresee an approximate number of vulnerabilities in software products. When allowed to choose from a set of software products, our proposed method shall guide a prospective buyer to look for software with a lower number of forecasted vulnerabilities, thus reducing his IT risk while doing business. Additionally, we demonstrate the computation of IT risk through vulnerability estimation for a set of software vulnerabilities with the help for a business scenario. We conclude this study with a future research direction in the possible exploration of nonlinear forecasting techniques including ANNs and threshold autoregression models.

Acknowledgments

The authors wish to express their sincerest thanks to the two anonymous reviewers for their valuable comments and feedback which was enormously helpful in improving the technical quality of the paper. The authors also wish to thank the Book Editor-in-Chief Dr. Brij B. Gupta for his inputs and constant support during the writing of this chapter.

Key Terminology and Definitions

Box–Jenkins Method: In econometric analysis, the Box–Jenkins method refers to the three-stage modeling approach consisting of model identification and selection, parameter estimation, and model validation with time-series data.

Computer Forensics: Also known as cyber forensics, it helps to gather evidence from an IT system or a computer device, or a smartphone in a structured manner after a cybercrime.

Cyber-physical cloud systems: Also known as CPCS, they are an advanced form of cyber-physical systems (CPS). CPCS is cloud-based and enables networking of IoTs, real-time analytics, and logistics management—to name a few.

Domain Name Server: Also known as the DNS server system, it helps to determine the user behind each IP address mapped to it. For example, IP 65.156.1.60 corresponds to the www.tandfonline.com, so that if one types 65.156.1.60 types in the web browser, it will redirect to www.tandfonline.com.

Information security management system: Also known as ISMS, it consists of a set of security policies and activities that must take place in an organization to maintain regular business and keep IT risk at the minimum. These activities may consist of regulatory exercises, security training, audits, and other procedures.

Intrusion Detection System: Also known as the IDS, an intrusion detection system recognizes malicious patterns (signature-based) or anomalies in traffic data to raise the alarm in case. It is of two primary categories: network-based IDS (NIDS) and host-based IDS (HIDS).

Intrusion Prevention System: Also known as the IPS, an intrusion prevention system recognizes malicious patterns or anomalies in traffic, tries to raise the alarm and stop it if required. Typically, it is of two primary categories: network-based IPS (NIPS) and host-based IPS (HIPS).

Open System Interconnection Protocol: Also known as OSI, is a theoretical framework proposed in the ISO/IEC 7498-1 manual to define network components into seven distinct layers. It has been replaced in most organizations with TCP/IP due to its rigidity and less flexibility to match technicality.

RACI: It is derived from the four key responsibilities in an organization responsible, accountable, consulted, and informed. RACI matrix helps to determine the relevant role(s) and duties in different departments and projects.

Software Vulnerability: A software vulnerability is a mistake in the system that can be used by an attacker to gain access to that system or network and thus break the defined security policy. Technically, they are seen as imperfections that may exist within the software codes due to mistakes made by the developers. They may also arise due to modifications in the program execution environment.

SQL Injection: It is a type of code injection vulnerability where a malicious user can insert some mischievous SQL commands which are then executed to extract some private information, access escalation attacks to the benign user.

Secure Socket Layer: It is also known as SSL, and was a cryptographic protocol used to authenticate data generated from the application(s) between client and server. They consist of a public key and private key. SSL ensures that emails, e-commerce transactions, etc. are securely executed.

Sybil Attack: Occurs mostly on a P2P network, where an attacker destabilizes its reputation system. The vulnerability level of the system determines how easily Sybil can be launched on that P2P network.

TCP/IP protocol: The Transmission Control Protocol/Internet Protocol is known as TCP/IP and the primary data transmission and exchange protocol in networks across the internet and other hosts. TCP/IP considers addressing, acknowledgment and mapping of IPs. It has four primary layers instead of seven layers of OSI.

Transport Layer Security: It is also known as TLS and is an up-to-date version of SSL. Most client-server applications resort to TLS to prevent eavesdropping and information altering.

Trojan horse: It is a type of malware that behaves in a naïve manner, but accomplishes malicious tasks such as theft of sensitive information, and data corruption.

VDMs: Based on historical disclosure data, VDMs take help of empirical methodology to estimate and forecast future vulnerabilities in software. In this manner, they can help the software users to identify the maturity of the software. VDMs essentially serve as black boxes for researchers to forecast and come up with a post-facto reliability analysis of the software.

References

Ab Rahman, N. H. and K. K. R. Choo. 2015. A survey of information security incident handling in the cloud. *Compu. Secur.* Vol. 49:45–69.

Ab Rahman, N. H., N. D. W. Cahyani, and K. K. R. Choo. 2017. Cloud incident handling and forensic-by-design: Cloud storage as a case study. *Concur. Comput. Pract. Exp*. Vol. 29 Ser. 14.

Ab Rahman, N. H., W. B. Glisson, Y. Yang, and K. K. R. Choo. 2016. Forensic-by-design framework for cyber-physical cloud systems. *IEEE Cloud Comp*. Vol. 3 Ser. 1: 50–59.

Alhazmi, O. H. and Y. K. Malaiya. 2005. Modeling the vulnerability discovery process. In *Proceedings of the 16th IEEE International Symposium on Software Reliability Engineering*. ISSRE 2005, Chicago, IL. pp. 1–10.

Alhazmi, O. H. and Y. K. Malaiya. 2006. Prediction capabilities of vulnerability discovery models. In *Proceedings of the IEEE Annual Reliability and Maintainability Symposium, 2006. RAMS'06*, Anaheim, CA. pp. 86–91.

Alhazmi, O. H. and Y. K. Malaiya. 2008. Application of vulnerability discovery models to major operating systems. *IEEE Trans. Reliab*. Vol. 57 Ser.1: 14–22.

Alhazmi, O. H., Y. K. Malaiya, and I. Ray. 2007. Measuring, analyzing and predicting security vulnerabilities in software systems. *Compu. Secur*. Vol. 26 Ser.3: 219–228.

Alomari E., S. Manickam, B. B. Gupta, S. Karuppayah, and R. Alfaris. 2012. Botnet-based Distributed Denial of Service (DDoS) Attacks on Web Servers: Classification and Art. *Int. J. Comp. Appl*. Vol. 49 no. 7, 24–32.

Al-Qurishi, M., S. M. Mizanur, M. S. Hossain, A. Almogren, M. Alrubaian, A. Alamri, and B. B. Gupta. 2017. An efficient key agreement protocol for Sybil-precaution in online social networks. *Future Gen. Comp. Sys*. Vol. 84: 139–148.

Alsmirat, M. A., Y. Jararweh, I. Obaidat, and B. B. Gupta. 2017. Internet of surveillance: A cloud supported large-scale wireless surveillance system. *J. Supercomput*. Vol. 73 Ser.3: 973–992.

Anderson, R. 2002. *Security in open versus closed systems—the dance of Boltzmann, Coase and Moore* (pp. 1–15). Technical report, England, Cambridge University.

Ardagna, D. 2015. Cloud and multi-cloud computing: current challenges and future applications. pp. 1–2. In *The Proceedings of the 7th International Workshop on Principles of Engineering Service-Oriented and Cloud Systems*, Florence, Italy, IEEE Press.

Badve, O., B.B. Gupta, and S. Gupta. 2016. Reviewing the Security Features in Contemporary Security Policies and Models for Multiple Platforms. pp. 479–504. In: B.B. Gupta, D. P. Agrawal and S. Yamaguchi [eds.] *Handbook of Research on Modern Cryptographic Solutions for Computer and Cyber Security*, IGI Global, Hershey, PA.

Bass, F. M. 1969. A new product growth for model consumer durables. *Manag. Sci*. Vol. 15 Ser 5: 215–227.

Box, G. E. P., and G. M. Jenkins. 1970. *Time Series Analysis, Forecasting and Control: Holden-Day*, San Francisco, U.S.A.

Box, G. E. P. and G. M. Jenkins and G. C. Reinsel. 1994. *Time Series Analysis, Forecasting and Control*, 3rd Ed., Prentice Hall, Englewood Cliffs, NJ.

Brockwell, P.J. and R. A. Davis. 1987. *Time Series: Theory and Methods*, Springer-Verlag, New York.

Brockwell, P.J. and R. A. Davis. 2002. *Introduction to Time Series and Forecasting*, 2nd Ed., Springer-Verlag, New York.

Cahyani, N. D. W., B. Martini, K. K. R. Choo, and A. K. B. P. Al-Azhar. 2017. Forensic data acquisition from cloud-of-things devices: Windows Smartphones as a case study. *Concur. Comput. Pract. Exp*. Vol. 29 Ser. 14, https://doi.org/10.1002/cpe.3855.

Chhabra, M., B.B. Gupta, and A. Almomani. 2013. A novel solution to handle DDOS attack in MANET. *J. Infor. Secur*. Vol. 4 Ser. 3: 165.

Chatfield, C. 1996. Model uncertainty and forecast accuracy. *J. Forecast*. Vol. 15 Ser.7: 495–508.

Daryabar, F., A. Dehghantanha, and K. K. R. Choo. 2017. Cloud storage forensics: MEGA as a case study. *Aust. J. Forensic. Sci*. Vol. 49 Ser. 3: 344–357.

Dickey, D. A., and W. A. Fuller. 1981. Likelihood ratio statistics for autoregressive time series with a unit root. *Econometrica J. Econ. Soc*. Vol. 49 Ser. 4: 1057–1072.

D'Orazio, C. J. and K. K. R. Choo. 2018. Circumventing iOS security mechanisms for APT forensic investigations: A security taxonomy for cloud apps. *Future Gen. Comp. Sys*. Vol. 79, Ser.1: 247–261.

Fernando, N., S. W. Loke, and W. Rahayu. 2013. Mobile cloud computing: A survey. *Future Gen. Comp. Sys*. Vol. 9 Ser. 1: 84–106.

Ginovsky, J. 2014. Under Attack. American Bankers Association. *ABA Bank. J.* Vol. 106 Ser 4: 30.

Gupta, B. B., R. C. Joshi, and M. Misra. 2012. ANN based scheme to predict number of zombies in a DDoS Attack. *Int. J. Netw. Secur.* Vol. 14 Ser. 2: 61–70.

Gupta, B. B, D. P. Agrawal, and S. Yamaguchi. (Eds.). 2016. *Handbook of Research on Modern Cryptographic Solutions for Computer and Cyber Security*, IGI Global, Hershey, PA.

Gupta, S. and B. B. Gupta. 2015. PHP-sensor: A prototype method to discover workflow violation and XSS vulnerabilities in PHP web applications. p. 59. In *Proceedings of the 12th ACM International Conference on Computing Frontiers*, Ischia, Italy, ACM.

Gupta, S. and B. B. Gupta. 2016. JS-SAN: defense mechanism for HTML5-based web applications against JavaScript code injection vulnerabilities. *Secur. Comm. Netw.* Vol. 9 Ser. 11: 1477–1495.

Gupta, S., and B. B. Gupta. 2017. Cross-Site Scripting (XSS) attacks and defense mechanisms: Classification and state-of-the-art. *Int. J. Syst. Assur. Eng. Manage.* Vol. 8 Ser. 1: 512–530.

Holt, C. C. 1957. Forecasting trends and seasonal by exponentially weighted averages. *Int. J. Forecast.* Vol. 20 Ser. 1: 5–13.

Jimenez, M., M. Papadakis, and Y. Le Traon. 2016. An empirical analysis of vulnerabilities in openSSL and the linux kernel. pp. 105–112. In *Proceedings of 23rd Asia-Pacific Software Engineering Conference (APSEC)*, Hamilton, New Zealand, IEEE.

Joh, H., J. Kim, and Y. K. Malaiya. 2008, November. Vulnerability discovery modeling using Weibull distribution. In *Proceedings of 19th IEEE International Symposium on Software Reliability Engineering*, ISSRE 2008, Seattle, WA. pp. 299–300.

Johnson, P., D. Gorton, R. Lagerström, and M. Ekstedt. 2016. Time between vulnerability disclosures: A measure of software product vulnerability. *Comput. Sec.* Vol. 62, 278–295.

Hwang, Y. H. 2015. IoT security & privacy: Threats and challenges. p. 1. In *Proceedings of the 1st Workshop on IoT Privacy, Trust, and Security*, Singapore, ACM.

Ibtihal, M. and N. Hassan. 2017. Homomorphic encryption as a service for outsourced images in mobile cloud computing environment. *Int. J Cloud Appl. Comp.* Vol. 7 Ser. 2: 27–40.

Jiang, R., R. Lu, and K. K. R. Choo. 2018. Achieving high performance and privacy-preserving query over encrypted multidimensional big metering data. *Future. Gen. Comp. Sys.* Vol. 78: 392–401.

Kayworth, T. and D. Whitten. 2012. Effective information security requires a balance of social and technology factors. *MIS Quart. Exec.* Vol. 9 Ser. 3: 165–182.

Kumari, S., X. Li, F. Wu, A. K. Das, K. K. R. Choo, and J. Shen. 2017. Design of a provably secure biometrics-based multi-cloud-server authentication scheme. *Future. Gen. Comp. Sys.* Vol. 68: 320–330.

Ljung, G. and G.E.P. Box. 1978. On a measure of lack of fit in time series models. *Biometrika* Vol. 65: 297–303.

Loch, K. D., H. H. Carr, and M. E. Warkentin. 1992. Threats to information systems: Today's reality, yesterday's understanding, *MIS Quart.* Vol. 16 Ser. 2: 173–186.

Makridakis, S., S. C. Wheelwright, and R. J. Hyndman. 2008. *Forecasting Methods and Applications*, John Wiley & Sons, New York.

Memos, V. A., K. E. Psannis, Y. Ishibashi, B. G. Kim, and B. B. Gupta. 2018. An efficient algorithm for media-based surveillance system (EAMSuS) in IoT smart city framework. *Future. Gen. Comp. Sys.* Vol. 83: 619–628.

Nguyen, V. H., and F. Massacci. 2012. An independent validation of vulnerability discovery models. In *Proceedings of the 7th ACM Symposium on Information, Computer and Communications Security*, pp. 6–7.

Odelu, V., A. K. Das, Y. S. Rao, S. Kumari, M. K. Khan, and K. K. R. Choo. 2017. Pairing-based CP-ABE with constant-size cipher-texts and secret keys for cloud environment. *Comp. Stand. Interf.* Vol. 54: 3–9.

Osanaiye, O., S. Chen, Z. Yan, R. Lu, K. K. R. Choo, and M. Dlodlo. 2017. From cloud to fog computing: A review and a conceptual live VM migration framework. *IEEE Access* Vol. 5: 8284–8300.

Osanaiye, O., K. K. R. Choo, and M. Dlodlo. 2016. Distributed denial of service (DDoS) resilience in cloud: review and conceptual cloud DDoS mitigation framework. *J. Netw. Comput. Appl.* 67: 147–165.

Patrikakis, C., M. Masikos, and O. Zouraraki. 2004. Distributed denial of service attacks. *The Internet Protoc. J.* Vol. 7 Ser. 4: 13–35.

Ransbotham, S., S. Mitra, and J. Ramsey. 2012. Are markets for vulnerabilities effective? *MIS Quart.* Vol. 36 Ser. 1: 43–64.

Rescorla, E. 2005. Is finding security holes a good idea? *IEEE Sec. Priv.* Vol. 3 no. 1, 14–19.

Ruohonen, J., S. Hyrynsalmi, and V. Leppänen. 2015. The sigmoidal growth of operating system security vulnerabilities: an empirical revisit. *Comp. Sec.* Vol. 55 no. 1, 1–20.

Scandariato, R., J. Walden, A. Hovsepyan, and W. Joosen. 2014. Predicting vulnerable software components via text mining. *IEEE Trans. Softw. Eng.* Vol. 40 no.10, 993–1006.

Sen, R., and S. Borle. 2015. Estimating the contextual risk of data breach: An empirical approach. *J. Manag. Inform. Syst.* Vol. 32 no. 2, 314–341.

Shin, Y., and L. Williams. 2011. An initial study on the use of execution complexity metrics as indicators of software vulnerabilities. In *Proceedings of the 7th International Workshop on Software Engineering for Secure Systems*, pp. 1–7.

Somani, G., M. S. Gaur, D. Sanghi, M. Conti, and R. Buyya. 2017. DDoS attacks in cloud computing: Issues, taxonomy, and future directions. *Compu. Comm.* Vol. 107: 30–48.

Stergiou, C., K. E. Psannis, B. G. Kim, and B.B. Gupta. 2018. Secure integration of IoT and cloud computing. *Future. Gen. Comp. Sys.* Vol. 78: 964–975.

Teing, Y. Y., A. Dehghantanha, K. K. R. Choo, and L. T. Yang. 2017. Forensic investigation of P2P cloud storage services and backbone for IoT networks: BitTorrent Sync as a case study. *Compu. Electr. Eng.* Vol. 58: 350–363.

Telang, R. and S. Wattal. 2007. An empirical analysis of the impact of software vulnerability announcements on firm stock price. *IEEE Trans. Softw. Eng.* Vol. 33 Ser. 8: 544–557.

Tewari, A. and B. B. Gupta. 2017. A lightweight mutual authentication protocol based on elliptic curve cryptography for IoT devices. *Int. J. Adv. Intell. Parad.* Vol. 9 Ser. 2: 111–121.

Tripathi, S., B.B. Gupta, A. Almomani, A. Mishra, and S. Veluru. 2013. Hadoop based defense solution to handle distributed denial of service (ddos) attacks. *J. Infor. Secur.* Vol. 4 Ser. 3: 150.

Tsay, R. S. 2005. *Analysis of financial time series*, John Wiley & Sons, New York.

Winters, P.R. 1960. Forecasting sales by exponentially weighted moving averages. *Manage. Sci.* Vol. 6 Ser. 3: 324–342.

Woo S-W, H. C. Joh, O. H. Alhazmi, and Y. K. Malaiya. 2011. Modeling vulnerability discovery process in Apache and IIS HTTP servers, *Comp. Sec.* Vol. 30 no. 1, 50–62.

Yang, Y., J. K. Liu, K. Liang, K. K. R. Choo, and J. Zhou. 2015. Extended proxy-assisted approach: Achieving revocable fine-grained encryption of cloud data. p. 146. In *Proceedings of the 20th European Symposium on Research in Computer Security*, Vienna, Austria, Springer.

Younis, A., H. Joh, and Y. Malaiya. 2011, July. Modeling learningless vulnerability discovery using a folded distribution. In *Proc. of International Conference of Security and Management SAM*, Vol. 11, pp. 617–623.

Younis, A., Y. K. Malaiya, and I. Ray. 2016. Assessing vulnerability exploitability risk using software properties. *Softw. Qual. J.* Vol. 24 no. 1, 159–202.

Younis, A., Y. Malaiya, C. Anderson, and I. Ray. 2016. To fear or not to fear that is the question: Code characteristics of a vulnerable function with an existing exploit. pp. 97–104. In *Proceedings of the 6th Conference on Data and Application Security and Privacy*, New Orleans, ACM.

Yu, C., J. Li, X. Li, X. Ren, and B. B. Gupta. 2017. Four-image encryption scheme based on quaternion Fresnel transform, chaos and computer generated hologram. *Multimed. Tools Appl.* Vol. 77 Ser. 4: 1–24.

Zhang, Z., and B. B. Gupta. 2016. Social media security and trustworthiness: overview and new direction. *Future Gener. Comp. Syst.* Vol. 86, 914–925.

Zhang, Z., R. Sun, C. Zhao, J. Wang, C. K. Chang, and B. B. Gupta. 2017. CyVOD: A novel trinity multimedia social network scheme. *Multimed. Tools Appl.* Vol. 76 Ser. 18: 18513–18529.

Zhou, L., Y. Zhu, and K. K. R. Choo. 2018. Efficiently and securely harnessing cloud to solve linear regression and other matrix operations. *Future. Gen. Comp. Sys.* Vol. 81: 404–413.

Zkik, K., G. Orhanou, and S. El Hajji. 2017. Secure mobile multi-cloud architecture for authentication and data storage. *Int. J. Cloud Appl. Comput.* Vol. 7 Ser. 2: 62–76.

Further Reading

Amin, A., L. Grunske, and A. Colman. 2013. An approach to software reliability prediction based on time series modeling. *J. Syst. Softw.* Vol. 86 Ser. 7: 1923–1932.

Arora, A., R. Telang, and H. Xu. 2008. Optimal policy for software vulnerability disclosure. *Manage. Sc.* Vol. 54 Ser. 4: 642–656.

Arora, A., A. Nandkumar, and R. Telang. 2006. Does information security attack frequency increase with vulnerability disclosure?—An empirical analysis. *Info. Sys. Front.* Vol. 8 Ser. 5: 350–362.

Arora, A., R. Krishnan, R. Telang, and Y. Yang. 2010. An empirical analysis of software vendors' patch release behavior: impact of vulnerability disclosure. *Info. Syst. Res.* Vol. 21 Ser. 1: 115–132.

Igure, V. M., S. A. Laughter, and R. D. Williams. 2006. Security issues in SCADA networks. *Comp. Secu.* Vol. 25 Ser. 7: 498–506.

Mitra, S. and S. Ransbotham. 2015. Information disclosure and the diffusion of information security attacks. *Info. Syst. Res.* Vol. 26 Ser. 3: 565–584.

Pang, Y., X. Xue, and A. S. Namin. 2015. Predicting vulnerable software components through n-gram analysis and statistical feature selection. pp. 543–548. In *Proceedings of the 14th International Conference on Machine Learning and Applications*. Varna, Bulgaria, Springer.

Rahimi, S. and M. Zargham. 2013. Vulnerability scrying method for software vulnerability discovery prediction without a vulnerability database. *IEEE Trans. Reliab.* Vol. 62 Ser. 2: 395–407.

Sen, R. and S. Borle. 2015. Estimating the contextual risk of data breach: An empirical approach. *J. Manage. Info. Sys.* Vol. 32 Ser. 2: 314–341.

Shin, Y., and L. Williams. 2013. Can traditional fault prediction models be used for vulnerability prediction? *Emp. Softw. Eng.* Vol. 18 Ser. 1: 25–59.

Stuckman, J., J. Walden, and R. Scandariato. 2017. The effect of dimensionality reduction on software vulnerability prediction models. *IEEE Trans. Reliab.* Vol. 66 Ser. 1: 17–37.

Chapter 4

Cyberspace and Cybersecurity in the Digital Age: An Evolving Concern in Contemporary Security Discourse

Sushma Devi and Mohd Aarif Rather

Central University of Gujarat

Contents

4.1 Introduction

The concept of security is one of the core concepts in the study of International Relations (IR). Traditionally, security analysis focused on the state security, viewing this security as a function of the levels of threats that states face from other states as well as the manner and effectiveness of state responses to such threats. The emphasis until recently has been what might be categorized as traditional security issues giving priority to states (Rather and Jose 2014). Under such purview, the concept of national security came into existence and attained top priority at the global level. It is defined as the ability of a state to pursue the development of its internal life without any interference or even threat of interference from external powers (Cooley 2011). During the Cold War period, the concept of national security centered on the realist paradigm under which states mainly relied on the military power to protect their political stability, territorial integrity, and sovereignty. Thus, national security was a simple strategy aimed to respond to activities arising out of aggression, territorial imperative, and expansionism (Goss 1999).

However, after the end of the Cold War, there was a shift of focus from the state-centric notion of security to protection of the individual. As such, the individuals became the referent objects of security (Buzan 1991). The nature of threats changed from external aggression to intra-state conflicts arising due to civil wars, environmental degradation, economic deprivation, and human rights violation. It is in this context that the national security came to include within its ambit other issues of security apart from territorial protection such as poverty, industrial competitiveness, educational crises, environmental hazards, drug and human trafficking, resource shortages. Apart from these threats, the age of Information, Communication and Technology (ICT) such as Internet, email, social websites, and satellite has revolutionized every aspect of human life. The Internet evolved as an icon of digital age and more particularly of cyberspace. The period of ICT also known as information or digital age has increased the significance of interest groups, firms (both private and public), social movements, individuals, and transnational networks.

At the same time, the arena of the national security in the digital age is confronted with new threats intended against destroying the technology infrastructure of a nation. It covers a wide range of issues like critical infrastructure protection, cyber terrorism, cyber threats, privacy issues, cybercrime, and cyber warfare. With the advent of globalization process, the world has become more interconnected, and the number of Internet hosts and personal computers industry has increased. The Internet and ICTs are essential for economic and social development and form a vital infrastructure. Economy, society, and governments become increasingly reliant on this digital infrastructure to perform their essential functions. Under such an open and wide platform, the Internet remained no longer safe (Pillai 2012). This information revolution has brought into forefront issues of privacy and security concerns and more significantly the concept of cybersecurity.

4.2 Cyberspace and Territorial State

Cyberspace is very different from the international political and geographic space and is subject to different rules, different potentialities, and different threats. Due to its ubiquitous nature and vast scope and scale, cyberspace transcends physical space where information is free to travel anywhere it is requested regardless of national borders. In recent times, the issues related to cyberspace and its uses have entered into realm of high politics. The capabilities of cyber have now become a source of vulnerability and thereby posing potential threats to national security as well as disturb-ing the familiar and traditional world order. The growth of cyber access has already started influ-encing the Westphalian-anchored global system in powerful ways (Choucri 2012). For instance, the Stuxnet worm marked a turning point into a new cyber conflict under which the states need to protect their territorial spaces as well as assure the safety and economic well-being of their citizens. Nowadays, all states are attempting to control anything that comes across their territory includ-ing cyberspace. As a result, a new "cyber Westphalian age" started emerging, and the states began to protect their economies as well as citizens and thereby the process of regulating the cyber-space initiated. In present times, the major powers such as United States and China are already started demonstrating basic elements of emerging cybered territorial sovereignty (Demchak and Dombrowski 2014).

Also, the interconnectedness imparted by cyberspace around the globe has also challenged the traditional understanding of national security, IR and power politics, boundaries and bor-ders vis-à-vis a host of other concepts and their parallel realities (Choucri 2012). On the other hand, cyberattacks on institutions resulting in the theft of valuable intellectual property rights have hit the financial services and defense industries. States have taken increasing notice, not simply because their own information systems are compromised but because government officials recognize their dependence on the private sector which has become the weaker link in national security and cyberspace (Demchak and Dombrowski 2011). In addition, the arena of cyberspace is assumed by many as the twenty-first-century battleground in which the next war among the developed world will be fought (Hughes 2010).

In recent decades, the information and technology has strongly intertwined in our lives inter-connecting people through Internet, satellite television, and mobile phones. It is making a great impact on the industry and trade by offering technological innovations. It also has the potential to change our learning and working patterns, social relationships, our business, and even our cultural spheres (Ram 2010). The reliance on these technologies has left the world open to a wide range of threats commonly known as cyber threats. However, the nature of such threats can vastly increase their reach as well as impact as the attackers need not to be physically close to their victims and can more easily remain unidentified. Also, the sophistication of cyberattack tech-niques which involve combined multiple techniques can target individuals, critical infrastruc-tures, businesses, and government organizations (Wilshusen 2012). The state which is seen as the core provider of security to its citizens is being increasingly challenged in its role by various non-state actors like business firms, transnational organizations, networks, and individuals. These channels can communicate information all over the world with great speed. What is different is the magnitude of information and the multiple entry points that have further exhausted the capabilities of states and their resources to block the penetration of that information (Eriksson and Giacomello 2007).

From the theoretical perspective of IR, not much study has been done with regard to under-standing the impact of informational revolution on security. Realist scholars like Barry Buzan and Kenneth Waltz assume that the IT-related security threats are largely economic in nature and such threats do not necessarily affect the security of states (Buzan 1991, Walt 1994). Therefore, these threats may not be considered as security threats and could not be included within the real-ist paradigm of IR. Contrary to realism, the liberals view not only states but also non-state actors as important players in international politics. Within this purview, liberals such as Joseph Nye and Robert Keohane believe in the emergence of a wide range of new threats emanating from transnational corporations, online groups, etc. (Keohane and Nye 1998). The constructivists, however, focus on identity and culturally related threats, and under this approach, it is possible to address the wide range of perceived security threats. In terms of threats to critical infrastructures, this could, for example, include not only digital attacks but also technical collapses and bugs as well as natural disasters such as volcanic eruptions and earthquakes (Eriksson and Giacomello 2007). The elaboration of theoretical perspectives of cybersecurity is dealt in detail separately in the following pages.

4.3 Challenges in Cyberspace

Cyberspace represents a unique feature of the contemporary life. Individuals, groups, and communities across the world connect, organize, and socialize themselves in and through the arena of cyberspace. Due to the enhancement of global access to Internet, cyberspace has been increasingly woven into the fabric of everyday life around the world. Also, it has become an incubator for new forms of entrepreneurship, transparent governments, the spread of free speech, strong militaries, advances in technology as well as new social networks. In addition, the modern critical infrastructures like energy, transportation, communication, banking and finance, and the defense industry largely rely on cyberspace. Apart from this, the political and social movements rely on the Internet in order to enable new forms of organization and action. At the same time, threats confronting the cyberspace present serious challenges to economy, national security, and public safety all over the world (U.S. Dept. of Defence 2011).

The challenges for security in cyberspace can be understood under three broad categories, i.e., threat, vulnerability, and consequences. In the arena of cyberspace, "threat" represents a wide range of ongoing malicious activities which are hard to attribute to specific attackers and sources. The "vulnerability" signifies the characteristics of the target as well as the probability of an attempted attack to be successful. Third, "consequence" is the social, political, or economic damage vis-à-vis costs inflicted by a successful attack (Willis et al. 2005).

4.3.1 Threats

The cyberspace is an arena where there are low-entry barriers. This allows multiple malicious actors like hackers, industrial spies, terrorists, organized crime groups, and even foreign state actors to carry out their activities. Among these, states are the most dangerous and capable actors in cyberspace as they possess the capabilities of manpower and resources. In the year 2011, the U.S. Defense Department estimated that more than 100 foreign intelligence agencies had attempted to disrupt into the U.S. networks (Nielsen 2012). Such types of activities were repeatedly noticed in the arena of cyberspace.

In addition, the presence of malicious actors in the cyberspace and the methods they use have become increasingly sophisticated over time. Cyber criminals have started adopting automated tools having the capacity of releasing very large volumes of malware with sophisticated features making it difficult for the antivirus software to keep up (GTISC 2010). The report prepared by the Symantec regarding the Internet security threat emphasized that cyber criminals have shifted their efforts toward creating new kits with the intention of selling them to new entrants in the underground economy. This provides the technical knowledge to relatively inexperienced attackers in order to carry attacks without too much difficulty (Symantec 2010). Apart from cybercrimes, there existed concerns about the threat activity primarily because of unauthorized intrusions, data compromise, or theft and persistent presence.

The nature of cyber threats primarily challenges the internal sovereignty of states, i.e., effective control over the national boundary as well as of the people living within it, but not principally external sovereignty, i.e., the formal recognition of independence by other states. Against these threats, not only the tangible and intangible values of information but also the ability of governments to control the course of events are at stake. Apart from this, cyber threats and other challenges of the information revolution are clearly visible in the general trends of globalization. In this context, the advent of Internet not only made real-time global communications possible for existing NGOs, but it also provided an opportunity for new online groups. These events have both negative and positive effects like transnational crime, acts of terrorism, and the destabilization of states began to appear while as cooperation, integration, and liberation may have eased (Eriksson and Giacomello 2006). As in Beck's (1992, 1999) analysis, the increasing reliance and the development on modern technologies like nuclear power have the effect of constantly producing new risks. In this perspective, the focus is on the side effects of new technologies (ICTs) for commerce, energy production, and communication in general and on cyber threats in particular.

4.3.2 Vulnerabilities

Vulnerability means identifying the weak points and reducing the effectiveness of the system's quality and standard. To break the security of the system, the attackers use the set of applications and rules in order to create the weak points in networks. The common tools practiced within such an operation include Trojan attacks, ethical hacking, and logical bombing. By doing so, it becomes easy for the attackers to create the unwanted data between the networks as well as to change or modify the original data or information (Mary 2010). Thus, these attacks have the potential to cause varying degrees of harm ranging from the manageable to the serious.

The states all over the world have vulnerabilities in cyberspace. Due to great reliance on cyberspace in terms of networked systems and devices, the security of technologies vis-à-vis cybersecurity is confronted with severe critical threats. Also, the non-state actors increasingly threaten to penetrate and disrupt the defense mechanisms of the countries operating in the cyberspace. In the year 2002, the U.S. Naval War College hosted a war game known as "Digital Pearl Harbor" in order to develop a scenario for a coordinated cyber terrorism event in which fake attacks by computer security experts against critical infrastructure systems were carried out. These cyberattacks revealed that the most vulnerable infrastructure was the Internet as well as the computer systems that are part of the financial infrastructure (Chen 2013). In the same year, a major vulnerability was revealed in switching equipment software intended to threaten the infrastructure for major portions of the Internet. Such a flaw in the network has enabled the cyberattackers to take over Internet routers and damage the network telecommunication equipment's globally. However, before the problem could be exploited by hackers, it was tackled. But had it not been solved, its flaws could have been exploited to cause many serious problems like bringing down widespread telephone networks as well as halting of information exchanged between ground and aircraft flight control (Gellman 2002).

Most of the control systems are exacerbated by insecure connections and are vulnerable to be attacked. The organizations often leave open access links for maintenance as well as examination of system status. The authentication of such links may not be protected which enhances the risk that hackers could use these insecure connections to break their controlled system. In addition, control systems often use wireless communications systems and are vulnerable to attack (Ghansah 2009). Such vulnerabilities may also pass through commercial telecommunications facilities and may cause severe damages to these facilities.

The vulnerability of cyberspace also involves a denial of service attack having the potential of affecting the availability of a network resulting in an interruption of business operations. The presence of unreliability may deter people from using the service which in the long run could drive companies out of business. For instance, if confidential information is publicized over the Internet, people as well as organizations would hesitate to use that source, due to the threat of leak (McGuinn 2004). Moreover, the countries around the world have started to combine advancements in information technology with energy sectors particularly electricity infrastructure. Such a system uses interconnected elements that improve the control and communications across the various segments of energy generation, circulation, and consumption. However, the grid becomes a prime target for cyberattacks as well as acts of terrorism because of the critical nature of the technology and the services that it provides (Wilson 2005).

4.3.3 Risks

The third challenge of the cyberspace is the risk factor behind the attacks. There are possibly many realms of consequences involved but among them, national security, economic well-being, and public safety are of utmost concern. Public safety means protecting the critical infrastructure, i.e., systems, assets, and networks of the country. Any damage to such infrastructure may lead toward harmful effects on national and economic security as well as public safety. The critical infrastructures cover a wide range of fields in our day-to-day lives like energy, transportation systems, energy, communication, emergency services, banking and finance, and the like. The operation of this infrastructure is increasingly dependent on cyberspace and thus vulnerable to cyberattack. Therefore, these attacks have the potential consequences to destroy the critical infrastructure as well as causing physical damage and economic costs (U.S. Homeland Security 2013).

Another consequence of risk associated with the cyberspace is destruction to the economy. According to the study conducted in 2010 on 45 companies, it was estimated that the average annual cost of cybercrime is $3.8 million, but could also range from $1 million to $52 million per year per company (Ponemon Institute 2010). The costs include the loss of data as well as of recovery and system cleanup. Also, the cyberattacks may have major consequences for individuals having their sensitive personal information stored in communication devices. During 2005–2010, over 345 million records were either changed, lost, or destructed (Nielsen 2012). However, instead of such huge scale, there are many incidents that are unreported either because they are not detected or because organizations want to avoid revealing vulnerabilities. Thus, the economic consequences of inadequate cybersecurity could ultimately result in the loss of confidentiality in the system.

The final set of consequences relates to the issue of national security. National security is dependent on internal cohesion, economic strength, and technological expertise. The defense establishments as well as military are dependent on information technology for almost everything ranging from weapons procurement to logistics and from command and control to intelligence (Lynn 2010). Developed nations around the world are developing their cyber capabilities in order to counter the conventional military strengths. For instance, many analysts across the globe believe that the China is developing cyber war capabilities as a means to counter U.S. conventional military strength (Nielsen 2012). On the other hand, it is believed that inadequacies in the realm of national security could result in the loss of military capabilities which could reduce the ability of the government to pursue its national security interests as well as defend the country from foreign threats (Nielsen 2012).

Networks are operated in cyberspace and are embedded in our social and political life as well as in our economies. Therefore, they have attained the status of central tool for human activity.

Such networks hold information of immense value to regulate the machinery that provides critical services. But instead of providing immense opportunities, the arena has also evolved as a major source of risk to nations. The governments across the globe have been hesitant to interfere with it, and the result is a weakly governed space. Also, due to the lack of explicit agreement among nations as well as extensive cybercrime and cyber espionage, this unstable environment invites misinterpretation, miscalculation, and accidental escalation of conflict (Lewis 2013). Thus, it becomes prerequisite condition for all nations to uphold the responsibility in order to protect the said cyberspace.

4.4 Evolution of Cybersecurity

The genesis of cybersecurity may be traced to the invention of Internet.[1] However, cybersecurity has its roots during the Cold War when the Soviet Union launched the first space satellite called *Sputnik I* on October 4, 1957. As a counterpart, the United States established the Advanced Research Projects Agency in order to promote research that would ensure the United States to compete with and surpass Soviet Union in any technological race (Almagor 2011). At that time, the networks mainly relied on a single central control function, and the major focus remained to protect such networks from the vulnerability of attack. The common myth goes that the entire network would become unusable if the network's central control point ceased to function. Therefore, the scientists intended to diffuse the network in order to sustain it even after attacking one or more of its communication centers (Schneider and Evans 2007). It is from that time when the issues of defense-related secrets during wartime associated with networks came into existence and received priority among the power blocs.

The attacks on telecommunications systems in the early 1960s eventually led toward subversion of the long-distance phone systems as a means of amusement as well as for theft of services. As technology of telecommunications progressed throughout the IT world, the persons commonly known as hobbyists with criminal tendencies learned to enter systems and networks. In 1970s, the first computer hackers appeared and tried to circumvent the system besides attempting to make free phone calls. Also, the protocol known as "Telnet" came into being which opened the door for public use of data networks that were primarily restricted to academic researchers and government contractors (Kabay 2009).

However, it was only after the mid-1980s that the first computer virus called "Brain" was created and as such the Computer Fraud and Abuse Act was created in 1986 (Symantec 2009). The act was enacted by the U.S. Congress in order to protect the federal and bank computers as well as computers connected to the Internet. Although it was not a comprehensive provision, it was an inception toward filling the gaps and flaws in the existing federal criminal laws (Doyle 2014). Also, the period saw the beginning of the hackers and crimes relating to computers. The FBI all over the world raided over 414 gangs after a nine-day cracking spree accused of breaking top-secret systems (Red Hat 2005). Thus, the decade witnessed programs with malicious software like self-replicating programs which were created with the intention of interfering with personal computers. Also, the period was marked by the invention of Internet. With the increased access to Internet, the number of users also increased providing a space to criminals to use unauthorized access to poorly protected systems for damage, financial gain, and political action (Kabay 2009).

---

[1] The first recorded description of the social interactions that emerged through networking was a series of memos written by J. C. R. Licklider of MIT in August 1962 discussing his "Galactic Network" concept (Leiner 2015).

During the 1990s, the Internet became available to the public along with the existence of the World Wide Web. The Internet started to grow exponentially, and surfing the Internet has become a day-to-day affair for many users. At the same time, the security concerns related to Internet started increasing tremendously. It is estimated that there are approximately 950 million people using the Internet worldwide. On any day, there are unit roughly 225 major incidences of a security breach (Gahlot et al. 2014). The presence of such security breaches has also resulted in monetary losses to a large extent. Thus, the decade witnessed several notable threats affecting the modern information security industry. The Distributed Denial of Service Attacks (DDoS) as well as the bots that made them possible also came into being. Presently, the most problematic and latest trends in network security threats are the Botnet-based DDoS attacks on the application layer. These attacks on the application layer curtail revenue, limit resources as well as yield customer dissatisfaction, among others. Besides, such attacks are among the most challenging problems to resolve online, especially, when the target is the Web server (Alomari et al. 2012).

Moreover, in early decades of the twenty-first century, this malicious Internet activity assumed the shape of a major criminal enterprise aimed at monetary gain (Symantec 2009). Such activities entered into mainstream by primarily targeting online banking and then moving onto social networking sites (Pillai 2012). In the context of online social networks, the most significant type of intrusion is the so-called Sybil attack, in which the attacker spawns multiple accounts with false credentials, along with initiates many connections with genuine accounts, thus artificially building up the relevance of the fake users on the network (Al-Qurishi et al. 2017). Nowadays, the cyber issues have assumed a much larger dimension and have a significant impact on the national security of states. The year 2001 is often proclaimed by the media as the year of first cyber world war. In this year, a U.S. surveillance plane was forced to land into the territory of China after a mid-air collision with a Chinese jet fighter. The event was marked with a quick response from both sides including the destruction of U.S. and Chinese websites and waves as well as DDoS attacks (Kessimeris and Buckley 2010).

In 2010, the most expensive malware of the computer worm called the Stuxnet was discovered. The Stuxnet was introduced as a precedent of new threat faced in the cyberspace, and it is being argued that it marked the creation of a new westphalian world of virtual borders as well as national cyber commands (Demchak and Dombrowski 2011). It was reported by the security company Symantec that 60% of the infected computers worldwide were in Iran. Also, the Iranian nuclear program had been delayed because some of its centrifuges had been damaged by this worm (Reardon 2012). It is reported that the worm has bypassed the controls of Internet security and only corrupted the precise computer DNA of Iranian nuclear reactors. Inspite of early denials, the nuclear community of Iran admitted that its plant has been infected and its filters were insecure. Apart from this, with the help of Stuxnet, the attackers can freely choose the scale of their own organization, the proximity of their targets as well as the accuracy necessary to achieve their desired effects vis-à-vis can use the Internet to collect data on projected targets (Demchak and Dombrowski 2011). Thus, it has created an era in which the complexity of national security challenges posed by cyberspace has generated a new level of insecurity (Brenner 2004).

Besides, the globalization process accelerated by Information, Communication and technology has resulted in more people coming online and more things connected to internet hosts and personal computers has increased. As a result, the everyday life witnessed more people coming online and more things connected to Internet. With the public sector increasingly leveraging ICTs, possibilities of cyberattacks raised manifold. Under such an open and wide platform, the Internet remained no longer safe (Andreasson 2012). The issues of privacy and security concerns emerged, and the concept of cybersecurity came more prominently into the picture. Presently, cybersecurity has become a global concern and includes within its ambit the issues like cyber warfare, cybercrime, and cyber terrorism.

4.4.1 Cyber Warfare

In contemporary times, computers play an important role in the battlefields in controlling targeting systems, managing logistics as well as relaying critical intelligence information. Also, at both the strategic and tactical levels, the battlefields stand to be fundamentally altered by the information technologies. Therefore, the increasing depth and breadth of this battlefield as well as the improving accuracy and destructiveness of even conventional weaponries have heightened the importance of control, command, communications, and intelligence matters. The dominance in this particular aspect may now yield the advantages of consistent war-winning (Arquilla and Ronfeldt 1993). Today, cyber is being considered as a war fighting domain after land, air, and sea.

Cyber warfare is comparatively a new type of weaponry having various effects on the target. It can be defined as the actions taken by a state in order to penetrate into another state's networks or computers for the purpose of causing disruption or damage (Clarke and Knake 2012). It is beyond any limitations of use and can be useful in achieving most of the set goals. The history revealed that military organizations, doctrines. and strategies have frequently undergone profound changes due to the technological breakthroughs. Also, the information revolution crosses across borders, and thus, it generally compels closed systems to open up. This led a direct impact on the future of the military as well as of conflict and warfare more commonly. Thus, cyber warfare revolves around information and communications matters at much deeper levels. The cyber war may be applicable in conventional and nonconventional environments, low- as well as high-intensity conflicts and for offensive or defensive purposes. In broader sense, cyber war indicates a transformation in the nature of war (Arquilla and Ronfeldt 1993). Recently, the First Gulf War witnessed the initiation of precision-guided weapons warfare.[2] By these weapons, every target was visible in Iraq as well as nearly every target attacked was destroyed by more than one precision weapons (Griggs 1996). Within this perspective, it can be assumed that cyber warfare also joins precision warfare.

As cyberattacks are less expensive and easy to conduct, they have assumed a primary priority in modern warfare. Also, the growing reliance and dependency on cyber infrastructure particularly on electronics and telecommunications in terms of energy, power, and financial sectors have opened ways to new security threats. The director and chief economist of the U.S. Cyber Consequences Unit Scott Borg argues that the dangers of cyberattacks have the potential to cause hundreds of billions of dollars worth of damage and to cause thousands of deaths (Caplan 2013). Besides causing damage, the cyber warfare is often supposed to be a one-sided battle where the attacker makes all the strikes and the target of the attack responds so slowly that it becomes difficult to identify the attacker. On the other hand, the networks act as a medium of storage of sensitive information which has given birth to cyber economic warfare against businesses and cyber espionage against governments. In this context, the states have been subject to various forms of cyberattack during crisis or conflict at both the operational and tactical levels of war. At the same time, there has been a major shift in the character of warfare as the military competition also expands into the cyber domain. As such, both the state and non-state rivals vis-à-vis powerful

---

[2] In the First Gulf War, more than 17,000 precision-guided weapons were expended over a period of roughly six weeks to destroy the targets in Iraq (Krepinevich 2012).

or less developed nations could be able to execute cyberattacks inflicting speedy and catastrophic levels of destruction upon their opponents (Krepinevich 2012).

In contemporary times, the cyber warfare has moved beyond the military dimension and entered into economic, political, criminal, security, and civilian dimensions (Knapp and Boulton 2006). The reason for attaining such widespread dimension lies in the reluctance imparted by the governments across the globe to share information regarding their cyber activities or weapons. It also becomes difficult to grasp such an information as cyber weaponry requires no large industrial base to produce as well as can be tested in relative secrecy. Therefore, there is no easy way to determine the true power of states regarding the cyber war potentialities and capabilities (Krepinevich 2012). Furthermore, cyber warfare permits the actors to achieve their strategic as well as political goals without any requirement to go for an armed conflict.

Apart from it, this sort of warfare provides disproportionate power to small and relatively insignificant actors. It can also operate behind false IP addresses and through foreign servers. Therefore, the attackers can act with almost complete secrecy and relative liberty. In addition, the power in such a warfare can be exercised either by states or by non-state actors or simply by means of proxy. Further, cyber warfare is considered as a "fifth battlefield" after land, water, air, and space and is best understood as an entirely separate component of having the multifaceted conflict environment. Also, the ways and means of cyber warfare remain indisputably distinctive from other modes of conflict (Cornish et al. 2010).

Cyber warfare has become a more powerful instrument in today's battlefield and had large impact on the development of armies as well as weapon technologies in many countries. In mid-2007, the Israeli cyber warriors hacked the Syrian anti-aircraft installations and reprogrammed their computers. The installation system of Syrian's computers displayed an empty sky. By doing so, the Syrian's allowed Israeli planes to bomb over a suspected nuclear weapons manufacturing industry being built by North Korea (Clarke and Knake 2012). The first among known cyberattacks was launched by Russia in 2008 under DDoS against "Paperless government" of Estonia.[3] After this attack, the DDoS emerged as a common platform of attack for countries such as United States, China, Russia, North Korea, Israel, and Pakistan (Singh 2009). In the same year, Russia launched another important cyber campaign against Georgia. It made several attacks against Georgia's cyber infrastructure in order to overload and ultimately shut down its critical servers. The impact of these attacks was so huge that no outbound traffic in Georgia could get through. Also, the hackers seized direct control of all the routers supporting traffic to Georgia. As a result, the Georgians could not connect to any information sources or outside news and even could not send email out of the state. Thus, the analysts around the globe became conscious about the fact that any large-scale future conflict will comprise cyber warfare as part of a combined arms effort (Clarke and Knake 2012).

4.4.2 Cybercrime

Cybercrime refers to any illegal activity by using computers as a primary mode of commission. Since the inception of cyber commerce in the late 1990s, cyber criminals appeared on the international scenario. During the earlier years, the most effective cyber criminal operations were carried through DDoS attacks which were followed by general efforts at identity theft (Krepinevich 2012).

---

[3] After the attack, the head of IT security at Estonia's defence ministry, Mikhail Tammet said that "Estonia depends largely on the internet. We have e-government, government is so-called paperless... all the bank services are on the internet. We even elect our parliament via the internet" (BBC News 2007).

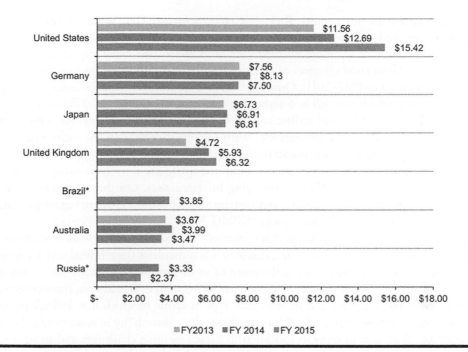

Figure 4.1   Total cost of cybercrime in seven countries.

Source: Ponemon Institute 2015.

Cyber criminals use computer technology to access business trade secrets, personal information, or using the Internet for malicious or exploitive purposes. It has been estimated that in 2012, 54 million people in Turkey, 40 million in the United States, 20 million in Korea, 20 million in China, and more than 16 million in Germany have been affected by the cybercrimes (Intel 2014). According to the report prepared by Norton on cybercrime, it is estimated that the highest number of cybercrime victims is found in Russia, i.e., 92%, followed by China's 84% and South Africa's 80% (Norton 2012). The growth is still alarming and is expected to be more than 800 million in 2013 at global level. Figure 4.1 shows the total costs of cybercrime as recorded in seven countries during 2013–2015.

The cybercrime is thus one of the biggest problems affecting both the developed and developing world. The consequences of cybercrime had bad implications on the trade, innovation, competitiveness, and global economic growth (Intel 2014). However, the problem associated with the cybercrime is that the perpetrators no longer require complex techniques or skills. On the other hand, the intensity and perceptions of relative risk and threat largely vary between governments and private sector enterprises. From the perspective of national security, almost two-thirds of countries view their systems of police statistics insufficient for recording cybercrime. According to the police-recorded cybercrime rates, the number of crimes is associated with levels of country's development vis-à-vis specialized police capacity rather than underlying crime rates (UNODC 2013).

In 2000, the first major instance of cybercrime took place when a mass-mailed computer virus affected around 45 million computer users worldwide (Bora and Singh 2013). However, the cybercrime landscape changed dramatically and began to attain politically motivated objectives. In the past decade, cyberattacks have evolved in utilizing the online weapons affecting several government entities. In this context, Richard Clarke, a former U.S. White House in charge of counter-terrorism and cybersecurity said that a full-scale cyberattack on a country's important infrastructure could have an unprecedented long-term effect. The cyber experts are of the view that the world has witnessed glimpses of cyber war with unethical cyber hackers stealing important state information (KPMG 2011). Quoting U.S. defense secretary Robert Gates, "cyberspace is the new domain in which war will be fought after land, sea, air and space" (Glenny 2010).

The digital age has witnessed online communication in which the Internet users as well as governments easily fall prey to cyberattack. With the advancement in the techniques of cyber criminals, their focus shifted from financial information to business espionage as well as accessing government information. The governments around the world are actively focusing on preventing and fighting the cyber criminals from damaging infrastructure. On the other hand, the cyber criminals are developing new techniques and thereby making it more challenging for governments and companies to cope up with such attacks (KPMG 2011).

However, there are several challenges that commonly confront in dealing with cybercrime. First, the investigation of criminals involved in cybercrimes is difficult as the criminal activity in itself is borderless by nature. Also, cybercrime is the result of an underground economy with many digital experts specializing in carrying out cyber operations (KPMG 2011). In addition, there exists a severe shortage of skills and expertise to fight with such type of crime in which it is difficult to trace its origin, and finally the use of pirated software increases the vulnerability of systems to cyberattacks (Kumar 2010). Therefore, in order to combat with these emerging challenges and to fight against fast-spreading cybercrime, governments must collaborate globally to develop an effective model that will control the threat Internet-based networking, cybercrime, and digital attack incidents.

4.4.3 Cyber Terrorism

Cyber terrorism is any deliberate attack against information of computer systems, programs, and data resulting in violence against noncombatant targets by secret agents or sub-national groups (Murrill 2011). The attacks are generally politically motivated. The cyberattacks are designed to cause extreme financial harm or physical violence. The thrust areas of cyber terrorist targets include military installations, banking industry, air traffic control centers, power plants, water systems, etc. The term "cyber terrorism" is sometimes referred to as information war or electronic terrorism (Rouse 2014).

Cyber terrorism allows terrorists to carry out their attacks from anywhere in the globe at relatively low costs, with a high level of secrecy as well as with no restrictions of time or space. It can arise from states, organizations, groups, or even individuals. It includes within its ambit a wide range of crimes like defacing of websites, creating worms and viruses, stealing sensitive information, and attacking infrastructures (Olmstead and Siraj 2009). The cyber terrorists often use information technologies and the Internet as a medium in conducting their plans in order to raise the financial funds, secure communications, and distribute their propaganda. In this context, George Tenet, the former director of the Central Intelligence Agency, in his statement in 2000 regarding "global security threats" described that the terrorist groups like Hezbullah, Al-Qaeda, and Hamas used computerized files, emails, and protection for supporting and carrying out their operations (Bogdanoski and Petreski 2013) (Figure 4.2).

The cyber terrorist also uses the Internet to reach out their audience without any need to use other media like television, radio, or holding of press conferences. To highlight the injustice, they design typical web pages vis-à-vis to recruit members and supporters. Such websites are often carrying instructions and content of procedures of making explosives and chemical weapons. By the

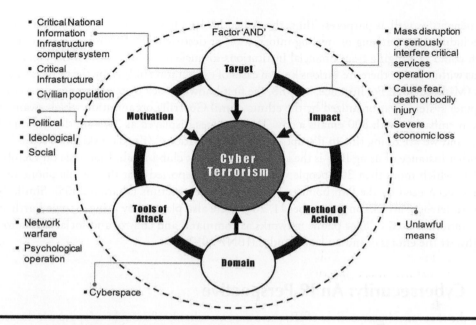

- Critical National Information Infrastructure computer system
- Critical Infrastructure
- Civilian population

- Political
- Ideological
- Social

- Network warfare
- Psychological operation

- Cyberspace

Factor 'AND'

Target

Motivation

Impact

Cyber Terrorism

Tools of Attack

Method of Action

Domain

- Mass disruption or seriously interfere critical services operation
- Cause fear, death or bodily injury
- Severe economic loss

- Unlawful means

Figure 4.2   Proposed cyber terrorism conceptual framework.

Source: Ahmad et al. 2012.

process, they also identify the most common users that can have sympathy for their cause as well as becomes an effective method for recruiting. This further supports individuals acting as terrorists to engage in terrorist activities (Bogdanoski and Petreski 2013).

Collin (1997) pointed out that the future cyber terrorists can attack the air traffic control systems by which two large civilian aircraft could collide. They can disrupt banks, stock exchanges, and international financial transactions. This may bring economic systems grind to a halt resulting in the loss of public confidence and ultimately the destabilization. The acts of cyber terrorists could lead to plane crashes, explosions, water contamination, economic losses, or even death. However, the motives behind these acts are largely political in nature and intended to cause grave harm like loss of life or severe economic damage (Awan 2014).

The present global era has witnessed more than one billion online users and 233 countries connected to the Internet (Turney 2008). In such an interconnected world, terrorism is flourishing through terrorist's use of ICTs. Today, nearly all the terrorist organizations either small or large have their own websites. The recent example of terrorist attacks includes attack on America's army deployment system during Iraq war. The terrorist organizations cooperate with organized crime vis-à-vis use technology to spread propaganda, recruit and train members, raise funds, communicate and launch attacks. Also, the governments face several difficulties in combating with terrorist's use of ICTs which include the lack of coordinated procedures and laws in investigating cybercrimes, ineffective or inadequate information sharing and complications in tracing and tracking cyber communications (Westby 2007).

Every technology developed so far has brought both benefits and risks; likewise, ICT has also revolutionized every aspect of human life but at the same time has boosted international terrorism. It has been exploited by the terrorist organizations in two different ways. First, as a tool in which the communications are used in support of their operations providing for control of all their activities. Also, the terrorists can operate in cyberspace to manipulate or destroy information for their own benefits as well as purposes. Thus, the skilled hackers having the terrorist intend can access all including the changing or stealing information or destroying it. Second, as a target of attack which could be ranging from financial institutions to nuclear installations. At the global level as well as within India, there are various known cases of exploitation of ICT by the terrorist organizations (Mishra 2003). For instance, in 1988, the first-known attack by terrorists against a country's computer systems was organized by the ethnic Tamil Guerrilla organization which swamped Sri Lankan embassies with 800 emails a day. The messages displayed as "We are the Internet Black Tigers and we are doing this to disrupt your communications" (Bogdanoski and Petreski 2013). The other instance of using ICT is the bombing of a night club in Bali, Indonesia on October 12, 2002 in which more than 200 people were killed. It is reported that the mobile phone technology has been used by the Bali bombers to massacre their victims (Sharma 2005). Similarly, the Mumbai terrorist attacks on September 11, 2008 were also planned by using Google Earth as well as the terrorists used cellular phone networks as command and control and social media to track and thwart the efforts of Indian commandos (IBN7 2012).

4.5 Cybersecurity: An IR Perspective

From the theoretical perspectives of IR, there are two schools of thought to approach the security in the digital age. One is traditionalists who mainly believe and practice realism and state-centric strategic studies, and the other is wideners who are a mixture of liberals and critical theorists. The traditionalists hold that in spite of the emergence of ethnic and religious insurgence, transnational crime, and global terrorism, there is no need to broaden the definition of security. However, some traditionalists have addressed the development of information technology, but only with regard to the material capabilities as they have always played a crucial role in a state-centric and military-oriented perspective on national security. Most traditionalists consider information technologies as merely a new fancy add-on (Eriksson and Giacomello 2006). On the other hand, the wideners claim that the conception of the security should be broadened to include new threats and challenges in social, political, economic, and environmental sectors (Buzan 1991). Also, they incorporate a range of new actors in their analyses particularly the NGOs, terrorist organizations, social movements, private firms as well as individuals. Eriksson and Giacomello (2006) argue that the wideners have very rarely addressed the information revolution like emergence of the Internet and its impact on security. Thus, to have a general understanding of the security in contemporary times, i.e., cybersecurity, there exists a need to address them according to three key IR perspectives, i.e., Realism, Liberalism, and Constructivism.

4.6 Realism and Cybersecurity

The post-Second World War period witnessed the emergence of realism in IR. Realism mainly focused on power politics, national security, and traditional warfare. However, access to cyber venues is possibly available to everyone and everywhere. Therefore, it becomes difficult to fully recognize what cybersecurity actually entails or what the cyber domain could signify in contemporary IR. Therefore, clarifications, theoretical innovations as well as adjustments are needed to hold the use of realist theory in any of its forms (Choucri 2012).

The arena of cyberspace is being treated as a new battleground, a new anarchy having no overarching authority to place limits on the behavior of actors (states). It is within this new anarchical system that new forms of capabilities could be found. For instance, state-sponsored hackers or cyber warriors can now break into the state institutions and thereby compromise the national security of that state. Also, the weapons of cyber war like denial of service attacks, information leakage, etc. have the capability to not only decrease the power of the state but also have the potential to render it under the control of another actor. The problem, however, exists in analyzing about the control, i.e., where it begins and where it ends. Thus, the arena of cyberspace witnesses that the power is neither more state-centric nor real, although it can be technological as well (Kremer and Muller 2014).

Realism treats cybersecurity mainly as a force-multiplier in the conventional state-centric perspective. It has received little or no attention in realist analyses besides the rise of non-state authority in cybersecurity as well as the perforation of sovereign boundaries in cyberattacks. Realism still considers state as the main and sometimes the only important actor in the IR even in the digital age (Mayer et al. 2014).

4.7 Liberalism and Cybersecurity

Liberalism focuses upon the plurality of international actors, the role of domestic political factors in shaping the international behavior of states, the role of international institutions in setting the rules of behavior for state actors and increasing the field of international studies by focusing on a broader set of issue areas in an anarchic international system. Liberals consider states as central actors in world politics but at the same time contend that other non-state actors like transnational corporations, pressure groups social movements are equally important and play significant roles in IR. Therefore, it takes into account emergence of new online groups and technologies having the impact on the structures and actors in global politics (Kremer and Muller 2014).

Generally, liberalism tends to avoid the security issues, but when some of its inherent features like idealism and fear of treading on realist ground (security studies) are removed, it helps to explain the complexity of security and power in the digital age. Also, the theory of liberalism sheds light on both the crises management and rise of private authority in security and on the merging of the civil and military spheres, which is particularly evident regarding cybersecurity (Mayer et al. 2014).

The arena of cyberspace comprises a border-free civil society where actors exchange information in a variety of structured or unstructured ways. It is generally viewed as an extra-territorial region and does not belong to any one actor or a group of actors. But, the liberals on the other hand claim that cyberspace could be both public and private and as such possesses both an economic and a national character. They, therefore, contend that international governmental regimes should play their due roles for the regulation of cyberspace as well as the actions of groups like social organizations and professionals. Moreover, liberals claim that in cyberspace, there exist several limitations on the mobilization of citizens through the establishment of local, national, and international norms. Cyberspace now known as "the virtual battle space" rather than "the global village" is territory with borders (Manjikian 2010). Thus, liberals accept that cyberspace possesses both the borders and has a national character where users are not netizens,[4] but subjects of their own governments.

In a broader perspective, the liberal theories of IR can help to explain how access to cyberspace can promote the growth and spread of political ideas, the development of transnational social networks and the organization of civil society. Liberals believe that the access and control of cyberspace can shape state's behavior as well as influence international politics. Liberal theories are also helpful in understanding international efforts to promote cooperation among states on issues related to the cybersecurity, control over cyberspace, and cyber arms control (Reardon and Choucri 2012).

---

[4] Netizens are the citizens of the Internet who assimilate community norms and behaviors as well as work to preserve its collective goods (Manjikian 2010).

4.8 Constructivism and Cybersecurity

Constructivism views IR in terms of social relations shaped by social interactions (Kubalkova et al. 1998). It is based on the assumptions that that knowledge and meaning are socially constructed and is a social reality. It further argues that identities and interests can never be seen as static but should be constantly produced and reproduced (Wendt 1992). In terms of threat perception, this theory highlights the identity and culturally related threats, particularly as these have been downplayed in realist and liberal accounts of security. Thus, the empirical openness of this theory allows one to address the widest possible range of perceived security threats. In addition, a notable contribution of this theory to security aspect is the concept of securitization as developed by the Copenhagen school (Buzan et al. 1998).

In terms of digital-age security, the constructivists mainly focus upon the challenges posed by the information warfare to a multitude of boundaries most particularly on boundary of identities. They are of the view that such warfare could formally penetrate into sovereign boundaries which may result into the emergence and articulation of new identities in cyberspace. Also, theorists like Der Derian (2000) showed a great concern about the effects of virtuality regarding the perception and conduct of warfare. Also, theorists like Der Derian (2000), showed a great concern about the effects of virtuality regarding the perception and conduct of warfare. He points out that one of many effects of war in the digital age is that it distances (some) actors from the reality of war by rendering geographical distance irrelevant (Eriksson and Giacomello 2006).

Constructivism also emphasizes that the study of symbolic politics[5] is very relevant for studying the security in the digital age. One study has been conducted about the digital symbolic politics in the presidential campaigning in United States, yet the symbolic politics approach has not earlier been applied in the studies of digital-age security. On the other hand, the defacing of websites constitutes a noteworthy practice of symbolic politics which has been practiced by the hackers of U.S. and Chinese governments in recent years. In the same manner, digital wars were going on between Pakistan and India as well as between Arab and Israel (Eriksson and Giacomello 2006).

Within the context of national scenario, the constructivist approaches in IR shift the focus of attention away from the states and their governments toward analyzing the agencies of multiple governments and nongovernmental actors. Thus, an analysis of IR has to be always an analysis of processes on the multiple local and global levels (Muller and Witjes 2014).

Thus, the literature on the digital-age security is generally policy oriented with little or no ambition to apply or contribute to theory, and with the few exceptions, IR scholars have paid only scant attention to the security problems of the digital age. However, the theories of liberalism and constructivism have contributed toward the security in the digital age. If stripped from its idealist and antirealist pretensions, liberalism focuses on many of the elements of digital age security like the multiplicity of non-state actors with transnational capacity, vulnerability interdependence, network economies, and the consequent perforation of formally sovereign boundaries. Similarly, constructivism's analysis focuses on several components such as the symbolic, identity-based and rhetorical aspects of digital-age security. Also, constructivist analysis can describe the role of language in digital-age security, including the meaning and function of rhetoric like cyber war and cyber terrorism. However, on the other hand, realism tackles the challenge of the digital age in the same way as it has tackled other features of globalization by

---

[5] It means the use as well as abuse of symbols for manipulating political discourse and public opinion. Such an approach is a constructivist contribution in social science that was introduced long before the information revolution (Merelman 1993).

largely ignoring it, or by subsuming information security to either domestic politics or political economy, none of which fit comfortably in the realist field of vision.

4.9 Conclusion

The exponential growth of ICTs and the expansion of cyberspace have possibly been one of the pioneering developments of the present century, but this development has also led to the misuse of cyberspace. It has also increased the vulnerability to a large number of attacks on crucial information infrastructure. The peculiar nature of cyberspace demands the states to enact laws and establish institutions in order to curb cybercrime and cyber terrorism. It is here that policy intervention becomes crucial by states. At the same time, the arena of cyber has attained significantly important position in contemporary security debate and is being considered as a fifth war fighting domain after land, air, and sea. It has moved beyond the military dimension and entered into economic, political, criminal, security, and civilian dimensions. Also, it becomes equally difficult to grasp such an information as cyber weaponry requires no large industrial base to produce as well as can be tested in relative secrecy. Thus, cyber war indicates a transformation in the nature of war in which there is no easy way to determine the true power of states regarding the cyber war potentialities and capabilities.

Similarly, cyber terrorism allows terrorists to carry out their attacks from anywhere in the globe at relatively low costs, with a high level of secrecy as well as with no restrictions of time or space. Internet is increasingly used by cyber terrorists to carry out deadly activities without using other media like television, radio, or holding of press conferences. For instance, in 2002, the U.S. Naval War College hosted a war game known as "Digital Pearl Harbor" in order to develop a scenario for a coordinated cyberterrorism event in which fake attacks by computer security experts against critical infrastructure systems were carried out (Chen 2013). It reveals that terrorism is flourishing through terrorist's use of ICTs. Likewise, cybercrime becomes an easy tool for criminals to affect trade secret and business strategy in the realm of cyber world. Although cybercrime seems to be increasing, the conventional methods (or techniques) are not able to detect, or even put records of it. In the sense, there is growing anxiety over failure that hovers around cybercrime. Thus, the crime and criminality in the cyber age seems to be changing in the direction that is underacted and vaguely defined. Presently, the most problematic and latest trends in network security threats are the Botnet-based DDoS attacks on the application layer. Presently, the most problematic and latest trends in network security threats is the Botnet-based DDoS attacks on the application layer, having the consequences of curtailing revenue, limiting resources, along with yielding dissatisfaction of customers. However, the most challenging problem confronting these attacks is to resolve them online, especially, when the target is the Web server.

References

Ahmad, et al. 2012. "Perception on cyber terrorism: A focus group discussion approach." *Journal of Information Security* 2012 (3): 231–237.

Almagor, R. C. 2011. "Internet history." *International Journal of Technoethics* 2 (2): 45–64.

Alomari, E., Manickam, S., Gupta, B. B., Karuppayah, S. and Alfaris, R. 2012. "Botnet-based distributed denial of service (DDoS) attacks on web servers: Classification and art." *International Journal of Computer Applications* 49 (7): 24–32.

Andreasson, K. J. 2012. *Cyber Security: Public Sector Threats and Responses*. Boca Raton, FL: Taylor & Francis Group.

Andy Whelan. 2015. DaviMUN 2015 Research Report: Measures to combat Cyber Warfare. Advisory Panel on the question of the Internet (APQi), Netherlands.

Arquilla, J. and Ronfeldt, D. 1993. "Cyberwar is coming." *Comparative Strategy* 12 (2): 141–165.

Awan, I. 2014. "Debating the term cyber-terrorism: Issues and problems." *Internet Journal of Criminology*. ISSN 2045 (6743): 1–14.

BBC News. 2007. "Estonia hit by 'Moscow cyber war'." *BBC News, UK*, May 17 Published: 2007/05/17 15:21:15 GMT. http://news.bbc.co.uk/go/pr/fr/-/2/hi/europe/6665145.stm.

Beck, U. (1992). *Risk Society: Towards a New Modernity*. London: Sage.

Beck, U. (1999). *World Risk Society*. London: Polity.

Bogdanoski, M. and Petreski, D. 2013. "Cyber terrorism-global security threat." *International Scientific Defence, Security and Peace Journal* 13 (24): 59–72.

Bora, M. S. and Singh, A. 2013. "Cyber threats and security for wireless devices." *Journal of Environmental Science, Computer Science and Engineering & Technology* 2 (2): 277–284.

Brenner, S. W. 2004. "Distributed security: Moving away from reactive law enforcement." *International Journal of Communications Law & Policy* 9 (2): 1–43.

Buzan, B. 1991. *People, States and Fear: An Agenda for International Security Studies in the Post-Cold War Era*. 2nd ed., London: Harvester Wheatsheaf.

Buzan, B., Waever, O. and De Wilde, J. 1998. *Security: A New Framework for Analysis*. Boulder, CO: Lynne Rienner.

Caplan, N. 2013. "Cyber war: The challenge to national security." *Global Security Studies* 4 (1): 93–115.

Chen, T. M. 2013. *An Assessment of the Department of Defense Strategy for Operating in Cyberspace*. Carlisle, PA: Strategic Studies Institute U.S. Army War College Press.

Choucri, N. 2012. *Cyberpolitics in International Relations*. London: MIT Press.

Clarke, R. A. and Knake, R. 2012. *Cyber War: The Next Threat to National Security and What to Do About It*. New York: Ecco Publications.

Collin, B. 1997. "The future of cyberterrorism: The physical and virtual worlds converge." *Crime and Justice International* 13 (2): 15–18.

Cooley, K. W. 2011. *Energy Security: Neglected Dimension of National Security?* Washington, DC: National Strategic Studies.

Cornish, P. et al. 2010. *On Cyber Warfare*. London: The Royal Institute of International Affairs.

Demchak, C. C. and Dombrowski P. J. 2011. Rise of a cybered westphalian age: The coming decades. In Mayer, M., Carpes, M. and Knoblich, R. (Eds.). *The Global Politics of Science and Technology* -Vol. 1. Berlin: Springer.

Demchak, C. C. and Dombrowski, P. J. 2014. Rise of a cybered westphalian age: The coming decades. In Mayer, M., Carpes, M. and Knoblich, R. (Eds.). *The Global Politics of Science and Technology*-Vol. 1. Berlin, Heidelberg: Springer, 91–113.

Derian, D. 2000. "Virtuous War/Virtual Theory." *Royal Institute of International Affairs* 76 (4): 771–788.

Detica. 2011. *The Cost of Cyber Crime: A Detica Report in Partnership with the Office of Cyber Security and Information Assurance in the Cabinet Office*. London: Detica Limited. https://assets.publishing.service. gov.uk/government/uploads/system/uploads/attachment_data/file/60943/the-cost-of-cyber-crime-full-report.pdf

Doyle, C. 2014. *Cybercrime: An Overview of the Federal Computer Fraud and Abuse Statute and Related Federal Criminal Laws*. Lexington, KY: Congressional Research Service.

Eriksson, J. and Giacomello, G. 2006. "The information revolution, security, and international relations." *International Political Science Review (SAGE) Publications* 27 (3): 221–244.

Eriksson, J. and Giacomello, G. 2007. *International Relations and Security in the Digital Age*. New York: Routledge.

Gahlot, D. et al. 2014. "Network security: It's time to take it seriously." *International Journal of Innovative Research in Science & Engineering* 2 (9): 613–620.

Gellman, B. 2002. The Washington post, cyber-attacks by Al Qaeda feared. *The Washington Post*, Washington.

Ghansah, I. 2009. *Smart Grid Cyber Security Potential Threats, Vulnerabilities and Risks.* PIER Energy-Related Environmental Research Program. Sacramento, CA: California Energy Commission.

Glenny, M. 2010. "Who controls the internet?" *The Financial Times*, Accessed October 05 2017.

Goss, P. 1999. "An introduction to the impact of information technology on national security." *Duke Journal of Comparative & International Law* 9 (2): 391–399.

Griggs, C. R. A. 1996. "Technology and Strategy." *Airpower Journal- Summer 1996* 10 (2): 105–113.

GTISC. 2010. *Emerging Cyber Threats Report 2011.* Atlanta: Georgia Tech Information Security Center.

Hughes, R. 2010. "A treaty for cyberspace." *Journal of International Affairs* 86 (2): 523–541.

IBN7. 2012. "Mumbai attack plan used Google Earth, says US commander." *IBN7 Live News*, Unites State, 16 May.

INTEL. 2014. *Net Losses: Estimating the Global Cost of Cybercrime, Economic impact of cybercrime II.* Center for Strategic and International Studies, Santa Clara, CA: McAfee, Centre for Strategic & International Studies.

Kabay, M. E. 2009. History of Computer Crime. In Bosworth, S. (eds.). *Computer Security Handbook*, 5 (1) New York: Wiley Publishing House.

Keohane, R. O. and Nye, J. S. Jr. 1998. "Power and interdependence in the information age." *Foreign Affairs* 77 (5): 81–94.

Kessimeris, G. and Buckley, J. 2010. *The Ashgate Research Companion Modern Warfare.* London: Ashgate Publishing Limited.

Knapp, K. J. and Boulton, W. R. 2006. "Cyber warfare threatens corporations: Expansion into commercial environments." *Information Systems Management* 23 (2): 76–87.

KPMG. 2011. Cybercrime: A growing challenge for governments. *KPMG International Issues Monitor* 8, Swiss: 1–15.

Kremer, J. and Muller, B. 2014. *Cyberspace and International Relations: Theory Prospects and Challenges.* Heidelberg: Springer.

Krepinevich, A. F. 2012. *Cyber Warfare: A "Nuclear Option"?* Washington, DC: Center for Strategic and Budgetary Assessments.

Kubalkova, V., Onuf, N. and Kowert, P. 1998. *International Relation in a Constructed World.* Armonk, NY: M. E. Sharpe.

Kumar, M. 2010. Cybercrime challenges in the GCC, *ITP.net.* Accessed October 28 2017. www.itp.net/580210-cybercrime-challenges-in-the-gcc.

Leiner B. M. et al. 2012. *Brief History of The Internet.* Geneva: Internet Society.

Lewis, J. A. 2013. *Report of the Technology and Public Policy Program: Conflict and Negotiation in CyberSpace.* Washington, DC: Center for Strategic and International Studies.

Lynn III, W. J. 2010. "Defending a new domain: The pentagon's cyberstrategy." *Foreign Affairs* 89 (5): 97.

Manjikian, M. M. 2010. "From global village to virtual battlespace: The colonizing of the internet and the extension of realpolitik." *International Studies Quarterly* 54 (2): 381–401.

Mary, S. C. 2010. "Evaluation of vulnerability assessment in system from hackers in cyber security." *International Journal of Engineering Science and Technology* 2 (7): 3213–3217.

Mayer, M., Carpes, M., Knoblich, R. 2014. *The Global Politics of Science and Technology- Vol. 1: Concepts of International Relation and Other Disciplines.* Berlin, Heidelberg: Springer-Verlag.

McGuinn, M. G. 2004. *Prioritizing cyber vulnerabilities final report and recommendations by the council.* National Infrastructure Advisory Council, Mellon, Mellon Financial Corporation, 1–14.

Merelman, R. M. 1992. *Language, Symbolism and Politics.* Boulder, CO: Westview press.

Mishra, S. 2003. "Exploitation of information and communication technology by terrorist organisations." *Institute for Defence Studies and Analyses* 27 (3): 439–462.

Muller, R. and Witjes, N. 2014. "Of red threads and green dragons: Austrian sociotechnical imaginaries about STI cooperation with China" in Mayer, M.; Carpes, M. Knoblich, R. (Eds.). *The Global Politics of Science and Technology- Vol. 2: Perspective, Cases and Methods.* Berlin, Heidelberg: Springer-Verlag.

Murrill, R. 2011. "The question of cyber terrorism." *Forensic Focus*, Accessed October 25, 2017. http://articles.forensicfocus.com/2011/07/23/the-question-of-cyber-terrorism/.

Nielsen, S. C. 2012. "Pursuing security in cyberspace: Strategic and organizational challenges." *Foreign Policy Research Institute* 66 (3): 336–356.

NIPP. 2013. Partnering for Critical Infrastructure Security and Resilience. *Homeland Security*, United States, pp 1–57.

Norton. 2012. "Cybercrime report", Symantec, Accessed October 18, 2017. http://now-static.norton.com/now/en/pu/images/Promotions/2012/cybercrimeReport/2012_Norton_Cybercrime_Report_Master_FINAL_050912.pdf.

Olmstead, S. and Siraj, A. 2009. "Cyberterrorism: The threat of virtual warfare." *The Journal of Defense Software Engineering* 23 (6): 16–18.

Pillai, P. 2012. "History of internet security." Accessed October 17, 2017. www.buzzle.com/articles/history-of-internet-security.html.

Ponemon. 2010. *First Annual Cost of Cyber Crime Study: Benchmark Study of US Companies*. USA: Ponemon Institute.

Ponemon. 2012. *Cost of Cyber Crime Study: United States*. USA: Ponemon Institute.

Ponemon. 2015. *2015 Cost of Cyber Crime Study: Global*, October, Research Report. USA: Ponemon Institute.

Al-Qurishi, M., Rahman, S.M.M., Hossain, M.S., Almogren, A., Alrubaian, M., Alamri, A., Al-Rakhami, M. and Gupta, B.B., 2017. An efficient key agreement protocol for Sybil-precaution in online social networks. *Future Generation Computer Systems* 84: 139–148.

Ram, C. S. 2010. "Impact of information technology on society: Visakhapatnam in India as a case study." *Indian Journal of Science and Technology* 3 (4): 475–482.

Rather, M. A. and Jose, K. 2014."Human security: Evolution and conceptualization." *European Academic Research* II (5): 6766–6797.

Reardon, R. and Choucri, N. 2012. "The role of cyberspace in international relations: A view of the literature." Paper Prepared on 1 April 2012 for the 2012 ISA Annual Convention San Diego: California.

Reardon, R. J. 2012. *Containing Iran: Strategies for Addressing the Iranian Nuclear Challenge*. Santa Monica: RAND Corporation.

Red Hat. 2005. "Red Hat Enterprise Linux 4: Security Guide". www.owlriver.com/issa/rhel-sg-en.pdf.

Rouse, M. 2014. Cyber terrorism, *Tech Target*, Accessed 23 October 2017. http://searchsecurity.techtarget.com/definition/cyberterrorism.

Sandeep, R. 2014. "A study of DOS & DDOS: Smurf attack and preventive measures." *International Journal of Computer Science and Information Technology Research* 2(4): 312–317.

Schneider, G. P. and Evans, J. 2007. *New Perspectives on the Internet: Comprehensive* (6th ed.). Boston, MA: Cengage Learning.

Sharma, D. P. 2005. *The New Terrorism: Islamist International*. New Delhi: APH Publishing Corporation.

Symantec. 2009. "A brief history of internet security." *SC Magazine*, Accessed October 22, 2017. www.scmagazine.com/a-brief-history-of-internet-security/article/149611/.

Symantec. 2010. Symantec global internet security threat report. Symantec Enterprise Security, United State.

Turney, J. 2008. *Technology: Ethical Debates about the Application of Science*. Nigeria: Evans Brothers.

UNODC. 2013. Comprehensive study on cybercrime. *United Nations office on Drugs and Crime*. Vienna, United Nations.

USDOD. 2011. *US Department of Defense Strategy for Operating in Cyberspace*. Washington, DC: Department of Defence United State of America.

Walt, S. 1994, "The renaissance of security studies." *International Studies Quarterly* 35 (2): 211–239.

Wendt, A. 1992. "Anarchy is what states make of it: The social construction of power politics." *International Organization* 46 (2): 391–425.

Westby, J. R. 2007. "Countering terrorism with cyber security." *Jurimetrics* 47 (3): 297–313.

Willis H. H., Morral, R. A., Kelly, K. T. and Medby, J. J. 2005. *Estimating Terrorism Risk*. Santa Monica, CA: The RAND for Terrorism Risk Management Policy.

Wilshusen, G. C. 2012. *Cybersecurity: Threats Impacting the Nation: Congressional Testimony*. United States: DIANE Publishing.

Wilson, C. 2005. *Computer Attack and Cyberterrorism: Vulnerabilities and Policy Issues for Congress*. Washington, DC: Congressional Research Service.

Chapter 5

A Systematic Review of Attack Graph Generation and Analysis Techniques

Urvashi Garg, Geeta Sikka, and Lalit K. Awasthi

Dr. B. R. Ambedkar National Institute of Technology

Contents

5.1 Introduction

As the technology is shifting toward IoT, cloud computing, high data management [69], etc. cyber security is becoming the major challenge these days. There are tremendous works that have been proposed to enforce security standards, i.e., encryption of data [67,68,70,71], web data protection [66,72,73], etc. These articles work well for web-based data security, but we need some separate mechanisms for securing systems in local organization network. While working with network security, attack graphs play a crucial role for analyzing attacker behavior in the network. Attacker may influence the target either through direct vulnerability exploitation on target or may follow indirect path approaching to target. Network can be easily secured against direct reachability as compared to indirect reachability because target machine vulnerabilities information can be easily gathered with the help of vulnerability scanners, but later one requires vulnerability information of multiple systems of network and their dependency upon each other. Indirect reachability information can be achieved through attack graphs. Attack graph is a combination of nodes and edges where nodes represent hosts or vulnerabilities and edges represent reachability from one host to another host or vulnerability that ultimately leads to target node.

With the drastic increase in vulnerabilities, the number of options for reaching the target is also increasing. This may increase the size and complexity of attack graphs. In this way, attack graph analysis and optimization become a significant topic for researchers these days. Researchers have been working upon this area since 1999 and proposed a lot of techniques and algorithms for attack graph analysis and optimization. This chapter delineates the review of some latest research works.

Various techniques are already there for representing the complexity of vulnerability, i.e., score, time involves in exploitation or patching, cost of exploitation, etc. These factors are responsible for vulnerability selection by attacker for exploitation. One of the techniques for assigning a score to vulnerability is Common Vulnerability Scoring System (CVSS) [11]. In this technique, the vulnerability score ranges from 1 to 10 depending upon its complexity, i.e., 0 means least severe and 10 mean most severe. In one of the works, the author proposed time to compromise model, for calculating time taken by attacker to exploit a system using vulnerability present on the system [16]. Cost of vulnerability exploitation and cost of patching can also be used as a factor for attack path prioritization [60].

These techniques work fine with individual vulnerability ranking, but they may fail to prioritize attack paths. In some of the cases, vulnerabilities are similar in behavior and characteristics; therefore, some techniques can not comply with such cases. Additionally, the size of attack graph is also a major challenge for researchers. To answer all these research questions, we need a systematic literature survey to find out which studies performed well in different scenarios and which studies can be further enhanced to solve above problems, etc.

The rest of this chapter is organized as follows. In Section 5.2, objectives of this research were specified. In Section 5.3, we provide the background of attack graphs and the motivation behind this systematic review. Section 5.4 discusses some of the major attack graph generation techniques and attack graph analysis techniques. Section 5.5 elaborates systematic review protocol. Section 5.6 depicts the discussion of research question. Various technical issues and challenges were examined in Section 5.7 followed by threats to the validity of results in Section 5.8. Finally, Section 5.9 concludes this systematic review while highlighting the future scope in this field, and Section 5.10 provides references used in this chapter.

5.2 Contributions

Attack graphs attract the researcher's attention these days as it is the most reliable method to identify network security breaches. Since every methodology has its own pros and cons, some problems are also there with attack graphs. The size of graph is the major issue for security administrators dealing with large network size. A considerable research is already going on dealing with the analysis of attack graphs because it is the need of today's vulnerable environment to improvise security-hardening strategies.

The review conducted in this chapter followed a systematic approach to gather an extensive database of literatures focusing on the generation and analysis of attack graphs. A detailed and planned process was followed to ascertain answers to research questions. The questions were answered from the data obtained from final articles. Only relevant articles from the best publishers were selected for this review. The major objectives for this review were as follows:

- Investigation of quality articles in the area of attack graphs.
- Analysis of attack graph generation strategies for their effectiveness in handling scalability problem of network.
- Analysis of vulnerability prioritization schemes to explore which scheme is best suited for a specific environment.
- Categorization of studies based on various parameters.
- Proposing future directions considering issues and limitations of the existing studies.

5.3 Background and Motivation

Attack graph portrays the information about a set of machines and their vulnerabilities that can be deleterious for network security. Attack graph generation and analysis can be divided into five phases. The details of each phase are as follows:

Phase 1: Preparation of prerequisites of attack graph. Basic requirements for attack graph generation are vulnerability dataset and a firewall rule file. The details of prerequisites are given below:

- Vulnerability dataset is a vector consisting of five variables:
  <cve, pre-privilege, pre-resource, post-privilege, post-resource>
  cve is the Common Vulnerability Exposure id [55] of vulnerability, *pre-privilege* is the privilege that is required on target machine to exploit a specific vulnerability, *pre-resource* represents the resource requirement on target machine for specific vulnerability exploitation, *post-privilege* is the privilege gained after vulnerability exploitation on target, and *post-resource* means resource access gained or resource affected after vulnerability exploitation on target.
- Firewall rule file consists of some statements in the following format:
  <source_ip, source_port, dest_ip, dest_port, action>
  source_ip and *source_port* specify the IP address and port number of source machine from which packet is coming, respectively. *dest_ip* and *dest_port* specify the IP address and port number of destination machine, respectively, and *action* specifies the action to be taken when a packet is coming from the source and approaching the destination.

Phase 2: Vulnerability scanning. In this phase, vulnerability scanners were used to get the vulnerability information of systems present in the network. Scanners provide information about vulnerability behavior, i.e., Vulnerability id, operating system requirement, CVSS score of vulnerability, etc.

Phase 3: Attack graph generation. In this phase, firewall rule file was scanned to get the information about the systems directly accessible from source node such that these systems are compromised to gain privileges. Then, postcondition of exploited systems is matched with preconditions of new system, and this process is repeated until target node is compromised.

Phase 4: Parameter calculation for attack paths. As the number of systems and vulnerabilities increases, the number of attack paths also increases. This may lead to state explosion problem [32]. Therefore, some parameters were required for attack path prioritization, i.e., cost, time, score, etc. Various algorithms and techniques have already been developed to evaluate such parameters.

Phase 5: Analysis of attack graph. Once the attack path is prioritized, riskier paths can be easily detected which needs to be patched immediately to secure network against attacks.

With the help of these five phases, network can be secured against direct and indirect attacks as attack graph portrays complete information about all attack paths followed by an attacker to approach the target machine.

5.3.1 Summary of Previous Studies

With the rise in the threat of vulnerabilities, researchers apparently have gained interest in attack graphs generation and analysis as an effective countermeasure for attacker's intentions. Initially, some descriptions about attack graph were found in some studies representing the dependencies among vulnerabilities [47,49]. A significant number of works have been published since then.

Lippmann elucidated a review of past papers published from 1999 to 2004 [37]. McQueen propounded a method to classify and analyze vulnerabilities of attack path [43]. They have introduced the time to compromise model for analyses of attack paths, i.e., the time taken by attacker to exploit the vulnerability. Wang resolved the issue of cycles in attack graphs [58]. They have also calculated a score metrics for analysis and prioritization of attack paths. Idika proffers a graph metrics for analyses of attack paths depending upon the length of attack paths [22]. In 2012, the idea about Vulnerability Rating and Scoring Scheme (VRSS) have been discussed to assign vulnerability score [38]. Wang discussed a method to generate attack graph [57]. They have also portrayed a technique for detecting a minimal set of vulnerabilities that must be patched to ensure network security. Zhao invented a new technique for attack path prioritization by calculating individual score (vulnerability impact rate [VIR] and vulnerability exploitability rate [VER]) for each path [65]. Poolsappasit employed Bayesian probability theorem for estimating next vulnerability exploitation depending upon previously exploited vulnerability [48]. Wang deployed hidden Markov model for estimation of the cost of attack paths [60]. Liu proposed plan recognition method for attack graph generation [40]. Almasizadeh relied on mean privacy metrics for analysis of attack graphs [6]. Kaynar suggested a time- and space-efficient approach to generate attack graphs using parallel agents [27]. None of the above works surveyed the relevant literature in systematic way.

In this chapter, we have done a systematic review of recent research studies that addresses the development and use of attack graphs. We have employed a rigorous and well-defined systematic review process that provides a comprehensive coverage of recent, relevant, and high-quality research results in this area. We have identified appropriate search keywords to find potential papers for inclusion in this survey from a wide array of reputed sources. After removing duplicates, we selected relevant works based upon our assessment of the articles, titles, and associated abstracts. We then reduced this set of papers by evaluating the content of the papers to ensure that our survey only included only high-quality research results. It's noteworthy that this systematic process should have the added benefit of minimizing the bias that could cause the inclusion of results that closely related to the author's research interests but also the exclusion of research that is not closely related. This final set of articles will be helpful in finding gaps in existing studies which will act as a base for future research.

Traditional reviews are very common as compared to systematic review as systematic review is a lengthy process where most of the time is elapsed in finding relevant literature.

5.4 Attack Graphs: Generation and Analysis

A number of techniques are already there to generate and analyze attack graphs. After surveying some latest works in this area, two factors became heart of our review:

- Attack graph generation and optimization techniques,
- Attack graph analyses techniques.

5.4.1 Attack Graph Generation and Optimization

Attack graphs can be represented in numerous ways. Some of the popular types of attack graphs presented in current literature are given below.

5.4.1.1 Attack State Transition Graph

Attack State Transition Graph (ASTG) is a combination of nodes and edges where node is the security state consisting of host id (where attacker is currently residing), vulnerability list (vulnerabilities present on the host), and host privilege gained by attacker. Two states are connected by an edge if attacker in one state progressively exploits vulnerability to get into next state with higher privileges [42]. Depth first search algorithm can be used to generate ASTG. Figure 5.1 represents ASTG in which attacker covets access to machine 3, progressing from machine 0 with vulnerability exploitation (complete information is not specified in the nodes).

Pros
- Real-time security state can be determined.
- Easy to develop ASTG.

Cons
- The size of attack graph is too large to understand and analyze.
- Unnecessary paths or vulnerabilities that are not very harmful or even not possible to be exploited are also included.
- Redundant states can cause state explosion problem [32].

5.4.1.2 Host-Level Attack Graph

In this case, node represents machines and edge represents vulnerability exploitation from one machine to other [41]. In Host-Level Attack Graph (HLAG), attacker first exploits the vulnerability on the machine that was directly reachable. In the next step, all machines where vulnerability preconditions match with postcondition of already-exploited machines were explored. This process continues till the target machine is compromised. In this model, scalability issues are much less than ASTG. Also, it was generated for every host separately, making it easier to understand. Figure 5.2 represents HLAG in which S1–S5 are machines and attacker can go from one machine to another depending upon the exploit execution as given in the table aside.

Pros
- Easy to understand and manage.
- Analysis is possible as numbers of nodes are less in comparison to ASTG.

Cons
- Difficult to manage preconditions and postconditions dataset for such numerous vulnerabilities.

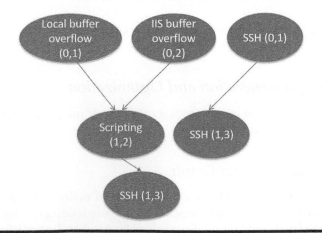

Figure 5.1   Attack state transition graph [42].

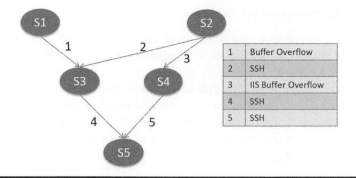

1	Buffer Overflow
2	SSH
3	IIS Buffer Overflow
4	SSH
5	SSH

Figure 5.2   Host-level attack graph [41].

5.4.1.3 Goal Plan Graph

The goal graph consists of a seven-tuple <P, O, A, Pa, Pg, G, E>, where P is the state nodes set, O is the observation nodes set, A represents actions, Pa is the predict action nodes set, Pg is the predict goal nodes set, G is the goal nodes set, and E is the set of edges which can be precondition edge, postcondition edge, action edge, goal edge, etc. [40]. Figure 5.3 portrays the complete information about all types of nodes and edges. Goal plan graph acts as a knowledge base to predict next moves of attacker. It is comparatively easier to detect valid and invalid paths in goal plan graph using temporal constraint.

Pros
- Easy to recognize and predict new attack.
- Easy to identify the weakest node.

Cons
- Unable to detect all possible paths for targeting goal.
- It is not an efficient graph to secure whole network.

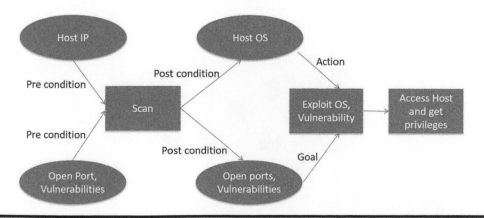

Figure 5.3   Goal plan graph [40].

5.4.1.4 Exploit Dependency Graph

These are the widely used graphs during attack graph analysis. In exploit dependency graphs, nodes were represented as exploits or conditions, and edges connects any exploit node with condition node or vice versa. It starts with an initial set of conditions or privileges that an attacker possesses which helps the attacker in vulnerability exploitation. In the next step, exploited vulnerability may provide further postconditions to attacker on a machine which will act as a precondition for the next exploit and the process continues until goal is achieved [14]. As shown in Figure 5.4, E_0 to E_3 are exploits and C_0 to C_4 are the conditions. Attacker starts from initial conditions C_0 and C_1 to achieve final goal condition C_4.

Pros
- Complexity of graph generation is reduced.
- Scalability issues are less than ASTG.

Cons
- Numbers of nodes are more than HLAG.
- Difficult to understand and analyze for large network consisting of enormous machines and vulnerabilities.

5.4.1.5 Network Attack Graph

Network graph delineates the information about complete network instead of single host. Initially, complete network was scanned for collecting vulnerability information. In the next step, attacker starts with a node that can be accessed directly and compromise it. After that, he approaches to all nodes reachable from every compromised node, and this process was repeated until all possible paths are traversed. Fayyad propound a technique to predict the next attack based upon the previous one using network attack graphs [10].

Pros
- Complete network analysis is possible.
- Attacker's moves can be analyzed with more efficiency as compared to other techniques because it represents all possible moves.

Cons
- Incurs scalability issues for large network size.
- Redundant paths caused memory and time wastage.

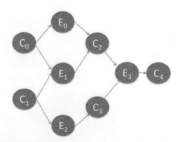

Figure 5.4 Exploit dependency graph [14].

5.4.1.6 Distributed Attack Graph

In 2015, a time- and space-efficient algorithm for generation of attack graph was proposed [27]. Distributed attack graph basically provides the solution to state explosion problem in large networks involving some advanced preconditions and postconditions. They have proposed parallel and distributed algorithm that necessitates the use of virtual shared memory and parallel agents to generate attack graph. In this case, software applications or machines involving vulnerabilities are distributed among agents such that agent uses the existing allowable privileges of the application and expand it in terms of the next gained privilege. Output received from all agents is combined to form a graph. As shown in Figure 5.5, P_1–P_8 are privileges gained on any system using application running on it. V_1–V_4 are vulnerabilities exploited on systems.

Each node contains some additional information related to system, i.e., IP address, Vulnerability id [55], application details, etc. Initially, P_1, P_2, and P_3 are assigned to different agents who perform their expansion parallelly. Each agent is having its own local memory page in virtual shared memory such that if one agent requires privilege information present in other agent's local memory, then it can be accessed without any read/write memory page headache.

Pros
- Graph generation is fast as compared to other techniques.
- State explosion problem is resolved.

Cons
- Difficult to manage and synchronize agents.
- Additional storage space is required.

5.4.1.7 Bayesian Attack Graph

Poolsappasit postulates a technique for calculation of conditional probability of the next exploit depending upon the previous exploit [48]. Initially, all atomic attacks were figured out and executed. In the next step, conditional probability of the next exploit was calculated using proposed algorithm and new node introduced in attack graph. This process was repeated until target is achieved. Conditional probability is based upon Bayesian theorem.

Pros
- Easy to implement.
- Provide different measures of graph optimization, i.e., conditional probability as well as preconditions, postconditions.

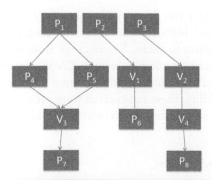

Figure 5.5 **Distributed attack graph [27].**

Cons
- Vulnerability exploitation depends upon attacker's capability and vulnerability complexity which was not considered.

5.4.1.8 Privilege Graph

Dacier proposed the concept of privilege graph [9]. Privilege graph consists of nodes and edges where nodes represent a set of privileges obtained by user and edges represent the possibility of a user to obtain the next privilege from the previous one.

Cons
- Incurs scalability issues.
- Difficult to identify critical nodes and vulnerabilities.

5.4.1.9 Scenario Graph

Jha proposed scenario graph for global analysis of systems [24]. Scenario graph is a compact representation of all the counterexamples of given property, e.g., if property says that buffer overflow attack should not be there, then this graph shows all the paths causing buffer overflow attack.

Cons
- Incurs scalability issues.
- Difficult to interpret.
- Does not consider chaining of vulnerabilities leading to target.

5.4.2 Attack Graph Analysis

Size and complexity of attack graph are growing rapidly with the increases in the size of network. It is not always possible to patch all the paths provided in such a perplexing attack graph. Therefore, some method is required to prioritize attack paths according to their cost, complexity, or any other factor. Various types of attack graph analysis techniques present in the current literature are given below.

5.4.2.1 Common Vulnerability Scoring System

The Forum of Incident Response and Security Teams is the custodian of CVSS scoring system, developed in 2005 by National Infrastructure Advisory Council [11]. It attempts to prioritize vulnerabilities by assigning scores to them. Scores range from 0 to 10 where 0 means the least severe vulnerability and 10 being the most severe one. CVSS consists of some metrics (base, temporal, and environmental), and each metrics is divided into various sub-metrics. Depending upon the characteristics of vulnerability, these sub-metrics were provided with some predefined values. Finally, these values were placed in a formula to calculate final score.

Pros
- Widely adopted standard till now.
- Easy to calculate and implement.
- Classify the vulnerability according to their behavior.

Cons

- Suitable for single vulnerability prioritization and cannot prioritize complete attack path effectively.
- Scores distribution among vulnerabilities (according to their severity level) is not uniform [38].

5.4.2.2 Minimal Attack Set

One of the best solutions to avoid attack chaining is to patch critical vulnerabilities [7,57]. To thwart to intruder from accessing and exploiting vulnerabilities on the system, the author proposes a technique to provide a minimal set of attacks to intruder [57]. In this technique, graph was divided into two types of nodes: black and white. White nodes represent the vulnerabilities that were not detected by Intrusion Detection System (IDS), and black ones are detected by IDS. Their main purpose was to provide a minimal number of white nodes to intruder such that attacker was unable to reach the target. Vulnerabilities that can be detected by IDS can be left unpatched. Chao proposed an algorithm to find a minimum critical set of initial conditions that should be patched to avoid attack path [7]. They have utilized ant colony optimization technique. These schemes are included in the category of miscellaneous schemes in Table 5.2.

Pros

- Easy to implement in small networks.
- Only some vulnerabilities need to be patched to prevent attack.

Cons

- Not suitable for large networks as it cannot be generalized.
- Does not consider false alarm conditions.
- Attack paths cannot be prioritized.

5.4.2.3 Vulnerability Rating and Scoring Scheme

VRSS was proposed in 2012 which uses CVSS as a baseline [38,39]. Since distribution of scores in CVSS was not uniform, VRSS comes into the picture to create a uniform distribution of score. VRSS score is a combination of qualitative and quantitative scores. Qualitative score is calculated from the impact score of CVSS, and quantitative score is calculated from both exploitability and impact scores of CVSS.

Pros

- Scores distribution among vulnerabilities (according to their severity level) is uniform.

Cons

- CVSS is a widely adopted standard, but VRSS is not.
- Completely based upon CVSS formulas.
- Attack paths cannot be prioritized.

5.4.2.4 Hybrid Technique

Hybrid technique combines two or more techniques at the same time to improve performance [46,65]. Zhao propound a hybrid ranking approach to calculate the score of vulnerability and expenditure incurred during attack [65]. They have employed CVSS ranking scheme and metrics group to calculate VIR and VER for each vulnerability instance (Vul_Inst is the action performed by the attacker to exploit the vulnerability). VIR and VER are used to calculate the crucial rate of attack paths which is further used to calculate expenditure incurred by the attacker during transition from one node to other. Steven Noel postulates the metrics that is grouped into four families: victimization family includes CVSS score, size family includes the size of attack graph ranked from 0 to 10, containment family includes risk in terms of resources which are affected by vulnerability exposure, and finally, topology family includes network topology which is used to calculate the number of connected components [46]. They have represented these families using graphs to represent network risk.

Pros
- Attack path prioritization is possible.
- Other factors along with score included in this scheme may further improve the results.

Cons
- Risk and size allotment in the range of 0–10 requires manual intervention, and no proper formula is given for the same.
- Neither efficient nor generalized for large network size.

5.4.2.5 Time to Compromise Model

In order to calculate the time consumed by attacker in exploitation of vulnerability, time to compromise model has been proposed [16,21,43]. Time to compromise a node is divided into three parts:

- Node in which attacker would have known at least one vulnerability for which exploit code is available.
- Node in which attacker would have known vulnerabilities for which exploit code is not available.
- Node which is exploited in the chaining of ancestor node.

The total time to compromise an attack path is the addition of time to compromise every node in that respective path. H. Holm derives the relationship between various scoring schemes and time to compromise value to state that only scoring technique is not sufficient for calculation of the weakest link efficiently [16]. Husni and Kurniati have calculated mean time to compromise a node by allocating some predefined values for probability of attacks being in nodes a, b, and c described above [21]. Also, they have calculated VEA-bility score for attack paths.

Pros
- Attack paths can be prioritized in terms of time taken by attacker to exploit the path which has never been done before.
- Easy to implement even in large network size.

Cons
- Time to compromise a node also depends upon attacker's capability which was not considered.
- Based on some assumptions which may be incorrect.

5.4.2.6 Bayesian Probability Model

Probability-based models can also be used for vulnerability prioritization [30,48]. Poolsappasit have used CVSS score to calculate probability of vulnerability exploitation [48]. They have also portrayed a formula for calculation of local conditional probability for path reaching target node. Finally, these values were used to calculate final posterior probability. They have also calculated the total cost of reaching the target by first assigning the initial cost of nodes and then calculating effective cost for complete path. Khosravi-Farmad uses temporal probability using base metrics of CVSS, which was further used for calculation of risk [30]. Bayesian probability scheme comes under the category of miscellaneous scheme in Table 5.2.

Pros
■ Easy to implement.
■ Cost as well as score is calculated for efficient analyses of attack graphs.

Cons
■ Vulnerability exploitation depends upon attacker's capability but not on probability.
■ Preconditions and postconditions have not been considered.
■ Method of assigning initial cost was not specified.

5.4.2.7 Attack Graph-Based Security Metrics

Several attack graphs-based security metrics schemes can be used for analysis of attack paths, i.e., Shortest Path metrics, Number of Paths metrics, and Mean of Path Lengths metrics. But these schemes were unable to adequately account for attack complexity. Therefore, these were extended to produce better results [22,35]. Idika and Bhargava have calculated normalized mean, median, mode, and standard deviation of path length metrics [22].

Kundu et al. posit an attack-resistant metrics and the weakest adversary metrics [35]. Attack-resistant metrics represents the difficulty level in execution of exploits, and the weakest adversary metrics is the minimal set of initial conditions required to initiate exploit. These schemes come under graph metrics scheme in Table 5.2.

Pros
■ Easy to calculate and understand.

Cons
■ Attack path complexity depends upon the most complex attack in the path. This condition has not been undertaken.
■ Preconditions and postconditions have not been considered.

5.4.2.8 Probability-Based Security Metrics

Score and cost can also be calculated using some probability values of vulnerability exploitation [28,60]. Wang has utilized hidden Markov model for cost estimation of attack paths [60]. Cost can be categorized into two types: attack execution cost and vulnerability patch cost. They have assigned some initial cost values to nodes using some probability measures which were further used to prioritize attack paths. Keramati and Akbari have used impact value of CVSS score [28]. Almasizadeh proposed Mean Privacy metrics (MP) for analysis of attack paths [6]. MP was divided into two phases: static and dynamic. In static phase, probability mass function value was assigned to each node so that entropy or initial uncertainty can be calculated, and in dynamic phase, final entropy value was calculated after propagating initial values of nodes to their parents. These schemes, where probability value is used for path prioritization, come under miscellaneous schemes in Table 5.2.

Pros
■ Double security measures, i.e., cost and score, can be calculated.

Cons
■ Attack path complexity depends upon attacker's capability and attack complexity. These constraints are not considered.
■ CVSS score is not a representation of probability of vulnerability exploitation. It is a measure of attack complexity depending upon different constraints.

5.4.2.9 Modified CVSS Score-Based Security Metrics

Some authors have modified CVSS metrics to improvise the ranking mechanism [1,8,29]. Cheng have modified CVSS base score metrics value to calculate effective base score [8]. They have generated a Bayesian network table whose values depend upon the path existence from one node to another node as well as effective base score. Abraham and Nair have calculated effective temporal exploitability score using base exploitability score and the temporal score of CVSS [1]. They have also used expected path length metrics and probabilistic path metrics. Another method is proposed in which confidentiality, integrity, and availability impact values of all vulnerabilities of attack path were added and then multiplied with Convenience Degree value (CD). CD is calculated using CVSS temporal score and length of attack path [29].

Pros
■ Easy to implement and understand.
■ Complete path score can be calculated.

Cons
■ Preconditions and postconditions have not been considered.

5.4.2.10 Node Rank Algorithm

Node ranking is the process of assigning ranks to attack nodes depending upon the capability of attacker [17,31,36]. Li and Qiu proposed a technique where root node was given an initial rank value depending upon some assumptions, and then ranks for other nodes were calculated depending upon parent node ranks [36]. Kijsanayothin and Hewett have given separate formula for rank calculation of initial and intermediate nodes [31]. Initial node can be root node or any node where we should start rescanning the network as the next attempt. Hong and Kim specified that node rank can be calculated using network centrality or location centrality [17]. Location centrality can be used when locations of attacker and target are specified initially, and depending upon the distance and number of hosts between attacker and target, rank is calculated, i.e., all those nodes that are closer to an attacker are assigned high rank than the other nodes. In network centrality, three metrics are used: degree (number of edges connecting to node), closeness (closeness of one node to other nodes), and betweenness (importance of node). These three metrics are used to calculate node rank. Rank of a node can be considered as score value in Table 5.2.

Pros
- Complete attack paths can be analyzed.
- Nodes can be easily prioritized depending upon their risk.

Cons
- Rank value for root node is based upon a guess.
- Exploit complexity has not been undertaken.
- Attack path complexity depends upon the most complex attack in the path. This condition has not been undertaken.

5.4.2.11 Genetic Algorithm

Genetic algorithms have been proposed in 2013 for the analysis of attack graphs [3,4]. Initially, probability of vulnerability exploitation and loss incurred at node after vulnerability exploitation was calculated which can be used to calculate final path risk value [3]. Here, genetic algorithm was used to find high-risk attack trees. Alhomidi and Reed propound genetic algorithm for calculation of minimum cut set (set of edges that divide the graph into two parts P and P' such that every edge passing through cut set has one end point in P and other one in P') such that network will be in secure state after removal of such edges [4].

Pros
- Genetic algorithms always prove to be the best in studies.
- Complete attack tree analysis is possible.

Cons
- Initial loss value is assigned manually which is not possible every time.

5.5 Review Protocol

Systematic review focuses on analyzing and characterizing research studies related to a specific topic using well-defined search strategy. Lippmann and Ingols review research works on attack graphs aiming to characterize research works on attack graph generation, goals of attacker, and attack graph scaling depending upon the size of network [37]. This report focuses on research work related to attack graphs till 2004. After that, there was hardly any systematic literature review for attack graphs.

In this chapter, we provide a systematic approach to comprehensively review and categorize research works related to attack graph generation and analysis. We have followed the review protocol as shown in Figure 5.6.

Figure 5.6 Review protocol.

5.5.1 Identify Research Question

Research question is the foremost step in systematic review process. In this chapter, the following research questions have been answered:

RQ1: What type of attack graph is widely followed to provide security and why?
RQ2: What percentage of works aims on analyzing attack graphs and how?

RQ1 specifies the techniques and types of attack graphs that have been used widely out of all discussed above and what are the pros and cons of that technique. RQ2 includes works that prioritize attack paths according to some factors: total cost incurred for either attacking or patching the attack path, score representing risk of attack path and time to exploit or patch the attack path, etc.

5.5.2 Specify Search Keywords and String

Manual searching of works using keywords and strings is performed to get relevant research papers. Keywords "Attack Graphs," "CVSS," and "Network Vulnerability Scoring" were used in searching process. These works were further filtered using advance search mechanisms.

5.5.3 Study Work Selection

The following criteria have been used to select relevant study work:

1. Research work on attack graphs involving software vulnerabilities was considered.
2. Works published in reputed journals and conferences were selected.

5.5.4 Research Work Inclusion/Exclusion

Inclusion and exclusion criteria were used to filter out works that were not relevant to research questions specified above. The following works are excluded:

- Tutorials,
- Duplicate studies,
- Studies in languages other than English,
- Research works in which complete and detailed information was not specified.

5.5.5 Final Study Selection

As we can see from Figure 5.7, the first phase includes exclusion of articles depending upon the author's reputation. In the second phase, duplicate works were removed. The third phase includes extraction of works based on title and abstract. In the fourth phase, a complete review of articles was performed to select a final set of articles in the fifth phase. After the fifth phase, we perform some reference-checking mechanism to proceed further with review process. Figure 5.8 represents the total number of articles at each phase. Articles that were found suitable for this review process depending upon title, abstract, and content were extracted.

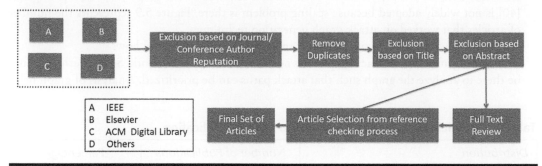

Figure 5.7   Systematic review process.

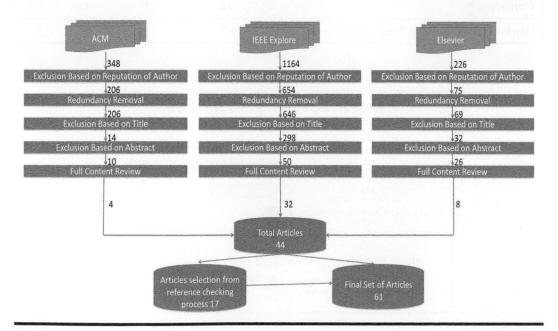

Figure 5.8   Article count for each phase of review process.

5.6 Discussion

The careful execution of review protocol summarized to some important and relevant articles that have been selected for review. In this section, we have concentrated on some tables and charts to represent answers to research questions and distribution of articles according to their publication source type and data content. In this review process, articles were selected from journals, conferences, workshops, and symposium that have been portrayed with the help of Table 5.1.

Here are the research questions and their answers:

RQ1: What type of attack graph is widely followed to provide security and why?

Seven types of attack graph generation schemes have already been specified earlier in this literature. Every scheme has its own pros and cons. But HLAG scheme [41] is better than others as in this case; size of attack graph is less than others which may avoid scaling problem of graph. But it should include additional preconditions to avoid irrelevant nodes. Network attack graph scheme is better if complete analysis of network is required in one graph [10]. Goal plan graph [40] is not widely adopted because scaling problem is there. Figure 5.9 represents the number of articles that worked on attack graph generation techniques.

RQ2: What percentage of works aims on analyzing attack graphs and how?

Merely generation of attack graph does not assure security of network. Some method should be there to analyze the graph such that attack paths can be prioritized. Analysis of graph helps

Table 5.1 Article Distribution According to Type of Publication

Distribution	Number of Publications	Percentage
Journal	18	29.5
Conference	26	42.6
Workshop/Symposium/Book/Report	17	27.8

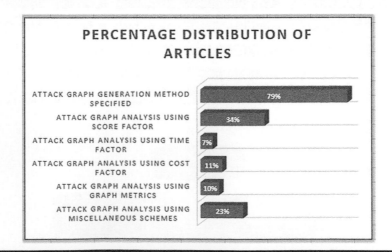

Figure 5.9 Frequency chart for article distribution according to idea proposed.

in taking decision of patching of the most risky path first. This analysis can be in the form of cost of attacking or patching of path [65], time taken to exploit or protect the attack path [43], attack graph metrics, i.e., path length metrics [6], or it can be in the form of any score also [11]. We have also categorized works according to the analysis technique they have proposed in Section 3.2. Article distribution according to the type of analysis technique has been given in Figure 5.9. Some works were there that propose more than one analysis method, and further details of these works are provided in Table 5.2.

5.6.1 Classification Results

We have classified all the works according to some classification factors. The classification of papers is summarized in Table 5.2.

5.7 Open Issues and Challenges

The major issue in attack graph generation is scaling and optimization. Attack graph optimization and scaling are possible when irrelevant nodes (e.g., CVE-2013-2465 is possible only if oracle is installed on system [56]) are avoided. Removal of such kind of nodes is possible when we have complete preconditions and postconditions for vulnerabilities. Detection of preconditions and postconditions for vulnerabilities is a challenging task. As the numbers of vulnerabilities are growing exponentially, it is becoming difficult to procure information about vulnerability precondition and postconditions. Also, there is no such online database available that can provide direct information about these conditions.

The next issue that comes into this field is attack graph analysis. Since the size of attack graph increases with the size of network, patching all vulnerabilities of attack graph is neither feasible nor possible. It is also a labor- and time-consuming process. Therefore, a proper method should be there to prioritize attack paths according to some parameters. The authors have focused on one or two parameters for graph analysis, i.e., cost, time, metrics, and score. But the problem arises when different attack paths possess the same value of any parameter. In such cases, hybrid technique is required that can combine more than two approaches. Also, majority of works are based upon probabilities and guesses irrespective of attack graph complexity or attacker's capability, which is not the relevant method for analysis. These issues and challenges must be addressed in the future work.

5.8 Threats to Validity

Although paramount care was taken while selecting the articles for review, still there might be threats to internal or external validity of this review process.

- **External Validity:** Threats can be there for external validity because of some articles might have been missed due to inappropriate selection criteria. The studies where the procedure for attack graph generation is not properly defined might have been excluded. Some studies that are difficult and unable to understand might have been left. One of the major issues is language also due to which numerous findings were also excluded.

Table 5.2 Article Classification Result

Author Name/ Reference Number	Year	Type of Attack Graph or Description of Paper	Attack Graph Generation						Attack Graph Analysis				
			Attack Graph Type Specified		Scaling and Optimization		Generation Method Specified		Graph Metrics Scheme	Score Scheme	Cost Scheme	Time Scheme	Misc. Scheme
			Yes	No	Yes	No	Yes	No					
Kaynar and Sivrikaya [27]	2015	Distributed attack graph	✓	–	✓	–	✓	–	–	–	–	–	–
Younis and Malaiya [64]	2015	–	–	✓	–	✓	–	✓	–	✓	–	–	–
Abraham and Nair [1]	2015	HLAG generated by MulVAL tool	✓	–	✓	–	–	✓	✓	✓	–	–	–
Huang et al. [19]	2015	HLAG generated by MulVAL tool	✓	–	✓	–	–	✓	–	✓	–	–	–
Husni and Kurniati [21]	2015	–	–	✓	–	✓	–	✓	–	✓	–	✓	–
Chao et al. [7]	2014	Exploit dependency graph	✓	–	–	✓	–	✓	–	–	✓	–	✓

(Continued)

Table 5.2 (Continued)   Article Classification Result

	Year	Type of Attack Graph or Description of Paper	Attack Graph Generation			Attack Graph Analysis				
			Attack Graph Type Specified	Scaling and Optimi-zation	Generation Method Specified	Graph Metrics Scheme	Score Scheme	Cost Scheme	Time Scheme	Misc. Scheme
Khosravi-Farmad et al. [30]	2014	Bayesian attack graph	✓	✓	–	–	–	–	–	✓
Kotenko et al. [34]	2014	–	–	✓	✓	–	✓	–	–	–
Noel and Jajodia [46]	2014	–	–	✓	✓	–	✓	–	–	✓
Almasizadeh et al. [6]	2014	HLAG	✓	✓	✓	✓	–	–	–	–
Keramati and Akbari [29]	2013	Exploit dependency graph	✓	✓	✓	–	✓	–	–	–
Wang et al. [60]	2013	HLAG generated by MulVAL tool	✓	–	✓	–	–	✓	–	–
Yi et al. [63]	2013	HLAG generated by various tools	✓	–	✓	–	–	–	–	–

(Continued)

Table 5.2 (Continued) Article Classification Result

			Attack Graph Generation			Attack Graph Analysis				
		Type of Attack Graph or Description of Paper	Attack Graph Type Specified	Scaling and Optimization	Generation Method Specified	Graph Metrics Scheme	Score Scheme	Cost Scheme	Time Scheme	Misc. Scheme
Alhomidi and Reed [4]	2013	HLAG generated by MulVAL tool	✓	✓	✓	–	✓	✓	–	–
Jin Bum Hong et al. [18]	2013	Goal plan graph	✓	✓	–	–	–	–	–	–
Alhomidi and Reed [3]	2013	HLAG	✓	–	✓	–	–	–	–	✓
Hong and Kim [17]	2013	HLAG generated by MulVAL tool+goal plan graph	✓	✓	✓	✓	✓	–	–	–
Fayyad and Meinel [10]	2013	Network attack graph	✓	–	✓	–	–	–	–	–
Kotenko and Chechulin [33]	2013	Network attack graph using AMSEC	✓	–	✓	–	–	–	–	–
Liu and Gu [40]	2013	Goal plan graph	✓	–	✓	–	–	–	–	–

(Continued)

Table 5.2 (Continued)   Article Classification Result

		Attack Graph Generation				Attack Graph Analysis				
	Year	Type of Attack Graph or Description of Paper	Attack Graph Type Specified	Scaling and Optimization	Generation Method Specified	Graph Metrics Scheme	Score Scheme	Cost Scheme	Time Scheme	Misc. Scheme
Ghosh and Bhattacharya [14]	2013	Exploit dependency graph	✓	–	✓	–	–	✓	–	–
Kijsanayothin and Hewett [31]	2013	HLAG	✓	–	✓	–	✓	–	–	–
Kundu et al. [35]	2012	Exploit dependency graph	✓	–	✓	✓	–	–	–	–
Alhomidi and Reed [2]	2012	Comparison of attack graphs types	✓	–	✓	–	–	–	–	–
Liu et al. [41]	2012	HLAG	✓	✓	✓	–	–	–	–	–
Wang et al. [57]	2012	HLAG	✓	✓	–	–	–	–	–	✓
Liu et al. [39]	2012	–	–	–	✓	–	✓	–	–	–
Lv and Wang [42]	2012	ASTG	✓	✓	✓	–	–	–	–	–

(Continued)

Table 5.2 (Continued)   Article Classification Result

			Attack Graph Generation			Attack Graph Analysis				
		Type of Attack Graph or Description of Paper	Attack Graph Type Specified	Scaling and Optimization	Generation Method Specified	Graph Metrics Scheme	Score Scheme	Cost Scheme	Time Scheme	Misc. Scheme
Cheng et al. [8]	2012	Exploit dependency graph	✓	–	✓	–	✓	–	–	–
Holm et al. [16]	2012	–	✓	–	✓	–	–	–	✓	–
Li and Qiu [36]	2012	ASTG	✓	–	–	–	✓	–	–	–
Poolsappasit et al. [48]	2012	Bayesian attack graph	✓	✓	–	–	–	–	–	✓
Marjan Keramati and Akbari [28]	2012	Exploit dependency graph	✓	–	✓	–	✓	–	–	✓
Holm [15]	2012	Comparison of scanners	–	–	✓	–	–	–	–	–
Allodi and Massacci [5]	2012	Compares CVSS scores of vulnerabilities	–	–	✓	–	✓	–	–	–
Shahzad et al. [50]	2012	Comparison of vulnerabilities on various factors	✓	–	✓	–	–	–	–	✓

(Continued)

Table 5.2 (Continued)   Article Classification Result

		Type of Attack Graph or Description of Paper	Attack Graph Generation			Attack Graph Analysis				
			Attack Graph Type Specified	Scaling and Optimization	Generation Method Specified	Graph Metrics Scheme	Score Scheme	Cost Scheme	Time Scheme	Misc. Scheme
Zhao et al. [65]	2011	HLAG generated by TVA–AG	✓	✓	–	–	✓	✓	–	–
Liu and Zhang [38]	2011	–	–	✓	✓	–	✓	–	–	–
Idika and Bhargava [22]	2010	Exploit dependency graph	✓	✓	✓	✓	–	–	–	–
Ghosh and Ghosh [13]	2009	Exploit dependency graph	✓	✓	✓	–	✓	–	–	✓
Wang et al. [58]	2008	Exploit dependency graph	✓	✓	✓	–	✓	–	–	–
Wing et al. [62]	2008	Scenario graph	✓	✓	✓	–	–	–	–	–
Mell et al. [45]	2007	CVSS scoring scheme	–	✓	✓	–	✓	–	–	–
Frei et al. [12]	2006	Comparison of vulnerabilities on various factors	–	✓	✓	–	–	–	–	✓

(Continued)

Table 5.2 (Continued)   Article Classification Result

			Attack Graph Generation			Attack Graph Analysis				
	Year	Type of Attack Graph or Description of Paper	Attack Graph Type Specified	Scaling and Optimization	Generation Method Specified	Graph Metrics Scheme	Score Scheme	Cost Scheme	Time Scheme	Misc. Scheme
Mehta et al. [44]	2006	Scenario graph	✓	–	✓	–	✓	–	–	–
Wang et al. [59]	2006	HLAG	✓	–	✓	–	–	–	–	✓
Lippmann and Ingols [37]	2005	Review of past papers on attack graph	✓	–	✓	–	–	–	–	–
McQueen et al. [43]	2005	–	–	–	✓	–	–	–	✓	–
Sheyner et al. [51]	2004	Scenario graphs	✓	✓	–	–	–	–	–	–
Sheyner et al. [53]	2004	Tool for generating HLAG	✓	✓	–	–	–	–	–	–
Wing et al. [61]	2003	Scenario graph	✓	✓	–	–	–	–	–	–
Hughes et al. [20]	2003	Scenario graph	✓	✓	–	–	–	–	–	–
Jha et al. [23]	2002	HLAG	✓	–	✓	–	–	–	–	✓

(Continued)

Table 5.2 (Continued)   Article Classification Result

		Type of Attack Graph or Description of Paper	Attack Graph Generation			Attack Graph Analysis				
			Attack Graph Type Specified	Scaling and Optimization	Generation Method Specified	Graph Metrics Scheme	Score Scheme	Cost Scheme	Time Scheme	Misc. Scheme
Sheyner et al. [52]	2002	Host-level graph generated using NuSMV	✓	–	✓	–	–	–	–	✓
Jha et al. [25]	2002	Host-level graph generated using NuSMV	✓	✓	✓	–	–	✓	–	✓
Jha et al. [26]	2001	Scenario graph	✓	–	✓	–	–	✓	✓	–
Swiler et al. [54]	2001	Tool for generating HLAG	✓	–	✓	✓	–	–	–	–
Jha et al. [24]	2000	Scenario graph	✓	–	✓	–	–	–	–	–
Schneier et al. [49]	1999	Attack trees	✓	–	✓	–	–	–	–	–
Phillips et al. [47]	1998	HLAG	✓	–	✓	–	–	–	–	–
Dacier et al. [9]	1996	Privilege graph	✓	–	✓	–	–	–	–	–

■ **Internal Validity:** Internal validity can also be affected due to some factors, i.e., we might have missed some relevant works. Due to some reference-checking mechanism, it might have been possible that any graph generation scheme is overlooked.

5.9 Conclusions and the Future Work

In this chapter, we have conducted a systematic review of attack graph generation and analysis techniques. A manual search has been conducted using IEEE Explore, ScienceDirect, and ACM Digital Library. We have also conducted a reference-checking mechanism to further advance our research to minimize the chances of missing relevant work.

In brief, this work focuses toward attack graph generation and analysis mechanism. The studies observed a growing interest in attack graph analysis using score calculation scheme. The results show that most of the works only specify analysis of graph without specifying attack graph generation technique. Although tremendous works have been proposed for attack graph optimization and prioritization, majority of the articles consist of some initial value guesses or probability-based calculations. It has also been observed that the size of attack graph is an issue for security administrators from the beginning of this field, but a few works have been proposed for optimizing the size of attack graph. We expect that this article will help the readers in getting brief understanding of attack graphs and its analysis. Additionally, the research questions and problems discussed in this chapter will help the researchers in getting idea about the future work.

References

1. Abraham, S., & Nair, S. (2015). Exploitability analysis using predictive cybersecurity framework. *Proceedings - 2015 IEEE 2nd International Conference on Cybernetics, CYBCONF 2015*, 317–323. doi:10.1109/CYBConf.2015.7175953.
2. Alhomidi, M. A., & Reed, M. J. (2012). Attack graphs representations. *2012 4th Computer Science and Electronic Engineering Conference, CEEC 2012 - Conference Proceedings*, 83–88. doi:10.1109/CEEC.2012.6375383.
3. Alhomidi, M., & Reed, M. (2013b). Risk assessment and analysis through population-based attack graph modelling. *World Congress on Internet Security (WorldCIS-2013)*, 19–24. doi:10.1109/WorldCIS.2013.6751011.
4. Alhomidi, M., & Reed, M. (2013a). Finding the minimum cut set in attack graphs using genetic algorithms. *International Conference on Computer Applications Technology, ICCAT 2013*. doi:10.1109/ICCAT.2013.6522000.
5. Allodi, L., & Massacci, F. (2012). A preliminary analysis of vulnerability scores for attacks in wild. *Proceedings of the 2012 ACM Workshop on Building Analysis Datasets and Gathering Experience Returns for Security - BADGERS '12*, 17. doi:10.1145/2382416.2382427.
6. Almasizadeh, J., & Abdollahi Azgomi, M. (2014). Mean privacy: A metric for security of computer systems. *Computer Communications*, 52, 47–59. doi:10.1016/j.comcom.2014.06.009.
7. Chao, Z., Huiqiang, W., Fangfang, G., Mo, Z., & Yushu, Z. (2014). A heuristic method of attack graph analysis for network security hardening. *2014 International Conference on Cyber-Enabled Distributed Computing and Knowledge Discovery*, 43–47. doi:10.1109/CyberC.2014.18.
8. Cheng, P., Wang, L., Jajodia, S., & Singhal, A. (2012). Aggregating CVSS base scores for semantics-rich network security metrics. *Proceedings of the IEEE Symposium on Reliable Distributed Systems*, 31–40. doi:10.1109/SRDS.2012.4.
9. Dacier, M., Deswarte, Y., & Kaâniche, M. (1996). Models and tools for quantitative assessment of operational security. *12th International Information Security Conference (IFIP/SEC'96)*, 177–186. doi:10.1007/978-1-5041-2919-0_15.

10. Fayyad, S., & Meinel, C. (2013). Attack scenario prediction methodology. *Proceedings of the 2013 10th International Conference on Information Technology: New Generations, ITNG 2013*, 53–59. doi:10.1109/ITNG.2013.16.

11. FIRST. (1989). Common vulnerability scoring system. Retrieved from www.first.org/cvss.

12. Frei, S., May, M., Fiedler, U., & Plattner, B. (2006). Large-scale vulnerability analysis. *SIGCOMM Workshop on Large-Scale Attack Defense (LSAD)*, 131–138. doi:10.1145/1162666.1162671.

13. Ghosh, N., & Ghosh, S. K. (2009). An approach for security assessment of network configurations using attack graph. *1st International Conference on Networks and Communications, NetCoM* 2009, 283–288. doi:10.1109/NetCoM.2009.83.

14. Ghosh, S. K., & Bhattacharya, P. (2012). Analytical framework for measuring network security using exploit dependency graph. *IET Information Security*, 6(4), 264–270. doi:10.1049/iet-ifs.2011.0103.

15. Holm, H. (2012). Performance of automated network vulnerability scanning at remediating security issues. *Computers and Security*, 31(2), 164–175. doi:10.1016/j.cose.2011.12.014.

16. Holm, H., Ekstedt, M., & Andersson, D. (2012). Empirical analysis of system-level vulnerability metrics through actual attacks. *IEEE Transactions on Dependable and Secure Computing*, 9(6), 825–837. doi:10.1109/TDSC.2012.66.

17. Hong, J. B., & Kim, D. S. (2013). Scalable security analysis in hierarchical attack representation model using centrality measures. *Proceedings of the International Conference on Dependable Systems and Networks*. doi:10.1109/DSNW.2013.6615507.

18. Hong, J. B., Kim, D. S., & Takaoka, T. (2013). Scalable attack representation model using logic reduction techniques. *2013 12th IEEE International Conference on Trust, Security and Privacy in Computing and Communications*, 404–411. doi:10.1109/TrustCom.2013.51.

19. Huang, Z., Shen, C.-C., Doshiy, S., Thomasy, N., & Duong, H. (2015). Difficulty-level metric for cyber security training. *2015 IEEE International Inter-Disciplinary Conference on Cognitive Methods in Situation Awareness and Decision Support (CogSIMA)*, 172–178. doi:10.1109/COGSIMA.2015.7108194.

20. Hughes, T., & Sheyner, O. (2003). Attack scenario graphs for computer network threat analysis and prediction. *Complexity*, 9, 15–18.

21. Husni, E., & Kurniati, Y. (2015). Application of mean time-to-compromise and VEA-bility security metrics in auditing computer network security. *Proceedings of 2014 8th International Conference on Telecommunication Systems Services and Applications, TSSA* 2014. doi:10.1109/TSSA.2014.7065960.

22. Idika, N., & Bhargava, B. (2012). Extending attack graph-based security metrics and aggregating their application. *IEEE Transactions on Dependable and Secure Computing*, 9(1), 75–85. doi:10.1109/TDSC.2010.61.

23. Jha, S., Sheyner, O., & Wing, J. (2002). Two formal analyses of attack graphs. *Proceedings of the Computer Security Foundations Workshop*, 2002–Janua, 49–63. doi:10.1109/CSFW.2002.1021806.

24. Jha, S., Wing, J., Linger, R., & Longstaff, T. (2000). Survivability analysis of network specifications. *Proceedings of the 2002 International Conference on Dependable Systems and Networks*, 613–622. doi:10.1109/ICDSN.2000.857597.

25. Jha, S., Wing, J., & Sheyner, O. (2002). Minimization and reliability analyses of attack graphs. *Citeseer*. Retrieved from http://citeseerx.ist.psu.edu/viewdoc/download?doi=10.1.1.61.1788&rep=rep1&type=pdf%5Cnpapers2://publication/uuid/BFFE4D66-6A9E-4144-B0E8-26AE7B3C0D81.

26. Jha, S., & Wing, J. M. (2001). Survivability analysis of networked systems. *Proceedings of the 23rd International Conference on Software Engineering. ICSE*.

27. Kaynar, K., & Sivrikaya, F. (2015). Distributed attack graph generation. *IEEE Transactions on Dependable and Secure Computing*, 13(5), 519–532. doi:10.1109/TDSC.2015.2423682.

28. Keramati, M., & Akbari, A. (2012). An attack graph based metric for security evaluation of computer networks. *2012 6th International Symposium on Telecommunications, IST 2012*, 1094–1098. doi:10.1109/ISTEL.2012.6483149.

29. Keramati, M., & Akbari, A. (2013). CVSS-based security metrics for quantitative analysis of attack graphs, (Iccke), 1–6.

30. Khosravi-Farmad, M., Rezaee, R., & Bafghi, A. G. (2014). Considering temporal and environmental characteristics of vulnerabilities in network security risk assessment. *2014 11th International ISC Conference on Information Security and Cryptology, ISCISC 2014*, 186–191. doi:10.1109/ISCISC.2014.6994045.

31. Kijsanayothin, P., & Hewett, R. (2013). Exploit-based analysis of attack models. *Proceedings - IEEE 12th International Symposium on Network Computing and Applications, NCA 2013*, 183–186. doi:10.1109/NCA.2013.18.

32. Kot, M. (2003). The state explosion problem, 1–6. Retrieved from www.cs.vsb.cz/kot/down/Texts/StateSpace.pdf.

33. Kotenko, I., & Chechulin, A. (2013). Computer attack modeling and security evaluation based on attack graphs. *Proceedings of the 2013 IEEE 7th International Conference on Intelligent Data Acquisition and Advanced Computing Systems, IDAACS 2013*, 2(September), 614–619. doi:10.1109/IDAACS.2013.6662998.

34. Kotenko, I., Doynikova, E., & Chechulin, A. (2014). Security metrics based on attack graphs for the Olympic games scenario. *Proceedings - 2014 22nd Euromicro International Conference on Parallel, Distributed, and Network-Based Processing, PDP 2014*, 561–568. doi:10.1109/PDP.2014.113.

35. Kundu, A., Ghosh, N., Chokshi, I., & Ghosh, S. K. (2012). Analysis of attack graph-based metrics for quantification of network security. *2012 Annual IEEE India Conference, INDICON 2012*, 530–535. doi:10.1109/INDCON.2012.6420675.

36. Li, P., & Qiu, X. (2012). NodeRank: An algorithm to assess state enumeration attack graphs. *2012 International Conference on Wireless Communications, Networking and Mobile Computing, WiCOM 2012*, 0–4. doi:10.1109/WiCOM.2012.6478585.

37. Lippmann, R., & Ingols, K. (2005). An annotated review of past papers on attack graphs. *(No. PR-IA-1). Massachusetts Inst of Tech Lexington Lincoln Lab.* Retrieved from http://oai.dtic.mil/oai/oai?verb=getRecord&metadataPrefix=html&identifier=ADA431826.

38. Liu, Q., & Zhang, Y. (2011). VRSS: A new system for rating and scoring vulnerabilities. *Computer Communications*, 34(3), 264–273. doi:10.1016/j.comcom.2010.04.006.

39. Liu, Q., Zhang, Y., Kong, Y., & Wu, Q. (2012). Improving VRSS-based vulnerability prioritization using analytic hierarchy process. *Journal of Systems and Software*, 85(8), 1699–1708. doi:10.1016/j.jss.2012.03.057.

40. Liu, Y., & Gu, W. X. (2013). An effective recognition method for network attack. *Optik*, 124(21), 4823–4826. doi:10.1016/j.ijleo.2013.02.036.

41. Liu, Z., Li, S., He, J., Xie, D., & Deng, Z. (2012). Complex network security analysis based on attack graph model. *2012 Second International Conference on Instrumentation, Measurement, Computer, Communication and Control*, 183–186. doi:10.1109/IMCCC.2012.50.

42. Lv, H. Y., & Wang, R. M. (2012). *Network Real-Time Threat Awareness and Analysis Based on Attack State Transition*, (1), 1–6.

43. McQueen, M. A., Boyer, W. F., Flynn, M. A., & Beitel, G. A. (2005). Time-to-compromise model for cyber risk reduction estimation. *Quality of Protection*, 49–64. doi:10.1007/978-0-387-36584-8_5.

44. Mehta, V., Bartzis, C., Zhu, H., Clarke, E., & Wing, J. (2006). Ranking attack graphs. *9th International Symposium on Recent Advances in Intrusion Detection (RAID'06)*, *4219*, 127–144. doi:10.1007/11856214_7.

45. Mell, P., Scarfone, K., & Romanosky, S. (2007). The common vulnerability scoring system (CVSS) and its applicability to federal agency systems. *NIST Interagency Report 7435*.

46. Noel, S., & Jajodia, S. (2014). *Metrics Suite for Network Attack Graph Analytics*, 10, 2–5. doi:10.1145/2602087.2602117.

47. Phillips, C., & Swiler, L. P. (1998). A graph-based system for network-vulnerability analysis. *Proceedings of the 1998 Workshop on New Security Paradigms*, 71–79. doi: 10.1145/310889.310919.

48. Poolsappasit, N., Dewri, R., & Ray, I. (2012). Dynamic security risk management using Bayesian attack graphs. *IEEE Transactions on Dependable and Secure Computing*, 9(1), 61–74. doi:10.1109/TDSC.2011.34.

49. Schneier, B. (1999). Attack trees. *Dr. Dobb's Journal*. Retrieved from www.schneier.com/academic/archives/1999/12/attack_trees.html.

50. Shahzad, M., Shafiq, M. Z., & Liu, A. X. (2012). A large scale exploratory analysis of software vulnerability life cycles. *Proceedings of the 2012 34th International Conference on Software Engineering (ICSE '12)*, 771–781. doi:10.1109/ICSE.2012.6227141.

51. Sheyner, O. M. (2004). Scenario graphs and attack graphs. *Architecture*, (October), 3–4. Retrieved from http://citeseerx.ist.psu.edu/viewdoc/download? doi:10.1.1.83.6220&rep=rep1& amp;type=pdf.

52. Sheyner, O., Haines, J., Jha, S., Lippmann, R., & Wing, J. M. (2002). Automated generation and analysis of attack graphs. *Proceedings—IEEE Symposium on Security and Privacy*, 2002(January), 273–284. doi:10.1109/SECPRI.2002.1004377.

53. Sheyner, O., & Wing, J. (2004). Tools for generating and analyzing attack graphs. *2nd International Symposium on Formal Methods for Components and Objects (FMCO'03)*, 3188, 344–371. doi:10.1007/978-3-540-30101-1_17.

54. Swiler, L. P., Phillips, C., Ellis, D., & Chakerian, S. (2001). Computer-attack graph generation tool. *Proceedings - DARPA Information Survivability Conference and Exposition II, DISCEX 2001*, 2, 307–321. doi:10.1109/DISCEX.2001.932182.

55. US-CERT. (1999). Common vulnerabilities and exposures. Retrieved from www.cve.mitre.org/.

56. US-CERT. (2015). Top 30 targeted high risk vulnerabilities. Retrieved from www.us-cert.gov/ncas/alerts/TA15-119A.

57. Wang, C., Du, N., & Yang, H. (2012). Generation and analysis of attack graphs. *Procedia Engineering*, 29, 4053–4057. doi:10.1016/j.proeng.2012.01.618.

58. Wang, L., Islam, T., Long, T., Singhal, A., & Jajodia, S. (2008). An attack graph-based probabilistic security metric. *Lecture Notes in Computer Science (Including Subseries Lecture Notes in Artificial Intelligence and Lecture Notes in Bioinformatics)*, 5094 LNCS, 283–296. doi:10.1007/978-3-540-70567-3_22.

59. Wang, L., Noel, S., & Jajodia, S. (2006). Minimum-cost network hardening using attack graphs. *Computer Communications*, 29(18), 3812–3824. doi:10.1016/j.comcom.2006.06.018

60. Wang, S., Zhang, Z., & Kadobayashi, Y. (2013). Exploring attack graph for cost-benefit security hardening: A probabilistic approach. *Computers and Security*, 32, 158–169. doi:10.1016/j.cose.2012.09.013.

61. Wing, J. M. (2003). Scenario graphs applied to security (summary paper). *Scenario*, 1–6.

62. Wing, J. M. (2008). Scenario graphs applied to network security. *Information Assurance*, 247–277. doi:10.1016/B978-012373566-9.50011-2.

63. Yi, S., Peng, Y., Xiong, Q., Wang, T., Dai, Z., Gao, H., Xu, L., Wang, J., & Xu, L. (2013). Overview on attack graph generation and visualization technology. *Proceedings of the International Conference on Anti-Counterfeiting, Security and Identification, ASID*. doi:10.1109/ICASID.2013.6825274.

64. Younis, A. A., & Malaiya, Y. K. (2015). Comparing and evaluating CVSS base metrics and microsoft rating system. *2015 IEEE International Conference on Software Quality, Reliability and Security*, (1), 252–261. doi:10.1109/QRS.2015.44.

65. Zhao, F., Huang, H., Jin, H., & Zhang, Q. (2011). A hybrid ranking approach to estimate vulnerability for dynamic attacks. *Computers and Mathematics with Applications*, 62(12), 4308–4321. doi:10.1016/j.camwa.2011.09.031.

References for Advance/Further Reading

66. Al-Qurishi, M., Rahman, S. M. M., Hossain, M. S., Almogren, A., Alrubaian, M., Alamri, A., ... Gupta, B. B. An efficient key agreement protocol for Sybil-precaution in online social networks. *Future Generation Computer Systems*, 2017, 84, 139–148.

67. Gupta, B., Agrawal, D. P., & Yamaguchi, S. (Eds.). *Handbook of Research on Modern Cryptographic Solutions for Computer and Cyber Security*. IGI Publishing, Hershey, PA, 2016.

68. Ibtihal, M., & Hassan, N. Homomorphic encryption as a service for outsourced images in mobile cloud computing environment. *International Journal of Cloud Applications and Computing (IJCAC)*, 2017, 7(2), 27–40.

69. Stergiou, C., Psannis, K. E., Kim, B. G., & Gupta, B. Secure integration of IoT and cloud computing. *Future Generation Computer Systems*, 2018, 78, 964–975.

70. Tewari, A., & Gupta, B. B. A lightweight mutual authentication protocol based on elliptic curve cryptography for IoT devices. *International Journal of Advanced Intelligence Paradigms*, 2017, 9(2–3), 111–121.

71. Yu, C., Li, J., Li, X., Ren, X., & Gupta, B. B. Four-image encryption scheme based on quaternion Fresnel transform, chaos and computer-generated hologram. *Multimedia Tools and Applications*, 2017, 77(4), 4585–4608.
72. Zhang, Z., Sun, R., Zhao, C., Wang, J., Chang, C. K., & Gupta, B. B. CyVOD: A novel trinity multimedia social network scheme. *Multimedia Tools and Applications*, 2017, 76(18), 18513–18529.
73. Zkik, K., Orhanou, G., & El Hajji, S. Secure mobile multi cloud architecture for authentication and data storage. *International Journal of Cloud Applications and Computing (IJCAC)*, 2017, 7(2), 62–76.

Chapter 6

Biometric-Based Authentication in Cloud Computing

Poonam Saini
Punjab Engineering College

Awadhesh Kumar Singh
National Institute of Technology, Kurukshetra

Contents

6.1 Introduction to Cloud Computing and Biometrics

6.1.1 Cloud Computing

In past few years, the emerging paradigm of cloud computing has extended the potential of information technology in the form of software, platform, and infrastructure. According to *National Institute of Standards and Technology* (NIST), the cloud computing model enables ubiquitous, convenient, and on-demand network access to a shared pool of configurable computing resources, e.g., network, servers, storage, applications, and services (Mell et al., 2011). Further, the resources can be rapidly provisioned to end-users and later released with minimal service provider interaction (Ertaul et al., 2010). The broader classification of cloud comprises deployment model and service layers. The placement and management of cloud's infrastructure is handled via a deployment model that can be categorized as public, private, community, or hybrid depending upon the need and requirement of a customer or company. Next, relying upon the kind of services being offered, cloud computing applications are executed within a service model, namely, *Software as a Service* (SaaS), *Platform as a Service* (PaaS), and *Infrastructure as a Service* (IaaS). Few examples of the services are Google App Engine (GAE), Microsoft Azure, and Amazon Web Services (AWS) (Xiao et al., 2013). Another notion that has become popular in recent years is *Anything as a Service* or *Everything as a Service* (XaaS). Figure 6.1 shows the standard framework of cloud computing (Singh et al., 2016). The inter- and intra-cloud communication makes it more vulnerable to attacks, and hence, the security model of cloud computing is distinguished from a traditional one based on different threats. Thus, the major point of concern is to identify various vulnerabilities and associated risks in a cloud computing system in order to optimize the performance and reliability of applications to be executed.

The ecosystem of cloud security as shown in Figure 6.2 depends mainly on factors like *confidentiality, integrity, availability,* and *accountability* (Adhikari, 2017). The significant areas that need to be addressed are network security, interfaces (authentication), data security, virtualization, governance, compliance, legal issues, information security, authentication, Identification, Authentication, Authorization, Auditing (IAAA) mechanisms, storage, management access, communication, computational resource, services and Application Program Interfaces (APIs) (Grobauer et al., 2011). Some of the important cloud-related standards, for example, Open Authentication (OAuth), OpenID, and Security Assertion Markup Language (SAML), provide optimal solution to security-related issues. However, the improper or lack of enforcement of such standards adds

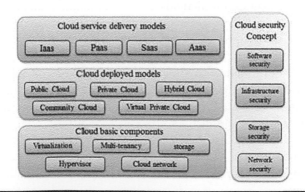

Figure 6.1   Generic framework of cloud computing.

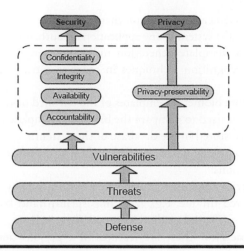

Figure 6.2   Ecosystem of cloud computing.

to the security concern. The first and foremost step in cloud communication is to authenticate a user in order to access the cloud services. This, in turn, may avoid major cloud-related attacks like account hijacking, data leakage, impersonation, etc. At the same time, the task of authenticating someone's identity has become tedious due to the enormous growth of fraudulent users.

6.1.2 Biometrics

The word "biometrics" refers to an old and simple concept of security called human identification. In scientific terms, biometrics is the technique used to match the physical or behavioral traits of a person with the already-existing database, to check for originality (Jain et al., 2004). Figure 6.3 shows a basic biometric system with different components (given below) that can be used by cloud or any computing platform:

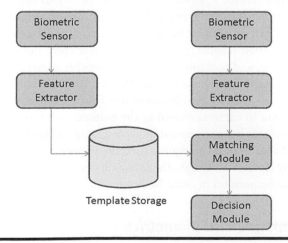

Figure 6.3   A basic biometric system.

■ A biometric sensor or a data acquisition unit that captures an image or video sequence of a user who want to enroll into the system or any application for authentication/identification purposes.

■ A feature extractor or template generation unit employing machine learning, computer vision, and pattern recognition techniques in order to retrieve a biometric template from the input data.

■ A database used to store biometric templates of the enrolled or registered users.

■ A matching component used to compare the biometric template taken from a real-time/live image with template(s) stored in the database of the system.

■ While considering biometrics as a mean to identify and authenticate human users, we generally use two classifications:

1. **Physical biometrics**: These are features inherent to the physical body of a person that could be considered unique, e.g., face, fingerprint, hand biometrics (hand geometry, palm print, hand vein), and ocular biometrics (iris, retina).

2. **Behavioral biometrics**: These are features of a person's actions that could uniquely distinguish a person, e.g., written signatures, keystroke patterns, gait, and voice.

A few biometric applications could be hybrid comprising both physical and behavioral traits, e.g., unique frequency characteristics of one's voice message, which could be physical, whereas the way a person speak could be behavioral (Dinca et al., 2017).The biological terms that qualify to be a biometric trait are human, physiological, and/or behavioral characteristic with following features:

i. *Universality*: Each person should have the features.

ii. *Distinctiveness*: Any two persons should be suitably different in terms of the features.

iii. *Permanence*: The features should be sufficiently uniform (with respect to the matching standard) over a span of time.

iv. *Collectability*: The features can be measured in quantifiable manner.

Common forms of biometrics control include fingerprint, facial, iris, palm print, finger vein, retina, voice, hand geometry, keystroke, and handwriting recognition (Albahdal et al., 2014). In past few years, face recognition has become a popular security tool in various applications like user authentication, hash tag, or person tag in social networks, gaming, and as criminal recognition. In recent decades, the reliability of face recognition has been improved considerably; however, there is a challenge to make face recognition reliable in unconstrained scenarios, like changes in lighting, head pose, facial expression, view, and occlusion. In addition, another constraint related to face recognition is high feature dimensionality inherent to face images. In the facial feature extraction process, even a single face image may lead to high-dimensionality feature vectors, which is aggravated by the increasing image resolution in cameras offered in the market. As a result, the direct processing of original face features involves a heavy computational processing and hence requires efficient machine learning methods to be used in facial recognition. As the enough number of face image samples is not available to properly represent the high-dimensionality face manifold (the space where the face images lie), biometric authentication in cloud becomes a major challenge (Soldera et al., 2017).

6.1.3 Cloud Computing and Biometrics

Cloud computing offers intriguing services; however, the issue of security, privacy, and reliability is an unresolved issue. With security encompassing all categories of threat, the problem needs to be handled primarily. In literature, multifactor authentication has been used as a potential solution to provide security with biometric-based, *physical* and *behavioral*, methods. Moreover, the dynamic environment of cloud computing needs a robust mechanism in order to avoid vulnerability into the services and maintain overall integrity of the communication process (Mihailescu and Nita, 2015). The traditional methods like passwords, PINs, encryption keys, codes, etc. require a user to have a sharp memory to remember and at the same time can be illicitly compromised. Hence, the need is to identify an individual in order to maintain privacy, thereby ensuring a secure environment. In the existing literature, *Biometrics* or *Biometrics as a Service* (Rose, 2016) in cloud has been proposed which solves the problem from user's perspective. As emphasized by Peer and Bule (2013), there are certain aspects of biometric systems that are specific to cloud computing. First, a biometric engine is already present in cloud that makes the cloud-based biometric technology accessible by every end-user. In addition, it can be easily integrated with other security applications. Second, the storage of biometric data in cloud ensures highly scalable system, thereby leading to reliable adaptation of the technology to an increasing user base. However, biometric data in cloud may raise privacy concerns too.

In the book chapter, we will deliberate upon classification of various authentication models along with their usage to handle different categories of threats. Further, we present a computational model based on feature selection to achieve authentication in cloud. The technology/technical terms used in the book chapter are explained wherever they appear or at the "Key Terminology & Definitions" section. Apart from regular references, additional references are included in the "References for Advance/Further reading" section for the benefit of advanced readers.

6.2 Background and Classification

6.2.1 Classical Authentication Methods

Authentication is a process of identifying and verifying the credentials submitted by the user. The authorization, authentication, and accounting (AAA) came into action when a user tries to authenticate itself for using cloud services. Earlier, the authentication methods revolve around the usage of secret knowledge-based approach like User ID/password, PIN (O'Gorman, 2003) (Crawford et al., 2014), where a user has to remember a secret keyword. The secret keyword could be a combination of words or phrases that must match with the already-stored values in the database. The method may not be efficient because a user cannot afford to forget the password or being stolen. Moreover, password needs to be updated frequently being the main target of social engineering attacks. The Public Key Infrastructure (PKI) (Haidar et al., 2009), a trusted third party, issues private keys for communication which cannot be shared; however, scalability is a major issue. Kerberos (Steiner et al., 1988) has been designed for mutual authentication between client and server where one trusted authority issues tickets. The limitation here is the lack of time synchronization. Further, Single Sign On (SSO) (Revar et al., 2011) has been proposed which works upon one time user authentication in order to access multiple applications. However, a single security loophole may prove fatal across multiple applications. Though, One Time Passwords (OTPs) (Aloul et al., 2009) can be used, in parallel, as a second factor for authentication, the application and management of OTP generation is difficult. Figure 6.4 outlines the classification of different authentication methods (Babaeizadeh et al., 2015).

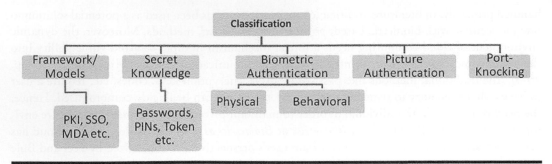

Figure 6.4   Classification of authentication methods.

Framework/Models: The categorization of authentication methods is based on the concept of the existing frameworks. Traditional frameworks comprise Open ID, PKI, Mobile-Trusted Module (MTM), SSO, TrustCube, NemoAuth, MDA, SeDici2 and many more. The standard PKI (Haidar et al., 2009 and Das, 2014) provides authentication, authorization, confidentiality, integrity, and accountability. The keys here can be hacked, forged, manipulated, or stolen. The concept of mobile cloud computing and the respective security vulnerabilities of mobile devices and cloud computing have been proposed (Jeong et al., 2014). Here, a multifactor authentication model is proposed to provide safety, efficiency, and user convenience. It combines basic user ID/password with a user's bio-information. The authentication methods could be added as needed, thus adding to flexibility into the model. However, the use of diverse authentication factors such as face, voice, IEMI, and password makes the processing delayed as well as complex. Another model (Choudhury et al., 2011) focuses on providing legitimate user authentication in order to restrict illegal access to the cloud servers. The deliverables are identity management, mutual authentication, and session key management between user and cloud server. It gives privilege to the user to change password at any point of time. The mechanism comprises two-step verification, i.e., password and smart card. A novel authentication method using Message Digest-based Authentication, MDA (Dey et al., 2016), targets the problem of accessing cloud services from non-trusted cloud locations. Here, the concept of hashing is incorporated with the password/Ids in a calculated way, thereby making it secure against phishing and eavesdropping attacks. Due to increase in the number of communication messages, the authentication overhead is high and user traceability is also an unresolved issue. An OpenID 2.0 platform for user-centric identity management (Recordon and Reed, 2009) is an open standard and decentralized authentication protocol. The framework works with four layers, namely, *Identifiers*, *Discovery*, *Authentication*, and *Data Transport*. The OpenId framework focuses on data exchange with address- and card-based identifiers to provide digital identity.

Secret Knowledge-Based Approach: The classification comprises combinations that are kept as secret by the user and needs to be provided at the time of authentication. Here, the input secret has to match with the already-stored values in the database for a valid authentication. The standard examples are passwords, PINs, tokens, and keys. An existing study (Acar et al., 2013) observes that on average, a user has only seven passwords that are reused to operate three different accounts. There are chances that a user forgets his password and hence uses other mode of authentication, which may be phished by an intruder. In order to avoid such issues, the authors proposed single-password authentication method. Though various protocols exist to restrain dictionary attacks, phishing, malware, and cross-site scripting attacks, the solution does not guarantee complete security. The usage of passwords and tokens (O'Gorman, 2003) is prone to repudiation and compromise of attacks but is inexpensive. Tokens can be used along with passwords to provide an additional layer of security. Understanding vulnerabilities of the system and continuous monitoring is suggested. Later, the concept of authentication using mobile device in the form of generation of OTP followed by SMS-based mechanism has been proposed (Aloul et al., 2009). The method is easy to use and is compatible with password authentication; however, proper generation and transmission of OTP are challenging.

Biometric-Based Authentication: The conventional authentication methods like pin, password, token, etc. must be memorized by a user which may be difficult when the number of applications to login is high. Here, biometrics is the best way to authenticate a legitimate user with the help of a unique set of biometric traits like face, voice, fingerprints, etc. Keystroke authentication being a behavioral biometric feature (Babaeizadeh et al., 2014) is the simplest and cost-effective method with no extra hardware. The results, however, may be affected by the varying pattern of a user. Biometrics has been used as a second factor for authentication (Yassin et al., 2012 and Ruj et al., 2014) where fingerprints and digital signatures have been used. The method possesses many security features such as user anonymity, mutual authentication, freely chosen password, revocation, and session key agreement. The only concern is with the chosen biometric trait being prone to forgery. Section 2.3 discusses a handful of the existing protocols that use biometric as a tool for user authentication.

Picture Authentication: In the method, the power of human mind to remember images as compared to alphabets or numbers is utilized as it is psychologically justified. The concept has been used in mobile cloud computing with the help of QR code (Oh et al., 2011). The property of data integration at higher level to authenticate any user makes the method more effective. The data is stored in a distributed fashion and offers fast processing. Here, Diffie–Hellman is used to mitigate phishing, replay, and eavesdropping attacks. However, the mutual authentication has not been implemented. Afterwards, the concept of graphical password (Gurav et al., 2014) has been introduced where the tedious task to remember passwords is replaced by images. A user can use more than one image as a password and makes the hacking process more difficult. However, choosing the right image needs user familiarity with the technique. Later, fuzzy picture password along with integration of various techniques like zero-knowledge authentication, fuzzy vault, and Diffie–Hellman key exchange has been discussed for secure channel communication (Schwab and Yang, 2013). The users must have a prior knowledge about the picture authentication method.

Port Knocking Authentication: The port-knocking authentication is achieved using the closed ports. The clients, essentially known as port-knocker, send non-reply synchronization packets to the specific closed ports of server, simultaneously, which is called a knocked process. The information is stored in a buffer as the server logs the incoming packets. Hence, for password purpose, port sequence is used. The sequence of keys is kept as secret and can be defined dynamically or statically. The length of the sequence is important from security point of view as short sequences could be easily hacked, whereas random increase may lead to buffer overflow, thereby resulting in increased time for authentication. The concept of virtualization for port-knocking decreases the load of buffering to cloud gateway (Boroumand et al., 2014).

6.2.2 Generic Security Challenges in Cloud Computing

In the existing literature, security in cloud computing has been a major point of concern due to its adaptability issue. As virtualization provides a way for resource sharing that includes software, platform, and infrastructure, security at both ends, *user* and *vendor*, is essential. A third-party certification and standardization have been suggested for the total acceptance from potential users (Ertaul et al., 2010). A quantitative analysis of current security concerns and solutions for cloud computing (Gonzalez et al., 2012) focuses on better understanding of the complex security scenario of cloud computing in the context of current security status. A reliable sphere must be provided to enable the use of cloud applications for moving data and business process to the virtualized infrastructure. The highlighted areas that need to be addressed are network security, interface authentication, data security, virtualization, governance, compliance, and legal issues. In understanding cloud computing vulnerabilities (Grobauer et al., 2011), the authors distinguish generic security concerns from cloud-specific issues. The core cloud computing technologies with their vulnerabilities such as unauthorized access, Internet protocol vulnerabilities, management interface, data recovery, billing, and metering evasion have been explained. The main areas are IAAA mechanism, storage, management access, communication, computational resource, services, and APIs. The formal modeling of PKI-based authentication (Haidar et al., 2009) provides authentication to users in distributed systems like as cloud computing, wireless sensor network, and mobile cloud computing. It is used in applications ranging from e-commerce to web services. However, proper formulation of the method is necessary to scrutinize its correctness and usability. A recent survey of authentication methods in mobile cloud computing (Reshmi and Rakshmy, 2015) proposes a new classification model. The broad categories of methods described are *user profile, port-knocking, cryptography-based,* and *image-based*. An efficient and user-friendly authentication mechanism in mobile cloud computing may be utilized as a trusted platform to deploy various applications. The system model consists of different parameters of security, privacy, and authentication.

6.2.3 Biometric-Based Authentication Schemes

In cloud security, authentication plays a major role, and thus, numerous solutions have been developed in order to prevent unauthorized access to the available resources. This, in turn, enhances the development of safety-critical applications that can be utilized by potential end-users. Most solutions are based on one-time authentication scheme and PKI-based where password is applicable only for one-time login. However, many schemes are prone to attacks such as privileged internal user, server/client impersonation, and replay attacks as well as these schemes suffer from significant key-management overhead. Ameen and Jin (2016) propose an efficient authentication scheme with Biometric key management in Cloud Environment. The proposed scheme is robust one-time authentication based on a noninteractive one-time biometric key to generate one-time login request message. The key used in the scheme consists of two strong building blocks. First, it is biometrically based on the extraction of features from the entities' irises. Second, it is cryptographically based on the strong key-based message authentication code MAC-SHA-512 and Rivest Cipher 4. The proposed scheme considers several important security attributes like key agreement, biometric key management and single authentication request for each user's login, mutual authentication, invulnerability, and efficiency. Wazid and Das (2016) proposed a new provably secure biometric-based user authentication and key agreement scheme for cloud computing. The scheme overcomes the weaknesses of the existing schemes and supports extra functionality features, *viz.* user anonymity, effective password, and biometric update phase for multi-server environment. The authors used AVISPA tool to analyze the various security aspects and formal verification. The results exhibits that the proposed scheme is secure against various known possible attacks with lower computation and communication overhead.

Recently, Cao and Ge (2015) analyzed various authentication schemes and found that a few existing schemes are susceptible to replay attack where an adversary is imposed as a legal server machine or as a legitimate and anonymous end-user. This allows an adversary to execute a password change process by intercepting the user's ID during login. Though the limitation of existing schemes was overcome, Cao and Ge's scheme is susceptible to a biometric recognition error, slow wrong password detection, offline password attack, user impersonation, and Denial of Service (DoS) attack. Moreover, the scheme cannot provide session-key agreement. Afterwards, (Choi et al., 2017) proposed a security-enhanced multifactor biometric authentication scheme. The security analysis and formal verification has been done using the Burrows–Abadi–Needham logic. The results show that the protocol is efficient and can protect against several possible types of attacks with slightly high computational cost. An efficient authentication system of smart device using multifactors in mobile cloud service architecture (Jeong et al., 2014) is another approach. Here, different authentication parameters like ID/password and mobile identification number are combined with bio-information of a user to ensure security. The bulk processing makes this approach different and more efficient, henceforth increasing the performance. The proposed architecture comprises four main entities, namely, mobile devices, management server, storage server, and a cluster host. However, using biometrics and password or other parameters parallelly demands more computational resources. An efficient biometrics-based remote-user authentication scheme using smart cards (Li and Hwang, 2010) provides a cost-effective solution in terms of computational cost. The proposed scheme gives an opportunity to end-user to change the password frequently with the use of one-way hash function, biometric identification, and smart card. The approach uses timestamps to resist replay attacks as well as ensures non-repudiation because of personal biometric attributes. The model has three phases, namely, *registration*, *login*, and *authentication*. The performance evaluation is compared with the existing methods.

Biometric authentication in cloud computing (Batool et al., 2015) emphasizes on security with authentication as a prominent issue. The authors analyze various authentication systems used by Cloud Service Providers (CSPs). Most of the techniques use fingerprint, face, and iris as biometric authentication tool. Biometric data has been compared on the basis of universality, distinctiveness, permanence, and collectability where the face data has proven efficient with high accuracy for these parameters. The problems and promises of using cloud and biometrics (Albahdal and Boult, 2014) explore the mutual benefits of biometrics technology and cloud computing. The strong authentication property of biometrics assures security in cloud computing. The new layer in service model, namely, Biometric authentication as a Service (BioAaaS), results as a combination of both technologies. On the other hand, biometrics technology can uplift the cloud's unbounded computational resources like processing power or data storage. This further helps to improve flexibility, scalability as well as reduce overall cost overhead. A secure biometric-based authentication scheme for cloud computing (Wong and Kim, 2013) ensures both *security* and *privacy*. Several components like client, service agent, and service provider have been incorporated and the protocol works in three phases, namely, *enrollment, transformation,* and *verification*. It accepts two credential information as input, i.e., *verification code* and *user's feature vector* that must be combined, transformed, and shuffled appropriately. In the solution, a match between query feature vector (Q) and biometric template (T) is essential. The protocol uses homomorphic encryption for its additive property, shuffle protocol for randomness, and squared Euclidean distance for code matching and correctness. Though random biometric traits have been used, the protocol does not consider in-depth security (misuse, theft, or loss) of templates stored in cloud. In addition, the complex computations in verification phase take more time, thus delaying the processing of results.

In early times, fingerprint authentication has been a popular and effective method to allow authorized users only to access the cryptographic keys. Later, the same method was adopted for authentication in cloud computing applications. A New Fingerprint Authentication Scheme Based on Secret-Splitting for Enhanced Cloud Security (Wang et al., 2011) presented a new remote authentication scheme based on a secret-splitting concept. In the proposed approach, a part of the biometric data is encrypted and stored on a smart card, while the other part of data is encrypted and stored on a server. The approach helped to protect the information of a user from different malicious attacks as well as safeguard from any internal data abuse by any staff within an organization. The hacking into Certificate Authority (CA) was overcome as in order to counterfeit the entire biometric information available, a dishonest staff or hacker must simultaneously decrypt two secret keys rather than just one. In addition to the secret-splitting concept, the proposed authentication scheme utilizes the Diffie–Hellman key exchange/agreement algorithm in order to ensure security of data transmission or communication between a terminal and the server. The major difference of the proposed scheme in comparison to existing ones can be summarized as follows:

i. The approach uses smart card that stores only part of the fingerprint template used in the identity authentication process. Hence, the user's identity is protected even in case the card is lost or stolen.

ii. In the proposed method, the template information stored on the smart card and server is encrypted independent of each other. As a result, after a successful attack on any authenticated database, the information retrieved by a hacker or dishonest staff member is insufficient to pass the liveness test.

In later work on same biometric feature, i.e., fingerprint (Jiang and Zheng, 2014) proposed an Indirect Fingerprint Authentication Scheme in Cloud Computing. However, the critical security issue in remote biometric cryptosystem is to protect the template of a user stored in a database. However, the biometric template is not robust enough and the stolen templates cannot be revoked, which makes it convenient for the intruder to breach the information and leak important credentials of an end-user. In order to overcome the shortcomings, (Wang et al., 2011) presented an indirect fingerprint authentication scheme and applied the same to the cloud system in combination with PKI mechanism.

An efficient privacy-preserving biometric identification in cloud computing (Yuan and Yu, 2013) presents a privacy-preserving biometric identification scheme which achieves efficiency by utilizing the power of cloud computing. The biometric database is encrypted and sent to the cloud servers. First, the database owner generates a credential for the candidate's biometric trait and forwards it to cloud server for biometric identification. Thereafter, cloud servers perform identification process over the encrypted database using credentials and return the result to the owner. The scheme is divided into three stages: *biometric database processing, privacy-preserving FingerCode comparison,* and *final result generation.* The scheme has been implemented on Amazon cloud and provides high level of privacy along with reliable results as compared with conventional cryptographic methods. However, the algorithm fails to handle multiple requests at the cost of hardware with high consumption of bandwidth. CloudID: Trustworthy cloud-based and cross-enterprise biometric identification (Haghighat et al., 2015) focuses on a cross-enterprise biometric identification solution and privacy-preserving scheme based on unique identifier i.e., CloudID. It links the confidential information of the users to their biometrics traits and stores it in an encrypted form. The proposed approach is a proven zero-data disclosure approach which is first of its kind in cloud computing security. The biometric identification in CloudID consists of two parts: (a) *training* and (b) *query.* Here, face images have been used as biometric identifier. In order to create encrypted search queries, a *k-d* tree structure in the core of the searchable encryption is proposed. The aspect of confidentiality in authentication system has been covered with more accurate results and minimum overhead. However, the lager cipher text size adds to complexity and makes it costlier for real-time applications with large databases.

Although, a multifunction biometric sensor may not readily available in current mobile phones, however, in future computing technologies, the scenario will change as per user's requirement and demand. Nevertheless, biometric authentication is gaining popularity, particularly to deal with crucial applications like bank transactions, online healthcare, education, etc. The existing work focuses on a hybrid approach to ensure higher level of security, thus, making it more difficult for an attacker to breach the user's critical information. Moreover, cloud computing, being rich in computational resources, can make the hybrid approach much easier and further improve security to access various cloud services. In literature, a cognitive authentication scheme called cloud cognitive authenticator (CCA) has been proposed (Jivanadham et al., 2013). The method uses cognitive biometrics as an authentication parameter due to the fact that cognitive biometrics may record both, the sentimental and cognitive status, of a user. CCA is the combination of biometrics, advanced encryption standard (AES) and zero-knowledge protocol (ZKP), thereby ensuring robust and rigid security with very lesser power as well as storage capacity. The CCA protocol executes in the following four steps, namely:

1. First, it reads the Electro Dermal Response (EDR) of the skin conductance of a user, which is further verified in order to determine the mental state of a user.
2. After successful verification, CCA generates an encrypted user id that is generated by merging the EDR reading, IP address, device details, and current timestamp.
3. Third, the user-id is transmitted to the cloud system for decryption.
4. Finally, connection with the hypervisor is established by using ZKP.[1]

6.2.4 AVISPA Tool

To design a secure protocol in order to ensure development and successful deployment of safety-critical applications is a hard problem. Moreover, in a network, messages may be eavesdropped or modified by an intruder, interchangeably, called as attacker or adversary. Hence, there is a need to develop tools to speed up the development of next-generation security protocols and improve their security. Optimally, the tools should be completely automated, robust, expressive, and user-friendly, so that they can be integrated into the protocol development and standardization processes.

Most of the existing protocols for biometric authentication in cloud computing have used AVISPA for automated security protocol analysis (L. Vigano, 2006). It is a push button tool for automated validation of Internet security-sensitive protocols and applications. The tool:

1. Provides a modular and expressive formal language for specifying security protocols and properties, the High-Level Protocol Specification Language (HLPSL),
2. Integrates different back-end to implement automatic analysis techniques ranging from protocol falsification to abstraction-based verification methods.

---

[1] In cryptography, a zero-knowledge protocol is a method by which one party can prove to another party (the verifier) that a given statement is true, without conveying any information apart from the fact that the statement is indeed true.

Architecture of AVISPA Tool: The architecture of AVISPA consists of various components with execution in following steps:

- First, a user interacts with the tool by specifying a security problem in the HLPSL. The language is formal, expressive, and role-based, which allows specifying control-flow patterns, data structures, and different cryptographic functions along with their properties. Also, an adversary model as well as complex security properties can be presented.
- Next, the AVISPA tool automatically translates a user-defined security problem into an equivalent specification written in Intermediate Format (IF). An IF specification describes an infinite-state transition system amenable to formal analysis: IF specifications are automatically input to the back-ends of the AVISPA tool, which implement different techniques to search the corresponding infinite-state transition system for states that represent attacks on the intended properties of the protocols.
- Upon termination, each back-end of the AVISPA tool exhibits the output in the form of analysis using a common, predefined format. It informs if the input problem was solved or not.

Table 6.1 summarizes and compares various authentication protocols that are important in cloud computing (discussed so far) along with description, authentication technique used, and trade-offs.

6.3 Proposed Work: Toward Biometric Authentication Scheme in Cloud Computing

6.3.1 System Model Assumptions

The proposed system model assumes secure storage of user data (*username, password*) and biometric template (*T*) in a trusted cloud server. The CSP is efficient enough to serve "*N*" number of users as per the enrollment. The input images are assumed under well-lit conditions refraining from any obfuscation. The proposed model is broadly divided into following three phases:

Phase 1: Biometric data acquisition: We propose to use face being a biometric trait in order to authenticate a user. Moreover, capturing a face image is easier due to availability of cameras in laptops, mobile phones, tablets, and PCs (may be termed as client in the system model). The collection of images is done in such a manner that each and every expression of user is captured and thus, reduces the chance of nonrecognition at the time of authentication.

Phase 2: Processing and matching of feature vector V: The phase works in following three steps:

Step I: The input image (face) is provided by the customer with the help of client machine and forwarded for step II processing.

Step II: The step extracts features using the simplest Principal Component Analysis technique. The necessary features are then stored in the form of templates with a trusted CSP.

Step III: The matching of feature vector is achieved by comparing the already-stored feature vectors in cloud DB with the feature vector of a user. This completes authentication process and helps to login the system.

Table 6.1   Comparison of Authentication Methods in Cloud Computing

Authentication Type	Authors	Description	Authentication Technique	Trade-offs
Framework/ Model based	Haidar et al. (2009)	Formal approach for modeling certificated-based PKI authentication is presented.	PKI	• Scalability issues • Trust issues
	Jeong et al. (2014)	Vulnerabilities related to mobile devices and Cloud Computing are discussed. A multifactor authentication framework is proposed.	Multifactor	• Processing delay due to large factors for authentication • Security issue for biometrics
	Choudhury et al. (2011)	Cloud server security is addressed by legitimate authentication of user.	Two-factor	• Formal security proofing technique needs to be explored
	Dey et al. (2016)	Risks involved in accessing cloud services using mobile devices through untrusted networks are countered.	MDA	• Efficiently handles attacks • Privacy issues not addressed
Port-Knocking based	Boroumand, Laleh et al. (2014)	Authentication using closed ports has been explained with different parameters involved.	Virtualization	• Sequence length issues hinder processing
Secret knowledge based	Acar et al. (2013)	Single-password authentication protocol.	Single password	• Prone to hacking • Social engineering attack
	Gorman (2003)	Focus on different user authentication methods like id, password, etc.	Authenticators	• Passwords can be easily compromised, stolen, or forgotten
	Aloul et al. (2009)	Uses OTP and SMS for authentication.	OTP/SMS	• Generation and transmission of OTP is a challenging task

(Continued)

Table 6.1 (*Continued*) Comparison of Authentication Methods in Cloud Computing

Authentication Type	Authors	Description	Authentication Technique	Trade-offs
Biometric based	Choi and Lee (2017)	A security-enhanced multifactor biometric authentication scheme.	Burrows–Abadi–Needham logic	• High computational cost
	Cao and Ge (2015)	Works against replay attack where an adversary imposes as a legal server machine or as a legitimate and anonymous end-user.		• Biometric recognition error • Slow wrong password detection, DoS attack • Offline password attack and user impersonation
	Babaeizadeh et al. (2014)	Authentication using keystrokes with 97% correctness.	Keystroke	• Explores new parameters for measuring keystrokes
	Yassin, Ali A. et al. (2012)	Two-factor authentication covering deployment complexity, high cost, and cloud security.	Fingerprint digital signature	• Better performance • Immune to various attacks
Picture based	Oh et al. (2011)	Authentication using two-dimensional QR code.	QR code	• Anonymity issues • Security issues
	Gurav, Shradda M. et al. (2014)	A user-friendly authentication method with the help of images to reduce the stress of remembering passwords.	Graphical password	• Implementation using cloud and security needs to be addressed
	Schwab, David and Yang, Li (2013)	Highlights the need of authenticating both, client and server with different techniques.	Digital signature and fuzzy picture password	• Implemented secure protocols against various attacks • Needs familiarity with technique in the beginning

***Phase 3: Decision module*:** The last phase grants or denies the permission to a user based on authenticity for further login.

6.3.2 Performance Metrics

Figure 6.5 shows the schematic view of proposed system model. As the model comprises both biometric and cloud computing, performance is analyzed for both. The biometrics is analyzed upon False Acceptance Rate (FAR) and False Rejection Rate (FRR), whereas cloud computing depends on cost and time for performance. The idea of cloud computing is to reduce cost and time for processing as well as availability of any data or service.

6.3.3 Working of the Algorithm

The cloud computing technology helps to utilize the abundant storage and computation power to execute different applications. In the proposed work, storage has been utilized from Microsoft Azure with its SQL server to which the application is linked. The computation is done using Aneka Management Studio as explained in the next section. The working of algorithm comprises two main steps as given below:

Step 1: Creation of application

The application named FaceAuth is designed using Microsoft Visual Studio 10 and C#. The application provides face recognition as a second factor of authentication along with traditional methods, i.e., username and password. The flow of the authentication procedure follows in the following manner:

- **Main window:** First, a main window appears with login, reset, login with face, and sign-up option. The new users have to enroll using *<sign up>* in order to avail other features.

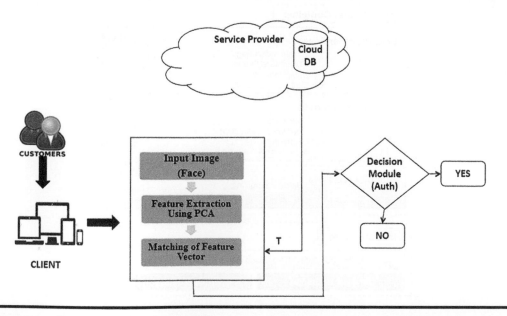

Figure 6.5   The proposed system model.

- **User sign-up window:** For signing up, a new user clicks on *<detect>* to start the webcam for capturing live image. Afterwards, the faces are added using *<add face>* followed with setting up of desired username and password. Lastly, on clicking *<save>*, all the data gets stored in the cloud storage. Meanwhile at the back-end, with the usage of Principal Component Analysis, Eigen faces are calculated which are prepared to be matched while login.
- **Face login window:** The option may reduce the efforts to remember tedious username and passwords. With face login window, a user can directly login into the application after authentication through *<detect>* and *<recognize>* that matches the currently displayed live image of the person with the already-stored images in the database. In case there is no mismatch, the name of the person is displayed on the box, otherwise shown as unknown person followed with a sign-up message again.

Step 2: Offloading application on Aneka Cloud

The main aim is to reduce the computation power involved in running the application, for which Aneka 4.0 is used. Aneka is a Cloud Application Development Platform (CAP) to develop and run compute and data-intensive applications. As a platform, it provides users with a runtime environment to execute applications developed using any programming model, namely, *Thread, Task,* and *MapReduce.* Here, Thread programming model has been used for implementation. The architecture of Aneka is given in Figure 6.6. The middleware container provides the basic management features of single node and leverages all the other operations on the services. It contains fabric, foundation, and execution services. At the application level, a set of different components and tools are provided to simplify the development of applications

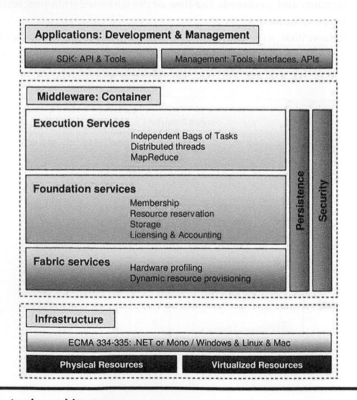

Figure 6.6 The Aneka architecture.

(SDK) monitoring and managing the Aneka Cloud (R. Buyya, Manjrasoft). The following set of functions can be executed through Management Studio:

- Quick setup of computing clouds,
- Distant installation and configuration of nodes,
- System tuning and load monitoring,
- Monitoring total dynamic numbers and searching individual nodes for CPU and memory load.

6.3.4 *Implementation and Simulation*

The offloading of application for proposed protocol uses Aneka SDK, Libraries and Configuration file being imported from the installed Aneka folder. Afterwards, the machine (nodes) is created along with a daemon to serve as a background process as shown in Figures 6.7 and 6.8. Further, in order to use more than one machine, a remote repository is mandatory which is shown in Figure 6.9. However, when the application has to be run on a single machine, local repository serves the purpose.

Next, we create *Master* and *Worker* containers. The same machine can be made master or worker depending on the CPU requirements of an application. The master container allocates the respective tasks to the workers and handles job distribution. The machines are installed using credentials such as IP address, username, and password. The CPU utilization may decide to create single or multiple nodes (machines). The master container is made on a machine with better configuration, and the rest of the machines are used as worker containers. We use both Visual Studio and Aneka Management Studio for authentication as well as increase computation time with reduced CPU utilization. The application is run on a single node first and then multiple nodes. The dynamic deployment of application is shown in Figure 6.10.

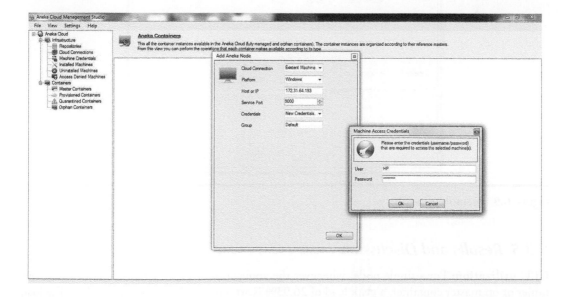

Figure 6.7   Installation of nodes.

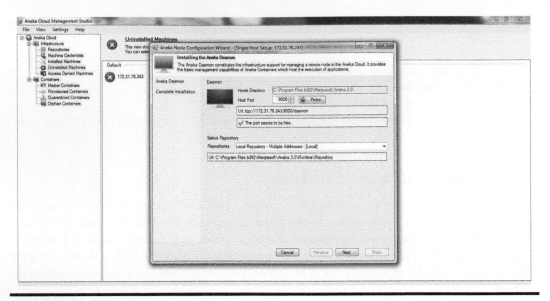

Figure 6.8 Creating Aneka Daemon.

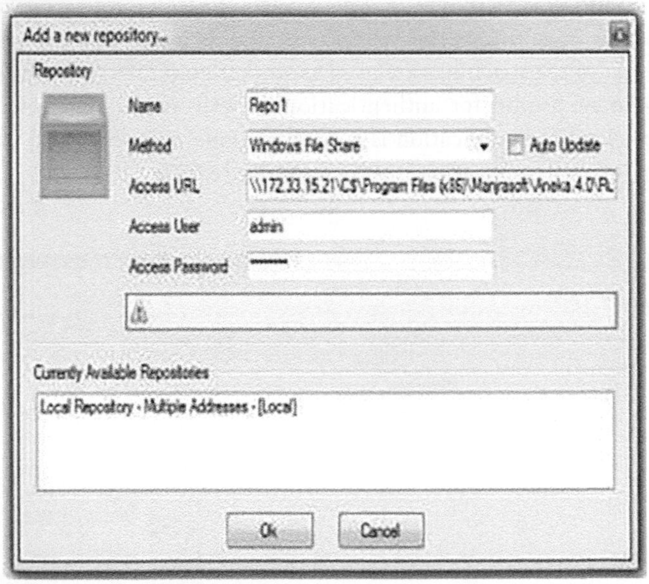

Figure 6.9 Remote repository.

6.3.5 Results and Discussion

CPU utilization: For a single node, whenever the application is executed either on worker container or on master container, a peak load of 26.93% is attained as shown in Figure 6.11. The load value may vary depending upon the specification of the selected machine. The better the processor used, the lower the peak load. Moreover, only single master or worker machine is allocated all

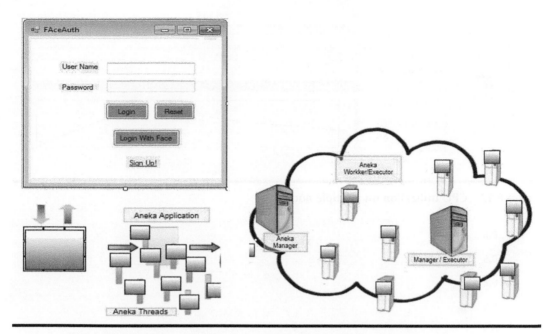

Figure 6.10   Aneka: dynamic deployment of application tasks on clouds.

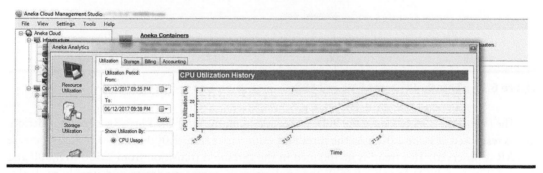

Figure 6.11   CPU utilization on single node.

tasks; thus, the performance may degrade in terms of execution time as well. On the other hand, with the multiple-node execution shown in Figure 6.12, CPU utilization reduces to a greater extent. Now, the peak load is 0.03% which is very less as compared to single-node execution. The additional machines with better configuration have substantially improved the CPU utilization.

FAR and FRR Analyses: After executing and testing the proposed application on a different set of users, FRR and FAR at different threshold values of EigenDistance have been plotted as shown in Figure 6.13. The formula used to calculate the values is:

FRR = Number of rejected attempts/Number of verification total attempts

FAR = Number of successful independent fraud attempts/Number of all independent fraud attempts against a person

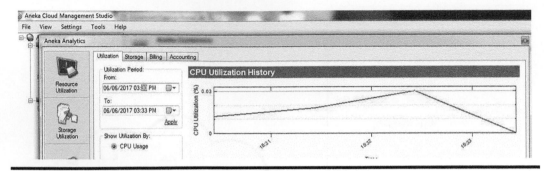

Figure 6.12 CPU utilization on multiple nodes.

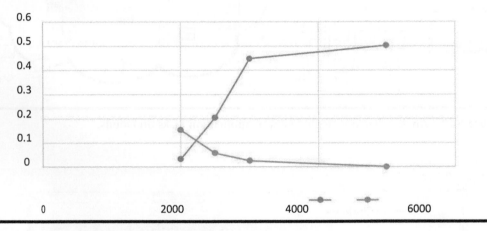

Figure 6.13 Threshold versus FAR and FRR.

The threshold is set based on the library used, i.e., EmguCV for the EigenRecognizer function, and is restricted at value 2,000. As the threshold value varies from 2,000 to 2,500, a slight increase in FAR is observed. This trend is maintained in the threshold transition from 2,500 to 3,000 and from 3,000 to 5,000. At value 5,000, the application becomes moderate and unable to distinguish a fraud person from a genuine person. Hence, after executing several runs of experiment with changing threshold values, 2,000 is assumed to be best suited for the proposed application to give desired results. On the other hand, the trend in FRR is seen to be descending because at value 5,000, the system is very relaxed and it matches the values as high as 5,000. Here, no rejection takes place, and original user is matched with other users, which is not acceptable. It can be observed that FRR is comparatively more when the system is made to restrict at threshold value 2,000. Here, the fraud person is rejected and not granted access to login.

Chapter Summary and Future Work

Security concerns like user authentication add more reliability to the use of cloud computing. The chapter discusses classical authentication schemes followed by the description of biometric authentication schemes in cloud computing. Afterwards, a framework has been designed to support biometrics-based user authentication in cloud computing. It involves extraction of biometrics trait (face in our proposed protocol) of the user and compare with already-stored images for further processing. We use cloud computing as a platform to implement the proposed work due to its storage and computational power. The output reflects that proposed solution results in user-friendly authentication. Also, with the use of Aneka Management Studio, the computation time is reduced. The future work focuses on the optimization of proposed model based on the issues related to forging of face images that are used for authentication and usage of Local Binary Patterns Histograms in order to resolve unknown person's login without sign-in.

Keywords/Terminology

Authentication: Authentication is a process to confirm the correctness of the claimed identity.

Authorization: Authorization is the approval, permission, or empowerment for a user.

Biometrics: Biometrics use physical characteristics of the users to maintain access control.

Confidentiality: Confidentiality is the need to ensure that information is disclosed only to those who are authorized to view it.

Cryptographic Algorithm or Hash: An algorithm that employs cryptography and includes encryption, cryptographic hash, digital signature, and key agreement.

Denial of Service: The prevention of authorized access to a system resource or the delaying of system operations and functions.

Dictionary Attack: An attack that combines all phrases or words in a dictionary and trying to crack a password or key. A dictionary attack uses a predefined list of words compared to a brute force attack that tries all possible combinations.

Diffie–Hellman: A key agreement algorithm published in 1976 by Whitfield Diffie and Martin Hellman. Diffie–Hellman performs key establishment but not encryption. However, generated key may be used for encryption and key management operations or any other cryptography.

Digest Authentication: Digest Authentication allows a web client to compute MD5 hash of the password.

Digital Certificate: A digital certificate is an electronic "credit card" that establishes a user's credentials to do transactions on the Web, issued by a certification authority. It contains name, serial number, expiration dates, certificate holder's public key, and digital signature of the certificate-issuing authority.

Hardening: Hardening is the process of identifying and fixing vulnerabilities into a system.

Hash Function: An algorithm that computes a value based on a data object, thereby mapping the data object to a smaller data object.

Host-Based ID: Host-based intrusion detection systems use information from the operating system audit records to watch all operations occurring on the host. These operations are further compared with a predefined security policy.

Identity: Identity is a parameter by whom someone or what something is known, for example, name of a person.

Kerberos: A system developed at the Massachusetts Institute of Technology that depends on passwords and symmetric cryptography (DES) to implement ticket-based, peer entity authentication service and access control service distributed in a client–server network environment.

Masquerade Attack: A type of attack in which one system entity illegitimately poses as (assumes the identity of) another entity.

National Institute of Standards and Technology (NIST): Formerly known as the National Bureau of Standards, NIST promotes and maintains measurement standards. It also has active programs for encouraging and assisting industry and science to develop and use these standards.

Phishing: The use of e-mails that appear to be originated from a trusted source to trick a user into entering valid credentials at a fake website.

Session Key: A security mechanism that uses a cryptographic hash function to generate a sequence of 64-bit, one-time passwords for remote-user login. The client generates a one-time password by applying MD4 cryptographic hash function multiple times to the user's secret key.

Symmetric Key: A cryptographic key that is used in a symmetric cryptographic algorithm.

Threat Model: A threat model is used to describe a given threat and harm for a system, in case the system is prone to vulnerability.

Token-Based Devices: A token-based device is triggered by the time of day. Hence, every minute the password changes and requires a user to possess the token whenever he/she logs in.

Zero-Day Attack: A zero-day (or zero-hour or day zero) attack or threat is a computer threat that tries to exploit computer application vulnerabilities that are unknown to others or undisclosed to the software developer.

References

Acar, T., Belenkiy, M. and Küpçü, A., Single password authentication. *Computer Networks*, 57(13), 2597–2614, 2013.

Albahdal, A.A. and Boult, T.E., Problems and promises of using the cloud and biometrics. *11th IEEE International Conference on Information Technology: New Generations (ITNG)*, 293–300, 2014.

Aloul, F., Zahidi, S. and El-Hajj, W., Two factor authentication using mobile phones. *IEEE/ACS International Conference on Computer Systems and Applications (AICCSA)*, 641–644, 2009.

Ameen, Z. and Jin, H., Towards efficient authentication scheme with biometric key management in cloud environment. *IEEE 2nd International Conference on Big Data Security on Cloud (BigDataSecurity)*, 146–151, 2016.

Babaeizadeh, M., Bakhtiari, M. and Maarof, M.A., Keystroke dynamic authentication in mobile cloud computing. *International Journal of Computer Applications*, 90(1), 2014.

Batool, R., Naveed, G. and Khan, A., Biometric authentication in cloud computing. *International Journal of Computer Applications*, 129(11), 6–9, 2015.

Boroumand, L., Shiraz, M., Gani, A., Khan, S. and Khokhar, R., Virtualization Technique for port-knocking in mobile cloud computing. *International Journal of Advanced Soft ComputingApplications*, 6(1), 2014.

Buyya, R., Aneka, Manjrasoft, www.manjrasoft.com/products.html.

Cao, L. and Ge, W., Analysis and improvement of a multi-factor biometric authentication scheme. *Security and Communication Networks*, 8(4), 617–625, 2015.

Choi, Y., Lee, Y., Moon, J. and Won, D., Security enhanced multi-factor biometric authentication scheme using bio-hash function. *PLoS ONE* 12(5), 2017.

Choudhury, A.J., Kumar, P., Sain, M., Lim, H. and Jae-Lee, H., A strong user authentication framework for cloud computing. *IEEE Asia-Pacific Services Computing Conference (APSCC)*, 110–115, 2011.

Crawford, H. and Renaud, K., Understanding user perceptions of transparent authentication on a mobile device. *Journal of Trust Management*, 1(1), 7–17, 2014.

Dey, S., Sampalli, S. and Ye, Q., MDA: Message digest-based authentication for mobile cloud computing. *Journal of Cloud Computing*, 5 (1), 18–28, 2016.

Dinca, L.M. and Hancke, G.P., The fall of one, the rise of many: A survey on multi-biometric fusion methods. *IEEE Access*, 5, 6247–6289, 2017.

Ertaul, L., Singhal, S. and Saldamli, G., Security challenges in cloud computing. *Security and Management*, 36–42, 2010.

Gonzalez, N., Miers, C., Redigolo, F., Simplicio, M., Carvalho, T., Näslund, M. and Pourzandi, M., A quantitative analysis of current security concerns and solutions for cloud computing. *Journal of Cloud Computing: Advances, Systems and Applications*, 1(1), 11–21, 2012.

Grobauer, B., Walloschek, T. and Stocker, E., Understanding cloud computing vulnerabilities. *IEEE Security & Privacy*, 9(2), 50–57, 2011.

Gurav, S.M., Gawade, L.S., Rane, P.K. and Khochare, N.R., Graphical password authentication: Cloud securing scheme. *IEEE International Conference on Electronic Systems, Signal Processingand Computing Technologies (ICESC)*, 479–483, 2014.

Haghighat, M., Zonouz, S. and Abdel-Mottaleb, M., CloudID: Trustworthy cloud-based and cross-enterprise biometric identification. *Expert Systems with Applications*, 42(21), 7905–7916, 2015.

Haidar, A.N. and Abdallah, A.E., Formal modelling of PKI based authentication. *Electronic Notes in Theoretical Computer Science*, 235, 55–70, 2009.

Jain A.K, Ross A. and Prabhakar S., An introduction to biometric recognition, *IEEE Transactions on Circuits and Video Technology*, 14(1), 4–20, 2004.

Jeong, Y.S., Park, J.S. and Park, J.H., An efficient authentication system of smart device using multi factors in mobile cloud service architecture. *International Journal of Communication Systems*, 28(4), 659–674, 2014.

Jiang, X.C. and Zheng, J.D., An indirect fingerprint authentication scheme in cloud computing, *Applied Mechanics and Materials*, 484, 986–990, 2014.

Jivanadham, L. and MuzahidulIslam, A.K.M., Cloud Cognitive Authenticator (CCA): A public cloud computing authentication mechanism, *IEEE International Conference on Informatics, Electronics Vision*, 1–6, 2013.

Li, C.T. and Hwang, M.S., An efficient biometrics-based remote user authentication scheme using smart cards. *Journal of Network and Computer Applications*, 33(1), 1–5, 2010.

Mell, P. and Grance, T., The NIST definition of cloud computing, 2011.

O'Gorman, L., Comparing passwords, tokens, and biometrics for user authentication. *Proceedings of the IEEE*, 91(12), 2021–2040, 2003.

Oh, D.S., Kim, B.H. and Lee, J.K., A study on authentication system using QR code for mobile cloud computing environment. *Future Information Technology*, 500–507, 2011.

Peer, P. and Bule, J., Buiding cloud-based biometric services. *Informatica*, 37, 115–122, 2013.

Recordon, D. and Reed, D., OpenID 2.0: A platform for user-centric identity management. *Proceedings of the Second ACM Workshop on Digital Identity Management*, 11–16, 2009.

Reshmi, G. and Rakshmy, C.S., A survey of authentication methods in mobile cloud computing. *IEEE 10th International Conference for Internet Technology and Secured Transactions (ICITST)*, 58–63, 2015.

Revar, A.G. and Bhavsar, M.D., Securing user authentication using single sign-on in cloud computing. *IEEE International Conference on Engineering (NUiCONE), Nirma University*, 1–4, 2011.

Rose, J., Biometrics as a service: The next giant leap? *Biometric Technology Today*, 3, 7–9, 2016.

Schwab, D. and Yang, L., Entity authentication in a mobile-cloud environment. *ACM Proceedings of the Eighth Annual Cyber Security and Information Intelligence Research Workshop*, 42, 2013.

Singh, S., Jeong, Y.S. and Park, J.H., A survey on cloud computing security: Issues, threats, and solutions. *Journal of Network and Computer Applications*, 75, 200–222, 2016.

Soldera, J., Schu, G., Schardosim, L.R. and Beltrao, E.T., Facial biometrics and applications. *IEEE Instrumentation & Measurement Magazine*, 20(2), 4–10, 2017.

Steiner, J.G., Neuman, B.C. and Schiller, J.I., Kerberos: An authentication service for open network systems. *Proceedings of Winter Usenix Conference*, 191–202, 1988.

Wang, P., Ku, CC. and Wang, TC., A new fingerprint authentication scheme based on secret-splitting for enhanced cloud security. *Recent Application in Bio-metrics*, 183–96, 2011.

Wazid, M., Das, A.K., Kumari, S., Li, X. and Wu, F., Provably secure biometric-based user authentication and key agreement scheme in cloud computing. *Security Communication Network*, 9(17), 4103–4119, 2016.

Wong, K.S. and Kim, M.H., Secure biometric-based authentication for cloud computing. *Proceedings of the 2nd International Conference on Cloud Computing and Services Science (CLOSER'12)*, 86–101, 2013.

Vigano, L., Automated security protocol analysis with the AVISPA tool. *Electronic Notes in Theoretical Computer Science*, 155, 61–86, 2006.

Xiao, Z. and Xiao, Y., Security and privacy in cloud computing. *IEEE Communications Surveys & Tutorials*, 15(2), 843–859, 2013.

Yassin, A.A., Jin, H., Ibrahim, A. and Zou, D., Anonymous password authentication scheme by using digital signature and fingerprint in cloud computing. *IEEE Second International Conference on Cloud and Green Computing (CGC)*, 282–289, 2012.

Yuan, J. and Yu, S., Efficient privacy-preserving biometric identification in cloud computing. *Proceedings IEEEINFOCOM*, 2652–2660, 2013.

Additional/Further Reading

Adhikari, M., Biometrics in cloud computing. In G. Deka & S. Bakshi (Eds.), *Handbook of Research on Securing Cloud-Based Databases with Biometric Applications*. IGI Global, Hershey, PA, 269–297, 2015.

Babaeizadeh, M., Bakhtiari, M. and Mohammed, A.M., Authentication methods in cloud computing: A survey. *Research Journal of Applied Sciences, Engineering and Technology*, 9(8), 655–664, 2015.

Choudhury, A.J., Kumar, P., Sain, M., Lim, H. and Jae-Lee, H., A strong user authentication framework for cloud computing. *IEEE Asia-Pacific Services Computing Conference (APSCC)*, 110–115, 2011.

Das, R., *Biometric Technology: Authentication, Biocryptography, and Cloud-Based Architecture*. CRC Press, 2014.

Mihailescu, M.I. and Nita, S.L., *Security of Biometrics Authentication Protocols: Practical and Theory Applications*. LAP LAMBERT Academic Publishing, Germany, 2015.

Ruj, S., Stojmenovic, M. and Nayak, A., Decentralized access control with anonymous authentication of data stored in clouds. *IEEE Transactions on Parallel and Distributed Systems*, 25(2), 384–394, 2014.

Reshmi, G. and Rakshmy, C.S., A survey of authentication methods in mobile cloud computing. *10th International Conference for Internet Technology and Secured Transactions (ICITST)*, 58–63, 2015.

Chapter 7

Analysis of Various Trust Computation Methods: A Step toward Secure FANETs

Kuldeep Singh and Anil Kumar Verma

Thapar University

Palvi Aggarwal

Indian Institute of Technology Mandi

Contents

7.1 Introduction to Flying Ad-Hoc Network

Flying Ad-hoc Network (FANET) [1] is a subclass of Mobile Ad Hoc Networks (MANETs). In FANET, a group of Unmanned Aerial Vehicles (UAVs) are communicating to execute a given task. They are connected through the wireless communication channel without any support of established infrastructure [2]. In FANET, UAVs can fly autonomously based on pre-programmed flight plans or can be operated using complex dynamic automation systems, and are versatile and flexible in implementation [3]. When ordinary communication infrastructure is out of service or simply not available, a group of small flying robots can provide a rapidly deployable and self-managed ad-hoc Wi-Fi network to connect and coordinate rescue teams on ground [4]. FANETs have a wide range of applications such as disaster management, location aware services, rescue operations, and security services. [5]. Similar to MANETs, FANET nodes are free to move in any direction to complete assigned task, due to which the network topology changes frequently. Nodes can join or leave the network as and when required. FANET is a subclass of MANETs that offer self-organized and independent behavior of nodes which may lead to malicious and selfish behavior of nodes in the network [3,6,7]. Due to heterogeneous applications of FANETs, it is mandatory for nodes to follow the protocols and cooperative behavior, highlighting the need of security of such networks. Classical methods of security, i.e., cryptographic techniques, demand more resource consumption [8]. Hence, securing FANETs with limited resources becomes an essential need to research. Past research has been done for trust management in the area of ad-hoc networks, indicating that trust management techniques are helpful in securing ad-hoc networks from various kinds of attacks [6]. Hence, in order to secure FANETs, the concept of trust management is viable [8]. Trust management systems maintain the trust relationships between participating nodes. This chapter focuses on various available trust computation methods for MANETs which can be adaptable for FANETs.

7.1.1 Common Features of MANET and FANET

MANET and FANET have certain common features, thus inviting to explore the possible usage of the existing solution to FANETs as well. The common features of MANETs and FANETs are listed below [2]:

- ■ *Multi-hop routing:* Both the networks follow multi-hop routing scheme in which they follow multiple hops to transfer a message rather than choosing a single long path.
- ■ *Infrastructure less:* Both MANETs and FANETs are infrastructure-less networks because there is no pre-established infrastructure available. They create network as per requirement.
- ■ *Dynamic topology:* Both of these networks do not follow one topology. Nodes leave and join the network so frequently; hence, topology remains dynamic.
- ■ *Random mobility pattern:* Mobility patterns for nodes are not fixed. Nodes can randomly move in any direction.
- ■ *Limited device capability:* Both of the networks have devices with limited computation power, load capacity, and energy.

- *Limited physical security:* In these networks, physical security is very less. This is because the nodes keep moving in different directions. So, it is difficult to provide them physical security.
- *Node density:* Both FANETs and MANETs have very low node density. Nodes are sparse in the network.
- *Message propagation model:* Both of the networks follow centralized and decentralized message propagation model.
- *Network scalability:* MANETs and FANETs are easily scalable. New nodes can be added into the network at any point of time as per requirement.
- *Threats from external and compromised nodes:* In both MANETs and FANETs, nodes are self-organized in nature. Nodes may get compromised easily due to no central control. Both of the networks have threats from such nodes.

7.1.2 Motivation

As we have already discussed the similarities between MANET and FANET, in both the classes high mobility nodes join and leave networks very frequently. This results in link breakage and packet losses. So, it requires some technique that can detect the behavior of nodes in the network. Another issue with ad-hoc networks is the decentralization. Each node decides itself that to which neighbor node, it should communicate based on their reputation. So, there is a need to define a system that can provide reputation feedback to the nodes in the network. Information forwarding and sharing is another important aspect in such a real-time ad-hoc networks. These networks become prone to various types of attacks due to malicious nodes in the network. These attacks aim to send false information, forged packets, and change routing information. In such environments, trust management systems can have an extremely important role in calculating the reputation of network nodes. Trust management systems are basically helping to detect untrustworthy network nodes and keep the records of activities performed by nodes to calculate trust values. In this book chapter, we analyze various trust computation techniques in order to answer few questions given in Table 7.1.

7.1.3 Our Contribution

We did a comprehensive analysis of various state-of-the-art trust management techniques in the area of ad-hoc networks. This review contributes to the research community focusing on the security aspect of FANETs.

- We identified various attacks that exploited the security of flying nodes, i.e., UAVs or on FANET itself.
- We investigated the complete process of trust management that includes various stages: trust composition, trust formation, trust computation, trust propagation, and trust updation.
- We investigate various trust management techniques on the basis of their contributions in ad-hoc networks in terms of complexity, dynamicity, scalability, and security.
- We suggest few best techniques that would help to build trust among flying nodes and prevent from various identified attacks in FANETs.
- We provide future research directions to the community to implement trust management solutions in FANETs.

Table 7.1 Research Question and Motivation

Research Question	Motivation
How trust management can help to achieve better security in FANETs?	FANETs are dynamic networks with limited energy and resources. Most of the tasks in FANETs require timely and accurate responses. In such situations, the security of a network becomes a major concern. In order to secure FANET, we need to identify a lightweight solution that can help to achieve most of the security aspects. Trust management has been identified as one of the lightweight solution. These questions will help to explore about the applicability of the existing trust management solution in the area of FANETs. This review article compares various existing trust management solutions on the basis of their contributions in other ad-hoc networks, complexity, dynamicity, scalability, and security. It is hard to conclude one best technique; however, we try to suggest a subset of techniques chosen for FANET.
What are various trust computational methods that can be applied to FANET?	
What would be the best way to compose trust in FANETs?	
Which trust computation techniques are best to deal with the uncertain network behavior?	
Which trust computation techniques are better in dealing with network scalability?	
Which trust computation techniques consume least resources?	
Which computation techniques are able to prevent multiple security attacks?	
Which trust computation technique most secure?	

In this book chapter, we have discussed about the potential attacks to which FANETs are vulnerable. As a solution to the potential attacks, trust mechanism has been discussed in details. Further, an analysis of various trust computation methods for ad-hoc networks has been represented. In the last section, a discussion on findings with future research direction of trust computation in FANETs is presented.

7.2 Potential Threats to FANETs

FANETs are prone to various security attacks due to inherited features from MANETs. These attacks target the integrity, confidentiality, and availability of nodes. Table 7.2 lists all the possible common attacks in FANETs [9–14]. To understand the importance of trust management scheme to secure from these attacks, first we should understand the attack behaviors and different consequences of these attacks to FANETs. Further, we will analyze various trust management techniques that can be helpful to mitigate such attacks in FANETs.

These attacks are very common in ad-hoc networks. Most of the attacks target availability and integrity of the network resources. FANET employs a group of UAVs, which coordinate and cooperate with each other to complete the mission. To identify and eliminate noncooperative and malicious nodes from the network, trust plays an important role. Trust not only identifies the malicious and selfish nodes in the network, but it also prevents other nodes to avoid communication with them. So, it is important to highlight the importance of trust management process and various trust computation methods for FANETs.

Table 7.2 Potential Attacks in FANETs

Attacks	Source	Target	Attacking Behavior	Attacks Consequences
GPS spoofing attack	Ex	Integrity	The local transmitter with stronger GPS signal is used to override original GPS satellite signal.	The false information about UAVs location by spoofed GPS signal.
GPS jamming attack	Ex	Availability	Flight control lost, not able to monitor its route, location, altitude, and the direction.	Rely on another source of information which may be vulnerable.
Malicious hardware/ software	In	Confidentiality	A Trojan of backdoor is installed in flight controller or ground control unit.	Loss of confidential mission data.
Man in the middle attack	Ex	Integrity	Directly on the communication link between UAV and its Ground Control Station.	Live data can be captured by the attacker.
(ADS-B) attack	Ex	Integrity	False information is injected into ADS-B data.	Collision due to false information about position, heading, speed, and intent of other UAVs.
Worm hole	In	Availability	Record packets at one place in the network and tunnel them to another place and retransmit them.	The whole network paralyzed and jam, cryptographic protection compromise.
Sybil	In	Confidentiality	A node uses multiple identities to pretend as multiple nodes in the networks.	Link eavesdropping between legitimate nodes.
Sniffing	Ex	Confidentiality	Monitor, capture, and read the data from proximity nodes.	Eavesdropping of sensitive information.

(Continued)

Table 7.2 (*Continued*) Potential Attacks in FANETs

Attacks	Source	Target	Attacking Behavior	Attacks Consequences
Grey hole	In	Integrity and availability	Packets dropping for a specific target node, after a certain time period/packets or randomly.	Drop data packets, data integrity issue, and increased cost and risk.
Black hole	In	Availability	Discard incoming and outgoing network packets without knowledge of the source.	Traffic blockage and extend crisis with other attacks.
Sinkhole	In	Availability	Attract all the network traffic by showing the best path through it.	Creation of false routing.
Denial of service	Both	Availability	The attacker tries to attack network resources unavailable, so that legitimate user cannot use it.	Network unavailability or network jam.
Alter, replay, and spoofed info.	Both	Integrity	Modify network data, repeatedly data transmission, and fabrication of messages.	False messages, shorten or extended routes and increase delay.
Energy drain attack	Both	Availability	Initiate a large amount of data to respond from other node in the network.	Paralyze whole network.
Flooding	In	Availability	Transmit or broadcast a huge amount of non-valuable and required data in the network.	Control the data flow for wastage of network resources.
Bad mounting attack	In	Availability	Attacker node spread false trust values of other nodes to decrease their trustworthiness.	Block genuine path.
Conflict behavior	In	Availability	Attacker node shows different behaviors for various nodes.	Conflict opinion leads to decreased trustworthiness.

(*Continued*)

Table 7.2 (*Continued*) Potential Attacks in FANETs

Attacks	*Source*	*Target*	*Attacking Behavior*	*Attacks Consequences*
intelligent behavior	In	Confidentiality and availability	According to trust threshold values, selectivity provides low or high recommendation value.	Disrupt trust system and reputation evaluation cost increment.
Packet injection	Ex	Integrity	An attacker can inject a packet with false or malicious data.	False information and unusual system behavior.
Selfishness	In	Availability	Attacker node can refuse to transmit data for saving the resources like battery.	End-to-end delay and packet drop rate increase.
On–off attack	In	Availability	Attacker node toggles its behavior between trustworthy and untrustworthy to keep its trust value above threshold.	Remain undetected after damage.
Routing loop	Ex	Integrity and availability	Routing information such as hop count is altered by the attacker node.	Difficult to find valid path.

ADS-B, automatic dependent surveillance broadcast; In, internal; Ex, external.

7.3 Trust: Concept–Process–Stages

Trust is the belief among two or more communicating parties. Trust is defined differently based on its utility in that domain. This section deals with application of trust in ad-hoc networks. Here, the concept of trust in ad-hoc networks, its process, and the various stages involved in trust management systems are discussed.

7.3.1 Concept of Trust

According to Mui et al. [15], "Trust is a subjective expectation an agent has about another's future behavior based on the history of their encounters." Another definition from Grandison and Sloman [16] refers to the "competence" to act, "Trust is the firm belief in the competence of an entity to act dependably, securely, and reliably within a specified context." In general computer science as well as defined by Mui et al. [15], trust is dependent on feedback based on past interactions. In online systems also, trust is built based on past interactions and experiences. Trust is considered as direct trust and indirect trust. Direct trust is that in which the user himself experience through communication with the system. In the case of indirect trust, some other user shares his/her experience. This is also called recommendation trust. Trust plays very important role in ad-hoc networks. Trust has been interchangeably used by reputation in some places in this chapter. Blaze et al. [17] defined "Trust Management" as different components of security in networks. Trust management is very important in the intrusion detection systems, access control systems, detection of selfish nodes, secure routing, and authentication. Trust management starts from trust establishment, then based on interactions updation of trust values and finally, if the trust values are not meeting the threshold, revocation of trust. This task is more challenging for ad-hoc networks than traditional centralized systems due to mobile nodes.

7.3.2 Trust Management Process

Trust management is about creating the trust, evaluating the trust values, and updating trust and revocation. The detailed explanation of trust management process follows the steps shown in Figure 7.1.

- **Trust Initialization:** Trust initialization is the first step in the trust management system. When two nodes start interaction, first time they have either no information or very less information about other nodes to decide trust. Based on this, these nodes are categorized into trusted, non-trusted, and undefined [18–20]. This value of trust status is updated more accurately based on record communications. The process of trust initialization is also called bootstrapping.
- **Evidence Space:** The second step in the trust management system is to gather evidences. Evidences can be gathered directly or indirectly. Direct evidences are those which are gathered by direct observation by node. Indirect evidences are those which are gathered through

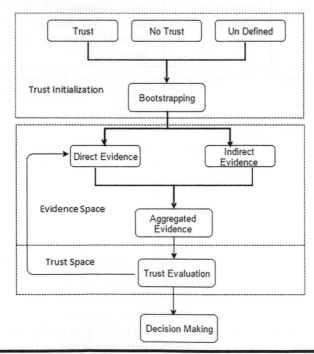

Figure 7.1 Trust management process.

others observations [21]. Based on these direct and indirect evidences, trust values are recalculated, which increase or decrease values. Based on this outcome, nodes are again classified as trusted or untrusted.

$$T_{updated} = T_{past} + T_{recent}$$

■ ***Trust Space:*** In ad-hoc networks, trustworthiness is calculated by individual nodes because there is no centralized node to calculate the trust value for the whole network. Trust is represented in different formats. For example <subject, agent, action, time, outcome> is a vector that represents the interaction at some particular point [22]. It shows that subjects consider that the agent done action successfully or failed at time t. <subject, agent, action, k, n> is another way to represent the number of successes, k, and failures, n, that a subject considers about an agent [23]. Mapping from evidence space to trust space is done by individual node based on the trust value calculated in the evidence space. This mapping can be done based on beta distribution also [23].

■ ***Decision-Making:*** In trust management process, decision is dependent on the kind of communication between nodes. A set of trustworthy nodes are updated based on the results calculated in previous phases. The decision-making process will classify the nodes as trustworthy or non-trustworthy nodes based on their trust values.

7.3.3 Stages of Trust Management

In mobile ad-hoc networks, trust computation involves various stages. These stages can be classified under different sections based on their purpose. Based on the literature, we have classified trust computation stages in five dimensions: trust composition, trust formation, trust calculation, trust propagation, and trust updation. Figure 7.2 shows various stages involved in trust management.

■ ***Trust Composition:*** Trust composition refers to the components which are to be considered for trust computation; it includes quality of service (QoS) and social trust.
  a. *Quality of Service Trust:* In mobile ad-hoc networks, QoS [24] trust refers to the performance of nodes in the networks in terms of node competence, cooperativeness among nodes, node reliability, and task performance (delay, PDR, throughput, and energy consumption) of a node.
  b. *Social Trust:* Social trust [25] of nodes in mobile ad-hoc network can be calculated on the basis of their social relationship with other nodes. The social relationship of network nodes can be measured through their privacy, honesty, friendship, similarity, selfishness, and centrality.

■ ***Trust Formation:*** Trust formation refers to the technique how trust value is identified for a node in the network. We have considered two factors (observation and property) on which trust formation completes in ad-hoc networks.
  a. *Based on Observation:* A node can calculate trust for another node in the network by three ways: direct observation, indirect observation, and through recommendation [26]. In direct observation, a trustor node observes the behavior of a node when having interaction with that node. In indirect observation, a trustor node observes the behavior of trustee node when trustee node having interaction with other node in the network. In the recommendation, trustor node gets information about trustee node from other nodes in the network.
  b. *Based on Property:* Trust of a network node can be calculated based on the number of properties; we have used two classes: single trust and multi-trust [27]. Single trust refers that only one trust property is being considered to calculate the trust of a node, whereas

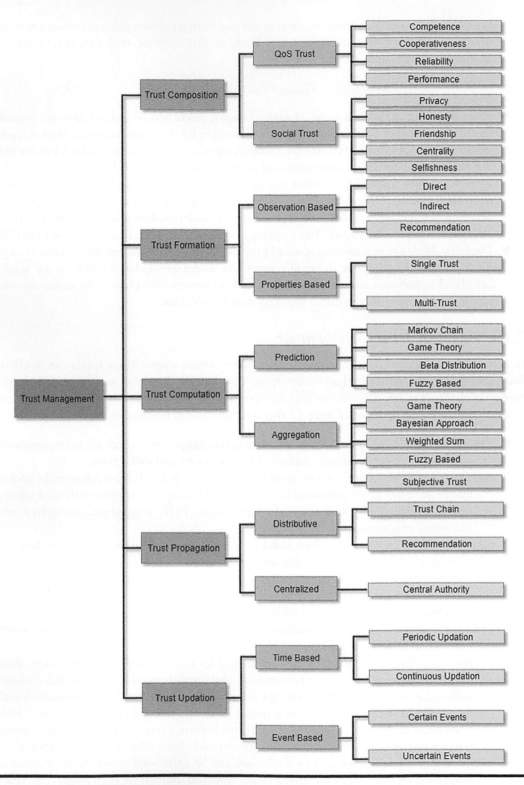

Figure 7.2   Stages in trust management.

multi-trust depicts that multiple trust properties are used to calculate the trust of a node in the ad-hoc network.

■ ***Trust Computation:*** Trust computation refers to the mechanism through which the total trust value of a network node is calculated. Two techniques, trust prediction and trust aggregation, are used to calculate trust value of a node in the ad-hoc network.

   a. *Trust Prediction:* Trust prediction is a technique to predict trust among node by using the past and current behaviors of nodes in the network. In trust prediction method, recommendation from other nodes is also considered to predict the trust value. In literature, Markov chain model [28], mathematical induction [29], and fuzzy-based [30] prediction models are discussed.

   b. *Trust Aggregation:* Trust aggregation methods are used to calculate trust when trust of a network node is propagated through multiple paths. So, aggregation technique combines these multiple values to obtain a single trust value of a node in the network. Literature consists of game theory, Bayesian approach, weighted sum, and fuzzy as aggregation methods [31–33].

■ ***Trust Propagation:*** Trust propagation is a technique through trust of network nodes are propagated in the network. Trust propagation is used to avoid the recalculation of trust for a node again and again through which resource can be conserved. There are two schemes, distributed and centralized, to propagate node trust in the network.

   a. *Distributed Trust:* In the distributed scheme, a node's trust can be shared either through trust chaining or through recommendation [34]. In chaining concept, trust is forwarded from a trusted node to another node in a chain fashion. In recommendation, a node trust value is shared by another node that has information about recommended node through direct or indirect methods.

   b. *Centralized Trust:* In centralized trust propagation scheme, a node in the network works as a central authority and work as a trust propagation entity in the network for every node in the network [35].

■ ***Trust Updation:*** Trust updation refers to the answer to a question that when trust of a network node will be updated. There are two schemes, time based and event based, that can be applied to update node trust in the network.

   a. *Time Based:* In the time-based approach [36], trust based on (observation or property) is updated in two ways: periodic updation and continuous updation. In periodic updation, trust value of a node updated after a certain time period, whereas continuous updation is to evaluate the trust of a node continuously without any time interval.

   b. *Event Based:* In event-based trust updation technique, trust of network nodes is updated when an event occurs [37]. Event-based updation technique can be further divided into two ways: certain event and uncertain event. In certain event-based scheme, trust will be updated only when a predefined or specific event will occur, whereas in uncertain scheme, trust of network node will be updated when any event will occur.

7.4 Trust Computation Using Various Methods

Trust management systems have wide applications in various fields like in e-commerce systems, distributed systems, sensor networks, ad-hoc network, and information technology. Trust and reputation have been calculated using various trust computation techniques, i.e., fuzzy model, Bayesian trust model, game theory model, etc. Here, we discussed popular trust computational methods that are already being implemented in MANETs and explain their applicability in FANET.

7.4.1 Fuzzy Model

Fuzzy model is one of the major techniques to estimate trust of mobile nodes in the network. RFSTrust [38], FuzzyTrust [39], and TSR [40] are some popular models that calculate trust scores using Fuzzy logic. Trust value can be classified into two ways: discrete trust values and continuous trust values. The common range of discrete trust values could be [−1, 0, 1], whereas continuous trust values range between [0–1]. Fuzzy logic deals with approximate values rather than exact values. Compared to binary set, fuzzy variables have values in range [0, 1]. Fuzzy logic is used to compute trust values and handle partial truth, their aggregation and dissemination [41]. In MANETs, node trust is symbolized by a fuzzy variable with membership function explaining the degree of node trust, e.g., if a node has trust value in the range [0, 0.2], then it may be considered as a less trusted node. If a node has trust value in range [0.3, 0.6], then it may be considered as a medium trusted node. If a node has trust value in range [0.7, 1], then it may be considered as a highly trusted node. The following are the steps for reasoning with fuzzy rules:

- First, define fuzzy sets and criteria of evaluation,
- Then, do variable initialization for fuzzy engine,
- Apply fuzzy rules to obtain output, and draw conclusions,
- Now, evaluate results and modify fuzzy rules according to requirement.

7.4.2 Bayesian Trust Model

Probabilistic trust methods are used to develop trust management models based on probability theory. Applying probability theory provides the opportunity to explore a wide range of possible derivation methods [42]. As trust is uncertain in nature, probabilistic models can offer better performance as compared to deterministic trust models to achieve the required security measures. The mechanism of trust calculation depends on the past behavior of a node and updated according to the current behavior in the network. Bayesian theory works on the same principal. Prior probability in Bayes' theorem considers the past behavior of nodes, and posterior probabilities represent the updated trust value based on the current behavior. Hence, Bayesian trust model is a suitable method for calculation of trust. Few researchers explored the concept of Bayesian trust models in various domains like Dong et al. [43] PTME for distributed e-commerce, Wang and Vassileva [44] in peer-to-peer networks, LogitTrust [45], Feng et al. [46], and Wei et al. [47] for MANETs, etc.

7.4.3 Game Theory Model

Game theory is the study of mathematical models where two decision makers either cooperate or conflict. This study helps to predict the future behavior of an entity. Srinivasan et al. [48] and Felegyhazi et al. [49] used game theoretic models for the development of a trust management system. Game theory captures the dynamic system behavior where the success of one player depends on the actions of another player. Game theory is a good technique to detect the selfish behavior of a node in the network and to design optimal strategies using the Nash equilibrium for gaining more benefits. In ad-hoc networks, nodes behave in a cooperative manner. Hence, any node playing in an uncooperative manner will be detected easily. In [50], the author used this technique to detect misbehaving nodes on the network. Interaction among nodes can be modeled as games such as Prisoner's dilemma. Game theory acts as a behavior analysis tool that can be used by policy makers of the network.

7.4.4 Subjective Trust

Due to network congestion or network unavailability, cooperative nodes are labeled as selfish nodes. This reduces the performance of the network. To solve such issues, Jøsang et al. [51] introduced the concept of subjective logic for calculating trust among communicating nodes. Subjective logic works on subjective beliefs about the object called an opinion. The opinion denoted by w_{yx} is a tuple defined in Equation 7.1.

$$w_{yx} \equiv b_{yx}, d_{yx}, u_{yx}, a_{yx} \qquad (7.1)$$

b: Belief, $b_{y:x} \in [0.0, 1.0]$ represents node y's belief in node x.
d: Disbelief, $d_{y:x} \in [0.0, 1.0]$ represents node y's disbelief in node x.
u: Uncertainty, $u_{y:x} \in [0.0, 1.0]$ denotes y's uncertainty value on node x.
a: Base rate, $a_{y:x} \in [0.0, 1.0]$ is the relative atomicity. It is used in the absence of evidence.

The relation between b, d, and u is defined as

$$b_{yx} + d_{yx} + u_{yx} = 1.0 \qquad (7.2)$$

7.4.5 Weightage Based

Weighted sum is a widespread technique to combine trust evidences. Many trust systems such as Xia et al. [52] and TRIP [53] are using a weighted sum for aggregating ratings and feedbacks. More trusted feedbacks are given higher weightage than less trusted. Nitti et al. [54] calculate trustworthiness which is obtained from QoS and social trust parameters. This trustworthiness is used as criteria to decide weightage of a rater for indirect trust aggregation. Chen et al. [55] also use similarity, which is derived from social trust as the criteria to decide weights for indirect trust aggregation. Weighted sum is also used for aggregating the direct and indirect trust values. Further research focuses on dynamic weight allocation.

7.4.6 Markov Chain Model

Andrey Markov discovered a Markov chain model which is also known as discrete-time Markov chain. It is a stochastic process that goes through transitions from one state to another state defined on a state space [56]. The probability of moving to next state depends only on the current state of the model, and previous events in the sequence do not play any role in deciding probability distribution values. Thus, Markov chain model possesses memoryless property. Markov model does not assume any fixed probability distribution about the behavior of a node. Markov-based trust models are helpful to decide the node's current status, because the Markov model predicts short-term trust values with the help of the current behavior of the node. Moe et al. [57] and Estahbanati et al. [58] used Markov chain model to predict the trust values in a network.

7.4.7 Beta Distribution

Beta distribution is a probabilistic model based on Bayesian probability. Similar to Bayesian model, the beta distribution model has been used to develop various trust models like HTMF [59], CONFIDANT [60], and OTMF [61]. This model gets the trust ratings as input and calculates the trust score using the probability density function of beta distribution [59–61] proposed trust and reputation models using the beta distribution. They used beta probability density function to compute the trust score. The beta distribution is estimated by α and β that represent the rating of positive and negative outcomes, respectively. The expectance of PDF of beta function is $\dfrac{\alpha}{\alpha + \beta}$.

After discussing the concept of the most commonly used trust computation methods, we provide the summary of an analysis of all the methods. Table 7.3 summarizes the main advantages, examples of trust models, and the context, i.e., what kind of security problem is handled, and it also lists the attacks considered by various methods.

Table 7.3 Comparison of Various Trust Computation Methods

Trust Computation Method	Advantages	Context	Attacks Considered	Example Trust Models
Fuzzy model	• Fuzzy logic handles uncertainty, incomplete information, and imprecision effectively. • Fuzzy model incorporates the feedback and improve its performance. • Fuzzy controller rules help to keep track of past information. • Human expert's knowledge can be fed into the model.	Secure route, malicious and selfish node detection.	Black, gray hole, worm hole, and message modification.	RFSTrust [38], FuzzyTrust [39,] and TSR [40]
Bayesian model	• The Bayesian model considers past and present behaviors to calculate trust. • However, the adversary may form its trust by providing a more number of truthful ratings within the short span of time.	Misbehaving node, secure routing	Bad mouthing, DOS, man in the middle attack	LogitTrust [45], Feng et al. [46], and Wei et al. [47]

(Continued)

Table 7.3 (*Continued*) Comparison of Various Trust Computation Methods

Trust Computation Method	Advantages	Context	Attacks Considered	Example Trust Models
Game theory	• Allow strategy-based analysis. • Helps to identify nodes, which are behaving rationally. • Allows to observe and update trust over the period of time using dynamic cyber security games.	Selfish node detection	Message forging, replication, modification, black hole, gray hole	Srinivasan et al. [48] and Felegyhazi et al. [49]
Subjective logic	• Can be used in situations of uncertainty and incomplete knowledge. • Partial ignorance and lack of information can be handled. • Representation of belief is human understandable.	Secure route	Spoofing, gray hole, and black hole	Jøsang et al. [51]
Weightage based	• Combination of direct and indirect trusts. • Helpful to construct hybrid models. • It cannot be used as a standalone model for complex applications.	Misbehaving nodes	DOS, link spoofing, black hole and jellyfish, selfish node	Xia et al. [52] and Mármol et al. [53]
Markov chain	• It can account for nodes whose behavior is not static with time. • It can estimate the rate with which an agent's behavior changes.	Secure routing	Selfish nodes, packet dropping	Moe et al. [57] and Estahbanati et al. [58]

(Continued)

Table 7.3 (*Continued*)   Comparison of Various Trust Computation Methods

Trust Computation Method	Advantages	Context	Attacks Considered	Example Trust Models
	• The Markov model considers time component so that a bad node cannot deceive by mimicking good for some time. • Large number of parameters			
Beta distribution	• Less resource-intensive method due to only two parameters. • Helps to evaluate trust accumulated over a number of experiences. • Addition of beta function property allows combination of direct experiences and recommendations. • This model does not consider time as component; it just relies on the number of rating for trust calculation.	Misbehaving nodes	Node misbehavior and bad mouthing	HTMF [59] and CONFIDANT [60]

In this book chapter, we have selected the few factors, i.e., scalability, dynamics, time complexity, space complexity, and security level, to compare various trust models selected above in Table 7.3 based on the FANET requirements. First, we give a brief description of the factors that we use to compare various models shown in Table 7.4.

- ■ ***Time Complexity:*** In FANETs, nodes move with high velocity resulting in frequent topology change. Hence, a computationally fast trust model is required. In this chapter, we consider the time complexity as an important factor for comparison of different trust models.
- ■ ***Space Complexity:*** Ad-hoc networks have limited resources. Therefore, the designed trust models should consume minimum space. We consider space complexity as another factor of comparison for trust models.

Table 7.4 Comparison of Various Trust Models

Trust Model	Computation Method	Scal-ability	Dynami-city	Time Complexity	Storage Complexity	Security Level
RFSTrust [38]	Fuzzy	High	High	Low	Low	High
FuzzyTrust [39]	Fuzzy	High	High	Medium	Low	High
TSR [40]	Fuzzy	High	High	Low	Medium	High
LogitTrust [45]	Bayesian	High	High	Medium	Medium	Low
Feng et al. [46]	Bayesian	Low	Low	High	High	Low
Wei et al. [47]	Bayesian	Low	Low	Medium	Medium	Low
Srinivasan et al. [48]	Game theory	High	High	Low	Low	High
Felegyhazi et al. [49]	Game theory	High	Medium	Low	Low	High
Jøsang et al. [51]	Subjective	High	Medium	High	High	Low
MTRA Xia et al. [52]	Weightage	Medium	Medium	Low	Low	Low
TRIP [53]	Weightage	High	Low	Low	Low	Medium
Moe et al. [57]	Markov chain	High	Medium	Low	Low	High
Estahbanati et al. [58]	Markov	High	High	Low	Low	High
HTMF [59]	Beta distribution	Low	Low	High	Medium	Medium
CONFI-DANT [60]	Beta distribution	High	Medium	Medium	Low	Medium

- **Dynamics:** Due to high speed and rapid network topology changes in FANETs, the trust models should be able to cope up with such a dynamic environments. We evaluate trust models based on whether they can adjust in such environment or not.
- **Scalability:** FANETs have a wide range of applications where based on the need of situation, nodes may be added or removed. Scalability is a way to handle extra nodes without any loss in the performance of the network. Hence, scalability plays a crucial role in FANETs.
- **Security Level:** Trust models are also prone to various attacks. Security level measures how secure the trust model is. We consider the security level as an important factor for comparison of trust models.

7.5 Discussion

Various trust computation techniques have been developed by various researchers to mitigate cyber-attacks for ad-hoc networks. Table 7.4 represents the advantages of various techniques, examples of each technique and quote in which domain it will provide security and which attacks it safe. It has been observed that Fuzzy logic, Game theory model, and Markov model are the best-suited models for FANETs. As it can be seen from the table, Fuzzy technique has been used in the environments that involve uncertainty and incomplete information. FANETs are highly dynamic in nature which involves more uncertainty and high chances of information loss. Fuzzy logic is a suitable trust management model for such dynamic environments. Fuzzy model can include knowledge of human experts which helps to deal with the unknown situation that may occur in disaster situations handled by FANETs. Major attacks in network communication happen on the routing, and Fuzzy model is able to mitigate major routing attacks, i.e., gray-hole, worm-hole, and black-hole attacks. Bayesian models are another category of trust management models which comes under probabilistic models. Although Bayesian model pay attention to the past and current behaviors of any node, this model cannot handle mimicking behavior of a bad node. A bad node may build a very good reputation before launching any attack. Trust decay based on current behavior is very slow. Hence, this is not suitable to FANETs. Next, we consider game theory-based models which help to understand the exact behavior of a node in the network. Any node going against the network strategy will be immediately detected using game theory. It also helps in developing strategies and policies for securing the network. So, this can be helpful in detecting selfish nodes in FANET. Markov models use stochastic processes to evaluate the trust of a node. This model is featured with calculation of the rate at which any node changes its behavior. It also helps to identify the deceptive nodes in the network. Hence, Markov model seems suitable for FANETs. Weightage-based model and subjective trust model are very straightforward models. They cannot capture the complexity of FANETs alone. Hence, they are not suitable for using in FANETs independently. Next, the beta distribution model has the same issues as faced by Bayesian models. They just consider trust ratings and do not take time component into consideration. Hence, beta distribution models are not well suited to be used in FANETs. Further, Table 7.3 describes the example models of various techniques and discusses their applicability with respect to FANET requirements. From both Tables 7.3 and 7.4, it is evident that Fuzzy, game theory, and Markov models are the most suitable models for FANETs. Table 7.5 gives brief comments about the main findings of this review of various trust computation methods.

7.6 Future Research Direction for Trust Management in FANETs

Trust management in ad-hoc networks is an inspiring area of research. Its adaptation and applications in various situations or task-specific ad-hoc networks make it more challenging and open new vistas for the research community. This survey of various trust computation methods will help the research community to implement trust-based security solutions for FANETs. However, while designing the trust management solution, the following are some open issues and research challenges that need to be considered in FANETs:

1. In a trust management system, trust metric should have used appropriate trust composition (i.e., Quality of Service and Social trust), trust formation (i.e., node observation and property base), and trust propagation (i.e., distributed and centralized) techniques according to the specific mission or task.

Table 7.5   Summary of Key Findings for Various Trust Computation Methods

Trust Computation Method	MANETs	FANETs	Comments
Fuzzy	Yes	Yes	The ability to handle incomplete information, uncertainty in dynamic environments, and inclusion of expert knowledge makes the Fuzzy model applicable for FANETs. Fuzzy trust models in literature have been identified as scalable, dynamic, and less complex with high security in nature.
Bayesian	Yes	No	Bayesian models require more continuous computation that increases the complexity and reduces dynamicity. The Bayesian models are prone to mimicking attacks and could give false alarms, which reduce their security level.
Game theory	Yes	Yes	Models in the literature support that game theory models are really successful for selfish node detection and strategy development with low complexity. High security, scalability, and dynamicity features make the game theory models suitable for FANETs.
Markov chain	Yes	Yes	Trust evaluation through Markov chain helps to investigate the rate at which a node changes its behavior. The Markov models for trust management are identified as low complexity, high dynamicity, and scalable models. Hence, Markov models are suitable for FANETs for belief propagation and evaluation.
Weightage based	Yes	No	These are very simple models, but they cannot handle the trust evaluation of complex and dynamic networks such as FANETs.
Subjective logic	Yes	No	Subjective logic can handle incomplete information and uncertainty. However, this has not been explored much in the domain of MANETs.
Beta distribution	Yes	No	Beta distribution is prone to deceptive attacks which reduce its security. The models found in literature are not very dynamic and scalable in nature. The computation complexity is also not suitable for FANETs.

2. A trust management should have appropriate mechanisms to compute the local and global trust of a node in the network because the local trust calculation is easy, whereas global trust calculation is difficult.

3. A trust management system should address false information provided in indirect or recommendation-based approach by a malicious neighbor (i.e., in cooperative attack scenario) to compute trust value for a node in the network.

4. Different operations or situation-specific task has different requirements. So, a trust management system should be specific to purpose or task. It should support requirement to the specific operation/mission such as performance, security, and reliability.

5. FANETs nodes have high mobility, so topology changes frequently. A trust management system should have quick trust computational (i.e., aggregation and prediction) techniques to cope with high mobility and frequent topology change.

6. A trust management system should be flexible to adapt changing network conditions such as network scalability, node density, routing scheme, and traffic pattern.

7. A trust management system should have provision to compute single-node trust value as well as group trust value.

8. Most of the existing trust management schemes aim to cope with selfishness and node misbehavior attack, other attacks such as message modification, false information forwarding and rushing, which should be addressed by a trust management scheme.

7.7 Conclusion

To prevent FANETs from various attacks due to node misbehavior and selfishness, trust management in the networks can play a significant role. Trust management schemes can help to identify malicious and noncooperative nodes in the network, can predict the future behavior of nodes, and discover trusted nodes. FANETs are highly dynamic in nature which involves more uncertainty and high chances of information loss. Hence, the use of trust management schemes in FANETs can be beneficial for successful mission accomplishment. In this chapter, we analyzed various trust management techniques that have already been implemented for traditional ad-hoc network. It has been observed that Fuzzy logic, Game theory, and Markov model-based trust schemes are best suited for FANETs. These techniques provide capability to handle uncertainty, noncooperativeness, and frequent behavioral changes. Further, we discussed future research directions and challenges for implementing trust schemes for FANETs.

Acknowledgment

This work is financially supported by The Ministry of Electronics and Information Technology, Government of INDIA as a part of the VISVESVERYA PHD Scheme for Electronics & IT under Ref. No. PHD-MLA/4(33)/2014–15.

References

1. Müller, M. (2012). Flying ad-hoc networks. *Institute of Media Informatics Ulm University*, 53.
2. Bekmezci, I., Sahingoz, O. K., & Temel, Ş. (2013). Flying ad-hoc networks (FANETs): A survey. *Ad Hoc Networks*, *11*(3), 1254–1270.
3. Sahingoz, O. K. (2014). Networking models in flying ad-hoc networks (FANETs): Concepts and challenges. *Journal of Intelligent & Robotic Systems*, *74*(1–2), 513–527.
4. Singh, K., & Verma, A. K. (2014, May). Applying OLSR routing in FANETs. In *2014 International Conference on Advanced Communication Control and Computing Technologies (ICACCCT)* (pp. 1212–1215). IEEE.

5. Singh, K., & Verma, A. K. (2015, March). Experimental analysis of AODV, DSDV and OLSR routing protocol for flying adhoc networks (FANETs). In *2015 IEEE International Conference on Electrical, Computer and Communication Technologies (ICECCT)* (pp. 1–4). IEEE.

6. Akbani, R., Korkmaz, T., & Raju, G. V. S. (2012). Mobile ad-hoc networks security. In *Recent Advances in Computer Science and Information Engineering* (pp. 659–666). Springer, Berlin, Heidelberg.

7. Sentürk, E. (2016). Security issues in flying ad-hoc networks (fanets). *Journal of Aeronautics and Space Technologies, 9*(2), 13–21.

8. Mohammed, F., Jawhar, I., Mohamed, N., & Idries, A. (2016, April). Towards trusted and efficient UAV-based communication. In *Big Data Security on Cloud (BigDataSecurity), IEEE International Conference on High Performance and Smart Computing (HPSC), and 2016 IEEE 2nd International Conference on Intelligent Data and Security (IDS)* (pp. 388–393). IEEE.

9. Kim, A., Wampler, B., Goppert, J., Hwang, I., & Aldridge, H. (2012). Cyber attack vulnerabilities analysis for unmanned aerial vehicles. In *Infotech@ Aerospace* (p. 2438).

10. Singh, K., & Verma, A. K. (2018). Flying ad hoc networks concept and challenges. In *Encyclopedia of Information Science and Technology*, Fourth Edition (pp. 6106–6113). IGI Global.

11. Altawy, R., & Youssef, A. M. (2016). Security, privacy, and safety aspects of civilian drones: A survey. *ACM Transactions on Cyber-Physical Systems, 1*(2), 7.

12. Javaid, A. Y., Sun, W., Devabhaktuni, V. K., & Alam, M. (2012, November). Cyber security threat analysis and modeling of an unmanned aerial vehicle system. In *Homeland Security (HST), 2012 IEEE Conference on Technologies for* (pp. 585–590). IEEE.

13. Hartmann, K., & Steup, C. (2013, June). The vulnerability of UAVs to cyber attacks-An approach to the risk assessment. In *Cyber Conflict (CyCon), 2013 5th International Conference on* (pp. 1–23). IEEE.

14. Mansfield, K., Eveleigh, T., Holzer, T. H., & Sarkani, S. (2013, November). Unmanned aerial vehicle smart device ground control station cyber security threat model. In *2013 IEEE International Conference on Technologies for Homeland Security (HST)* (pp. 722–728). IEEE.

15. Mui, L., Mohtashemi, M., & Halberstadt, A. (2002, January). A computational model of trust and reputation. In *System Sciences, 2002. HICSS. Proceedings of the 35th Annual Hawaii International Conference on* (pp. 2431–2439). IEEE.

16. Grandison, T., & Sloman, M. (2000). A survey of trust in internet applications. *IEEE Communications Surveys & Tutorials, 3*(4), 2–16.

17. Blaze, M., Feigenbaum, J., & Lacy, J. (1996). Decentralized trust management. In *Security and Privacy, 1996. Proceedings, 1996 IEEE Symposium on* (pp. 164–173). IEEE.

18. Nguyên, C. T., & Camp, O. (2008, October). Using context information to improve computation of trust in ad hoc networks. In *2008 IEEE International Conference on Wireless and Mobile Computing, Networking and Communications* (pp. 619–624). IEEE.

19. Chen, R., Bao, F., Chang, M., & Cho, J. H. (2010, December). Trust management for encounter-based routing in delay tolerant networks. In *Global Telecommunications Conference (GLOBECOM 2010), 2010 IEEE* (pp. 1–6). IEEE.

20. Chen, A., Xu, G., & Yang, Y. (2008, October). A cluster-based trust model for mobile ad hoc networks. In *Wireless Communications, Networking and Mobile Computing, 2008. WiCOM'08. 4th International Conference on* (pp. 1–4). IEEE.

21. Wang, Y., & Singh, M. P. (2007, January). Formal trust model for multiagent systems. In *IJCAI* (Vol. 7, pp. 1551–1556).

22. Buchegger, S., & Boudec, J. Y. L. (2002). Nodes bearing grudges: Towards routing security, fairness, and robustness in mobile ad hoc networks. In *Proceedings. 10th Euromicro Workshop on Parallel, Distributed and Network-Based Processing, 2002* (pp. 403–410). IEEE.

23. Jsang, A., & Ismail, R. (2002, June). The beta reputation system. In *Proceedings of the 15th Bled Electronic Commerce Conference* (Vol. 5, pp. 2502–2511).

24. Singh, K., & Verma, A. K. (2018). A fuzzy-based trust model for flying ad hoc networks (FANETs). *International Journal of Communication Systems, 31*(6), e3517.

25. Yan, Z., & Holtmanns, S. (2008). Trust modeling and management: From social trust to digital trust. In *Computer security, privacy and politics: Current issues, challenges and solutions* (pp. 290–323). IGI Global.

26. Nguyen, C. T., Camp, O., & Loiseau, S. (2007, March). A Bayesian network based trust model for improving collaboration in mobile ad hoc networks. In *Research, Innovation and Vision for the Future, 2007 IEEE International Conference on* (pp. 144–151). IEEE.

27. Li, W., Parker, J., & Joshi, A. (2012). Security through collaboration and trust in MANETs. *Mobile Networks and Applications, 17*(3), 342–352.

28. Chatterjee, P., Sengupta, I., & Ghosh, S. K. (2012). STACRP: A secure trusted auction oriented clustering based routing protocol for MANET. *Cluster Computing, 15*(3), 303–320.

29. O'Donovan, J., & Smyth, B. (2005, July). Trust no one: Evaluating trust-based filtering for recommenders. In *IJCAI* (Vol. 5, pp. 1663–1665).

30. Dai, H., Jia, Z., & Qin, Z. (2009). Trust evaluation and dynamic routing decision based on fuzzy theory for MANETs. *Journal of Software, 4*(10), 1091–1101.

31. Govindan, K., & Mohapatra, P. (2012). Trust computations and trust dynamics in mobile adhoc networks: A survey. *Communications Surveys & Tutorials, IEEE, 14*(2), 279–298.

32. Cho, J. H., & Swami, A. (2009). *Towards Trust-Based Cognitive Networks: A Survey of Trust Management for Mobile ad hoc Networks*. Army Research Lab Adelphi md Computational and Information Sciences Directorate. Defense Technical Information Center, Ft. Belvoir.

33. Li, J., Li, R., & Kato, J. (2008). Future trust management framework for mobile ad hoc networks. *Communications Magazine, IEEE, 46*(4), 108–114.

34. Theodorakopoulos, G., & Baras, J. S. (2006). On trust models and trust evaluation metrics for ad hoc networks. *Selected Areas in Communications, IEEE Journal on, 24*(2), 318–328.

35. Park, S. S., Lee, J. H., & Chung, T. M. (2008, November). Cluster-based trust model against attacks in ad-hoc networks. In *ICCIT'08. Third International Conference on Convergence and Hybrid Information Technology, 2008* (Vol. 1, pp. 526–532). IEEE.

36. Ferdous, R., Muthukkumarasamy, V., & Sithirasenan, E. (2011, November). Trust-based cluster head selection algorithm for mobile ad hoc networks. In *2011 IEEE 10th International Conference on Trust, Security and Privacy in Computing and Communications (TrustCom)* (pp. 589–596). IEEE.

37. Kute, D. S., Patil, A. S., Pardakhe, N. V., & Kathole, A. B. (2012). A Review: MANET routing protocols and different types of attacks in MANET. *International Journal of Wireless Communication, 2*(1), 26.

38. Luo, J., Liu, X., & Fan, M. (2009). A trust model based on fuzzy recommendation for mobile ad-hoc networks. *Computer Networks, 53*(14), 2396–2407.

39. Song, S., Hwang, K., Zhou, R., & Kwok, Y. K. (2005). Trusted P2P transactions with fuzzy reputation aggregation. *IEEE Internet computing, 9*(6), 24–34.

40. Xia, H., Jia, Z., Li, X., Ju, L., & Sha, E. H. M. (2013). Trust prediction and trust-based source routing in mobile ad hoc networks. *Ad Hoc Networks, 11*(7), 2096–2114.

41. Singh, K., & Verma, A. K. (2018). FCTM: A novel fuzzy classification trust model for enhancing reliability in flying ad hoc networks (FANETs). *Adhoc & Sensor Wireless Networks, 40*.

42. Jøsang, A. (2007). Trust and reputation systems. In *Foundations of security analysis and design IV* (pp. 209–245). Springer, Berlin, Heidelberg.

43. Dong, P., Wang, H., & Zhang, H. (2009, November). Probability-based trust management model for distributed e-commerce. In *2009 IEEE International Conference on Network Infrastructure and Digital Content* (pp. 419–423). IEEE.

44. Wang, Y., & Vassileva, J. (2003, September). Trust and reputation model in peer-to-peer networks. In *Proceedings. Third International Conference on Peer-to-Peer Computing, 2003. (P2P 2003)* (pp. 150–157). IEEE.

45. Wang, Y., Lu, Y. C., Chen, I. R., Cho, J. H., Swami, A., & Lu, C. T. (2014, December). Logittrust: A logit regression-based trust model for mobile ad hoc networks. In *6th ASE International Conference on Privacy, Security, Risk and Trust* (pp. 1–10). Boston, MA.

46. Li, F., & Wu, J. (2010). Uncertainty modeling and reduction in MANETs. *IEEE Transactions on Mobile Computing, 9*(7), 1035–1048.

47. Wei, Z., Tang, H., Yu, F. R., Wang, M., & Mason, P. (2014). Security enhancements for mobile ad hoc networks with trust management using uncertain reasoning. *IEEE Transactions on Vehicular Technology, 63*(9), 4647–4658.

48. Srinivasan, V., Nuggehalli, P., Chiasserini, C. F., & Rao, R. R. (2003, March). Cooperation in wireless ad hoc networks. In *INFOCOM 2003. Twenty-Second Annual Joint Conference of the IEEE Computer and Communications. IEEE Societies* (Vol. 2, pp. 808–817). IEEE.
49. Felegyhazi, M., Hubaux, J. P., & Buttyan, L. (2006). Nash equilibria of packet forwarding strategies in wireless ad hoc networks. *IEEE Transactions on Mobile Computing*, 5(5), 463–476.
50. Komathy, K., & Narayanasamy, P. (2008). Trust-based evolutionary game model assisting AODV routing against selfishness. *Journal of Network and Computer Applications*, 31(4), 446–471.
51. Jøsang, A., Hayward, R., & Pope, S. (2006, January). Trust network analysis with subjective logic. In *Proceedings of the 29th Australasian Computer Science Conference* (Vol. 48, pp. 85–94). Australian Computer Society, Inc.
52. Xia, H., Jia, Z., Ju, L., & Zhu, Y. (2011, November). Multicast trusted routing with QoS multi-constraints in wireless ad hoc networks. In *2011 IEEE 10th International Conference on Trust, Security and Privacy in Computing and Communications* (pp. 1277–1282). IEEE.
53. Mármol, F. G., & Pérez, G. M. (2012). TRIP, a trust and reputation infrastructure-based proposal for vehicular ad hoc networks. *Journal of Network and Computer Applications*, 35(3), 934–941.
54. Nitti, M., Girau, R., & Atzori, L. (2014). Trustworthiness management in the social internet of things. *IEEE Transactions on Knowledge and Data Engineering*, 26(5), 1253–1266.
55. Chen, R., Guo, J., & Bao, F. (2016). Trust management for SOA-based IoT and its application to service composition. *IEEE Transactions on Services Computing*, 9(3), 482–495.
56. Zhang, F., Jia, Z. P., Xia, H., Li, X., & Edwin, H. M. S. (2012). Node trust evaluation in mobile ad hoc networks based on multi-dimensional fuzzy and Markov SCGM (1, 1) model. *Computer Communications*, 35(5), 589–596.
57. Moe, M. E., Helvik, B. E., & Knapskog, S. J. (2008, October). TSR: Trust-based secure MANET routing using HMMs. In *Proceedings of the 4th ACM symposium on QoS and security for wireless and mobile networks* (pp. 83–90). ACM.
58. Estahbanati, M. M., Rasti, M., & Hamami, S. M. S. (2014, September). A mobile ad hoc network routing based on energy and Markov chain trust. In *2014 7th International Symposium on Telecommunications (IST)* (pp. 596–601). IEEE.
59. Li, R., Li, J., Liu, P., & Kato, J. (2009, June). A novel hybrid trust management framework for MANETs. In *2009. ICDCS Workshops' 09. 29th IEEE International Conference on Distributed Computing Systems Workshops* (pp. 251–256). IEEE.
60. Buchegger, S., & Le Boudec, J. Y. (2002, June). Performance analysis of the CONFIDANT protocol. In *Proceedings of the 3rd ACM international symposium on Mobile ad hoc networking & computing* (pp. 226–236). ACM.
61. Li, J., Li, R., & Kato, J. (2008). Future trust management framework for mobile ad hoc networks. *IEEE Communications Magazine*, 46(4), 108–114.

Chapter 8

Security in Wireless LAN (WLAN) and WiMAX Systems

Shashank Gupta
Birla Institute of Technology and Science Pilani

Brij B. Gupta
National Institute of Technology Kurukshetra

Contents

8.1 Introduction..196
    8.1.1 Traditional10/100 BaseT Ethernet Wired LAN 196
    8.1.2 Advantages of WLANs...197
    8.1.3 WLAN Components..197
    8.1.4 Wireless Protocol Stack..198
    8.1.5 IEEE 802.11 Standards...198
8.2 Authentication Mechanism in WLAN..201
    8.2.1 Open System Authentication 201
    8.2.2 Shared System Authentication 201
    8.2.3 Vulnerabilities of WLAN 202
8.3 Encryption on a WLAN 203
    8.3.1 WEP Encryption 203
    8.3.2 WPA Encryption 203
    8.3.3 AES Encryption...203
    8.3.4 Tools for Attacking the WLAN 204
    8.3.5 WLAN Threats..204
8.4 Bluetooth Ad-Hoc Network 204
    8.4.1 Bluetooth Architecture 204
    8.4.2 Bluetooth Security Features 206
    8.4.3 Bluetooth Threats 208
    8.4.4 WiMAX Security 209

8.1 Introduction

Network security is regularly ignored or may be in complete well-thought-out, while install-ing the wireless network. People purchase essential network devices, link it, switch on the power, and finally have unrestricted wireless connectivity for the entire fellow citizen within its communication range. The only effort required in such an unsafe wireless network is to get inside range and start your desktop to get connected. That could be a normal behavior with a palmtop or possibly your friend who is continuously inside the range of the wireless network. The flora of created wireless networks encourages us to confront and formally address them. Hence, the security of wireless network is subsequently essential if you need to thwart other people from gaining access to your wireless network. The main contributions of this chapter are as follows:

■ The basic terminology of WLAN has been discussed starting with its traditional version, needed components and their different modes, underlying protocol stacks and several exist-ing WLAN standards.
■ Numerous categories of authentication mechanism have also been presented in WLAN including several emerging vulnerabilities in WLANs and possible encryption mechanism in WLAN.
■ Some of the attacking tools for WLAN and WLAN threats are also explained.
■ The concept of Bluetooth ad-hoc network has also highlighted with its secured infrastruc-ture and numerous vulnerabilities are also presented.
■ Lastly, the concept of Worldwide Inter-operability for Microwave Access (WiMAX) security has also been presented including its protocol architecture, its security vulnerabilities, and its possible countermeasures.

8.1.1 Traditional10/100 BaseT Ethernet Wired LAN

A conventionally wired 10/100 BaseT setup of Ethernet LAN is very expensive for a large number of people and necessitates several days to install. Figure 8.1 illustrates the structure of a traditional 10/100 BaseT Ethernet LAN. Numerous organizations that utilize such Ethernet LAN also incur extra expenses due to alteration in the physical structure of the organization [1]. The cost differs as per the physical structure and the features of the apparatus put in service.

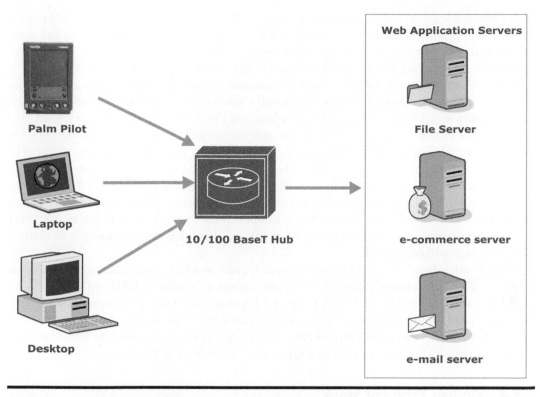

Figure 8.1 Overview of traditional 10/100 baseT ethernet LAN.

8.1.2 Advantages of WLANs

On the other hand, WLANs are not as much as expensive and less sensitive to sustain needed modifications. The following are some of the specific advantages of WLAN:

- It has streamlined preservation requirements as access points can be placed in any corner of the building. In addition to this, it can be easily moved from one location to another.
- WLANs assist in accessing their resources from any position inside the transmission range of the access point.
- This high level of accessibility can directly increase employee's efficiency.
- The roaming characteristics of a WLAN can be used across multi-standard organization.
- The aggregate advantages of streamlined accessibility and preservation, and the autonomy to roam reduce expenditure and provide administrative simplicity and enhance productivity of employees.
- Therefore, the ultimate result is the total budget of proprietorship and involved procedure.

8.1.3 WLAN Components

WLANs are clusters of wireless networked devices inside a restricted geographical zone, like an apartment or university campus, that allow proficient transmission of radio waves [2]. WLANs are typically employed as a substitute to the current wired LANs to support unrestricted user movement within network transmission area. This provides administration a flexibility to its personnel travel everywhere inside a wide range of exposure zones and still be linked to the WLAN. WLAN enables a quick and operational addition of a standard LAN. Setting up a WLAN is without any stress and eradicates the requirement to burry cable wires through floors and walls. The two main essential components in a WLAN are Wireless Access Points (WAPs) and Wireless Clients. A WAP is mounted as base stations for the WLAN and transmit and accept radio wave frequencies from wireless clients to link with Internet. On the other hand, wireless clients can be any interrelated apparatus device such as palmtops, PDA, and fixed workstations that have a Network Interface Card [3].

A WLAN can be designed in both ad-hoc and infrastructure method. An ad-hoc WLAN mode permits wireless clients to link directly to each other to share different types of data [4]. The ad-hoc mode does not entail a WAP. Therefore, in ad-hoc mode, the wireless clients link and interconnect straight to each other by utilizing the wireless client device like PCI, PC card adapters, etc. This mode is recognized by numerous wireless clients, which have a similar Service Set Identifier (SSID) and radio channel for peer-to-peer message mode. In addition to this, every wireless client communicates directly with other wireless client. Figure 8.2 illustrates an abstract view of wireless ad-hoc network.

On the other hand, in an infrastructure mode, every wireless client talks to other wireless client via WAP. The wireless client can be on the network of similar WLAN or linked to other outside network through the WAP [5]. Figure 8.3 highlights the view of infrastructure mode of WLAN. In addition to this, every wireless station can simultaneously operate in the ad-hoc as well as infrastructure mode. This type of network is known as a mixed network or Extended Basic Service Set (EBSS). Figure 8.4 shows an abstract view of wireless fixed network.

8.1.4 Wireless Protocol Stack

The WLAN protocol stack is aimed such that prevailing applications can utilize them with slight modifications. The uppermost three layers of the WLAN protocol stack are identical as the additional networks. Figure 8.5 presents an overview of protocol stack for WLAN.

8.1.5 IEEE 802.11 Standards

Table 8.1 sums up numerous characteristics of IEEE 802.11 standards [6,7]. The table also covers an explanation, comments, and overall accessibility present in each IEEE 802.11 standard.

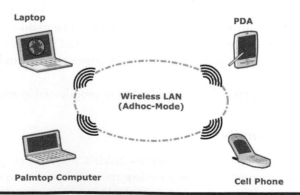

Figure 8.2 Abstract view of wireless ad-hoc network.

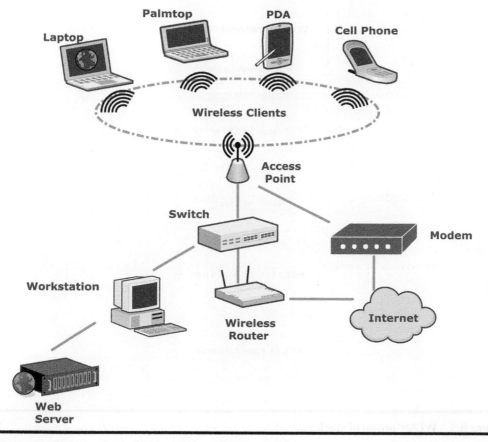

Figure 8.3 Abstract view of infrastructure mode of WLAN.

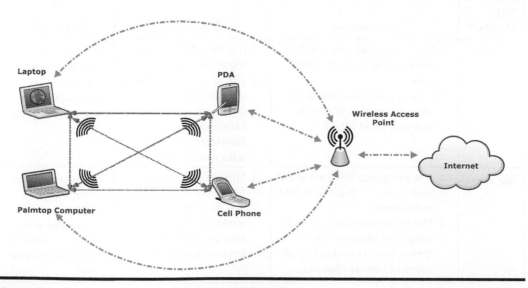

Figure 8.4 Abstract view of wireless fixed network.

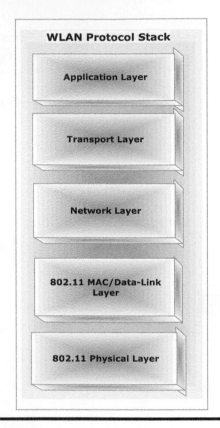

Figure 8.5   WLAN protocol stack.

Table 8.1   Summary of IEEE 802.11 Standards

IEEE Standard	Explanation	Comments	Accessibility
802.11a	1. It is a physical criterion that is executed in 5 GHz radio band. 2. It incorporates eight radio channels with a maximum link rate of 54 Mbps.	1. It generally delivers higher performance. 2. The increased number of radio channels facilitates optimized protection against interference from adjacent access points.	The related standard product has been accessible from the market since 1999.
802.11b	1. It is a physical layer standard that operates in 2.4 GHz ISM radio band. 2. The maximum link rate is 11 Mbps per channel. The throughput is utilized by all users of similar channel.	1. The overall data rate degrades as the distance between the wireless clients and access points goes beyond the limit.	This product was completed in 1999. Several related products are accessible in the market since 2001.

(Continued)

Table 8.1 (*Continued*)   Summary of IEEE 802.11 Standards

IEEE Standard	Explanation	Comments	Accessibility
802.11d	1. This product is treated as an additional component to the MAC layer in 802.11 for the efficient utilization of 802.11 WLAN by the global users. 2. The main rationale behind this standard is to operate lawfully by following some of its rules and restrictions within the boundary of the country.	1. It is well accepted worldwide in those countries depending on the requirements of physical layer radio.	This standard was completed in 2001. Several related products are accessible from the market since then.
802.11e	1. This standard is treated as an additional support to the MAC layer for QOS feature in several applications of WLAN. 2. The main motto is to facilitate the WLAN users with QOS-enabled audio and video web applications.	1. This QOS-enabled feature standard provides some useful benefits for differentiating various levels of traffic streams, especially audio and video streams.	This standard was completed in 2005, and it is available in market now.
802.11f	1. The key aim of this standard is to facilitate AP interoperability within a multi-vendor WLAN. 2. This standard performs an interchange of useful data between several APs, when a wireless client is shifted from one access point to another.	1. This standard provides good quality of handover operation to facilitate multi-vendor infrastructures.	This standard product was finished in 2003, and it is available in the market now.

8.2 Authentication Mechanism in WLAN

WLAN specifies two authentication mechanisms: open system authentication and shared system authentication [8,9].

8.2.1 Open System Authentication

This authentication system does not provide security at all. A wireless client station requests SSID for an effective association. If any new wireless client approaches within the EBSS zone, it will be facilitated with one SSID. Figure 8.6 highlights WLAN open system authentication.

8.2.2 Shared System Authentication

In this authentication system, a wireless client station cannot authenticate automatically unless the wireless client does not possess Wired Equivalent Privacy (WEP)-shared secret key. WEP protocol

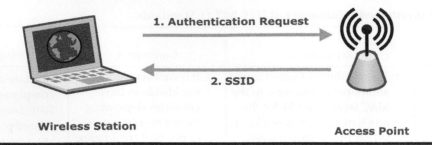

Figure 8.6   WLAN open system authentication.

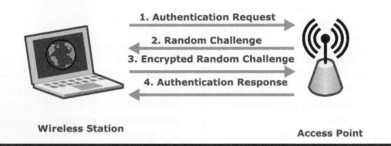

Figure 8.7   WLAN shared system authentication.

is utilized for encryption of messages shared between the wireless station and the access point. Figure 8.7 shows the view of WLAN shared system authentication.

8.2.3 *Vulnerabilities of WLAN*

A link to a WLAN is established via a WAP (also known as AP). Any workstation with a WLAN card that is inside the range of the WLAN can endeavor to link to the wireless network. For home-based clients, this depicts that neighbors can directly gain access to the WLAN if it is not safeguarded. WLAN security is still a puzzling issue for both the trade and industries. An open WLAN is vulnerable to attackers, resulting in theft which possibly could destruct an industry or an individual if crucial statistics are stolen [10].

The notion of war driving exemplifies the easiness with which unsolicited people can come into your WLAN if it is not protected [11]. War drivers move around many places in a car, examining for open WLAN via laptop or palmtop [13]. Not every war drivers always link to your WLAN, but they could start if they start hunting for. As soon as they discover an unsafe WLAN, they link to get it, gaze all over the place, utilize your WLAN connection, and flow on to the subsequent unsafe WLAN. This type of uninvited use is not safe all the times. But you must select if you desire to leave your WLAN and/or WLAN link exposed to other visitors.

A broadly used method of WLAN is "Encryption." Encryption is a technique to encrypt data beforehand it is transmitted over the network so that it is unreadable to attackers. A distinct key phrase is utilized to decode the info once data is received. Fragile encryption categories are already proven to be moderately informal as an attacker can acquire the key phrase and gain admittance to your WLAN. It is consequently recommended to utilize the toughest possible encryption category that a WLAN apparatus could support.

8.3 Encryption on a WLAN

WAP generally provides numerous categories of encryption. These algorithms scramble documents beforehand it is sent over the WLAN, creating it indecipherable to the attackers [12]. Encryption can effectively mend the safety of your WLAN. Most WAPs for home-based use provide the following two categories of encryption [14,15]. Presently, they are the utmost collective categories of encryption techniques. Figure 8.8 illustrates several types of WLAN encryption techniques. Both WEP and Wi-Fi Protected Access (WPA) have several subtypes that each deals with a diverse level of safety.

8.3.1 WEP Encryption

It is a slightly fragile category of encryption; however, it is presented in almost all WAPs [15]. This encryption is frequently measured to be weak option for an appropriate safety of WLAN. It is comparatively simple to guess WEP key by utilizing several programs like Airsnort, etc. A WEP key comprises two portions. First is a shared key, which is identical for all computers in the WLAN, and the next is an initialization vector (IV). The IV is a flexible portion of the key which is of length 24 bits slightly smaller for WEP. It naturally consumes a comparatively smaller time as similar IV is utilized for several times. In a busy WLAN, an attacker may examine the match between these packets and discern their mutual value: the shared key. In addition to this, WEP does not encode headers of the packets, making them clear to anybody in the range of WLANs.

8.3.2 WPA Encryption

WPA resolves the problem of weak headers. By utilizing autonomous rekeying technique, the Temporal Key Integrity protocol of WPA occasionally alters the key value that is utilized to encode the document, making it difficult for the attackers to discover resemblances between messages in transit.

8.3.3 AES Encryption

The hardest encryption category currently available is the so-called Advanced Encryption Standards (AESs) or "Rijndael" encoding procedure. The American government has selected AES encryption algorithm as conventional standard for safeguarding delicate information in all government organizations. AES is presently the robust category of encryption technique for WLAN.

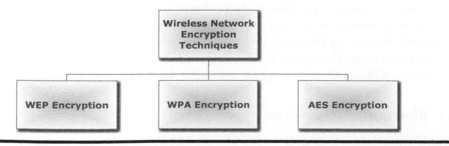

Figure 8.8 WLAN encryption techniques.

Table 8.2   Tools for Attacking the WLAN

WLAN Attack Tools	Operating System	Description
WEPCrack	Linux	Breaks the WEP Key
Airsnort	Linux	Cracks the WEP key
NetStumbler	Windows	Reveals the sensitive network parameters
Kismet	Linux	A WLAN Sniffer
Thc-Wardrive	Linux	Utilized for war driving
Dstumbler	FreeBSD	Similar version of netstumbler
Dsniff	Linux	Corresponding counterpart of netstumbler

8.3.4 Tools for Attacking the WLAN

Table 8.2 lists some of the tools for exploiting vulnerabilities of WLANs.

8.3.5 WLAN Threats

As many administrations have deployed WLAN and as current utilization is expected to raise, it is critical for them to study and recognize the categories of vulnerabilities in a WLAN [16, 17, 30–40]. Therefore, administrations need to comprehend the threats before deploying the WLAN by performing supplementary studies in identifying the risks linked with a WLAN. Figure 8.9 illustrates some of the threats associated with WLANs.

8.4 Bluetooth Ad-Hoc Network

Bluetooth wireless technology is generally utilized for small-range radio frequency (RF) communication message in creating Personal Area Networks (PANs). This technology has been incorporated into several categories of commercial and customer equipment, which comprises smart phones, laptops, mice, headsets, etc. This scheme allows the users to create ad-hoc networks between a several range of equipment to transmit voice and files. Bluetooth offers a mechanism designed for generating small wireless networks on an ad-hoc basis, called as piconets [18]. A piconet is a collection of two to eight Bluetooth gadgets in physical nearness that run on the similar channel by utilizing the same frequency hopping sequence. An example of a piconet is a Bluetooth-reliant association between a headset and a smartphone.

Bluetooth piconets are frequently formed on a provisional and dynamic base, which delivers communications tractability and scalability between numerous smart phones. Several important characteristics of Bluetooth technology are as listed in Table 8.3.

8.4.1 Bluetooth Architecture

Bluetooth technology allows gadgets to create an ad-hoc network that permits easy establishment of links between the gadgets in the same physical location deprived of employing any

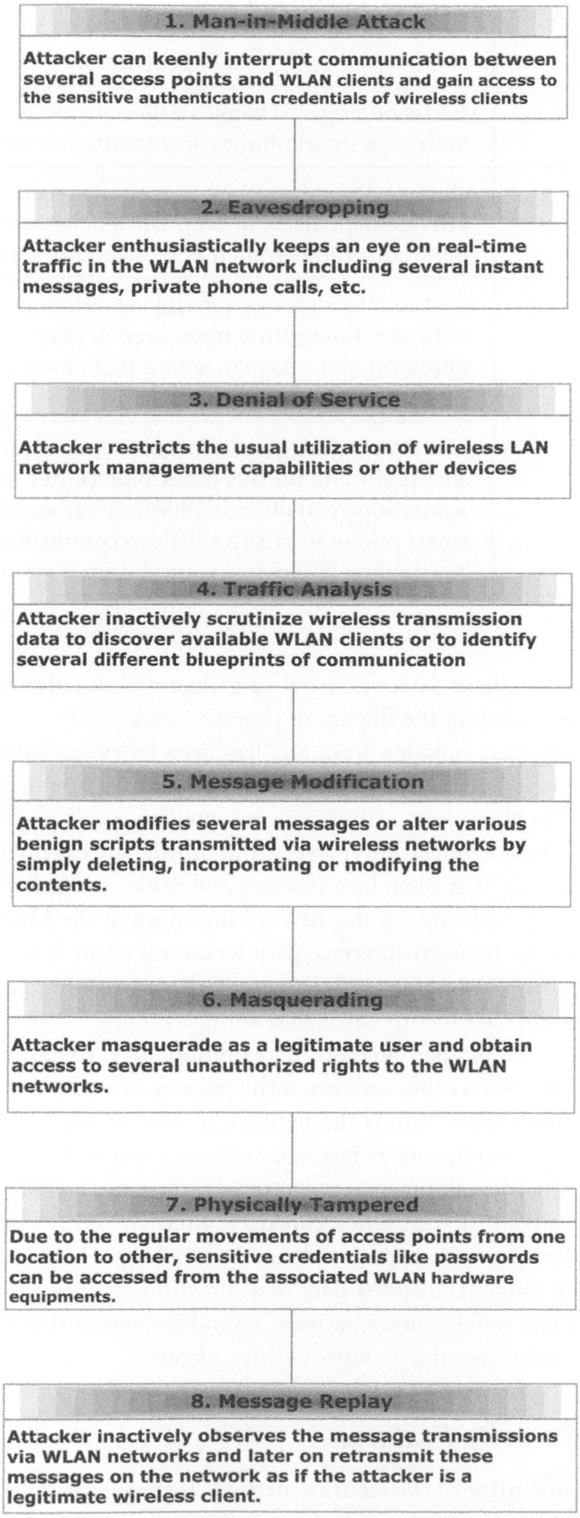

1. Man-in-Middle Attack

Attacker can keenly interrupt communication between several access points and WLAN clients and gain access to the sensitive authentication credentials of wireless clients

2. Eavesdropping

Attacker enthusiastically keeps an eye on real-time traffic in the WLAN network including several instant messages, private phone calls, etc.

3. Denial of Service

Attacker restricts the usual utilization of wireless LAN network management capabilities or other devices

4. Traffic Analysis

Attacker inactively scrutinize wireless transmission data to discover available WLAN clients or to identify several different blueprints of communication

5. Message Modification

Attacker modifies several messages or alter various benign scripts transmitted via wireless networks by simply deleting, incorporating or modifying the contents.

6. Masquerading

Attacker masquerade as a legitimate user and obtain access to several unauthorized rights to the WLAN networks.

7. Physically Tampered

Due to the regular movements of access points from one location to other, sensitive credentials like passwords can be accessed from the associated WLAN hardware equipments.

8. Message Replay

Attacker inactively observes the message transmissions via WLAN networks and later on retransmit these messages on the network as if the attacker is a legitimate wireless client.

Figure 8.9   WLAN encryption techniques.

Table 8.3   Important Characteristics of Bluetooth Technology

Characteristics	Description
Cable replacement	This technology exchanges a diversity of cables, like those earlier utilized in smart phones, keyboards, mouse, headsets, etc.
Easiness of Data Sharing	A Bluetooth-empowered gadget can create a piconet to provide data distribution proficiencies with several other Bluetooth gadgets such as PCs and notebooks.
Wireless Synchronization	Bluetooth technology can deliver automated management between Bluetooth-empowered gadgets. For instance, Bluetooth permits management of contact info enclosed in e-address records and diaries.
Internet Connectivity	A Bluetooth gadget with Internet connection can share that access with numerous other Bluetooth gadgets. For example, a notebook can utilize a Bluetooth association to redirect a smart phone to create a dial-up connection and subsequently a notebook could access the Internet via smart phone.

infrastructure. A Bluetooth client device is merely a gadget with a radio and software and their corresponding interfaces including the Bluetooth protocol stack.

The Bluetooth design offers isolation from any liabilities by executing stack utilities between a client and a device controller. The client host, commonly known as a master, is accountable for upper-layer protocols. The client host utilities are executed in a cell phone or a notebook. The device controller is accountable for the lower layers, and utilities are executed through a combined USB adapter of the Bluetooth. The client host (master) and device controller transmit the information to all others (slaves) by utilizing regular networking through the Host Controller Interface. This regular Host Controller (master) Interface permits several client hosts and device controllers (slaves) from diverse retailers to interoperate. In many other circumstances, both the client host and device controller utilities are incorporated into a single gadget.

Figure 8.10 illustrates the simple Bluetooth network topology. In a piconet, one gadget functions as a master by using several other gadgets in the piconet, which are called "slaves".

The master gadget governs and forms the network by broadcasting the network's frequency hopping sequence. Though merely one gadget can assist as a master for every piconet, time division multiplexing permits a slave in one piconet to serve as a master for other piconet, thus constituting a number of networks [19]. This series, called a scatternet, permits interaction of numerous other gadgets in a wider space to support a dynamic topology which could be altered in any specified period. Since a gadget transports data in a direction away from the master gadget, the topology might modify due to interaction between several gadgets of this instantaneous network. Figure 8.11 illustrates a scatternet that comprises three piconets.

8.4.2 Bluetooth Security Features

This segment presents an outline of the security methods incorporated in the Bluetooth specifications by exemplifying their drawbacks and offer advantages in terms of security endorsements. Figure 8.12 illustrates the security infrastructure of the Bluetooth radio. The following instance of

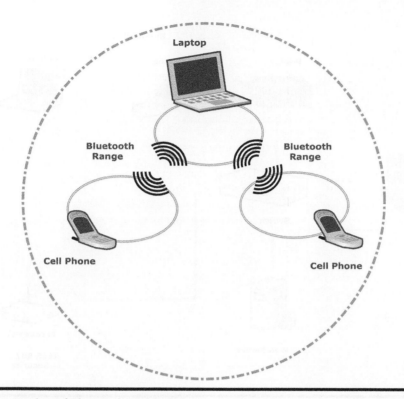

Figure 8.10   Design of Bluetooth architecture.

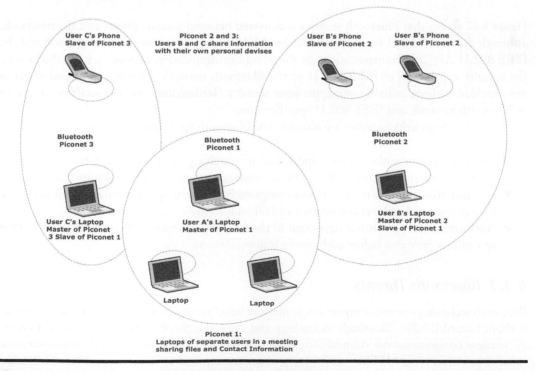

Figure 8.11   Multiple scatternets of Bluetooth architecture.

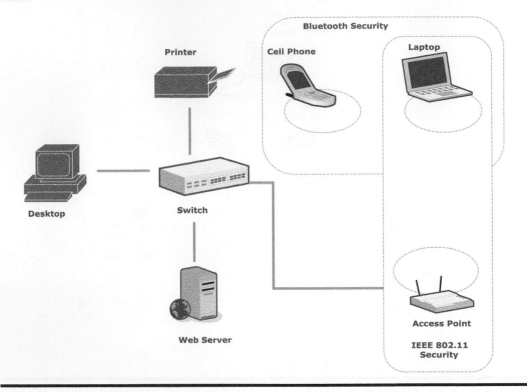

Figure 8.12   Setup of Bluetooth security infrastructure.

Figure 8.12 shows that Bluetooth security is delivered between a smart phone and the notebook, although the IEEE 802.11 security defends the WLAN association between the notebook and the IEEE 802.11 AP [20]. Transportations on the wired communication network are not shielded by the security capabilities of IEEE 802.11 or the Bluetooth network. Hence, end-to-end safety is not provided without utilizing any upper-layer security clarifications over the security structures of Bluetooth network and IEEE 802.11 specifications.

Three simple security facilities are stated in the Bluetooth specifications of the standard:

■ **Authentication:** authenticating individual interactive gadgets is created by their specific address of Bluetooth gadget. Bluetooth technology does not offer inherent user verification.
■ **Confidentiality:** thwarting data loss instigated by eavesdropping through confirming that merely approved gadgets can retrieve and outlook transferred information.
■ **Authorization:** permitting restriction of the assets by confirming that a gadget is certified to utilize a provision before authorizing it to perform so.

8.4.3 Bluetooth Threats

Bluetooth technology provides numerous profits and benefits; however, the profits are not delivered without hazard [19,20]. Bluetooth technology and their associated gadgets are exposed to over-all wireless communication vulnerabilities, like DoS attacks, plain-text modifications, resource misuse, eavesdropping, MITM attacks, etc. and are too exposed by numerous explicit Bluetooth-associated attacks whose illustrations are highlighted in Table 8.4.

Table 8.4 Tools for Attacking the WLAN

Attack	Exploitation
Bluesnarfing	This attack permits the malicious attackers to retrieve the access to a Bluetooth gadget via utilizing a firmware fault in earlier gadgets. This attack makes a link to a Bluetooth gadget, permitting the access to information saved on the gadget containing the gadget's international mobile equipment identity.
Bluejacking	An attacker exploits the bluejacking attack via transmitting unwanted plain-text messages to the client of a Bluetooth-empowered gadget. The real plain-text messages do not produce any loss to the client's device; however, they might lure the client to reply in some manner.
Bluebugging	Bluebugging utilizes a security weakness in the firmware of certain earlier Bluetooth-enabled gadgets to obtain access to the gadget and their commands. This attack utilizes the commands of Bluetooth-enabled gadget devoid of notifying the client, permitting the malicious attacker to retrieve the information, transmit the messages, and exploit additional facilities or features accessible by the gadget.
Car Whisperer	Car Whisperer [21] is a tool designed by European security investigators that utilizes a key implementation problem in hands-free Bluetooth tools mounted in cars. The Car Whisperer tool permits a malicious attacker to transmit to or obtain audio from the car tools. A malicious attacker could transfer the audio to the speakers of the car or obtain audio from the microphone in the car.
Denial of Service	Comparable to other wireless technologies, Bluetooth technology is vulnerable to DoS attacks. Effects comprise creating a device's Bluetooth interface inoperative and exhausting the gadget's battery.
Fuzzing Attacks	Bluetooth fuzzing attacks comprise transmitting twisted or else non-average information to a gadget's Bluetooth radio and perceiving how the gadget responds. If a gadget's task is slowed down or clogged via such attacks, a severe susceptibility possibly occurs in the protocol stack.
Paring Eavesdropping	LE Pairing (Bluetooth 4.0) is vulnerable to eavesdropping attacks. The popular eavesdropper who gathers all coupling frames could decide the top-secret key given in an appropriate period, which permits trustworthy device imitation and data decoding.
Secure Simple Pairing Attacks	Several wide varieties of practices can provoke a distant gadget to utilize any pairing method and then try to exploit the man-in-the-middle attack. Moreover, static keys can permit a malicious attacker to execute man-in-the-middle attacks as well.

8.4.4 WiMAX Security

WiMAX is based on the IEEE 802.16 standard which offers wireless communication of information by means of communication ways and provides complete access to mobile Internet. The WiMAX is maintained by the WiMAX environment that is a nonrevenue association designed to encourage the acceptance of WiMAX well-suited commodities and amenities. It supports a very capable skill using several key types. For example, WiMAX system has the proficiency of operating on numerous open access bands: 2.3, 2.5 GHz, etc., and delivers flexibility by using high data rates. It correspondingly offers robust security and resilient Quality of Service (QOS)-based facilities for numerous categories of data. However, to attain a development level in WiMAX and turn out to be an effective expertise, additional investigation on security risks and explanation to these risks are needed.

8.5 IEEE 802.16 Protocol Design Architecture

The IEEE 802.16 protocol design architecture is organized into two main layers: the Medium Access Control (MAC) layer and the Physical (PHY) layer, which is shown in Figure 8.13.

MAC layer comprises three main sub-layers. The primary sub-layer is Service-Specific Convergence Sub-layer (CS) that transforms higher-level information services to MAC layer service movement and links [22]. The next subsequent sub-layer is a Common Part Sub-layer (CPS) that is central to this standard as well as strongly tied to security sub-layer. This layer describes the policies and several procedures for method access, bandwidth distribution, and linking management. The MAC protocol is located in this sub-layer. The final sub-layer of MAC layer is the Security Sub-layer that is placed between the MAC CPS and the PHY layer, addressing the verification, key formation and exchange, encryption, and decryption of data swapped between the MAC and PHY layers.

The PHY layer offers a two-way transformation between the MAC protocol data units and the PHY layer frames communicated via coding of several RF signals.

8.5.1 WiMAX Security Solutions

By understanding the finest expertise available nowadays, the WiMAX has been designed on the foundation of IEEE 802.16e standard that offers robust provision for validation, key administration, encoding and decoding, mechanism and administration of plain-text defense, and security procedure optimization [23]. In WiMAX, all of the security problems are reported and controlled in the MAC security sub-layer, which is shown in Figure 8.14.

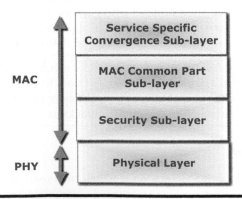

Figure 8.13 IEEE 802.16 protocol architecture.

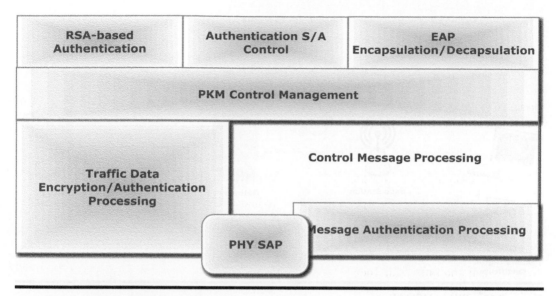

Figure 8.14 MAC security sub-layer.

Two key objects in WiMAX, together with Base Station (BS) and Subscriber Station (SS), are secured via resulting WiMAX safety features.

8.5.2 Security Association

A Security Association (SA) is a category of security-related constraints that a BS and one or more of its client SSs commonly acquire known as Mobile Stations (MSs). Each SA has its own specific identifier (SAID) and comprises a cryptographic suite identifier, encryption keys, and IVs.

8.5.2.1 Public Key Infrastructure

WiMAX utilizes the Privacy and Key Management (PKM) protocol regarding safe key administration, transmission, and interchange between several MSs. This protocol likewise validates an MS to a BS. The PKM utilizes X.509 digital certificates, Rivest, Shamir, Aldeman (RSA) algorithm, and a robust encoding algorithm (AES). The first draft kind of WiMAX utilizes PKMv1 which is a one-way validation technique as well as includes a threat for man-in-the-middle attack. To handle this problem in the advanced version 802.16e, the PKMv2 was utilized to deliver two-way validation procedures. Figure 8.15 highlights the general idea of Public Key Infrastructure (PKI) in WiMAX.

8.5.2.2 Device/User Authentication

WiMAX provides three categories of authentication that are controlled in the security sub-layer. The primary category is RSA-based authentication that utilizes X.509 certificates along with RSA encoding scheme. The X.509 certificate is allotted by the SS producer and encompasses the SS's public key and their associated MAC address. On demanding an authorization key, the SS transmits their certificate to the BS, and the BS certifies the digital certificate and then utilizes the

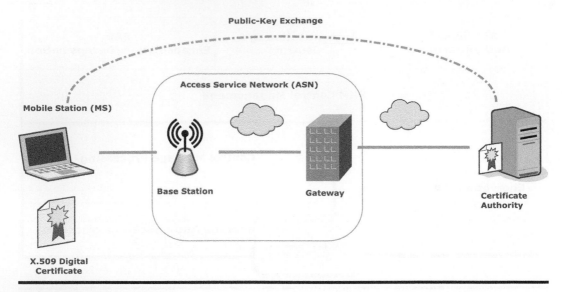

Figure 8.15   PKI in WiMAX.

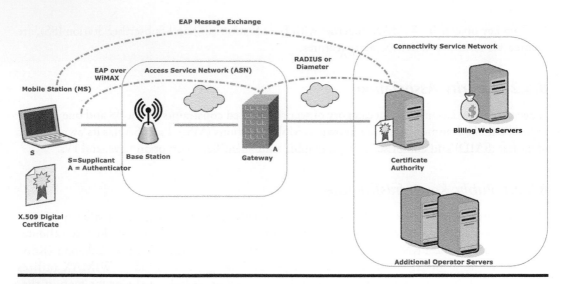

Figure 8.16   EAP-based authentication.

certified public key to encode an authorization key and transferred it to the SS. The second category is Extensive Authentication Protocol-based authentication (shown in Figure 8.16) in which the SS is verified through X.509 certificate. The final category of authentication is the RSA-based authentication monitored by the EAP authentication.

8.5.2.3 Authorization

Subsequent to the validation step is the authorization procedure in which SS demands for an Authentication Key as well as SAID from the BS via transferring an Authorization Request communication message. This communication message contains SS's X.509 digital certificate, encoding algorithms and cryptographic identifier [24]. The BS then interacts with an authentication web server to certify the request through the SS and transmits back an Authorization Reply message that incorporates the Authentication Key encoded with the SS's public key, a lifetime key and an Service Authentication Identifiers.

8.5.2.4 Data Privacy and Integrity

WiMAX utilizes the AES algorithm for encoding of plain-text messages. The AES secret message is stated as a quantity of reiterations of alteration sequences which transform the plain-text message into the concluding output of secret message [25,26]. All rounds comprise numerous handling phases and are based on the encoding key. A category of converse series is utilized to convert cipher message into novel plain-text message via the similar encoding key. As Data Encryption Standard algorithm provides no further enough protection, AES algorithm is suggested in WiMAX through several reinforced methods [27–29].

8.5.2.5 WiMAX Security Vulnerabilities and Countermeasures

Exploitation techniques of WiMAX attacks and their solutions are listed in Table 8.5.

Table 8.5 Exploitation Techniques of WiMAX Attacks and Their Solutions

Attack	Exploitation	Solution
Jamming attack	This attack can be accomplished by bringing together a cause of noise resilient enough to considerably shrink capability of the network.	We can thwart this attack by growing the influence of signals or the bandwidth of signals by utilizing spreading practices. For example, direct sequence spread spectrum.
Scrambling attack	Scrambling is a category of jamming attack, however, simply triggered for small intermissions of period and targeted for explicit WiMAX frames or portions of frames in the physical layer.	As scrambling is discontinuous, it is additionally challenging to discover scrambling as compared to a jamming attack. In a practical situation, a user can utilize the variances observed beyond the performance standard to discover scramblers.
Water torture attack	A malicious attacker forces an SS to consume its battery or computing resources via transmitting a sequence of spurious frames. This attack is well-thought-out even additional harsh than a usual DoS attack as an SS that is typically movable device, is expected to possess inadequate resources.	To thwart such category of attack, a refined mechanism is needed to remove spurious frames, therefore circumventing any shortage of adequate resources.

(Continued)

Table 8.5 (*Continued*)   Exploitation Techniques of WiMAX Attacks and Their Solutions

Attack	Exploitation	Solution
Forgery and replay attack	802.16 is also susceptible to forgery attacks in which a malicious attacker possessing a suitable radio receiver can write to a wireless station. In the mesh mode, 802.16 is also exposed to replay attacks in which a malicious attacker retransmits effective frames which the attacker has captured in the mid of previous transmission.	WiMAX has addressed this security weakness of 802.16 by delivering shared authentication to guard against both categories of attacks.
Masquerading attack	Masquerade attack is a kind of attack in which one station predicts the identity of another station.	WiMAX provides one-sided, scheme-level authentication which is a X.509 digital certificate dependent authentication. This digital certificate can be automated in a device through the manufacturer.
Man-in-the-middle attack (MIMA)	MIMA necessitates a malicious attacker to possess the capability of observing and inserting messages into a network station.	Though WiMAX can thwart MIMA attack through rogue BS by utilizing PKMv2, it is still exposed to MIMA attack.

8.6 Concluding Remarks

With recent advances in wireless technology, WLAN has created an equal amount of prospects and threats. These radical changes can exemplify a great accomplishment to an administration's networking competence, permitting enhanced employee efficiency and decreasing IT expenses. To minimize the associated dangers, IT supervisors can device a variety of methods, comprising of confirming several policies for wireless security, researches, as well as carrying out implementation of several designs of LAN and implementation. Achieving this level of prospects and threats permits organizations to assertively deploy WLAN technology and recognize the advantages this progressive technology offers. The security of WLAN will drive to a far distance. Additional incentives to initiate several standards that are vigorous and deliver sufficient safety are required. In this chapter, we have presented basic terminologies of WLAN, comprising traditional versions, its numerous components, their different operating modes, protocol stacks, and several WLAN standards. There are numerous WLAN threats, emerging vulnerabilities in Bluetooth ad-hoc network and several open issues in WiMAX security. It is significant that customers must recognize the WLAN technology and the associated threats involved in the utilization thereof. Most of these vulnerabilities can be simply alleviated by following explicit security guidelines when it comes to the use of WLAN ad-hoc network capabilities.

Key Terminology and Definitions

Cyberattacks: Cyberattacks are the attacks that are carried through Internet that are targeted on individual machine, servers of corporation or government, military services with the aim of gaining private information, altering or destroying important data, or just creating havoc. These attacks are carried out by spreading malwares, phishing websites, or any other means of stealing private information. Some attacks are done just for pleasure and satisfaction purpose, and the other types of attacks are done for acquiring some important information or having financial gain. Another way for categorizing the cyberattacks are denial-of-service attacks that achieves the unavailability of the services for legitimate users and targeted attack that are concentrated on one particular organization, service providers and try to obtain the private, technical, or institutional information. Some of the attacks are very persistent and are targeted on particular entity. Such kinds of attacks are called as advanced persistent threat. These advanced persistent threats may include attacks that are carried out through social media or e-mails containing malicious programs.

Contribution of the malwares in the world of cyberattacks is more than any other cyberattack. Malwares include computer viruses, worms, Trojan horse, etc. Another major type of cyberattack is insider criminal's attack, which means attack is carried out onto the servers and private data by the employees or internal workers of the victim company. Data breaching, which includes unauthorized access of private data, is also a great danger. SQL injection is also another type of attack that is made on applications that are database driven. Malicious SQL code is inserted into the input field to perform malicious activity. Phishing attack is done by mimicking the websites interface where the attacker tries to acquire the user's credentials or tries to acquire financial gain. The following sections discuss these various cyberattacks in detail.

Malwares: Malware is a software or piece of software that is used to interrupt the normal behavior of the computer system for gaining important private information from the victim machine. Malware is the short form of malicious software, and it can penetrate into the victim's system in the form of executables. These are downloaded from the websites or from attractive ads intentionally or unintentionally by the victim. These include computer viruses, worms, spywares, and Trojans.

Computer Virus: Computer viruses are malicious programs that are written to replicate themselves into multiple modified copies without the user's knowledge and harm the victim's computer by altering, damaging, or deleting important data; occupying hard disk space or consuming processor's time; accessing private information; and displaying irrelevant message on the computer screen. They enter into a victim's computer via malicious e-mails, instant message services, downloads on the Internet as an attachment of images, audio or video files, or hidden in free or trial software programs. Therefore, it is always advisable not to open the e-mail attachments if the source of the e-mail is not known. Most of the viruses are attached with some legitimate-looking executable programs, and when they are run by the user, viruses become active. Therefore, viruses cannot spread in a computer system without the involvement of its user, such as opening the executable file.

File Virus: File virus is attached with the binary executable files or .COM files. Once this virus stays in memory, it tries to infect all programs that load on to memory.

Macro Virus: Some of the applications such as Microsoft Word, Excel, or PowerPoint allow macro to be added in the document so that when document is opened that macro code is automatically executed. Macro virus is written in macro code and is spread when such infected document is opened. Once infected, repairing these files is very much difficult.

Master boot record Virus: Master boot record (MBR) is the record of the information regarding the operating system's location so that it can be booted from that location. MBR virus infects MBR information and creates problems in the booting procedure. To remove the virus from system, MBR area is cleared from the disk.

Multipartite Virus: It is the combination of MBR virus and file virus. It is attached to the binary executable file at an initial stage. When user runs this file, virus gets inserted inside the boot record and when next time computer is booted, virus is loaded into memory and infects other files and programs on computer.

Polymorphic Viruses: These types of viruses change their forms each time they attach on the system. This property of these viruses makes them very difficult to detect and find cure for them.

Stealth Viruses: These viruses affect the files, directory entries of file systems, disk head movement, etc. Their effect is hidden from the user's perspective, but it affects the memory storage or processing speed.

Computer Worms: Worms are the types of malware that spreads across the computer and network by self-replication. Computer worms are different from the computer viruses, as they are not attached to any files; they do not need anyone to trigger their spreading; and generally they do not harm any file or program, but they consume a large amount of memory or network bandwidth. Many worms that have been created are designed only to spread, but they do not attempt to change the systems they pass through. They use communication networks for sending a large volume of data to other computers. This consumes bandwidth which may result in deleting or discarding files. It may also harm the computer by sending documents via e-mail. In November 2008, computer worm named Conficker was detected in Microsoft Windows operating system. It used the flaws in Windows operating system dictionary and attacked administrator passwords to propagate. It formed botnet to attack from distributed sources. It used many advanced malware techniques which made finding any efficient cure for fighting against Conficker harder. It infected millions of computers from over 200 countries.

Spyware: Spyware is another type of malware which gathers private and confidential information from victim's machine without their knowledge or consent. Information collected may vary significantly as per the motivation of the attacker. Information may include the web browsing history which may be the password of the victim. It may change computer's desktop and system files. It may have the ability to store the keystroke information and send it to the third party for gaining business-related information or for having financial gain. Spywares are bundled with other free downloadable software applications to enter and infect a computer machine. Another way of infecting with spywares is pop-up ads that are displayed on various websites. They show the message box that looks like Windows box and no matter which button gets clicked spyware gets installed on victim's machine. Spyware is difficult to remove and detect. It can reinstall itself even after it appeared to be removed. Therefore, it is advisable to have installed good anti-spyware software and update the Windows security updates time to time and always scan for spywares. Adware, which is a type of spyware, also accomplishes the same thing that spyware does. It shows the unwanted pop-ups for advertisement or banners on computer screen and attracts the user to click on them. Adwares are also called as Advertising Supported Software.

Trojan Horse: Trojan horse is a type of malware which provides unauthorized and remote access to a user's machine. They do not spread by replicating themselves like computer viruses and worms, but they have the ability to open the gates for viruses that are installed since the attacker has the remote access to the computer with the help of Trojan. The term Trojan came from old Greek war story. Greek offered Trojan horse, a large wooden horse, as a peace offering to the city of Troy. When the night fell, soldiers, those were hidden in the horse, opened the gate for the army waiting outside to attack the city. The function of Trojan malwares is almost the same. It first enters the computer machine with legitimate-looking application program. Then, it gives the unauthorized remote access to the attacker, and then the attacker attacks on the machine as mentioned above. It steals the information that is very much confidential to the user like credit card information, e.g. password. It may install other malware causing system to go in havoc. It may also install keyloggers that log the information of keys pressed. Attacker can search the infected computer with Trojan by simply performing port scanning.

Backdoor: Backdoor attack is a malware that bypasses the security authentication in the computer system and offers unauthorized remote access to the attacker.

Rootkit: Rootkit is another type of malware that enables privileged access to the computer while hiding the existence of certain processes and programs. Once the attacker has administrator access or root access to the computer, he can obtain the confidential information which was otherwise not possible to access with simple user access.

Logic Bombs: Logic bombs starts infecting the system when certain conditions are satisfied. It is a piece of code that remains hidden until desired circumstances are not met. For example, on some particular day, it will start showing messages or start deleting the files, etc.

Denial of Service: Denial-of-service attack compromises service availability by sending voluminous data to the server that is supposed to work for other legitimate requests. Victim server becomes unavailable to work for other users and gets busy in servicing the attacker's packets. Also, some attacker sends malicious requests so that system's resources overflow with the data and then tries to drop the packets belonging to the legitimate users.

Distributed Denial of Service: Distributed denial-of-service (DDoS) attack is a dangerous and disastrous type of attack which is targeted from distributed source instead of single source as in the case of DoS attack. In DDoS, attacker creates its army to attack in the form of bots or zombies. The network of such zombies is called as botnet. All these bots are instructed to attack on victim at the same time, to cripple down the victim's functionality. They use the resources provided by the server and try to overflow them. Target resources may include processing element, memory storage, or even the network in which it works. If victim server does not have enough resources to fulfill these requirements, then that server may become slow and unavailable to other users. There are various types of DoS attacks performed through Internet. Some of them are SYN Flood, XML-DoS, HTTP-DoS, ICMP-DoS, and Teardrop attack.

Phishing: Phishing is a type of cyberattack in which attacker creates an entity such as bank website, social media website, or online payment-processing website that is exactly similar in look as legitimate website. Then, attacker makes the user to enter the confidential information such as bank account password and credit card information, and uses the information for his financial gain or any other motive. Phishing is carried out with the help of spam e-mails or instant messaging services and are sent in bulk to thousands of users. Users are made attracted to such phishing e-mails by announcing, for example, they may get a reward of money if they login to their bank website, but once logged in, the webpage of phishing website gets opened.

In 2003, many eBay users suffered from phishing attack. eBay users received e-mails in which attackers claimed that the user's eBay account was about to be suspended unless they clicked on the provided link and updated the credit card information that the genuine eBay already had. The scam counted on people being tricked into thinking they were actually being contacted by eBay and were subsequently going to eBay's site to update their account information. More than 160 people fell for this scam. In 2012, Syrian activists attempted to perform phishing attack on Facebook to steal username and password of the Facebook users.

Cross-Site Scripting (XSS): Cross-site scripting (XSS) is a type of computer security vulnerability typically found in web applications. XSS refers to the hacking technique that makes use of vulnerabilities in the code of a web application to allow hacker to send malicious content from an end-user and collect some type of data from the victim. Web applications that take input from user side and then generate output without performing any validation are vulnerable to such attacks. Attacker injects client-side script into web pages that are accessed by other users. When browser of that user executes the script, it may perform malicious activities, like access cookies, session tokens, or other sensitive information that is supposed to remain with the user.

Man-in-the-Middle Attack: The man-in-the-middle attack is a form of active eavesdropping. Attacker makes independent connections with the victims and relays messages between them, making them believe that they are talking directly to each other. But, in fact, the entire conversation is controlled by the attacker. Consider victims A and B are communicating with each other about bank transaction and attacker is eavesdropping on their communication. A may send the message to transfer an amount of Rs. 1000 to user C. Attacker gets this message, and it will change the content of the message to transfer the money to attacker's account. Victim B won't be having any idea about the changes made in transit and consider that message is sent by A and carry out the transferring of the money.

Spoofing: In spoofing attack, one person or program pretends to be another user or another device and then tries to perform some malicious activities like launching denial-of-service attacks, stealing data, spreading virus or worms, bypassing access controls, etc. There are various types of spoofing techniques like IP spoofing, ARP spoofing, DNS server spoofing, and e-mail address spoofing.

IP Spoofing: IP address spoofing is the most common and widely used spoofing among other spoofing attack types. Attacker spoofs the source address of the attack packet with other IP address. So, when attack is detected, true source of the attack packet could not be found out. For example, in the case of DDoS attack, a large number of attack packets are sent to the victim server with spoofed source address. Another way of IP spoofing is to spoof the target address. When service packets are replied back to target address, they go to the spoofed address, i.e., the address of victim.

ARP Spoofing: Address resolution protocol (ARP) is used to resolve IP addresses into link layer addresses when packet is received from outside the network. In ARP spoofing, attacker sends spoofed ARP message across LAN so that link layer address of the attacker gets linked with IP address of some machine in network. This results into redirection of the messages from legitimate source to attacker instead of legitimate destination. Attacker, then, is able to steal information or alter the data that is in transit or prohibit all the traffic that is coming in the LAN. ARP spoofing is also used to perform other types of attacks like DoS, man-in-the-middle attack, session hijacking, etc.

DNS Server Spoofing: Domain Name Server (DNS) maps domain names with IP addresses. When user enters the website address into the browser, it is the responsibility of the DNS to resolve that domain name address into IP address of the server. In DNS spoofing attack, attacker changes entries in the DNS server, so that when user enters the particular website address, it gets redirected to another IP address that generally belongs to attacker or it can also be related to victim to which attacker may want to flood the traffic. Attacker may reply to these messages with malicious programs that are sent to harm the victim's computer.

E-mail Address Spoofing: E-mail address spoofing uses different e-mail address instead of true source of the e-mail. Recipient cannot know the actual sender of the e-mail, since they can only see the spoofed e-mail address. Since Simple Main Transfer Protocol (SMTP) does not provide any proper authentication, attacker is able to perform the e-mail address spoofing. Generally, prevention is assured by making the SMTP client to negotiate with the mail server, but when this prevention is not taken, anyone who is familiar with the mail server can connect to the server and use it to send messages. E-mail information that is stored and forwarded to the recipient can be changed and modified as attacker wants it to be. And therefore, it is possible for the attacker to send the e-mail with spoofed source address.

Zero-Day Attack: Zero-day or day zero attack, vulnerability or exploit is a security hole or security vulnerability in the software, website, or any other application that remained unknown to the vendor until attacker tries to exploit that vulnerability for performing attack. "Zero day" refers to the fact that the attack was unknown to the people, i.e., developer and vendors, and it is the first occurrence of its kind. Zero-day attacks can be applied to insert computer viruses, worms, and spyware, or they may allow unauthorized access to private information. Recently, Adobe Flash Player experienced zero-day attack via malicious advertisements observed in dailymotion.com website. Such new types of attacks are filtered with the help of security update patches that are made available on a regular basis by security provider companies. Therefore, to prohibit the attack from further affecting the system, it is always advisable to update the antivirus patches, browser plug-ins, etc. regularly.

References

1. Caswell, W. Wireless home networks: Disconnected connectivity. *Home Toys*, Apr. 2000. Accessed from: www.hometoys.com/mentors/caswell/apr00/wireless.htm.
2. Conover, J. Wireless LANs work their magic. *Networking Computing*, July 2000. Accessed from: www.networkcomputing.com/1113/1113f2full.html.
3. Molta, D. The road ahead for wireless. Network Computing, July 9, 2001. Accessed from: www.networkcomputing.com/1214/1214colmolta.html.
4. Conover, J. First things first—Top 10 things to know about wireless. *Networking Computing*, July 2000. Accessed from: www.networkcomputing.com/1113/1113f2side2.html.
5. Cox, J. LAN services set to go wireless. *Network World*, Aug. 20, 2001. Accessed from: www.nwfusion.com/news/2001/0820wireless.html.
6. Dornan, A. Emerging technology: Wireless LAN standards. Feb. 6, 2002, NetworkMagazine.com. Accessed from: http://networkmagazine.com/article/NMG20020206S0006.
7. IEEE Working Group for WLAN Standards. Accessed from: http://grouper.ieee.org/groups/802/11/index.html.
8. Vicomsoft Wireless Networking Q&A. Accessed from: www.vicomsoft.com/knowledge/reference/wireless1.html.

9. Wireless within corporate reach. eWeek, May 3, 2000. Accessed from: http://techupdate.zdnet.com/techupdate/stories/main/0,14179,2530201-1,00.html.

10. Gardner, D. Wireless Insecurities. *Information Security Magazine*, Jan. 2002. Accessed from: www.infosecuritymag.com/articles/january02/cover.shtml.

11. Practically Networked. Should I use NetBeui? Accessed from: www.practicallynetworked.com/sharing/netbeui.htm.

12. Borisov, N., I. Goldberg, and D. Wagner, UC Berkeley. Security of the WE Algorithm, Accessed from: www.isaac.cs.berkeley.edu/isaac/wep-faq.html.

13. Practically Networked. Wireless encryption help. Accessed from: www.practicallynetworked.com/support/wireless_encrypt.htm.

14. Practically Networked. Securing your wireless network. Accessed from: www.practicallynetworked.com/support/wireless_secure.htm.

15. Practically Networked. Mixing WEP encryption levels. Accessed from: www.practicallynetworked.com/support/mixed_wep.htm.

16. Rysavy, P. Break free with wireless LANs. *Network Computing*, Oct. 29, 2001. Accessed from: www.networkcomputing.com/1222/1222f1.html.

17. Search Networking.com. *Wireless LAN Links*. Accessed from: http://searchnetworking.techtarget.com/bestWebLinks/0,289521,sid7_tax286426,00.html.

18. Cordeiro, C., and D. P. Aggarwal. *Adhoc and Sensor Networks*, 2nd Ed. World Scientific, Singapore, 2011.

19. Yan, G., and S. Eidenbenz. Modeling propagation dynamics of bluetooth worms (Extended Version). *IEEE Transactions on Mobile Computing*. Mar. 2009, 8 (3): 353–367.

20. Tan, M., and K. A. Masagca, An investigation of bluetooth security threats, In *Proceedings of the International Conference on Information Science and Applications* (pp. 1–7). Jeju Island, South Korea, Apr. 2011.

21. Car Whisperer Definition from PC Magazine Encyclopedia. Accessed from: www.pcmag.com/encyclopedia/term/59746/car-whisperer.

22. IEEE 802.16-Wikipedia. Accessed from: http://en.wikipedia.org/wiki/IEEE_802.16.

23. Barbeau, M. WiMAX/802.16 threat analysis. In *Proceedings of 1st ACM International Workshop on Quality of Service and Security for Wireless and Mobile Networks (Q2SWinet)* (pp. 8–15). Oct. 2005.

24. Barbeau, M. and C. Laurendeau. Analysis of threats to WiMAX/802.16 security. In *Mobile WiMAX: Toward Broadband Wireless Metropolitan Area Networks*, ser. Wireless Networks and Mobile Communications Series (pp. 347–362). 2007.

25. Han, T., N. Zhang, K. Liu, B. Tang, and Y. Liu, Analysis of Mobile WiMAX Security: Vulnerabilities and Solutions, In *MASS 2008. 5th IEEE International Conference on Mobile Ad Hoc and Sensor Systems, 2008. MASS 2008* (pp.828–833). Sep. 29–Oct. 2, 2008.

26. Bhargava, B., Y. Zhang, N. Idika, L. Lilien, and M. Azarmi, Collaborative attacks in WiMAX networks. *Security and Communication Networks*. 2009, 2: 373391.

27. McHugh, K., W. Akpedeye, and T. Hayajneh. Next generation wireless-LAN: Security issues and performance analysis. In *Computing and Communication Workshop and Conference (CCWC), 2017 IEEE 7th Annual* (pp. 1–7). IEEE, 2017.

28. Coleman, D. D., D. A. Westcott, and B. E. Harkins. Wireless LAN security auditing. In *CWSP®: Certified Wireless Security Professional Study Guide CWSP-205: Certified Wireless Security Professional Study Guide CWSP-205* (pp. 439–468). 2017.

29. Zhan, G. and A. H. K. Wong. Consumer adoption of Wi-Fi network: The role of security knowledge, perceived threat and security measures. In *Proceedings of the 8th International Conference on E-Education, E-Business, E-Management and E-Learning* (pp. 1–5). ACM, 2017.

30. Gupta, S. and B. B. Gupta. XSS-secure as a service for the platforms of online social network-based multimedia web applications in cloud. *Multimedia Tools and Applications*. 2016, 77: 1–33.

31. Gupta, S., B.B. Gupta, and P. Chaudhary. Hunting for DOM-Based XSS vulnerabilities in mobile cloud-based online social network. *Future Generation Computer Systems*. Jun. 12, 2017, 79: 319–336.

32. Chaudhary, P., S. Gupta, B. B. Gupta, V. S. Chandra, S. Selvakumar, M. Fire, R. Goldschmidt, Y. Elovici, B. B. Gupta, S. Gupta, and S. Gangwar. Auditing defense against XSS worms in online social network-based web applications. *Handbook of Research on Modern Cryptographic Solutions for Computer and Cyber Security*. 2016, 36 (5): 216–245.

33. Chaudhary, P., B. B. Gupta, and S. Gupta. Defending the OSN-based web applications from XSS attacks using dynamic javascript code and content isolation. In *Quality, IT and Business Operations* (pp. 107–119). Springer, Singapore, 2018.

34. Gupta, S. and B. B. Gupta. Smart XSS attack surveillance system for OSN in virtualized intelligence network of nodes of fog computing. *International Journal of Web Services Research (IJWSR)*. Oct. 1, 2017, 14 (4): 1–32.

35. Gupta, B. B., S. Gupta, and P. Chaudhary. Enhancing the browser-side context-aware sanitization of suspicious HTML5 code for halting the DOM-based XSS vulnerabilities in cloud. *International Journal of Cloud Applications and Computing (IJCAC)*. Jan. 1, 2017, 7 (1): 1–31.

36. Gupta, S. and B. B. Gupta. An infrastructure-based framework for the alleviation of javascript worms from OSN in mobile cloud platforms. In *International Conference on Network and System Security* (pp. 98–109). Springer International Publishing, Sep. 28, 2016.

37. Gupta, S. and B. B. Gupta. XSS-immune: A google chrome extension-based XSS defensive framework for contemporary platforms of web applications. *Security and Communication Networks*. Nov. 25, 2016, 9 (17): 3966–3986.

38. Gupta, S. and B. B. Gupta. Alleviating the proliferation of JavaScript worms from online social network in cloud platforms. In *Information and Communication Systems (ICICS), 2016 7th International Conference on* (pp. 246–251). IEEE, Apr. 5, 2016.

39. Gupta, S. and B. B. Gupta. JS-SAN: Defense mechanism for HTML5-based web applications against javascript code injection vulnerabilities. *Security and Communication Networks*. 2016, 9: 1477–1495.

40. Gupta, S. and B. B. Gupta. XSS-SAFE: A server-side approach to detect and mitigate cross-site scripting (XSS) attacks in JavaScript code. *Arabian Journal for Science and Engineering*. 2016, 41 3: 897–920.

References for Advance/Further Reading

Pan, Chien-Yuan, Tzyy-Sheng Horng, Wen-Shan Chen, and Chien-Hsiang Huang. "Dual wideband printed monopole antenna for WLAN/WiMAX applications." *IEEE Antennas and Wireless Propagation Letters* 6 (2007): 149–151.

Pei, Jing, An-Guo Wang, Shun Gao, and Wen Leng. "Miniaturized triple-band antenna with a defected ground plane for WLAN/WiMAX applications." *IEEE Antennas and Wireless Propagation Letters* 10 (2011): 298–301.

Dang, Lin, Zhen Ya Lei, Yong Jun Xie, Gao Li Ning, and Jun Fan. "A compact microstrip slot triple-band antenna for WLAN/WiMAX applications." *IEEE Antennas and Wireless Propagation Letters* 9 (2010): 1178–1181.

Hu, Wei, Ying-Zeng Yin, Peng Fei, and Xi Yang. "Compact triband square-slot antenna with symmetrical L-strips for WLAN/WiMAX applications." *IEEE Antennas and Wireless Propagation Letters* 10 (2011): 462–465.

Moosazadeh, Mahdi, and Sergey Kharkovsky. "Compact and small planar monopole antenna with symmetrical L-and U-shaped slots for WLAN/WiMAX applications." *IEEE Antennas and Wireless Propagation Letters* 13 (2014): 388–391.

Pan, Yong, Kaihua Liu, and Ziye Hou. "A novel printed microstrip antenna with frequency reconfigurable characteristics for Bluetooth/WLAN/WiMAX applications." *Microwave and Optical Technology Letters* 55, no. 6 (2013): 1341–1345.

Naidu, Praveen Vummadisetty, and Raj Kumar. "Design of a compact ACS-fed dual band antenna for Bluetooth/WLAN and WiMAX applications." *Progress in Electromagnetics Research C* 55 (2014): 63–72.

Li, Wen Tao, Yong Qiang Hei, Wei Feng, and Xiao Wei Shi. "Planar antenna for 3G/Bluetooth/WiMAX and UWB applications with dual band-notched characteristics." *IEEE Antennas and Wireless Propagation Letters* 11 (2012): 61–64.

Cai, L. Y., Guang Zeng, and Hong Chuan Yang. "Compact triple band antenna for Bluetooth/WiMAX/WLAN applications." In *2010 International Symposium on Signals Systems and Electronics (ISSSE)*, vol. 2, pp. 1–4. IEEE, 2010.

Kaur, Jaswinder, Rajesh Khanna, and Machavaram Kartikeyan. "Novel dual-band multistrip monopole antenna with defected ground structure for WLAN/IMT/BLUETOOTH/WIMAX applications." *International Journal of Microwave and Wireless Technologies* 6, no. 1 (2014): 93–100.

Bakariya, Pritam Singh, Santanu Dwari, Manas Sarkar, and Mrinal Kanti Mandal. "Proximity-coupled microstrip antenna for Bluetooth, WiMAX, and WLAN applications." *IEEE Antennas and Wireless Propagation Letters* 14 (2015): 755–758.

Li, Yingsong, Wenxing Li, and Raj Mittra. "A Compact ACS-FED Dual-Band Meandered Monopole Antenna for Wlan and WiMax Applications." *Microwave and Optical Technology Letters* 55, no. 10 (2013): 2370–2373.

Chapter 9

Botnet Behavior and Detection Techniques: A Review

Ammar Almomani and Osama M. Dorgham
Al-Balqa Applied University

Mohammad Alauthman and Mohammed Al-Refai
Zarqa University

Nauman Aslam
Northumbria University

Contents

9.1 Introduction

Botnet hazards have increased in the Internet environment subsequent to the first-known Botnets found at the beginning of the 1990s based on the Internet Relay Chat (IRC). The IRC was set up in the late 1980s to allow the computer user to connect to the Internet anywhere and to join live chats. Botnets exploited the benefits of this channel so as to set up communication between the Botmaster and the Bot in the victim's computer.

This chapter began by introducing the history of Botnets. The following section gives definitions of terms related to Botnets and explains the life cycle. Section 9.3 introduces the threats from Botnets, and Section 9.3 illustrates Botnet evolution. Sections 9.4 and 9.5 classify Botnets and Botnet detection approaches, respectively. A summary of this chapter and its relevance to the present study are given in Section 9.6.

9.2 Background of Botnets

This section describes Bots, Botnets, Command and Control (C&C), and victim hosts, and then it elaborates on the role of Botnet in cybercrime.

9.2.1 Definitions Related to Botnet

■ Bot: the word Bot derives from the word robot, which means "worker." In the world of computers, a Bot is a general term adopted to describe an automated operation (Schiller and Binkley, 2007). In other words, a Bot refers to a malicious code on victim computer that allows the attacker to control the computer remotely and perform specific operations (Silva, Silva, Pinto, and Salles, 2013).

■ Botnet: is a collection of compromised computers (zombies) connected through the network, and it is under the control of a Botmaster via a C&C channel (Huy, Xuetao, Faloutsos, and Eliassi-Rad, 2013; Lashkari, Ghalebandi, and Reza Moradhaseli, 2011). The Bot is commonly installed on the victim's computer in several ways, such as when an untrusted website is surfed or a malicious email attachment is open. Generally, the Bot is configured to be launched when it infects the victim's machine, and then the Bot will be ready to receive a command from the Botmaster through the C&C server (Silva et al., 2013).

■ C&C: is a communication channel used to transfer orders between the Botmaster and Bots to achieve various distributed attacks remotely (Feily, Shahrestani, and Ramadass, 2009; Nagaraja et al., 2011). Furthermore, the interaction between the Botmaster and Bots through the C&C communication channel can be classified into three groups: message types, message directions, and communication protocols (Rodríguez-Gómez, Maciá-Fernández, and García-Teodoro, 2013). C&C message types can be classified as command or control messages. A command message is used by the Botmaster to send an order to the Bots to execute an action on the victim's computer. The other type of C&C message is a control message that gives the Botmaster information about the status of Botnets, such as the number of active Bots. What is more, C&C message directions may be divided into two categories: pulls and pushes (Gu, Zhang, and Lee, 2008). In a pull style, the C&C server sends a command to Bots and waits for them to respond before sending the second order. On the other hand, if the C&C server sends a command and it does not wait for a response, this is a push case message. These approaches are used by centralized Botnet structures such as IRC and HTTP Botnet-based. The communication protocols perform a significant part of the communication between the C&C server and the Bots. IRC, HTTP, and P2P protocols are the most common types of protocol used in C&C server communications (Rodríguez-Gómez et al., 2013).

■ The Botmaster (attacker): is the person who creates the Bots and coordinates all the operations going on between the Bots and the C&C server. In addition, the Botmaster builds and develops the ability of the Bots to infect a victim's machine as well as coordinating the communication between Botnet system components (Boshmaf, Muslukhov, Beznosov, and Ripeanu, 2013). However, on the Internet, there are many toolkits that can be used to build and manage Botnet systems (Boshmaf et al., 2013).

■ The victim: the main aim of the Botmaster is to spread the Bot code to infect any connected computer and then control these computers via the C&C server. For instance, system, person, or network could be a Botnet target. The victims vary depending on the objective of the attacks or the Botnet type, for example, receiving spam email or stealing confidential information from the victim's machine. In another example, distributed denial-of-service (DDoS) attacks have played a key role in companies losing millions of dollars (Rodríguez-Gómez et al., 2013).

9.2.2 Generic Botnet Life Cycle

This section reviews the main stages of the Botnet life cycle. Botnet behavior is addressed in terms of the set of operations used by a Botnet during its life cycle phase. The majority of Botnet detection approaches focus on the specific stage of a Botnet life cycle via studying its behavior during these phases. As a result, the analysis of the Botnet life cycle is also important in understanding the previous work on Botnet detection and Botnet behavior. Zhaosheng et al. (2008), Feily et al. (2009), and Silva et al. (2013) addressed Botnet life cycles in similar ways with slight differences, dividing it into three stages: infection, communication, and attack. However, the Botnet life cycle can be described in detail in five phases: initial infection, secondary injection, connection, C&C, and updating and maintenance (Feily et al., 2009), as illustrated in Figure 9.1.

The first phase of creating a Botnet is a critical phase; the Botmaster tries to exploit a known computer operating system's vulnerability to infect the user's machine. Moreover, scanning techniques are used by an attacker to insert the Bot into the target's machine (Feily et al., 2009). There

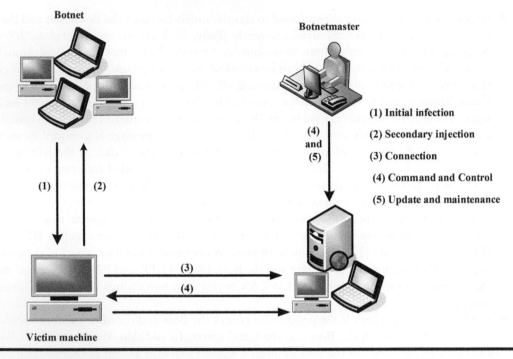

Figure 9.1 Generic botnet life cycle (Feily et al., 2009).

are several methods for installing Bots in end-user computers, such as opening malicious spam email attachments or browsing malicious webpages (Lu, Rammidi, and Ghorbani, 2011).

When the initial infection is accomplished, then the secondary injection phase starts by executing the dropper script code in the infected machine. The execution of the dropper script code starts by downloading the Bot binary from a specific Internet server using a File Transfer Protocol (FTP), HTTP, or Peer-to-Peer (P2P), and then setting up a newer Bot code on the victim's machine. At the end of this phase, the infected machine turns into a zombie (Bot).

After that, the third phase begins by launching the C&C server to issue the communication channel with an army of recruited Bots which gives the Botmaster control ever the Botnet network (Feily et al., 2009). The fourth phase starts when the Botmaster has the ability to use the C&C server to send commands to the Bot in order to execute it on the target's machine. The final phase of the Botnet's life cycle is updating and maintenance, where the Botmaster updates the Bot software for several reasons. For instance, the Botmaster may need to add a new function to enhance the Botnets future attacks or to improve the evasion methods. In addition, the IP address of a new C&C server can be updated to keep it working and thus then prevent it from being blocked due to the evolution of Botnet detection techniques.

9.2.3 P2P Botnet Life Cycle

The life cycle of the P2P Botnet consists of four primary phases, namely, initial infection, peer propagation, secondary injection, and attack. These phases are shown in Figure 9.2 (Felix, Joseph, and Ghorbani, 2012). First, the Bot code is created for insertion into an end-user computer using different techniques such as vulnerability exploitation, web downloads, automatic scanning, and email attachments (Chao, Wei, and Xin, 2009).

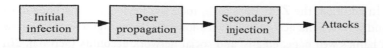

Figure 9.2 P2P Botnet life cycle.

Second, the Bot tries to connect with other Bots on infected hosts based on its own hard-coded peer list. Third, the Bot downloads the latest update of the Bot code through the C&C channel, which will update it for future tasks. In this phase, a host is considered a Bot in the Botnet network. Finally, the Bot initiates malicious activities such as spam or phishing emails, DDoS, stealing information, and scanning activities.

9.3 Botnet Threats

A Botnet is more dangerous than previous more traditional threats such as worms and viruses. The Honeynet project listed many kinds of Botnet attacks, including DDoS, Spam, stealing information, and exploiting resources (Bacher, Holz, Kotter, and Wicherski, 2005). Moreover, Lanelli et al. reported that Botnets can be exploited in several kinds of cybercrimes (Ianelli and Hackworth, 2005).

9.3.1 Distributed Denial of Service

The DDoS is one of the most potent threats produced by Botnets. In the 2014 Information Security Breaches Survey report in the UK, 38% of big organizations were attacked by DDoS in the previous year (Mille, Horne, and Potter, 2014). The massive number of members in a Botnet network gives the DDoS considerable destructive power. The Botmaster uses the Botnet network to take down the victim system of control as the Bots members send huge numbers of requests to this system. In addition, some massive Botnets can even be harmful to Internet Service Providers (ISPs).

9.3.2 Spam

Spam is an operation where an overwhelming quantity of email messages containing advertisements or malicious links are sent to a large number of users. A Botnet is the best choice for an attacker's use as a tool to send spam emails. The spam attacks start by sending commands to the Bots from Botmaster before they begin sending spam email to the victim's address. In this case, the detection approaches that used a blacklist technique become useless and hereby hard to detect a real attacker.

Ramachandram et al. identified Botnets as the major cause of email spam problems (Ramachandran and Feamster, 2006). In a study that set out to determine the source of email spam, John et al. (2009) found that Botnets were responsible for 79% of the spam emails received at the University of Washington (John, Moshchuk, Gribble, and Krishnamurthy, 2009).

9.3.3 Stealing Information

A Botmaster employs Bots to collect secret information from victim hosts by using techniques such as key logging, reading log files, and screen capture. For example, the SDBot is a type of Botnet that employs a keylogging technique to gather users' sensitive information. This can then be sold to others in order to perform illegitimate actions (Bailey, Cooke, Jahanian, Yunjing, and

Karir, 2009). In addition, the Zeus Bot's main tools use keylogging methods to steal credit card information and private bank accounts, which allows the Botmaster to extract passwords and usernames from a bank's web page, emails, and social network accounts (Selvaraj, 2014). Moreover, this Bot exploits the Windows application program interface (API) to extract private user information before the web browser can encrypt it (Hannah and Gianvecchio, 2015).

9.3.4 Exploiting Resources

Bot hosts are controlled to perform illegal activities. For example, the Bot uses the victim's computer to visit a website periodically to increase the number of website visitors without the user's permissions. In addition, they can be used to cast fake votes or to grow the number of followers on Twitter and Facebook.

9.4 Botnet Classification

As can be seen from the Botnet life cycle, the C&C server mechanism is the most important component of a Botnet system. Based on the C&C mechanism, the Botmaster is able to communicate with Bots, and infrastructure of the C&C communicational channel is the main difference between a Botnet and other malwares (Zeidanloo, Bt Manaf, Vahdani, Tabatabaei, and Zamani, 2010). In contrast to other malwares that are used to perform malicious behaviors individually, a Botnet works as a group of infected hosts based on the C&C communication channel. Therefore, the Botmaster can use this channel to deliver a command to thousands of Bots in order to launch an attack or receive information from victim computers. In 2005, Cooke and co-workers classified Botnets depending on their C&C mechanism into three different groups: centralized, distributed, and random. This paper also contained the first academic analysis of the P2P Botnet (Cooke, Jahanian, and McPherson, 2005). Dittrich and Dietrich grouped Botnets into four classes in terms of their development environments as IRC, HTTP, P2P, and hybrid Botnets (Dittrich and Dietrich, 2008). However, in this chapter, the Botnet network is described based on the structure of its C&C channels and the type of protocol used in Botnet communications as follows.

9.4.1 Botnet Classification According to Control and Command Structure

The C&C server is what makes Botnets more powerful than other types of malicious malware. Botnet structure based on the C&C server can be classified into centralized, decentralized, and unstructured C&C architectures (Chao et al., 2009).

- Centralized architecture: Here, all Bots members are connected to one or many C&C servers as shown in Figure 9.3, such as in HTTP and IRC Botnets. The C&C server plays a significant role in delivering commands from the Botmaster to Bots, and there are no direct connections between Bots. In addition, the centralized architecture is considered to be the easiest type of Botnet to construct, but it does suffer from the fact that it has a single point of failure in the C&C server. A shutdown of the C&C server would result in the loss of communication between the Bots and Botmaster (Ludl, McAllister, Kirda, and Kruegel, 2007). In spite of this weakness, it is widely used in cybercrimes because the commands are sent more quickly with low latency. However, it is not so difficult to detect the C&C server, and thus to crush the whole Botnet network.

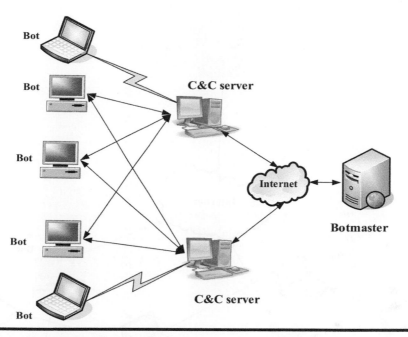

Figure 9.3 A typical centralized Botnet structure.

■ Decentralized (P2P) Botnet: In this architecture, there is no centralized point for the C&C, so mitigating or detecting these Botnets is very challenging. Due to the distributed network structure of P2P systems, all peers in the network work as a Bot (client) and C&C (server) at the same time. In this case, the Botmaster plays the main role by sending commands to any infected peers to execute any order or requesting information at any time as shown in Figure 9.4. However, in order to avoid the weakness of a single point of failure, Botnet attackers have recently started to build Botnets based on decentralized C&C infrastructures such as the P2P Botnet (Felix et al., 2012), and the P2P model was adopted by many types of Botnet, for example Storm Bot, Conficker Bot, and Waledac Bot (Davis, Fernandez, and Neville, 2009).

In 2007, the Storm Botnet showed that the power of decentralizing C&C structure to protect the viability of a Botnet. Decentralizing the C&C introduces a serious challenge to defenders who cannot remove an individual set of points to destroy a Botnet (Grizzard, Sharma, Nunnery, Kang, and Dagon, 2007; Stover, Dittrich, Hernandez, and Dietrich, 2007). A decentralized Botnet architecture is hard to detect as a result of the anonymity involved and the dispersed nature of the P2P network's design (Han and Im, 2012).

■ Unstructured C&C (hybrid) architecture: As demonstrated in Figure 9.5, this model is considered an extreme form of P2P Botnet, where every Bot has a connection with one peer and it does not own information about other peers in the Botnet network. Furthermore, the Bots are organized randomly in this architecture (Silva et al., 2013). In this type, there cannot be a direct communication between the Botmaster and the Bot where it has to search randomly on the Internet to find a Bot in order to submit a new task. What is more, it is not affected by a single point of failure, as is centralized architecture. In addition, Wang et al. (2010) introduced a hybrid Botnet model as a new idea that combined

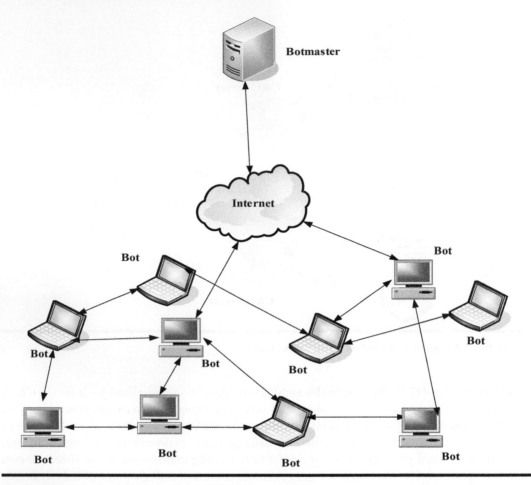

Figure 9.4   A typical decentralized (P2P) Botnet architecture.

the fundamental characteristics of centralized and decentralized C&C mechanisms in order to gain the benefits of both a low latency of communication and P2P flexibility (P. Wang, Sparks, and Zou, 2010). However, this architecture does not have a warranty for the message delivery, and it suffers from a high rate of C&C message latencies (Bailey et al., 2009).

The general properties of the different Botnet structures are summarized in Table 9.1 (Bailey et al., 2009).

9.4.2 Botnet Classification Based on the Communication Protocols

It is necessary to own a communication channel linking the Botmaster with their Bots inside victim machines in order to facilitate the flow of send/receive information between them. Based on the existing network communication protocols, Botnets can be categorized according to protocols such as IRC-based, Web-based, P2P-based, and Custom protocols (Tyagi and Aghila, 2011). Table 9.2 shows a comparison of Botnet communication protocols.

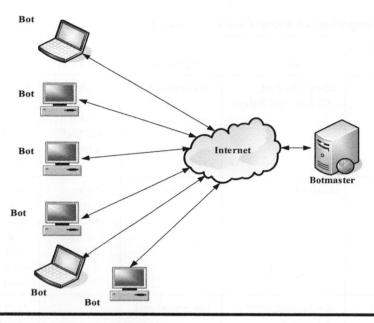

Figure 9.5   Unstructured C&C architecture.

Table 9.1   C&C Structures and Basic Properties

Topology	Complexity	Detectability	Message Latency	Survivability
Centralized	Low	Medium	Low	Low
Decentralized (P2P)	Medium	Low	Medium	Medium
Unstructured	Low	High	High	High

Source: Bailey et al. (2009).

■ IRC-based: In this type of Botnet, an IRC channel plays a key role in Botnets development. Initially, the idea of IRC Bots was developed to support chatting services, not taking into account the fact that this idea was utilized by malicious developers, and then the first IRC-based Botnet appeared. The Botmaster used the IRC Botnet to bring the victim machine under control and to exploit it to execute malicious activities. According to Trend Micro report, few examples of IRC Botnets are Rbot, Phatbot, GTBot, and Sdbot (Trend-Micro, 2006). Nevertheless, the IRC can be efficiently identified by configuring the devices of network security in order to hinder IRC traffic.

■ Web-based: HTTP is used by this type of Botnet as the main communication channel, as the basis of the widespread HTTP. The Botmaster uses this protocol to spread malicious activities, which is difficult to detect and capable of bypassing network security devices. Through the World Wide Web, the Botmaster uses HTTP to manage its Bots. The Botmaster identifies a web server, and then the Bots periodically connect to the specific web server in order to receive commands or send information. Unlike IRC Botnets, HTTP Botnet communication can be hidden in legitimate HTTP traffic in order to evade detection systems. There are many examples of this Botnet such as the Rustock Bot (Chiang and

Table 9.2 Comparison of Botnet Communication Protocols

Communication Protocols	Example	Topology	Weakness	Advantages
IRC-based	Rbot, Phatbot, GTBot, and Sdbot	Centralized	Single point of failure in the C&C server	It is widely used in cybercrimes because the commands are sent quickly with low latency.
Web-based (HTTP)	Rustock	Centralized	Single point of failure in the C&C server	HTTP Botnet communication can be hidden in legitimate HTTP traffic to evade detection systems.
P2P-based	BlackEnerg,Storm, and Zeus	Decentralized	–	Avoid the weakness of a single point of failure.

Lloyd, 2007) and blackEnergy Bot (Daswani and Stoppelman, 2007). However, HTTP Botnets and IRC Botnets suffer from the disadvantage of a single point of failure in the C&C server (K. Wang, Huang, Lin, and Lin, 2011).

■ P2P-based: Napster was one of the first P2P networks; P2P protocols then became popular. The main concept of the P2P network is that every node works as a server and client at the same time. Several protocols may be followed such as Gnutella, eDonkey, BitTorrent, and Kademlia. The core of these protocols is totally decentralized and that attracted the attention of Botmasters (Mukamurenzi, 2008). P2P Botnets adopt a decentralized architecture using an overlay network to exchange C&C data making their detection even more difficult. So, the P2P Botnet is named based on its use of P2P mechanisms or protocols. Many Botnets utilize the P2P network, such as Conficker (R. Weaver, 2010), Storm (Holz, Steiner, Dahl, Biersack, and Freiling, 2008), Nugache (Stover et al., 2007), and Waledac (Stock et al., 2009).

■ Custom protocols: In addition to the previously listed types, there are some kinds of Botnets that use their own protocols based on the TCP/IP stack, and they only use transport-layer protocols such as UDP, TCP, and ICMP.

9.5 Taxonomy of Botnet Detection

Recent years have witnessed several Botnet detection techniques which can be classified as signature-based, anomaly-based, Domain Name System (DNS)-based, and data mining-based (Feily et al., 2009). Other researchers, such as Han et al., have classified P2P Botnet detection systems into three general types: data mining, machine learning, and network behavior and traffic analysis

(Han and Im, 2012). What is more, Zeidanloo and colleagues classify the Botnet detection system as Honeynets or intrusion detection systems (IDS), and they also divide the IDS into three subgroups of anomaly-based, specification-based, and signature-based. In addition, the Botnet detection system can be classified based on its installation point as host-based, network-based, and hybrid systems (Zeidanloo, Shooshtari, Amoli, Safari, and Zamani, 2010). Lu et al. (2011) have classified Botnet detection techniques on the basis of machine learning type as supervised or unsupervised Botnet detection (Lu et al., 2011).

9.5.1 Honeynet-Based Detection

Honeynets are one of the most common detection methods used by many researchers recently. This technique imitates an infected machine so as to convince the Botmaster that there is a Bot in its Botnet in order to record all communication and actions between them. This mechanism is commonly used in the initial phase of Botnet detection. A Honeynet method contains two components: Honeypot and Honeywell (Bacher et al., 2005). The Honeypot points out a vulnerable host. What is more, the Honeywell refers to the group of tools used to capture and analyze the sent and received traffic from the Honeypot. By utilizing the information gathered by a Honeynet, it is possible to perform a comprehensive analysis and to extract the main features of a Bot to understand its technology and therefore use the extracted features in improving Botnet detection. GenIII (Balas and Viecco, 2005) and Honeyd (Provos, 2003) are two popular Honeynets in the field of malware detection.

In 2006, Baecher et al. introduced a Nepenthes platform as a framework for collecting information from self-replicating malware based on the Honeypot. The Nepenthes framework is one of the most practical ways to provide the developer of an antivirus system with information about unknown malware (Baecher, Koetter, Holz, Dornseif, and Freiling, 2006). Rajab and co-workers proposed distributed multifaceted Honeynets, effectively capturing the activities of IRC Bots (Rajab, Zarfoss, Monrose, and Terzis, 2006). Moreover, the Honeypot mechanism was used in the Botminer method to understand the behavior of two Botnets, Nugache and Storm. However, there are many Botnet detection techniques which utilize Honeynets such as (Barford and Yegneswaran, 2007; Cooke et al., 2005; Freiling, Holz, and Wicherski, 2005; Kang et al., 2009; Pham and Dacier, 2011).

Despite the success of the Honeynet in reducing the effects of Internet malware, it has some shortcomings. It takes time to analyze information about the malware binaries. Moreover, if an attacker has knowledge of the existence of the Honeypot, he/she will not send anything to it or may send fake commands in order to give the Honeypot the wrong information.

Table 9.3 summarizes Botnet detection methods that utilize Honeynet.

Table 9.3 Summary of Honeynet Detection Methods

Method	Technique	Shortcoming
Baecher et al. (2006)	Collecting information from self-replicating malware based on the Honeypot.	• Malware binaries analyzing time. • Providing false attack information by the attacker.
Rajab et al. (2006)	Distributed multifaceted Honeynets.	

9.5.2 Signature-Based Detection

Signature-based detection includes exploring the traffic in the network to find a set of traits such as a series of bytes or sequences of packets and a matching set of pre-specified signature lists. Whenever there is a match in particular network traffic, the administrators are alerted or a predefined action will be taken by the system. Some IDS, applying the signature approach, use a repository to store signatures. The repository is frequently explored to match predefined patterns such as the content of payload packets or system activities to determine whether it contains known signatures. So, the quality of signatures plays a significant role in the performance of signature-based detection. Despite an attempt to generate automatic signatures for malware (Kreibich and Crowcroft, 2004), it is still a restricted to human expertise and knowledge.

Unfortunately, signature-based detection does not have the ability to detect an unknown Botnet. For example, Lu et al. (2011) proposed an approach for detecting the Botnet's malicious traffic by using an n-gram feature selection algorithm to analyze payload content. Then, they clustered P2P applications into groups based on payload content using a decision tree model to distinguish between known applications and malicious Botnet traffic. In the clustering stage, three clustering algorithms used in the approach are K-means (Jain, Murty, and Flynn, 1999), merged X-means and un-merged X-means (Pelleg and Moore, 2000). Moreover, the approach is based on the hypotheses that the diversity of Botnet packet content is less than that of legitimate traffic. Although the approach is able to detect Botnets independently of protocol and network structure, it is vulnerable to methods of encryption of payload content and authorization to read the actual content of the packets. Clearly, this method will no longer work because today's Botnets are much more sophisticated.

SNORT is one of the popular network intrusion detection schemes. It examines the network traffic and applies certain rules/patterns to identify well-known signatures of Bots (Alder et al., 2007). SNORT is suitable for detecting Bots that have information about it, with low false positive rate (FPR) and instant detection. However, it fails to classify similar Bots with hardly changed signatures or new types of Bots till their signatures have been determined and attached to the rule set database.

In 2007, Goebel and Holz presented another technique of using a signature-based approach called Rishi. The method works by comparing the IRC communication traffic with known IRC Bot nickname patterns, or using unusual channels for communication (Goebel and Holz, 2007). But the Rishi approach fails to detect non-IRC Bots or new (unknown) nicknames, or if the Bot applies an encryption algorithm in communication.

In 2007, Gu and colleagues suggested a BotHunter that utilizes the correlation analysis of malicious behavior. It correlates SNORT (Roesch, 1999) alarms in the bidirectional communication between external and internal hosts to detect the C&C communication and malicious activities such as scanning and exploited usage. Then, this evidence is used in a rule-based system to detect the host infected by Botnet (Gu, Porras, Yegneswaran, Fong, and Lee, 2007). BotHunter also has its weaknesses. This method will be avoided if Botnets update their predefined infection procedures or if the frequency of C&C interactions is very low (Gu, Zhang, et al., 2008). In general, the main advantage of signature-based approaches is to achieve a high detection rate since it uses the signature found in the database. However, a major drawback is its incapability to detect new Bot attacks, or so-called zero-day attacks (N. Weaver, Paxson, Staniford, and Cunningham, 2003). Another drawback of signature-based detection is that it needs the involvement of human expertise to create the signatures (Table 9.4).

Table 9.4   Summary of Signature-Based Methods

Method	Technique	Shortcoming
Lu et al. (2011)	K-means, Un-merged X-means, Merged X-means clustering	• Payload encryption content. • Privacy issue.
Goebel and Holz (2007)	N-gram analysis	• Fail to detect non-IRC Bots. • Payload encryption. • Detect zero-day attack.
BotHunter (Gu et al., 2007)	Correlation analysis	• Detect zero-day attack. • Need human expertise to create the signatures.

9.5.3 Anomaly-Based Detection

Anomaly-based detection techniques have been explored a lot in the past decade, and they are the most general detection technologies. They try to determine the "normal" behavior of the system to be protected and then look for any considerable changes in network behaviors (García, Zunino, and Campo, 2014). This includes any behavior that is considered an unusual activity such as traffic at uncommon ports, network traffic with high volumes, latency with high network traffic, and abnormal system behavior based on a predefined pattern of normal system behavior. These approaches attempt to build a model of abnormal system behavior in order to find any similarities with previously expected malicious behavior located in the range of a given threshold. According to Zeidanloo and co-workers, anomaly-based methods are classified on the basis of data collection location into host-based and network-based. Network-based techniques can be broken down into active and passive (Zeidanloo et al., 2010). The main advantage of anomaly-based methods is their ability to detect new types of attacks, known as zero-day attacks. These attacks are malicious activities that are not already known by the detection system and cannot be detected by signature-based approaches. However, the quality of the features selected for use in the detection system and high-false alarm rates are the most common limitations of such detection approaches which apply anomaly-based techniques (Weaver et al., 2003).

9.5.3.1 Host-Based

A host-based Botnet technique attempts to detect a Bot binary as a virus, and so, it treats the infected machine in the same way an antivirus software does. This approach is based on the hypothesis that a Bot program executes a series of calls to system libraries which are dissimilar to those performed using normal processes (Micro, 2006). Host-based techniques monitor the machine activities and record system events such as remote-control activities, register updates, file deletion, and traffic sent to or received from a host. An alert is activated when it detects Botnet activities on the host.

In 2007, Stinson and Mitchell proposed a BotSwat as a host-based detection technique based on the above premise. BotSwat has tools to monitor and track the interactions of computer program calls with system libraries that receive data from the untrusted network in order to discriminate between Botnet command responses from normal host activities. Moreover, this method was created with the aim to detect Botnets independent of C&C architectures or communication protocols (Stinson and Mitchell, 2007).

EFFORT (Seungwon, Zhaoyan, and Guofei, 2012) is a host-based detection approach that collects Bot characteristics at client and network levels, and correlates Bot-related information by monitoring local computer activity such as keystrokes and monitoring connections with other computers. This approach applies one class of supervised support vector machine (SVM) algorithms to model legitimate user behavior (Witten and Frank, 2005). Furthermore, 15 Bot samples were used to evaluate the method, and a 100% true positive rate was achieved with less than 1% FPR. The main advantage of this method is that it does not depend on the protocol and communications topology used. In addition, it is able to detect Bots that use encryption techniques to hide malicious behavior. The major limitations of this method are critical to evasion techniques, such as Fast-flux, and it also cannot be proven as a real-time detection approach.

In 2008, Liu and colleagues introduced a BotTracer as a Botnet detection tool based on a virtual machine. This method is based on the idea that a Bot has three features. First, the Bot has automatic startup activities without involving any user actions. Second, the Bot must establish C&C a communication channel with its Botmaster. Finally, a Bot must launch an attack remotely or locally. These features represent the three basic stages of a Bot attack: injection, update, and attack. Besides this, a Bot should communicate with a rendezvous point in order to launch a C&C channel with its Botmaster, and BotTracer catches these channels and analyses them to identify the Bot C&C channels. The BotTracer runs a virtual machine on the host that contains a copy of the host system file that automatically starts without human interaction. Then, it will monitor all auto-start communication processes to find a Bot C&C channel fingerprint (Liu, Chen, Yan, and Zhang, 2008). Therefore, it will detect the Bot when it begins a malicious activity. This is a real-time technique that is capable of detecting unknown Bots without considering the communication protocol. Moreover, it achieves a low FPR regardless of the encryption of Botnet communication traffic. However, in BotTracer, high levels of computation are required due to the virtual machine's degradation of host performance. What is more, many Bots have the ability to check for the presence of a virtual machine, so, in this case, the BotTracer will not work.

Al-Hammadi and Aickelin proposed a P2P Botnet detection approach by correlating behavioral features. The approach developed a program to monitor and extract suspicious API function calls in order to use these features as input to the correlation algorithm. Moreover, the Storm P2P Bot was used as a case study (Al-Hammadi and Aickelin, 2010). However, the main shortcomings of this technique are that the detection threshold is undefined, and it is evaluated using only one type of Bot. Another host-based study in Botnet detection introduced by Nummipuro presented some of the P2P Botnet's behavioral characteristics such as using the System Service Table (SST) Hooking (Nummipuro, 2007). Although this host-based approach achieved satisfactory results in reducing the spread of malware, it works as an individual host, and so the monitoring and analysis operation is costly, complex, and non-scalable.

Table 9.5 summarizes host anomaly-based Botnet detection methods.

9.5.3.2 Network-Based

Nowadays, network-based approaches are widely used for Botnet detection by analyzing the entire network traffic (Barsamian, 2009). Furthermore, this technique is installed at the end of the network such as in the firewall or router unlikely host-based methods which analyze individual host activities. Network-based approaches have been further divided into active and passive monitoring.

In passive monitoring techniques, information about traffic on the network is gathered to find suspicious communications in order to detect Botnets. A key idea behind passive monitoring is that Bots create communication behavior different from that of a normal host and Bots belong to

Table 9.5 Summary of Host Anomaly-Based Methods

Method	Technique	Shortcoming
EFFORT (Seungwon et al., 2012)	SVM and one-class SVM	• Critical to evasion techniques, such as Fast-flux. • Not proven as a real-time detection approach.
BotTracer (Liu et al., 2008)	Virtual machine	• Virtual machine's degradation of host performance. • Providing false attack information by the attacker.
Al-Hammadi and Aickelin (2010)	Correlation algorithm	• The detection threshold is undefined. • Evaluated using only one type of Bot.
Nummipuro (2007)	Using the SST Hooking	• The leak of scalability.

a Botnet network that presents similar communication patterns (Micro, 2006). The Botmaster has to make connections with its Bots to issue an attack or update command. Moreover, because the Bot is pre-programmed, they react with the Botmaster using a similar pattern. Furthermore, the Botnet uses the same protocol in each phase of the Botnet life cycle (Micro, 2006). Many researchers have investigated such similarities in network traffic to identify Bot behavior.

For example, Gu and colleagues (2008) use the fact that Bot is a pre-programmed software and has a similar pattern to the C&C server to develop a BotSniffer detection method based on the spatial–temporal correlation. It depends on the hypothesis that Botnets favor to contact in an extremely synchronized way, unlike human activities. BotSniffer can identify C&C servers and a compromised host based on the similarity of spatial–temporal data. Additionally, it can recognize C&C channels for IRC-based and HTTP-based Botnets. What is more, this technique is network-based, so it can identify a host with comparable suspicious network behavior such as spamming and scanning (Gu, Zhang, et al., 2008). However, Botsniffer was developed to detect Botnets with a centralized architecture. Consequently, it cannot identify Bots that use a different architecture for the C&C server, and it is not able to recognize an individual infected host. Moreover, it was developed to identify a Botnet in a local area network, so it is not applicable at the Internet level. Also despite having a low FPR, the Botsniffer can be avoided by utilizing encoded channels or using a decentralized architecture for the C&C server as in P2P Botnets.

In 2007, Karasaridis et al. presented an anomaly-based algorithm for detecting IRC Botnet controllers using the transport-layer data in the backbone of the network, such as Tier-1 ISP networks. The statistical characteristics of the C&C server traffic are used to find considerable quantities of the data of the network traffic. This data is gathered by utilizing the skeptical host activity findings (ports scan, email spam, and generating DDoS attack traffic) collected from chosen network connections by matching a well-known IRC traffic signature, such as the low amount of network traffic, chat-like, or a network traffic that has a PING-PONG pattern. After collecting network data, methods are applied to detect the connections of candidate controllers that use unusual IRC ports. First, it finds the suspected Bot flow with a remote machine that acts as a server. Second, it identifies flows whose behavior is within the range of normal IRC traffic. Finally, they analyze the conversation of a candidate control to recognize suspicious controllers and their ports (Karasaridis, Rexroad, and Hoeflin, 2007). However, although the Karasaridis technique is

Table 9.6 Summary of Network Anomaly-Based Methods

Method	Technique	Shortcoming
BotSniffer (Gu, Zhang, et al., 2008)	Spatial–temporal correlation	• Payload encryption content. • Privacy issue. • Detect single Bot infection.
Karasaridis et al. (2007)	Correlation algorithm	• Fails to detect non-IRC Bots. • Detect zero-day attack.
BotProbe (Guofei et al., 2009)	Injecting packets in a communication session.	• Increasing network traffic. • Injecting packets to facilitate detection may lead to legal issues.

able to work passively with large-scale networks and achieve less than 2% FPR and so it is suitable to detect IRC Bots, it may not be able to detect modern kinds of Botnet such P2P and HTTP.

As opposite to passive monitoring that interacts with Botnet behavior, active monitoring techniques interact with a Botnet directly by probing the network host with active communication and analyzing its responses. Moreover, it actively confuses Botnet activity by meddling with the Bots' communication with the C&C server. The majority of detection techniques are passive, while only a few, such as BotProbe (Guofei, Yegneswaran, Porras, Stoll, and Wenke, 2009), are active.

BotProbe was introduced by Gu and colleagues as an active detection mechanism. The main target of BotProbe is to determine whether or not a Bot or user is using the host at that side by injecting packets dynamically in a communication session. The authors noted that a Bot is a pre-programmed reply to any contact based on a set of predefined rules. So, they discriminate the human client from a Botnet with regard to the frequency and pattern of responses. This technique was tested on a number of IRC Bots and around 100 real users (Guofei et al., 2009).

However, active techniques have the serious shortcoming of greatly increasing network traffic by sending extra packets to suspicious clients. Furthermore, and most essentially, injecting packets to facilitate detection may be lead to legal issues. In addition, the passive detection approach has the advantage of detecting a Botnet without any direct interaction with the Bot, but only using the Bots behavior within a network.

Table 9.6 summarizes network anomaly-based Botnet detection methods.

9.5.4 Machine Learning-Based Detection

Machine learning plays a significant role in the domain of artificial intelligence because it has excellent performance, and so it is widely used in many fields such as data mining, pattern recognition, and medical diagnosis. Machine learning algorithms extract hidden relationships and rules within data, which can be used to create models for prediction and classification, and thus its goal is to construct systems which have the ability to learn from data (Mitchell, 1997; Witten and Frank, 2005). Learning in this context indicates the ability to identify complicated patterns and utilize labeled data to make qualified decisions. One of the main challenges in machine learning is how to make a generalization of knowledge extracted from a previous dataset or derived from a limited set of previous experiences, in order to construct a prediction system for new and unseen datasets. To deal with this problem, algorithms are developed based on statistical, artificial intelligence, information theory, biology, philosophy, cognitive science, control theory, and computational principles (Mitchell, 1997). Machine learning algorithms are classified in terms of the type of learning involved, which are supervised learning, unsupervised learning, and reinforcement learning (RL).

Supervised learning algorithms use a labeled dataset to generate a model that is able to classify an unlabeled dataset in the future. It is as if a supervisor is helping you out, to be able to classify in the future, which is why it is called supervised. The principle of supervised learning is used by popular machine learning algorithms, for example, in Classification and Regression Trees (Breiman, Friedman, Olshen, and Stone, 1984), neural networks (Gurney, 1997), and SVMs (Cristianini and Shawe-Taylor, 2000). The field of supervised learning may be divided into classification and regression problems. In Botnet detection problems, supervised machine learning mechanisms are employed to train with both Botnet traffic datasets and normal traffic datasets in order to construct classifiers.

Compared to supervised learning, unsupervised learning algorithms do not require a labeled dataset for training. The goal of unsupervised learning methods is to divide an unlabeled dataset into different subgroups depending on specific metrics. Furthermore, the dataset is learned from in order to understand its structure and to find patterns, instead of creating a generalization model from an available labeled dataset as in supervised learning approaches. Nilsson defined unsupervised learning as the use of "procedures that attempt to find natural partitions" (Nilsson, 1996). The most common unsupervised learning algorithms used to detect Botnets are hierarchical clustering, X-means and K-means algorithms.

In RL approaches, an agent learns what to do via some experiences including trial and error (Barto and Andrew, 1998). RL agents modify themselves according to the states of the environment to increase the number of rewards gained in the long run. To maximize the gains, RL agents estimate action-value function, which are specified as the relationships between state-action pairs and the measures of returns that the agents will obtain in the future.

A recent study in the field of P2P Botnet detection by Babak et al. (2014) proposed a PeerRush, which uses a one-class classification approach to classifying various types of normal and abnormal P2P traffics. One-class classifications including the k-Nearest Neighbors (KNN) algorithm, Parzen, and Gaussian data description classifiers (TAX, 2001) are used. An application profile is initially created by learning traffic samples of known P2P applications. Moreover, features such as interval delays between packets and flow duration are used to classify P2P applications (Babak, Roberto, Andrea, and Kang, 2014). This approach achieves high accuracy rates in classifying P2P applications depending on the features selected. On the other hand, this method does not show clearly how to detect P2P Botnets, and also detection can be easily avoided by changing the delay between packets.

Garg et al. (2013) presented several machine learning algorithms, such as KNN, Naive Bayes, and J48. These were analyzed for the detection of P2P Botnets using various network traffic features. The results show that the accuracy of the classifiers trained using the Nearest Neighbor and J48 is good (Garg, Singh, Sarje, and Peddoju, 2013). However, the detection of legitimate traffic is very weak.

Jiang and Shao (2012) presented a method that focuses on the C&C traffic of P2P Bots regardless of how they perform their malicious activity. This method developed a detection mechanism based on Bots that exhibit connection flow dependency with other Bots in the same Botnet network. According to the flow dependency behavior, this approach uses a single-linkage hierarchical clustering mechanism to differentiate between P2P Bots and normal hosts (Jiang and Shao, 2012). This method was built based on the similarity of Botnet traffic, and so it will fail to detect Botnets that use the irregularity of traffic flow, such as Storm Bot (Li, Hu, and Yang, 2012). Also, it has a limitation in identifying individual Bot behavior.

One study by Junjie et al. (2011) introduced a P2P Botnet detection system that can identify stealthy P2P Botnets. The proposed approach focuses on identifying Bots based on the monitoring of C&C traffic. They extracted four features for each traffic flow, including the numbers of bytes received and sent and the numbers of packets received and sent. The hierarchical clustering (Jain et al., 1999) and BIRCH algorithms (Zhang, Ramakrishnan, and Livny, 1997) were used to cluster network flow (Junjie, Perdisci, Wenke, Sarfraz, and Xiapu, 2011). Furthermore, the approach is independent of payload signatures and has also achieved high detection rates of both malicious and legitimate hosts, with an FPR of 0.2% and a TPR of 100%. Although this system can detect Botnets regardless of how they perform their malicious activities, it focuses only on P2P Botnets and cannot detect other types such as IRC or HTTP Bots. However, the proposed technique is vulnerable to some evasion methods such as flow disturbance packets and using the DGA and Fast-flux algorithms as a communication facility to provide a high level of C&C privacy.

Wen-Hwa and Chia-Ching (2010) used a methodology based on packet size to distinguish between P2P Botnet traffic and legitimate P2P traffic. They presented the following observations. First, P2P Bots try to update information for other Bots rather than staying idle. Second, the Bot mainly transmits data with a minimum rate of connections. Bayesian networks, Naive Bayes, and J48 are used to classify network traffic (Wen-Hwa and Chia-Ching, 2010). Furthermore, the accuracy rates for these three algorithms are 87%, 89%, and 98%, respectively. However, it was found that the size of P2P Botnet packets is smaller than that of any other P2P applications.

Zhao and co-workers (2010) introduced a P2P Botnet detection system using machine learning techniques based on the flow intervals of network traffic. In addition, they applied a Bayesian network and decision tree (REPTree) as a classification method to investigate online P2P Bot detection (Zhao et al., 2013). The main drawback of this technique was its sensitivity to evasion methods such as the random connection interval. For example, the connection interval of the Srizbi Bot is random in the interval from 60 to 1200 s (Dae-il, Kang-yu, Minsoo, Hyun-chul, and Bong-Nam, 2010).

Nogueira et al. (2010) introduced a Botnet detection approach based on the identification of traffic using artificial neural networks to classify legal and illegal patterns (Nogueira, Salvador, and Blessa, 2010). This technique has several advantages, such as being independent of protocol and network structure and having the ability to detect encrypted Bot traffic. Nevertheless, the trained neural network was able to classify only 87% of network traffic. The main drawback is the need for external judgment in order to provide adaptive operation.

In 2012, F. Tegeler et al. introduced a network Botnet detection approach called BotFinder, which detects separate hosts infected by Bots focusing on the statistical features of network flow based on frequent Bot C&C communications constructed in a controlled environment. Additionally, they used clustering based on a local Shrinking algorithm (X. Wang, Qiu, and Zamar, 2007) as the machine learning method used to separate the captured network flow into legitimate and malicious classes where the final model will decide whether the flow generated by hosts is malicious or not (Tegeler, Fu, Vigna, and Kruegel, 2012). On the other hand, BotFinder has detection rates varying from 49% for the Bifrose Bot to 100% for the Banbra Bot. This technique has several advantages such as IP address blacklisting or deep packet inspection of contents being unnecessity.

The detection system introduced by Fedynyshyn et al. (2011) uses a host-based approach to detect Bots using the property of temporal persistence. They utilized a J48 classifier and a Random Forest algorithm to sort various kinds of Botnet infection categorized according to C&C model (HTTP, IRC, and P2P). Moreover, they found similarities in C&C structures for different categories of Bots that are different from those of legitimate network traffic (Fedynyshyn, Chuah, and Tan, 2011).

A recent study in the Botnet detection field by Saad et al. (2011) addresses the P2P Botnets detection problem by using several machine learning techniques, including an artificial neural network (ANN), linear SVM, a Gaussian-based classifier, Nearest Neighbor classifier, and a Naive Bayes classifier (Witten and Frank, 2005). The study evaluated the ability of these machine learning techniques in terms of online Botnet detection requirements such as adaptability, novelty detection, and early detection (Saad, 2011). They showed that all the machine learning algorithms had great potential for detecting patterns of Botnet traffic, achieving detection rates greater than 89%. However, SVM and ANN took the most time in the training phase. Furthermore, the performance of these techniques is highly dependent on the features selected for classification or cluster analysis, and they often have high computational requirements.

Strayer et al. (2006) introduced one of the first techniques that utilize machine learning for the purpose of Botnet detection in network traffic. This approach is an extension of Strayer's previous work (Strayer, Walsh, Livadas, and Lapsley, 2006) and works conducted by Livadas et al. (Livadas, Walsh, Lapsley, and Strayer, 2006). Bayesian network, C4.5 tree and Naive Bayes classifiers as machine learning approaches were evaluated in classifying IRC traffic as legitimate or malicious flows (Timothy, David, Robert, and Carl, 2008). Although these methods were effective in detecting Botnets, the techniques are still restricted to particular types of Botnets such as IRC Botnets or specific architectures such as centralized hierarchies. Furthermore, they need human experts to make the final decision.

Masud et al. (2008) introduced an approach to Botnet detection based on the observation that a Bot has many reaction patterns that are different from those of humans. This approach can detect Bots by correlating incoming packets with outgoing packets, new outgoing connections, and application startup in hosts. Several machine learning algorithms such as the C4.5 decision tree, support vector machine, Naive Bayes, Bayes network classifier, and Boosted decision tree (Witten and Frank, 2005) were compared and evaluated in the detection of IRC Botnets. The result of the evaluation showed that all machine learning algorithms achieved over 95% detection rates, less than 3% FPR, and under 5% false negative rates. The greatest overall performance was reached by a Boosted decision tree (Masud, Al-khateeb, Khan, Thuraisingham, and Hamlen, 2008). However, one major drawback of this approach is that it cannot detect Botnets that use encrypted communication due to the need to access the contents of payload packets. On the other hand, the method has been tested on IRC Bots, so it is unable to deal with modern types of malware such as P2P Botnets.

Gu et al. (2008) introduced Botminer as a network-based detection method which detects Botnet by correlating machines with comparable malicious activities and comparable C&C communications. Botminer utilizes X-means and hierarchical clustering methods to identify a Botnet using the observation that a Botnet is a collection of malware instances that are administered through the C&C channel and it has a similarity of the temporal behavior. The detection process operates by detecting hosts with activities of similar communications in the C-plane where hosts are communicating with different hosts, in other words, hosts which its traffic flows are related in respect of flows per hour (fph), bytes per second (bps), bytes per packet (bpp), and packets per flow (ppf). Besides this, hosts are defined with traffic of similar attacks in the A-Plane showing which host is doing what, such as hosts performing ports scan, downloading the same files, and spamming. The detection results are obtained by creating a cross-correlation between the A-Planes and C-Planes in order to classify machines that share similar malicious activity patterns and similar communications (Gu, Perdisci, Zhang, and Lee, 2008). The main advantages of Botminer is that it can identify several Botnet kinds such as IRC-based, P2P-based, and HTTP-based Botnets with 99% true positive rate and low FPR around 1%. Nevertheless, correlating activities that generated by various hosts needs at least two machines on the network be infected by the similarly Bot type. Consequently, Botminer fails in the situation of an individual machine is infected by Bot or when several machines inside the network are infected with diverse Bots types. Furthermore, Botminer fails to detect Bots that exchange C&C messages without any suspicious activity.

In Wei et al.'s (2009) study, they suggested BotCop as an online Botnet traffic detection system. In this method, network traffic is categorized into various applications using a decision tree technique. The network's payload characteristics are utilized, and then, based on each application community obtained, the temporal frequency properties of their flows are examined to classify a communication as malicious or legitimate traffic (Wei, Tavallaee, Rammidi, and Ghorbani, 2009). Table 9.7 summarizes machine learning-based Botnet detection methods.

Table 9.7   Summary of Machine Learning-Based Detection Methods

Method	Technique	Shortcoming
PeerRush (Babak et al., 2014)	One-class classification including the KNN algorithm, Parzen, and Gaussian data description classifiers	• Evaded by changing the delay between packets.
Garg et al. (2013)	KNN, Naive Bayes, and J48	• Detection of legitimate traffic is very weak.
Jiang and Shao (2012)	Single-linkage hierarchical clustering mechanism	• Detection single Bot infection.
Junjie et al. (2011)	The hierarchical clustering and BIRCH algorithms	• Fail to detect non-P2P Bots. • Evaded by DGA and Fast-flux algorithms.
Wen-Hwa and Chia-Ching (2010)	Bayesian networks, Naive Bayes, and J48	• NAT technology makes it difficult to detect P2P flows.
Zhao et al. (2013)	Bayesian network and REPTree decision tree	• Sensitivity to evasion methods such as the random connection interval.
Nogueira et al. (2010)	Artificial neural networks	• Need an external judgment to provide adaptive operation.
Timothy et al. (2008)	Bayesian network, C4.5 Tree, and Naïve Bayes classifiers	• Fail to detect non-IRC Bots. • Need human experts to make the final decision.
Masud et al. (2008)	C4.5 decision tree, SVM, Naive Bayes, Bayes network, and Boosted decision tree	• Payload encryption content. • Privacy issue.
Botminer (Gu, Perdisci, et al., 2008)	Spatial–temporal correlation	• Detection single Bot infection. • Detect Bots that exchange C&C messages without any suspicious activity.

9.5.5 DNS-Based Detection

At the same time, as efforts to detect Botnet are passively based on network traffic, other research-ers started to look for suspicious Botnet behaviors in DNS traffic. The DNS is a distributed nam-ing system for devices that are connected to the Internet; the DNS is responsible for converting domain names to IP addresses (Goerzen and Brandon, 2010). Bots exploit the DNS to find the Botmaster IP address, and the DNS responds by giving IP addresses that connect the compro-mised computers with the C&C server.

Accordingly, Kristoff (2005) introduced a technique that can identify a Botnet by monitoring the DNS traffic, and the technique blacklists any connected servers that spread malicious malware (Kristoff, 2005). In 2005, Dagon detected the activity of Botnets using a comparison of the rate of malicious DNS to legitimate DNS traffic (Dagon, 2005). However, both approaches can easily be avoided, whenever the Botmaster generates a fake DNS query or applies DDNS queries.

Choi et al. (2009) introduced BotGAD as an anomaly detection approach based on group activi-ties on Botnet DNS traffic (Choi, Lee, and Kim, 2009). The authors indicated that the group activities of DNS were key features of traffic used to differentiate a Botnet DNS from a normal DNS request. BotGAD is capable of detecting novel Botnet attacks on networks of huge scale in real time. The main weakness of the method is that it requires a long time for processing to monitor large volumes of network traffic (Han and Im, 2012). What is more, it is able to detect Botnets that execute group DNS traffic activities. Thus, it cannot detect Bots, which use the DNS once and never return to it.

Some of the common DNS-based techniques try to detect Botnets by detecting anomalies in DNS traffic (Villamarin-Salomon and Brustoloni, 2008), or detecting Bots based on DNS group behavior (Choi and Lee, 2012), using DNSBL (DNS Black List) (Ramachandran, Feamster, and Dagon, 2006), or constructing a reputation system for DNS queries (Antonakakis, Perdisci, Dagon, Lee, and Feamster, 2010). But many new models of Botnets as P2P and hybrid P2P do not involve DNS services in their operation, and so these approaches are significantly limited in detecting such Bots (Stevanovic, Revsbech, Pedersen, Sharp, and Jensen, 2012). Table 9.8 sum-marizes DNS-based Botnet detection methods.

9.5.6 Hybrid Botnet Detection Approaches

In parallel with standard network-based and client-based detection techniques, a new class of hybrid detection methods has appeared. This type of method detects Botnets by collecting the features of Bots at both client and network levels. The main reason behind hybrid strategies is that

Table 9.8 Summary of DNS-Based Detection Methods

Method	Technique	Shortcoming
Kristoff (2005)	White and black lists	• Avoided by generating a fake DNS query. • Avoided by using Dynamic DNS queries.
Dagon (2005)	Correlation algorithm	• Avoided by generating a fake DNS query. • Avoided by using DDNS queries.
BotGAD (Choi et al., 2009)	Monitoring group behavior through DNS traffic	• Detection single Bot infection. • Processing time.

it is likely to afford increases in performance in Botnet detection by connecting findings from client-based and network-based detection systems.

For example, Yuanyuan et al. (2010) proposed a hybrid detection approach that detects Botnets by combining the host- and network-level behaviors. The approach is based on the hypothesis that two sources of Bot observations will complement each other in making detection decisions. The structure of the approach consists of three parts: network analysis, host analysis, and a correlation engine (Yuanyuan, Xin, and Shin, 2010).

9.6 Summary

The existing Bot and Botnet detection systems described above have advantages and shortcomings compared to others. Different Botnet detection methods can be categorized based on various measures, such as being host-based or network-based, detecting individual Bots or Botnet networks, machine learning-based, anomaly-based, or signature-based Bot detection. They may be limited to one class of C&C topology or can detect Bots that apply multiple C&C structures.

References

Al-Hammadi, Y., & Aickelin, U. (2010). Behavioural correlation for detecting P2P bots. *Paper presented at the Second International Conference on Future Networks (ICFN)*, Sanya, Hainan.

Alder, R., Burke, J., Keefer, C., Orebaugh, A., Pesce, L., & Seagren, E. S. (2007). Chapter 4: Introducing snort. In R. Alder, J. Burke, C. Keefer, A. Orebaugh, L. Pesce & E. S. Seagren (Eds.), *How to Cheat at Configuring Open Source Security Tools* (pp. 181–212). Syngress, Burlington.

Antonakakis, M., Perdisci, R., Dagon, D., Lee, W., & Feamster, N. (2010). Building a dynamic reputation system for DNS. *Paper presented at the Proceedings of the 19th USENIX conference on Security*, Washington, DC.

Babak, R., Roberto, P., Andrea, L., & Kang, L. (2014). PeerRush: Mining for unwanted P2P traffic. *Journal of Information Security and Applications*, 19(3), 194–208. doi:10.1016/j.jisa.2014.03.002.

Bacher, P., Holz, T., Kotter, M., & Wicherski, G. (2005). Know your enemy: Tracking botnets. *The Honeynet Project and Research Alliance*.

Baecher, P., Koetter, M., Holz, T., Dornseif, M., & Freiling, F. (2006). The nepenthes platform: An efficient approach to collect malware. In D. Zamboni & C. Kruegel (Eds.), *Recent Advances in Intrusion Detection* (Vol. 4219, pp. 165–184). Springer, Berlin/Heidelberg.

Bailey, M., Cooke, E., Jahanian, F., Yunjing, X., & Karir, M. (2009). A survey of botnet technology and defenses. *Paper Presented at the Cybersecurity Applications & Technology Conference for Homeland Security*, Washington, DC.

Balas, E., & Viecco, C. (2005). Towards a third generation data capture architecture for honeynets. *Paper Presented at the In Proceedings of the 2005 IEEE Workshop on Information Assurance and Security*, New York.

Barford, P., & Yegneswaran, V. (2007). An inside look at botnets. In M. Christodorescu, S. Jha, D. Maughan, D. Song & C. Wang (Eds.), *Malware Detection* (Vol. 27, pp. 171–191). Springer, New York.

Barsamian, A. V. (2009). Network characterization for botnet detection using statistical-behavioral methods. *PhD Thesis*, Thayer School of Engineering Dartmouth College, Hanover, New Hampshire.

Barto, A. G., & Andrew, R.S. (1998). *Reinforcement Learning: An Introduction*. MIT Press, Cambridge, UK.

Boshmaf, Y., Muslukhov, I., Beznosov, K., & Ripeanu, M. (2013). Design and analysis of a social botnet. *Computer Networks*, 57(2), 556–578.

Breiman, L., Friedman, J. H., Olshen, R. A., & Stone, C. J. (1984). *Classification and Regression Trees*. Wadsworth & Brooks, Monterey, CA.

Chao, L., Wei, J., & Xin, Z. (2009, December 7–9). Botnet: Survey and case study. *Fourth International Conference on Paper Presented at the Innovative Computing, Information and Control (ICICIC)*, Kaohsiung, Taiwan.

Chiang, K., & Lloyd, L. (2007). A case study of the rustock rootkit and spam bot. *Paper Presented at the First Workshop in Understanding Botnets*, Cambridge, MA.

Choi, H., & Lee, H. (2012). Identifying botnets by capturing group activities in DNS traffic. *Computer Networks*, 56(1), 20–33. doi:10.1016/j.comnet.2011.07.018.

Choi, H., Lee, H., & Kim, H. (2009). BotGAD: Detecting botnets by capturing group activities in network traffic. *Paper Presented at the Proceedings of the Fourth International ICST Conference on Communication System Software and Middleware*, Dublin, Ireland.

Cooke, E., Jahanian, F., & McPherson, D. (2005). The zombie roundup: Understanding, detecting, and disrupting botnets. *Paper Presented at the Proceedings of the USENIX SRUTI Workshop*.

Cristianini, N., & Shawe-Taylor, J. (2000). *An Introduction to Support Vector Machines and Other Kernel-Based Learning Methods*. Cambridge University Press, Cambridge, UK.

Dae-il, J., Kang-yu, C., Minsoo, K., Hyun-chul, J., & Bong-Nam, N. (2010). Evasion technique and detection of malicious botnet. *Paper Presented at the International Conference for Internet Technology and Secured Transactions (ICITST)*, London, UK.

Dagon, D. (2005). Botnet detection and response, the network is the infection. *Paper Presented at the OARC Workshop*. www.caida.org/workshops/dns-oarc/200507/slides/oarc0507-Dagon.pdf.

Daswani, N., & Stoppelman, M. (2007). The anatomy of clickbot. A. *Paper Presented at the Proceedings of the First Conference on First Workshop on Hot Topics in Understanding Botnets*.

Davis, C. R., Fernandez, J. M., & Neville, S. (2009). Optimising Sybil attacks against P2P-based botnets. *Paper Presented at the 4th International Conference on Malicious and Unwanted Software*, Montreal, QC.

Dittrich, D., & Dietrich, S. (2008). Discovery techniques for P2P botnets. *Stevens Institute of Technology CS Technical Report 2008* (Vol. 4).

Fedynyshyn, G., Chuah, M., & Tan, G. (2011). Detection and classification of different botnet C&C channels. In J. A. Calero, L. Yang, F. Mármol, L. García Villalba, A. Li & Y. Wang (Eds.), *Autonomic and Trusted Computing* (Vol. 6906, pp. 228–242). Springer, Berlin/Heidelberg.

Feily, M., Shahrestani, A., & Ramadass, S. (2009). A survey of botnet and botnet detection. *SECURWARE '09. Third International Conference on Paper Presented at the Emerging Security Information, Systems and Technologies*, Athens, Glyfada, Greece.

Felix, J., Joseph, C., & Ghorbani, A. (2012). Group behavior metrics for P2P botnet detection. In T. Chim & T. Yuen (Eds.), *Information and Communications Security* (Vol. 7618, pp. 93–104). Springer, Berlin/Heidelberg.

Freiling, F., Holz, T., & Wicherski, G. (2005). Botnet tracking: Exploring a root-cause methodology to prevent distributed denial-of-service attacks. In S. di Vimercati, P. Syverson & D. Gollmann (Eds.), *Computer Security: ESORICS 2005* (Vol. 3679, pp. 319–335). Springer, Berlin/Heidelberg.

García, S., Zunino, A., & Campo, M. (2014). Survey on network-based botnet detection methods. *Security and Communication Networks*, 7(5), 878–903. doi:10.1002/sec.800.

Garg, S., Singh, A. K., Sarje, A. K., & Peddoju, S. K. (2013). Behaviour analysis of machine learning algorithms for detecting P2P botnets. *2013 15th International Conference on Paper Presented at the Advanced Computing Technologies (ICACT)*.

Goebel, J., & Holz, T. (2007). Rishi: Identify bot contaminated hosts by IRC nickname evaluation. *Paper Presented at the Proceedings of the First Conference on First Workshop on Hot Topics in Understanding Botnets*, Cambridge, MA.

Goerzen, J., & Brandon, R. (2010). Domain name system. In *Foundations of Python Network Programming* (2nd ed., pp. 65–85). Apress. ISBN 1430230037, 9781430230038.

Grizzard, J. B., Sharma, V., Nunnery, C., Kang, B. B., & Dagon, D. (2007). Peer-to-peer botnets: Overview and case study. *Paper Presented at the Proceedings of the First Conference on First Workshop on Hot Topics in Understanding Botnets*, Cambridge, MA.

Gu, G., Perdisci, R., Zhang, J., & Lee, W. (2008). BotMiner: Clustering analysis of network traffic for protocol-and structure-independent botnet detection. *Paper Presented at the USENIX Security Symposium*, San Jose, CA.

Gu, G., Porras, P., Yegneswaran, V., Fong, M., & Lee, W. (2007). BotHunter: Detecting malware infection through IDS-driven dialog correlation. *Paper Presented at the Proceedings of 16th USENIX Security Symposium on USENIX Security Symposium*, Boston, MA. http://portal.acm.org/citation.cfm?id=1362915#.

Gu, G., Zhang, J., & Lee, W. (2008). BotSniffer: Detecting botnet command and control channels in network traffic. *Paper Presented at the 15th Annual Network & Distributed System Security Symposium*, San Diego, CA.

Guofei, G., Yegneswaran, V., Porras, P., Stoll, J., & Wenke, L. (2009). Active botnet probing to identify obscure command and control channels. *Paper Presented at the Computer Security Applications Conference, 2009. ACSAC '09. Annual*, Honolulu, HI, USA.

Gurney, K. (1997). *An Introduction to Neural Networks.* Taylor & Francis, Bristol, PA.

Han, K.-S., & Im, E. (2012). A survey on P2P botnet detection. In K. J. Kim & S. J. Ahn (Eds.), *Proceedings of the International Conference on IT Convergence and Security 2011*, Suwon, South Korea (Vol. 120, pp. 589–593). Springer, Netherlands.

Hannah, K., & Gianvecchio, S. (2015). Zeuslite: A tool for botnet analysis in the classroom. *Journal of Computing Sciences in Colleges*, 30(3), 109–116.

Holz, T., Steiner, M., Dahl, F., Biersack, E., & Freiling, F. C. (2008). Measurements and mitigation of peer-to-peer-based botnets: A case study on storm worm. *LEET*, 8(1), 1–9.

Huy, H., Xuetao, W., Faloutsos, M., & Eliassi-Rad, T. (2013). Entelecheia: Detecting P2P botnets in their waiting stage. *Paper Presented at the IFIP Networking Conference*, Brooklyn, NY.

Ianelli, N., & Hackworth, A. (2005). Botnets as a vehicle for online crime. *CERT Coordination Center*, 1(1), 28.

Jain, A. K., Murty, M. N., & Flynn, P. J. (1999). Data clustering: A review. *ACM Computing Surveys*, 31(3), 264–323. doi:10.1145/331499.331504.

Jiang, H., & Shao, X. (2012). Detecting P2P botnets by discovering flow dependency in C&C traffic. *Peer-to-Peer Networking and Applications*, 7(4), 320–331.

John, J. P., Moshchuk, A., Gribble, S. D., & Krishnamurthy, A. (2009). Studying spamming botnets using Botlab. *Paper Presented at the 6th USENIX Symposium on Networked Systems Design and Implementation (NSDI)*, Boston, MA.

Junjie, Z., Perdisci, R., Wenke, L., Sarfraz, U., & Xiapu, L. (2011). Detecting stealthy P2P botnets using statistical traffic fingerprints. *Paper Presented at the IEEE/IFIP 41st International Conference on Dependable Systems & Networks (DSN)*, Hong Kong.

Kang, B. B., Chan-Tin, E., Lee, C. P., Tyra, J., Kang, H. J., Nunnery, C., . . . Kim, Y. (2009). Towards complete node enumeration in a peer-to-peer botnet. *Paper Presented at the Proceedings of the 4th International Symposium on Information, Computer, and Communications Security*, Sydney, Australia.

Karasaridis, A., Rexroad, B., & Hoeflin, D. (2007). Wide-scale botnet detection and characterization. *Paper Presented at the Proceedings of the First Conference on First Workshop on Hot Topics in Understanding Botnets*.

Kreibich, C., & Crowcroft, J. (2004). Honeycomb: Creating intrusion detection signatures using honeypots. *SIGCOMM Computer Communication Review*, 34(1), 51–56. doi:10.1145/972374.972384.

Kristoff, J. (2005). Botnets, detection and mitigation: DNS-based techniques. *NU Security Day*, 23.

Lashkari, A., Ghalebandi, S., & Reza Moradhaseli, M. (2011). A wide survey on botnet. In H. Cherifi, J. Zain & E. El-Qawasmeh (Eds.), *Digital Information and Communication Technology and Its Applications* (Vol. 166, pp. 445–454). Springer, Berlin/Heidelberg.

Li, H., Hu, G., & Yang, Y. (2012). Research on P2P botnet network behaviors and modeling. In C. Liu, L. Wang & A. Yang (Eds.), *Information Computing and Applications* (Vol. 307, pp. 82–89). Springer, Berlin/Heidelberg.

Liu, L., Chen, S., Yan, G., & Zhang, Z. (2008). BotTracer: Execution-based bot-like malware detection. In T.-C. Wu, C.-L. Lei, V. Rijmen & D.-T. Lee (Eds.), *Information Security* (Vol. 5222, pp. 97–113). Springer, Berlin/Heidelberg.

Livadas, C., Walsh, R., Lapsley, D., & Strayer, W. T. (2006). Using machine learning techniques to identify botnet traffic. *Paper Presented at the Proceedings 2006 31st IEEE Conference on Local Computer Networks*, Tampa, FL.

Lu, W., Rammidi, G., & Ghorbani, A. A. (2011). Clustering botnet communication traffic based on n-gram feature selection. *Computer Communications*, 34(3), 502–514. doi:10.1016/j.comcom.2010.04.007.

Ludl, C., McAllister, S., Kirda, E., & Kruegel, C. (2007). On the effectiveness of techniques to detect phishing sites. In B. Hämmerli & R. Sommer (Eds.), *Detection of Intrusions and Malware, and Vulnerability Assessment* (Vol. 4579, pp. 20–39). Springer, Berlin/Heidelberg.

Masud, M. M., Al-khateeb, T., Khan, L., Thuraisingham, B., & Hamlen, K. W. (2008). Flow-based identification of botnet traffic by mining multiple log files. *Paper Presented at the First International Conference on Distributed Framework and Applications*, Penang, Malaysia

Micro, T. (2006). Taxonomy of botnet threats, *A Trend Micro White Paper*.

Mille, A., Horne, R., & Potter, C. (2014). Information security breaches survey (technical report). PriceWaterhouseCoopers.

Mitchell, T. M. (1997). *Machine Learning*. McGraw-Hill, New Delhi.

Mukamurenzi, N. M. (2008). Storm worm: A P2P botnet. Master of Science in Communication Technology, Norwegian University of Science and Technology, Norway.

Nagaraja, S., Houmansadr, A., Piyawongwisal, P., Singh, V., Agarwal, P., & Borisov, N. (2011). Stegobot: A covert social network botnet. In T. Filler, T. Pevný, S. Craver & A. Ker (Eds.), *Information Hiding* (Vol. 6958, pp. 299–313). Springer, Berlin/Heidelberg.

Nilsson, N. J. (1996). *Introduction to machine learning: An early draft of a proposed textbook*. Stanford University, USA.

Nogueira, A., Salvador, P., & Blessa, F. (2010). A botnet detection system based on neural networks. *Paper Presented at the Fifth International Conference on digital Telecommunications (ICDT)*, Athens, TBD, Greece.

Nummipuro, A. (2007). Detecting P2P-controlled bots on the host. *Paper Presented at the Seminar on Network Security*, Espoo, Helsinki.

Pelleg, D., & Moore, A. W. (2000). X-means: Extending K-means with efficient estimation of the number of clusters. *Paper Presented at the Seventeenth International Conference on Machine Learning (ICML)*, Stanford University, USA.

Pham, V.-H., & Dacier, M. (2011). Honeypot trace forensics: The observation viewpoint matters. *Future Generation Computer Systems*, 27(5), 539–546.

Provos, N. (2003). Honeyd-a virtual honeypot daemon. *Paper Presented at the 10th DFN-CERT Workshop*, Hamburg, Germany.

Rajab, M. A., Zarfoss, J., Monrose, F., & Terzis, A. (2006). A multifaceted approach to understanding the botnet phenomenon. *Paper Presented at the Proceedings of the 6th ACM SIGCOMM Conference on Internet Measurement*, Rio de Janeiro, Brazil.

Ramachandran, A., & Feamster, N. (2006). Understanding the network-level behavior of spammers. *SIGCOMM Computer Communication Review*, 36, 291–302. doi:10.1145/1151659.1159947.

Ramachandran, A., Feamster, N., & Dagon, D. (2006). Revealing botnet membership using DNSBL counter-intelligence. *Paper Presented at the Proceedings of the 2nd conference on Steps to Reducing Unwanted Traffic on the Internet—Volume 2*, San Jose, CA.

Rodríguez-Gómez, R. A., Maciá-Fernández, G., & García-Teodoro, P. (2013). Survey and taxonomy of botnet research through life-cycle. *ACM Computing Surveys (CSUR)*, 45(4), 45. doi:10.1145/2501654.2501659.

Roesch, M. (1999). Snort: Lightweight intrusion detection for networks. *Paper Presented at the 13th USENIX Conference on System administration*, Seattle, WA, USA.

Saad, S., Traore, I., Ghorbani, A., Sayed, B., Zhao, D., Lu, W., Felix, J., & Hakimian, P. (2011). Detecting P2P botnets through network behavior analysis and machine learning. *Paper Presented at the Ninth Annual International Conference on Privacy, Security and Trust (PST)*, Montreal, QC.

Schiller, C., & Binkley, J. R. (2007). *Botnets: The Killer Web Applications*. Syngress.

Selvaraj, K. (2014). A brief look at zeus/Zbot 2.0. *Symantec Security Response*.

Seungwon, S., Zhaoyan, X., & Guofei, G. (2012). EFFORT: Efficient and effective bot malware detection. *Paper Presented at the INFOCOM, 2012 Proceedings IEEE*, Orlando, FL.

Silva, R. S. C., Silva, R. M. P., Pinto, R. C. G., & Salles, R. M. (2013). Botnets: A survey. *Computer Network*, 57(2), 378–403. doi:10.1016/j.comnet.2012.07.021.

Stevanovic, M., Revsbech, K., Pedersen, J., Sharp, R., & Jensen, C. (2012). A collaborative approach to botnet protection multidisciplinary research and practice for information systems. In G. Quirchmayr, J. Basl, I. You, L. Xu & E. Weippl (Eds.), *Multidisciplinary Research and Practice for Information Systems* (Vol. 7465, pp. 624–638). Springer, Berlin/Heidelberg.

Stinson, E., & Mitchell, J. C. (2007). Characterizing Bots' remote control behavior. *Paper Presented at the Proceedings of the 4th International Conference on Detection of Intrusions and Malware, and Vulnerability Assessment*, Lucerne, Switzerland.

Stock, B., Go, X., Bel, J., Engelberth, M., Freiling, F. C., & Holz, T. (2009). Walowdac: Analysis of a peer-to-peer botnet. *Paper presented at the European Conference on Computer Network Defense (EC2ND)*, Milan, Italy.

Stover, S., Dittrich, D., Hernandez, J., & Dietrich, S. (2007). Analysis of the storm and nugache trojans: P2P is here. *USENIX; Login*, 32(6), 18–27.

Strayer, W. T., Walsh, R., Livadas, C., & Lapsley, D. (2006). Detecting botnets with tight command and control. *Paper Presented at the 31st IEEE Conference on Local Computer Networks*, Tampa, FL.

Szymczyk, M. (2009). Detecting botnets in computer networks using multi-agent technology. *Paper Presented at the Fourth International Conference on Dependability of Computer Systems*, Brunow, Germany.

TAX, D. (2001). One-class classification. *PhD Thesis*, TU Delft University.

Tegeler, F., Fu, X., Vigna, G., & Kruegel, C. (2012). BotFinder: Finding bots in network traffic without deep packet inspection. *Paper Presented at the Proceedings of the 8th International Conference on Emerging Networking Experiments and Technologies*, Nice, France.

Timothy, S. W., David, L., Robert, W., & Carl, L. (2008). Botnet detection based on network behavior. In W. Lee, C. Wang & D. Dagon (Eds.), *Botnet Detection* (Vol. 36, pp. 1–24). Springer, Boston, MA.

Tyagi, A. K., & Aghila, G. (2011). A wide scale survey on botnet. *International Journal of Computer Applications*, 34(9), 9–22.

Villamarin-Salomon, R., & Brustoloni, J. C. (2008). Identifying botnets using anomaly detection techniques applied to DNS traffic. *Paper Presented at the 5th IEEE Consumer Communications and Networking Conference (CCNC)*, Las Vegas, NV.

Wang, K., Huang, C.-Y., Lin, S.-J., & Lin, Y.-D. (2011). A fuzzy pattern-based filtering algorithm for botnet detection. *Computer Networks*, 55(15), 3275–3286. doi:10.1016/j.comnet.2011.05.026.

Wang, P., Sparks, S., & Zou, C. C. (2010). An advanced hybrid peer-to-peer botnet. *Dependable and Secure Computing, IEEE Transactions on*, 7(2), 113–127.

Wang, X., Qiu, W., & Zamar, R. H. (2007). CLUES: A non-parametric clustering method based on local shrinking. *Computational Statistics & Data Analysis*, 52(1), 286–298. doi:10.1016/j.csda.2006.12.016.

Weaver, N., Paxson, V., Staniford, S., & Cunningham, R. (2003). A taxonomy of computer worms. *Paper Presented at the Proceedings of the 2003 ACM Workshop on Rapid Malcode*, Washington, DC.

Weaver, R. (2010). A probabilistic population study of the Conficker-C botnet. *Paper Presented at the Proceedings of the 11th International Conference on Passive and Active Measurement*, Zurich, Switzerland.

Wei, L., Tavallaee, M., Rammidi, G., & Ghorbani, A. A. (2009). BotCop: An online botnet traffic classifier. *Paper Presented at the Seventh Annual Communication Networks and Services Research Conference (CNSR)*, Moncton, NB.

Wen-Hwa, L., & Chia-Ching, C. (2010). Peer to peer botnet detection using data mining scheme. *Paper Presented at the International Conference on Internet Technology and Applications*, Wuhan, China.

Witten, I. H., & Frank, E. (2005). *Data Mining: Practical Machine Learning Tools and Techniques* (Morgan Kaufmann Series in Data Management Systems), 2nd Ed. Morgan Kaufmann, Boston, MA.

Yuanyuan, Z., Xin, H., & Shin, K. G. (2010). Detection of botnets using combined host- and network-level information. *Paper Presented at the IEEE/IFIP International Conference on Dependable Systems and Networks (DSN)*, Chicago.

Zeidanloo, H. R., Bt Manaf, A., Vahdani, P., Tabatabaei, F., & Zamani, M. (2010). Botnet detection based on traffic monitoring. *Paper Presented at the International Conference on Networking and Information Technology (ICNIT)*, Manila, Philippines.

Zeidanloo, H. R., Shooshtari, M. J. Z., Amoli, P. V., Safari, M., & Zamani, M. (2010). A taxonomy of Botnet detection techniques. *Paper Presented at the 3rd IEEE International Conference on Computer Science and Information Technology (ICCSIT)*, Chengdu, China.

Zhang, T., Ramakrishnan, R., & Livny, M. (1997). BIRCH: A new data clustering algorithm and its applications. *Data Mining and Knowledge Discovery*, 1(2), 141–182. doi:10.1023/a:1009783824328.

Zhao, D., Traore, I., Sayed, B., Lu, W., Saad, S., Ghorbani, A., & Garant, D. (2013). Botnet detection based on traffic behavior analysis and flow intervals. *Computers & Security*, 39, Part A(0), 2–16. doi:10.1016/j.cose.2013.04.007.

Zhaosheng, Z., Guohan, L., Yan, C., Zhi, F., Roberts, P., & Keesook, H. (2008). Botnet research survey. *Paper Presented at the 32nd Annual IEEE International Computer Software and Applications*, Turku.

Chapter 10

Overview of Smartphone Security: Attack and Defense Techniques

Diksha Goel and Ankit Kumar Jain

National Institute of Technology

Contents

10.1 Introduction

Nowadays, mobile devices especially smartphones are increasingly being used by the users due to a wide range of functionalities they provide. Apart from basic services, such as calling, Short Message Service (SMS), audio, video, Multimedia Messaging Service (MMS), and other multimedia services, these devices also provide a variety of other services like Internet, office applications, Wi-Fi, etc. These devices are very compact and provide functionalities similar to those of traditional desktop computers along with a variety of connectivity options, such as Global System for Mobile (GSM) communications, General Packet Radio Service (GPRS), IEEE 802.11, Bluetooth, HSPA, and Universal Mobile Telecommunications System (UMTS) due to which attackers are now targeting the mobile users. In addition, smartphones also consist of many sensors like microphone, Global Positioning System (GPS), accelerometers, camera, and speakers. Moreover, small screen size, portability, ease of use, and longer battery life of smartphones have also attracted users.

Smartphone devices have become dominant for accessing the Internet. Since users frequently use smartphones for carrying out their online sensitive transactions like Internet banking or online shopping, more attacking opportunities are created for the attackers. As a result, the mobile platform has become a new focus point for the attackers. Not only the device but also the information contained in it presents an attractive target for the attackers. Mobile applications are getting popularity among the users. Users may download an application while browsing or from third-party application store, which may result in download of malware. Once the malicious application enters your device, it collects sensitive information of the users and transmits it to attackers. Login and account details are the prime targets for the attackers. Consequently, a malicious application may cause financial loss to the users by stealing personal information. Recent studies have shown that over 70% of mobile applications request for the permissions that are not relevant for the working of application and can result in leakage of personal information or improper use of resources. Once the device is compromised, it can be used to perform a number of malicious activities.

A study reveals that 44% of users are not even aware of security solutions available for mobile devices [1]. The first attack against the smartphone was launched in March 2010. It was a drive-by download attack on iPhone 3GS that targeted the SMS database. Resource management process of smartphone devices varies from that of desktop devices, due to which the existing security solutions for desktop systems are not compatible with mobile devices [2]. Antivirus software is available for mobile devices. According to International Data Corporation (IDC) research report, only 5% of smartphones have an antivirus program installed in them [3]. Therefore, security solutions are required in order to address the security issues of the smartphone devices.

Researchers and software development organizations have understood that traditional static analysis methods are inefficient and vulnerable, whereas techniques like encryption and code conversion approaches are capable of protecting users from well-known malware. So, anomaly detection and dynamic analysis-based approaches should be used. The existing techniques focus on securing operating system (OS) of smartphone, but with the increasing malware attacks, there is a tremendous need for anti-malware techniques. The exponential increase in the number of malicious applications has attracted the focus of anti-malware industry to come up with robust and efficient methods. Manual analysis and extraction process need adequate time and skills. Furthermore, the mobile OS enforces restrictions on mobile applications. Security solutions for mobile devices must defend them from viruses, malware, intrusion attacks, other threats incurred.

iOS, as well as Android mobile OS, implements application privilege separation model, i.e., sand-box shields the applications from unauthorized access to data.

The chapter is structured as follows. Section 2 describes OSs for the smartphones where we have discussed Android and iOS architectures in detail. Section 3 discusses background notions on mobile technologies for both wireless telecommunication technologies and networking technologies. Section 4 presents various security concerns of smartphones. Section 5 discusses different types of attacks against smartphone devices. In Section 6, various defense approaches are discussed. In Section 7, the existing countermeasures proposed by researchers are discussed. In Section 8, various reverse-engineering tools and attack detection tools are discussed. In Section 9, open issues and challenges are discussed. Finally, Section 10 concludes the chapter.

10.2 OSs for Smartphones

The mobile OS [4] is a software platform on top of which other applications or programs run such as Mobile phones and Personal Digital Assistant (PDA). Initially only standardized OSs were used for the smartphones, but nowadays, a number of Oss are available such as Android, iOS, and Windows. The OS has evolved over the years, from desktop-based OS to embedded OS to smartphone-oriented OS. Moreover, this evolution has decreased the complexity of OS and is driven by development in hardware, software, and the Internet.

Hardware: Form factor size of microprocessor and peripherals is reduced in order to design mobile devices. It is only when factor size was reduced that mobile devices are able to achieve small size along with high processing capabilities. Earlier there were either big size desktop computers or low processing PDAs. Also, earlier mobile OSs were not multitasking and did not support 3D graphics. But now with the evolution of hardware, it is possible to design small smart devices with high processing power.

Software: Software is mainly focused on the productivity of the user. The software for smart-phones helps users to manage personal data on the device, such as contacts, images, and emails. There are many application software developed to make the task of user easy, e.g., banking application and shopping application.

Internet: After the development of Web 2.0, an enormous amount of information is available on the network for the users. This information includes business information, educational data, organizational information, etc. Users are now dependent on the Internet for a variety of tasks.

10.2.1 Android OS

Android OS was developed by the Open Handset Alliance headed by Google in 2007. By 2013, Android device market was more than the other OSs like Windows and iOS [5]. For Android platform, applications are developed in Java, and these applications run with Dalvik Virtual Machine (DVM). DVM is an Android virtual machine optimized for mobile devices. Every application in Android platform runs with a unique User ID (UID) and with distinct permissions. The architecture of Android platform is shown in Figure 10.1 and layers are discussed below:

Linux Kernel: Android platform depends on Linux for fundamental system services such as process management, memory management, and security.

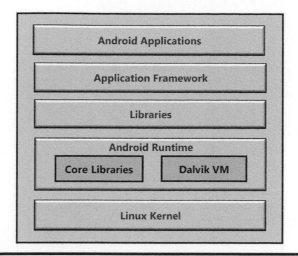

Figure 10.1   Android OS architecture.

Android Runtime: A set of core libraries are provided by the Android runtime, and it supports many functionalities in the core libraries of Java. Android Virtual Machine is also known as DVM, and it depends on the Linux kernel for performing core functionalities.

Libraries: Android consists of a set of C or C++ libraries. Android application framework presents these libraries to the developers. These libraries include system C libraries, media libraries, surface manager, SQLite, and so on.

Application Framework: It provides access layer to the Application Program Interface (API) used by the core applications. It allows the developers to use the components of the device.

10.2.2 *iOS*

iOS, previously known as iPhone OS, is an OS for mobile devices developed by Apple, Inc. and was developed solely for Apple hardware. It is not an open source platform. It can also be regarded as a variant of UNIX. It consists of four layers: Core OS, Core Services, Media, and Cocoa Touch. The architecture of iOS platform is shown in Figure 10.2 and layers are discussed below:

Core OS: The kernel of the OS includes basic fundamental features, such as system support for threads, sockets, input/output, memory management, general security services like certificates, private/public keys, Bluetooth, encryption, image processing, and hardware management.

Core Services: There are various fundamental services that are subdivided into frameworks based on C. These services include basic application services such as contacts, accounts, data management, networking, calendar events, location information, store purchasing, XML support, and SQLite.

Media Layer: It includes high-level frameworks that are responsible for the use of graphics, audio and video technologies.

Cocoa Touch: The UIKit provides a number of functionalities that are required for the development of an iOS application. It also includes API such as touch input, multitasking, interface views, notifications, and access to device data for building applications.

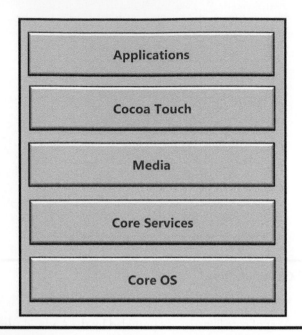

Figure 10.2 iOS architecture.

10.3 Mobile Technologies

Mobile technology is used for cellular communication. The mobile devices have evolved from being a two-way pager to a smartphone with embedded features. This section briefly describes wireless network technologies that have contributed to the increase in the usage of smartphone devices.

10.3.1 Wireless Telecommunication Technologies

Wireless technology has put an end to the costly process of using cables wires for establishing the connection between different locations. Wireless technology is implemented using radio technology. In Open System Interconnect model, it is implemented at the physical layer. In this subsection, wireless telecommunication technologies such as GSM, GPRS, Enhanced Data rates for GSM Evolution (EDGE), and UMTS that are used for mobile communication are discussed.

10.3.1.1 GSM Communications

GSM is a standard for telecommunication system used in Europe and other parts of the world. It is a Second-Generation (2G) technology. GSM facilitates the formation of a cellular network where the mobile stations (also called mobile phones), with the help of base stations and network, communicate with each other. It uses the variation of Time Division Multiple Access. GSM in collaboration with other technologies, such as High Speed Circuit Switched Data, UMTS, GPRS, and EDGE, is part of the development of wireless mobile telecommunications [6].

10.3.1.2 GPRS and EDGE

Both GPRS and EDGE standards are the stems of GSM. GPRS is General Packet Radio Service, also called 2.5 Generation (2.5G). It was an initiative to increase the data rate and decrease access time by improving the performance of the GSM network. Packet switching mechanism is used by GPRS for data transmission. EDGE stands for Enhanced Data rates for GSM Evolution. It is a standard, designed to improve the GPRS by providing higher reliability and transmission rate [7]. It was launched by Cingular in United States in 2003. It is also known as 2.75 Generation (2.75G). It was developed to deliver various multimedia services, such as audio and videos, to mobile phones at a faster rate. It provides speed up to 384 Kbps.

10.3.1.3 Universal Mobile Telecommunications System

UMTS was introduced in 2002 and is also known as Third-Generation (3G) network. It is based on GSM standard. Its transmission rate is more than 2G and 2.5G, and it provides transmission speed up to 2 Mbps. UMTS provides a set of services to the users and supports circuit switching connections along with packet switching. It supports data applications as well as voice applications. UMTS is a complete network system and is also called as Freedom of Mobile Multimedia Access. UMTS has increased the quality of the voice and reduced the round trip packet delay [8].

10.3.1.4 Long-Term Evolution

Long-Term Evolution (LTE) is a wireless communication standard for mobile devices. This standard is developed by the Third-Generation Partnership Project (3GPP). LTE is commonly known by the name "4G LTE". LTE is based on Orthogonal Frequency Division Multiple Access and has achieved data rates of 300 Mbps. The design goal behind LTE is to increase the speed and capacity of wireless network using digital signal-processing techniques [9].

10.3.2 Networking Technologies

With the increase in the popularity and usage of laptop computers, the popularity of Wireless Local Area Network (WLAN) has also increased. With the help of this technology, users can move in the local area network without being disconnected to the network. Various standards are there in WLAN that regulate the communication. For the mobile environment, Bluetooth and IEEE 802.11 are the popular ones.

10.3.2.1 Bluetooth

It was developed in 1999 by Bluetooth Special Interest Group (SIG). It enables transfer of data among the devices that are present within a short range (i.e., 1–100 m) and have low processing capabilities. It was designed to support networking among portable devices that run on battery. Currently, many devices support Bluetooth such as cell phones, printers, computers, speakers, and wireless keyboards. There has been much revision in the Bluetooth standards starting from version 1 to version 5 [10]. Earlier Bluetooth standards supported connections below 1 Mbps, whereas current versions support connections up to 50 Mbps.

10.3.2.2 WLAN IEEE 802.11

It is a standard of WLAN, developed in 1997 by Institute of Electrical and Electronics Engineers (IEEE). It uses radio waves to connect the devices such as laptops and mobile phones to the Internet. It supports a network bandwidth of up to 2 Mbps. It comprises various communication protocols operating at different frequencies, such as 2.4, 3.6, and 5 GHz. It basically operates in two modes. First, in infrastructure mode, a device denoted as an access point is a referee and controls access to the network. Second, in infrastructure-less mode, also called an ad-hoc mode, there is no referee, and devices themselves observe the network. Other protocols included in 802.11 standards are 802.11b and 802.11g [11].

10.4 Security Concerns of Smartphones

In this section, we discuss various security concerns related to the smartphones that include the goals of attackers, assets of smartphones, reason of smartphone vulnerabilities, and various threats to smartphones.

10.4.1 Goal of Attackers

Attackers take advantage of vulnerabilities found in the device as well as the careless behavior of the user. This section discusses the goal of the attackers:

- Attack on the privacy of user: Smartphones are comparatively smaller in size than laptops, so chances of these devices getting stolen is more. In privacy attacks, the integrity and confidentiality of the smartphones are violated. There are many methods, such as cross-site scripting or phishing attacks to steal data from smartphone device.
- Overbilling: Many wireless services follow the pay-per-use system. The attacker may target the victim to charge additional amount by showing more usage of the service and then transfer this extra amount to his own account.
- Denial of service (DoS) attack: In DoS attack, the attacker affects the availability of device or service. Due to hardware limitation of mobile devices, DoS attack on a mobile device can be launched by the traffic generated by one attacker only. An attacker can initiate the DoS attack by sending a large number of SMSs or MMSs to the device of user, preventing him from performing any task. This attack can also drain the device battery by carrying out CPU-intensive tasks that lead to consumption of energy.
- Selling user information: Sometimes attackers steal user's credentials not for personal use but for selling it to other users who might use these credentials to hide their identity.
- Eavesdropping: It is an unauthorized interception in the personal communication, such as voice calls, messages, and video conferencing. An attacker attempts to intercept the communication between mobile phone and the base station in order to gain sensitive credentials of the user.
- Ransom: Attackers attack smartphone devices in order to get ransom from the users who can pay the ransom. Ransomware is a virus which when downloaded restricts access to data or services and threatens user to block the device unless a ransom is paid.

10.4.2 Assets of Smartphones

Assets can be regarded as one of the targets for the attackers for launching attack against the device. Table 10.1 shows some of the smartphone assets along with their description. These assets

Table 10.1   Assets of Smartphone

Assets	Description
Private information	It comprises data stored in the mobile device as well as data transferred from the device, e.g., SMS, location information, passwords for login, contacts, call history, and other information.
Applications	Applications installed by the user on the device.
Device	Lost smartphone can be used for performing malicious activities.

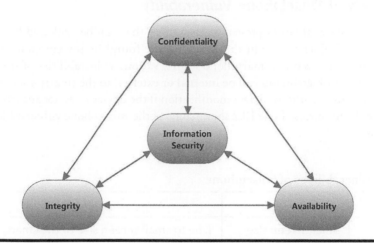

Figure 10.3   CIA triad.

include private information stored in the device, applications of the device, and the device itself. Resources of the smartphone are considered as an asset. Sensitive information stored in the device is also an important asset. This information includes contacts, messages, login ids, passwords, emails, etc. The application installed in the device can also be considered as an asset. Applications store login ids and passwords for the online authentication process for the corresponding applications. Due to inconvenience experienced by the users in providing login details each time he wants to access service, they save the credentials in the application. In addition, smartphone device itself is an asset. The lost device can be used by the attacker to perform illegal activities.

10.4.3 Security Objectives

Confidentiality, integrity, and availability are the basic security objectives that need to be attained for information security [12]. These three security objectives are popularly known as CIA triad and are shown in Figure 10.3. These security objectives are violated whenever an attacker attacks the device.

Confidentiality: Confidentiality is essential in order to establish trust between the communicating parties. It determines who is authorized to access how much amount of information. It is nearly same as privacy. Data encryption is a commonly used method to ensure confidentiality.

Integrity: Integrity is maintained when the data remains the same during transmission and usage unless an authorized modification is done by authorized users. Integrity ensures that only authorized users are allowed to access or modify the resources. It ensures that the data is precise, consistent, and accurate.

Availability: Availability ensures that services or resources should be available to the authorized users at any time of their requirement without any delay. Since effective security solutions protect the components of the system, ensuring the availability of the resources is directly related to information security.

10.4.4 Reason of Smartphone Vulnerability

Vulnerabilities are the weaknesses present in the device that can be exploited by the attacker to perform the attack. Vulnerabilities in the device can be found in any components, procedures, designs, etc. In order to keep the smartphone secure, various vulnerabilities of smartphone need to be identified [13]. Vulnerabilities can be internal or external to the smartphone. For example, a device is vulnerable to unauthorized data modification if the device does not authenticate the users before accessing the resources. Table 10.2 shows some of the smartphone vulnerabilities along with their description.

Table 10.2 Vulnerabilities of Smartphone

Vulnerability		Description
Internal of smartphone	Small screen size	Due to small screen size of the smartphone, browsers and other application have to change or remove many security features which help attackers to bypass the security mechanism.
	Open source platform	Many OS have an open source platform which helps attacker to bypass the security checks.
	Implementation error	Attacker can take advantage of implementation errors (arbitrary code, type safety, execution).
	Incompatibility	Attacker can take advantage of incompatibility between two applications or between application and platform.
	User unawareness	Unawareness of user may lead to installation of malicious applications, connecting device to untrusted networks, improper configuration, social engineering attacks, and misplace of smartphone.
External of smartphone	Vulnerabilities of wireless network	Attacker can take advantage of vulnerabilities of wireless network by corrupting or modifying the information using sniffing or eavesdropping.
	Vulnerabilities of external objects	Attacker can take advantage of vulnerabilities of external objects of smartphone environment like web server, access point, or base station.

10.4.5 Threats to Smartphones

Threat exploits the vulnerability in order to perform the attack and directly affects the security of the device. It is a potential occurrence of an event that may compromise the objectives or assets of the smartphone device. There are many threats to the smartphone devices such as malware, wireless network attack, DoS attacks, spyware, break-in, loss of device, and phishing attacks. The threat to the smartphone can be caused by the attacker or user. By controlling the vulnerability, a threat can be blocked. Some threats along with their vulnerabilities are shown in Table 10.3.

10.5 Attacks against Smartphones

Attacks on mobile devices can be classified into various categories. In this section, various types of attacks against the smartphone devices are discussed.

10.5.1 Social Engineering Attacks

Social engineering attack tricks users into revealing their credentials. These attacks over mobile phones can be carried out through SMS, voice calls, emails, etc. This attack targets the vulnerabilities present in users rather than that of system due to which technical protection is not effective. This attack takes advantage of ignorance and carelessness of the users. Social engineering attack cycle includes gathering information about the victim, developing relation with the victim, after that the attacker exploits the relationship and executes the attack to achieve the objectives. The social engineering attack cycle is shown in Figure 10.4. Some of the social engineering approaches are social approach, technical approach, and physical approach.

Table 10.3 Threats to Smartphone

Caused by	Threat	Vulnerability
Attacker	Malware	Implementation error User unawareness Vulnerabilities of external objects
	Wireless network attack	Vulnerabilities of wireless network
	DoS	Vulnerabilities of wireless network Vulnerabilities of external objects
	Spyware	User unawareness
	Botnet attack	Implementation error
	Eavesdropping	Vulnerabilities of wireless network
	Break-in	Implementation error

(Continued)

Table 10.3 (*Continued*)   Threats to Smartphone

Caused by	Threat	Vulnerability
User	Malfunctioning	Incompatibility User unawareness
	Phishing	User unawareness
	Loss of device	
	Loss of information	
	Ad and click fraud	
	Dead applications	
	Platform alteration	

10.5.2 Wireless Attacks

There are various kinds of wireless attacks that target the sensitive information of the user. Attackers spy on the data transmitted through the wireless medium to gain sensitive information of the user. These attacks can manipulate the hardware identification of the devices in order to spy on the user. Different security challenges in the wireless environment are discussed in [14]. Wireless attacks on mobile devices can be launched through Wi-Fi or Bluetooth.

10.5.2.1 Attack through Bluetooth

Bluetooth technology is used to share the data using wireless links between devices that are present within a short range. Bluetooth attack is used to spread malware from one device to another. When two devices come in range, the compromised device gets connected to the target device using default Bluetooth passwords and malicious content is sent to that device without owner's permission [15]. Once the attacker gains access to the device of the user, he can monitor the activities performed by the user.

10.5.2.2 Attack through Wi-Fi

Wi-Fi is a wireless networking technology, which is used to provide Internet and network connection over wireless links. As the number of devices that support Wi-Fi is increasing, wireless hotspot providing free connection is also increasing. Users are not aware that all the hotspots do not have same security level and rogue access point also exists. It is an easy task for an attacker to set up a

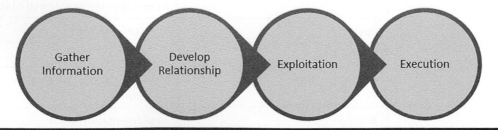

Figure 10.4   Social engineering attack cycle.

rogue access point that looks similar to authentic one. The architecture of Hotspot is vulnerable, and it does not perform any encryption to protect the transferred data.

10.5.3 Man-in-the-Middle Attacks

In man-in-the-middle (MITM) attack, the attacker intercepts between the legitimate user and the server, and listens their communication or impersonates as legitimate user. User believes that he is directly communicating with the server, but in actual, the attacker is sitting between the user and the server as shown in Figure 10.5. The details submitted to server are received by the attacker, and the attacker continues to pass the details to the server so that user's transaction is not affected. The goal of attacker is to steal personal information such as card details and login information from the user. Target victims may be the financial application users [16].

10.5.4 Break-in Attacks

In Break-in attack, the attacker gains control over the target device by exploiting the flaws present in the code such as buffer overflow or format string vulnerability. Break-in attacks are used as an initial step for performing further attacks such as identity theft and spying on the user [17]. An attacker may install a corrupted file into the user's device which may contain Trojan to spy on activities of the user.

10.5.5 Mobile Application Attacks

Application-based attacks on mobile phone have become one of the major problems faced by mobile phone users. Once the malicious application enters the device, it may collect personal information of the user and transmit the same to attacker. Attacker may gain complete control over the device by installing the malicious application into the device of the user. Attacker may also install backdoor. Malicious application can be of two types. First is when a malicious application pretends to be a legitimate application [9]. Second is when a malicious application attempts to

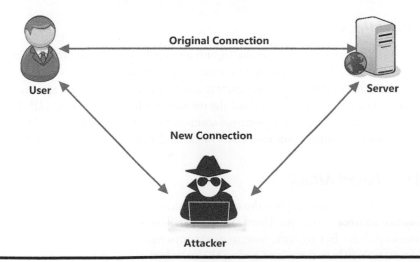

Figure 10.5   **Man-in-the-middle attack.**

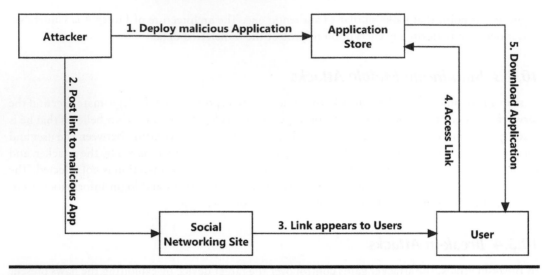

Figure 10.6   Distribution of malicious applications in mobile phones.

hijack the existing legitimate applications. Figure 10.6 describes the distribution process of malicious applications in mobile phones.

10.5.6 Infrastructure-Based Attacks

Infrastructure provides basic services for the essential working of the smartphones, such as making or receiving calls, emails, and SMS, but the social and economic impact of the attack on infrastructure is very large [18]. Security impacts of SMS interface on the availability of network are discussed in [19]. For example, if an attacker sends messages by using some available ports into the network, this aggregated load can block the legitimate communication. As the architecture of GPRS is based on GSM, so its security architecture is also based on the security measures of GSM. The attack on GPRS may target the interface that connects GPRS network with the Internet.

10.5.7 DoS Attack

In DoS attack [20], an attacker prevents the legitimate user from accessing the services, resources, or devices. In this attack, the attackers flood the network, server, or systems with a large amount of traffic, making it difficult for the legitimate users to access the services. In DoS attack, one computer and one Internet connection are used to flood the network with bogus requests [21]. In Distributed Denial of Service attack, multiple compromised computer systems (slaves) are used to flood the network with Transmission Control Protocol/User Datagram Protocol packets as shown in Figure 10.7.

10.5.8 User-Based Attack

In user-based attacks, attackers exploit the vulnerabilities caused due to the behavior of the users, e.g., ignoring the security warnings. There are some malwares that are not designed to exploit the technical vulnerabilities but to trick user so as to outweigh the technical security mechanism. These malwares aim to lure users into giving their credentials to the attackers. Various surveys have been conducted to determine the security awareness of the users. Many times users ignore

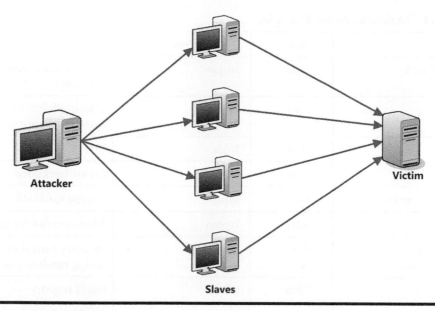

Figure 10.7 DoS attack.

the permissions requested by the application and grant access to contacts and messages which are not even relevant as per the functionality of the applications. So, the user must actively participate in the installation process of the applications.

10.5.9 Mobile Malware-Based Attack

Malware is a malicious software that enters the device without permission of the user. Generally, it is distributed as a malicious attachment with the spam. Malware in mobile phones can spread through various vectors such as via MMS having a malicious attachment, SMS containing a link to the malicious website, or malicious program received through Bluetooth. The aim of malware is to steal sensitive information from the user [22]. Table 10.4 presents some examples of mobile malware. Figure 10.8 shows the distribution of mobile malware for the years 2015 and 2016. This section provides an overview of mobile malwares.

10.5.9.1 Virus

It is a malicious piece of code that replicates by copying itself to another document or program. Attackers make use of security vulnerabilities to infect the device and spread the virus. Virus results into failure of device, corrupting data and consuming device resources. The virus also performs some harmful activities on the host device, such as consuming disk space, accessing sensitive information, logging their keystrokes, and even rendering the device useless [24].

10.5.9.2 Trojan

It is a malicious application that claims to perform some useful functionality in front of the user but instead contains malicious program and performs malicious actions in the background.

Table 10.4   Mobile Malware Examples

Name	Year	Type	Effects
Liberty Crack	2000	Trojan	Remove third-party software
Cabir	2004	Worm	Scan of Bluetooth, drain battery of phone
Skulls	2004	Trojan	DoS
Brador	2004	Trojan	Create backdoor
CommonWarrior	2005	Worm	Charge for MMS
Locknut	2005	Trojan	Allows entries for new apps
Cardblock	2005	Virus	Memory card is encrypted using random passwords
Letum	2006	Worm	Infect registry
Redbrowser	2006	Trojan	Send SMS
Feak	2007	Worm	Send SMS to contact list along with URL
Flocker	2007	Trojan	Send SMS to contact list
InfoJack	2008	Trojan	Security settings are disabled
Yxe	2009	Worm	Send contact list to server
Ikee	2009	Worm	Alter wallpaper
FlexiSpy	2009	Spyware	Track usage of device
ZeuS MitMo	2010	Worm	Steal bank details
iSAM	2011	Multifarious malware	DoS, send malicious SMS
Shamoon	2012	Virus	Delete files from the system
CryptoLocker	2013	Ransomware	Encrypts user's files
Regin	2014	Trojan horse	Download various extensions
Tiny Banker Trojan	2016	Trojan horse	Converts the host machine into botnet
Pegasus	2016	Spyware	Access messages, calendar and others
Xafecopy	2017	Trojan	Wireless Application Protocol billing

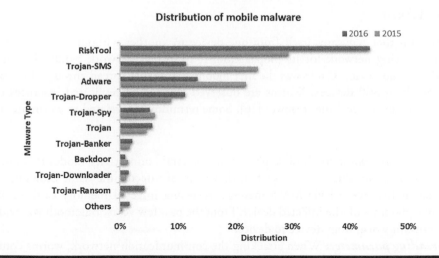

Distribution of mobile malware

Figure 10.8 Distribution of new mobile malware by types in 2015 and 2016 [23].

Trojan is used to gain sensitive credentials of the user. Attacker installs a malicious application in the device of the user to gain control over the device. Trojan can corrupt the file, overwrite data, spy on user's activities, spread malware, install backdoors, log keystrokes, and send these reports secretly to the attacker.

10.5.9.3 Rootkits

Rootkit attacks the system by compromising the OS of the device, and users remain unaware of this fact. It deactivates the antivirus and the firewall of the device, and installs malicious applications that run under the privileged mode. Rootkits are not detected by the antiviruses. The rootkit does not harm the device but is used by the attacker to install malicious applications in the device so as to gain control of the device.

10.5.9.4 Backdoor

Backdoor does not itself harm the device but helps other malware to bypass the security mechanism and enter the device. Developers often create backdoors so that applications can be accessed for troubleshooting purposes. In order to gain super-user privilege, backdoor exploits root account; sometimes even anti-malware scanners are not able to detect backdoor.

10.5.9.5 Botnet

Botnet is a network of compromised computers. Attacker installs a malware "bot" in the vulnerable devices turning these devices into a network of compromised machines. Earlier, mobile network was isolated from the Internet, but now mobile networks are combined with the Internet, so mobile devices may be the target for the attackers that aim to turn the smartphone devices into bot-client. These devices may be used to launch DoS attack. Command and control (C&C) networks are used to circulate the messages, responsibilities and payload to the bots, and the bot masters. Communication with mobile-based botnet can be carried out through Bluetooth C&C or SMS C&C [25].

10.5.9.6 Worm

It is a program that replicates itself from one device to another without human intervention. It uses the existing network for its propagation. It consumes network bandwidth and affects the security of the device. Cabir was the first mobile worm that spread through Bluetooth and attacked Symbian S60 devices. Worms are observed when their replicated instances consume resources of the device making it slower [26]. Some terminologies related to worm are described below:

- *Transmission channels:* Mobile phones have several connectivity modes that are used by the worm as spreading vectors, such as download of infected file while browsing, opening malicious file received via MMS message, accessing infected memory card, or attaching mobile phones with the infected device. From the past few years, Bluetooth was widely used to transmit worm from device to device.
- *Spreading parameter:* When attacking the communication network, worms compromise the network along with user's ability to use the device. The worms that use messaging service as route to spread infectious files have more speed and hence are more virulent. The worms can be sent using only one click and can be propagated to any part of the world with higher success rate.
- *User mobility model:* Networks of mobile phones have different characteristics in terms of capacity, services, topology, and communication pattern. There are some worms that do not require Internet connection for their propagation, and as a result, they spread and propagate without being detected by the security mechanism of the network. Mobile worms may use proximity attack to infect the vulnerable devices.

10.6 Defense Approaches

In this section, various static, dynamic, and hybrid defense approaches for protecting mobile phone devices are discussed.

10.6.1 Static Approach

Techniques based on static analysis approach [27] use structure code of the application. These approaches work using disassembly and de-compilation. Table 10.5 presents some of the security mechanisms. This section discusses some of the static analysis techniques.

10.6.1.1 Signature-Based Detection Approach

Signature-based detection approach works by extracting syntactic and semantic features, and on the basis of these features, signatures are created. Signature-based solutions search for the signature of the application in the pre-stored set of malware signatures. If a match is found, an action is performed. The limitation of this method is that it can identify only a limited number of threats or malware. Most of the Android applications are associated with a unique signature. Hardman and Steinberger-Wilckens developed a robust signature-based technique called "AndroSimilar" in order to detect zero-day malware attacks [27].

Table 10.5   Applicable Security Mechanisms

Types	Mechanism	Description
System Add-on	Anti-Virus Solution	Antivirus solution protects form malware, access to phishing site. Scan files, memory, SMSs, and MMS.
	Secure API	Secure APIs helps in developing secure functionalities and provide cryptographic functionality for application developers.
	Spam Filter	Spam filtering application prevents and blocks SMS, phone calls, MMS, and emails from unwanted source.
System Modification	Firewall	Firewall prevents network-related attacks by refusing connection with untrusted network.
	Access Control	Access control restricts the access of user and process to resources or services.
	Authentication	Authentication process prevents unauthorized access to the device.
	Pre-testing	Pre-testing prevents users from malware and ensures security of applications by authorizing the developers.
	Regular Update	Regular update of mobile platform and applications of the smartphone prevents the user from various attacks.
	Remote Access Control	Using remote access control, configuration, and management damage due to lost smartphone can be reduced.

10.6.1.2 *Permission-Based Analysis Approach*

This analysis method depends on the permissions granted to the applications. In this method, the risk of permissions granted to applications and security of resources is analyzed. Based on the risk level, the malicious applications are analyzed and detected. None of the applications have default permissions that can affect the security of the user, so it is important to identify dangerous permissions. In [28], the authors have mapped the requested and the used permissions, and their corresponding APIs. These features are then used with machine learning algorithms for detecting malware.

10.6.1.3 Control-Flow Analysis Approach

In this technique, Control-Flow Graph (CFG) of the application is extracted which checks for the possibility of resource misuse and the presence of a vulnerability in application code. On the basis of discovered threats and vulnerabilities, the decision is taken. The control-flow analysis determines all probable paths that can be taken by the application during execution. Dalvik byte code contains branch, jump, and methods that can alter the order of execution. An intra- or inter-procedural CFG is generated for further analysis. The Tech2 Poll Outcome performed the control-flow analysis on the basis of semantic signatures to identify malicious applications [29].

10.6.1.4 Component-Based Analysis Approach

For a detailed analysis and assessment of application, disassembling of application is performed in order to extract some components like resources or bytecodes. With the help of definition and bytecode, component-based analysis technique analyses the components to recognize the vulnerabilities.

10.6.1.5 System Isolation-Based Approach

It is the ability of the OS to isolate the applications and preventing it from compromising the security of the device. System isolation is low in the case of iPhone platform because several applications run at the same privilege level. Hence, if any vulnerability exists in one such application, other applications are also compromised. Whereas system isolation is high in the case of Android platform, due to which even if the attacker is able to access the data of an application due to the presence of a vulnerability in that application, it cannot affect other applications as each application runs with unique UID.

10.6.2 Dynamic Approach

Static analysis techniques work well and are fast but do not detect encrypted and transformed malware. Dynamic analysis techniques analyze the applications and identifying their malicious actions. Due to limitations of resources in mobile devices, dynamic analysis methods are not executed properly. The limitation of dynamic analysis approach is that if the technique is not triggered at the proper time, some malicious activities may get missed. Dynamic approaches are further divided into these categories [17].

10.6.2.1 Profile-Based Anomaly Detection Approach

Profile-based anomaly detection techniques maintain a history of the normal behavior of the applications using application profile and treat any activity deviating from it as a possible intrusion [30]. Malicious applications may launch DoS attacks against the smartphone by overusing the resources. Various factors like network traffic pattern, CPU usage, battery usage, memory utilization statistics, and system-calls for legitimate and malicious application are collected from the Android subsystem. Some of the profile-based techniques along with machine learning techniques are discussed in [31] and [32].

10.6.2.2 Malicious Behavior-Based Detection Approach

Behavior-based detection evaluates an object on the basis of its action or behavior. Various malicious behaviors like information leakage, sending SMS, and calling without user permission can be discovered by observing some particular features. Various features are taken into consideration, and on the basis of these features, applications are checked for the malicious behavior. An application that performs some abnormal or unauthorized actions indicates that the instance is malicious.

10.6.3 Hybrid Analysis Approach

This section discusses the various existing mechanisms developed to prevent different types of threats and attacks on the mobile device.

10.6.3.1 Intrusion Detection System

It is a device or software that analyzes the network traffic and detects malicious traffic. An Intrusion Detection System (IDS) consists of three components, i.e., sensors, console, and detection engine. IDS is generally used along with other preventive mechanisms. IDS can be of two types: detection based and prevention based.

10.6.3.1.1 Detection-Based IDS Approach

IDS first serves as a line of defense and defends the device from the malicious activities. There are two main types of detection:

- **Anomaly-based detection:** It is used for detecting network as well as device intrusions. The detection is based on heuristics instead of the signature. To identify the attack traffic accurately, the system is trained to identify the normal activity of the system. Anomaly-based detection consists of two phases, i.e., training phase and testing phase. The limitation of this mechanism is that it has a high false positive rate.
- **Signature-based detection:** It detects malicious behavior based on well-known attack patterns. These patterns are called as signatures. When an exploit is found, its signature is recorded and stored. IDS scans the traffic in order to find a match for the known patterns. The advantage of this scheme is that false positive is very low, but the drawback is that it can detect only known attacks, i.e., those attacks for which signature is stored.

10.6.3.1.2 Prevention-Based IDS Approach

Prevention-based IDS analyzes the traffic flow in order to detect and prevent vulnerability exploits. These exploits are malicious inputs to target services and applications used by the attackers to intrude and gain control of the device. It is a control-based system which sits between the two networks and analyses the traffic passing through them. In prevention-based IDS, some rules are specified related to traffic on the basis of which traffic is allowed to pass. It ensures confidentiality, integrity, and authentication by using cryptographic algorithms, hash functions, and digital signature. Preventive-based IDS can either run online or in real time.

10.7 Existing Countermeasures

Since software architecture of smartphones is similar to that of desktop computers, so smartphones are also vulnerable to security risks faced by desktops. Resource-constrained nature of these devices prevents advanced security solution to be implemented for the smartphones. Based on the defense approaches discussed above, the current section highlights some of the countermeasures proposed by different authors.

In [33], a dynamic analysis technique is given for detecting the malicious behavior of the applications. The framework collects traces from a large number of users with the help of crowdsourcing. The framework is described by examining the data gathered in the server with the help of two types of datasets: first is artificial malware dataset created for testing, and second is real malware dataset. The proposed technique is effective in isolation of malware and warning the users about the presence of malware. In order to prevent the attacks on Android platform, a cloud-based reputation security model is given [34]. This model makes use of the unique UID for each application in order to calculate the reputation index of each application. With the help of computational index matrix, the user is notified about the probable risk associated with the application even before the installation. In [35], a security model "Secloud" implemented in the cloud environment is presented. Secloud keeps registered smartphone devices coordinated by constantly giving the inputs of the device and network to the cloud. This helps Secloud to implement resource-intensive security analysis on the emulated model which otherwise would not be possible to run on the device.

In [36], a general OS framework "L4Android" for securing smartphone devices is given. This framework is capable of achieving security without requiring hardware extensions. OS of the device is encapsulated in the virtual machine, and highly secured applications can be used simultaneously using virtual machine. This framework ensures isolation between secure applications and the virtual machine. "Andromaly," a behavioral malware detection framework for Android devices, is proposed in [37]. The framework implements a host-based malware detection system and analyses various events and features of the smartphones by using machine learning detection algorithms to classify the data as suspicious or normal. Due to lack of malicious application dataset, the authors themselves developed malicious applications and assessed the ability of Andromaly in the detection of malware. The results show that Andromaly is effective in the detection of malware on mobile devices.

An empirical analysis of permission-based security model that uses Self-Organizing Map (SOM) algorithm of Kohonen is presented in [38]. To enhance the quality of the permission model for Android devices, some potential points have been identified that increase the quality of the model without increasing any type of permissions or complexity. A fine-grained security system better than the permission-based system is proposed in [39]. The system protects users against malicious users and applications. The system is capable of implementing complex policies based on time, cardinality, and space conditions by modifying or inhibiting various actions and executing supplementary actions. Leveraging the recent advances in information flow tracking technology, the given policies also relate to data instead of a single representation of data.

Mobile application sector is one of the rapidly growing sectors in the worldwide mobile market. The applications are developed at a faster pace to give a good experience to the users. A layered approach for the development of Android applications which can download data from the server is discussed in [40]. It also discusses Android application sandbox which performs static as well as dynamic analysis of Android applications in order to detect suspicious applications. For the detection of illegal use of smartphones, the scheme proposed in [41] is used to log data of iPhone along with four machine learning algorithms, i.e., Random Forest, Bayesian Networks, K-Nearest Neighbors, and Radial Basis Function. Calls, SMSs, and web browsing are used to classify the behavior of the user. SHA-1 algorithm is used to hash the records of users in order to preserve anonymity, and data can be analyzed either independently or in a multimodal fashion. Android-based security solution for the smartphone devices has been proposed in [42], which exploits Security-Enhanced Linux. In [43], the authors have studied many popular Android applications and analyzed millions of lines of code in order to recover source code of Java applications from its Dalvik installation image. The result shows that some applications exploit private information, such as phone identifiers, International Mobile Subscriber Identity, Integrated Circuit Card ID and location information by sending information through HTTP GET/POST requests, in turn stalking users.

Even though power consumption is considered as a drawback, [44] takes positive impacts of this for preventing malware on mobile devices. Depending upon the limitation of the smartphone, three techniques are proposed by the authors. The first technique is for observing power consumption which deals with the ability of the device in detecting an attack based on battery usage of the device. The second technique is for imposing hardware sandbox where the hardware modules that are not frequently used are switched off so that they cannot be used for malware propagation. The third technique is for increasing platform diversity in which various APIs are used for development and execution of an application. In [45], a SBVLC-secure, barcode-based, visible-light communication mechanism for smartphones is given. The authors have analyzed the security of SBVLC and proposed a mechanism by manipulating angles of screen view and controlling user-induced motions. They have also developed three schemes for exchanging data securely by encoding the data in barcode streams. In [46], the authors have analyzed the amount of information leakage during the installation of the application. The authors have used man-in-the-middle proxy to interrupt the traffic generated by applications installed in the smartphones.

The security models of smartphone platform allow users to take security-related decisions while performing various tasks. This delegation ranges from giving access of protected resources to allowing the users to infer if the application damages the security mechanism or not. The survey finding [47] shows that the users are not properly ready for taking accurate security decisions and download the applications from the app store without checking whether applications are tested or not. Moreover, in permission-based security models, users ignore the security warnings prompted to them and tend to overlook all the messages shown by the applications. This is where security model fails as these security models assume that users carefully read displayed messages so as to take right decisions. It has been seen that only technical users are likely to check these messages. A majority of security controls are disabled due to which mobile device users are more vulnerable to privacy and security threats. Most of the users make use of the same device for business as well as personal purpose. As a result, the threat to information stored in the device is increased. Additionally, a large number of users believe that security solutions for the smartphones are not much necessary.

10.8 Tools

In this section, some reverse-engineering tools are discussed. Tables 10.6 and 10.7 discuss free and commercial attack detection security tools, respectively, along with their description.

Table 10.6 License-Free Attack Detection Tools for Smartphones

Tool	Description
Sophos [54]	• 100% malware detection rate, 0% false positive rate. • Provides robust scanning during installations, scans the existing applications and storage media, web filtering, password protection. • Consume less battery and processing power.
Lookout [55]	• Protects against unsecure Wi-Fi connections, malicious applications, deceitful links, and other mobile threats. • Automatic backups. • In case of loss of device, locate the device on a Google map even when GPS is off.

Table 10.7 Commercial Attack Detection Tools for Smartphones

Tool	Description
Snap Secure [56]	• Protects against unsecure Wi-Fi connections, malicious applications, deceitful links, and other mobile threats. • Automatic backups. • In case of loss of device, locate the device on a Google map even when GPS is off.
LastPass [57]	• Contains antivirus and anti-spyware. • Call- and SMS-blocking feature. • Back up data to online account to restore data if required.
OWASP Zed Attack Proxy Project [58]	• Third-party password generator (generates safe password and saves them so that users do not have to remember them). • Supports platform including iOS, Android, and Blackberry.
HP Enterprise Software [59]	• Static security testing tool. • Assess security of a variety of mobile applications. • Assess the vulnerability of the applications using reverse engineering.
WaveSecure [60]	• Security testing of applications, dynamic scans at regular intervals. • Supports platform iOS, Android, Windows Phone, and Blackberry. • Analyze the static resources of the mobile applications.
BullGuard Mobile Security 10 [61]	• Lock and Wipe • Provide localization and SIM tracking • Backup and Restore
ESET Mobile Security [62]	• Antivirus, Anti-spyware, Anti-theft • Parental Control and basic backup • Firewall • Spam filter

(Continued)

Table 10.7 (*Continued*)   Commercial Attack Detection Tools for Smartphones

Tool	Description
Trend Micro [63]	• Firewall • Antivirus • Anti-theft • SMS/MMS Anti-spam
Avast Mobile Security [64]	• Protects against phishing sites, privacy scanners. • Malware blocking and cleaning, application locking, call filtering, and anti-theft tools. • 99% malware detection rate and 0% false positive rate.
Cheetah [65]	• Antivirus (scans applications and URLs). • Wi-Fi scanning. • Firewall to control network traffic.

10.8.1 *Reverse-Engineering Tools*

Reverse engineering is the procedure of extracting information from the product and rebuilding it on the basis of extracted information. This process was earlier applied to hardware only, but now it is applied to database and software also. Reverse engineering can be used to detect the breaches about how attacker entered the device and steps followed by the attacker. This section discusses some of these tools.

- **Apktool:** Apktool [48] is an open source reverse-engineering tool that can decode APK binary content or resources into original form and rebuild the code after making some changes. In order to make reading and manipulations easy, the tool disassembles the binary code and converts byte code present in classes .dex into smali byte code. After all these modifications, the code is repackaged again into an APK by the tool.
- **Dex2jar:** Dex2jar [49] contains components named dex-reader, dex-translator, dex-ir, dex-tools, d2j-smali, and dex-writer. Dex2jar is used to convert Dalvik Executable (.dex/.odex) format to jar files by retargeting the Dalvik byte code into Java byte code. Also, after modifications, it assembles jar files back into the .dex format.
- **Dare:** Dare [50] is a tool that retargets Android applications in. dex or .apk format to traditional .class format. Java tools can be used to preprocess the .class files. The .class files can be analyzed further by using various traditional techniques that were developed initially for Java applications. Octeau et al. [51] have proved that Dare tool is 40% more precise than dex2jar.
- **Dedexer:** Dedexer [52] is used to disassemble .dex file into "assembly-like format" which is influenced by Jasmin syntax. It generates a separate file for each class for easy reading as well as manipulation. But the limitation is that it does not reassemble the disassembled class files.
- **JEB:** JEB [53] is a reverse-engineering tool available for Windows, Macintosh, and Linux platforms. It is Graphical User Interface-based de-compiler that analyses the reversed malware application content. This tool converts the Dalvik code into Java source code. It supports Python scripts and plugins.

10.9 Open Security Issues and Research Challenges

Many security solutions have been proposed by the researchers to detect and prevent attacks on mobile devices. But still, no single solution is there that can protect users from all the attacks.

Every time researchers come up with any idea or technique, attacker finds the weaknesses in the current solution. In this section, some open challenges that are needed to be addressed are discussed.

10.9.1 Resource Constraints

Smartphones are the resource-constrained devices that consist of a limited battery life and low computational power. If the proposed solution requires more computational power, then the impact may be so high that the device may become unusable for the users. Complex computations may also drain the battery. So, security solutions for mobile devices are designed as per these limitations, which reduces the effectiveness of the solutions.

10.9.2 Permission Escalation

In permission escalation attacks, open kernel vulnerabilities or flaws in OS and applications are exploited to access the resources or services that are otherwise protected by the application. Permission escalation may lead to unauthorized actions by an application getting more privileges than required causing sensitive information leakage [66]. Malicious application and even legitimate application may escalate permissions granted to them.

10.9.3 Colluding

Colluding is a client-side attack. It occurs when a user installs a set of applications developed by a developer, signed with same certificates but grant different permissions to applications. These applications collude with each other so as to enhance their privileges rights by sharing their permissions. In this case, these applications can make use of shared UID and get access to various sensitive and nonsensitive permissions and resources. This attack imposes a serious threat to the privacy of smartphone users [67].

10.9.4 Repackaging Applications

Repackaging is the process of injecting malicious code into the original code by decompiling APK files with the help of reverse engineering. This vulnerability is caused by the structural characteristics of bytecode that runs on a virtual machine [68]. It is an important security issue for mobile applications. Using repackaging, a malicious application may pretend to be a legitimate application. It is hard to differentiate between genuine application and repackaged malicious application as both seem to be legitimate [69,70].

10.9.5 Information Leakage

In the OS architecture of smartphones, applications can access the resources and other applications only when authorized by the users. Users grant usage rights before installing the applications. When a user allows applications to access various resources without any constraint, then information leakage occurs. Various studies show that 70% of smartphone applications request for the permissions irrelevant to the main functionality of the application [71]. Moreover, a large number of applications are available at third-party application store, but a very small number of users read the permissions being requested [72]. Unaware users do not realize that these irrelevant requests may compromise their privacy.

10.9.6 Update Issues

Android Open Source Project is responsible for upgrade and maintenance of application source-code. Original Equipment Manufacturers (OEMs) is responsible for the release of patches, or any major updates. Moreover, OEM OS is customized by the wireless carriers to suit their requirements due to which sometimes an update chain may take months to reach the end users. Due to unavailability of updates, different versions of Android remain scattered, and this process is called Fragmentation.

10.9.7 Platform-Oriented Breaches

Smartphones comes with the preinstalled OS. Different OS provide different functionalities and applications. But raise a challenge for hardware and software developers whose products must support all mobile OSs. Since OSs are vulnerable to security breaches, security solutions should precisely address these issues. Software must be customized by the developers for various mobile platform OS.

10.9.8 Management of Sensitive Information

Applications and web browsers store sensitive information of the user. Also, in order to avoid entering login details repeatedly, users store these details in apps or browsers. In addition, a lot of information is stored in the storage units of the smartphone. This information includes private information such as contacts, home address, email, text, call logs, and messages. Disclosure of this information results in an invasion of user privacy, leading to financial losses. So, management of sensitive information is an important issue.

10.10 Conclusion

A smartphone is a device that offers more functionalities than those of a basic feature phone. With the increasing usage of smartphones that are equipped with a variety of features, there is also an increase in the development of malware for these devices. Due to the limitations of mobile devices in terms of computing power and hardware, mobile devices are more vulnerable to malware attacks. Attackers can exploit the privacy of the user by spying on them. Recent development in mobile computing technology has gained the attention of malicious attackers. Malware for the desktop OS is currently migrating to mobile platform due to which there is a severe increase of mobile malware. Currently, various researches are in progress for smartphone security. But still, all the security threats have not been addressed. In order to establish security of smartphone device, security threats of smartphone environment need to be identified.

In this work, various mobile technologies that are used for cellular communication are discussed. Wireless Telecommunication Technologies have enabled the users to communicate over wireless links. We have discussed some of the wireless telecommunication technologies such as GSM, GPRS, EDGE, and UMTS. Various security concerns of the smartphones such as assets of smartphones, security objectives, smartphone vulnerability, and threats of smartphones are discussed in detail. Then, we have discussed some attacks against smartphones followed by defense approaches and existing countermeasures propose by researchers. Lastly, some open security issues and challenges are discussed.

Key Terminology and Definitions

Malware: Malware is a malicious software designed to harm the computer or smartphone devices. Malware may steal sensitive information from the device, delete files, make the device slow, or monitor the activities of the user. Malware includes viruses, spyware, worms, etc. Once malware enters the device, attacker can gain complete control over the device.

Mobile security: Mobile security is protecting the smartphones, laptops, and other portable devices. Security of mobile devices has become an important issue due to various security concerns such as loss of device, application security, data leakage from the device, and malware attacks. There are many threats that exploit the security of smartphone due to which security solution are designed to protect the sensitive data of users.

Smartphones: Smartphone is a small handheld device having functionalities similar to desktop computers. These devices provide features such as calling, SMS, audio, video, gaming, and web browser. Smartphones also come with the touchscreen feature. We can install a number of applications in the smartphone.

Unauthorized access: Unauthorized access is when someone attempts to access a device, application, or the resources without permission. For example, if the user tries to access some files to which he/she is not permitted to access then this is unauthorized access. To prevent unauthorized access, proper authentication mechanism should be used.

References

1. Fernandes, G., Rodrigues, J. J., & Proença, M. L. (2015). Autonomous profile-based anomaly detection system using principal component analysis and flow analysis. *Applied Soft Computing*, 34, 513–525.
2. Cambiaso, E., Papaleo, G., & Aiello, M. (2017). Slowcomm: Design, development and performance evaluation of a new slow DoS attack. *Journal of Information Security and Applications*, 35, 23–31.
3. Gartner Research. "Gartner says worldwide sales of smartphones grew 9 percent in first quarter of 2017". www.gartner.com/newsroom/id/3725117. Accessed 27/10/2017.
4. Zaidi, S. F. A., Shah, M. A., Kamran, M., Javaid, Q., & Zhang, S. (2016). A survey on security for smartphone device. *International Journal of Advanced Computer Science and Applications*, 7(4), 206–219.
5. Moore, D., & Shannon, C. (2002, November). Code-Red: A case study on the spread and victims of an Internet worm. In *Proceedings of the 2nd ACM SIGCOMM Workshop on Internet Measurement* (pp. 273–284). ACM.
6. Bellalta, B. (2016). IEEE 802.11 ax: High-efficiency WLANs. *IEEE Wireless Communications*, 23(1), 38–46.
7. Reina, A., Fattori, A., & Cavallaro, L. (2013). *A System Call-Centric Analysis and Stimulation Technique to Automatically Reconstruct Android Malware Behaviors*. EuroSec, April, Prague, Czech Republic.
8. Huang, C. Y., Tsai, Y. T., & Hsu, C. H. (2013). Performance evaluation on permission-based detection for android malware. In *Advances in Intelligent Systems and Applications*-Volume 2 (pp. 111–120). Springer, Berlin, Heidelberg.
9. Akyildiz, I. F., Gutierrez-Estevez, D. M., Balakrishnan, R., & Chavarria-Reyes, E. (2014). LTE-Advanced and the evolution to beyond 4G (B4G) systems. *Physical Communication*, 10, 31–60.

10. Mylonas, A., Kastania, A., & Gritzalis, D. (2013). Delegate the smartphone user? Security awareness in smartphone platforms. *Computers & Security*, 34, 47–66.
11. Symantec Internet Security Threat Report 2014, Vol. 19. www.symantec.com/content/en/us/enterprise/other_resources/b-istr_main_report_v19_21291018.en-us.pdf. Accessed 20/7/2017.
12. Kataria, A., Anjali, T., & Venkat, R. (2014, February). Quantifying smartphone vulnerabilities. In *2014 International Conference on Signal Processing and Integrated Networks (SPIN)* (pp. 645–649). IEEE.
13. He, D., Chan, S., & Guizani, M. (2015). Mobile application security: Malware threats and defenses. *IEEE Wireless Communications*, 22(1), 138–144.
14. Zou, Y., Zhu, J., Wang, X., & Hanzo, L. (2016). A survey on wireless security: Technical challenges, recent advances, and future trends. *Proceedings of the IEEE*, 104(9), 1727–1765.
15. Delac, G., Silic, M., & Krolo, J. (2011, May). Emerging security threats for mobile platforms. In *MIPRO, 2011 Proceedings of the 34th International Convention* (pp. 1468–1473). IEEE.
16. Singh, R. S., Prasad, A., Moven, R. M., & Sarma, H. K. D. (2017, March). Denial of service attack in wireless data network: A survey. In *Devices for Integrated Circuit (DevIC), 2017* (pp. 354–359). IEEE.
17. La Polla, M., Martinelli, F., & Sgandurra, D. (2013). A survey on security for mobile devices. *IEEE Communications Surveys & Tutorials*, 15(1), 446.
18. Enck, W., Traynor, P., McDaniel, P., & La Porta, T. (2005, November). Exploiting open functionality in SMS-capable cellular networks. In *Proceedings of the 12th ACM Conference on Computer and Communications Security* (pp. 393–404). ACM, Alexandria, VA.
19. Is mobile anti-virus even necessary? www.csoonline.com/article/2134001/mobile-security/is-mobile-anti-virus-even-necessary-html. Accessed 27/10/2017.
20. Haataja, K. M., & Hypponen, K. (2008, March). Man-in-the-middle attacks on Bluetooth: A comparative analysis, a novel attack, and countermeasures. In *Communications, Control and Signal Processing, 2008. ISCCSP 2008. 3rd International Symposium on* (pp. 1096–1102). IEEE.
21. Von Solms, R., & Van Niekerk, J. (2013). From information security to cyber security. *Computers & Security*, 38, 97–102.
22. Karim, A., Shah, S. A. A., & Salleh, R. (2014). Mobile botnet attacks: A thematic taxonomy. In *New Perspectives in Information Systems and Technologies* (Vol. 2, pp. 153–164). Springer, Cham.
23. Lifewire, what is Bluetooth wireless networking. www.lifewire.com/definition-of-bluetooth-816260. Accessed 27/10/2017.
24. Mouly, M., Pautet, M. B., & Foreword By-Haug, T. (1992). *The GSM System for Mobile Communications*. Telecom publishing.
25. He, D., Chan, S., & Guizani, M. (2015). Mobile application security: Malware threats and defenses. *IEEE Wireless Communications*, 22(1), 138–144.
26. Yang, L. X., Yang, X., Zhu, Q., & Wen, L. (2013). A computer virus model with graded cure rates. *Nonlinear Analysis: Real World Applications*, 14(1), 414–422.
27. Hardman, S., & Steinberger-Wilckens, R. (2014). Mobile phone infrastructure development: Lessons for the development of a hydrogen infrastructure. *International Journal of Hydrogen Energy*, 39(16), 8185–8193.
28. Wognsen, E. R., & Karlsen, H. S. (2012). Static analysis of Dalvik bytecode and reflection in android. *Master's Thesis*, Department of Computer Science, Aalborg University, Aalborg, Denmark.
29. Tech2 Poll Outcome: Android OS made biggest impact in 2011. www.firstpost.com/tech/news-analysis/tech2-poll-outcome-android-os-made-biggest-impact-in-2011-3591613.html. Accessed 20/10/2017.
30. Chadza, T. A., Aparicio-Navarro, F. J., Kyriakopoulos, K. G., & Chambers, J. A. (2017, May). A look into the information your smartphone leaks. In *2017 International Symposium on Networks, Computers and Communications (ISNCC)* (pp. 1–6). IEEE.
31. Damopoulos, D., Kambourakis, G., & Portokalidis, G. (2014, April). The best of both worlds: A framework for the synergistic operation of host and cloud anomaly-based IDS for smartphones. In *Proceedings of the Seventh European Workshop on System Security* (p. 6). ACM.
32. Burguera, I., Zurutuza, U., & Nadjm-Tehrani, S. (2011, October). Crowdroid: Behavior-based malware detection system for android. In *Proceedings of the 1st ACM workshop on Security and privacy in smartphones and mobile devices* (pp. 15–26). ACM, Chicago, IL.

33. Tesfay, W. B., Booth, T., & Andersson, K. (2012, June). Reputation based security model for android applications. In *2012 IEEE 11th International Conference on Trust, Security and Privacy in Computing and Communications (TrustCom)* (pp. 896–901). IEEE, Liverpool, England.

34. Barrera, D., Kayacik, H. G., van Oorschot, P. C., & Somayaji, A. (2010, October). A methodology for empirical analysis of permission-based security models and its application to android. In *Proceedings of the 17th ACM Conference on Computer and Communications Security* (pp. 73–84). ACM, Chicago, IL.

35. Shabtai, A., Kanonov, U., Elovici, Y., Glezer, C., & Weiss, Y. (2012). "Andromaly": A behavioral malware detection framework for android devices. *Journal of Intelligent Information Systems*, 38(1), 161–190.

36. Feth, D., & Pretschner, A. (2012, June). Flexible data-driven security for android. In *2012 IEEE Sixth International Conference on Software Security and Reliability (SERE)* (pp. 41–50). IEEE, Gaithersburg, MD.

37. Shabtai, A., Fledel, Y., & Elovici, Y. (2010). Securing android-powered mobile devices using SELinux. *IEEE Security & Privacy*, 8(3), 36–44.

38. Lange, M., Liebergeld, S., Lackorzynski, A., Warg, A., & Peter, M. (2011, October). L4Android: A generic operating system framework for secure smartphones. In *Proceedings of the 1st ACM Workshop on Security and Privacy in Smartphones and Mobile Devices* (pp. 39–50). ACM, Berlin, Germany.

39. Holla, S., & Katti, M. M. (2012). Android based mobile application development and its security. *International Journal of Computer Trends and Technology*, 3(3), 486–490.

40. Zonouz, S., Houmansadr, A., Berthier, R., Borisov, N., & Sanders, W. (2013). Secloud: A cloud-based comprehensive and lightweight security solution for smartphones. *Computers & Security*, 37, 215–227.

41. Digital Vaccine Labs. http://dvlabs.tippingpoint.com/blog/2010/02/15/pwn2own-2010. Accessed 22/10/2017.

42. Enck, W., Octeau, D., McDaniel, P. D., & Chaudhuri, S. (2011, August). A study of android application security. In *USENIX security symposium* (Vol. 2, p. 2).

43. Yan, Q., Deng, R. H., Li, Y., & Li, T. (2010). On the potential of limitation oriented malware detection and prevention techniques on mobile phones. *International Journal of Security and Its Applications*, 4(1), 21–30.

44. Damopoulos, D., Menesidou, S. A., Kambourakis, G., Papadaki, M., Clarke, N., & Gritzalis, S. (2012). Evaluation of anomaly-based IDS for mobile devices using machine learning classifiers. *Security and Communication Networks*, 5(1), 3–14.

45. Trend Micro, Business support. https://success.trendmicro.com/business-support. Accessed 20/10/2017.

46. Silberschatz, A., Galvin, P. B., & Gagne, G. (2014). *Operating System Concepts Essentials*. John Wiley & Sons, Inc, New York, NY.

47. Davi, L., Dmitrienko, A., Sadeghi, A. R., & Winandy, M. (2010, October). Privilege escalation attacks on android. In *International Conference on Information Security* (pp. 346–360). Springer, Berlin, Heidelberg.

48. Dex2Jar, Android Decompiling with Dex2jar. http://code.google.com/p/dex2jar/. Accessed 22/10/2017.

49. DARE: Dalvik Retargeting. http://siis.cse.psu.edu/dare. Accessed 22/10/2017.

50. Dedexer. http://dedexer.sourceforge.net/. Accessed 22/10/2017.

51. Zhang, B., Ren, K., Xing, G., Fu, X., & Wang, C. (2016). SBVLC: Secure barcode-based visible light communication for smartphones. *IEEE Transactions on Mobile Computing*, 15(2), 432–446.

52. JEB Decompiler. www.android-decompiler.com/. Accessed 22/10/2017.

53. Octeau, D., Jha, S., & McDaniel, P. (2012, November). Retargeting android applications to Java bytecode. In *Proceedings of the ACM SIGSOFT 20th International Symposium on the Foundations of Software Engineering* (p. 6). ACM.

54. Cheetahmobile. www.cmcm.com/en-us/. Accessed 20/10/2017.

55. Snap Secure Anti Virus and Mobile Security. www.getjar.com/categories/tool-apps/snapsecure-antivirus-mobile-security-414072. Accessed 27/10/2017.

56. Lastpass. lastpass.com/features/. Accessed 29/10/2017.

57. OWASP Zed Attack Proxy Project. www.owasp.org/index.php/OWASP_Zed_Attack_Proxy_Project. Accessed 22/10/2017.

58. Hewlett Packard Enterprise, Enterprise IT Management Software. www.hpe.com/in/en/software. html. Accessed 15/10/2017.
59. McAfee, WaveSecure. www.wavesecure.com/. Accessed 20/10/2017.
60. BullGuard Ltd, BullGuard Mobile Security 10. www.bullguard.com. Accessed 20/10/2017.
61. ESET, ESET Mobile Security. www.eset.com/us/home/products/mobile-security/. Accessed 20/10/2017.
62. Liu, H., Li, R., Pan, Y., Quan, X., Yang, L., & Zheng, L. (2014). A multi-broadband planar antenna for GSM/UMTS/LTE and WLAN/WiMAX handsets. *IEEE Transactions on Antennas and Propagation*, 62(5), 2856–2860.
63. Avast, Avast mobile security. www.avast.com/en-in/free-mobile-security. Accessed 20/10/2017.
64. Sophos. www.sophos.com/en-us.aspx. Accessed 20/10/2017.
65. Lookout. www.lookout.com/. Last accessed 20/10/2017.
66. Huang, H., Zhu, S., Liu, P., & Wu, D. (2013, June). A framework for evaluating mobile app repackaging detection algorithms. In *International Conference on Trust and Trustworthy Computing* (pp. 169–186). Springer, Berlin, Heidelberg.
67. Kashefi, I., Kassiri, M., & Salleh, M. (2015). Preventing collusion attack in android. *International Arab Journal of Information Technology*, 12(6A), 719–727.
68. Jung, J. H., Kim, J. Y., Lee, H. C., & Yi, J. H. (2013). Repackaging attack on android banking applications and its countermeasures. *Wireless Personal Communications*, 73(4), 1421–1437.
69. Zhou, W., Zhou, Y., Jiang, X., & Ning, P. (2012, February). Detecting repackaged smartphone applications in third-party android marketplaces. In *Proceedings of the Second ACM Conference on Data and Application Security and Privacy* (pp. 317–326). ACM.
70. Gunasekera, S. (2012). Android Architecture. In *Android Apps Security* (pp. 1–12). Apress, Berkeley, CA.
71. Felt, A. P., Chin, E., Hanna, S., Song, D., & Wagner, D. (2011, October). Android permissions demystified. In *Proceedings of the 18th ACM Conference on Computer and Communications Security* (pp. 627–638). ACM, Chicago, IL.
72. Faruki, P., Ganmoor, V., Laxmi, V., Gaur, M. S., & Bharmal, A. (2013, November). AndroSimilar: Robust statistical feature signature for Android malware detection. In *Proceedings of the 6th International Conference on Security of Information and Networks* (pp. 152–159). ACM, Aksaray, Turkey.

Chapter 11

Cryptography for Addressing Cloud Computing Security, Privacy, and Trust Issues

Mustapha Hedabou

Cadi Ayyad University

Contents

11.1 Introduction

Cloud computing services are in high demand because they can reduce the cost and complexity of owning and managing computers and networks. Customers have no investment in information technology infrastructure, purchase hardware, or buy software licenses because these charges are covered by cloud providers. On the other hand, they can benefit from rapid return on investment, rapid deployment, and customization. Moreover, cloud providers that have specialized in a particular area (such as e-mail) can bring advanced services that a single company might be unable to develop or implement. Cloud computing is often considered efficient because it allows organizations to devote their resources only to innovation and product development [1,3,7,32,70].

Nowadays, cloud services are widely used by businesses [66]. More than 3 million businesses have adopted Google Apps, Googles' cloud e-mail, calendar, and collaboration solutions for businesses. This rate is expanding at 3,000 users a month [76].

Despite its potential benefits, many chief executives and IT managers are not willing to lose the control of their data by offloading it to cloud computing platforms. Their main concerns are about confidentiality and privacy of the outsourced data. Their fear is amply justified because cloud provider employees can either accidentally or intentionally tamper with the hosted data. This violation can occur without the knowledge of the data's owner.

Cloud computing services are delivered to the end users through tree types of models, namely, Software as a Service (SaaS), Platform as a Service (PaaS), and Infrastructure as a Service (IaaS) that provide infrastructure resources, application platform, and software as services. The requirements of security level depend drastically on the cloud services delivery model. The location of the SaaS model in the higher layers increases the difficulty of guaranteeing the security of hosted data because cloud and service providers have full control over the software and operating environment that manipulate the customers' data. In PaaS model, the end users may have some control over the security of their build applications on top of the platform, but all the security privileges under the application level will still have the exclusive right of the cloud provider [63]. These privileges include host configuration and network intrusion prevention. Security in IaaS services is under the end user control as long as the hypervisor virtualization is not compromised since it cannot be reasonably possible to protect a virtual machine if there is a security hole in the virtualization manager [27].

Many security concerns in traditional information systems including authentication, authorization, and availability apply to cloud computing [54]. These concerns are amplified by the cloud conception architecture that does not provide security managers in cloud users' side the ability to access system hardware physically. Usual authentication and authorization solutions for on-premise environments may need to be strengthened in order to meet cloud security requirements. Cloud providers cannot be entrusted upon users' credentials; therefore, a trusted authority may be leveraged for maintaining and checking all users' credentials [42,17]. Availability of data in cloud computing is also of a big concern than in enterprise environments as the number of affected consumers is significantly higher in case of cloud service unavailability. The disruption of the Amazon cloud service in 2011 has caused the breakdown of many websites such as Reddit. Cloud security researchers advise to adopt more solutions against hardware, software failure, and denial of service attacks [61].

There are other security risks that apply exclusively to cloud computing services. Virtualization is a great security issue since multiple virtual machines belonging to different users may share the same physical machine. A single infected virtual machine can affect the other VMs. Assuring an absolute isolation between VMs on the same physical server is a major task of virtualization, which is not completely satisfied by today's architecture. Another vulnerability related to virtualization technology lies in the procedure for controlling administrator on virtual machines and guest operating systems [37,54]. Data location of hosted data in cloud may represent a serious problem for the end cloud users who are unable to determine exactly where their data is stored. This problem can be exacerbated by compliance and data privacy laws in force in some countries, which may prohibit the transfers of some type of data to some specific countries [26].

Data access control management is a lot more challenging task in cloud computing than within a single enterprise. The risk of an unauthorized access is a matter of concern for cloud consumers who are totally conscious about the existence of backdoors established by cloud provider for maintenance and support legitimate purposes. It is difficult, if not impossible, for cloud consumers to know employees and their granted privileges having access to hosted data, such information is not provided by the cloud providers [40]. A typical example is an instance of Office 365; Microsoft database administrators have full access to all resources in their database including consumers' data [68]. Checking whether cloud providers infrastructure is compliant with standards and certification is also of a great concern for cloud consumers [65]. Many cloud providers can claim that they are compliant with certain standards, but it is very complicated for customers to make sure that they match the kind of security they are looking for.

Other security issues related to cloud computing include the use and deletion of consumers' data by the cloud providers who have full control over hosted data in their platforms even if cloud consumers still have the ownership of the data. Requests to delete users' data in cloud provider platforms may not be done in desired way. This can result either from the existence of extra copies of stored data or because the deleted disk also stores data from other clients. Storing data in cloud platforms in encrypted format and managing the corresponding encryption keys in the cloud consumers' side can help to mitigate this issue [60]. A big cloud provider such as Amazon cannot afford to allow any consumer's demand to inspect their data centers since they could have tens of thousands, if not millions of consumers. Hence, cloud consumers are unable to check how cloud providers deal with incident in preparation, detection, reaction, and investigation phases [68]. These concerns can be categorized into auditing security testing, incidents management, and risk of data loss issue. Lock-in and portability is one of the top concerns of cloud consumers toward cloud providers [61]. Cloud consumers are worried about time allocated and tools or API made at their disposable for migrating their data to another location. Office 365 instance gives 90 days to cloud users in order to export their data by themselves. The format of the recovered e-mail data may not allow to be imported into other e-mail services.

Many efforts have been taken by cloud providers in order to strengthen the security and the privacy of their platforms by minimizing the threat of the insider attacks. For example, they protect and restrict access to the hardware facilities, adopt stringent accountability and audit procedures, and minimize the number of staff who have access to critical components of the infrastructure [56]. Despite these efforts, many attacks remain a serious threat on hosted data. In 2007, attackers targeted the prominent cloud service provider (CSP) Salesforce.com, and succeeded in stealing customer e-mails and addresses using a phishing attack [47]. In 2017, it was reported that Verizon Enterprise was a victim of a data breach that allowed hackers to steal information on an estimated 1.5 million enterprise clients. The stolen data was proposed for seal on an underground cyberforum [39].

Cryptography can help in mitigating the security, privacy, and trustiness issues related to the large adoption of cloud computing. The major levels of security and privacy aspects where cryptography can be involved are secure storage [6,16,64,67,75] and secure computation [8,9,19,45,62]. We should notice that there are already some commercial offers of secure storage services with encrypted data. The most known secure storage services, which encrypt data in the client side prior to outsourcing it, are Spideroak and Dropbox.

The main goal of the secure storage is to protect the outsourced data from unauthorized access. For achieving this purpose, the cloud user encrypts data before uploading it to the cloud storage by using well-known symmetric algorithms for ensuring the confidentiality and the integrity of his/her data. The key management remains the main issue in the concept of secure storage. Indeed, decryption keys must be at cloud providers' disposal in order to process data on behalf of the user. This means that users agree implicitly to lose control of their data. Companies with high expectation of security and privacy requirements, such as financial firms and health service providers, are not willing to lose control over their sensitive data.

To allow companies to outsource confidential data in the cloud computing platforms while still being able to process it without having to decrypt it, secure computation can be used to provide efficient solutions for performing computations over encrypted data. Secure computation is an approach for delegating to the cloud providers the task of processing encrypted data without being decrypted. This is done without revealing any information about the data or the decrypting key. A large set of secure computation techniques have been proposed. Secure multiparty computation (MPC), homomorphic encryption, and predicate encryption are the most popular among these.

11.2 Privacy, Security, and Trust in Cloud Computing

In 2009, a Gartner report argued that security, privacy, and trust issues are among the top inhibitors to cloud computing large adoption [23]. First, it is difficult for users to test whether countermeasures for mitigating security risks have been taken by the cloud providers since they cannot conduct an audit on the cloud provider platforms. The data location rises another risk since the users are unable to know where their data is stored and under what jurisdiction law. A third risk is about the control over their data since users may be unable to reach, retrieve, or remove their data. A fourth risk concerns the destruction of user's data that may be caused by intentional or accidental behavior. Finally, Gartner mentioned the security risk related to unauthorized access to the hosted data.

All these risks related to cloud computing can be categorized in privacy, security, and trust issues. The terms privacy, security, and trust may have many definitions, and their meaning and currency can change according to context. Furthermore, there is some interdependency between these terms.

Privacy. In the European context, privacy is often understood as compliance with European data protection regulations regarding the right to private life [48]. The context of privacy in cloud computing differs according to the type of the cloud. Typically in a public cloud, data is stored in machines owned by a cloud provider in unencrypted form, which raises many great privacy concerns. Major concerns are about the unauthorized use of data, the assurance if data has been properly destroyed and compliance with desired requirements.

According to Pearson [48], the most relevant privacy issues in cloud computing are lack of user control, potential unauthorized secondary usage, regulatory complexity (especially due to the global nature of cloud, complex service ecosystems, data proliferation, and dynamic provisioning and related difficulties meeting transborder data flow restrictions), litigation, and legal uncertainty. Privacy issue for sensitive data is certainly the most critical case in cloud computing. Special laws concerning treatment of sensitive data, data leakage, and loss of privacy may be a major hurdle for hosting sensitive data to a public cloud platform.

Due to the cloud computing design, the users' data can be stored in multiple data centers within different jurisdictions. It may be difficult for users to know where their data actually resides, which regulators have jurisdiction and what regulations apply. The jurisdictional issue affects directly the protection of personally identifiable information (PII) and the law enforcement access to this data, since there is a divergence across countries in law investigation and enforcement, including access to encrypted data and investigation of extraterritorial offenses.

Users have to verify the specific laws or regulations that apply to the cloud services related to data retention, data protection, interoperability, medical file management, and disclosure to authorities before migrating their data to a cloud computing platform. On the other hand, cloud providers can demonstrate that they are compliant with an established set of security controls as a useful approach for giving more confidence to users. Depending on cloud service models (IaaS, PaaS, SaaS), regional location, and business, there are a number of useful certifications which can be appropriate for a cloud service.

The most widely recognized international standard for information security compliance is ISO/IEC 270014 which includes national variants and well-developed certification regimes [35]. ISO is currently developing new standards, ISO/IEC 270175 "Security in Cloud Computing" and ISO/IEC 270186 "Privacy in Cloud Computing," which will specifically address cloud security and privacy considerations that built upon ISO/IEC 27001.

Security. The meaning of the term information security has evolved in recent years. In the past, most people's idea of computer security focused on the physical machines. Regarding the recent advances, information security may be defined as "Preservation of confidentiality, integrity and availability of information; in addition to other properties such as authenticity, accountability, non-repudiation and reliability can also be involved" [36].

In traditional security models, the great concerns are about unauthorized access, destruction, and modification of data, usurpation of identity and unavailability of systems. Many techniques including Firewalls, IPS, IDS, access control, and authentication are used to address these security issues.

In cloud computing, security challenges are the same in traditional non-cloud services. However, security concerns are increased by the loss of control over the owner's data and the possible misuse of these data. Indeed, outsourcing data to a cloud computing involves the transfer of the responsibility and control of the owner's data to cloud providers which means the loss of direct control over operations performed on data in the future.

In addition to the traditional security issues, there is a non-exhaustive list of new security risks inherent to the cloud computing [60]. The most critical among them are as follows:

■ Responsibility ambiguity. The responsibility for maintaining security feature is spread across users and cloud providers with the potential risk that essential countermeasures will not be implemented. Undoubtedly, there will be a failure to determine clearly the responsibility of each actors.

■ Isolation failure. Due to multi-tenancy and shared resources, which are defining characteristics of cloud computing, there is a serious risk that arises from the failure of mechanisms separating the usage of storage, memory, and routing.

- Malicious behavior of insiders. Cloud provider employees with some admin's privileges can tamper with the outsourced data or damage it. Damage can also be caused by the people working within the cloud customer's organization. Cloud computing architecture allows such attacks to be conducted from either or both the consumer organization and the provider organization sides.
- Management interface vulnerability. The management of the public interfaces of a cloud provider poses increased risks especially regarding remote access and web browser vulnerabilities. Risks can come either from the consumer organization or the provider organization sides or both.
- Handling of security incidents. Users must rely on the cloud providers for detecting, reporting, and managing security breaches on their data without any proof that the adequate actions have been taken.
- Loss of governance. Public cloud consumers cede the control of their data to the cloud providers who are theoretically responsible for addressing issues that may affect security. Service-level agreements (SLAs) should seal explicitly this agreement; otherwise, there will be holes in security defenses.
- Data protection. Cloud consumers and providers are both very preoccupied by the hosted data protection. Disclosure and release of sensitive data are on top of these preoccupations. This is amply exacerbated by the transfer of data between federated cloud services.

Trust. Trust is a complex concept for which there is no universally accepted scholarly definition. Among standard-used definitions, trust can be defined as the expectation that a system will operate as it is expected to operate or the expectation that the trustee will not engage in opportunistic behavior [49]. Trust in cloud computing can be seen as a guarantee ensured by a known trusted authority, which is usually the cloud provider, that a platform with a particular identity can be trusted to operate in an expected behavior.

Trust in a cloud provider is mainly based on its reputation which is perhaps a company's most valuable asset. Indeed, cloud providers have no interest in the behavior of the service instance it hosts. They can strengthen assurances of trustworthiness to its customers by issuing attestations of its own software stack based on a hardware root of trust. The cloud provider is also responsible for granting the privilege access of the admin's interface to the service provider; thus, it can limit the control of the service provider on the application after it was launched to only the legitimate operations (launch, stop, etc.). In addition, cloud computing providers can use trusted computing technologies for reinforcing trust in their services.

Trusted computing technology is built to ensure an execution of arbitrary software on any platform, without being able to tamper with the confidentiality and integrity of information on the platform. With such technology, even if executing programs have access to information protected by the trusted module, they cannot interpret the data since the data protected by the trusted module is encrypted. Pearson [48] defined a trusted platform as "a computing system that has a trusted component, in the form of built-in hardware which it uses to create a foundation of trust for software process." The basic goal of trusted computing, as defined by the Trusted Computing Group (TCG), is to ensure trust in software processes executing on a platform with the trust being rooted in hardware.

There is no way to distinguish arbitrary software from trusted software other than to measure the executing software. Typically, this involves creating a hash of the executable and associating a secret with the measured hash. Trusted platforms provide a way to measure and store the resulting digest in a tamper-resistant environment. When queried by a remote party, a trusted platform has a way to provide proof of its capabilities as well as its capacity to provide the measured digests to the remote party in an assured way.

Addressing the security, privacy and trust issues which result from hosting data in cloud platforms must be assured by cloud providers. Nevertheless, users still need to take responsibility for their use of cloud computing services in order to guarantee security and privacy of their data in the best interest of their organization. They have to ensure that the contract with the provider and its associated SLA has appropriate provisions for security and privacy. Moreover, users must also ensure appropriate integration of the cloud computing services with their own systems for managing security and privacy.

11.3 Cryptographic Techniques for the Cloud Security

This section introduces the advanced cryptographic primitives and protocols that are designed to strike a balance between security, efficiency, and functionality in cloud computing environments. These techniques provide a variety of computations on encrypted data, ranging from general-purpose computations to special-purpose computations. We discuss fully and functional encryption, secure MPC, and searchable encryption.

11.3.1 Fully Homomorphic Encryption

While fully homomorphic encryption (FHE) schemes are new, the concept is not. In 1978, Rivest, Adelman, and Dertouzos [53] were the first to investigate the design of a homomorphic encryption scheme based on the multiplicative homomorphic properties of the Rivest, Shamir and Adelman (RSA) cryptosystem. Their main goal was to achieve the ability to execute queries on encrypted data as a perfect solution for the scenario where a financial company wants to outsource its sensitive data to an offsite location. For security and privacy purposes, data must be encrypted before offloading it. Obviously, this approach grants the confidentiality and integrity of data, but it has a serious drawback: the company cannot query it. Rivest et al. proposed the privacy homomorphism, a theoretical encryption scheme for queering data in completely encrypted environments. Unfortunately, their privacy homomorphism was broken a couple of years later by Brickell and Yacobi [10].

A lot of articles have proposed solutions dedicated to numerous application contexts: secret sharing scheme, threshold schemes, zero-knowledge proofs, commitment schemes, protection of mobile agents, MPC, and so forth [21]. A little progress have been made until 2009 when Craig Gentry [28] constructed a FHE scheme capable of evaluating an arbitrary number of additions and multiplications (and thus, compute any function) on encrypted data.

Unfortunately, Gentry's fully encryption scheme introduces noise in the ciphertexts as computations are performed on it. Every multiplication operation increases the noise by a significant amount, meaning that at some point, the noise will be too big and decryption will become invalid. Gentry proposed to overcome this limitation by doing noise reduction and then make his scheme bootstrappable, which means that it can evaluate its own decryption circuit. This allows its original scheme to support an arbitrary number of computations on the ciphertexts. It turns out that any computable function can be performed on the encrypted data.

In the last five years, many homomorphic schemes have been proposed to improve the efficiency of the fully homomorphic scheme introduced by Gentry. There are also much informal discussions in the industry environment about whether FHE is efficient to be implementable or practicable. While the initial Gentry's scheme was considered as being infeasible for practical deployments, other significant developments produced other schemes [19,59,62] leading up to the most recent solutions of Brakerski and Vaikuntanathan [8,9].

11.3.1.1 Introduction

In this section, we present the basic definition related to the homomorphic encryption. Let P be plaintexts space with addition operator + and multiplication operator × and C the ciphertexts space with addition operator + and multiplication operator ×. Let E: $P{\rightarrow}C$ be a (probabilistic) encryption scheme and D: $C{\rightarrow}P$ the corresponding decryption scheme. A public key cryptosystem is homomorphic under addition and multiplication, if

$$D\big(E(m_1) + E(m_2)\big) = m_1 + m_2$$

and

$$D\big(E(m_1) \times E(m_2)\big) = m_1 \times m_2$$

for all $m_1, m_2 \in P$.

Less formally, these definitions mean that it is equivalent to perform operations on the plaintexts before encryption or on the corresponding ciphertexts after encryption. It turns out that there is a kind of commutativity between encryption and some data-processing operations.

To extend this definition, consider the constraint that

$$D(f\big(E(m_1), E(m_2), \ldots, E(m_n)\big) = f(m_1, m_2, \ldots, m_n)$$

for some set of functions f and for all m_i in the plaintexts space. We say that an encryption scheme is *partially homomorphic* if f is a finite or infinite subset of computable functions and that it is *fully homomorphic* if f is a set of all computable functions.

Since 1978, a number of encryption schemes have been proven to be partially homomorphic, which means only under multiplication or under addition. The most known under addition is Pallier [46] and under multiplication are El Gaml [25] and RSA [53].

11.3.1.2 Homomorphism under Multiplicative: RSA

In this section, we discuss the basic multiplicative homomorphism based on RSA. First, we recall the RSA scheme:

Parameters: Let n be a product of two big prime numbers p et q and e a number such as
  $gcd(e,(p{-}1)(q{-}1)) = 1$
Private key: d such as $d = e^{-1}$ mod $(p{-}1)(q{-}1)$, Public key: (e,n)
Encryption: $E(m) = m^e$ mod n
Decryption: $D(C) = C^d$ mod n.

As stated below, the decryption of a multiplication of two ciphertexts yields the multiplication of the corresponding plaintexts:

$$E(m_1) \times E(m_2) = m_1^e m_2^e \bmod n$$

$$D(E(m_1) \times E(m_2)) = m_1 m_2^d \bmod n = m_1^{de} m_2^{ed} \bmod n = m_1 m_2 \bmod n$$

The RSA encryption is not known to be homomorphic under addition.

11.3.1.3 Gentry's Partially Homomorphic Encryption

This section introduces Gentry's basic partially scheme over integers [21].

- Key generation: choose a random odd integer p with λ^2 bits, where λ is an integer.
- Encryption: a single bit $m \in \{0,1\}$ can be encrypted by c = $pq + m'$, where p is the private key, m' is a random bit integer with the same least bit as m, and q is a random λ^5 bit integer.
- Decryption: $m = (c \bmod p) \bmod 2$.

The security of this scheme is based on the approximative GCD problem. The best-known algorithm for solving this problem is exponential in time with respect to the size of inputs, which means that without p the decryption process is intractable.

It is easy to show that this scheme is homomorphic under addition and multiplication:

Addition:

$$E(m_1) + E(m_2) = m_1 + pq_1 + m_2 + pq_2$$

$$D(E(m_1) + E(m_2)) = (m_1 + m_2 + pq_1 + pq_2 \bmod p) \bmod 2$$

$$= m_1 + m_2 \bmod 2$$

Multiplication:

$$E(m_1) \times E(m_2) = (m_1 + pq_1)(m_2 + pq_2)$$

$$D(E(m_1) + E(m_2)) = (m_1 m_2 + m_1 pq_2 + m_2 pq_1 + p^2 q_1 q_2 \bmod p) \bmod 2$$

$$= m_1 m_2 \bmod 2$$

As many operations are performed on the ciphertext, the introduced noise on it grows. For example, if a single addition and multiplication are performed:

$$(E(m_1) + E(m_2)) \times E(m_3) = (m_1 + pq_1 + m_2 + pq_2)(m_3 + pq_3)$$

$$= m_3(m_1 + m_2) + p^2(q_1 q_3 + q_2 q_3)$$

The resulted noise is $p^2(q_1 q_3 + q_2 q_3)$.

When the noise is too big, a problem comes in. The parity of the plaintext is corrupted, and the resulting decryption is invalid. To reduce the growing noise, Gentry proposed to encrypt the ciphertext before a specific number of operations, and before the noise is too big, the encrypted ciphertext will be decrypted. This operation is called bootstrapping. However, encryption and the decryption functions with the bootstrapping process have too many operations so that the homomorphic scheme cannot handle it. Gentry introduces a new technique named "squash the decryption circuit" to address this problem. The idea behind it is to add to the public key a hint about the secret key, so anybody can post-process the ciphertext leaving less work for the decryption. The scheme of Brakerski and Vaikuntanathan [8] is a significant improvement upon Gentry's scheme since it introduces the relinearization and modulus switching, removing the need of a squashing step. Later, the scheme of Brakerski, Gentry, and Vaikuntanathan [9] improves upon Brakerski and Vaikuntanathan's scheme to obtain FHE without bootstrapping.

In spite of its promising benefits, current implementations of homomorphic encryption schemes are not sufficiently efficient to be used for real deployment. Recent result analysis showed that key generation in Halevi's lattice-based scheme may take place from 2.5 s to 2.2 h [29] and a homomorphic evaluation of AES using FHE by Gentry et al. [30] requires up to 36 h. The large amount of required memory is another barrier to the adoption of fully homomorphic schemes since the used ciphertext and the public key must be of a very large size in order to avoid possible lattice-based attacks [41], namely the public key sizes of the Gentry and Halevi's FHE scheme [29] ranging from 17 MB to 2.25 GB.

11.3.1.4 State of the Art

Even if the almost FHE schemes remain prohibitively slow for use in practice, there exist few prototypes of implementation. The foremost among these is HElib, a library developed by IBM which is based on the Halevi and Shoup's [34] scheme. Bootstrapping was introduced to HElib in 2014, but the secure Gaussian randomness distribution is not yet implemented which means that there is no security proof for this library [34]. Currently, HElib performs a matrix vector multiplication for a 256-integer vector in approximately 26 s.

Recently, other hardware approaches for improving the efficiency of the fully homomorphic schemes have been proposed. Optimized architectures based on GPU technology [73] or FPGA technology [18] are most promising among them. The implementation proposed by Coron et al. [18] over Xilinx Virtex-7 FPGA speeds up the running time of the encryption phase by a factor up to 40 times. These results point out that a further research work can lead to more efficient FHE schemes that can be used in real applications.

11.3.2 Functional Encryption

Traditional encryption schemes are all-or-nothing, meaning one can either decrypt and read the entire plaintext or cannot learn anything at all about the plaintext. For many emerging applications in cloud computing services, there are specific needs that cannot be met by traditional encryption schemes. For example, the encryptor would say that only individuals who satisfy some specific conditions described in policy sealed with the ciphertext can decrypt it. More formally, we want to allow access to a function of the plaintext not to its entirety depending on a specific policy.

Consider the situation where a cloud provider storing encrypted medical records and a medical researcher who wants to fetch among the databases for a link between a genotype and a type of cancer in a particular ethnic group without having access to all patients' medical information. If the traditional encryption is used for encrypting the medical records, there is no way for the researcher to carry out his work. With the functional encryption paradigm, the administrator can define a function for testing only this link without revealing any detail about patients' medical conditions. By giving the researcher the secret key corresponding to this function, this task can be accomplished.

The Functional Encryption (FE) concept was only recently formalized by Boneh, Sahai, and Waters [4] and O'Neil [45]. For a functional encryption, the secret keys are associated with families of functions $\{F\}$. For each function $f()$, there exists a secret $k_s(f)$ that allows its owner to compute the value of $f(x)$ from an encryption of x. Typically, if $E(k_p,x)$ is an encryption of any x with any public key k_p, the decryption of $E(k_p,x)$ with a secret key $k_s(f)$ outputs $f(x)$. This means that the decryptor holding the secret key $k_s(f)$ obtains $f(x)$ even if the encryption of x is only available.

Functional encryption requires four algorithms:

■ Set up algorithm which outputs the secret and public keys. The secret key is called the master key (k_m).
■ Key Generation algorithm which takes as input the master key k_m and a function $f()$, and outputs the key $k_s(f)$ specific to the function $f()$.
■ Encryption algorithm which takes as input a message x and a public key k_p and outputs the obtained ciphertext c.
■ Decryption algorithm which takes as input the ciphertext and the secret key corresponding to public key used in the encryption process, and outputs the plaintext of the message. The decryption of c by using the secret key $k_s(f)$ outputs $f(x)$.

We should notice that the traditional public key encryption is a special case of the functional encryption where the only supported function is the identity function. The result of the decryption process is the entire message if the decrypting key is valid or nothing otherwise. Moreover, functional encryption encompasses many advanced encryption concepts like identity- or attribute-based encryption.

11.3.2.1 Attribute-Based Encryption

Attribute-based encryption (ABE) was first proposed by Sahai and Waters [58]. This concept allows users to encrypt and decrypt messages based on user attributes by specifying complex access policies. It comes in two different formulations of ABE: key policy ABE and ciphertext-policy ABE [24].

In the ciphertext-policy encryption, the policy that gives access to decryption process depends upon the recipient's attributes such as the country where he/she lives, his/her sex, or his/her age. These attributes are a boolean formula. For example, the encryptor can encrypt messages to anyone who lives in New York, who are females and over 30 years old. The encryption of a message m with policy ϕ is obtained by $E(k_p,(\phi,m))$ where k_p is the used public key.

For a recipient with attributes u, the Key Generation issues a corresponding secret key $k_s(f_u)$, where

$$f_u(\phi,m) = m \text{ if } \phi(u) = 1$$

The condition $\phi(u) = 1$ yields if all the attributes specified in the encryption process are satisfied. With a valid secret key, the recipient can decrypt ciphertexts where the user's attributes satisfy the decryption policy but learns nothing about the decryption of other ciphertexts.

11.3.2.2 Identity-Based Encryption

Identity-based encryption (IBE) uses a public key generated from publicly identifiable information such as an e-mail address or a telephone number in order to simplify public key cryptography. The idea was first proposed by Shamir in 1984. The fully schemes that achieve this idea was proposed by Boneh and Franklin in 2001 [5]. Their scheme uses bilinear functions defined on elliptic curve such as Weil Pairing and Tate Pairing.

IBE public keys are often called "identities" and denoted by id. The corresponding private key can only be generated by a Private Key Generator (PKG) who has knowledge of a master secret k_m. Using IBE, anyone can encrypt messages or verify signatures without prior public key distribution. This is useful where the deployment of the traditional certificate authority (CA)-based PKI is inconvenient or infeasible.

The IBE can be seen as a special case of the functional encryption where the function is the testing equality. By using the same notation, to encrypt a message m to identity id the encryptor runs the encryption algorithm:

$$E\left(k_p,(id,m)\right)$$

We should notice that the data being encrypted is the pair (id, m). For a recipient with identity id^*, Key Generation algorithm issues a secret key $k_s(f_{id^*})$ where the function f_{id^*} is defined as

$$f_{id^*}\left(id,m\right)=m \text{ if } id=id^*$$

Recall that the global public key k_p and the master key k_m result from the set up algorithm.

11.3.2.3 Boneh and Franklin's Basic Scheme

This section introduces the Boneh and Franklin's basic scheme [14] which is not secure against an adaptive chosen ciphertext attack.

Let G_1, G_2 be two cyclic groups of prime order q, P be a generator of G_1, and H:$\{0,1\}^* \rightarrow G_1$ be a secure cryptographic hash function. Let e be an admissible map from $G_1 \times G_2$ to G_2, which satisfies the following properties:

■ Bilinearity: for any $u,v \in G_1$ and $a,b \in \mathbb{Z}_q^*$, $e\left(u^a,v^b\right)=e(u,v)^{ab}$,
■ Nondegenerate: there exists $P,Q \in G_1$ such that $e\left(P,Q\right) \neq 1$,
■ Computability: there is an efficient algorithm to compute $e(u, v)$ for $u,v \in G_1$.

In the basic implementation, G_1 is an elliptic curve subgroup $E\left(\mathbb{F}_q\right)$ with points of order p, and G_2 is the group of the $p^{\text{éme}}$ roots of the unity.

■ Setup: the Public Key generator chooses a random point $P \in G_1$, an integer $s \in \mathbb{Z}_p$, and a hash function H, and computes $P_{pub} = sP$. The public parameters are $\langle p, G_1 = E[P], G_2 = \mu_p, P, P_{pub}, e, H \rangle$, and the master key is s.
■ Extraction: The PKG puts the ID into a point of the elliptic curve Q_{ID} of order p and generates $d_{ID} = sQ_{ID}$.
■ Encryption: Alice chooses a random integer r and computes $U = rP$, $g_{ID} = e(P_{pub}, Q_{ID})$. The ciphertext is $C = \langle U,V \rangle$ where $V = M \oplus H\left(g_{ID}^r\right)$.
■ Decryption: Boob computes $V \oplus H\left(e(U,d_{ID})\right)$.

The decryption process outputs the plaintext M since

$$e(U, d_{ID}) = e(rP, sQ_{ID}) = e(P, Q_{ID})^{rs} = e(sP, Q_{ID})^r = e(P_{pub}, Q_{ID})^r = g_{ID}^r$$

$$\text{Consequently } V \oplus H\left(e(U, d_{ID})\right) = M \oplus H\left(g_{ID}^r\right) \oplus H\left(g_{ID}^r\right) = M$$

11.3.2.4 State of the Art

Despite its promising interest, generic functional encryption currently exists only on the academic research. Most known constructions focus on restricted class of scheme with only a single functional key [57,60] or with a bounded number of key [33]. Another approach was introduced by Naveed et al. [43], which requires an interaction between the data's owner and any party performing a function on encrypted data. To our knowledge, the existing schemes are proven to be inefficient and hence cannot be used in practice [43].

In the last few years, many propositions for ABE have been introduced. The first one is Bethencourt's et al. over pairing-based cryptography library [2]. The most relevant implementation was proposed by Khoury et al. [38]. The encryption phase is conducted in 3 ms, whereas the decryption process is achieved in 6 ms, which is fairly preferable for use in practice.

Nowadays, several IBE implementations are available; the most practicable among them are based upon elliptic curves quadratic residues. Hardware implementations of IBE such as on FPGA and on smart cards are widespread in real applications [51]. Voltage security claims that there are more than 505 million Voltage Secure Mail users worldwide.

11.3.3 Secure MPC

In many situations, there are several players P_1, P_2,..., P_n that want to compute some function $f(x_1, x_2, ..., x_n)$ on their data in a secure way. Each player i has its own private data x_i. Security means that the process guarantees that the output function is correct and the privacy of their data is assured. The obvious way to solve this dilemma is to mandate a third trusted party to compute the agreed function on their behalf. This approach implicitly assumes that all the players trust the third party on their private information since all these information must be on its possession in order to perform the computation. In real world, players with very sensitive data are not willing to trust other parties on their data. Furthermore, it is very unlikely that there will be a single party that everyone can trust.

Due to the complexity to set up a solution with a trusted party, finding efficient algorithms that address this situation is known to be a very challenging problem. In cryptography, this problem is called secure multiparty computation (MPC). As a relevant example of secure MPC are medical companies that aim to conduct medical research on their patients' data without revealing any private information of their patients to the other companies. Another example is electronic voting where there are electors with an integer (vote) for each one as their secret data. Computing the score of each candidate without revealing the vote of each elector is the goal of the MPC. Secure benchmarking, electronic auctions, and secure signal processing are also applications that can be addressed by secure MPC.

For many years, researches of MPC have shown that general purpose of MPC protocols allowing to compute any functions exist for only theoretical interests. Practicable protocols were designated for particular tasks such as voting or data mining. Yao [74] was the first to introduce a two-party protocol based on the use of boolean circuits. Since then, a lot of MPC protocols based on the boolean circuits have been proposed. They are all based on Yao's one. Recently, the use of the arithmetic circuits, namely secret sharing or homomorphic encryption techniques, has emerged as promising approach for building efficient MPC protocols.

Boolean circuits: Yao's MPC works as follows for two parties: A the circuit initiator, and B the circuit evaluator. A chooses two secret keys, each one corresponds to the bit input 0 and 1. A truth table consisting of encrypted wire key stored in a random way. The encryption is made under the pair of the corresponding input wire keys. A sends the truth table to B with the corresponding input wire keys. The evaluator B is unable to learn any information about the inputs since the keys are stored in a random way. Thanks to the oblivious transfer, the corresponding key to each A's inputs are at the disposal of B without revealing any information about its input. For each gate, B gets the output wire key from the truth table by decrypting the appropriate entry. At the end of the process, the evaluator B announces to initiator A the output key which determines if the output is 0 or 1.

Arithmetic circuits: MPC protocols based on homomorphic encryption. Let E be some FHE, i.e., if $C_1 = E(x)$ and $C_2 = E(y)$ then $C_1 + C_2 = E(x + y)$ mod p where p is some integer. The initiator A sends $C_1 = E(a)$ to the evaluator B. By using the functionalities of the homomorphic encryption, the evaluator B can compute $C_2 = E(ab - r)$ and returns it to A. By decrypting it, the initiator A obtains $s = ab - r$ and hence both A and B have at their disposal r and s. To our knowledge, the most accomplished of this setting is the one proposed by Bendlin et al. [13].

11.3.3.1 State of the Art

In the past years, a lot of work has been done to improve the implementation of the MPC protocols. In 2009, the first implementation of two parties with active security was proposed by Pinkas et al. [52]. It allows to compute a circuit of 310^3 gates in 10^3s. Later, Nielsen et al. [44] reduced this time to 5 s. The first-time use of MPC in real application was in 2008 for moving the real money in the context of a nationwide auction for sugar beets contracts between farmers in Denmark [22].

11.3.4 Searchable Encryption

The concept of Search in Encrypted Data (SED) has become a relevant topic for the cloud security field since it provides a higher level of protection for hosted data. It has already captured the attention of many researchers in the cryptography area working on the advanced and efficient techniques that can be implemented in the near future.

With searchable encryption, a client is able to authorize a third party to search on its encrypted data without allowing himself/herself to have access to his plaintext data. More precisely, the third party can process queries in the encrypted data on behalf of the data's owner without being able to learn any information about the plaintext data. For achieving more privacy, many searchable encryption schemes go one step further and prevent the third party to learn any information about queries that it processes on behalf of the clients.

As a relevant scenario for an application of the SED, suppose that a frequent traveler has a data that he needs to have access anytime during his travel and from anywhere around the world. He can outsource his data in encrypted manner with an SED scheme to a third-party cloud service provider such as Amazon'S3 or Dropbox. With this approach, the outsourced data can be accessible at any time and from anywhere while the privacy of his data is preserved. Indeed, the user can issue any search query in encrypted way to cloud service provider which will process it and return the obtained results that match the search criteria. We should notice that the obtained result is also encrypted which prevents any leakage of information.

One of the most relevant challenges in the searchable encryption is the Private Information Retrieval (PIR) [16] where a user needs to retrieve information from a database outsourced in a third-party server without revealing any information about the requested data to the server. Advanced searchable encryption schemes go one step further and allow the user to search in the recovered data. The first searchable encryption scheme was defined in 2000 [64]. It uses symmetric encryption and provides query isolation, controlled searching, and hidden queries.

In [6], the authors proposed a scheme called public key encryption with keyword search (PEKS). A user can make his public key available to any entity that can encrypt messages for him. The user can also issue a token to third-party server in order to search in his encrypted data. A lot of work has been done to improve the concept of searchable encryption in many aspects [67,75].

In this section, we describe a variant of noninteractive searchable symmetric encryption based on the paper of Chase and Kamara [15]. The description assumes that the users documents are encrypted using some symmetric encryption scheme and that the documents can be identified with a unique identifier that is independent of their content. Such assumption is made in order to prevent any information leakage about a file's contents from the knowledge of its identifier.

Let us suppose that a user has a data collection $\mathbf{D} = (D_1, \ldots, D_n)$, he sets up a database DB that maps keyword w in the collection to the identifiers of the documents that contain it. The term DB[w] will refer to a list of identifiers of documents that contain keyword w. In the present context, the term database is used loosely to refer to a data structure optimized for keyword search (i.e., a search structure).

The searchable symmetric encryption scheme consists of three algorithms: Set up, Token, and Search:

- Set up: the client runs the algorithm that takes as input a security parameter 1^k and a database DB; it returns as output secret key K and an encrypted database EDB.
- Token: the client runs the algorithm that takes as input K and a keyword w; it returns as output a token t_k.
- Search: the cloud provider runs the algorithm that takes as input an encrypted database EDB and a token t_k; it returns as output a set of identifiers DB[w].

In addition to the security requirements, the search complexity of a searchable encryption scheme must be low. Sublinear in the number of documents and, ideally, linear in the number of documents that contain the search term since at a minimum the server needs to fetch the relevant documents just to set them back. Requiring sublinear search complexity is crucial for practical purposes unless the work is done on small dataset. Linear search would not be realistic to imagine if the desktop search application or e-mail search function did sequential search over the hard drive or e-mail collection every time a search is performed.

11.4 State of the Art

In the past years, a lot of methods based on preprocessing and parallelization have been proposed in order to improve the performance and scalability of searchable encryption. First, Freedman et al. [22] introduced a new technique based on achieving some preprocessing operations between the querier and the server, and Papas et al. [50] exploited the opportunities of parallelization within a single execution. According to [23], these improvements make the searchable encryption technology very close to commercial interest.

CryptoDB, developed by Popa et al. [51], is a library allowing queries over encrypted data. The main idea behind it is that many encryption forms provide the possibility to perform different queries directly on encrypted data. This client side library shows that it is really possible to achieve search over encrypted data.

11.5 Hardware Approach for Cloud Security

In the past decade, many approaches have been proposed to enhance security in computer systems via the use of special-purpose hardware devices. These hardware devices range from simple devices with limited computational power, like cryptographic smart cards, to sophisticated high-end devices like secure co-processors that come with powerful processors and provide a high degree of tamper resistance. Trusted Platform Module (TPM), introduced by TCG [72], is the most notable approach among them. This section discusses how TPM can be used for enhancing security in cloud computing environments.

11.5.1 Trusted Platform Module

The idea behind the TPM architecture for hardware-based security was motivated by increasingly sophisticated malware attacks in the late 1990s. Antivirus software was and is still the most efficient solution against these attacks on the computer systems. Sophisticated malware gains execution on a computer at the same privilege level as the antivirus software, and it can simply disable the program to conceal its existence, which means that the software cannot verify itself. This is the fundamental flow with the software-only defense. To overcome this limitation and ensure software configuration integrity, there is a need to a trusted neutral device in the computing platform which is able to record and verify the state of the software.

The TPM is a security specification defined by the TCG. It is usually installed on the motherboard of a computer or laptop and communicates with the rest of the system through hardware bus by using well-defined commands. The TPM provides cryptographic operations such as encryption, decryption, and signing as well as random number generation. It also provides space for the storage of a small amount of information such as cryptographic keys. Since it was implemented carefully in the hardware, the TPM is resistant to software attacks.

The specification for TPMs is produced by the TCG, an industry consortium. TPM chips are produced by a variety of vendors including Infineon, Broadcom, Atmel, STMicroelectronics, and Nuvoton. PC manufacturers shipping TPM-enabled PCs include Dell, Lenovo, HP, Toshiba, and Fujitsu. The current specification version is TPM 2.0. Microsoft has announced that all systems submitted to the Windows Certification Program after January 1, 2015 will be required to have TPM 2.0. TPMs have been used in a wide variety of applications from secure military platforms, to secure industrial control systems, as well as to secure electronic voting systems [71].

TPM offers additional capabilities including secure storage where the user can store data that is encrypted by keys available only to the TPM; Platform Integrity Measurement and Reporting, which enables the platform to create reports of its integrity and configuration state using the Platform Configuration Registers, that can be relied on by a remote verifier through a remote attestation; and Platform Authentication that allows the user to authenticate the platform via the TPM signature [71].

The TPM contains two important functional components: cryptographic engine that can perform cryptographic operations and a small amount of nonvolatile random access memory, which can be used to store keys or data. The TPM 1.2 specification has had cryptographic limitations: only RSA and SHA-1 have been supported, whereas the TPM 2.0 has been written to allow for flexibility in encryption algorithms. It supports elliptic curve encryption and signature and SHA-256 which should replace SHA-1 that begins to show some signs of weakness.

Due to space storage limitation, the TPM does not normally store keys permanently. Rather, it contains a Storage Root Key that is stored persistently. When a new key is required by a software, the TPM creates a new key, concatenates it with a value known only to the TPM, adds any authorization information, and then encrypts these data with the public portion of the Storage Root Key. The program is responsible for storing this new key and loading it into TPM memory after a software request. Prior to this, TPM decrypts the key with the Storage Root Key, checks that the proof value is its own, and checks that the supplied password matches. Software can then specify this loaded key in an encryption or digital signature command.

Each TPM is associated with a number of signing keys. The endorsement private key (EK) identifies the TPM and thus, the physical host. The EK stands for the validity of TPM [71]. The respective manufacturers sign the corresponding public key to guarantee the correctness of the chip and validity of the key. Related to the EK are attestation identity keys (AIKs). An AIK is created by the TPM and linked to the local platform through a certificate for that AIK. This latter certificate is created and signed by a CA. In particular, the CA allows a platform to present different AIKs to different remote parties, so that it is impossible for these parties to determine that the AIKs are coming from the same platform.

11.5.1.1 Remote Attestation Based on the TPM

In cloud computing environments, the remote attestation is responsible for assessing the integrity of the nodes in the cloud infrastructure. It allows cloud users to deploy their virtual machines and applications on a physical host that meets their security requirements represented by the integrity levels. Furthermore, the remote attestation can help administrators to monitor the status of the node in an efficient way and to take appropriate countermeasures once a compromised host has been detected [55].

Remote attestation is a mechanism that allows a software to prove its executing state on a device to a verifier. It can offer assurance of software invocation, delivery of content to trusted clients, and mitigation of mutual suspicion between clients. The verifier trusts that attestation because it is signed by the TPM's keys which are certified by a trusted CA.

The TPM attestation consists of several steps of cryptographic authentication by which the specification for each layer of the platform is checked from the hardware up to the operating system and application code. At a high level, the TPM attests the source code of service application by signing its hash with an AIK. This will be done by following the trust chain TPM → BIOS → BootLoader → OS → Application. Direct Anonymous Attestation [11] can be used to protect the privacy of the TPM in such a way that a user will be able to verify the validity of attestation without linking it to the platform that contains the TPM.

Trust in a cloud provider is mainly based on its reputation; therefore, it has no interest in the behavior of the service instance it hosts. It can strengthen the confidence of users by certifying the software running on its platform through a hardware root of trust. The cloud provider is also responsible for granting the privilege access the admin's interface to the service provider. Thus, it can limit the control of the service provider on the application after it was launched to only the legitimate operations (launch, stop, etc.). For all these reasons, the cloud provider itself can be seen as a trusted platform that runs a well-tested software stack and offers hosting platform for multi-tenants users. By using remote TPM attestation, the cloud provider can serve as a guarantor for preventing attackers from tampering with application services after it was launched on their platforms.

11.5.2 Trusted Network Connect

TCG has provided Trusted Network Connect (TNC) [69] as an industry standard approach to network security and network access control (NAC) that works with leading providers, including Cisco and Microsoft. TNC is an open and vendor-neutral specification for the integrity check of communication endpoints, which requests access to a resource. The TCG's TNC uses the TPM to guarantee the accuracy of the platform integrity information used in the NAC process which gives administrators facilities to control network access based on user and device credentials, while they are monitoring behavior on the network and they can immediately respond to problems as they occur.

The main special aspect of the TNS is its capability to provide a strong solutions against "Lying Endpoint" which is a serious issue for the software-based NAC systems. In "Lying Endpoint" scenario, an endpoint infected or compromised may lie about its health state and thus can gain access to the network and infect other systems. Usual endpoint security solutions can mitigate this issue but not eliminate it. By performing a system monitoring, they can detect infected endpoint and eliminate it, but only after spreading the infection. Furthermore, the endpoint security solutions will miss stealthy infections like keystroke loggers and rootkits.

The TNC's solution for preventing the lying endpoint problem is based on the TPM facilities. During the endpoint's boot, the TPM measures (hashes) all the critical software and firmware components before they are loaded: BIOS, boot loader, operating system kernel, etc. and send them to the TNC server in order to be compared to values for proper configurations already stored in the server. An endpoint is declared infected if the comparison does not match, and thus it can be moved to the quarantine. We should notice, however, that TPM-based verification is optional with TNC.

In cloud computing environments, maintaining virtual machines across multiple systems presents different administrative challenges to traditional physical systems deployment. For example, virtual machines can be suspended or powered of or even moved to other servers during a patch application process. Moving a virtual machine, for example, might open a window of vulnerability by potentially having a different patch level than is required on a target physical system.

Combined with patch management tools, TNC can help to detect virtual machines that do not meet the corporate policies that are established for a visualized data center [12]. Alerts are triggered if noncompliant virtual machines are detected. TNC and patch management analyze data from both the service update manager and the network installation manger to check each virtual machines during activation.

11.6 Cryptography and Cloud Security Challenges

The SLAs are a contract between users and cloud service providers that aim to protect users' interests. The SLA can mitigate the trust, security, and privacy issues, but it is not totally satisfactory in the perspective of users who are looking for better technical controls to get guaranteed protection for their data in cloud platforms. As mentioned before, cryptography is one of the most valuable solutions for providing technical controls over outsourced data in cloud computing platforms.

In this section, we sketch some cryptographic solutions used to address privacy, security, and trust issues in cloud computing.

■ Secure deletion: All implemented solutions for deletion of data in cloud computing platforms are proposed and totally controlled by the cloud services provider companies. This is the case of the "Inactive Account Settings" solution offered by Google. Performing cryptographic operation of encryption and managing keys can achieve secure deletion. Indeed, if data is stored in encrypted format and keys used in the encryption are locally destroyed once data deletion in need, the remaining data in cloud platform are encrypted. Encrypted data with a strong encryption algorithm are useless as deleted data.

   Another proposed cryptographic solution for secure deletion is the use of method based on policy control. Cloud's users define a policy launching the deletion process of encryption keys when policy expiry criteria are met. FADE [60] is by far the most accomplished policy-based file deletion scheme for achieving both access control and assured deletion for outsourced data.

■ Secure storage. Encryption is the obvious solution for securing the stored data at rest. This will ensure that data do not get compromised, even if unauthorized access or insider abuse takes place in cloud platforms. However, traditional encryption algorithms are not practical since indexing or searching in encrypted data cannot be achieved. Searching and FHE can be used for accomplishing secure storage in cloud computing provided that research advances made significant progress in implementing efficient algorithms.

■ Communication security. In cloud computing, sensitive data needs to be transmitted between cloud users and cloud platforms or within components distributed in a cloud platform. Cryptographic techniques play a major role for protecting data in transit. Well-known and widely adopted SSL, SSH, and VPN protocols are used to mitigate and prevent threats on transmitted data over unsecure public network.

■ Virtualization security. For ensuring tight access control to virtual machines, Secure Shell or SSH are used to provide access for users to their virtual machines. The use of private keys allows that only authorized and legitimate customers are able to access and manage their virtual images hosted in cloud platform. In addition, well-known cryptographic-based countermeasures can be used for preventing side channel attacks. Cryptographic operations related to hashing and message authentication code (MAC) can ensure that no violation of virtual machines integrity occurs.

■ Privacy. In addition to the recognized international standard for information security compliance, FHE can help to mitigate privacy issue in cloud computing. Van Dijk and Juels [20] argued, however, that even the most powerful cryptographic techniques cannot alone enforce the privacy demanded by cloud services. They proposed to spread the outsourced data among a collection of cloud providers platforms in such a way that one cloud provider can have the full control over the consumer data.

■ Trust: by ensuring the execution of a given software stack, TPM can help to address trust problems in cloud computing. The cryptographic functionalities of the TPM allow to issue a remote attestation about the state of the software, executed on a cloud platform, to the cloud users, which help to increase their trust on the cloud services. This approach has been used by Santos et al. [56] to design a trusted cloud computing platform based on TPM attestation chains. In [31], the authors have proposed Terra, a trusted platform based on a virtual machine. Terra is able to prevent insider attacks from tampering with the users' data. Terra also provides a remote attestation capability that enables a customer to determine upfront whether the host can securely run the computation on their data.

Figure 11.1 summaries the cryptographic techniques used for cloud security.

Undoubtedly, cryptographic solutions can help to mitigate security, privacy, and trust issues in cloud computing environments. Traditional techniques like encryption, MAC, and access control are used to address the security issues shared with conventional information systems. For example, the well-known SSL, SSH protocols, and VPN tunnels can be used to establish secure channels. In many cases, these techniques must be adapted to meet the specific security requirements of cloud computing architecture. Users' authentication is a relevant example of these cases since users credentials cannot be stocked securely in the cloud providers' side. Therefore, a trusted authority may be used for maintaining and checking all users' credentials.

Advanced cryptographic techniques can be reserved for specific security requirements in cloud computing. Fully homomorphic, searchable encryption can be applied to achieve secure storage and secure computation provided that sufficient advances will be made in their implementation. Cryptographic-based hardware can turn out to be a satisfactory solution to address trust needs. TPMs, the most prevalent form of trusted hardware, are built to reinforce users' trust in cloud computing platforms.

Despite its valuable support, it is an established fact that cryptography cannot alone deal with all security, privacy, and trust issues in cloud computing environments. Cloud consumers still have to take more responsibility for protecting their data by contracting an appropriate SLA and ensuring an adequate integration of the cloud services systems of management and security. They have

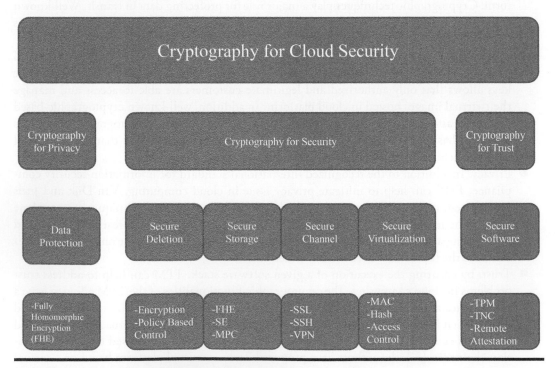

Figure 11.1 Cryptography for cloud privacy, trust and security.

also to adopt other solutions of security enforcement including tamper proof hardware, distributed computing, and multiple trust ecosystems [20].

11.7 Summary

In this chapter, we surveyed some of the important security, privacy, and trust issues related to the cloud computing model and introduced the cryptographic solutions used to mitigate these issues. We focused on the specific security challenges such as service unavailability, insecure or incomplete data deletion and handling of security incidents that cannot be addressed by traditional cryptographic solutions. Our aim was not an exhaustive survey of the area, but an exposition of the advanced cryptographic techniques including homomorphic and searchable encryption and a study of their ability to provide appropriate solutions for the most challenging security vulnerabilities. The study of the current state of the art in implementing these advanced protocols has shown that further progress needs to be made before consideration for a large adoption in real applications. Along with the protocols, we prospected the most relevant cryptographic-based hardware solutions, namely, TPM and TNC, and explored their impact on helping to fulfill the cloud privacy and trust requirements. Finally, we discussed how valuable is cryptography in providing cloud consumers with technical controls over hosted data in cloud computing platforms. We conclude that despite its contribution, cryptography alone cannot address all the cloud privacy and trust concerns.

References

1. F. Armknecht, C. Boyd, C. Carr, K. Gjøsteen, A. Jäschke, C.R. euter M. Str. A guide to fully homomorphic encryption. In *Cryptology ePrint Archive*. Report 2015/1192, 2015, Available at: https://eprint.iacr.org/2015/1192.
2. J. Bethencourt, A. Sahai, B. Waters. Ciphertext-policy attribute-based encryption. In *IEEE Symposium on Security Privacy*, pp. 321–334, 2007.
3. A. Bentajer, F. Ennaama, M. Hedabou, S. Elfezazi. Enhancing trust in cloud's SPI stack. In *4th International Conference on Computational Experimental Science Engineering*. Antalya-Turkey, 2017.
4. D. Boneh, A. Sahai, B. Waters. Functional encryption: Definitions challenges. *TCC*, 6597, 253–273, 2011.
5. D. Boneh, M. Franklin. Identity based encryption from the Weil pairing. *Journal of Computing*, 32(3), 586–615, 2003.
6. D. Boneh, G. Di Crescenzo. Public key encryption with keyword search. *Proceedings of Eurocrypt*, 3027, 506–522, 2004.
7. P. Bogetoft, D. Christensen, I. Damgard, M. Geisler, T. Jakobsen, M. Krøigaard, J. Nielsen, J. Nielsen, K. Nielsen, J. Pagter, M. Schwartzbach, T. Toft. Secure multiparty computation goes live. In *Cryptology ePrint Archive*. Report 2008/068, 2008.
8. Z. Brakerski, V. Vaikuntanathan. Efficient fully homomorphic encryption from (stard) LWE. *SIAM Journal of Computing*, 43(2), 831–871, 2014.
9. Z. Brakerski, G. Gentry, V. Vaikuntanathan. (Leveled) Fully homomorphic encryption without bootstrapping. In *ITCS 2012*, pp. 309–325, 2012.
10. E. Brickell, Y. Yacobi. On privacy homomorphisms. *Advances in Cryptology*, 304, 117–125, 1987.
11. E. Brickell, J. Camenisch, L. Chen. Direct anonymous attestation. In *ACM Conference on Computer Communications Security*, pp. 132–145, 2004.
12. A. Buecker, F. Costa, R. Davidson, E. Matteotti, G. North, D. Sherwood, S. Zaccak. Managing security compliance in cloud or virtualized data centers using IBM PowerSC. In *IBM Red Books*, January 2013.

13. R. Bendlin, I. Damgrd, C. Orli, S. Zakarias. Semi-homomorphic encryption multiparty computation. In *EUROCRYPT*, pp. 169–188, 2011.

14. D. Boneh, M. Franklin. Identity based encryption from the Weil pairing. *Journal of Computing*, 32(3), 586–615, 2003.

15. M. Chase, S. Kamara. Structured encryption controlled disclosure. *Advances in Cryptology-ASIACRYPT*, 6477, 577–594, 2010.

16. B. Chor, E. Kushilevitz, O. Goldreich, M. Sudan. Private information retrieval. *Journal of ACM*, 6, 965–981, 1998.

17. A. Choudhury, P. Kumar, M. Sain, H. Lim, H. Jae-Lee. A strong user authentication framework for cloud computing. In *IEEE Asia -Pacific Services Computing Conference*, IEEE, 2011. doi:10.1109/APSCC.2011.14

18. J.-S. Coron, D. Naccache, M. Tibouchi. Public key compression modulus switching for fully homomorphic encryption over the integers. In *EUROCRYPT*, pp. 446–464, 2012.

19. M. van Dijk, G. Gentry, S. Halevi, V. Vaikuntanathan. Fully homomorphic encryption over the integers. In *29th Annual International Conference on the Theory Applications of Cryptographic Techniques*, pp. 24–43, 2010.

20. M. van Dijk, A. Juels. On the impossibility of cryptography alone for privacy-preserving cloud computing. In *USENIX Conference*, pp. 1–8, 2010.

21. C. Fontaine, F. Gal. A survey of homomorphic encryption for nonspecialists. *Journal of Information Security*, 1, 41–50, 2009.

22. M. Freedman, Y. Ishai, B. Pinkas, O. Reingold. Keyword search oblivious pseudorom functions. In *Second Theory of Cryptography Conference*, vol 3378, pp. 303–324, 2005.

23. Gartner. Top five cloud computing adoption inhibitors. 2009. Available at: www.gartner.com/doc/977217/top-cloudcomputing-adoption-inhibitors.

24. V. Goyal, O. Pey, A. Sahai, B. Waters. Attribute-based encryption for fine-grained access control of encrypted data. In *ACM Conference on Computer Communications Security*, pp. 89–98, 2006.

25. T. El Gamal. A public key cryptosystem a signature scheme based on discrete logarithms. *CRYPTO*, 196, 10–18, 1984.

26. European Union. Directive 95/46/EC of the European parliament of the council of 24 October 1995 on the protection of individuals with regard to the processing of personal data on the free movement of such data. 1995.

27. B. Gupta, D. Agrawal, S. Yamaguchi. *H and book of Research on Modern Cryptographic Solutions for Computer Cyber Security*. IGI Global press, Hershey, PA, 2016.

28. G. Gentry. Fully homomorphic encryption using ideal lattices. In *Proceedings of the Annual ACM Symposium on Theory of Computing*, pp. 169–178, 2009.

29. C. Gentry, S. Halevi. Implementing gentry's fully-homomorphic encryption scheme. In *EUROCRYPT*, pp. 129–148, 2011.

30. C. Gentry, S. Halevi, N. Smart. Homomorphic evaluation of the AES circuit. *Advances in Cryptology*, 2012, 9–23, 2012.

31. T. Garfinkel, B. Pfaff, J. Chow, M. Rosenblum, D. Boneh. Terra: A virtual machine-based platform for trusted computing. In *Proceedings of SOSP*, pp. 12–37, 2003.

32. S. Goldwasser, Y. Tauman Kalai, R. Popa, V. Vaikuntanathan, N. Zeldovich. Reusable garbled circuits succinct functional encryption. In *Symposium on Theory of Computing Conference*, pp. 555–564, 2013.

33. S. Gorbunov, V. Vaikuntanathan, H. Wee. Functional encryption with bounded collusions via multiparty computation. In *Advances in Cryptology*, pp. 162–179. 2012.

34. S. Halevi, V. Shoup. HElib: An implementation of homomorphic encryption. Available at: www.github.com/shaih/HElib.

35. ISO/IEC 27018. Available at: www.iso27001security.com/html/27018.html.

36. ISO 27001. Information security management specification with guidance for use. 2005. Available at: www.iso.org/isoiec-27001-information-security.html.

37. M. Jouini, A. Rabai. A security framework for secure cloud computing environments. *International Journal of Cloud Applications Computing*, 6(3), 32–44, 2013.

38. J. Khoury, G. Lauer, P. Pal, B. Thapa, J. Loyall. Efficient private publish-subscribe systems. In *17th IEEE International Symposium on Object, Component, Service Oriented Real Time Distributed Computing*, pp. 64–71, 2014.

39. S. Kura. The 10 biggest data breaches of 2016. Available at: www.crn.com/news/security/300080151/ telecom-partners-say-cloud-security-is-top-of-mind-in-wake-of-verizon-breach.htm.

40. D. Kormann, A. Rubin. Risks of the passport single sign on protocol. *Computer Networks Journal*, 33(16), 51–58, 2000.

41. C. Moore, M. O'Neill, M. O'Sullivan, Y. Doröz, B. Sunar. Practical homomorphic encryption: A survey. In *Circuits Systems (ISCAS)*, pp. 2792–2795, 2014.

42. P. Murukutla, K. Shet. Single sign on for cloud. In *International Conference on Computing Sciences*, IEEE, 2012. doi:10.1109/ICCS.2012.66

43. M. Naveed, S. Agrawal, M. Prabhakaran, X. Wang, E. Ayday, J.-P. Hubaux, C. Gunter. Controlled functional encryption. In *Conference on Computer Communications Security*, pp. 1280–1291, 2014.

44. J. Nielsen, P. Nordholt, C. Orli, S. Sheshank Burra. A new approach to practical activesecure two-party computation. In *Cryptology ePrint Archive*. Report 2011/091, 2011.

45. A. O'Neill. Definitional issues in functional encryption. *Cryptology ePrint Archive*, Report 2010/556, 2010.

46. P. Paillier. Composite-residuosity based cryptography: An overview. *RSA Cryptobytes*, 5(1), 20–26, 2002.

47. S. Pearson, G. Yee. Privacy security for cloud computing. In *Computer Communications Networks*, pp. 4471–4489, 2013.

48. S. Pearson. Trusted computing platforms, the next security solution. Technical report, Hewlett-Packard Laboratories, 2002. Available at: www,hpl.hp.com/techreports.

49. S. Pearson, A. Benameur. Privacy, security trust issues arising from cloud computing. In *2nd IEEE International Conference on Cloud Computing Technology Science*, pp. 693–702, 2010.

50. V. Pappas, F. Krell, B. Vo, V. Kolesnikov, T. Malkin, S. Geol Choi, W. George, A. D. Keromytis, S. Bellovin. Blind seer a scalable private DBMS. In *EEE Symposium on Security Privacy*, pp. 359–374. 2014.

51. R. Popa, C. Redfeld, N. Zeldovich, H. Balakrishnan. Protecting confidentiality with encrypted query processing. In *ACM Symposium on Operating Systems Principles*, Cascais, Portugal, 2011.

52. B. Pinkas, T. Schneider, N. Smart, S. Williams. Secure two-party computation is practical. In *ASIACRYPT*, pp. 250–267, 2009.

53. R. L. Rivest, L. Adleman, M. L. Dertouzos. On data banks privacy homomorphisms. *Foundations of Secure Communication*, 4(11), 169–177, 1978.

54. R. Rai, G. Sahoo, S. Mehfuz. Securing software as a service model of cloud computing: Issues solutions. *International Journal on Cloud Computing: Services Architecture*, 3(4), 2013.

55. Remote Attestation Service. Available at: www.tclouds-project.eu/downloads/factsheets/tclouds-factsheet-07-attestation.pdf.

56. N. Santos, K. P. Gummadi, R. Rodrigues. Towards trusted cloud computing. In *Proceedings of 9th the Workshop on Hot Topics in Cloud Computing*, San Diego, CA, 2009.

57. A. Sahai, H. Seyalioglu. Worry free encryption functional encryption with public keys. In *Proceedings of Conference on Computer Communication Security*, pp. 463–472, 2010.

58. A. Sahai, B. Waters. Fuzzy identity-based encryption. In *Proceedings of EUROCRYPT*, pp. 457–473, 2005.

59. N. Smart, F. Vercauteren. Fully homomorphic encryption with relatively small key ciphertext sizes. In *International Workshop on Public Key Cryptography*, 6056, 420–443, 2010.

60. Security for cloud computing 10 steps to ensure success. Available at: www.cloud-council.org/ deliverables/CSCC-Security-for-Cloud-Computing-10-Steps-to-Ensure-Success.pdf.

61. A. Seccombe, A. Hutton, A. Meisel, A. Windel, A. Mohammed, A. Licciardi. Security guidance for critical areas of focus in cloud computing. *Cloud Security Alliance*, Available at: https:// cloudsecurityalliance.org/csaguide.pdf.

62. N.P. Smart, F. Vercauteren. Fully homomorphic simd operations. In *Cryptology ePrint Archive*, Report 2011/133, 2011.

63. S. Subashini, V. Kavitha. A survey on security issues in service delivery models of cloud computing. *Journal of Network Computer Applications*, 34, 1–11, 2011.

64. D.X. Song, D. Wagner, A. Perrig. Practical techniques for searches on encrypted data. In *21st Symposium on Security Privacy*, pp. 44–55, 2000.

65. Softlayer. Service level agreement master service agreement. Availaible at: www.softlayer.com/sla.htmlS, 2012.

66. C. Stergiou, K. Psannis, B. Kim, B. Gupta. Secure integration of IoT cloud computing. *Future Generation Computer Systems*, 78, 964–975, 2018.

67. H.S. Rhee, J.H. Park, W. Susilo, D.H Lee. Improved searchable public key encryption with designated tester. In *ASIACCS*, pp. 376–379, 2009.

68. Telenor Research. A briefing on cloud security challenges opportunities. Availaible at: www.telenor.com/wp-content/uploads/2013/11/TelenorWhitepaperCloud-V30v.pdf.

69. Trusted Computing Group. TCG trusted network connect TNC architecture for interoperability. Available at: www.opus1.com/nac/tnc/tnc-architecture-v1-1-r2.pdf.

70. Y. Tang, P. Lee, J. Lui, R. Perlman. Secure overlay cloud storage with access control assured deletion. *IEEE Transactions Dependable on Secure Computing*, 9, 903–916, 2012.

71. Trusted platform module evolution. Available at: www.jhuapl.edu/techdigest/TD/td3202/32-02-Osborn.pdf.

72. Trusted Computing Group. TPM main specification. Available at: www.trustedcomputinggroup.org/resources/tpmmainspecification.

73. W. Wang, Y. Hu, L. Chen, X. Huang, B. Sunar. Accelerating fully homomorphic encryption using GPU. In *HPEC*, pp. 1–5, 2012.

74. A. Yao. Protocols for secure computations. In *SFCS'08*. *23rd Annual Symposium on Foundations of Computer Science (FOCS)*, Washington, DC, 1982.

75. G. Yang, C. Tan, Q. Huang, D. Wong. Probabilistic public key encryptionwith equality test. *Topics in Cryptology-CT-RSA*, 598, 119–131. 2010.

76. R. Zalkind. Protecting your data in google docs compliance in the cloud. Available at: www.cloudlock.com/pdf/Protecting-Your-Data-In-Google-Docs.pdf.

Chapter 12

Medical Image Enhancement Techniques: A Survey

Sonali Maharajan and Satya Prakash Ghrera
Jaypee University of Information Technology

Amit Kumar Singh
National Institute of Technology, Patna

Sima Sahu
Dr. A.P.J. Abdul Kalam Technical University

Contents

12.1 Introduction

During communication, the data parameters of digital images suffer from different types of noise [1]. Imperfect gadgets and atmospheric turbulence are the main cause of noise generation, and this conveys wrong information about the image. Other sources of noise are noisy channel, faulty pixels in camera sensors, and faulty memory location. The noise degrades the quality of image and leads to the loss of important information [25]. Digital image processing is the processing of digital images for storage, transmission, and representation for human interpretation and machine perception. The area of digital image processing has developed vastly and plays a key role in the processing of digital medical images for diagnosing diseases. Recently, digital image processing gained a vast area of applications. One of the most important applications is in medical science. A lot of study has been done to enhance the image quality and remove noise. Recently, medical image processing and their enhancement are the most significant trend in modern medicine [2]. Further, a current 3D medical imaging technique offers advances in science, and as a result, higher dependability medical images are created. Different types of noise like Gaussian noise, impulse noise, Poisson noise, Rician noise, and Speckle noise corrupt the medical images [38,45]. Medical images such as X-ray, magnetic resonance imaging (MRI), computed tomography (CT), ultrasound, optical coherence tomography (OCT), single-photon emission computed tomography (SPECT), Heidelberg retina tomography, and fundus usually have very low contrast, and the work of image enhancement algorithms is to sharpen them. Medical image enhancement aims to improve the contrast of medical image and reduce noise level [2]. Figure 12.1 shows the effect of medical image enhancement.

This chapter is organized as follows. After the Introduction section, medical image processing along with different medical image modalities, important medical image noises, major performance parameters, and image quality parameters are discussed in Section 12.2. Section 12.3 discusses the image enhancement techniques followed by related state-of-the-art techniques. Different research challenge issues are discussed in Section 12.4. Comparison summary of various existing techniques is also provided in this section. Section 12.5 concludes the chapter followed by references to benefit researchers for further detailed study.

12.2 Medical Image Processing

Medical image processing is the processing of medical images whose inputs and outputs are images that extract essential data and features from medical images. Figure 12.2 shows the basic building

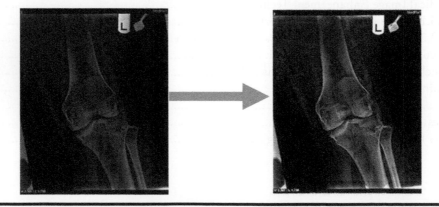

Figure 12.1 Showing effect of medical image enhancement on MRI image of the left knee.

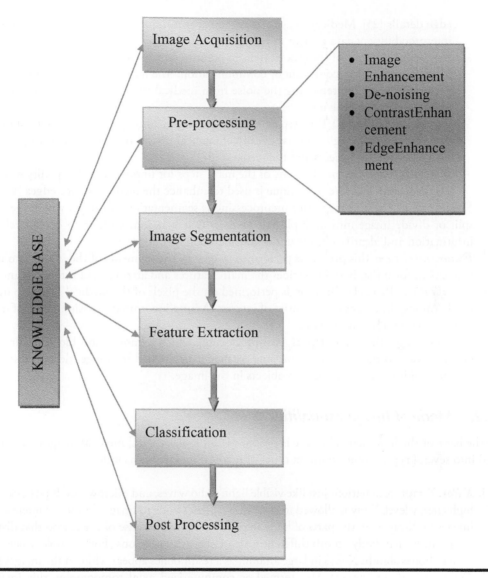

Figure 12.2   Building blocks of medical image processing.

blocks of medical image processing. The fundamental steps vary from type to type of medical image modality. Some of the basic steps in medical image processing are briefly explained below.

  i. *Image acquisition*: Image acquisition is the first step in medical image processing. In this step, the image is retrieved from the source for further processing.
 ii. *Preprocessing*: After acquiring the image, preprocessing is done at the basic level of abstraction of image, and it envelops various further steps to enhance medical image or to remove noise or distortion from medical image for further processing of image. Some of the preprocessing steps are explained below.
      – *Image enhancement*: This step is an important and most challenging area in medical image processing. The main aim of this step is to suppress the noise while preserving the

edge details [25]. Medical image enhancement techniques enhance the perception and interpretability of data present in the image [38].

- *De-noising*: It is one of the crucial steps in preprocessing of medical image. Noise occurs in an image during acquisition or communication. The main motive of de-noising is to preserve edges while removing the noise from medical image. Different types of filters are used to remove the noise.
- *Contrast enhancement*: This step converts a low-contrast image to a high-contrast image. It aims at improvising the visual quality of medical image. It improves the brightness of image between its objects and background [37].
- *Image edge enhancement*: It is one of the main steps for improvising the quality of medical image. Guided filter technique is used to enhance the medical image edges [43].

iii. *Segmentation*: The next step after preprocessing is segmentation of image, which means to split or divide image into multiple sub-parts so that it becomes easier to extract relevant information and identify objects under consideration from image.

iv. *Feature extraction*: This process is performed to change the segments of the image into more convenient form that better describes the main features and attributes of interest of image.

v. *Classification*: Then, classification is performed on the pixels of the medical image to divide pixels among the classes or categories of interest. A function is used to assign pixels of image to its respective class or domain.

vi. *Post-processing*: The final step is post-processing, which removes the blocking artifacts occurred due to transformation method (orthogonal) applied to image, decompresses the compressed image, and recognizes objects in the image.

12.2.1 Medical Image Modalities

On the basis of the how medical image is produced and looks, digital medical images are categorized into several types. Some common types of medical images are as follows:

i. *X-Ray*: X-rays are radiations just like visible light, radio waves, and microwaves. It possesses very high energy level. X-ray is allowed to enter into patient's body to image the area of interest. The images by X-ray show the parts of body in different shades because of the reason that distinct tissues in human body absorb different scale of energy's radiations. For example, calcium in human bones absorbs X-rays in large amount as a result bones appear white in the images [44].

ii. *Computerized tomography*: Also termed as computerized axial tomography, this imaging technique uses X-rays to create detailed cross-sectional images of internal organs of human body such as blood vessels, bones, and organs.

iii. *Magnetic resonance imaging*: Strong magnets and radiofrequency pulses are used in this imaging technology to create images. These signals are detected by a radio antenna. This imaging method can acquire 3D images. MRI has gained a large popularity among the modalities. MRI is used to take the images of internal organs such as breast tissues, brain, spinal cord, heart, bones, joints, and blood vessels.

iv. *Ultrasound*: High-frequency sound waves are used to capture ultrasound images. It is vastly used due to its simplicity and less expensiveness. A transducer is used to send and receive the signal. The transducer transmits the high-frequency sound waves into the human body, which are then reflected back according to the density of the tissues they strike. Then, the reflected sound waves are transformed into electric signals, and thus moving images shows up on the display screen.

v. *Optical coherence tomography*: OCT is the latest technology in the field of medical imaging. Like ultrasound, it also uses light waves to scan body parts and take cross-sectional higher-resolution images. It is basically used to examine parts of eye (specifically retina).

vi. *Single-photon emission computed tomography*: It is a new technology in the area of medical imaging that uses radioactive materials and a specific-purpose camera that takes 3D images of the body parts. SPECT imaging can visualize the actual functioning of internal organs, for example, the flow of blood in human heart.

Table 12.1 shows the comparison of different medical image modalities based on their resolution, speed of acquisition, cost, rate of data acquisition, effects on human body, and availability. Figure 12.3 shows different image modalities.

12.2.2 Noise in Medical Images

Noise may be introduced in medical images during the acquisition or transmission processes. Different types of noises, such as Gaussian, impulse, Poisson, and speckle, degrade the quality of medical images. Figure 12.4 shows the degradation and reconstruction model of medical

Table 12.1 Comparison of Various Medical Images

Properties	*Modality*					
	X-ray	*CT scan*	*MRI*	*Ultrasound*	*OCT*	*SPECT*
Image resolution	Normal	Moderate	High	Depends upon transducer selection	Better than MRI and ultrasound	High
Time required for acquisition	Less	Moderate	Long	Depends on operator	Less	Moderate
Cost	Low	Costlier	Costlier	Moderate	Costlier	Costlier
Data acquisition	Less	Improved	Improved	Less	Improved	Improved
Effects on human body	Harmful to human body due to ionization effect	Harmful to human body due to ionization effect	No effect	Harmful to human body due to non-ionization radiation effect	No effect	Harmful to human body due to ionization effect
Implementation	High	High	Less than CT	High	Moderate	Moderate

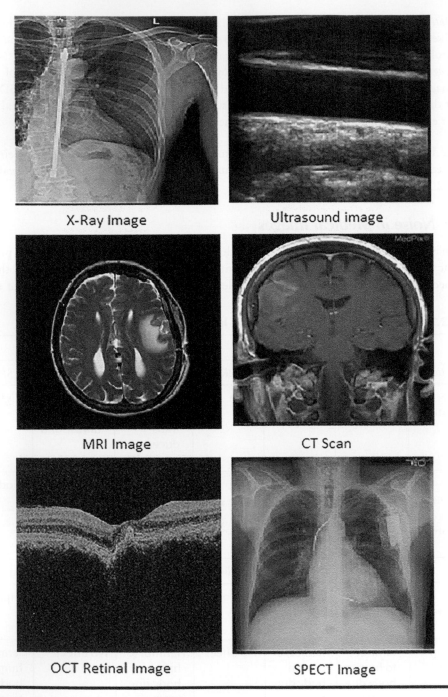

X-Ray Image   Ultrasound image

MRI Image   CT Scan

OCT Retinal Image   SPECT Image

Figure 12.3   Important image modalities.

images. The noise in the medical image may be additive noise or multiplicative noise depending on the image acquisition system. An example of additive noise is Gaussian noise, which is mostly found in all kinds of medical images. It is uniformly added with the pixel intensity in

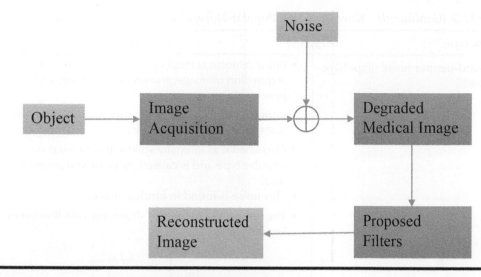

Figure 12.4   Image degradation and reconstruction model.

the medical image. Speckle noise is a multiplicative noise affecting mostly ultrasound and OCT images. Multiplicative noise is multiplied with the pixel intensity of the medical image. Different medical image noises and their characteristics are listed in Table 12.2. Figure 12.5 shows the effect of noise in medical image.

Table 12.2   Showing Some Popular Noises Found in Medical Images

Noise type	Description
Gaussian noise (amplifier noise)	• Thermal vibration of atoms, amplifier noise, and radiation of warm objects are the main cause of the generation of Gaussian noise. • It is also known as white noise or amplifier noise. • It changes the pixel values in digital images. • Gaussian noise spreads evenly on the image and has Gaussian distribution in structure. • This noise is found in MRI image. • The probability distribution function is of bell shape [1] and is expressed by $$W(f) = \frac{1}{\sqrt{2\pi\sigma^2}} e^{-\frac{(f-n)^2}{\sigma^2}}$$ Here f = gray level, n = mean value of probability density function, σ = noise standard deviation,

(Continued)

Table 12.2 (*Continued*) Showing Some Popular Noises Found in Medical Images

Noise type	Description
Salt-and-pepper noise (impulsive noise)	• Impulse noise is most commonly acquired in acquisition of image, transaction, storage, and processing of images. • Impulse noise degrades the quality of image as well as loses the information details. • Also known as intensity spikes, this noise is of impulse type and is caused by error in transmission of data. • This noise is found in fundus image. • The following expression shows the distribution of impulse noise: $$f(N) = \begin{cases} p_a & \text{for } N = a \\ p_b & \text{for } N = b \\ 0 & \text{otherwise} \end{cases}$$ where $a, b \in R$ p_a = probability of a, p_b = probability of b, N = random variable.
Speckle noise	• Speckle noise is multiplicative in nature, so multiplied with the image pixel values. • Medical images such as ultrasound image and OCT image are suffered from speckle noise. • The degraded image resulting from speckle noise is expressed as $$G(n, m) = X(n, m) \times S(n, m) + \eta(n, m)$$ where $G(n, m)$ = observed image with pixel values (n, m), $X(n, m)$ = original image, $S(n, m)$ = speckle noise, $\eta(n, m)$ = additive noise.
Poisson noise (photon noise)	• X-rays, visible lights, and gamma rays are the causes of the generation of Poisson noise. • These sources are having random fluctuation of photons. Result gathered image has spatial and temporal randomness. This noise is also called as quantum (photon) noise or shot noise [46].

(Continued)

Table 12.2 (*Continued*)   Showing Some Popular Noises Found in Medical Images

Noise type	Description
	• This noise caused due to the insufficient capture of photons, which do not provide sufficient statistical information. • The distribution of Poisson noise is given by $$P(k) = \frac{\left(\lambda^k e^{-\lambda}\right)}{k!}$$ where λ = number of events occurred during the considered time interval, e = Euler's number, k = the event index or number.

12.2.3 Performance Metrics

Performance metrics are used to evaluate the efficiency of different types of image enhancement techniques. Some of the most commonly used performance metrics are described in Table 12.3. Table 12.4 shows the image quality parameters used to evaluate the performance by comparing the input pixels with the corresponding output pixels.

12.3 Medical Image Enhancement Techniques

Figure 12.6 shows the major classification of medical image enhancement techniques. The enhancement techniques can be classified into two main domains: 1) spatial domain and 2) transform domain.

12.3.1 Image Enhancement in Spatial Domain

In this type of enhancement technique, the process is based on direct manipulation of pixels in an image. Spatial domain techniques can be expressed as

$$O(x, y) = T\big[I(x, y)\big] \qquad (12.1)$$

where $I(x,y)$ is the input image, $O(x,y)$ is the processed image, and T is the transformation operator on 'T, defined over some neighborhood of (x,y).

Bhattacharya et al. [30] developed a single-value decomposition (SVD) to enhance the contrast of an image. This technique worked on enhancement of visual information of an image using multiple steps such as contrast enhancement, de-blurring, and de-noising. Yiwen Dou et al. [6] presented an image enhancement method based on hue and chroma constraint to extract visual attention focus in accuracy. In this method, initially the RGB color space is translated to YCbCr, and after that, the iteration image enhancement model is applied in constraint of chroma and hue.

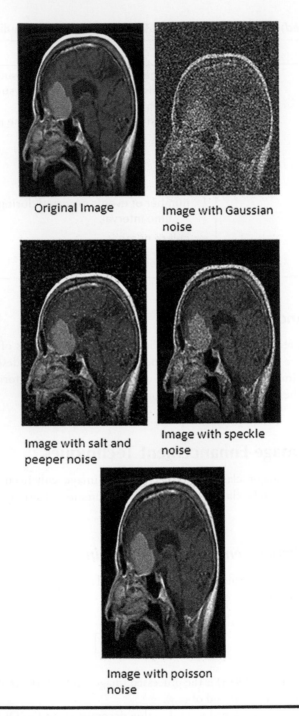

Figure 12.5 Effect of noise in medical image.

Then, the remaining image evaluation function implements closed-up control to adjust the iteration step and enhancement of performance. Some of the popular spatial domain enhancement techniques are explained below.

Table 12.3 Different Performance Metrics to Evaluate Enhancement Techniques

Metric	Characteristics
Mean square error (MSE)	• This metric shows the difference of original image and recovered image. • A low value of MSE indicates high performance. • MSE can be defined by the following expression: $$\text{MSE} = \frac{1}{m \times n} \sum_{i=1}^{m \times n} \left(\hat{y}(i,j) - y(i,j) \right)^2$$ where $m \times n$ is the size of image, $\hat{y}(i,j) = $ recovered image, $y(i,j) = $ original image.
Peak signal-to-noise ratio (PSNR)	• PSNR can be expressed as $$\text{PSNR} = 20 \log_{10} \frac{255}{\sqrt{\text{MSE}}}$$ • High value of PSNR is required for high performance.
Root mean square error (RMSE)	• RMSE can be expressed as $$\text{RMSE} = \sqrt{\frac{1}{m \times n} \sum_{i=1}^{m} \sum_{j=1}^{n} \left(\hat{y}(i,j) - y(i,j)^2 \right)}$$ • Less value is required for high performance.
Mean absolute error (MAE)	• MAE can be expressed as $$\text{MAE} = \frac{1}{m \times n} \sum_{i=1}^{m} \sum_{j=1}^{n} \left| \hat{y}(i,j) - y(i,j) \right|$$ • A small value is required for good performance.

i. *Gray-level transformation*: One of the basic spatial domain image enhancement techniques is gray-level transformation. Pixel values before and after processing are correlated by an equation in the following form:

$$s = T(r) \tag{12.2}$$

Here, 'T' is a transformation function which corresponds to a pixel value in original image 'r' into a pixel value in processed image 's.'

Table 12.4 **Different Image Quality Parameters**

Metric	Characteristics
Structural similarity index (SSIM)	SSIM can be expressed as $\mathrm{SSIM}(X,Y) = \left[l(X,Y)^{\alpha} \cdot c(X,Y)^{\beta} \cdot s(X,Y)^{\gamma} \right]$ where '*X, Y*' are two windows of the same dimension of original and reconstructed images, respectively. α, β, and γ are the weights assigned to these parameters. *l*, *c*, and *s* are the luminance, contrast, and structure, respectively, which together combine with certain weights to form SSIM and are computed as $$l(X,Y) = \frac{2\mu_X \mu_Y + c_1}{\mu_X^2 + \mu_Y^2 + c_1}$$ $$c(X,Y) = \frac{2\sigma_X \sigma_Y + c_2}{\sigma_X^2 + \sigma_Y^2 + c_2}$$ $$s(X,Y) = \frac{\sigma_{XY} + c_3}{\sigma_X \sigma_Y + c_3}$$ Here, μ_X is the average of *X*, μ_X is the average of *Y*, σ_X^2 is the variance of *X*, σ_Y^2 is the variance of *Y*, σ_{XY} is the covariance of *X* and *Y*, c_1 and c_2 are the two parameters to stable the division with poor denominator, $c_3 = \frac{c_2}{2}$, When value of SSIM approaches to 1 shows better similarity between original image and recovered image.
Edge preserving index (EPI)	EPI can be expressed as $$\mathrm{EPI} = \frac{\left(\displaystyle\sum_{m=1}^{M} \sum_{n=1}^{N-1} \left\| X'(m, n+1) - X'(m,n) \right\| \right)}{\left(\displaystyle\sum_{p=1}^{M} \sum_{q=1}^{N-1} \left\| X(m, n+1) - X(m,n) \right\| \right)}$$ where *X'* is the reconstructed image, while '*X*' is the original image, '*M*' is the rows count in image, '*N*' is the column count in image.

(*Continued*)

Table 12.4 (*Continued*)   Different Image Quality Parameters

Metric	Characteristics
Correlation coefficient (CoC)	when value of EPI approaches to 1 shows better preservation of edges in the image. CoC can be expressed as $$\text{CoC}_{X,X'} = \frac{\left(E\left[(X - \rho_X) \cdot (X' - \rho_{X'}) \right] \right)}{\sigma_x \sigma_{X'}}$$ where ρ_X and $\rho_{X'}$ are the average of the original and recovered images, respectively. σ_X and $\sigma_{X'}$ are standard deviation of original and recovered images, respectively. When value of CoC approaches to 1 shows the better corelation between images under consideration.

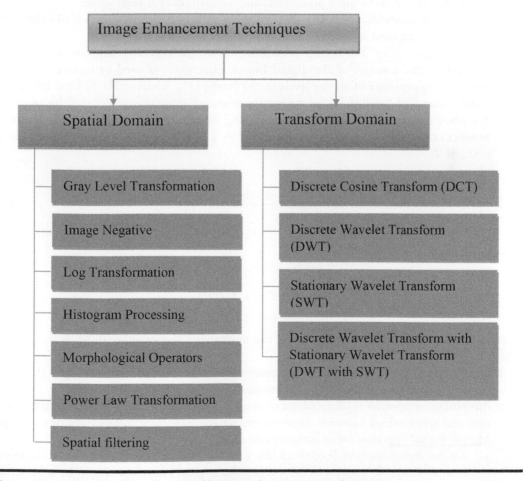

Figure 12.6   Classification of medical image enhancement techniques.

ii. *Image negative*: The image negative is obtained by the negative transformation given by the following equation:

$$O = M - 1 - I \tag{12.3}$$

I = input image
O = output image

The gray level ranges from 0 to $[M-1]$

Equation (12.3) reverses the values of intensity levels of an image and gives an equivalent of negative image. This enhancement technique enhances white or gray pixels encapsulated in dark regions, particularly when black areas are the principal ones [25].

iii. *Log transformation*: The log transformation technique limits the range of images with changes in intensity values [16]. It is formulated as

$$O = c \log(1 + I) \tag{12.4}$$

Here 'c' is a constant, 'I' is the input pixel value, and 'O' is the output pixel value.

This transformation widens the dark pixel values in an image while low gray level values into a broad range and vice versa for higher values [25].

iv. *Histogram processing*: Histogram processing technique regulates the image intensities to enhance the contrast of the digital image. Histogram is used to represent the frequency of appearance of all the levels in the image [37]. Khan et al. [8] used histogram equalization (HE) technique for the enhancement of image contrast. Let 'I' be an image described as a matrix of integer pixels varying from 0 to $M-1$. Here, 'M' is the total number of possible intensity values, mostly 256. Let 'O' designate the normalized histogram of 'I'.

$$O_n \left(\text{normalized histogram} \right) = \frac{\text{number of pixels with intensity}\,(n)}{\text{total number of pixels}} \tag{12.5}$$

HE is denoted by 'g' and is formulated as

$$g_{i,j} = (M-1) \sum_{n=0}^{f_{i,j}} (O_n) \tag{12.6}$$

Here, '$g_{i,j}$' is the equalized histogram, 'O_n' is the normalized histogram, and 'M' is the interval value, i.e., $[0, M-1]$.

Liang Hua et al. [32] proposed an enhancement method for color medical image. This technique used HE to obtain enhanced intensity numbers matrix.

v. *Morphological operators*: Morphological operators are based on the mathematical axioms and relationships between classes to extract the important information of an image. Morphological operators are of basically two types:

a. *Top-hat transformation*: It operates like a high-pass filter and extracts the small details from an image. It is found by subtracting the original image opening 'I' by some structural element 'b' from image itself. Top-hat transformation is defined as

$$T_{\text{th}}(I) = I - I \circ b \tag{12.7}$$

Here 'T_{th}' is the image after top-hat transformation, '$I \circ b$' is the opening of image 'I' by structural element 'b'.

b. *Bottom-hat transformation*: It is used for dark objects on light background and is found by subtracting the original image from its closing.

$$T_{\text{bh}}(I) = I - I \cdot b \tag{12.8}$$

Here 'T_{bh}' is the image after bottom-hat transformation.

'$I \cdot b$' is the closing of image 'I' by structural element 'b'.

Rajendran et al. [43] combined the morphological transformation technique with edge filter to solve the issue of the edge degradation in medical images. This methodology put into use the combination of guided filter with edge enhancement and contrast stretching, and hence the results obtained were lesser noise in CT images as well as X-ray images as compared with other enhancement methods. Kurt et al. [36] proposed an enhancement technique of medical images which was based on top-hat morphological transform, contrast-limited histogram equalization, and anisotropic filter to improve the contrast and also to enhance the quality of specific visual areas that are of particular interest. When Measure of enhancement of original image and enhanced image was compared, this method gives very beneficial results.

vi. *Power law transformation*: It is a category of gray-level transformation. Mathematically, it is written as

$$O = cI^{\gamma} \tag{12.9}$$

Here 'c' and 'γ' are constants, 'I' is normalized input pixel values, and 'O' is normalized output pixel values. Power law transformation removes the drawbacks of log transformation with the help of different 'γ' values.

vii. *Spatial filtering*: Filtering in the spatial domain enhancement method involves the determination of the processed values of the prevailing pixel based on the value of the neighboring pixels [1]. Mean filtering and median filtering are of this type. These filters are broadly classified as linear and nonlinear filters based on the method how current and neighbor pixels are correlated.

Gerig et al. [47] presented a spatial filtering technique (i.e., post-processing technique) for de-noising and boundary enhancement of medical image (MRI) based on the technique of "Nonlinear Anisotropic Filtering." Output of this technique is quite impressive as it satisfies all the parameters for which it was developed, i.e., the output filtered image was quite clear than before and also image boundaries were more precise than before.

12.3.2 Image Enhancement in Transform Domain

This processing technique is based on transforming the image from one form to another by applying some filter functions to the image and returning to the original form that results enhanced image [17]. Different transform functions, such as discrete cosine transform (DCT), Fourier transform, discrete wavelet transform (DWT), and stationary wavelet transform (SWT), are used to enhance the images [13–19]. The transform coefficients are manipulated to improve the quality

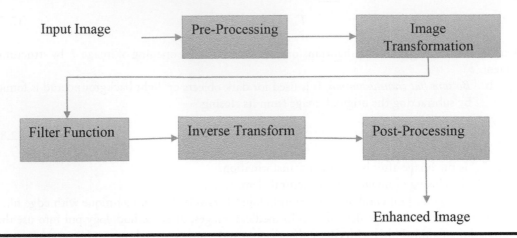

Figure 12.7 Block diagram of transform domain image enhancement technique.

of an image. The block diagram of transform domain image enhancement technique is shown in Figure 12.7.

Qin Xue in 2013 [31] proposed a new methodology for medical image enhancement by imposing local range modification in shearlet domain using "Shearlet Transformation." Some of the popular enhancement techniques in transform domain approach are discussed below.

i. *Discrete cosine transform*: This method enhances image resolution by image stretching with minor or slight loss. In DCT, most of the power is concentrated in lower-frequency bands, and also DCT has efficient energy compaction property. These properties of DCT help in human visual system (HVS) as HVS is highly sensitive to chrominance than luminance. Poor contrast is the main limitation of DCT [42]. Figure 12.8 shows the block diagram of DCT-based image enhancement technique. In this figure, input image is subjected to DCT, and then filter function is applied on it. Inverse DCT (IDCT) is then applied to get back the output image.

ii. *Discrete wavelet transform*: DWT basically conserves the high-frequency components. First, the input image is classified into four sub-bands by applying the DWT to image. The four sub-bands are low-low (LL), high-low (HL), low-high (LH), and high-high (HH). For a two-level DWT, the LL sub-band is further divided into four sub-bands (LL_1, HL_1, LH_1, and HH_1). For next higher levels, the abovementioned procedure continues

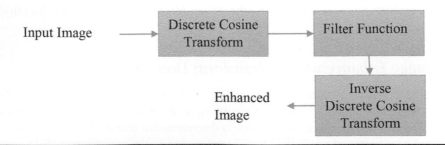

Figure 12.8 Block diagram of DCT-based image enhancement technique.

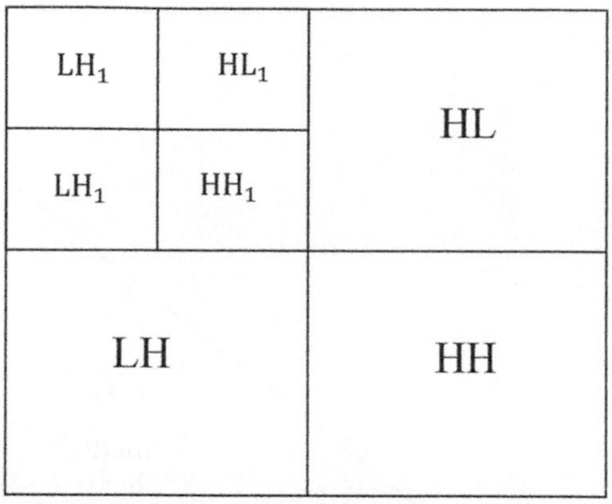

LH$_1$	HL$_1$	HL
LH$_1$	HH$_1$	
LH		HH

Figure 12.9   Sub-band decomposition of two-level DWT.

recursively. Figure 12.9 shows the sub-band decomposition of a two-level DWT. Then, thresholding is further applied to the sub-band coefficients to enhance the wavelet coefficients. There are two major categories of thresholding: they are soft thresholding and hard thresholding.

Hard and soft thresholding functions are formally expressed as

$$\text{Hard thresholding: } H_{\text{th}}(x) = \begin{cases} x & \text{if } x \geq Th \\ 0 & \text{otherwise} \end{cases} \tag{12.10}$$

$$\text{Soft thresholding: } S_{\text{th}}(x) = \begin{cases} x - Th & \text{if } x \geq Th \\ 0 & \text{if } x < Th \\ x + Th & \text{if } x \leq -Th \end{cases} \tag{12.11}$$

where 'Th' is the given threshold level parameter for wavelet coefficients. Hard thresholding basically keeps the coefficients above the threshold while attenuates the coefficients below that threshold level, whereas soft thresholding narrows the coefficients above the threshold level. The continuity feature of soft thresholding is quite advantageous over the features of hard thresholding. Figures 12.10–12.12 show the original signal, hard thresholding signal, and soft thresholding signals, respectively. After shrinkage of wavelet coefficients inverse DWT (IDWT) is applied to recover the enhanced image [20–22]. DWT gives more sharp images with edge information but losses content at higher frequencies [42]. Figure 12.13 shows the block diagram of DWT-based image enhancement technique.

iii. *Stationary wavelet transform*: In this technique, the input image is converted to coefficients by taking the SWT. The LH, HL, and HH sub-band coefficients are manipulated to get the enhanced image. Bi-cubic interpolation is done for enhancing image resolution as it gives smooth edges with less blurring. High-frequency components are conserved by this technique. Compared to DWT, SWT has more complexity [42]. Figure 12.14 shows the block diagram of SWT-based enhancement method.

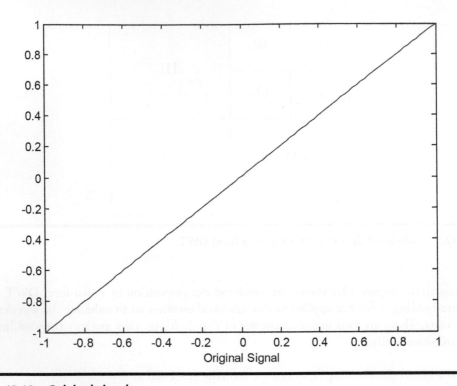

Figure 12.10   Original signal.

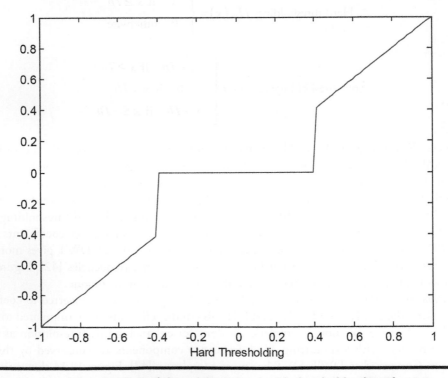

Figure 12.11   Hard thresholding of the original signal with threshold value *Th* =0.4.

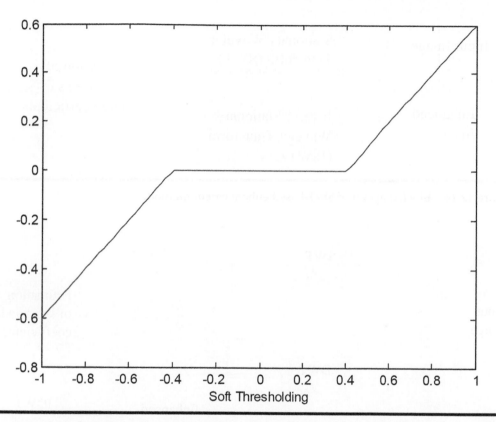

Figure 12.12 **Soft thresholding of the original signal with threshold value *Th* = 0.4.**

iv. *Discrete wavelet transform with stationary wavelet transform*: In this technique, both DWT and SWT are implemented to divide the image into four sub-bands, namely, LL, HL, LH, and HH. High-frequency components are undergone through bi-cubic interpolation obtained using DWT. Summations of the interpolated sub-bands are made with the sub-bands generated from SWT. Next, the enhanced image is recovered by applying IDWT. The advantage of this technique is that it prevents the information loss [42]. Figure 12.15 shows the block diagram of the SWT with DWT-based image enhancement method.

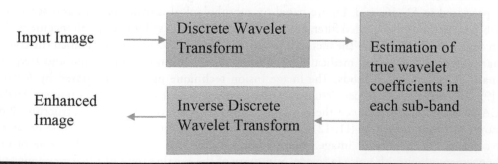

Figure 12.13 **Block diagram showing DWT-based image enhancement technique.**

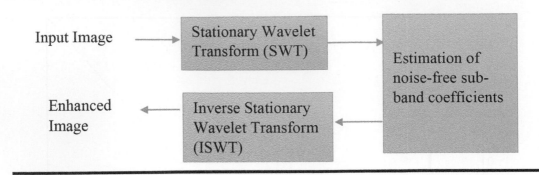

Figure 12.14 Block diagram of SWT-based enhancement method.

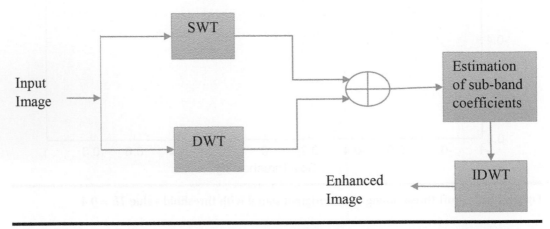

Figure 12.15 Block diagram showing SWT with DWT-based image enhancement method.

12.4 Discussion and Research Issues

Medical image enhancement techniques have been found to give high-contrast, noise-free, edge-preserving, and high-quality medical images. A lot of studies have been done in the enhancement of medical images while considering both the de-noising and edge preservation concept and by combining different types of enhancement techniques. The edge preservation or enhancement is achieved by Rajendran et al. [43] along with low noise quantity. The methods proposed in [2, 36, and 43] are based on morphological transformation, and some other combined methods like guided filter, contrast stretch, etc. are used for edge enhancement along with contrast enhancement. The methods proposed in [7, 27, 28, 30, and 37] embed the contrast enhancement techniques in medical images using combination of both spatial and frequency domain enhancement methods. The image fusion technique used was proposed by Atyali et al. [9], for detection of cancer tissues uses the combination of Principal Component Analysis (PCA) with DWT to enhance the results and also to preserve the original structure. Noise removal techniques used in [11, 12, 29, and 34] embed the removal of noise while preserving the contrast and quality of image. The method proposed in [11] removes the issue of over-enhancement along with noise in image. Summary of the existing state-of-the-art enhancement techniques is given in Table 12.5.

Table 12.5 Summary of the Existing Medical Image Enhancement Techniques

Ref. no.	Proposed objective	Techniques used	Results	Other important consideration
[2]	Medical image enhancement using morphological transformation	Top- and bottom-hat transform and morphological transformation	For different radius of masks, CNR and PSNR are higher than original image	As radius of mask increases PSNR decreases and SNR increases considerably
[3]	Low-contrast image enhancement using fuzzy set theory	Fuzzy measures and membership functions	Processing time: 0.062 s, PSNR = 22.039	Processing time of proposed method is greater than NINT technique
[5]	Multiscaleretinex (MSR)-based image enhancement method	MSR enhancement algorithm and wavelet transformation	For panchromatic as well as colored image, higher mean value is obtained and lower entropy and definition	MSR has better effect than wavelet transformation
[6]	Enhancement of color image by iterative and self-adapting method based on hue and chroma constraints	Chroma and hue constraint	Focus overage FO(%) = 97 Computational time = 570 ms	Only limited for robot visual servo use
[7]	TV-homomorphic filter-based image enhancement for X-ray image	Total variation and homomorphic filter	Higher average gradient and Laplacian, whereas only slight change in values of mean and entropy	
[8]	Image enhancement technique based on HE for contrast enhancement and brightness preservation	HE	Maximum standard deviation (SD) = 27.15 Minimum absolute mean brightness error (AMBE) = 0.05	

(Continued)

Table 12.5 (Continued) Summary of the Existing Medical Image Enhancement Techniques

Ref. no.	Proposed objective	Techniques used	Results	Other important consideration
[9]	Enhancement technique for brain tumor detection through image fusion	DWT and PCA	MSE (max) = 1424.44 PSNR (max) = 25.21 Structural content (SC)-(max) = 2.17 Standard deviation (SD)-(max) = 80.4 Entropy (max) = 1.83	
[10]	Image enhancement based on combined opportunity cost and image classification for nonlinear images	Opportunity cost, NIE algorithm, optimal parameter combination, and image classification	PSNR (max) = 33.6757 Mean opinion score (MOS)-(max) = 4.6 Reliability of measure (r) = 0.78627	
[11]	Enhancement of medical images based on averaging methods in cluster	Averaging method	PSNR (max) = 25.43	Easy to implement and give noise-free enhanced image and also removes over-enhancement
[12]	Enhancement of THz image based on the multi-scales nonlinear method of enhancement	Nonlinear filter	Better enhancement and more detailed edges	No quantitative parameter is used to evaluate the results
[23]	Medical image enhancement based on nonlinear technique and logarithmic transform coefficient histogram matching	DCT, logarithmic transformation, HE, and orthogonal transformation	Greater value of EME (i.e., 121.71) as compared to original as well as image after applying HE	Can be greatly used for face detection

(Continued)

Table 12.5 (*Continued*) Summary of the Existing Medical Image Enhancement Techniques

Ref. no.	Proposed objective	Techniques used	Results	Other important consideration
[24]	Fuzzy-based fingerprint enhancement technique based on adaptive thresholding	Fuzzy-based filtering, adaptive thresholding, and morphological operation	Highest PSNR (38.24) as compared to other classical methods	
[27]	Medical image enhancement based particularly for preserving the brightness and enhancement of contrast	Adaptive gamma correction, homomorphic filtering, and image normalization	Absolute mean brightness error (AMBE) (avg.) = 1.8792 PSNR (avg.) = 28.151	Enhances both global and local contrasts
[28]	Fuzzy image enhancement for low-contrast and nonuniform illumination images	Gaussian membership function	Quality index (Q) = 0.92 PSNR = 33 Computational time (s) = 0.95	Computational time of algorithm is higher than other methods (i.e., FHE and HE)
[29]	Image enhancement and de-noising based on removal of random impulse noise in images	Decision tree and DCT	PSNR (max) = 37.41 for 5% noise PSNR (max) = 34.43 for 10% noise PSNR (max) = 32.53 for 15% noise PSNR (max) = 30.92 for 20% noise	As percentage of noise increases, PSNR falls significantly

(*Continued*)

Table 12.5 (Continued) Summary of the Existing Medical Image Enhancement Techniques

Ref. no.	Proposed objective	Techniques used	Results	Other important consideration
[30]	Localized image enhancement with the technique of depth map	Depth map and localized image enhancement	PSNR = 15.28 Contrast enhancement metric (F) = 39.79 Image quality index (Q) = 10.35 Color enhancement factor = 21.33 Computational time = 26.57	Proper illumination model and reflectance model is needed to enhance radiometrically similar objects
[33]	Medical image enhancement based on non-subsampled contourlet transform (NSCT)	NSCT	Image of spine MSE = 621.4015 PSNR 726.322	
[34]	Medical image enhancement using adaptive multiscale product thresholding	2D wavelet transform (DWT) and Canny edge detection algorithm	Image of cameraman PSNR = 25.0251 SNR_original image = 14.5896 SNR_enhanced image = 22.1015	For all images under consideration, the proposed technique gives best result for only Poisson noise
[35]	Biomedical image enhancement using the techniques of spatial domain	Laplacian filter, HE, and nonlinear transformation	Lowest gamma = 0.8 Highest entropy = 5.4701	This technique can be further enhanced using logarithmic transformation or any other suitable one
[37]	Medical image enhancement based on histogram to focus particularly on contrast enhancement	Histogram processing	Contrast of image is increased as compared with other methods	

Figure 12.16   Showing various prominent research issues in the area of image enhancement.

Noise and different environmental conditions degrade medical images. Several studies have been proposed in the literature to reduce noise and enhance the quality of medical images. Still there are some research issues that need to be considered as shown in Figure 12.16. They are discussed below:

  i. *Edge degradation*: Edges play the most representative role in image processing, but image enhancement technique may corrupt the edges too. Therefore, it can result in degradation of edges.
 ii. *Illumination*: The maximum number of processes relies upon specific pre-defined norms to concentrate on the objects or regions in particular image. This may cause "imbalance in the illumination" of the output image after enhancement.
iii. *Artifacts*: Predominantly, image enhancement methods are of "transform domain" type, so this may cause certain "artifacts" to occur in output image after enhancement. To get rid of these artifacts, some specific assistance is required.
 iv. *Lost pixels*: Due to transform domain methods of image enhancement, some specific pixels get lost during transformation either "original to transform" or "transformed signal to original pixel values." It is one of the main issues that should be majorly taken into consideration.
  v. *Computational complexity*: The best technique is that which requires minimum computation, and hence to minimize computational complexity is one of the key factors in image enhancement techniques for its better real-time implementation.

Depending upon the application requirements, there can be trade-off between the above factors. Further, the contrast factor of enhancement methods can also differ slightly depending on the applications.

12.5 Conclusions and Future Directions of Research

The role of medical image processing has increased in the clinical applications. However, for computer-aided analysis, the incorporated noise during acquisition and transmission degrades its ability. Therefore, medical image enhancement techniques are required to improve the medical image quality for accurate disease diagnosis, detection, and treatment. The aim of this chapter is to provide an overall idea of available medical image enhancement techniques. A brief description of medical image processing along with its processing steps is discussed in this chapter. Different medical image modalities and their comparison in terms of acquisition, speed, resolution, cost, effects on body, and availability are presented in this chapter. Medical enhancement methods require prior knowledge of noise. Medical image noises and their characteristics are provided in this chapter. Image performance parameters are required to evaluate the effectiveness of the enhancement techniques. Different performance parameters are briefed. This chapter summarizes the existing image enhancement techniques in detail. State-of-the-art techniques are compared with one another based on their performance parameters. At the end, research issues of medical image enhancement techniques are introduced. Consideration of those issues supports researchers to develop improved adaptive enhancement techniques.

In future, this survey chapter will motivate researchers to develop new hybrid medical enhancement techniques and help in improving the diagnostic quality assessment of medical images.

Key Terminology and Definitions

Image enhancement: Image enhancement is a methodology that makes digital images more suitable for further analysis. It involves brightening or sharpening the image or removing noise from the image.

Noise: Noise in digital images is the variation in pixel intensities. It is caused due to the noisy sensors, digital camera and scanner circuitry, and environmental disturbances.

PSNR: Peak signal-to-noise ratio (PSNR) is a performance metric used for comparing reconstructed image with original image.

SSIM: Structural similarity index (SSIM) is an image quality measurement parameter. It is used for comparing the similarity between two images on pixel-by-pixel basis.

Database

■ Ultrasound database [online] Available: http://splab.cz/en/download/database/ultrasound
■ Osirix.2014. OSIRIX DICOM image library. [ONLINE] Available at: http://www.osirix-viewer.com/resources/diacom-image-library/

References

1. Narasimha C., and A. Nagaraja Rao (2015), A comparative study: Spatial domain filter for medical image enhancement. In: *2015 International Conference on Signal Processing and Communication Engineering Systems (SPACES)*, IEEE, pp. 291–295.
2. Firoz R., M. MdShahjahan Ali, N. Uddin Khan, M. Khalid Hossain, M. Khairul Islam, and M. Shahinuzzaman (2016), Medical image enhancement using morphological transformation. *Journal of Data Analysis and Information Processing*, 4, no. 1: 1.

3. Hasikin K., and N.M. Isa (2012), Enhancement of the low contrast image using fuzzy set theory. In: *Computer Modelling and Simulation (UKSim), UKSim 14th International Conference on*, IEEE, pp. 371–376.

4. Arun R., M.S. Nair, R. Vrinthavani, and R. Tatavarti (2011), An alpha rooting based hybrid technique for image enhancement. *Engineering Letters*, 19, no. 3. 159–168.

5. Henan W., Y. Guang, X. Zhonglin, L. Dejun, and Y. Yuwei (2011), Remote sensing image enhancement method based on multi-scale Retinex. In: *Information Technology, Computer Engineering and Management Sciences (ICM), 2011 International Conference on*, IEEE, vol. 3, pp. 15–18.

6. Dou Y., J. Wang, G. Lu, and C. Zhang (2017), Iterative self-adapting color image enhancement base on chroma and hue constrain. In: *Image, Vision and Computing (ICIVC), 2017 2nd International Conference*, IEEE, pp. 303–308.

7. Rui W., and W. Guoyu (2017), Medical X-ray image enhancement method based on TV-homomorphic filter. In: *Image, Vision and Computing (ICIVC), 2017 2nd International Conference*, IEEE, pp. 315–318.

8. Khan M.F., E. Khan, and Z.A. Abbasi (2012), Multi segment histogram equalization for brightness preserving contrast enhancement. In: *Advances in Computer Science, Engineering & Applications*, Springer: Berlin, Heidelberg, pp. 193–202.

9. Atyali R.K., and S.R. Khot (2016), An enhancement in detection of brain cancer through image fusion. In: *Advances in Electronics, Communication and Computer Technology (ICAECCT), 2016 IEEE International Conference*, IEEE, pp. 438–442.

10. Wang L.-J., and Y.-C. Huang (2012), Combined opportunity cost and image classification for nonlinear image enhancement. In: *Complex, Intelligent and Software Intensive Systems (CISIS), 2012 Sixth International Conference*, IEEE, pp. 135–140.

11. Govind V., and A.A. Balakrishnan (2013), Medical image enhancement by applying averaging method in clusters. In: *Advanced Computing and Communication Systems (ICACCS), 2013 International Conference*, IEEE, pp. 1–3.

12. Peng Z., H. Weiliang, L. Wenjian, and Z. Zhihui (2013), The multi-scales nonlinear enhancement method of THz image. In: *Microwave Technology & Computational Electromagnetics (ICMTCE), 2013 IEEE International Conference*, IEEE, pp. 341–344.

13. Netravali A.N., and B. Prasada (1977), Adaptive quantization of picture signals using spatial masking. *Proceedings of the IEEE*, 65, no. 4: 536–548.

14. Agaian S.S., K. Panetta, and A.M. Grigoryan (2001), Transform-based image enhancement algorithms with performance measure. *IEEE Transactions on Image Processing*, 10, no. 3: 367–382.

15. Lin T.-H., and T. Kao (2000), Adaptive local contrast enhancement method for medical images displayed on a video monitor. *Medical Engineering and Physics* 22, no. 2: 79–87.

16. McClellan J (1980), Artifacts in alpha-rooting of images. In: *Acoustics, Speech, and Signal Processing, IEEE International Conference on ICASSP'80*, IEEE, vol. 5, pp. 449–452.

17. Aghagolzadeh S., and O.K. Ersoy (1992), Transform image enhancement. *Optical Engineering*, 31, no. 3: 614–627.

18. Ramponi G., N.K. Strobel, S.K. Mitra, and T.-H. Yu (1996), Nonlinear unsharp masking methods for image contrast enhancement. *Journal of Electronic Imaging*, 5, no. 3: 353–366.

19. Polesel A., G. Ramponi, and V. John Mathews, (2000) Image enhancement via adaptive unsharp masking. *IEEE transactions on image processing*, 9, no. 3: 505–510.

20. Prager K.E., and P.F. Singer (1991), Image enhancement and filtering using wavelets. In: *Signals, Systems and Computers. 1991 Conference Record of the Twenty-Fifth Asilomar Conference*, IEEE, pp. 169–174.

21. Mallat S., and S. Zhong (1992), Characterization of signals from multiscale edges. *IEEE Transactions on Pattern Analysis and Machine Intelligence*, 14, no. 7: 710–732.

22. Laine A., J. Fan, and W. Yang (1995), Wavelets for contrast enhancement of digital mammography. *IEEE Engineering in Medicine and Biology Magazine*, 14, no. 5: 536–550.

23. Hossain M.F., M.R. Alsharif, and K. Yamashita (2010), Medical image enhancement based on nonlinear technique and logarithmic transform coefficient histogram matching. In: *Complex Medical Engineering (CME), 2010 IEEE/ICME International Conference*, IEEE, pp. 58–62.

24. Selvi M., and A. George (2013), FBFET: Fuzzy based fingerprint enhancement technique based on adaptive thresholding. In: *Computing, Communications and Networking Technologies (ICCCNT), 2013 Fourth International Conference*, IEEE, pp. 1–5.

25. Malik S.H., and T. Ahmad Lone (2014), Comparative study of digital image enhancement approaches. In: *Computer Communication and Informatics (ICCCI), 2014 International Conference*, IEEE, pp. 1–5.

26. Tripathi A.K., S. Mukhopadhyay, and A.K. Dhara (2011), Performance metrics for image contrast. In: *Image Information Processing (ICIIP), 2011 International Conference*, IEEE, pp. 1–4.

27. Tiwari M., and B. Gupta (2016), Brightness preserving contrast enhancement of medical images using adaptive gamma correction and homomorphic filtering. In: *Electrical, Electronics and Computer Science (SCEECS), 2016 IEEE Students' Conference*, IEEE, pp. 1–4.

28. Hasikin K., and N.M. Isa (2013), Fuzzy image enhancement for low contrast and non-uniform illumination images. In: *Signal and Image Processing Applications (ICSIPA), IEEE International Conference*, IEEE, pp. 275–280.

29. Rajesh R., and P. Malathi (2016), An effective denoising and enhancement technique for removal of random impulse noise in images. In: *Advances in Electronics, Communication and Computer Technology (ICAECCT), 2016 IEEE International Conference*, IEEE, pp. 256–261.

30. Bhattacharya S., S. Gupta, and K.S. Venkatesh (2014), Localized image enhancement using depth map. In: *Signal Processing and Information Technology (ISSPIT), 2014 IEEE International Symposium*, IEEE, pp. 000195–000200.

31. Xue Q (2013), Enhancement of medical images in the shearlet domain. In: *Computer Science and Network Technology (ICCSNT), 2013 3rd International Conference*, IEEE, pp. 235–238.

32. Hua L., Z. Zhou, H. Feng, and L. Ding (2012), A new color medical image enhancement method. In: *IET International Conference on Information Science and Control Engineering 2012 (ICISCE 2012)*, IEEE, pp. 1–5.

33. Z. Feng, X. Ma, Y. Li, and X. Zhou (2013), Medical image enhancement based on NSCT. In: *IET International Conference on Smart and Sustainable City 2013 (ICSSC 2013)*, IEEE, pp. 166–169.

34. Aggarwal A., and A. Garg (2014), Medical image enhancement using adaptive multiscale product thresholding. In: *2014 International Conference on Issues and Challenges in Intelligent Computing Techniques (ICICT)*, IEEE, pp. 683–687.

35. Jindal K., K. Gupta, M. Jain, and M. Maheshwari (2014), Bio-medical image enhancement based on spatial domain technique. In: *IEEE International Conference on Advances in Engineering & Technology Research (ICAETR-2014)*, IEEE, pp. 1–5.

36. Burçin K., V.V. Nabiyev, and K. Turhan (2012), Medical images enhancement by using anisotropic filter and CLAHE. In: *2012 International Symposium on Innovations in Intelligent Systems and Applications*, IEEE, pp. 1–4.

37. Yelmanova E.S., and Y.M. Romanyshyn (2017), Medical image contrast enhancement based on histogram. In: *2017 IEEE 37th International Conference on Electronics and Nanotechnology (ELNANO)*, IEEE, pp. 273–278.

38. Panetta K., S. Agaian, Y. Zhou, and E.J. Wharton (2011), Parameterized logarithmic framework for image enhancement. *IEEE Transactions on Systems, Man, and Cybernetics, Part B (Cybernetics)*, 41, no. 2: 460–473.

39. Verma R., and J. Ali (2013), A Comparative Study of Various Types of Image Noise and Efficient Noise Removal Techniques. *International Journal of Advanced Research in Computer Science and Software Engineering (IJARCSSE)*, 3: 617–622.

40. Yu S., and H.H. Muhammed (2016), Noise type evaluation in positron emission tomography images. In: *2016 1st International Conference on Biomedical Engineering (IBIOMED)*, IEEE, pp. 1–6.

41. Rathod M., and J. Khanapuri (2017), Satellite image resolution enhancement using SWT and DWT with SWT. In: *2017 International Conference on Nascent Technologies in the Engineering Field (ICNTE-2017)*, IEEE, pp. 1–5.

42. Rathod M., and M. Rathod (2017), A comparative study of transform domain methods for image resolution enhancement of satellite image. In: *2017 11th International Conference on Intelligent Systems and Control (ISCQ)*, IEEE, pp. 287–291.

43. Rajendran R., S.P. Rao, S.S. Agaian, and K. Panetta (2016), A versatile edge preserving image enhancement approach for medical images using guided filter. In: *2016 IEEE International Conference on Systems, Man, and Cybernetic*, IEEE, pp. 002341–002346.

44. Goel N., A. Yadav, and B. Mohan Singh (2016), Medical image processing: A review. In: *2016 Second International Innovative Applications of Computational Intelligence on Power, Energy and Controls with their Impact on Humanity (CIPECH-16)*, IEEE, pp. 57–62.

45. Gupta M., and A. Garg (2017), An efficient technique for speckle noise reduction in ultrasound images. In: *2017 4th International Conference on Signal Processing and Integrated Networks (SPIN)*, IEEE, pp. 177–180.

46. Rodrigues I., J. Sanches, and J. Bioucas-Dias (2008), Denoising of medical images corrupted by poisson noise. In: *2008 15th IEEE International Conference on Image Processing*, IEEE, pp. 1756–1759.

47. Gerig G., O. Kubler, R. Kikinis, and F.A. Jolesz (1992), Nonlinear anisotropic filtering of MRI data. *IEEE Transactions on Medical Imaging*, 11, no. 2: 221–232.

References for Advance/Further Reading

Pieciak T., G. Vegas-Sánchez-Ferrero, S. Aja-Fernández (2016), Variance stabilization of noncentral-chi data: Application to noise estimation in MRI. In: *IEEE International Symposium on Biomedical Imaging (ISBI)*, pp. 1376–1379.

Pieciak T., S. Aja-Fernández, G. Vegas-Sánchez-Ferrero (2017), Non-Stationary Rician Noise Estimation in Parallel MRI Using a Single Image: A Variance-Stabilizing Approach. *IEEE Transactions on Pattern Analysis and Machine Intelligence*, 39, no. 10: 2015–2029.

Pieciak T., I. Rabanillo Viloria, S. Aja-Fernández (2018), Bias correction for non-stationary noise filtering in MRI. In: *IEEE International Symposium on Biomedical Imaging (ISBI)*.

Sahu S., H.V. Singh, B. Kumar, A.K. Singh (2017) *De-noising of Ultrasound image using Bayesian approached heavy-tailed Cauchy Distribution, Multimedia Tools and Applications*, Springer. doi: 10.1007/s11042-017-5221-9.

Sahu S., H.V. Singh, B. Kumar, A.K. Singh (2018), A Bayesian Multiresolution Approach for Noise Removal in Medical Magnetic Resonance Image, *Journal of Intelligent Systems*, Walter de Gruyter GmbH & Co. KG, Germany, doi: 10.1515/jisys-2017-0402.

Chapter 13

Extraction of Malware IOCs and TTPs Mapping with CoAs

Shiza Hasan, Masoom Alam, Tanveer Khan,
Nadeem Javaid, and Abid Khan
COMSATS Institute of Information Technology

Contents

13.1 Introduction

Threat intelligence is the evidence-based facts, related to emerging threats, and consists of indicators, context, inferences, and actionable intelligence. Threat intelligence gathering and management is the current trend as the number of cyber incidents and breaches is increasing immensely [1]. Attackers are increasingly becoming agile and advanced. In addition to it, they are collaborating with one another by sharing knowledge, tools, techniques, and services [2,3]. In cyber threats, malwares are most commonly used by attackers against the government, individuals, or corporate sector to steal financial, business, or personal information. According to Verizon's 2017 Data Breach Investigation Report, 51% breaches include malwares. A recent attack of WannaCry ransomware malware spread across 150 countries, including UK, USA, France, Russia, and Spain [33]. UK National Healthcare Service (NHS) was unable to access patient's record as systems were locked by ransomware malware [34].

Due to the increase in complexity of current cyber security operations [37], it is growingly becoming necessary for organizations to have cyber threat intelligence management capability. Exchange of threat intelligence with other partners or organizations is the observable trend for managing cyber threat response activities and to mitigate the incidents [4,5]. Threat intelligence sharing can be useful for foreseeing major threats that can have disrupting effect on society, for increasing situational awareness and observing changes in threat landscape.

A large amount of malware threat intelligence available on open, public, or community sources includes indicators of compromise (IOCs) [25] such as malware hashes, IP addresses, and malicious domain names. This intelligence often has short lifespan as to target a specific organization, its simple for an attacker to modify malware through some obfuscation techniques or conceal the Command and Control (CnC) communication. In this way, attackers can bypass the efforts made against this threat intelligence. The existing threat intelligence management systems are lack of tactic techniques and procedures (TTPs) and suggested course of actions (CoAs) [30] for managing response activities, i.e. detection, prevention, and incident response. There is need to include advance parameters and to dig more about malware for gathering information such as TTPs, complex IOCs [26], different malware families, network infrastructure used by the threat actors, attack methods, and motivation can be vital for predicting future attacks and threat developments [27].

Unfortunately, the number of malware samples that need to be analyzed is increasing constantly, and this large quantity of malwares requires an automated behavior analysis approach [9,10], to quickly distinguish the samples that deserve a manual analysis [11]. Some malware samples may use anti-VM, anti-sandboxing [10], or evasion techniques to avoid analysis process. In these situations, automated behavior analysis is accompanied by manual analysis.

A number of platforms are available, which provide threat data aggregation, management, and exchange, with other communities. The number of observed platforms primarily focuses on the sharing of IOC, e.g., the Open Threat Exchange (OTX), the Model-based Analysis of Threat Intelligence Sources (MANTIS), Collective Intelligence Framework (CIF) and HP Threat Central. IOC includes information that enables the identification of potentially malicious activities. For example, indicators of compromise are malicious IP addresses, anomalous user activities, descriptions of malicious files, etc. While the OpenIOC standard is primarily designed to share them, the analyzed platforms use the Structured Threat Information Exchange's (STIX) observable and indicator construct to describe them. Other solutions offered threat intelligence management options by deriving valuable intelligence from collected information through different sources. Malware Information Sharing Platform (MISP), Combine and Soltra Edge comes in this category. Intelworks, ThreatStream, ThreatConnect, Collaborative Research into Threats (CRITs), ThreatQuotient, and Vorstack also provide threat management options.

We used STIX standard to represent threat information in a common structured format. STIX is a flexible and promising structured language for the representation of cyber threat information relevant to a variety of use cases. STIX document is a detailed schema with almost the whole lot optional, so that specified portions related to a use case could be leveraged. There are three considerations for us to use STIX for threat representation: first, it is becoming de facto standard for automatic cyber threat information management and exchange; second, it is used to deliver structured threat information along with detailed contextual information; and third, it can represent the exploit information in a way that it can be used for their prevention and detection on a targeted system along with CoAs to prevent and remediate that threat. Our contributions in this research work are as follows:

- Proposing architecture for threat intelligence management system with organization specific data gathering and automated real-time malware analysis.
- Extraction of IOCs and TTPs for proactive defensive measures and situational awareness.
- Defining some general CoAs with response type.
- IOCs and TTPs mapping with suggested CoAs.

Remaining of this chapter is organized as follows: Section 13.2 consisted of background knowledge of current research. Section 13.3 includes extraction of IOCs, TTPs, and their mapping with CoAs along with mathematical model. Section 13.4 based on ransomware malware case study. Section 13.5 includes limitations and use cases. Section 13.6 discusses related work with previous investigations, existing threat intelligence management systems, critical analysis, and comparison of existing open source threat intelligence management systems. The chapter concludes in Section 13.7.

13.2 Background

13.2.1 Cuckoo—Malware Analysis Engine

Malware analysis engine is used for automated malware analysis to quickly infer that how it works and what it intends to do. Cuckoo is an automated malware analysis engine which is based on host–guest architecture. Cuckoo Linux host is connected to both guest virtual machine (VM) and external Internet connection. Guest VM is used by the host to execute malware sample. The host manages the overall processing of cuckoo sandbox and collects the results from guest VM to generate the detailed analysis report.

The report provides the detailed and fast understanding of a malware sample, which is necessary for generating countermeasures in an efficient and timely manner. Analysis report comprises file detailed, registry keys, accessed or deleted files, network activity, and static analysis sections. Cuckoo generates analysis report in HTML and JSON and export to MongoDB or ElasticSearch to display results on a web page. Cuckoo also provides a web interface for submitting samples, browse the reports, and search across the analysis reports. The analysis report can be used to extract observables, indicators, incidents, and TTPs for their further mapping with CoAs.

13.2.2 Cyber Observable Expression

Cyber Observable Expression (CybOX) provides the capability to automate the sharing of threat intelligence. It is one of the initiatives for storing and sharing of threats data in a common format. CybOX is the dictionary of objects that can be used to define stateful properties or measurable events (e.g., domain name, IPs, HTTP, mutex, file, registry keys) of an attack. Objects can

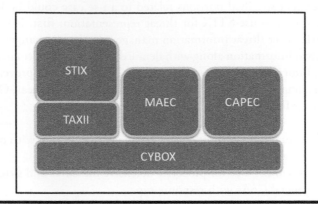

Figure 13.1   MITRE threat intelligence formats.

be useful for sharing threat intelligence and supporting advanced analysis of cyber threats. The higher-level schemas (e.g., STIX, MAEC, and CAPEC) used objects defined in CybOX for adding additional context. Figure 13.1 [14] depicts that how the other standards, designed by the MITRE, based on the CybOX.

13.2.3 *Structured Threat Information Exchange*

STIX is a flexible and promising standard for the representation of cyber threat information that tends to a variety of use cases. STIX document is a detailed schema so that specified portions related to a use case could be leveraged. STIX leverages the CyboX for observables and also provides a loose coupling mechanism for leveraging CAPEC, MAEC, and Common Vulnerability Reporting Framework (CVRF).

In Figure 13.2 [15], the detailed STIX architecture is depicted. It represents the core concepts of cyber threats with detailed constructs and content of each. The arrows between the constructs indicate the relationship in the form of content elements between these constructs. The asterisk on each of the arrow labels indicates that each relationship may exist zero to many times.

The eight high-level constructs of STIX are as follows:

i. *Observables*: are the measurable events or stateful properties that are considered the base constructs of STIX architecture. Some examples of common observables are IP address, domain, file (name, size, hash), and registry key value. STIX leverages CybOX to represent observables.

ii. *Indicators*: are specific observable patterns with contextual information, i.e., indicated TTP, confidence matrix, valid time window, suggested CoAs, related campaigns, etc.

iii. *Incidents*: are distinct instances of indicators which represent an ongoing threat with a specific adversary behavior, related observables, related indicators, threat actor, TTPs, kill chains, nature of compromise, CoAs requested, CoAs taken, etc.

iv. *Tactic techniques and procedures*: are the characterizations of adversary behavior about what it does and how it does in series of detailed steps. TTPs represent the adversary behaviour including malware, exploit target, attack pattern, kill chain, and used tools, etc.

v. *Exploit target*: are vulnerabilities or weaknesses used by threat actor for exploitation. STIX leverages Common Vulnerabilities and Exposures (CVEs), Open Source Vulnerability

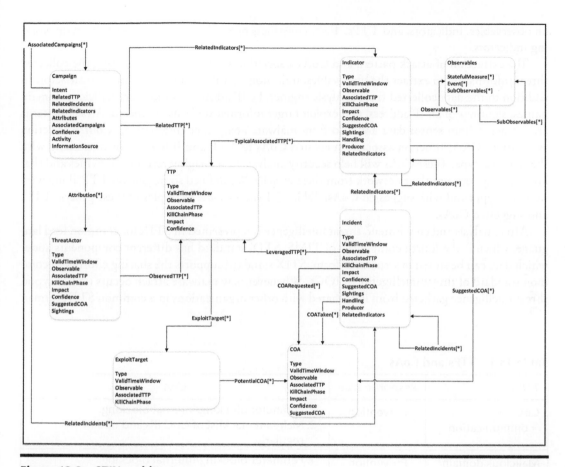

Figure 13.2 STIX architecture.

Database, CVRF, and Common Configuration Enumeration to identify publicly disclosed vulnerabilities, weaknesses, and configuration issues.

vi. *Course of action*: are specific measures for defense against known cyber threat indicators, TTPs, or incident. The CoAs fall under three categories, investigation, mitigation, and remediation, that can be deployed on endpoints or network.

vii. *Threat actor*: characterization of an adversary including categorization of identity, historically observed TTP and behavior, intended motivation and effect, etc.

viii. *Campaign*: the objective of an adversary concentrating on specific threat motive and mission across the organization described by series of incidents, TTPs, intended effect of adversary, etc.

13.3 Extraction of IOCs, TTPs, and Mapping with CoAs

Malware is analyzed in a virtualized environment to analyze that how this malware works and what is its malicious intent. After analysis, it provides file detail, dropped files, network activity, static, and behavior analysis. This detailed report is in a large size, in some cases, of 20 megabytes or more. It is not possible to quickly take decision on the basis of such lengthy reports. We focused on observables, indicators, and TTPs. These constructs of STIX standard showed the main working indicators.

The extraction of attack pattern and CoAs association is in charge of processing the collected threat information to extract the observables, indicators, TTP, exploit target, and threat actor. In addition to the data collected from analysis engine, the IP addresses of known malicious domain names, sightings of an IP address, and exploit target information is also gathered. Attack patterns are extracted from sensor data and also from malware analysis engines report. Course of action association (CAA) function associate suggested CoAs to TTP and IOCs at run time along with the response type. These CoAs will help security analysts in managing response activities and that how they can prevent their network from these attacks. We defined some general TTP along with response types and with suggested CoAs. Table 13.1 shows some examples of these generic TTPs and suggested CoAs.

After analysis and enrichment, threat intelligence is represented in STIX for common feed language, which is the fourth component of TIMS. STIX standard has different components about which data can be stored in structured form. STIX standard supports the sharing efforts as a common standard of threat intelligence or IOCs. Whenever new malware attack occurs on honeypot, threat intelligence gathered from it, is shared with other organizations in a common STIX format.

Table 13.1   TTPs and CoAs

TTP	Response type	CoA
CnC communication	Prevention	1. Perimeter blocking/internal blocking. 2. Maintain blacklist of CnC IPs and update it regularly.
Malicious domain/ URL	Prevention	1. Perimeter blocking/internal blocking. 2. Maintain blacklist.
Steal browser information	Prevention	1. Do not accept or open suspicious error dialogs from within the browser. 2. Install product updates and security patches before using the Internet. 3. Keep web browser up to date with the latest patches.
Steal browser passwords	Prevention	1. Do not allow browser to remember passwords. 2. Use password managers to keep passwords encrypted with a master password to save them locally.
Make entry in Autorun	Prevention	1. Disable autoplay feature on the system and network drives.
Use autoplay feature	Prevention	1. Disable autoplay to prevent the automatic launching of executable files on network and removable drives, and disconnect the drives when not required. 2. If write access is not required, enable read-only mode if the option is available.

(Continued)

Table 13.1 (*Continued*)   TTPs and CoAs

TTP	*Response type*	*CoA*
P2P connection to infect other computers on your network	Prevention	1. Scan all files with any Internet security solution before transferring them to your system. Only transfer files from a well-known source. 2. Protect personal data by limiting the folders and files that can be shared on a peer-to-peer network. 3. Turn off file sharing if not needed. If file sharing is required, use ACLs and password protection to limit access. Disable anonymous access to shared folders. Grant access only to user accounts with strong passwords to folders that must be shared. 4. Block all unwanted outbound communication.
Keystrokes/ keylogger activity	Containment	1. Run a full system scan and repair or delete all the files detected. 2. Navigate to the following keys, delete any value that contains the name of the file that was detected by antivirus or anti-keylogger. HKEY\LOCAL\MACHINE\Software\Microsoft\ Windows\CurrentVersion\Run HKEY\CURRENT\USER\Software\Microsoft\ Windows\CurrentVersion\Run
Use of conficker variants	Prevention	1. Use strong administrator passwords that are unique for all computers. 2. Do not log onto computers by using Domain Admin credentials or credentials that have access to all computers. 3. Make sure all systems have the latest security updates applied. 4. Disable the autoplay features. 5. Remove excessive rights to shares. This includes removing write permissions to the root of any share. 6. Block CnC IP on the gateway.
Use of backdoor variants	Detection	1. Navigate to the following keys, delete any value that contains the name of the file that was detected by antivirus: HKEY\LOCAL\MACHINE\Software\Microsoft\ Windows\CurrentVersion\Run HKEY\CURRENT\USER\Software\Microsoft\ Windows\CurrentVersion\Run

Before formalizing the concept, we classify and categorize some basic notations and concepts. The following are the key concepts used in the algorithm:

- M_{art} represents a finite set of artifacts of malware.
- A_i, A_u, A_d, A_m, A_r, A_s, and A_f represent the finite artifact sets of IP, url, domain, mutexes, registry key, services, and file, respectively.
- $A_{d,i} \subseteq (d \times i)$ represents a binary relation between domain name and IP.

- $A_{s,r} \subseteq (s \times r)$ represents a binary relation between service and registry key.
- $A_{u,d,i} \subseteq (u \times_d \times i)$ represents a triple relation between a url, url's domain name, and its registered IP.
- $P(n)$ is a quantified propositional function "n is 0 or greater than 0," where n is the number of elements of a set.
- SOB represents a finite set of observables.
- OBI_i, OBI_u, OBI_d, OBI_r, OBI_s, OBI_m, and OBI_f represent the finite artifact sets of observable's ID of IP, url, domain, mutexs, registry key, services, and file, respectively.
- T represents the used TTP by malware.
- $\mathcal{F}$ represents the malware family.

Definition 1: $A_{d,i}$ is a finite set of domain d and IP i, there exists an enrichment function E such that E: $d \rightarrow i$. With every new pair (d,i), conjunction holds between pair and the set $A_{d,i}$. Formally defined as

$$A'_{d,i} = A_{d,i} \cup (d,i)$$

Example: Domain name observable includes the value and type of domain. To add context in indicator, domain names resolved IP is accessed through enrichment like IP address for "dvdcdk. com" is "104.239.213.7."

Definition 2: A finite set $A_{d,i}$ is a subset of A_i if and only if the cardinality of their intersection is equal to the cardinality of $A_{d,i}$. Formally defined as

$$A_{d,i} \subseteq A_i \Leftrightarrow |A_{d,i} \cap A_i| = |A_{d,i}|$$

Definition 3: $A_{s,r}$ is a finite set of service s and registry key r such that s 2 $A_s(9!r$ 2 $A_r)$. Conjunction holds between the pair (s,r) and the $A_{s,r}$. Formally

$$A'_{s,r} = A_{s,r} \cup (s,r)$$

Example: For each service, there might exist a registry key in the set. To add context to service indicator, relevant entry in registry could be seen through registry key. As for service "sysdrv32" entry in registry is "HKEY\LOCAL\MACHINE\SYSTEM\ControlSet001\Services \sysdrv32\ Start."

Definition 4: A finite set $A_{s,r}$ is a subset of A_r if and only if the cardinality of their intersection is equal to the cardinality of $A_{s,r}$. Formally defined as

$$A_{s,r} \subseteq A_r \Leftrightarrow |A_{s,r} \cap A_r| = |A_{s,r}|$$

Definition 5: For the elements of set A_m, a quantified propositional function $\mathbf{P(x)}$ exists such that "there is possibility that a malware have no mutex or it can have more than more one mutexes." Formally defined as

$$\forall A_m \in M_{art} P(n)$$

Definition 6: For a malware artifact, there may exist an IP or domain artifact or may not exist. Formally defined, for IP and domain, respectively, as

$$\forall_{\text{art}} \in M_{\text{art}} \left((i \in A_i)(i \in A_i) \right)$$

$$\forall_{\text{art}} \in M_{\text{art}} \left((i \in A_d)(i \in A_d) \right)$$

Definition 7: CAA is a function that maps related TTP T and family F with suggested CoA in combination of response type. We formally defined this process as follows:

$$CAA : T \vee F \angle CoA$$

Where $\angle$ represents the CoA association relation.

Algorithm 1 Algorithm for observable's generation

Input: $M_{art} = A_i, A_u, A_d, A_r, A_s, A_m, A_f$
Output: $SOB = OBI_i, OBI_u, OBI_d, OBI_r, OBI_s, OBI_m, OBI_f$

1:   **if** $!(A_f = \phi)$ **then**
2:     $M'_{an} = M_{an} \cup A_f$
3:     **for** $a = 1$ to n **do**
4:       –a represents no. of artifacts of malwre˜
5:       **if** $!(A_i = \phi)$ **then**
6:         $M'_{art} = M_{art} \cup A_i$
7:         **if** $!(A_d = \phi)$ **then**
8:           $A_i = (E: d \mapsto i)$
9:           $M'_{an} = M_{an} \cup A_{d,i}$
10:         **end if**
11:         **if** $!(A_u = \phi)$ **then**
12:           $A_d = (E: u \mapsto d)$
13:           $A_i = (E: d \mapsto i)$
14:           $M'_{an} = M_{an} \cup A_{u,d,i}$
15:         **end if**
16:         **return** $OB - ID(A_i), OB - ID(A_d), OB - ID(A_u)$
17:         **return** OBI_u, OBI_d, OBI_i
18:       **end if**
19:       **if** $!(A_r = \phi)$ **then**
20:         $M'_{art} = M_{art} \cup A_r$
21:         **if** $!(A_s = \phi)$ **then**
22:           $M'_{an} = M_{an} \cup A_{s,r}$
23:         **end if**
24:         **return** OBI_r, OBI_s
25:       **end if**
26:     **end for**
27:     **return** OBI_f
28:   **else**
29:     do nothing
30: **end if**

The main purpose of this algorithm is collection of malware artifacts as observables for their further use as a reference in indicators, incidents, and campaigns. STIX observables generation algorithm takes artifacts related to a specific malware as input for generating observables. It returns observable ID for each specific observable on execution.

13.4 Case Study

In this section, we have provided analysis of a botnet malware and a ransomware with their extracted observables, IOCs, TTPs, and CoAs.

13.4.1 Usecase—I

A botnet is a collection of infected and controlled devices that are connected through Internet to launch a Distributed Denial of Service attack. The word botnet consists of two words "robot" and "network." Each device in a botnet, referred to as bot, is remotely controlled by a CnC server. Botnets are normally used for data theft, email spam, DOS attack, click fraud campaign, or other fraudulent activities. Botnet has gone through from almost three decades, but still it is one of the serious attacks in cybercrimes. The first botnet, called IRC, was created in 1988 [32] by Jarkko Oikarinen. After this, a number of botnets were created, and the first malicious bot, GT-BOT, was found in April 1998 [32].

We used a botnet sample of virut family, to extract IOCs and TTPs, and their mapping with CoAs. Observables collected for this botnet are file, IP addresses, domain names, registry keys, services, and mutexes. Each observable is assigned a unique ID which is used as a reference in indicator or TTP. For file observable, file name, type of file, size in bytes, packer, Md5 hash, and SHA1 are extracted. File indicator consists of file observable's ID as reference and Indicated_TTP to add context that the file is a "virut family." This threat intelligence is of high importance for security defenders and incident response teams. Suggested CoAs are assigned to both indicator and TTP. The following list shows the full traces of file artifacts:

```
# Malware executable file
—TTP1: 'Virut-Family'
—Indicator: 'virut-rbot'
—Observable:'File'
name:svchost.exe
size—in—bytes:6728545
file—type:window—executable
packed:no
md5:325ef85abc2de3dcebfdf6be232aaeaf
SHA1:6d2621336def778ef59197beefe44eef7
—CoAs:
```

IP address observable consisted of address_value, is_source, is_destination, and category. Category for an IP address could be ipv4 or ipv6. IP address is the most common form of indicators which describe the TCP traffic. This indicator consists of indicator ID, title "IP address of CnC server," description, IP address's observables_id, and context of this indicator. Indicated_TTP is used to add TTP for context with the indicator. In this scenario, TTP is "if IP address is found in TCP traffic it means that it might be a CnC server." This information is necessary to understand the adversary's infrastructure. A CoA is associated with TTP under Suggested_CoAs field, which will suggest what steps should be taken if this IP found on the network. In this scenario, CoA is "perimeter\ internal blocking of IP."

```
# IP-Watchlist
-TTP2: 'C2-Behavior'
-Indicator: 'IP-Watchlist'
-Observable:'IP'
value:51.141.32.52
type:ipv4
value:212.61.180.100
type:ipv4
value:198.105.244.11
type:ipv4
value:104.239.213.7
type:ipv4
-CoA:'Perimeter blocking'
-CoA:'Maintain blacklist of CnC IPs and update
      it regularly.'
```

For domain name, observable value and type of domain are collected. Domain name is a commonly observed indicator. In current scenario, domain name, type, description, observable_id, and domain value is collected from the report. As a number of domain names are observed, a composite indicator is generated under "domain watchlist" title.

```
# Domain-Name
-TTP3: 'Run service sysdrv32.sys'
-Indicator: 'run service'
/*Composite indicator*/
-Observable:'registry-key'
value:ilo.brenz.pl
value:dvdcdk.com
value:gasymd.com
value:ftuaaq.com
-CoA:'Perimeter blocking'
```

Executable files create the mutex to ensure that there is only one instance running in the memory.

```
# Mutex
—Indicator: 'mutex'
—Observable:'mutex'
value:x9JKdhdUnm0963x
```

We observed one service created by botnet "sysdrv32.sys." A registry key entry is also found to create this service, which add context to the indicator.

```
# Registry-Key
—TTP4: 'Run service sysdrv32.sys'
—Indicator: 'run service'
—Observable:'registry-key'
value:HKEY LOCAL MACHINE SOFTWARE ControlSet001
      Services sysdrv32.sys start
—CoA:'Remove registry key entry.'
```

Registry keys observable characterizes the registry keys and key/value pairs. Different registry key entries are observed from analysis report as the registry key is created to run the svchost.exe as a service on startup. Registry keys indicator consists of observable ID as reference, and indicated_TTP is "the malware trying to make an autorun entry."

```
# Registry-Key
—TTP5: 'Run executable as a service on startup'
—Indicator: 'regitry-key indicateing malware'
—Observable:'registry-key'
value:HKEY LOCAL MACHINE SOFTWARE Microsoft
      Windows CurrentVersion Run WSVCHO
—CoA:'Remove autorun entry'
—CoA:'Disable auto-play feature on the system
      and network drives.'
—CoA:'Disable AutoPlay to prevent the automatic
      launching of executable files on network and
         removable drives, and disconnect the drives
      when not required.'
```

And the following entries of registry keys are created to run the service SVCWINSPOOL in safe mode. For other four keys, indicated_TTP is "registry keys are created to run the service SVCWINSPOOL in safe mode."

```
# Registry-Key
-TTP6: 'run the service in safe mode'
-Indicator: 'registry-key'
-Observable1:'registry-key'
key:HKEY LOCAL MACHINE SYSTEM ControlSet001
    Control SafeBoot Minimal SVCWINSPOOL
-Observable2:
value:HKEY LOCAL MACHINE SYSTEM ControlSet001
    Control SafeBoot Minimal SVCWINSPOOL (
    Default)
-Observable3:
key:HKEY LOCAL MACHINE SYSTEM ControlSet001
    Control SafeBoot Network SVCWINSPOOL
-Observable4:
key:HKEY LOCAL MACHINE SYSTEM ControlSet001
    Control SafeBoot Network SVCWINSPOOL (
    Default)
-CoA:'Remove registry key entry.'
-CoA:'Clean system for the removal of botnet
    variant.'
```

13.4.2 Usecase—II

Ransomware is one of the pervasive computer malwares first appeared in 2005 [34]. A number of ransomware variants came in the wild. WannaCry ransomware is the recent ransomware variant which hit across multiple countries and locked thousands of computers.

We used WannaCry ransomware sample to extract IOCs and TTPs, and their mapping with CoAs.

Observables collected for this WannaCry are file, IP addresses, domain names, registry keys, services, and mutexes. Each observable is assigned a unique ID which is used as a reference in indicator or TTP. For file observable, file name, type of file, size in bytes, packer, Md5 hash, and SHA1 are extracted. File indicator consists of file observable's ID as reference and indicated_TTP to add context that the file is a "ransomware family." This threat intelligence is of high importance for security defenders and incident response teams. Suggested CoAs are assigned to both indicator and TTP. The following list shows the full traces of file artifacts:

```
# Malware executable file
-TTP1: 'Ransomware-Family'
-Indicator: 'ransomware'
-Observable:'File'
name:winword.exe
size in bytes:81920
file type:window executable
packed:no
md5:c008729ea6b0c307b8dd5ba9fc18482
```

```
# IP-Watchlist
–TTP2: 'C2-Behavior'
–Indicator: 'IP-Watchlist'
–Observable:'IP'
value:
type:ipv4
value:
type:ipv4
value:
type:ipv4
value:
type:ipv4
–CoA:'Perimeter blocking'
–CoA:'Maintain blacklist of CnC IPs and update
     it regularly.'
```

13.5 Use Cases and Limitations

Threat intelligence use cases are important to effectively manage cyber threat response activities. A threat intelligence management and sharing system can have many use cases, but we focus specifically on threat prevention, threat detection, and incident response. The response systems will take actions according to specific feeds and mentioned attack w.r.t use cases. Figure 13.3 depicts the flow diagram for managing response activities.

Following are the use cases of threat intelligence:

13.5.1 Threat Prevention

Security personnel analyze the identified threats and select the relevant preventative CoAs in order to harden the systems and network. As newly learned IOCs and TTPs with suggested CoAs could be implemented in the network. Threats are received from sensors/honeypots and analyzed

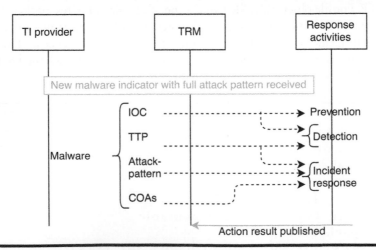

Figure 13.3   Flow managing response activities.

for IOCs and other interesting facts. IOCs, TTPs, and other contextual information along with suggested CoAs are represented in STIX reports. The suggested CoAs for specific threats can be implemented as rules in SIEM and endpoints, i.e., block an IP address on the firewall, implement a blocking rule at email gateway in case of a confirmed phishing attack, or implement a blocking rule at web security gateway for a new botnet attack, etc.

13.5.2 Threat Detection

Security personnel may use automated, semiautomated, or manual ways to evaluate the network and endpoints to detect the occurrence of a particular attack through observed IOCs in history or ongoing dynamic situational awareness. Threat detection is brought through the specific threat indicators and attack pattern. The observed IOCs with related TTPs and COAs are applied as rule in SIEM and endpoints. In case a rule is matched against indicator or TTP, for any suspicious activity on the network, then an incident is represented through STIX. After that, mitigation and removal CoAs are implemented.

13.5.3 Incident Response

To detect a potential cyber threat, a cyber-operations personnel investigates what has occurred or is occurring, tries to identify the nature of the threat, and carries out mitigation and remediation CoAs to mitigate the attack. Mitigation is necessary so that threat can be blocked from affecting the neighbors. In the case of a confirmed phishing attack, TIMS will receive the incident report and will put it for analysis. It will extract the observables from this specific incident for correlation with any available context. Actionable details can then be added with this contextual information by the SIEM automatically or manually by the incident responder. Incident responder can also add 'taken of CoAs' for the future help of such type of attacks.

13.5.3.1 Limitations

Anti-VM or anti-sandbox techniques are used by malwares to evade the behavior analysis. There exist a number of such techniques through which a malware can detect the virtual environment. These types of malware then stop working, or they unhook the processes that are keeping eye on their activity. We observed that our technique is not working fine for these malware because they stop working in virtualized environment. Table 13.2 shows some of these malwares.

Table 13.2　Malware Using Anti-VM/Sandbox Techniques

Md5 Hash	File name	File type
701fbdc24ec274d5afcecc0145a37f9e	http-OhSa1l	Window executable
8fda455a6488a272834c29c99b63d244	8fda455a6488a272834c29c99b63d244	Window executable
7e25c2c0977526d844aa212a69a2e132	http-ZE36Pl	Window executable
66d31fc52e0b2f3344be18343a85a61f	smb-owr30kg0.tmp	Data
cbe6efc32092be7a4f0ea8a09d5eea9b	http-fg48pt	Window executable
430811e62ba43a3b6219448553d20601	http-Rimxhh	Window executable
e44bc0ea44810143b9e0077946c2146a	e44bc0ea44810143b9e0077946c2146a	Window executable

13.6 Related Work

In the past years, traditional communication solutions were used to exchange threat intelligence between organizations, i.e., through email, telephone, or face-to-face meetings. Exchange of cyber threat intelligence through automated or semiautomated platforms is the current trend [8]. Moreover, not every organization has threat intelligence capability, so that they can protect their assets by using knowledge and efforts of other organizations [36]. Standard and structured representation of cyber threat intelligence is the recent trend in cyber security community [12]. A number of standards are the result of community efforts, e.g., OpenIOC [13], CybOX [14], STIX [15], MAEC [16], CAPEC [17], and TAXII [18]. These standards are the initiatives to exchange IOC and other contextual information in a common format. Burger et al. [28] provide agnostic framework to assess and evaluate these standards according to particular use cases.

Cyber security threat intelligence management is also an important research topic in various research communities. Threat intelligence collection, analysis, and distribution idea were presented in a U.S. patent [6], and Dandurand [7] was the first to present cyber threat intelligence management platform. There are different key elements that have been proposed [4,7] for a threat intelligence management and sharing system.

There are a number of platforms available that allow data aggregation from different threat intelligence communities [21,29] and exchange which exclusively target the cyber security community. For example, CIF allows combining known threat information from different sources independent of the data models [22] and using this information for prevention, detection, and incident response. Likewise, the MANTIS offer a flexible data model [23], which accepts different formats and revisions. MANTIS provide repository and support management of cyber threat intelligence which is expressed in standards such as CYBOX, STIX, OpenIOC, and IODEF. It allows filtering, browsing, and searching of stored threat information. Alienvault OTX, HP Threat Central, and IBM X-Force Exchange also come in this category.

Other solutions offered threat intelligence management options by deriving valuable intelligence from collected information through different sources. MISP allows effective sharing of malware information [31]. MISP lets us to automatically import data in intrusion detection systems for faster and better detection. Combine collects threat intelligence from public sources, enriches data, and represents the threat intelligence in CSV format [31]. It supports IP addresses and domain names only. Soltra Edge is a platform for automated standard threat intelligence sharing. Soltra Edge takes threat intelligence from any source in any format, and it aggregates and distributes threat intelligence within and outside of an organization in STIX standard format [5,30]. It uses TAXII server for sharing standard STIX content. Intelworks, ThreatStream, ThreatConnect, CRITs, ThreatQuotient, and Vorstack also provide threat management options. Table 13.3 shows the comparison of TIMS platform with open source and freely available platforms.

A variety of sources provide cyber threats information, i.e., open source, commercial source, and sharing communities, which spans different timescales and levels. A large amount of threat intelligence available on open, public, or community sources includes IOCs [25] such as malware hashes, CnC IP addresses, and malicious domain names, where responses can be executed automatically by a response system. This intelligence often has short lifespan as to target a specific organization, it's simple for an attacker to modified malware through some obfuscation techniques or conceals the CnC communication. In this way, attacker can bypass the efforts made against this threat intelligence. The existing threat intelligence management systems are lack of TTPs and suggested CoAs for managing response activities, i.e., incident response and security monitoring activities.

Table 13.3 Comparison with the Existing Open Source Systems on the Basis of Features

	CIF	MANTIS	Combine	MISP	SOLTRA EDGE	CRITS	OTX	Proposed system
Organization-specific data gathering [16]	✓	×	×	×	✓	✓	×	✓
Malware analysis [13]	×	×	×	×	×	×	×	✓
Correlation [18]	✓	–	×	✓	✓	✓	×	×
Data enrichment [18]	✓		✓	×	✓	×	✓	×
Confidence matrix [16]	✓	×	×	×	✓	×	×	×
STIX standard threat intelligence [21]	×	✓	–	✓	✓	✓	✓	✓
Automation [16]	✓	×	×	✓	✓	–	✓	*
Integration [32]	✓	×	×	×	✓	✓	✓	×
TTPs extraction [13]	×	×	×	×	×	×	×	✓
Suggested CoAs [13]	×	×	×	×	×	×	×	✓
Visual dashboard [16]	×	×	×	×	✓	✓	×	×
✓, fully exist; ×, not exist; *, partially exist; –, could not deduce.								

There is need to include advance parameters and to dig more about malware for gathering information such as TTPs [26], different malware families, network infrastructure used by threat actors, attack methods and motivation. This information can be vital for predicting future attacks and threat developments [27]. This information is valuable for longer timescale and also necessary for cyber defenders and incident responders to ensure that their network defense, detection, and investigation are up to date according to these tactics and suggested CoAs. Table 13.4 shows the comparison of the existing platforms on the basis of some prominent features.

Table 13.4 Comparison with the Existing Open Source Systems on the Basis of Observables

	CIF	MANTIS	Combine	MISP	SOLTRA EDGE	CRITS	OTX	Proposed system
File name	✓	×	×	✓	×	✓	×	✓
File type	×	×	×	✓	×	×	×	✓
File size	×	×	×	×	×	×	×	✓
Packer	×	×	×	×	×	×	×	✓
Hash	×	✓	✓	✓	✓	×	✓	✓
Malware family	×	×	×	×	×	×	×	✓
Mutex	×	×	×	×	×	×	✓	✓
IP address	✓	✓	✓	✓	✓	✓	✓	✓
Domain name	✓	✓	✓	✓	✓	✓	✓	✓
CVE number	×	×	×	×	×	×	✓	×
Registry key entries	×	×	×	×	×	×	×	✓
Email	×	×	×	×	×	✓	✓	×
Started services	×	×	×	×	×	×	×	✓
Autorun location	×	×	×	×	×	×	×	✓

✓, fully exist; ×, not exist.

13.7 Conclusion

Threat intelligence is the verified knowledge, about an emerging threat, including indicators, context, inferences, and actionable intelligence for proactive defensive measures. In cyber threats, malwares are involved in 51% of the breaches. It is the need of the hour to move on complexed malware IOCs and TTPs like malware family, created services, autorun entries, registry keys, attacker motivation, and network infrastructure. The current proposed and implemented study provides IOCs, TTPs along with suggested CoAs to provide a broad view of the threat landscape and situational awareness to organizations and incident response teams. And standard threat representation in STIX can be used to share it in near real time with other communities.

Bibliography

1. Marinos L., Belmonte A., Rekleitis E., "ENISA Threat Landscape 2016". In: *Technical Report*, ENISA – The European Union Agency for Network and Information Security, Heraklion, Greece, (2016).
2. Miller A., Horne R., Porter C., 2016 information security breaches survey. In: *Technical Report*, PWC – PrisewaterhouseCoopers, London, UK, (2016).
3. PWC: The Global State of Information Security Survey 2017. In: *Technical Report*, PWC-PrisewaterhouseCoopers, London, UK, (2017).
4. Fenz S., Heurix J., Neubauer T., Pechstein F., Current challenges in information security risk management. *J. Information Management and Computer Security*, 22, 410–430, (2014).
5. Fransen F., Smulders A., Kerkdijk R., Cyber security information exchange to gain insight into the effects of cyber threats and incidents. *e i Elektrotechnik und Informationstechnik*, 132(2), 106–112, (2015, February).
6. Aziz A., System and method of detecting malicious traffic while reducing false positives, U.S. Patent No. 8,776,229. 8, (2000).
7. Dandurand L., Serrano O.S., Towards Improved Cyber Security Information Sharing, In: *5th Int. Conf. Cyber Confl.*, Tallinn, Estonia, pp. 1–16, (2013).
8. Brown S., Gommers J., Serrano O., From Cyber Security Information Sharing to Threat Management, In: *Proceeding 2nd ACM Workshop on Information Shararing and Collaborative Security – WISCS'15*, Denver, CO, pp. 43–49, (2015).
9. Wagener G., State R., Dulaunoy A., Malware behaviour analysis, *J. Comput. Virol.*, 4(4), 279–287, (2007, December).
10. Joo J., Shin I., and Kim M., Efficient Methods to Trigger Adversarial Behaviors from Malware during Virtual Execution in SandBox, *Int. J. Secur. Its Appl.*, 9(1), 369–376, (2015).
11. Egele M., Scholte T., Kirda E., Kruegel C., A survey on automated dynamic malware-analysis techniques and tools, *ACM Comput. Surv.*, 44(2), 1–42, (2012, February).
12. Kampanakis P., Security Automation and threat information-sharing options, *IEEE Comput. Reliab. Soc.*, 12(5), 42–51, (2014).
13. OpenIOC. [Online]. Available: www.openioc.org/.
14. Cyber Observable eXpression (CybOX). [Online]. Available: http://cybox.mitre.org/.
15. Barnum S., Standardizing cyber threat intelligence information with the Structured Threat Information eXpression (STIX™). In: *Technical Report*, MITRE Cooperation, McLean, VA, (2012).
16. Maware Attribute and Enumeration Characterization (MAEC). [Online]. Available: https://maec.mitre.org/.
17. Common Attack Pattern Enumeration and Classification (CAPEC). [Online]. Available: https://capec.mitre.org/.
18. Trusted Automated Theat eXchange of Indicator Information. [Online]. Available: http//taxii.mitre.org.
19. Appala S., Cam-Winget N., Mcgrew D., Verma J., An Actionable Threat Intelligence System using a Publish-Subscribe Communications Model, In: *Proc. 2nd ACM Work. Inf. Shar. Collab. Secur. – WISCS'15*, Denver, CO, pp. 61–70, (2015).
20. Rhoades D., Machine actionable indicators of compromise, In: *2014 Int. Carnahan Conf. Secur. Technol.*, Italy, pp. 1–5, Oct. (2014).
21. Serrano O., Dandurand L., Brown S., On the Design of a Cyber Security Data Sharing System. In: *Proc. 2014 ACM Work. Inf. Shar. Collab. Secur. – WISCS'14*, Scottsdale, AZ, pp. 61–69, (2014).
22. Ren-Isac G.I., Ren-Isac K.B., *Federated Threat Data Sharing with the Collective Intelligence Framework*, Honolulu, U.S., pp. 1–27, (2013).
23. Grobauer B., Schreck T., The MANTIS Framework: Cyber Threat Intelligence Management for CERTs. Boston, MA, (2014).
24. Issa A., Anti-virtual machines and emulations, *J. Comput. Virol.*, 8(4), 141–149, (2012, June).
25. Catakoglu O., Balduzzi M., Balzarotti D., Automatic Extraction of Indicators of Compromise for Web Applications. In: *Int. World Wide Web Conference Committee*, Switzerland, pp. 333–343, (2016).
26. Jasper S.E., U.S. Cyber Threat Intelligence Sharing Frameworks, *Int. J. Intell. CounterIntell.*, 30(1), 53–65, 2017.

27. Liao X., Yuan K., Wang X., Li Z., Xing L., Beyah R., Acing the IOC Game: Toward Automatic Discovery and Analysis of Open-Source Cyber Threat Intelligence, In: *Proc. 2016 ACM SIGSAC Conf. Comput. Commun. Secur.*, Vienna, Austria, pp. 755–766, (2016).

28. Burger E.W., Goodman M.D., Kampanakis P., Zhu K.A., Taxonomy model for cyber threat intelligence information exchange technologies. In: *ACM Workshop on Information Sharing and Collaborative Security*, Scottsdale, AZ, pp. 51–60, (2014).

29. Sander T., Hailpern J., Ux aspects of threat information sharing platforms: An examination and lessons learned using personas. In: *2nd ACM Workshop on Information Sharing and Collaborative Security*, ACM: New York, pp. 51–59, (2015).

30. Sauerwein, C., Sillaber, C., Mussmann, A., Breu, R., Threat Intelligence Sharing Platforms: An Exploratory Study of Software Vendors and Research Perspectives. In: *Proceedings der 13. Internationalen Tagung Wirtschaftsinformatik (WI 2017)*, St.Gallen, Switzerland, pp. 837–851, 2017.

31. Wagner C., Dulaunoy A., Wagener G., Iklody A., MISP: The Design and Implementation of a Collaborative Threat Intelligence Sharing Platform, In: *Proc. 2016 ACM Work. Inf. Shar. Collab. Secur.*, Denver, CO, pp. 49–56, (2016).

32. Li C., Jiang W., Zou X., Botnet: Survey and Case Study, In: *4th International Conference on Innovative Computing, Information and Control*, Kaohsiung, Taiwan, (2009).

33. www.bbc.com/news/technology-39920141.

34. www.bbc.com/news/health-39899646.

35. Amin K., Robertson W., Balzarotti D., Bilge L., Kirda E., Cutting the gordian knot: A look under the hood of ransomware attacks. In: *International Conference on Detection of Intrusions and Malware, and Vulnerability Assessment*, Springer: Cham, pp. 3–24, (2015).

36. Gupta B, Agrawal D.P., Yamaguchi S., *Handbook of Research on Modern Cryptographic Solutions for Computer and Cyber security*, IGI Global, Hershey, PA, (2016).

37. Zhiyong Z., Gupta B.B., Social media security and trustworthiness: overview and new direction. *Fut. Gen. Comput. Syst.*, (2016).

Chapter 14

Implementing a Secure Web-Based Application Using Microsoft SDL

Swapnoneel Roy and Pavan S. Mudundi

University of North Florida

Contents

14.1 Introduction

Web applications have become a major source of interaction in the 21st century. Most of the applications now being used have been developed since 2012. More information is now exchanged through web applications than ever before. After the dot com revolution (1995–2001), the web became the primary means of sharing and accessing information. Since the introduction of Web 2.0 in late 2004, information is accessed and simultaneously updated through the Internet. More organizations are moving their businesses online by building stand-alone and dynamic web applications to better connect with their clients. With the smartphone revolution, mobile applications are being developed at a furious pace. Every company is developing mobile apps to reach their customers and provide seamless service. Banking and financial transactions used to be done only at physical locations of the companies. But now, with every service available on your smartphone, consumers can order checks in just a few clicks and get them delivered to their door. They can also deposit checks from their phones using an app rather than going to the physical location of the bank. E-commerce is one of the fastest growing markets. Every day millions of transactions are done on e-commerce and m-commerce (mobile) applications. Applications now store user information such as personal data, credit card information, and medical data for faster communication and to improve service to users. But such storage of user data carries a great risk in terms of information protection and privacy of the individual user. Threats are common in the computing world. Such threats include stealing of and preventing access to the information.

Security in the computing world has gained importance, and research on security has become more urgent as the number of security threats grows. It is important to consistently maintain confidentiality, integrity, and accessibility of information. Threats like buffer overflow, denial of service (DoS), SQL injection, and cross-site scripting compromise personal and corporate resources. Investments in security are small compared to the total cost of a software project. In this fast-paced economy, companies want to be ahead of their rivals and develop software quickly. As a result, they sometimes shortchange the most important aspect of software development: security.

14.2 Problem Statement

Securing web applications is important since they contain sensitive and confidential information. Vulnerabilities are frequently discovered in software applications due to developers considering security as a nonfunctional requirement or not investing much effort in designing security features during application development.

The problem addressed in this chapter is to integrate security as a functional requirement during the design and implementation phases of the software development lifecycle for a web application. The goal of this chapter is to identify a good Security Development Lifecycle (SDL) which implements security as functional requirement, and apply it to the development of a web application to make it secure against common software vulnerabilities. The contribution of this research will be to provide a base for future work in expanding software development lifecycle security concepts into other software development processes.

14.3 Purpose of the Application

The application developed in the research work as illustrated in this chapter was for a research study called *Diversity and Inclusion*. This research has as its goal a more diverse and inclusive academic environment for students, which will ultimately benefit the college community and prepare students to live and work effectively in a diverse world. This research is conducted for an important aspect of building an academic community that promotes mutual respect and courtesy and development of trust among various members of the community. Behavioral economists have recognized that trust plays a major role in promoting cooperation among different communities to produce positive economic, social, cultural, and political outcomes. To recognize the factors that contribute to trust among different communities, the Diversity and Inclusion research utilizes a variant of a trust game, that is a decision-making experiment that allows researchers to identify the determinants of a student's choice to invest resources in other students. The Diversity and Inclusion researchers are particularly interested in understanding the extent to which racial and gender biases among UNF students influence the decisions they make. For this purpose, a web application for conducting this research was needed to capture the user/participants' opinions and analyze their behavior using responses they provide when participating in a survey using the application. All the responses were stored into a database. This database consists of demographic information of enrolled participants who are interested in taking part in this study/research. Information regarding attitudes, behaviors, and emotional, mental, behavioral, and physical profile are stored in the database.

14.4 Motivation

Security has become an important aspect of software development. With more corporations moving their businesses online, there is a need to develop interactive and useful web interfaces and applications to better serve their users. Current web application interactions include collecting, processing, storing, and retrieving data. These applications may contain sensitive data such as user personal and financial information, corporate assets, and medical data. Software can be vulnerable to security threats, and the cost of damages could be staggering if these applications are compromised. To save time and money, firms incorporate off-the-shelf security components into their software products, even though they may not be compatible. These measures have not helped the software industry to overcome the most common attacks on web applications (Siddharth and Doshi, 2006). The fundamental problem is that security must be implemented as part of software development, not as an add-on feature.

14.5 Background

Software development usually consists of analysis, design, development, and delivery of software without considering security as part of it and adds security as an add-on in later iterations (Devanbu and Stubblebine, 2000; Mouratidis, 2006). Security is a term used frequently in reference to software. It is an essential element that must be incorporated into software development. When compared to software without security incorporated into its development, software that goes through a SDL tends to experience a lower rate of discovery of software vulnerabilities (Lipner, 2004). Attacks on software occur because vulnerabilities are present in software architecture, design, and implementation (Al-Ahmad, 2011).

Security-related vulnerabilities are categorized into two major areas: technical problems and social engineering challenges (Jürjens et al., 2006). Technical challenges are related to technology used in developing the software. Social engineering attacks consider an intruder who poses as a doctor in emergency hospital and asks personal information about patient medical records. This shows that security is not always considered as technical implementation. To avoid both the scenarios from happening, security should be considered as an important feature in software development lifecycle (Jürjens et al., 2006). The task of designing software can also be done by researching between various security professionals, with an end goal of improving the quality of security to be implemented in software development (Miller et al., 2013). This helps to quantify the opinions of experts, examine aggregating opinions, and produce an assessment on attacks

(Miller et al., 2013). It also assesses two important topics of interests, measuring factors in security and quantitative security management. Measuring factors in security method uses human experts to assess software systems. Perceptions between both individual expert and professional expert vary and are used to produce an assessment that accounts for it. Quantitative security management uses an expert opinion on security of the system including measuring uncertainty factor (Miller et al., 2013).

14.5.1 Security in Software Development Lifecycles

A traditional software development lifecycle includes the following phases:

- Requirements
- Design
- Implementation and coding
- Testing and results gathering
- Release and maintenance.

These five phases are common to any software development lifecycle. But when security is considered as an important aspect, few software development lifecycles incorporate security-related activities in their development processes. Software development lifecycles that incorporate security as functional requirement are listed here:

1. *Microsoft SDL*: SDL is a software development process proposed and used by Microsoft to reduce maintenance requirements and increase the reliability of software. It uses security as a main functional requirement with security features incorporated in each phase of the software development. A paper called Secure Software Development (Ahmed, 2007) is based on Microsoft SDL, which elaborates each phase in a more specific and detailed way to help developers make use of it with ease. Microsoft SDL was used in developing Microsoft products such as Windows Vista and SQL server (Microsoft Corporation, 2012).

2. *NIST 800-64*: National Institute of Standards and Technology (NIST) is a premium institute under the U.S. Dept. of Commerce, which is responsible for issuing federal standards. NIST considers that implementing security is essential to a comprehensive strategy for managing risk in the systems development lifecycle. NIST special publication 800–864 (Kissel, et al., 2008) is intended to assist federal agencies to implement security compliance in their system development lifecycles (Kissel, et al., 2008). This publication describes the security roles and responsibilities that should be part of the software development process. A brief description of Software Development Lifecycle (SDLC) is provided along with guidelines to allow persons with no knowledge of SDLC to understand the relationship between information security and SDLC.

3. *Open Web Application Security Project (OWASP) Comprehensive Lightweight Application Security Process (CLASP)*: OWASP CLASP is an activity-driven, role-based set of process components guided by formalizing best practices (Graham, 2006). CLASP helps software development teams implement security in the early stages of new and existing software development lifecycles in a structured, repeatable, and measurable way. Many software development employees in which software resources from many development lifecycles were decomposed to create a CLASP on extensive work. These resulting requirements form the

basis for CLASP's components which, when implemented, can help organizations address vulnerabilities in a systematic way. The CLASP process is based on five high-level perspectives called CLASP views. These views help users to understand how CLASP components interact in a specific software development lifecycle.

4. *Cigital's Security Touchpoints*: Touchpoints are both destructive and constructive (McGraw, 2004. Destructive touchpoints deal with attack vulnerabilities and their exploitation, whereas constructive touchpoints deal with design, implementation, defense, and functionality. Touchpoints are presented in the order of their effectiveness and how they should be implemented. They include code review, architectural risk analysis, penetration testing, risk-based security tests, abuse cases, security requirements, and security operations.

A common aspect of these models is security. Though they differ with respect to implementation, all have as their goal the optimization of security practices. Although there are many security development models, in this search no SDL was identified that was used to develop a web application such as that mentioned in Section 14.2. So, one of these models was used to develop this application and to test whether the developed application was free from common vulnerabilities (described in Section 2.2).

Even though no software is completely secure, understanding how systems will be deployed and their risks and vulnerabilities can facilitate process-oriented software development that has a more secure outcome (Mouratidis, 2006). Because security is a nonfunctional requirement, presently most applications are secured using a firewall, an antivirus or commercially available off-the-shelf component. But in the Next Generation Internet, software and web applications are connected to the Internet and interact with each other. Whether it is a mobile or computer or platform-specific environment, all future software will be connected using the Internet. This connectivity can benefit users and hackers alike, so the only option will be to build secure software—thus the need to incorporate security in the development process for web applications. This need is addressed by the security-aware software development lifecycle (Talukder, 2009).

14.5.2 Security Development Lifecycle

There are many procedures in developing software or applications. One of the common processes is the standard SDLC, a well-known development methodology used to develop applications. It consists of at least five important phases to develop software or an application from initial concept to a working product: planning, designing, building, testing, and deployment. Additional phases may be added depending upon the scope of the project. To develop secure applications, security must be incorporated into every phase of software development. However, traditional SDLC procedures don't include security. To develop secure applications, Microsoft has developed an SDL and implemented it in developing products like the SQL server (Howard and Lipner, 2005). For this research, Microsoft SDL was selected as the security development model. This model was selected from those described in Section 2.1 because SDL is straightforward and all the phases are elaborated, helping users to comfortably implement security concepts while developing the application. When compared to other models, SDL is easier to understand and less complex. For the application developed in this research, Microsoft SDL is well suited because of its close integration with standard SDLC.

14.5.3 *Common Security Threats*

Security threats are inevitable. They can originate from any source and can exist in the software without being noticed if no precautions are taken. The most common errors include considering security as a nonfunctional requirement, employing developers who lack knowledge and awareness of security concepts, and investing as little as possible in security architecture, all of which lead to security vulnerabilities. Common security vulnerabilities of web applications are DoS attack, SQL injection, cross-site scripting, and buffer overflows.

- *DoS Attacks*: DoS is the most common and sophisticated form of attack. This attack sends more requests than a system or network can handle. Attackers try to overwhelm the network or server on which the application runs with fake requests. Due to the high volume of requests, the system starts to deny all requests; thus, legitimate users are denied access (McDowell, 2009). Dedicated DoS is an extension of DoS, which takes control of a second system to start a DoS attack on the target system. Such attacks are mainly due to security vulnerabilities in the target systems (McDowell, 2009).
- *SQL Injection*: SQL injection is a popular attack on databases in which special SQL commands are executed to get unauthorized access to sensitive information. This attack can be used to access, modify, delete, and perform special operations on databases. After successful injection, they damage the confidentiality, authentication, authorization, and integrity of the databases. SQL injections occur when an unauthorized source injects data into programs and dynamically constructs an SQL query by entering special SQL commands into the input areas of an application or by manipulating URLs. SQL injections are common in web applications that contain unsafe coding and lack form validation so that they accept undesired input. Any website or application with such flaws can be easily identified and exploited. The severity of SQL injection depends on the attacker's expertise and imagination (Halfond, Viegas, and Orso, 2006).
- *Cross-Site Scripting (XSS)*: XSS is another well-known attack on web applications. This type of attack tries to execute client-side scripts on web pages viewed by users. When a user tries to access a web page that uses an unsafe URL, a script that is predefined by the attacker and which can contain malicious code is executed on the user browser. XSS consists mainly of two types. Persistent XSS, which is the most devastating, permanently stores predefined data or scripts on servers and returns them on the user browser whenever the server is accessed. In nonpersistent XSS, the most common type, server-side scripts directly use information, usually an http request provided by the web client to process and display results to users without proper validation of requests. This lack of validation helps attackers execute malicious scripts on user browsers (Spett, 2005).
- *Buffer Overflow*: Buffer overflow (Cowan, 2011) is an odd behavior that occurs in the source code when writing data to buffer, overruns the buffer's boundary, and writes to the adjacent memory locations. This is mainly done on applications with code written in C/C++. This programming languages have no built-in protection against accessing or overwriting of data and no automatic checking whether the data written to array is within the boundaries of that array. Programming languages like java have inbuilt checking of array bounds. Buffer overflows can happen only when native code is called via Java native interface or in the JVM itself and if the interpreter or just in time compiler does not work properly.

14.5.4 Microsoft SDL

Microsoft recommends Microsoft SDL for developing secure applications. It is like the traditional SDLC, but it has security as the main feature. SDL helps developers build secure applications by addressing security requirements in parallel to the development process, thus reducing future failures and extra costs. Microsoft implements this model throughout their ecosystem and believes that SDL plays a critical role in embedding security and privacy in software development. SDL implements security in all phases of the development process and reduces the occurrence of vulnerabilities in software.

Microsoft has created an SDL Optimization Model to help organizations address security issues. This Optimization Model is organized into five capability areas that generally correspond to phases of the SDLC (Howard, 2010). These phases include the following:

1. Training, policy, and organizational capabilities
2. Requirements and design
3. Implementation
4. Verification
5. Release and response.

Furthermore, this Optimization Model defines four maturity levels for practices and capabilities: Basic, Standardized, Advanced, and Dynamic (Figure 14.1). The Basic level of maturity is characterized by little or no process, training, and tooling. Organizations follow this model progress to the Dynamic level, which is characterized by SDL compliance. A complete SDL includes efficient and effective processes, highly trained entities, special tools, and strong responsibility that have effects both internally and externally (Howard, 2010).

Like other maturity models, the SDL Optimization Model is focused on developing process improvements and moving organizations from lower to higher levels of process maturity. Microsoft SDL also suggests indicators of when an application or project should adopt SDL:

■ Deployed in business or enterprise environment,
■ Deals with personal or sensitive information,
■ Communicates over the Internet or other networks.

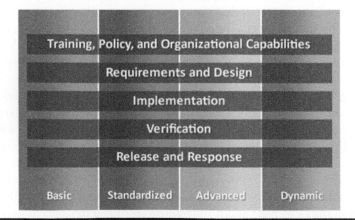

Figure 14.1 The SDL Optimization Model. (Adapted and modified from https://www.owasp. org/images/4/45/SDL_in_practice.pdf)

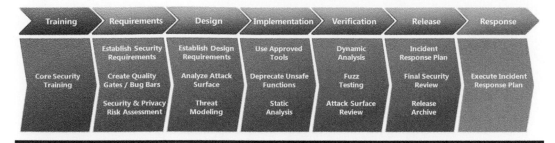

Figure 14.2 Simplified Microsoft SDL Optimization Model. (https://www.owasp.org/images/4/45/ SDL_in_practice.pdf)

Microsoft SDL provides a simplified collection of security activities, presented in the order in which they occur by phase of the SDLC. Many security features, when implemented on a stand-alone basis, provide some degree of security. However, practical experience has shown that if security is considered as part of software development, security is improved compared with implementing security features separately or on an ad-hoc basis (Howard, 2010). Other security activities can be added based on project needs or to achieve additional security objectives.

To maintain security throughout software development, organizations should focus on completeness of output at each phase. For example, the requirements phase is the most important. Using the SDL Optimization Model, the desired output for a requirements phase would be identification of all security threats and improving the requirements using misuse cases. This process will ensure that there are no unsafe requirements that may cause security issues in later phases. The SDL provides benefits by implementing effective tools, but the real value lies in precise results in every phase.

14.6 Microsoft SDL Optimization Model

The Microsoft SDL Optimization Model is like a traditional software development process with steps that include requirement gathering to verification and deployment phases. Figure 14.2 depicts the important elements of each stage. The sections that follow describe each stage.

14.7 Pre-SDL Requirements: Security Training

14.7.1 Core Security Training

Members of software development teams must receive training in security basics and recent trends in security and privacy. Developers, testers, and other individuals who are involved in software development must attend at least one security training class each year. Training in software security must cover fundamental concepts such as

- Secure design, including
  - Attack surface reduction,
  - Defense in depth,
  - Principle of least privilege,
  - Secure defaults;

- Threat modeling, including:
  - Overview of threat modeling,
  - Design implications of a threat model,
  - Coding constraints based on a threat model;
- Secure coding, including
  - Buffer overruns (for applications using C and C++),
  - Integer arithmetic errors (for applications using C and C++),
  - Cross-site scripting (for managed code and web applications),
  - SQL injection (for managed code and web applications),
  - Weak cryptography;
- Security testing, including
  - Difference between security testing and functional testing,
  - Risk assessment,
  - Security testing methods;
- Privacy, including
  - Types of privacy-sensitive data,
  - Privacy design best practices,
  - Risk assessment,
  - Privacy development best practices,
  - Privacy testing best practices.

The preceding activities provide adequate knowledge to developers and stakeholders. Advanced concepts of training, including but not limited to the following, can be provided if time permits:

- Advanced security design and architecture,
- Trusted user interface design,
- Security vulnerabilities in detail,
- Implementing custom threat mitigations.

14.7.2 Requirements Phase

14.7.2.1 Establish Security Requirements

Security and privacy is a fundamental aspect of developing secure software. Identifying requirements early will help develop software that will function as planned. The important point is to define trustworthiness requirements for a software project in the initial stages. Security and privacy requirements assessment is done at the beginning of the project. The process includes establishing minimum-security requirements and identifying insecure requirements using misuse cases.

14.7.2.2 Create Quality Gates/Bug Bars

Quality gates and bug bars set minimum requirements for security and privacy quality. A bug bar is a quality gate, which applies to the entire software development project. Bug bars are used to set a threshold for security vulnerabilities (Howard, 2010). Once set, these should never be reduced.

These criteria improve the overall understanding of security risks and enable project teams to fix security bugs before checking the code (Howard, 2010). The project team should negotiate quality gates for each development phase and then get approval from the security advisor, who can add more stringent security requirements and measures as needed.

14.7.2.3 Security and Privacy Risk Assessment

Security and privacy risk assessments are mandatory to identify any vulnerability that might occur in later stages. These assessments must include the following considerations:

- Which portion of the project will require threat models before release?
- Which portions of the project will require security design reviews before release?
- Which portions of the project will require penetration testing by a manual agreed upon group that is external to the project team?
- Are there any additional testing or analysis requirements the security advisor deems necessary to mitigate security risks?
- What is the specific scope of fuzz testing requirements?
- What is the privacy impact rating?

Since all the above assessments relate to any future risks that might occur, these questions are addressed in future phases once the scope of the software development is established.

14.7.3 Design Phase

14.7.3.1 Establish Design Requirements

It is important to address security and privacy concerns in the design phase because mitigating security and privacy concerns is less expensive when done in the early stages of the project lifecycle. In the design phase, teams should differentiate between security features and secure features. Security features may be implemented which, in fact, are not secure enough. Secure features are well defined with respect to security, including validation of all data before implementing them. The design requirements should include creation of security and privacy design specifications and specification of cryptographic design requirements. All design specifications should describe how secure the implementation of all functionality provided by a given feature or function will be.

14.7.3.2 Analyze Attack Surface

Analysis of attack surface is used to reduce attacks by identifying potential risks and vulnerabilities. This type of analysis identifies the attacks that might occur on the application. This analysis also includes what type of attacks can occur, and what damage it can create to the software when attacked. Limiting or restricting access to the system, applying user privileges, follows up analysis and implementing layered defense wherever necessary.

14.7.3.3 Threat Modeling

Threat modeling is similar to attack surface reduction, but with a different approach to security issues. Threat modeling is used to consider security issues at the application level. Development teams usually do threat modeling, with project managers, developers, and testing teams addressing primary security analysis tasks during the design phase.

14.7.4 Implementation Phase

14.7.4.1 Use Approved Tools

Developers should define a list of approved tools, such as compiler/linker options and warnings, for security checks (Howard, 2010). The project security advisor should approve this list. All development teams should use the latest development environments and approved tools to take advantage of new security functions.

14.7.4.2 Deprecate Unsafe Functions

Most common risks arise due to use of unsafe functions or application program interfaces (APIs). Project teams should analyze all functions and APIs to be used in software development and prohibit those determined to be unsafe. Header files such as "banned.h" should be used by the project teams with code scan tools to check for any deprecated methods in the code or APIs and replace them with the latest and approved functions and APIs.

14.7.4.3 Static Analysis

Software project teams should perform static analysis of source code. This provides project teams the opportunity to ensure that only secure coding practices are followed. Static analysis by itself is like manual code review where checking code manually is not recommended because checking thousands of lines of codes is time consuming. Security teams should be aware of the strengths and weaknesses of static analysis and implement automated tools or human review as appropriate (Howard, 2010).

14.7.5 Verifications Phase

14.7.5.1 Dynamic Analysis

Dynamic program analysis is necessary to verify that the program functions as designed. This analysis should specify application behavior for user privilege issues, access controls, memory management, and other security-related functions. SDL uses run-time tools such as App verifier (Phillips, 2002), along with other fuzz techniques, to test the level of security.

14.7.5.2 Fuzz Testing

Fuzz testing is a specialized form of dynamic code analysis used to test the program by deliberately injecting random or malformed data into an application to observe its behavior. It is a planned test of the actual function of an application. The security expert may require additional tests or increase the scope and duration of the tests.

14.7.5.3 Attack Surface Review

It is common for the actual behavior of applications to deviate from their initial design specifications. Therefore, it is necessary to review the threat model and attack surface of an application when the code is complete. This will ensure that any design or implementation changes done on the application will be reviewed again so that their desired functionality does not change, and any new attacks or risks can be reviewed and mitigated.

14.7.6 Release Phase

14.7.6.1 Incident Response Plan

Every software release must include an incident response plan. Even programs with no vulnerabilities or risks during release may succumb to new threats that arise over time. An incident response plan should include the following:

- A sustained engineering team, or if the project team is too small, an emergency response plan that identifies appropriate engineering, marketing, communications, and management staff to act as the point of first contact in a security emergency;
- A 24/7 on-call contact with decision-making authority;
- A security servicing plan for code inherited from other groups within the organization;
- A security servicing plan for licensed third-party code, including file names, versions, source code, third-party contact information, and contractual permission to make changes.

14.7.6.2 Final Security Review

Final security review (FSR) is the final examination of all security-related aspects of the software before its release. The security advisor with the help of developers and privacy team leaders conducts this review. The FSR is not penetration and patchwork, nor is it a security exercise to correct features, which were ignored or forgotten. It involves examining threat models, exception results, tool outputs, and performance with respect to previously defined quality gates and bug bars. The FSR results in one of the following outcomes.

- *Passed FSR*: All security and privacy issues identified by the FSR process are fixed or mitigated.
- *Passed FSR with Exceptions*: All security and privacy issues identified by the FSR process are fixed or mitigated with all exceptions resolved. Any unresolved issues that cannot be addressed or fixed in the current release are pushed to the next release.
- *FSR with Escalation*: If the project team does not meet all SDL requirements and the security advisor cannot accept the project or approve it for release, the team must either address the issues according to SDL requirements prior to launch or escalate to executive management for a decision.

14.7.6.3 Release/Archive

Software release to manufacturing or release to web is conditional on completion of the SDL process. The security advisor assigned to the release must certify that the project team has satisfied all security requirements (Howard, 2010). Moreover, for all products that have at least one component with a privacy rating of p1, the project's privacy advisor must certify that the project team has satisfied the privacy requirements before the software can be shipped. Here, privacy impact rating is the degree of risk the software possesses. In addition, the release must include all specifications, source code, binaries, threat models, documentation, emergency response plans, licensing and servicing terms for any third-party software, and any other data necessary to perform post-release servicing tasks (Howard, 2010).

14.7.6.4 Response

This is the final phase, in which the incident response plan comes into effect. This phase concentrates on support of the software. Once the software is deployed and running, issue related to system outages and exceptions, which may occur during the operation, should be monitored frequently. The incident response plan is executed in this phase to support the software.

14.7.7 Web Application Development using Microsoft SDL

14.7.7.1 Objective

This section describes how the web application for the Diversity and Inclusion project was developed, from the initial requirements phase through design, development, implementation, and finally testing phases, embedding security as a main feature. The application developed in this chapter was a data-gathering application, which collects user responses and stores them in a database. Traditional data-gathering applications consist of data collected from the participants and stored in the database. In contrast, this application consists of user data that is stored in the database, and the data is dynamically rendered on user pages according to the choices made by the survey participant while using the application.

14.7.7.2 Technology

Web developers have a choice of many programming languages. Java is a strong object-oriented programming language that was used to develop this application. It is flexible, robust, and easy to implement for dynamic web applications. Java is supported in most modern integrated development environments (IDEs), and there exist a plethora of Java libraries, which have been tested. These factors make Java an important and favored language for developing secure web applications. The Java database connection (JDBC) driver was chosen for the core logic of the database connection, to store persistent data in the databases. Java server pages were used for developing user interfaces, and MS Access was used for the database. The Java Platform Enterprise Edition (Java EE) Java Development Kit JDK 8, the latest version available at the time of development, was used. Eclipse was chosen as the Java IDE. Eclipse offers two editions: the standard edition for beginners and the enterprise edition for enterprise developers. The latest version of the Java Development Kit is supported by the Eclipse enterprise edition and was used in this application development. Development was done in a Microsoft Windows environment. All the source codes were run and tested on Windows 8 and Windows 10 operating systems.

14.7.7.3 Application Development

Application development was done by implementing secure software development methods defined by Microsoft SDL. A similar work (Ahmed, 2007) elaborates much of the Microsoft SDL methodology. This section starts with the requirements phase in which functional and security requirements were defined using misuse cases. The design phase consisted of wireframes of the application, security architecture, threat models, user interaction areas, and application access points. In the implementation phase, code was written, and a comparison was made between how code looked before and after implementing security testing using a static code analyzer. In the testing phase, various tests were done, including functional and security testing.

14.7.8 Requirements Phase

Defining requirements is a key element in software development. Project success is dependent on how requirements are described and implemented. In this section, functional and security requirements were identified for the development of the application.

The functional requirements were defined as follows:

1. *User interface*: The user is presented with a landing page with introductory information about the application. The user authenticates on the second page, and the pages that follow each contain instructions on how to use that page.
2. *Hardware interface*: The application must run on most browsers. The application interface should run continuously on the server and should be accessed remotely using a URL. The application sends and receives data from the database, which is stored on the server's disk. The user computer/browser transfers data to the server using secure network protocols.
3. *Security requirements*: Only valid users should be able to access the application. Every valid user must authenticate using an identification number. The user must be allowed to enter only valid inputs, so restrictions on user inputs must be applied. The database should be accessible only through the application. These requirements are depicted in a use case (Figure 14.3), which shows how user and application interact with each other. This use case specifies the series of processes that are combined into one single use case. First, the user authenticates with the application using a unique identification number, which is shown in the first use case. Once the user is validated and granted access to the application, then the user requests the data and views it. Finally, the user saves his responses in the final step and submits the responses to the application to be stored in the database.

Security requirements are depicted in a misuse case in Figure 14.4. This misuse case is similar to the use case from Figure 14.3, but the difference is that it defines a new user called "intruder" who performs malicious activities on the application. These activities can be any kind of attack.

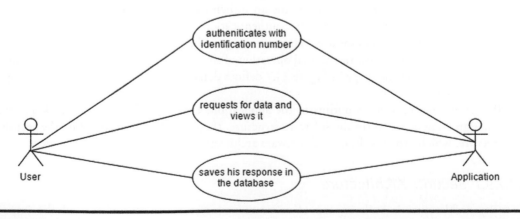

Figure 14.3   Use case diagram.

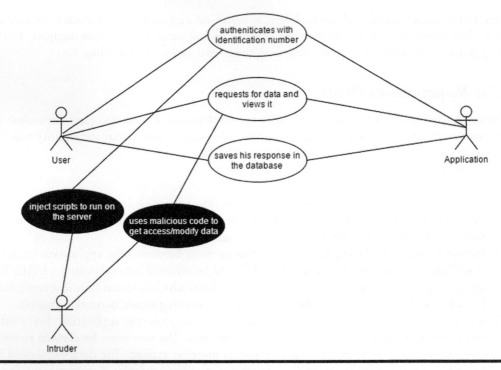

Figure 14.4   Misuse case.

14.7.9 Design Phase

In this phase, all the requirements are analyzed and elaborated into one or more designs. The design phase is a blueprint for the implementation phase. After requirements are analyzed, preliminary designs such as sketches and wireframes are developed using use cases and misuse cases. The application developed in this chapter contains multiple pages, starting with the landing page, and followed by the instructions page, characteristics page, participants' page, and responder page. Wireframes were developed to give a rough outline of the application.

As shown in Figure 14.5, the landing page is the first point of interaction, where the user is presented with instructions on how to use the application.

Figure 14.6 contains a few instructions and an authentication field where the user is prompted to enter his/her identification number. After authentication, the user is directed to the third page. Failure to validate will result in the user being redirected to the landing page with an alert message.

Figures 14.7 and 14.8 show the normal operation of the application after the authentication of the user. The characteristics page in Figure 14.7 defines demographics of participants such as age, gender, and race.

The wireframes provide an outline of the application. Even though sketches, mockups, and other design components form the software structure, there is still a need to define the security architecture, which explains the overall software architecture from a security point of view.

14.7.9.1 Security Architecture

Security architecture is built on top of software architecture. In this phase, all the important components of the security architecture along with their properties and interactions are

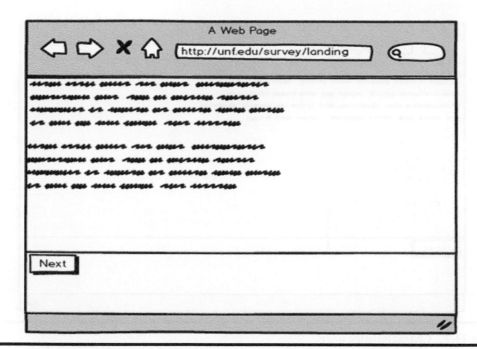

Figure 14.5 Landing page.

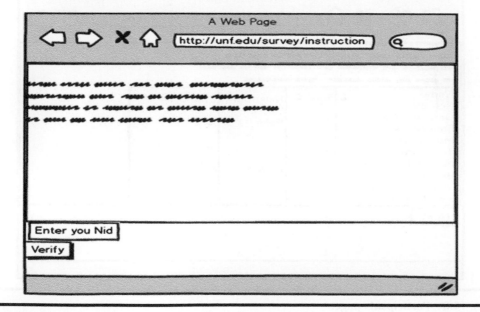

Figure 14.6 Authentication page.

identified. For this application, the security architecture consists entirely of in-app interactions. No application-to-application interactions take place as this application deals only with its own data, accessible over the Internet as a dynamic application. All the main interaction points are discussed. The application was developed using a top-down design approach because this application was developed from scratch.

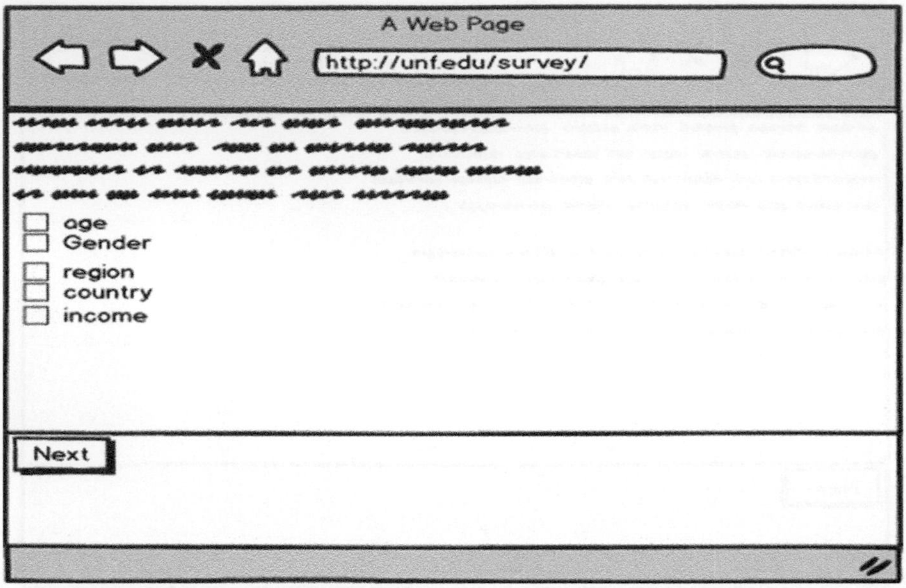

Figure 14.7 Characteristics page.

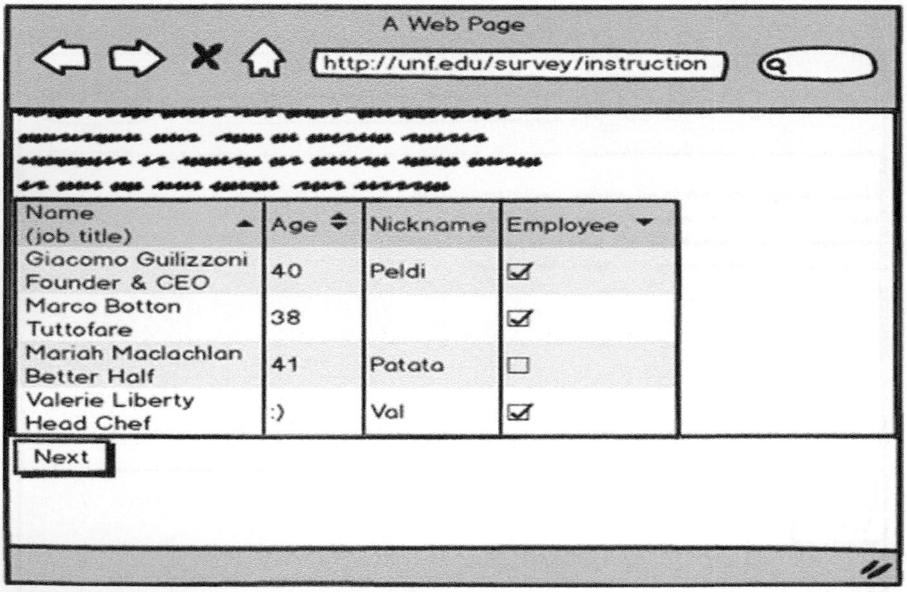

Figure 14.8 Participants page.

There are many access points in the application where it interacts with the data in the database. So, user privileges must be strictly enforced so that only authorized functions can access the source systems, in this case the database. Identifying possible attacks and minimizing the likelihood of their occurrence will increase the overall security of the application. Applications have multiple input fields where an attacker can inject malicious code. These are the starting point for attackers to take control of or compromise an application. With this in mind, all input fields are

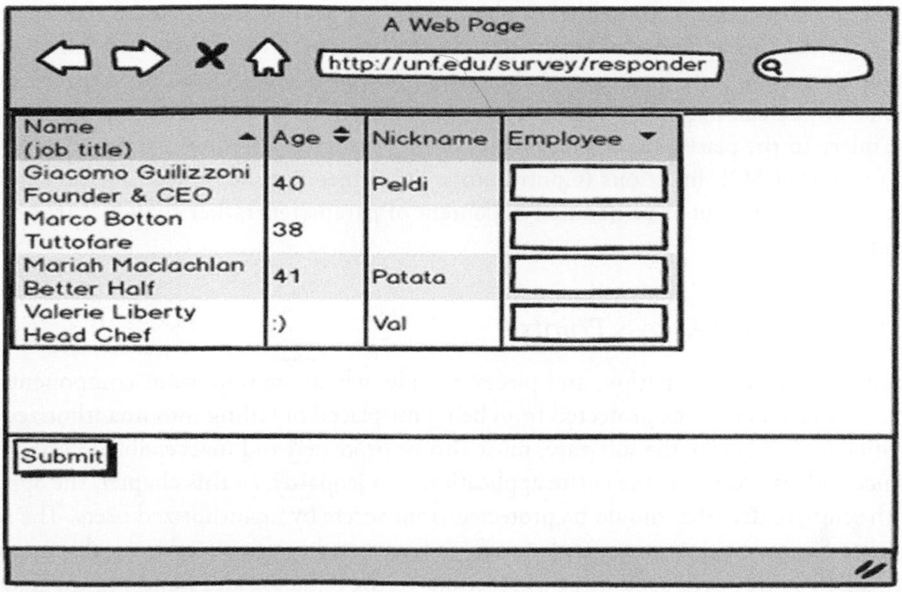

Figure 14.9 Respondent page.

restricted with form filters by validating only desired input and rejecting any other inputs. All the data moves through the network over the Internet. Using unsecured protocols will eventually give attackers an opportunity to tap into the network flow and alter the data passing through it. This issue was addressed using secure transport protocols like http and https to communicate between the browser and the server.

14.7.9.2 Interaction Points

Most software interacts with other software. Interaction between components within software is also common. Applications use the session ID, which is passed on to each page, to track a specific user.

Other common interaction points consist of user interaction with the application. In the work described in this chapter, the application requires user authentication using a unique identifier, in this case a student ID number. This interaction consists of an input field for entry of the student ID. This input field is the one of the user interaction fields in which external data is passed to the application. This input field will accept only a specific format for the student ID number. Security threats such as SQL injection or script injection can be present in the input fields. These should be eliminated by imposing restrictions on input fields by implementing filters in the form of format validators. Form validators are simple java script functions that define specific formats to accept as input. For example, a UNF student identification number consists of a letter followed by eight numbers, e.g. N01234567. To accept only this format as input requires a special JavaScript attribute called a pattern. This pattern attribute can be used to define a specific format to be implemented against the input field, in this case "[N] [0–9] {8}." This pattern will accept only the defined ID number format, and any other input will be rejected with an alert message. With the help of these validators, the application was made secure from malicious scripts getting injected into the software.

There is another important interaction point in the application. All the data that is requested by the user or the user responses is stored in a database. There are also pages on which database interaction is done to query data from the database. These queries are processed using "prepared statements," which can be parameterized. Here, "parameterized" means substituting the values in the SQL query in the place of a "?" placeholder. Using prepared statements adds an extra level of security to prevent SQL injections (Contributors, SQL injection, 2017) because prepared statements can force user input to be handled as content of parameters rather than as part of an SQL command.

14.7.9.3 Assets and Access Points

Assets consist of data, information, and pieces of code, which are important components of any software. All the data must be protected from being misplaced or falling into unauthorized hands. Code, which is the brain of the software, must also be protected and inaccessible to unauthorized users. Once code is accessible, the entire application is in jeopardy. In this chapter, the application deals with sensitive data that should be protected from access by unauthorized users. The sensitive data consists of participants' personal data, which is accessed by the users using this application. The application source code consists of connections to the database and handling the data that is processed and displayed to the user. This part of the source code must be private and protected from unauthorized access.

14.7.9.4 Minimize Attack Surface

No software is secure enough. All software can be attacked. Minimizing attack surface is key to software security. To do this, common security attacks on web applications are identified and security measures are implemented to minimize vulnerability. This is done by implementing secure source code, analyzing the code using static and dynamic analysis tools, and testing to check if the software is secure from common security attacks.

14.7.9.5 Threat Models

Threat models help software developers identify areas of attacker interest. They also consider functionalities of the software, technologies to be used, and the operating environment where the software will function. These combine to give a software developer an idea of possible types of attacks on a software application.

In the work described in this chapter, potential attacks were identified from the attacker's point of view. The most common security attacks on web applications include SQL injection and XSS (Ionescu, 2015). These two attacks and their risks are described in Tables 4.1 and 4.2. Since Java is used as the development language for this project, and buffer overflow occurs only in unusual cases for Java, buffer overflow is not considered for the overall implementation. The application described in this chapter contains one access point where the user enters a student ID number. The attacker can use this input field to inject malicious code and run it on the server. There is also the possibility that an attacker could input malicious SQL commands into the input fields that can threaten the database. These potential threats, their descriptions, target, risk, defensive technique, and risk management strategies are described in the sections that follow. Such detailed definition gives a clear picture of what the risks are, how they can occur, and what measures can be taken to prevent them.

Table 14.1   Risk 1: SQL Injection

Description	A code injection technique that inserts nefarious SQL statements into an input field. Once the SQL code is successfully executed, data can be accessed illegally, altered, or deleted.
Target	Web applications.
Risk	Illegal access to (sensitive) data, alteration, deletion.
Defensive Techniques	1. Use parameterized statements in SQL queries with placeholders, which store a value of a given type, rather than an arbitrary SQL command. 2. Use a pattern attribute to check if the inputs are valid. 3. Impose restrictions on input fields by allowing only a specific format to be accepted.

Table 14.2   Risk 2: XSS

Description	A security vulnerability typically found in web applications. It enables injection of client-side scripts into web pages. It is mainly used by the attackers to bypass access controls such as same origin policy (Contributors W., Cross-site scripting, 2016).
Target	Web applications.
Risk	Stealing of session cookies, storage of malicious scripts on the servers.
Defensive Technique	Proper sanitization of input before it is processed and executed.

14.7.10 Implementation Phase

In the implementation phase of software development, the requirements and design artifacts, including threat models, use case diagrams, wire frames, and security architecture, are incorporated into one working model. Implementation is the final phase in which security flaws can be introduced into the software. These flaws are most commonly introduced when writing code, due to poor coding, lack of knowledge of security principles, and use of unsafe methods. Using safe coding practices, employing a secure programming language, and performing static code analysis after the code is written can prevent such flaws. Static code analysis begins with identifying possible static code analysis tools, differentiating between them, and choosing the most appropriate tool to apply to the application.

14.7.10.1 Static Code Analysis

Static analysis is used to analyze the code for any flaws that can be detected after writing the code. Static code analysis can be done manually or using automated tools. Manual reviews are done by debugging the code and seeing how the system behaves during compilation.

Many static code analysis tools are available for testing web applications. A few of them are described here:

■ *FindBugs*: An open source Java source code analyzer. It classifies the severity of bugs into four ranks: Scariest, Scary, Troubling, and Of Concern, indicating possible impact. These ranks are customizable by the developer to avoid identifying bugs that are not considered damaging.
■ *PMD*: A static code analyzer, which scans the code for any potential bugs and flaws in the application. It identifies bugs including naming conventions and unused code. PMD operates on a set of defined rules. Not all issues reported by PMD are errors. The program can still run even if the detected errors are not corrected.
■ *Checkstyle*: A Java source code analyzer, which checks if the source code complies with good programming standards. The analysis is limited to presentation rather than content analysis. Not all the presentation standards can be achieved.

There are many static code analysis tools, but only a few were available to be implemented because they are not freely available. For this chapter, the static analysis tool FindBugs (Pugh and Hovemeyer, 2016) was selected from among the open source tools because it classifies the bugs into ranks. For the application developed in this chapter, classification of bugs according to severity was deemed to be important to addressing them. The presence of FindBugs does not have any impact on overall code functioning. This tool operates on Java bytecode rather than on source code. The tool is open source and distributed as a stand-alone GUI application. Plugins are available for almost every IDE, including Eclipse, IntelliJ, Gradle, Jenkins, Maven, NetBeans, Bamboo, and Hudson. For this chapter, FindBugs was installed on Eclipse as a plugin. Scariest, Scary, and Troubling bugs were chosen for this analysis.

14.7.10.2 Source Code Implementation

The source code of the application consists of four important packages. The "Validation" package consisted of the "UserValidation" class, which was used to validate the user; the "ParticipantsData" package consisted of the "GetParticipantsData" class, which was used to present characteristics of students; the "ParticipantsResponse" package consisted of the "GetParticipantsDetails" class, which was used to get details from the database based on the characteristics selected on the previous page; and finally the "StoreData" package consisted of the "SaveParticipantsData" class, which was responsible for recording responses from the user and storing them on the database. These class files are important because all the database connections and data storage happen in these classes.

Figure 14.10 shows one of the class files that is used for the database connections. Here, a driver manager that hardcodes the username and password into the source code itself defines authentication rules.

This is a common way to define a connection to a database. But the database connection is public, and authentication information is public. Anyone with access to the source code can gain access to the database. This unauthorized access can be avoided by defining all the database connections in a property file. FindBugs was used to analyze the source code of this class to find vulnerabilities and bugs. Running FindBugs on this class resulted in throwing bug report, i.e., database password is hardcoded in the class GetParticipants.doGet() method.

Figure 14.11 shows the FindBugs report in which there were bugs detected, one ranked as Scary. The bug was described as "Hardcoded constant database password." It states that the password is

```
77    String nId = (String)request.getSession().getAttribute("Nid");
78    String[] cbks = request.getParameterValues("cbk");
79    request.setAttribute("values", cbks);
80    System.out.println(nId);
81    String rd1 = request.getParameter("radio");
82    PrintWriter out = response.getWriter();
83    try {
84        Class.forName("net.ucanaccess.jdbc.UcanaccessDriver");
85        String url ="jdbc:ucanaccess://C:/Users/Deepu/Desktop/Database1.accdb";
86        conn = DriverManager.getConnection(url, "pavan", "test");
87        System.out.println("connection establised");
88    } catch (Exception e) {
89        e.printStackTrace();
90    }
91    StringBuilder builder1 = new StringBuilder();
92    ArrayList<String> list = new ArrayList<String>();
93    for (int i = 0; i < cbks.length; i++) {
94        builder1.append(cbks[i] + ",");
95    }
96    if(rd1!=null){
97    builder1.append(rd1 + ",");
98    }
99
```

Figure 14.10   Connections to the database.

not protected and anyone with access to source code can retrieve the password. To prevent unauthorized access, database connection details can be stored in a property file and imported when appropriate into the class file. Figure 4.10 shows how the database connection details can be stored securely in a properties file and imported to their respective class file. By storing the sensitive information in a properties file, unauthorized access to the database was prevented. When the revised code was tested using FindBugs, it detected no errors.

Figure 14.12 shows how the username and password of the database connection are now hidden in a property file and imported into the class, as compared with the previous hardcoded approach shown in Figure 14.11.

Another similar issue arises when the data from the input field is used to prepare SQL statements to query the database. When the user enters an authentication number, it is stored in a session object and used for both authenticating and in subsequent queries to the database. SQL statements are called using the JDBC Statement Interface. This interface is responsible for providing methods to execute the query. In the application, data is retrieved from the database and updated back into the database using Statement Interfaces. But Statement Interfaces can be vulnerable because they do not prevent SQL injection (Contributors, SQL injection, 2017). Statement Interfaces directly substitute the data from the input field into the SQL query without any validation. A better JDBC interface is Prepared Statement, which extends the Statement Interface and prevents SQL injection by avoiding the quotes and special characters. This strategy can avoid any malicious scripts being included directly in the query.

Figure 14.13 shows an SQL query with values directly substituted into the query. Statement Interface was used to create the statement, and the query was executed with ResultSet. But this implementation could allow SQL injection into the database. An attacker could include malicious code in the input field, which would be substituted directly into the SQL query. FindBugs threw an error and instead use PreparedStatement to avoid SQL injection.

Figure 14.11   FindBugs analyzer performed on database connection.

```
43   throws ServletException, IOException {
44   String nId = (String)request.getSession().getAttribute("Nid");
45   String[] cbks = request.getParameterValues("cbk");
46   request.setAttribute("values", cbks);
47   String rd1 = request.getParameter("radio");
48   PrintWriter out = response.getWriter();
49   try {
50       InputStream inputStream = GetParticipantsData.class.getClassLoader()
51           .getResourceAsStream("db.properties");
52       Properties properties = new Properties();
53       if (properties != null) {
54           properties.load(inputStream);
55
56           String dbDriver = properties.getProperty("dbDriver");
57           String connectionUrl = properties
58               .getProperty("connectionUrl");
59           String userName = properties.getProperty("userName");
60           String password = properties.getProperty("password");
61
62           Class.forName(dbDriver).newInstance();
63           conn = DriverManager.getConnection(connectionUrl,
64               userName, password);
65       }
```

Figure 14.12   Importing database connections using the properties file.

Figure 14.14 shows a warning and brief description of the error and suggestions for remedying it given by FindBugs. In the revised version of the code, PreparedStatement was used to build a query. FindBugs tested it again and showed no warnings. Figure 14.15 shows the same code with PreparedStatement used instead of Statement Interface to build and execute the SQL query.

```
58        ArrayList<String> list1 = new ArrayList<String>();
59        for(int j=0;j<cbks1.length;j++){
60            builder.append("'"+cbks1[j]+"'"+",");
61        }
62        for( int i = 0 ; i < 1; i++ ) {
63            builder1.append( cbks+",");
64        }
65        try{
66            String characters = builder1.deleteCharAt(builder1.length() -1 ).toString();
67            String Nnumbers = builder.deleteCharAt(builder.length() -1 ).toString();
68            Statement pst = conn.createStatement();
69            ResultSet rs = pst.executeQuery("SELECT "+characters+" FROM Registration where Nnumber in("+Nnumbers+")");
70            String temp="";
71            String[] headerValues = cbks.split(",");
72            System.out.println(headerValues.length);
73            if(headerValues.length==1){
74                list1.add(headerValues[0]+","+"Transfer");
75            }
76            if(headerValues.length==2){
77                list1.add(headerValues[0]+","+headerValues[1]+","+"Transfer");
78            }
79            if(headerValues.length==3){
80                list1.add(headerValues[0]+","+headerValues[1]+","+headerValues[2]+","+"Transfer");
81            }
82            if(headerValues.length==4){
```

Figure 14.13   SQL query.

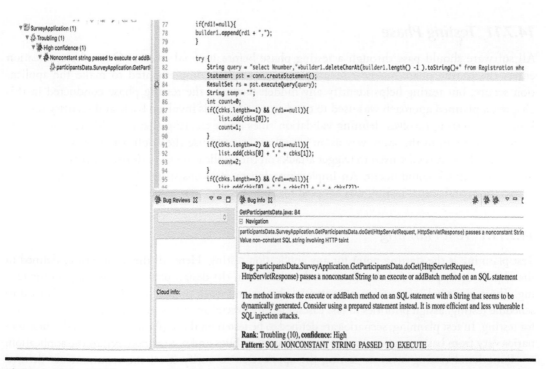

Figure 14.14   FindBugs warning for using Statement Interface.

```
78    try {
79        PreparedStatement pst = conn.prepareStatement("select Nnumber,? from Registration where NOT Nnumber=?");
80        pst.setString(1, builder1.deleteCharAt(builder1.length() -1 ).toString());
81        pst.setString(2, nId);
82        ResultSet rs = pst.executeQuery();
83        String temp = "";
84        int count=0;
85        if((cbks.lenath==1) && (rd1==null)){
```

Figure 14.15   Using prepared Statement Interface.

14.7.10.3 Performing Code Review

During code review, developers and analysis teams manually review each line of source code and perform step-by-step debugging to see how the revised code behaves. Manual code reviews are performed after static code analysis. Experienced developers perform code reviews to prioritize their work on certain parts of code where bugs are detected during static code analysis. Code reviews are also used to identify common vulnerabilities like buffer overflow, arithmetic issues, and SQL injections. Manual code review is not generally recommended because going through thousands of lines of code is time consuming and costly. Due to the relatively small scale of the application developed in this chapter, manual code review was performed. Since the work described in this chapter concentrated on building secure software, the areas where bugs were discovered during static code analysis were stressed to make sure those issues were fixed. When necessary, static code analysis was rerun to verify that bugs were fixed.

14.7.11 Testing Phase

All software should pass through a testing phase before its final release. Once the application enters the testing phase, no new security measures will be implemented to make the application secure, but testing helps identify any hidden flaws. In the testing phase conducted in this chapter, a planned approach was used to conduct testing. This involved basic and security testing. Functional testing involves defining validation rules and executing them on different scenarios, performing them in the same way as an actual user would use the application. In security testing, defined test cases are used to trigger attacks on the application to perform a real-time scenario of how the attack could occur. An implementation model consisting of test planning, test bed preparation, and actual testing was adopted for this chapter.

14.7.11.1 Test Planning

Test planning is the starting point for any application testing. Here, all the misuse cases defined in the requirements phase and the threat models defined in the design phase are used to plan the testing. These give vital information on potential threats and weak points. This information is used to schedule testing, assign priorities to test cases, identify execution orders for test cases, and select tools for testing. In test planning, scenarios are defined to be tested on the application developed. These scenarios vary from basic testing to security tests that inject bugs and vulnerabilities into the application.

Functional testing involves testing the application to verify if all the requirements defined in the use cases are functioning and whether all the functions of the application are performing their intended tasks. In functional testing, developers verify that all preconditions defined for pages adhere to requirements defined in the requirement phase, and check whether the database transaction is returning correct data and saving the data correctly from the application into the database. For this testing, an automated testing suite consisting of Selenium and Cucumber was used. Selenium (Contributors, Wikipedia, 2017) is a portable software-testing framework for web applications. Selenium provides drivers for different browsers to load appropriate URLs and execute the test cases. Cucumber (Contributors W., *Cucumber software*, 2017) is a behavior-driven language in which test cases are written in human understandable language and the subsequent methods are developed to implement the test cases. These two tools form an automated testing suite for web application testing and were used to both define the conditions to be tested and the methods to be executed. They were chosen for testing because they are open source, can be used to test web applications on multiple browsers, and are easy to implement because all the test cases are written in human understandable language. Both tools were run on Junit (Louridas, 2005), a Java-based unit-testing framework. This testing framework used a scenario-based approach, in which all the statements can be defined in a feature file, imported into a main class file as methods, and implemented. When the test is run on Junit, it will execute every method and provide failure reports if there are any errors while using the application.

Security testing involves testing the application from the security point of view. The main goal of this test is to act like an attacker and test the application to find if the application can be successfully attacked. Misuse cases that were defined in the earlier stages are used to define the attack vector. These include injecting scripts into input fields and using sophisticated SQL scripts to perform SQL injection. The application developed in this chapter was tested to see if any attacks could compromise the application. For this purpose, predefined attacks were built and tested on this application to see if this application was secure enough. There are different types of attacks that can be applied on a web application. For this chapter, two most common types of attacks, SQL injection and XSS (described in Section 2.2), were tested on the application.

■ *SQL injection attack*: SQL injection is a sophisticated attack performed on web applications, concentrated mainly on their data sources. The scripts can be of any kind. They are not predefined and can be built differently by each attacker. One attacker can use these to validate him to enter into an application, and another attacker can try to alter or delete the data by using a predefined script to execute the delete query. For the purposes of this testing, a series of malicious scripts were created. These included attempts to authenticate the user with invalid credentials and a malicious script that was set to run on the input fields to alter the database. In this application, on the instructions page where the user enters a user ID to authenticate and proceed to use the application, the application validates the user and grants or denies access. Sample scripts were defined for testing purposes. 'N01' or '1 = 1', (select top 1 number from table name). Since the input validations are strictly enforced, these inputs are rejected or an alert popped up when to check the user input.

■ *Cross-Site Scripting (XSS)*: XSS injects malicious scripts into web-based applications with attacks ranging from petty nuisance to significant security risk. The attacker injects specially formatted custom logic implemented scripts into web applications, mainly into input fields from which they are stored internally and triggered later. The application developed in this chapter was tested to see if the input fields were accepting or rejecting any scripts that might be used to perform XSS. A test script was developed and injected into the input field where user uses the input field to authenticate for using the application.

14.7.11.2 Test Bed Preparation

Test bed preparation is used to set up the environment to implement the test planning phase. In this case, "environment" refers to the hardware setup, software and network environment in which the software will be used. For this chapter, all tests were conducted on the local machine running Windows 10 operating system. Eclipse IDE was used to load and test the source code. The application was debugged and tested with the inputs defined in the test planning phase.

14.7.11.3 Testing

All the environments and test scripts that were defined in test planning and test bed preparation phases were applied to test the application's functionality and completeness in this phase. Additionally, the application completeness and its functionalities are tested as per the requirements.

14.7.11.4 Application Release and Deployment

Release is the final phase in the application development process. Once the development process reaches the release phase, it is assumed that most of the security bugs have been identified and the application software is now stable and ready to deploy. This phase consists of two important activities before the application is deployed: security review and security audit. Since this application is small and not enterprise level, security review and audits were limited. The basic level of security review consisted of final checks for any remaining flaws with thorough checks to see if input validations are placed correctly, data is stored in the database in the right format, and the application is functioning correctly. These questions were reviewed in the audit session to see if all the requirements are implemented and working.

1. Is the user able to validate with a correct user ID?
2. Is the user able to see the web pages in a right order as defined in the requirements phase?
3. Is the data requested by the user coming from the database correct?
4. Is the data saved correctly into the database?

Finally, the application was deployed on a secured server to be used by the users and researchers over the Internet.

14.7.11.5 Application Maintenance

Application maintenance is used to monitor the functioning of the application while it is deployed. This is an important phase where support is provided for the application when any unusual events occur, such as application failure due to system shutdown and server access issues. The application developed in this chapter was deployed on the university server and is being maintained by an IT support team.

14.8 Results

This research aimed to develop a secure web application. For this, Microsoft SDL was chosen to implement security measures in the software development lifecycle to ensure that it was secure from common security vulnerabilities, in this case, SQL injection and XSS.

14.8.1 Application Developed

The application developed in this chapter is used by a research project called Diversity and Inclusion. The application helps the researchers gather information from the participants. The application is named "Survey Application" since it is similar to a survey in which information is gathered from the participants. But unlike other survey applications, this one is dynamic, that is, pages are rendered according to user choices. Here, "choices" means information displayed in the application, which is used by the participants to complete the survey.

This application consists of five user interface pages. First is the application landing page (Figure 14.16). This page consists of information about the research study on Diversity and Inclusion, including the purpose of the study, number of participants, duration of the study, procedures, risks and discomforts, benefits and compensation, alternatives, confidentiality, costs, right to decline or withdraw, research contact information, institutional review board information, and participant agreement.

After reading the information and indicating agreement, the participant is directed to the "instructions/authentication" page (Figure 14.16). This page contains instructions on how to proceed through the application and complete the survey. The participant then enters his/her UNF ID number to authenticate. If the participant gives invalid or incorrect authentication details, an "invalid authentication" alert is displayed and the user is redirected to the instruction page.

Once the participant is authenticated, he/she is directed to the "characteristics" page (Figure 14.17). This page lists 31 different characteristics such as age, gender, race, financial information, and personal information, and five characteristics are to be selected by the participant. More information regarding these characteristics is provided if the cursor is hovered over the characteristic.

Once the participant selects a maximum of five characteristics and clicks "next," he/she is redirected to the "select participants" page (Figure 14.18). All the information regarding characteristics

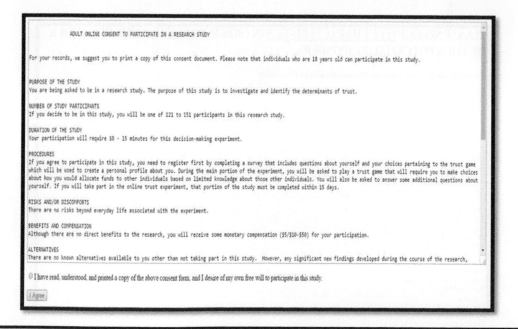

Figure 14.16 Landing page.

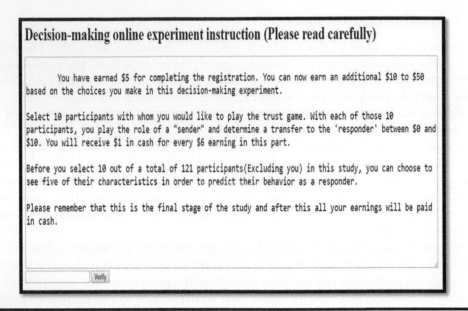

Decision-making online experiment instruction (Please read carefully)

You have earned $5 for completing the registration. You can now earn an additional $10 to $50 based on the choices you make in this decision-making experiment.

Select 10 participants with whom you would like to play the trust game. With each of those 10 participants, you play the role of a "sender" and determine a transfer to the 'responder' between $0 and $10. You will receive $1 in cash for every $6 earning in this part.

Before you select 10 out of a total of 121 participants(Excluding you) in this study, you can choose to see five of their characteristics in order to predict their behavior as a responder.

Please remember that this is the final stage of the study and after this all your earnings will be paid in cash.

Verify

Figure 14.17   Instruction/authentication page.

selected on the previous page is displayed for each person listed, with a "select" option for each person. On this page, there are a total of 121 people with the selected characteristic information displayed accordingly (Figure 14.19).

A participant can select a maximum of ten people. Then, the participant is directed to the "responder" page (Figure 14.20) once the "next" option is clicked. The responder page displays the people selected on the previous page along with their characteristics. Input fields are provided in

PLEASE SELECT FIVE CHARACTERISTICS IN ORDER TO PREDICT THE BEHAVIOUR OF YOUR POTENTIAL RESPONDERS.

For explaination, please hover on the checkbox next to the variable

☐ Age
☐ Gender
☐ Siblings
☐ Race
☐ State, Country, Continent
☐ University Enrollment
☐ College
☐ Major
☐ Source of Support
☐ Source of Self Income
☐ Household Income
☐ Dependents
☐ Moods
☐ Sensitive To
☐ Express Affection
☐ Feelings Hurt
☐ Confidence Level
☐ Mental Activity
☐ Thoughts
☐ Sleep
☐ Speech
☐ Voice
☐ Achieving Goals
☐ Donations
☐ Relationships

Figure 14.18   Characteristics page.

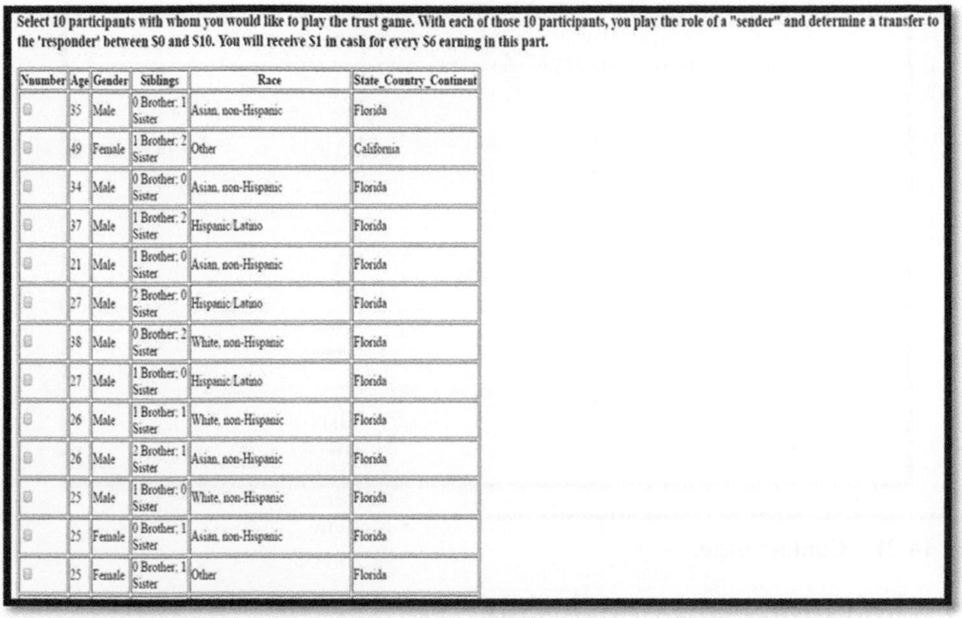

Nnumber	Age	Gender	Siblings	Race	State_Country_Continent
⊙	35	Male	0 Brother; 1 Sister	Asian, non-Hispanic	Florida
⊙	49	Female	1 Brother; 2 Sister	Other	California
⊙	34	Male	0 Brother; 0 Sister	Asian, non-Hispanic	Florida
⊙	37	Male	1 Brother; 2 Sister	Hispanic/Latino	Florida
⊙	21	Male	1 Brother; 0 Sister	Asian, non-Hispanic	Florida
⊙	27	Male	2 Brother; 0 Sister	Hispanic/Latino	Florida
⊙	38	Male	0 Brother; 2 Sister	White, non-Hispanic	Florida
⊙	27	Male	1 Brother; 0 Sister	Hispanic/Latino	Florida
⊙	26	Male	1 Brother; 1 Sister	White, non-Hispanic	Florida
⊙	26	Male	2 Brother; 1 Sister	Asian, non-Hispanic	Florida
⊙	25	Male	1 Brother; 0 Sister	White, non-Hispanic	Florida
⊙	25	Female	0 Brother; 1 Sister	Asian, non-Hispanic	Florida
⊙	25	Female	0 Brother; 1 Sister	Other	Florida

Select 10 participants with whom you would like to play the trust game. With each of those 10 participants, you play the role of a "sender" and determine a transfer to the 'responder' between $0 and $10. You will receive $1 in cash for every $6 earning in this part.

Figure 14.19   Select participants page.

which the participant enters a value between one and ten for each person. Once the participant enters the value in the input field and clicks "submit," the participant is directed to a final "contact" page (Figure 14.21) to receive instructions for collecting compensation.

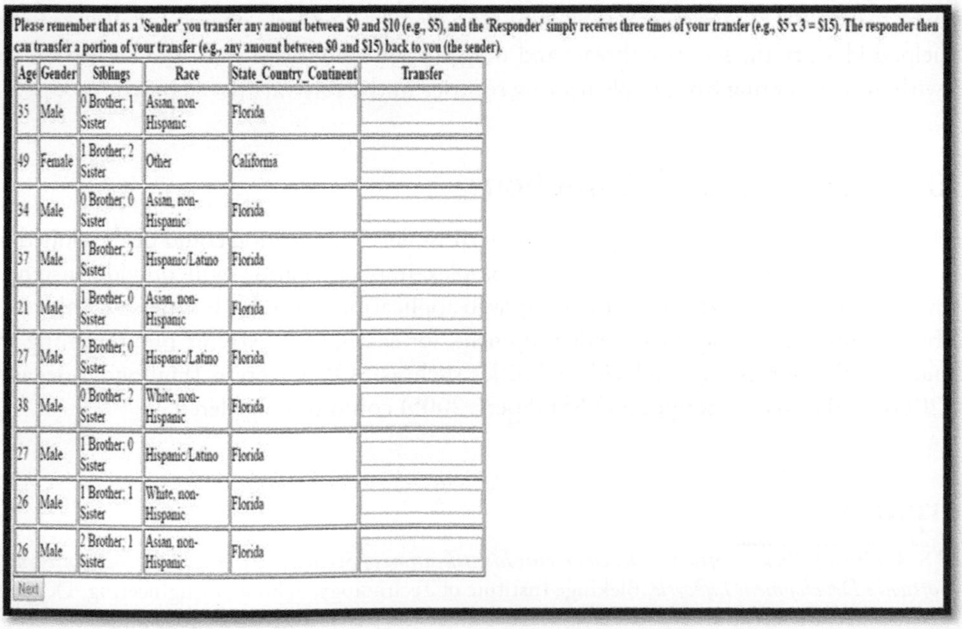

Please remember that as a 'Sender' you transfer any amount between $0 and $10 (e.g., $5), and the 'Responder' simply receives three times of your transfer (e.g., $5 x 3 = $15). The responder then can transfer a portion of your transfer (e.g., any amount between $0 and $15) back to you (the sender).

Age	Gender	Siblings	Race	State_Country_Continent	Transfer
35	Male	0 Brother; 1 Sister	Asian, non-Hispanic	Florida	
49	Female	1 Brother; 2 Sister	Other	California	
34	Male	0 Brother; 0 Sister	Asian, non-Hispanic	Florida	
37	Male	1 Brother; 2 Sister	Hispanic/Latino	Florida	
21	Male	1 Brother; 0 Sister	Asian, non-Hispanic	Florida	
27	Male	2 Brother; 0 Sister	Hispanic/Latino	Florida	
38	Male	0 Brother; 2 Sister	White, non-Hispanic	Florida	
27	Male	1 Brother; 0 Sister	Hispanic/Latino	Florida	
26	Male	1 Brother; 1 Sister	White, non-Hispanic	Florida	
26	Male	2 Brother; 1 Sister	Asian, non-Hispanic	Florida	

Next

Figure 14.20   Responder page.

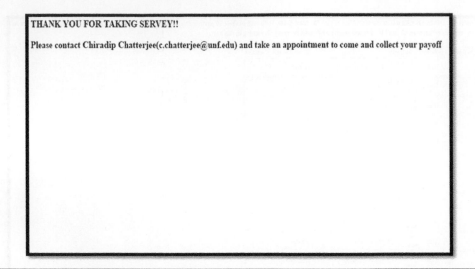

Figure 14.21   Contact page.

14.9 Limitations and Conclusion

In this chapter, security was implemented as a functional requirement in the software development lifecycle. The application developed in this chapter was not enterprise level, that is, it did not deal with multiple web services and applications interacting with each other. The attack vectors were also limited to those vulnerabilities that may occur in this application.

We narrowed our focus to secure software development (Ahmed, 2007), which more specifically implements security measures into each phase of software development, thus making sure that common security threats are mitigated during the development itself. This proved that considering security as functional requirement and incorporating right from early phases of software development helped identify the security threats and mitigate the amount of security threats that might occur without considering from implementing security in the software development process.

14.10 Future Research Directions

Extending this research, a more complex and enterprise-level application could be developed using secure software development. Such a more complex implementation will provide insight into implementation in organizations that develop web applications for their businesses. This research could be extended into agile software development, for example to extreme programming where continuous evaluation is key, and vulnerabilities such as SQL injection (Halfond, Viegas, and Orso, 2006) and cross-site scripting (XSS) (Spett, 2005) could be considered.

References

Ahmed S.R. (2007). *Secure Software Development: Identification of Security Activities and Their Integration in Software Development Lifecycle*, Blekinge Institute of Technology, School of Engineering, Department of Systems and Software Engineering. Retrieved from https://pdfs.semanticscholar.org/d0be/605180 eb14926e91003715cb3f535503aecb.pdf

Al-Ahmad W. (2011). Building Secure Software Using XP. *International Journal of Secure Software Engineering*, 63–76. Retrieved from https://dl.acm.org/citation.cfm?id=2441400

Contributors, Wikipedia (2017, February 22). *Cucumber (software)*. Retrieved from Wikipedia, The Free Encyclopedia: https://en.wikipedia.org/w/index.php?title=Cucumber_(software)&oldid=766926061

Contributors, Wikipedia (2017, March 28). *Selenium (software)*. Retrieved from Wikipedia, The Free Encyclopedia: https://en.wikipedia.org/w/index.php?title=Selenium_(software)&oldid=769282654

Cowan C. (2011). Buffer overflow attacks. StackGuard: Automatic Adaptive Detection and Prevention of Buffer-Overflow Attacks. Retrieved from https://www.usenix.org/legacy/publications/library/proceedings/sec98/full_papers/cowan/cowan.pdf

Crowe P. (2015, November 10). *Business Insider Inc.* Retrieved from Business Insider: www.businessinsider.com/jpmorgan-hacked-bank-breach-2015-11

Graham D. (2006, November 16). *US-CERT.* Retrieved from Department of Homeland Security: www.us-cert.gov/bsi/articles/best-practices/requirements-engineering/introduction-to-the-clasp-process

Halfond W.G., Viegas J., Orso A. (2006). A classification of SQL-injection attacks and countermeasures. *Proceedings of the IEEE International Symposium on Secure Software Engineering, IEEE*, vol. 1, pp. 13–15.

Howard M. (2010, November 4). *Security Development Lifecycle.* Retrieved 2016, from Microsoft Corporation: www.microsoft.com/en-us/download/confirmation.aspx?id=12379

Howard S., Lipner M. (2005, March). *Microsoft Corporation.* Retrieved from Microsoft Corporation website: https://msdn.microsoft.com/en-us/library/ms995349.aspx

Ionescu P. (2015, April 8). *Securityintelligence.* Retrieved from A. Security Intelligence Website: https://securityintelligence.com/the-10-most-common-application-attacks-in-action/

Jürjens J., Mouratidis H., Fox J. (2006). *Towards a Comprehensive Framework for Secure*, Berlin, pp. 48–62. Retrieved from https://pdfs.semanticscholar.org/a576/ab59380710e6ce9d817011edf9698c64ee1a.pdf

Kissel R., Stine K., Scholl M., Rossman H., Fahlsing J., Gulick J. (2008, October). *Security Considerations in the System Development Life Cycle.* Retrieved from National Institute of Standards and Technology: http://nvlpubs.nist.gov/nistpubs/Legacy/SP/nistspecialpublication800-64r2.pdf

Lipner S. (2004). The trustworthy computing security development lifecycle. *Computer Security Applications Conference, 2004. 20th Annual, IEEE*, pp. 2–13. Retrieved from https://dl.acm.org/citation.cfm?id=1038296

Louridas P. (2005). JUnit: unit testing and coiling in tandem. *IEEE Software*, 22, pp. 12–15. Retrieved from http://ieeexplore.ieee.org/stamp/stamp.jsp?tp=&arnumber=1463200&isnumber=31459

McDowell M. (2009, November 9). *United States Computer Emergency Readiness Team.* Retrieved 2016, from us-cert: www.us-cert.gov/ncas/tips/ST04-015

McGraw G. (2004). *Software Security.* Retrieved from Seven Touchpoints for Software Security: www.swsec.com/resources/touchpoints/

Microsoft Corporation (2012). *Microsoft Security Development Lifecycle (SDL) – Process Guidance.* Retrieved from Microsoft Corporation: https://msdn.microsoft.com/en-us/library/windows/desktop/84aed186-1d75-4366-8e61-8d258746bopq.aspx

Miller S., Appleby S., Garibaldi J.M., Aickelin U. (2013). Towards a More Systematic Approach to Secure Systems Design and Analysis. *International Journal of Secure Software Engineering*, 11–30. Retrieved from http://eprints.nottingham.ac.uk/3341/1/aickelin_article_IJSSE_4%281%29.pdf

Mouratidis H. (2006). Integrating Security and Software Engineering: Advances and Future Visions: Advances and Future Visions. IGI Global.

Phillips, T. (2002, January 1). *Microsoft Corporation.* Retrieved from https://technet.microsoft.com/en-us/library/bb457063.aspx

Pugh B., Hovemeyer D. (2016, October 5). *FindBugs*, 742697797. Retrieved 2017, from wikipedia: https://en.wikipedia.org/w/index.php?title=FindBugs&oldid=742697797

Siddharth S., Doshi P. (2006, April 27). *Symantic Corporation.* Retrieved from Symantic Corporation Website: www.symantec.com/connect/articles/five-common-web-application-vulnerabilities

Spett K. (2005). Cross-site scripting. *SPI Labs*, 1, 1–20.

Stubblebine S., Devanbu P. (2000). Software engineering for security: a roadmap. *ICSE '00 Proceedings of the Conference on The Future of Software Engineering*, Limerick, pp. 227–239.

Talukder A.K. (2009). Security-aware software development life cycle (SaSDLC)-processes and tools. *2009. WOCN'09. IFIP International Conference on Wireless and Optical Communications Networks, IEEE*: Cario, pp. 1–5.

Williams J. (2016, April 10). *SQL Injection*. Retrieved 2016, from owaps website: www.owasp.org/index. php/SQL_Injection

Chapter 15

Preserving Privacy for Trust-Based Unwanted Traffic Control with Homomorphic Encryption

Lifang Zhang, Zheng Yan, and Raimo Kantola

Aalto University

Contents

15.1 Introduction

Nowadays, we rely more and more on the Internet due to the great convenience it has brought to our daily life. As a result, the Internet is ubiquitous and has become an essential infrastructure of our society. However, the ubiquitous Internet has also made it much easier for spammers to spread unwanted traffic to a large number of Internet users. For example, it has been shown that the Internet, especially online social networks (OSNs), is overwhelmed with malicious content [1]. As reported in [2, 3], 21% of the surveyed teenage users of OSN web applications have encountered a harmful content and 6% of them has received malicious messages over the Internet. Unwanted traffic is undesired or harmful to its recipients because it is commonly used to spread unsolicited advertisements, malicious malware, or infectious virus. The undesirables of unwanted traffic over the Internet are further exacerbated by the following facts. First, it intrudes user devices and occupies the device memory. Second, unwanted traffic increases the burden of Internet Service Providers (ISPs) with extra useless traffic load, which also leads to a higher possibility of normal traffic congestion. Third, the recipients would be irritated and have to spend their precious time to filter out spams, install firewalls, scan virus and malware to detect intrusions, and clean up after infection. In other words, the unwanted Internet traffic consumes three most precious resources in the computational world, namely, storage space, bandwidth, and time, and thus must be controlled. Moreover, security has been recognized as one of the major issues in the emerging Internet-based technologies such as Internet of Things (IoTs) and Cloud Computing and their integration [4, 5]. As a result, research communities have been highly motivated to develop an efficient solution to prevent unwanted traffic over the Internet.

To reduce and control unwanted traffic over the Internet, technologies such as firewalls, Intrusion Detection System (IDS), and Intrusion Prevention System (IPS) have been widely used, achieving certain positive effects. However, for IDS/IPS to work effectively, extra administrative efforts are required in order to timely upgrade new intrusions. Thus, a variety of new approaches have been put forward in order to control the rapidly evolving attacks in the Internet, especially in Cloud Computing, IoT, and multimedia social networks [6–9]. A very promising approach among them is trust and reputation management [10]. As a result, literature has proposed many different variants of trust and reputation mechanisms to control different types of unwanted traffic, such as Email spam [11–16] and web page spam [17–24]. However, none of them preserve the privacy of unwanted traffic reporters, who are encouraged by these mechanisms to report their accusation against another Internet entity for spreading unwanted traffic. More specifically, the IDs of unwanted traffic reporters and the reporting content have not been protected from unauthorized access and modification, which has the following drawbacks:

- Without privacy protection, unwanted traffic reports can be disclosed to ISPs; thus, malicious hosts can easily collude with ISPs to block or modify legitimate and useful reports, degrading the performance in detecting unwanted traffic.
- The accusation may incur quarrels to unwanted traffic reporters with the accused entities, which is not in the interests of the reporter. As a result, users would be discouraged by the quarrels to report unwanted traffic, which also degrades the system performance.
- Current privacy laws do not allow ISPs to perform traffic monitoring and controlling without sufficient evidence. For example, the European privacy law allows an ISP (the same goes with any other parties) to monitor its traffic only when the ISP network itself is under attack or the attack is so severe that a part of the ISP network is under imminent threat. Specifically, it is illegal for the ISPs to provide their network monitoring reports (in plain text) to their customers unless they provide sufficient reasons to justify this action. Thus, the trust and reputation systems that ignored the privacy of unwanted traffic reporters cannot be legally deployed in practice.

Motivated by the serious threads of unwanted traffic over the Internet and the lack of privacy protection to the promising trust-based mechanisms, we propose in this chapter to integrate the privacy-preserving property to our previous Global Trust Management (GTM) system, which executes accurate, effective, and robust Unwanted Traffic Control (UTC) based on trust evaluation and management [10, 25, 26]. More specifically, we protect the privacy of unwanted traffic reporters by encrypting their reports with the homomorphic public key of Global Trust Operator (GTO). Homomorphic Encryption (HE) is applied herein because it enables ISPs to aggregate the encrypted reports without decryption. In this way, ISPs cannot access or modify unwanted traffic reports, thus guaranteeing the privacy of reporters. Moreover, GTO decrypts the unwanted traffic reports, and based on these decrypted reports, GTO evaluates the global trust of the accused entity in order to decide if it is really an unwanted traffic source. If the reports were consistent with the decision, GTO would increase the detection trust of their reporters, and vice versa. In this way, our system encourages honest reports and penalizes indifferent and dishonest reports. In addition, our proposed system discloses only anonymous reporter ID to GTO. As a result, even though GTO knows the report content, it has no idea who is accusing whom, and thus further protecting the privacy of unwanted traffic reporters. Once the unwanted traffic source has been detected, ISPs perform unwanted traffic control accordingly. To conclude, our proposed system can control unwanted traffic and meanwhile protect the privacy of unwanted traffic reporters, thus fulfilling current privacy laws.

15.2 Related Work Overview

15.2.1 UTC via Trust and Reputation Mechanisms

Recent years have witnessed an increasing number of advanced techniques in improving network security, such as Internet traffic classification with machine learning [27, 28] and UTC via trust and reputation [10, 25, 26]. Among them, controlling unwanted traffic via trust and reputation has attracted extensive research interest recently due to its effectiveness. For example, a number of trust-based solutions have been proposed to reduce different types of unwanted traffic, e.g., email spam [11–16] and web page spam [17–24].

15.2.1.1 Solutions for Email Spam

Email spam has been the focus of security research for a very long time. Moreover, it is capricious due to the fact that spammers are adopting increasingly sophisticated methods and applying new strategies [29]. Thus, most current trust- and reputation-based UTC solutions target email spam. For example, a reactive spam-filtering system based on reporter reputation was proposed in [11]. It introduces a trust-maintenance component to record the spam-reporting behaviors and filters spam according to the feedback from trustworthy users. In order to help email receivers to eliminate their unwitting trust and provide them with accountability support, a layered trust management framework was proposed in [12]. MailTrust was proposed in [13] to compute the trust of a mail server based on its credibility. The system then filtered out emails sent from mail servers with low trust. SocialFilter decided if a host is a spammer or not by weighting spam reports according to the trustworthiness of report senders accessed from OSNs [14]. LENS, a novel spam protection system based on a recipient's social network, was proposed to mitigate email spam with the social networks of email recipients and the assumption that all friends or friends-of-friends are trustable [15]. Moreover, in order to avoid incorrect filtering of legitimate emails sent from outside the social circles of email recipient, LENS further introduced trusted nodes to vouch for these non-malicious senders. Thus, only emails from the social networks of email recipients or emails vouched by the trusted nodes can be transmitted into the network. A personalized email spam cleaner named "Soap" was developed by integrating adaptive trust management, social interest, and social closeness spam-filtering approaches into a basic Bayesian filter [16].

The above work evaluates trust by collecting reports or feedback for the purpose of UTC. However, none of them handle privacy intrusion problem during the process of evidence collection. As a result, they cannot resist attacks caused by the collusion between ISPs and hosts, e.g., ISPs could illegally modify the negative feedback associated with the hosts that collude with them.

15.2.1.2 Solutions for Web Page Spam

Web spam refers to the immoral manipulation of search engine results that intentionally mislead search engines to rank certain web pages higher than they deserve. Since the web spam causes great nuisance to the Internet users by degrading searching quality, it has been identified as one of the top challenges faced by search engine providers. Thus, research community has made great efforts to develop effective countermeasures for combating the web spam.

The web spam can be classified into link spam, content-based spam, and spam that utilizes hiding techniques. Link spam boosts the ranking of a target web page by making use of a link-based ranking algorithm, such as PageRank [17]. For example, link spammers can fool PageRank to rank a spam page without useful information higher than it should be by creating a considerable number of extraneous and misleading links pointing to them. Normally, the link spam is very difficult to catch, thus deserving special attention. Many trust-based techniques have demonstrated their effectiveness in combating the link spam, thus representing the most promising countermeasures. TrustRank was the first trust mechanism to combat the link spam based on the fact that reputable websites seldom point to spam websites [18]. In TrustRank, a certain number of good seeds are first selected, and their trust values are then propagated through their links to the entire web recursively. However, TrustRank is biased to popular topics. To overcome this bias, Topical TrustRank was proposed to partition a seed set according to topical information and calculate trust scores for each seed set separately [19]. Instead of selecting a seed set of trusted pages, Anti-TrustRank proposed to propagate distrust from a set of known spam pages along incoming links [20]. However, propagating just trust of a good page excludes the advantages of propagating distrust of a spam page. In order to address this issue, LCRank linearly combines TrustRank and Anti-TrustRank, gaining better performance in combating web spam [21]. However, such simple linear combination of trust and distrust can only gain limited improvement since the trust and distrust are propagated separately. Good-Bad Rank (GBR) algorithm was proposed to overcome this limitation by propagating trust and distrust simultaneously and taking into consideration the probability of a source being trusted or distrusted [22]. However, the GBR algorithm suffers from a nontarget differential problem that a source blindly propagates the same amount of trust and distrust to both a spam page and a good page. Zhang et al. addressed the nontarget differential issue by penalizing the propagation of trust and distrust to a spam page, improving the web spam detecting effectiveness [23]. Trust mechanism can also be applied to combat content-based spamming. For example, Wang et al. proposed to construct a trust model based on the actual content of a web page to detect spam information [24].

However, the above solutions about controlling email spam and web page spam cannot preserve the privacy of network entities and resist attacks caused by the modification of feedback or reports. Moreover, they cannot comply with the legal requirements about privacy for telecommunications. Privacy preservation and the trustworthiness of system entities have not been seriously studied. Literature still lacks a trustworthy solution, which is efficient, accurate, and robust to control unwanted traffic with privacy preservation.

15.2.2 Privacy-Preserving Solutions and Their Pros and Cons

A good privacy-preserving solution should be able to protect personally identifiable information and ensure data secrecy, anonymity, and unlinkability in a certain degree. Privacy concerns thwart various new technologies such as IoT and data mining from being adopted, thus inviting vigorous research from both academia and industry. As a result, many privacy-preserving solutions have been proposed in the literature, including general and advanced cryptographic approaches. General solutions consist of random data perturbation, k-anonymity, and traditional standard encryption schemes. This group of techniques has been regarded as the basic and naive methods in protecting privacy. Meanwhile, the advanced cryptographic approaches include HE, group signatures, and attribute-based signatures.

As mentioned before, the privacy-preserving system we are designing needs to hide the report content from ISPs and the identity of an unwanted traffic reporter from GTO. Thus, we need to investigate both data secrecy and anonymity.

15.2.2.1 Data Secrecy

Random data perturbation technique hides sensitive data by adding random noise to the original sensitive data. This method is often applied to preserve privacy in data-collecting systems where many distributed data providers send their data to a centralized data center for analyzing and mining. However, random data distortion has been demonstrated to have little use from the perspective of privacy preserving [30].

Encryption technique has often been used to ensure the secrecy of different types of digital data, such as digital images in the cloud storage system [31, 32]. Even though an increasing number of new encryption algorithms (e.g., high-throughput encryption [33]) have been proposed in recent years, classic encryption schemes such as Advanced Encryption Scheme (AES) have still been playing the major role in protecting sensitive data because they are more mature. However, one inherent limitation of the classic encryption is that an information system working with encrypted data can at most store and retrieve the data. The limitation arises because such classic encryption schemes disable computations on encrypted data. In these schemes, decryption is needed before performing any computation on encrypted data, and without decryption, even a simple statistical analysis becomes impossible. Therefore, this approach is inapplicable for applications that require aggregation or computation on the sensitive data.

Homomorphic encryption enables meaningful computations on encrypted data without decrypting it. The fact that encrypted data can be processed without decryption by untrusted third parties or service providers ensures data privacy in applications that require data computation such as our system. Thus, our system applies homomorphic encryption to preserve the privacy of unwanted traffic reporters. Therefore, homomorphic encryption deserves further discussion, which will be presented in Section 15.4.

15.2.2.2 Anonymity

k-Anonymity prevents an identity from being disclosed by ensuring that each released record is indistinguishable from at least $k - 1$ other records regarding certain identifying attributes. k-Anonymity has gained popularity in the field of data-publishing applications where the anonymity of an individual data owner must be assured. However, this approach has some problems. For example, when sensitive attributes vary a little, an attacker can discover their values. Moreover, k-anonymity cannot protect privacy against attacks utilizing background information that is often known to the attackers. Because of this, l-diversity was proposed to preserve privacy beyond k-anonymity [34]. However, neither k-anonymity nor l-diversity offers protection against attribute disclosure.

A digital signature scheme ensures the authenticity of a digital message by providing a recipient sufficient reason to believe that the message was created by the claimed sender. Moreover, digital signatures can provide both non-repudiation and integrity. Non-repudiation herein means that the signer of a message cannot successfully deny the fact that he has signed the message. Integrity guarantees that a message was not modified during transmission and thus is useful in systems that involve nonsecure transmission channels. Classic digital signatures are realized by asymmetric cryptography such as Rivest–Shamir–Adleman (RSA). In such classic digital signatures, a signature is linkable and traceable to the identity of its signing user since a signature is usually combined with the identity of its owner. Group signature decouples the identity of a signing user from a verification procedure, thus ensuring unlinkability and providing better privacy protection. Group signature realizes such unlinkability by allowing a group member to anonymously sign a message on behalf of the group without involving the identity of the group member. The group member utilizes a group secret member key to produce a signature that can be verified using the public key of the group. Group signature can be applied in such applications where both the privacy and the anonymity of a sender are required. However, group signature is inefficient and produces a large signature and generates a longer key than classic signature schemes such as RSA. Because of this, group signature is not used as commonly as RSA.

On the other hand, attribute-based signature decouples a signature from the identity of its owner by allowing its owner to generate a signature using their attributes. In this way, a user can remain anonymous and is indistinguishable from all other users. Moreover, a user cannot forge a signature with attributes he does not possess. Attribute-based signatures are usually applied in such an authentication system where users are required to prove the possession of some attributes. However, attribute-based signature involves expensive operations and creates long signatures. In addition, it takes more time to provide user attributes than to compute the common cryptographic primitives such as RSA digital signature [35].

According to the above discussion, RSA is more suitable for our system to provide anonymity, authentication, non-repudiation, and integrity.

15.3 Problem Statement and Design Goal

15.3.1 System and Security Model

The proposed system contains three types of entities, as shown in Figure 15.1.

Host: A networking host subscribes to a local ISP and detects unwanted traffic by monitoring its inbound and/or outbound traffic, tracking host behaviors toward its received messages, checking message similarity, and reporting its local unwanted traffic detection results to its ISP in an encrypted form in order to protect the report from the ISP.

ISP: ISP cooperates with GTO to conduct UTC by collecting encrypted detection reports from its local hosts, monitoring the outbound traffic of suspicious local hosts if authorized by GTO, and taking some administrative action to control/filter the traffic from malicious hosts or impose penalties on malicious sources.

GTO: GTO collects evidence from ISPs based on which GTO evaluates the global trust (that indicates the possibility of an unwanted traffic source) and the detection trust (that specifies the quality of the unwanted traffic detection) of each entity. It also generates a gray list, sends it to all ISPs, and recommends control strategies to ISPs based on detection reports.

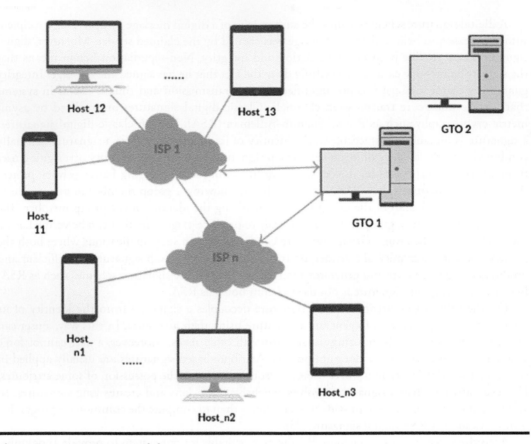

Figure 15.1 A system model.

15.3.2 Trust Relationship between Different Types of System Entities

Trust relationships between different types of system entities are described below.

Hosts could be malicious or benign. They could report unwanted traffic dishonestly. Secure and dependable communication channels are applied (e.g., using SSL) in the system for unwanted traffic reporting and controlling.

ISPs are curious for collecting the intrusion information and preference (like or dislike) of their hosts. They may disclose this private information to a third malicious party to gain extra profits. More importantly, due to Communications Privacy Regulation, ISPs and customer networks are disallowed to freely monitor traffic to find malicious contents if there is no sufficient evidence to support this action. Therefore, host reports should be protected. ISPs should support privacy-preserving reporting and report aggregating. Traffic monitoring is performed according to the instruction of GTO with sufficient evidence support. However, due to business incentives, ISPs try to offer sound networking services, e.g., providing qualified network access services, ensuring bandwidth, acting on intrusion attacks, and controlling/filtering unwanted traffic if needed.

GTOs are fully trusted to perform trust evaluation and management based on collected data (i.e., detection and monitoring reports from hosts and ISPs). GTO behaves as an authorized party to collect trust evidence and conduct trust evaluation on different system entities honestly due to business incentive and possible regulation to offer this service. Multiple GTOs could exist in the system, each supporting their own alliance of ISPs. The GTOs can collaborate together to exchange trust information and instruct UTC by applying a trusted collaboration protocol. Each GTO processing result can be shared with other GTOs through secure transmission channels. GTOs do not collude with any ISPs. Herein, we treat all GTOs as one authorized party and simplify them as one GTO in our presentation.

15.3.3 Design Goal

Due to the curiousness of an ISP, its potential cooperation with some malicious attackers and Communications Privacy Regulation, the content of host reports should not be disclosed to the local ISP. Since GTO is only trusted for trust evaluation, it should not know the real identity of each system entity being evaluated. For the purpose of security and privacy, the content of traffic and the real ID of each system entity should not be disclosed to GTO, either.

Based on the above problem description and design expectation, ISP should have no way to know the real content of any detection report sent by a host. It should be able to perform correlation and aggregation without knowing the plaintext of any report. GTO knows the aggregation results of reports, but it is better to hide the sources of the reports from it for the sake of security and privacy. This approach supports the confidentiality of the subscription relation of the ISP and its customer. The aim is to achieve privacy-preserving reporting and aggregating at ISP and preserve identity privacy at GTO. Traffic monitoring at ISP should be performed only when the judgment on the possibility of intrusion is positive with the authorization of GTO. Traffic is controlled by ISPs according to the instruction issued by GTO only when sufficient evidence is available.

15.4 Preliminaries in HE

As mentioned in Section 15.2.2.1, for our system, HE is a more desirable technique to ensure the secrecy of the host detection reports and achieve privacy-preserving report aggregating at ISPs. Thus, we present herein some preliminary knowledge about HE for the purpose of motivating the selection of a suitable HE scheme for our system.

15.4.1 Basic Knowledge about HE

15.4.1.1 Encryption Basics

In cryptography, an encryption scheme encrypts a message that a sender wishes to transmit to a receiver, referred to as plaintext, to a ciphertext that can only be read if decrypted. We can classify the encryption systems as symmetric and asymmetric according to the identicalness of their encryption key and decryption key. In symmetric encryption, a decryption key is the same as its corresponding encryption key. Thus, a key must be agreed among the communicating parties before exchanging any message. Therefore, it is impossible for two people who have never met to directly use such a scheme. In contrast, asymmetric encryption, also known as public-key encryption, uses two different keys for encryption and decryption. Although different, the two keys are mathematically linked. The encryption key is made public, whereas the decryption key remains private. Such a scheme is more functional than a symmetric one since there is no need for the sender and the receiver to agree on anything before communications. However, public-key encryption schemes are much slower than the symmetric ones. For example, AES, a widely used symmetric scheme, is typically 100 times faster than RSA encryption, which is one of the most prominent public-key cryptosystems, and 200 times faster than RSA decryption [36].

15.4.1.2 Security Notions of Encryption Schemes

We define a cryptosystem here as a tuple consisting of message space, ciphertext space, a key space, encryption and decryption functions. A cryptosystem is computationally secure if it is secure due to the computation cost of cryptanalysis, but would succumb to an attack with unlimited computation capacity. In contrast, a cryptosystem is unconditionally secure if it can resist any cryptanalytic attacks, no matter how strong computation capacity an opponent may possess. The one time pad that combines a plaintext with a randomly chosen key of the same length is the only unconditionally secure cryptosystem in common use. Although such a cryptosystem is provably secure, it is impractical due to the requirement on key size. No other cryptosystems have been proven unconditionally secure. Therefore, the security of any encryption scheme is evaluated based on the computing power of an opponent if one time pad is omitted. To assess the adequacy of a cryptographic system, the first step is to classify the threats to which it is to be subjected. The following threats are some that may apply to a cryptosystem and distinguished according to the capacity of an attacker [37].

A chosen-plaintext attack (CPA) is an attack model where an attacker can choose an unlimited number of plaintexts and obtain corresponding ciphertexts.

Nonadaptive chosen-ciphertext attack (CCA1) is an attack model where an attacker has access to a decryption oracle that takes a ciphertext as input and outputs its corresponding plaintext. However, the opponent can only access the decryption oracle before a challenging ciphertext is given. The feature of nonadaptive comes from the fact that queries to the decryption oracle cannot depend on the challenging ciphertext.

Adaptive chosen-ciphertext attack (CCA2) is an attack model where an attacker again can access a decryption oracle, but this time she can use the decryption oracle even after the challenging ciphertext is given, as long as the attacker does not ask for the decryption of the challenging ciphertext.

We consider two different goals of the cryptosystem here: indistinguishability (IND) and nonmalleability (NM). IND describes the inability of an adversary to learn any information about plaintext underlying a challenge ciphertext. NM describes the inability of an adversary to output a ciphertext y', given a challenge ciphertext y, such that the corresponding plaintexts x and x' are meaningfully related (e.g., $x' = 2x$).

Naor suggested a convenient way to organize the definitions of secure encryption: consider various possible goals and various possible attack models separately, and then obtain each definition as a pairing of a particular goal and a particular attack model. The two goals and the three attack models can be mixed and matched in any combination, giving rise to six security notions [38]. For example, notion IND-CPA means indistinguishability under a chosen plaintext attack. From the weakest to the strongest, we have IND-CPA, IND-CCA1, IND-CCA2, NM-CPA, NM-CCA1, and NM-CCA2. Thus, the strongest security level for an encryption scheme is IND-CCA2, which in particular implies NM.

15.4.1.3 Definition of HE

A formal definition of homomorphic encryption is as follows. Let M and C denote the plaintext and ciphertext set, respectively. We define a probabilistic encryption scheme, which encrypts the same plaintext into many different ciphertexts while keeping the plaintext decodable, to be homomorphic if the encryption function ε satisfies Formula (15.1) for any given encryption key k and some mathematical operators $\odot_M$ in M and $\odot_C$ in C:

$$\forall m_1, m_2 \in M, \varepsilon(m_1 \odot_M m_2) \leftarrow \varepsilon(m_1) \odot_C \varepsilon(m_2) \tag{15.1}$$

In Formula (15.1), $\leftarrow$ denotes "can be directly computed from without any intermediate decryption." For example, we say an encryption scheme is additively homomorphic if we consider $\odot_M$ as an addition operator $\oplus_M$, that is,

$$\forall m_1, m_2 \in M, \varepsilon(m_1 \oplus_M m_2) \leftarrow \varepsilon(m_1) \odot_C \varepsilon(m_2) \tag{15.2}$$

Similarly, a scheme is said to be multiplicatively homomorphic if $\odot_M$ is a multiplication operator $\otimes_M$ [36].

The homomorphic encryption schemes that support either addition or multiplication on plaintext are called partially homomorphic encryption (PHE). In contrast, an encryption scheme is called a fully homomorphic encryption (FHE) if it allows $\odot_M$ to be any arithmetic operator including both addition and multiplication. Many PHE schemes have been published and widely applied in many applications. However, the usage of FHE schemes is limited due to low efficiency, even though many FHE schemes have been constructed recently in the literature.

Most of the HE schemes are asymmetric, which means they are much slower than the symmetric encryption schemes. Note also that a homomorphic cryptosystem cannot achieve NM. Since under a homomorphic cryptosystem, a ciphertext y' can be computed from a given ciphertext y and decrypted to x' which is meaningfully related to the plaintext of y, violating the definition of NM. Thus, an HE scheme cannot reach IND-CCA. IND-CPA is the highest security level it can achieve [36].

15.4.1.4 Criteria to Evaluate HE Schemes

To evaluate an HE scheme, it is necessary to study its efficiency and security as both of them are essential in practice.

When it comes to efficiency, we observe the length of keys and ciphertext encrypted from a single bit. The length of a ciphertext can be expressed by message expansion, which is defined as the ratio of the length in bits of ciphertext to that of plaintext. The message expansion should not be too large since large message expansion will create heavy communication overhead and considerable storage consumption. In addition, we consider the time it takes in encrypting and decrypting a message and the time it takes to perform homomorphic operations on ciphertexts. These times are especially important in highly constrained devices such as personal digital assistants, mobile devices, smart cards, and radio frequency identification tags. Moreover, they are highly important when an HE scheme is utilized to process a huge amount of data, since in this situation slow operations (e.g., encryption, decryption, and homomorphic computation) will incur intolerable processing time. Normally, a computationally complex algorithm involves more time-consuming computations (e.g., modular exponentiation). Thus, we should evaluate these times according to the computation complexity of their corresponding algorithms.

The security of any encryption scheme is crucial since it describes how well an encryption scheme can keep our data confidential and private. Usually, an encryption scheme with higher security level can secure our data in a better way. The security of HE schemes can be evaluated by their mathematical structure since most of them belong to public-key encryption that is based on well-defined mathematical problems.

The range of homomorphic operations ($\odot_M$) supported by an HE scheme affects the possible range of application scenarios. For example, an FHE scheme that allows $\odot_M$ to be any arithmetic operator can better support sophisticated algorithms. Therefore, an FHE scheme can be used in many application scenarios where there is a need to perform complex computations on encrypted data. In contrast, PHE schemes can only be used to calculate a limited number of simple algorithms such as sum and average, confining its application scenarios.

Therefore, a desirable HE scheme should be able to support complicated algorithms while at the same time provide high efficiency and security. Thus, we suggest evaluating an HE scheme from the perspective of the following six parameters:

- *Message expansion (ME)*: the ratio of the length in bits of ciphertext to that of plaintext,
- *Security*: it can be evaluated according to the security notions defined in Section 15.4.1.2 such as IND-CPA,
- *Encryption computation complexity (ECC)*: the computation complexity of the encryption algorithm,
- *Decryption computation complexity (DCC)*: the computation complexity of the decryption algorithm,
- *Homomorphic operation computation complexity (HCC)*: the computation complexity of the homomorphic operation algorithm,
- *Supported homomorphic operations (SHO)*: the arithmetic operations on a plaintext set supported by the cryptosystem.

15.4.2 The State of the Art of PHE Schemes

In this section, we study the state of the art of PHE schemes according to the criteria described above. However, this section does not introduce their underlying mathematical theories. Instead, we discuss their advantages and disadvantages from the perspective of practical usage.

15.4.2.1 RSA Cryptosystem

Detailed RSA algorithms are as follows.

RSASetup: The algorithm randomly selects two large prime numbers p and q with equal length in bits. It first computes $n = q \times p$ and picks a large random integer d such that d is relatively prime to $(p-1) \times (q-1)$. The algorithm then computes e such that $ed = 1 \mod(p-1) \times (p-1)$. Then, it outputs public key RSA_PK = (e,n) and secret key RSA_SK = (d,n).

RSAEncrypt: Take as input $m \in \mathbb{Z}_n$ and RSA_PK, the algorithm outputs $c = E(m) = m^e \mod n$ where $c \in \mathbb{Z}_n$.

RSADecrypt: Take as input $c \in \mathbb{Z}_n$ and RSA_SK, the algorithm outputs $m = D(c) = c^d \mod n$, where $m \in \mathbb{Z}_n$ [40].

RSAMul: Take as input $c_1 \in \mathbb{Z}_n$ and $c_2 \in \mathbb{Z}_n$ and RSA_PK, the algorithm outputs $E(m_1) \times E(m_2) = c_1 \times c_2 = (m_1 \times m_2)^e \mod n = E(m_1 \times m_2)$.

As shown in algorithm *RSAEncrypt*, the ME of RSA cryptosystem is 1. Both RSA encryption and decryption algorithms require only 1 modular exponentiation. Thus, RSA cryptosystem is efficient. However, it only supports homomorphic multiplication. What is worse, it is not IND-CPA secure unless a message is randomly padded, but the padding variant loses the property of multiplicative homomorphism. Because of this, RSA cryptosystem is seldom used, although it has a multiplicative homomorphic property.

15.4.2.2 ElGamal Cryptosystem

ElGamal cryptosystem works as follows.

ElGSetup: The algorithm first selects p such that $p - 1$ has at least one large prime factor. It then chooses a generator $g \in Z_p$ and a number s uniformly from Z_p, and then computes $h = g^s$. The algorithm outputs public key $ElG\_PK = (h, g, p)$ and secret key $ElG\_SK = s$.

ElGEncrypt: Take as input $m \in Z_p$ and Elg_PK, the algorithm computes $c_1 = g^a \bmod p$ and $c_2 = h^a m \bmod p$ where a is randomly selected from Z_p. It outputs $c = E(m) = \{c_1, c_2\}$ where $c_1 \in Z_p$, $c_2 \in Z_p$.

ElGDecrypt: Take as input $c \in Z_p$ and ElG_SK, it outputs $m = D(c) = c_2 / c_1^s \bmod p$ where $m \in Z_p$ [41].

ElGMul: Take as input $c_1 \in Z_p$, $c_2 \in Z_p$, and ElG_SK, the algorithm outputs $c_1 \times c_2 = \left\{ g^{a_1 a_2}, g^s g^{a_1 a_2} m_1 m_2 \right\} = E(m_1 \times m_2)$.

The ME of ElGamal cryptosystem is 2, as the size of ElGamal ciphertext is double the size of its corresponding plaintext. ElGamal encryption algorithm ElGEncrypt needs two modular exponentiations and one modular multiplication, and its decryption algorithm ElGDecrypt requires one modular exponentiation and one modular multiplication. Therefore, the ElGamal cryptosystem is not as efficient as RSA. It also only supports homomorphic multiplication. On the other hand, the ElGamal cryptosystem offers a security level of IND-CPA, which is the highest security level an HE scheme can reach. In addition, it works for any family of groups for which the discrete logarithm problem is considered intractable. Therefore, ElGamal is a promising candidate for practical HE schemes. Normally, homomorphic addition is more useful than homomorphic multiplication in practical applications. Thus, Cramer et al. [42] proposed an additively homomorphic variant of ElGamal, but this variant suffers from inefficiency when decrypting big data. Moreover, the variant does not preserve the multiplicatively homomorphic property of the original ElGamal cryptosystem.

15.4.2.3 Paillier Cryptosystem

Paillier cryptosystem is constructed by following algorithms.

PailSetup: The algorithm randomly chooses two large primes p and q with equal lengths (in bits). It calculates $n = pq$ and selects a random integer $g \left(g \in \mathbb{Z}_{n^2}^* \right)$ such that n divides its order, namely n divides the smallest positive integer o satisfying $g^o = e$, where e is a unique identity element of group $\mathbb{Z}_{n^2}^*$. Next, it computes λ according to equation $\lambda = lcm(p - 1, q - 1)$, where function lcm calculates the least common multiple of $p - 1$ and $q - 1$. Then it outputs homomorphic public key $HE\_PK = (n, g)$ and homomorphic private key $HE\_SK = \lambda$.

PailEncrypt: Take as input $m \in \mathbb{Z}_n$ and HE_PK, the algorithm returns ciphertext $c = E(m) = g^m \times r^n \bmod n^2$, where $c \in \mathbb{Z}_{n^2}$ and r is randomly selected from $\mathbb{Z}_n^*$.

PailDecrypt: Take as input $c \in \mathbb{Z}_{n^2}$, HE_PK, and HE_SK, the algorithm returns plaintext $m \in \mathbb{Z}_n$ according to $m = \dfrac{L\left(c^\lambda \bmod n^2 \right)}{L\left(g^\lambda \bmod n^2 \right)} \bmod n$, where $L(u) = (u - 1)/n; \forall_u \in \left\{ u \left\langle n^2 \right| u = 1 \bmod n \right\}$ [43].

PailMul: Take as input $c_1 \in \mathbb{Z}_{n^2}$, $c_2 \in \mathbb{Z}_{n^2}$, and HE_PK, the algorithm outputs $c_1 \times c_2 \bmod n^2 = g^{m_1 + m_2} \times r_1 r_2^n \bmod n^2 = E(m_1 + m_2)$.

PailExp: Take as input $c \in \mathbb{Z}_{n^2}$, constant k and HE_PK, the algorithm outputs $c^k \bmod n^2 = g^{km} \times r^{kn} \bmod n^2 = E(km)$.

As shown in algorithm *PailEncrypt*, the ME of Paillier cryptosystem is 2. Paillier encryption algorithm *PailEncrypt* needs two modular exponentiations, one of which is based on g; its computation cost is not too high by judicious choice of *g* and applying computing constant parameters in advance. Paillier decryption algorithm *PailDecrypt*, requiring two exponentiation modulo n^2 to power λ and a low-cost multiplication modulo n, may also be achieved efficiently through Chinese Remainder Theorem and constant parameter pre-computation [43]. In addition, Paillier cryptosystem supports homomorphic addition (shown in *PailMul*) and homomorphic constant multiplication (shown in *PailExp*), which suffice to a number of practical applications (e.g., secure electronic voting and Private Information Retrieval). Moreover, Paillier encryption scheme can reach IND-CPA, the highest security level for HE schemes. Because of this, Paillier cryptosystem is one of the most widely known and used HE schemes.

Table 15.1 summarizes the analysis of the above PHE schemes.

15.4.3 *The State of the Art of FHE Schemes*

As mentioned before, an FHE scheme enables arbitrary computation to be performed on encrypted data. FHE has been regarded as the holy grail of cryptography for a long time. However, it was not until 2009 that an FHE scheme was construable, thanks to the breakthrough work of Gentry [44]. Gentry proposed the first FHE scheme with a blueprint to construct such a system. Even though Gentry's first proposal based on lattice was rather theoretical than implementable, this blueprint has been instantiated with a number of cryptographic assumptions, yielding progressively simpler and more efficient schemes. In this section, we first describe the ideas and methods behind Gentry's blueprint and its open issues. We then present current three main families of FHE schemes (i.e., FHE based on ideal lattices, FHE over the integers, and FHE based on learning with errors) and discuss the practical developments of FHE. Moreover, in order to better compare the efficiencies of different FHE schemes, we summarize their performance in Table 15.2.

15.4.3.1 *Gentry's Blueprint and Its Open Issues*

Gentry's construction consists of three main building blocks, starting with the construction of a somewhat homomorphic encryption (SWHE) scheme. A SWHE scheme is one that can homomorphically evaluate "low-degree" polynomials. More specifically, SWHE schemes allow only a limited number of homomorphic computations (e.g., many additions and a small number of multiplications) on ciphertexts. In all the proposed FHE schemes, encryption is a process of adding

Table 15.1 The Comparison of Different PHE Schemes

PHE Scheme	ME	Security	ECC	DCC	SHO	HCC
RSA	1	Not IND-CPA	1 ModExp	1 ModExp	Mul	1 ModMul
ElGamal	2	IND-CPA	2 ModExp + 1 ModMul	1 ModExp + 1 ModMul	Mul	1 ModMul
Paillier	2	IND-CPA	2 ModExp + 1 ModMul	2 ModExp + 1 ModMul	Add	1 ModMul
					CMul	1 ModeExp

ModExp, modular exponentiation; *Mul*, multiplicative; *CMul*, constant multiplicative; *ModMul*, modular multiplication; *Add*, additive.

Table 15.2 The Performance Comparison of Different FHE Schemes

Scheme Implementation	Encryption	Decryption	KeyGen	PK Size
Paillier (1024 b) [43]	20 ms	45 ms	—	—
Gentry–Halevi [49]	3 min	—	2.2 h	2.3 GB
Coron [50]	2 min 57 s	0.05 s	43 min	802 MB

KeyGen, key generation; *PK*, public key.

noise to plaintexts, thus resulting ciphertexts to carry a certain amount of built-in noise. This noise would increase in the process of any homomorphic computation, and when it becomes too large, correct decryption is impossible even with the right decryption key. Thus, the purpose of limiting the number of homomorphic operations on ciphertexts in SWHE schemes is to avoid decryption failure resulting from the noise growing too much. To overcome such limitations on the number of homomorphic operations and realize FHE, Gentry's construction proceeds to refresh ciphertexts constantly to reduce noise. Such a process is very costly and called bootstrapping. The final step is to squash the SWHE decryption circuit. Squashing aims to simplify the decryption circuit of a SWHE scheme so as to allow bootstrapping while keeping the homomorphic capacity of the scheme at the same time. Following this framework, several other works [45–47] construct FHE schemes by building various SWHE schemes. To construct FHE, all these schemes then progress to the squash and bootstrapping transformations.

Even though Gentry's blueprint and its various instantiations can achieve FHE, they also leave a number of important questions unsolved. First, construction based on Gentry's blueprint inherently suffers from the disadvantage of low efficiency. The most efficient FHE scheme currently known is still very expensive. More importantly, the per-gate evaluation overhead—namely, the ratio of the time in evaluating a circuit homomorphically to the time in computing it on plaintext inputs—remains as the bottleneck of FHE practical deployments. Second, all the schemes following the blueprint depend on multiple new and relatively unproven cryptographic assumptions. The most problematic one is the non-standard sparse subset sum assumption (SSSA) used in the squashing part. More open issues regarding FHE can be found in a paper authored by Vaikuntanathan [48]. It walks us through the development of FHE from the mathematic point of view and gives some insightful thoughts about future research directions of FHE schemes. Refer to [48] for more details.

15.4.3.2 FHE Based on Ideal

Gentry constructed the first FHE scheme based on ideal lattices about which we know relatively little [47]. Stehlé and Steinfeld improved the scheme by analyzing the SSSA against lattice attacks more aggressively and introducing a probabilistic decryption algorithm with low multiplicative degree, thus producing a faster FHE scheme of lower bit complexity [45]. Moreover, by optimizing the key generation and applying batching technique for encryption, Gentry and Halevi [49] implemented a variant of Gentry's FHE scheme [47], which represents the first implementation of Gentry's blueprint. The authors tested the implementation with four parameter settings ranging from "toy" to "large." For the "large" setting, the public-key size is 2.3 GB, and it takes 2.2 hours to generate keys, 3 min to encrypt a message, and 30 min to refresh ciphertext. In addition to the poor efficiency, this family of FHE encounters two more difficulties. First, it relies on multiple new and untested complexity assumptions associated with ideals in various rings. Second, it has to depend on the most problematic SSSA assumption.

15.4.3.3 FHE over the Integers

Instead of utilizing ideal lattices as in [45, 47], Dijk et al. published an FHE scheme over the integers [46]. FHE over the integers has the advantage of conceptual simplicity. However, this scheme is far from practical since it involves large public-key size and suffers from low efficiency. In order to reduce the public-key size of the scheme, Coron et al. [50] proposed to generate a public key from its smaller subset on the fly and implemented their system comparable to that of Gentry–Halevi implementation [49]. Specifically, for the "large" setting, their implementation generates 802 MB public key and takes 43 min to generate a key, 2 min and 7 s to encrypt a message, and 3 min 55 s to refresh ciphertext, as shown in Table 15.2. However, this family of FHE schemes also encounters the difficulty of having to rely on the most problematic SSSA assumption.

15.4.3.4 FHE based on Learning with Errors

Aiming to base FHE schemes on well-studied mathematical problems, Brakerski and Vaikuntanathan demonstrated the first FHE scheme deviating from Gentry's blueprint [51]. Such a new FHE scheme is based on the standard learning with errors (LWEs) assumption. They avoided the untested assumptions on ideal lattices by introducing a technique called re-linearization. Moreover, they applied a technique called dimension-modulus reduction to remove the indispensable squashing procedure of Gentry's blueprint, thus preventing its most problematic SSSA. However, this BV scheme suffers from poor efficiency by having to depend on the costly bootstrapping, and thus it has high per-gate evaluation overhead. In order to improve the efficiency of BV scheme, Gentry et al. constructed a leveled FHE scheme to replace bootstrapping with "modulus switching" technique in managing ciphertext noise [52]. In this scheme, the authors apply bootstrapping and batching to optimize the per-gate evaluation overhead, thus improving the efficiency.

15.4.3.5 HE Scheme for Our System

After getting familiar with HE and its state-of-the-art schemes, we can now select a suitable HE scheme for our system. In our previous GTM system, the aggregation of host reports at ISPs involves addition and multiplication by constant values. In order to preserve privacy, the host reports will be encrypted in our newly proposed system. Thus, the proposed scheme needs to integrate a cryptosystem that supports computation on encrypted data, namely HE, and whose SHO includes both addition and constant multiplication. Among the abovementioned cryptosystems, Paillier cryptosystem and all the FHE schemes can satisfy these two requirements. However, as discussed above, current FHE cryptosystems have the disadvantage of low efficiency. As a result, we rule out all the FHE schemes as a suitable choice for our new system in order to ensure its high efficiency. Therefore, we choose to adopt the Paillier cryptosystem to preserve the privacy of unwanted traffic reporting hosts in our system.

15.5 System Design

15.5.1 Basic Principles

In the proposed system, we apply unique host anonymous IDs at GTO for trust evaluation and utilize RSA for signature generation and verification on reports. The unique anonymous ID could be generated based on the IP address of the host and a shared system credential. The RSA public keys of hosts are shared with their local ISPs. The RSA public key of an ISP is shared with GTO. The GTO HE public key is globally available in all hosts and ISPs, and its RSA public key is shared with ISPs.

Anonymous authentication on reporting is applied by GTO when calculating the detection trust of system entities according to their detection performance. The host reports go to the local ISP first and are then forwarded to GTO if needed. The local ISP knows the real IDs of the reporters, which are hidden from GTO in order to enhance privacy. However, GTO can only see the anonymous IDs of the reports senders and uses them to perform trust evaluation. The report providers should sign their reports before sending. In this way, the sources of unwanted traffic evidence are trackable at ISPs.

15.5.2 Operations and Procedures

The procedure of our new privacy-preserving UTC system is illustrated in Figure 15.2. During system setup, each entity generates its own RSA public key PK and privacy key SK. GTO generates an HE key pair: HE_PK and HE_SK. ISPs and hosts share a system secret used for generating anonymous IDs. A reporting host encrypts its report using the GTO HE public key HE_PK and sends the encrypted report to its local ISP. ISP aggregates host reports complaining on a same source and sends the aggregation result to GTO to decide if further monitoring at ISP serving the source is needed. ISP would monitor the traffic of suspicious hosts indicated by GTO and forward relevant host detection reports to GTO. Furthermore, ISP provides its own monitoring report to GTO if the host being monitored is suspicious. Upon receiving the host detection reports and ISP monitoring results, GTO first decrypts the host reports and then updates the global and detection trust of corresponding system entities. GTO further generates a gray list according to the value of global trust to indicate the suspicious unwanted traffic sources. By sharing the gray list signed by GTO with all ISPs, the traffic from the suspicious sources in the gray list can be filtered and controlled.

15.5.3 Unwanted Traffic Detection at a Host

We apply a number of local hints to detect potential unwanted traffic intrusion at a host. These hints include local traffic deviation, host behaviors toward the received messages, and content similarity. All the above hints deduced from the inbound traffic are aggregated together in order to decide if the host should deliver the detection result to its local ISP. The concrete methods to quantify such hints from the received messages are described below.

Local Traffic Monitoring: The purpose of monitoring the inbound traffic $tr_k^{in}(t)$ of a host $U_k(k = 1,...,K)$ is to check whether the host has been intruded or not. The increase of inbound traffic of the host indicates the possibility of being intruded. An unwanted traffic indicator φ^k contributed by the local traffic monitoring can be formulated as Equation (15.3), which applies the Sigmoid function $f(x) = \dfrac{1}{1+e^{-x}}$ to normalize the traffic deviation into the interval of (0, 1).

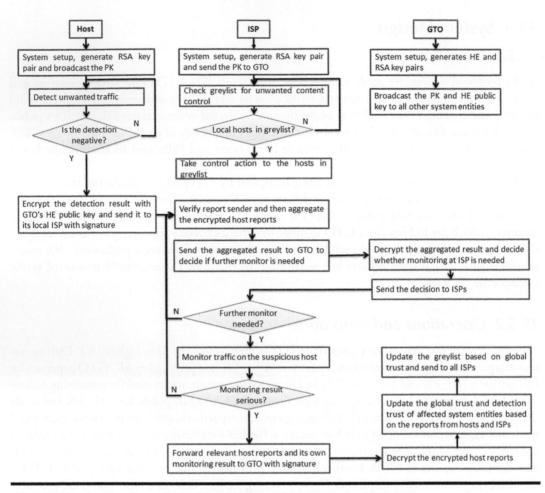

Figure 15.2 A procedure of our privacy-preserving system for UTC [54].

$$\varphi^k = \left| 1 - 2f\left\{ d_t\left[tr_k^{in}(t) \right] \right\} \right| \tag{15.3}$$

In Formula (15.3), $tr_k^{in}(t)$ denotes inbound traffic of host U_k at time t and $d_t\left\{ tr_k^{in}(t) \right\} = \dfrac{tr_k^{in}(t) - tr_k^{in}(t-\tau)}{\rho}$, $\rho \to 0$. The bigger φ^k is, the more probably U_k could be intruded.

Similarity Check: Most network intrusions send similar contents or the same contents to a single host multiple times. Therefore, we further check the similarity of contents received by U_k if $\varphi^k \geq thr1$, where $thr1$ is a threshold to trigger similarity check at host. For contents with similar size $E_k = \left\{ e_i^k \right\}, i = \{1,\ldots,I\}$ received by U_k within a time window $\left(w = \left[t - \dfrac{T}{2}, t + \dfrac{T}{2} \right] \right)$, we calculate their similarity according Formula (15.4):

$$\text{sim\_in}_i^k = \frac{\theta(I)}{(I-1)} \sum_{i' \neq i}^{I} \left(1 - \left| e_i^k - e_{i'}^k \right| \right) \tag{15.4}$$

In Formula (15.4), e_i^k represents the ith content received by host U_k and $e_i^k - e_{i'}^k$ is the difference between e_i^k and $e_{i'}^k$; T is the time window used to normalize the time of content processing. The similarity can be quantified based on a semantic relevance measure [32]. Our implementation applies cosine similarity to calculate content similarity. The cosine similarity measures the cosine of the angle between Term Frequency-Inverse Document Frequency (TF-IDF) vectors of two messages. Obviously, U_k could receive multiple sets of similar traffic intrusions. To calculate the similarity of U_k inbound traffic with regard to all similar contents, we design Equation (15.5) as below:

$$\text{sim\_in}^k = \frac{1}{S} \sum_S \left[\theta(I)/(I-1) \sum_{i' \neq i}^{I} \left(1 - \left| e_i^k - e_{i'}^k \right| \right) \right] \tag{15.5}$$

S denotes the number of the sets of similar contents. Notably, the bigger the number of similar contents in a set, the more possible that the similar content is unwanted. Thus, in (15.4) and (15.5), we consider the influence of integer I by using the Rayleigh cumulative distribution function $\theta(I) = 1 - \exp\left(\frac{-I^2}{2\sigma^2}\right)$.

Traffic Process: The behaviors of a host in processing the received traffic imply its likes or dislikes. Such a fact can be utilized to indicate whether the traffic is unwanted subjective to personal preference. Our system aims to support personalized unwanted traffic control based on subjective processing of a received message, please refer to [3, 32] for more detailed explanation. This chapter focuses more on the privacy-preserving property. Specifically, if the receiving time of a content e_i^k is r_t^i and its discarding time (e.g., the time to move it to a spam folder or specify it as unwanted) is d_t^i, the interval between r_t^i and d_t^i implies the user preference on the traffic. The unwanted traffic indicator τ_i contributed by the content processing behavior of a host can be described as in Formula (15.6):

$$\tau_i = 1 - \frac{d_t^i - r_t^i}{T}, \quad \text{when } d_t^i - r_t^i < T \tag{15.6}$$

T in Formula (15.6) has the same meaning as that in Formula (15.4). The bigger τ_i is, the more possible e_i^k would be unwanted by U_k. Note that if $d_t^i - r_t^i \geq T$, τ_i will not be counted.

Unwanted Traffic Reporting: A host can complain about unwanted traffic to its local ISP. The complaint is based on the inbound traffic deviation, content similarity, and the host processing behaviors toward the received traffic. Thereby, we formulate the unwanted traffic detection value $v_k^i(t)$ at time t by U_k about traffic e_i^k as in Formula (15.7):

$$v_k^i(t) = \text{sim\_in}_i^k \times \varphi^k \times \tau_i \tag{15.7}$$

As we mentioned in Formulas (15.3)–(15.6), the bigger φ^k, sim_in_i^k, and τ_i are, the more probably U_k is be intruded. Thus, the bigger the $v_k^i(t)$ is, the more possible that U_k has received unwanted traffic.

An unwanted traffic detection report containing $v_k^i(t)$ is automatically sent to the local ISP of the host if $v_k^i(t) \geq thr$, where thr is the threshold to trigger reporting. The report from host U_k to ISP is packaged as below:

$$\left\{ \begin{array}{l} R_{\mathrm{Enc}}(k) = \left\{ gh(k),\ E\left(v_k^i(t)\right),\ gh(k'),\ e_i^k,\ t \right\}, \\ \\ Sign\left(h\left(R_{\mathrm{Enc}}(k)\right),\ SK_k\right) \end{array} \right\}, (nr)$$

where $h()$ is a hash function, such as SHA-1; signature $Sign(h(R_{\mathrm{Enc}}(k)),\ SK_k)$ is signed on the hash code of the encrypted reporting message that includes host unique anonymous ID $gh(k)$, encrypted detection value $E\left(v_k^i(t)\right)$ obtained by calling *PailEncrypt* algorithm with HE_PK, unique unwanted traffic source anonymous ID $gh(k')$, content ID e_i^k and reporting time t. Function $gh(k)$ generates unique anonymous ID of U_k based on its unique real ID and the system secret known by hosts and ISPs.

15.5.4 Traffic Monitoring at ISP

ISP Process on Host Reports: Upon receiving a host report, ISP first verifies the reporter and checks the integrity of the report. ISP then aggregates relevant host reports complaining against a same source by applying the global trust ut_k^t and detection trust dt_k^t as the credibility of a complaining report. Formula (15.8) describes the equation to aggregate reports that are not encrypted:

$$s_i(t) = \sum_k v_k^i(t) \times ut_k^t \times dt_k^t \Big/ \sum_k ut_k^t \times dt_k^t \tag{15.8}$$

However, since $v_k^i(t)$ in our proposed system is encrypted as $E\left(v_k^i(t)\right)$ with the Paillier cryptosystem, ISP needs to convert Formula (15.8) to an encrypted version. The conversion can be based on the homomorphic properties of the Paillier cryptosystem as described in Section 15.4.2.4. More specifically, the multiplication of $ut_k^t \times dt_k^t$ and $v_k^i(t)$ is mapped into $C\exp_k^i(t) = E\left(v_k^i(t)\right)^{ut_k^t \times dt_k^t}$ with the *PailExp* algorithm. On the other hand, the addition of reports multiplied by the global trust and the detection trust is mapped into its encrypted version with the *PailMul* algorithm. Namely, when aggregating reports, ISP first transforms each encrypted report $E\left(v_k^i(t)\right)$ to $C\exp_k^i(t)$, then adds all $C\exp_k^i(t)$ together to *CMul*, which is finally divided by the sum of credibility (i.e., *Den* in Algorithm 15.1). Algorithm 15.1 demonstrates the encrypted version of Formula (15.8). Therefore, $es_i(t)$ from Algorithm 15.1 represents the encrypted version of plaintext aggregation result $s_i(t)$ in Formula (15.8).

After executing Algorithm 15.1, ISP sends the encrypted aggregation result $es_i(t)$ to GTO and hides its own ID and the real ID of the suspicious unwanted traffic source with their corresponding hash ID.

Algorithm 15.1: Aggregating the Encrypted Host Reports Complaining against the Same Source at ISP

Input: HE_PK, a set of N_r encrypted reports $ev_k^i(t) = E\left(v_k^i(t)\right)$ complaining against the same source from different host U_k, a set of global trust ut_k^t, and detection trust dt_k^t of host U_k.

Output: Encrypted aggregation result $es_i(t)$.

$Den = 0$;

For k = 1, 2,..., N_r

      $C\exp_k^i(t) = \mathrm{PaillierExp}\left(ev_k^i(t), ut_k^t \times dt_k^t, \mathrm{HE\_PK}\right)$;

      $Den = Den + ut_k^t \times dt_k^t$;

End

$Ctmp$ = PaillierEncrypt(HE_PK, 0);
For k = 1, 2,..., N_r
    $Cmul$ = PaillierMul$\left(C\exp_k^i(t), Ctmp, \text{HE\_PK}\right)$;
    $Ctmp$ = $Cmul$;
End

$es_i(t)$ = PaillierExp($Cmul$,1/Den,HE_PK)

Traffic Monitoring at ISP: GTO decrypts the aggregated results $es_i(t)$ with *PailDecrypt* algorithm to get $s_i(t)$ and decides whether the host being complained is suspicious. If the decision is positive, i.e., $s_i(t) \geq$ thr0, GTO authorizes ISP to monitor the traffic of the host being suspected, thr0 herein denotes the threshold to trigger ISP monitoring. The purpose of monitoring the traffic of a host U_k at its local ISP is to find the sources of unwanted traffic with such credibility that the ISP can either take administrative action or impose contractual penalties on the sources. Particularly, it can detect an infected host that has become a source of unwanted traffic. U_k can be any entity that links to the ISP, thus its traffic can be monitored by the ISP. It is efficient for the ISP to monitor its own subscribers because it sees all traffic sourced from them while other ISP subscribers are numerous and the ISP can only see a fraction of their traffic. Therefore, from the scalability point of view, the monitoring of other ISP subscribers should be very selective. Similar to (15.3), an unwanted traffic indicator $\varphi_{sp}^k(t)$ contributed by the ISP traffic monitoring on the outbound traffic $tr_k^{out}(t)$ of host U_k is formulated as in Equation (15.9):

$$\varphi_{sp}^k(t) = \left|1 - 2f\left\{d_t\left[tr_k^{out}(t)\right]\right\}\right| \tag{15.9}$$

Similar to (15.5), the similarity of S' sets of unwanted contents sent from U_k can be designed as in Formula (15.10):

$$\text{sim\_out}^k = \frac{1}{S'}\sum_{S'}\left[\theta(I)/(I-1)\sum_{i'\neq i}^{I}\left(1-\left|e_i^k - e_{i'}^k\right|\right)\right] \tag{15.10}$$

We quantify the unwanted traffic monitoring result (denoted by $sp_k^n(t)$) on host U_k from the nth ISP at time t according to Formula (15.11), which shows that ISP monitors the increase of outbound traffic and examines the content similarity:

$$sp_k^n(t) = \varphi_{sp}^k(t) \times \text{sim\_out}^k \tag{15.11}$$

If the monitoring result at ISP is serious, i.e., $sp_k^n(t) \geq$ thr1, ISP sends it (in plaintext) to GTO along with relevant host reports (in ciphertext). This package to be sent is signed by the ISP in order to ensure the integrity and non-repudiation of reporting. Parameter thr1 denotes the threshold to trigger an ISP to send its monitoring result to GTO. The reporting package from ISP is packed as below:

$$\left\{R_{isp}(n) = \left\{gh(n), sp_k^n(t), \{R_{Enc}(k)\}\right\}, \text{Sign}\left(h\left(R_{isp}(n)\right), SK_n\right)\right\}$$

It is noteworthy to mention that ISP monitoring in reality may (and will) differ from the methods shown above. We use the described methods as examples, and they can be replaced by any effective unwanted traffic detection approach.

15.5.5 Unwanted Traffic Control at GTO

Detection Credibility: The credibility of a detection report should be analyzed in order to fight against the malicious reporter behavior due to many reasons. For example, the complainer may be intruded; the host or ISP intentionally frames other hosts; the detection tools installed in the reporting host are broken or poor. Therefore, we apply detection trust to indicate the quality of reports since we cannot ensure that the unwanted traffic detection is always trustworthy. When generating the detection trust at GTO, we apply y to indicate detection performance and further introduce to record the number of bad detections in order to detect on–off and conflict behavior attacks. If the detection report from host U_k does not match the final evaluation result, $y = -1$ and γ++. On the other hand, when the detection report matches the fact, $y = 1$ and γ is not changed. If no detection report is provided, $y = 0$ and γ is not changed. In this way, good detecting performance increases the detection trust dt_k^t; otherwise, dt_k^t will be decreased. The detection trust dt_k^t of host U_k at time t is formulated based on Formula (15.12):

$$
dt_k^t = \begin{cases} dt_k^t + \delta y, (\gamma < thr3) \\ dt_k^t + \delta y - \mu\gamma, (\gamma \geq thr3) \end{cases} = \begin{cases} 1 \left(dt_k^t > 1 \right) \\ 0 \left(dt_k^t < 0 \right) \end{cases} \tag{15.12}
$$

In Formula (15.12), $\delta > 0$ is a parameter to control the change of dt_k^t. $thr3$ is a threshold to indicate the on–off and conflict behavior attacks. $\mu > 0$ is a parameter to control bad detection punishment. The optimal values of $thr3$, δ, and μ can be decided through simulations.

Trust Evaluation: The GTO evaluates the global trust of each entity based on the collected reports from the hosts and ISPs in order to find the sources of unwanted traffic. Obviously, a host $U_k(k = 1,...,K')$ could report many times at different time t. Considering the time influence and potential on-off and ballot stuffing attacks, we pay more attention to the recent reports. We use $e^{-|t-t_p|^2/\tau}$ to decay $V_k^i(t)$, where t_p is the trust evaluation time and τ is a parameter to control time decaying. GTO aggregates all the reports $v_k^i(t)$ from K' hosts that blamed $U_{k'}$ by considering both the global trust and the detection trust according to Formula (15.13):

$$
rt_{k'}^{t_p} = \frac{\displaystyle\sum_{k=1}^{K'} dt_k^{t_p} \times ut_k^{t_p} \times v_k^i(t) \times e^{-\frac{|t-t_p|^2}{\tau}}}{\displaystyle\sum_{k=1}^{K'} dt_k^{t_p} \times ut_k^{t_p} \times e^{-\frac{|t-t_p|^2}{\tau}}} \tag{15.13}
$$

In Formula (15.13), $rt_{k'}^{t_p}$ represents the aggregation result of host detection reports that blame host $U_{k'}$ as the source of unwanted content. In addition, GTO aggregates the monitoring reports from ISPs to calculate their contributions to the global trust of host $U_{k'}$ with Formula (15.14). Since ISP reporting immediately triggers the trust evaluation at the GTO, we do not apply time decaying in Formula (15.14):

$$mt_{k'}^{t_p} = \frac{\sum_{n=1}^{N} dt_n^{t_p} \times ut_n^{t_p} \times sp_{k'}^{n}\left(t_p\right)}{\sum_{n=1}^{N} dt_n^{t_p} \times ut_n^{t_p}} \tag{15.14}$$

where $mt_{k'}^{t_p}$ stands for the aggregation of ISP reports from monitoring on host $U_{k'}$. The global trust value of the blamed host $U_{k'}$ can be updated by deducting $mt_{k'}^{t_p}$ and $rt_{k'}^{t_p}$ from the original $ut_{k'}^{t_p}$. Meanwhile, we model the influence of the number of reporters with the Rayleigh cumulative distribution function. Specifically, the updating process of $ut_{k'}^{t_p}$ is designed as in Formula (15.15):

$$ut_{k'}^{t_p} = ut_{k'}^{t_p} - \theta(K') \times rt_{k'}^{t_p} - \theta(N) \times mt_{k'}^{t_p} \tag{15.15}$$

Gray List Generation: GTO collects reports from ISPs and hosts, and aggregates them for trust evaluation. If the global trust of the complained host is less than *thr2*, GTO adds the host into its gray list. *thr2* is the upper limit for $ut_{k'}^{t_p}$ to gray list its owner $U_{k'}$. Namely, if $ut_{k'}^{t_p} \leq thr2$, host $U_{k'}$ should be gray listed.

According to the evaluation result, GTO also evaluates the detection trust evaluation for the entities that sent reports according to Formula (15.12). GTO will then issue the updated global trust and detection trust value, and the gray list to all ISPs. The functionalities of GTO can be implemented in the control plane of the Software-Defined Networking. Upon receiving the gray list from GTO, ISPs will take control actions on the hosts in the gray list.

15.6 Performance Evaluation

15.6.1 Testing Environment

To evaluate the practicality of the proposed system, we conducted a number of experiments on a workstation with Intel(R) Xeon(R) CPU E31235@3.20 GHz, running Ubuntu 14.04.2 LTS in Oracle VirtualBox. In the subsequent experimental results, the execution time of RSA signature signing and verification and SHA-1 hash function was obtained using OpenSSL's built-in benchmarking suite openssl speed. All other experimental results represent the mean of 200 trials.

15.6.2 Security and Privacy Analysis and Proof

15.6.2.1 Security Analysis and Proof

In the proposed system, RSA signature is mainly responsible for assuring report integrity and ensuring non-reputation, thus protecting the detection reports from being maliciously tampered during transmission. Secure communication channels between ISPs and GTO are assumed in our design, ensuring the security of ISP reports sent to GTO. Thus, confidentiality of host reports is our main concern of system security. The security of host reports is ensured by the Paillier cryptosystem whose security level is analyzed as below.

Due to the homomorphic properties, the Paillier cryptosystem is malleable. In other words, an adversary of the Paillier cryptosystem can transform a ciphertext into another ciphertext that can be decrypted to a related plaintext. Therefore, the Paillier cryptosystem is not semantically secure against IND-CCA, but it is semantically secure against IND-CPA. We prove this by employing a game model. More specifically, we define the security model of our system as follows between adversary A and challenger C.

Setup: The challenger, who plays the role of GTO, runs the PailSetup algorithm and gives the resulting public key HE_PK to adversary $\mathcal{A}$ but keeps the private key HE_SK only to itself.

Phase 1: Adversary $\mathcal{A}$, who plays the role of curious ISPs or malicious hosts, runs the PailEncrypt algorithm for arbitrary input plaintext $m \in \mathbb{Z}_n$ for ln times that is polynomially bounded.

Challenge: When Phase 1 is over, adversary $\mathcal{A}$ submits two distinct plaintexts m_0 and m_1 to challenger $\mathcal{C}$. Challenger $\mathcal{C}$ picks a random bit $b \in \{0,1\}$, sets $c = E(m_b)$ and then sends c as the challenge to adversary $\mathcal{A}$.

Phase 2: As in Phase 1, adversary $\mathcal{A}$ runs the PailEncrypt algorithm for more times.

Guess: Adversary $\mathcal{A}$ outputs a guess $b' \in \{0, 1\}$. The adversary wins the game if $b = b'$.

We refer to such an adversary $\mathcal{A}$ as a chosen-plaintext (IND-CPA) attacker. According to Lemma 5 and discussions in Section 4 in [43], c is the ciphertext of m_1 if and only if $cg^{-m} \bmod n^2 = r^n \bmod n^2$ is an nth residue. c is said to be an nth residue modulo n_2 if a number $\varphi \in z_{n^2}^*$ exists such that $c = \varphi^2 \bmod n_2$. Given an integer c and a composite n, the problem of deciding nth residues, i.e., distinguishing nth residues from non-nth residues, is defined as Composite Residuosity Class Problem $CR[n]$. However, Computational Composite Residuosity Assumption (CCRA) assumes that there exists no probabilistic polynomial time algorithm that can solve $CR[n]$. Thus, adversary $\mathcal{A}$ cannot determine whether c is an encryption of m_1 and m_2. Therefore, the Paillier cryptosystem is semantically secure against IND-CPA if and only if CCRA holds.

As proved in [43], the Paillier probabilistic encryption scheme is one-way on the condition of CCRA. Moreover, no adaptive chosen ciphertext attack recovering factorization of the modulus is known with regard to the Paillier encryption scheme. Therefore, the Paillier cryptoscheme provides a high security level for host reports. In conclusion, our system is semantically secure against IND-CPA and one-way if and only if CCRA holds.

15.6.2.2 Privacy Protection

The proposed system assumes that ISPs are semi-trusted. They are curious to know the content of host reports and might disclose this private information to a third malicious party for gaining extra profits. However, due to business incentive, ISPs try to offer sound networking services, act on intrusion attacks, and control unwanted traffic if needed. Apart from the above, ISP performs host detection report aggregation. The proposed system assures the privacy of hosts at ISP by hiding plaintext reports from ISPs, even though the hosts rely on ISPs to aggregate and forward the reports.

GTO is assumed trusted for trust evaluation and does not collude with ISPs in the proposed system. Even though GTO knows the plaintext of detection reports from hosts and the plaintext of monitoring reports from ISPs, hiding the real IDs of hosts and ISPs from GTO can still protect the privacy of hosts and ISPs. A plaintext report is valuable to a malicious third party only when it is accompanied with the real ID of a report sender or the real ID of a complained host. So even though GTO colludes with other third malicious parties, without any privacy-sensitive information such as the real IDs of the report senders and the complained hosts, the threat of GTO to the privacy of other system entities is limited. In summary, our proposed scheme protects the privacy of hosts, thus encouraging them to report unwanted traffic honestly and actively.

In addition, the attacks caused by the collusion between ISPs and hosts can be restrained. ISPs cannot illegally monitor the traffic of a host without sufficient evidence and authorization. This is because GTO is the only party in the system to authorize the rights of such monitoring and the authorization is based on trust evaluation and management. Malicious and indifferent hosts can be kicked out in the trust evaluation.

15.6.3 Performance Analysis

The proposed system aims to avoid the disclosure of detection reports at ISPs and ensures the non-repudiation of reporting. However, encrypting reports at hosts, aggregating encrypted reports at ISPs and decrypting reports at GTO, as well as security verification would incur computation costs, thus increasing processing burden in the system. In addition, network overhead is inevitable because of the increased size of a report introduced by HE and the signature attached to each report, as well as the need to distribute public keys to other system entities. The need to store public keys consumes more storage than the original system [10]. Therefore, the proposed system fulfills legal requirements and user demands by preserving privacy at the cost of system performance in terms of computation cost, communication overhead, and storage consumption. We assess the performance of our system by adopting the GTM system previously proposed in [10] as a baseline system. We have proven the high detection accuracy of our system by extensive experiments in [10, 25] through both simulations and implementation on SMS spam control; thus, the evaluation of detection accuracy is omitted herein. And in this section, we focus on studying the extra costs introduced by privacy preservation from the point of view of computation complexity, communication overhead, and storage consumption.

15.6.3.1 Computation Complexity

We do not illustrate the computation cost of algorithms for unwanted traffic detection at host (Formulas 15.3–15.7), unwanted traffic monitoring at ISP (Formulas 15.8–15.11), and trust evaluation at GTO (Formulas 15.12–15.15), since they are negligible compared to cryptographic operations. Table 15.3 summarizes the operation time of 1024-bit key cryptographic operations spent in the proposed system. From this table, we can see that the computation cost depends mainly on the Paillier operations; thus in the following analysis, we omit RSA Sign, RSA Verify, and hash function SHA-1 in the computation complexity analysis. Figure 15.3 shows the execution time of the Paillier algorithms with different key lengths.

At system setup, GTO runs the *PailSetup* algorithm to generate HE_PK and HE_SK. Hosts and ISPs generate their RSA key pairs and a system secret. The system setup process is not affected by the number of encrypted reports generated and received; thus, its computation complexity is (1).

Extra computation cost at hosts comes from encrypting the detection reports using the *PailEncrypt* algorithm that takes about 2.7 ms for 1024-bit security parameter, as shown in Table 15.3. The computation complexity at a host depends on the number of unwanted traffic reports to ISP. Let N_u denote such a number, and the computation complexity at the host is (N_u).

As for ISP, it aggregates homomorphically encrypted reports according to Algorithm 15.1 that contains the *PailMul* and *PailExp* algorithms. For each malicious source, ISP needs to perform N_r times of *PailMul* and *PailExp*, where N_r is the average number of received reports complaining against such a malicious source. If the number of malicious sources is N_m, the computation complexity at ISP is $(N_m \times N_r)$.

GTO is responsible for decrypting the reports from hosts using the *PailDecrypt* algorithm that takes about 2.1 ms, as shown in Table 15.3. If there are N_m malicious sources and N_s out of N_m aggregation reports is serious, $N_s \times N_{rs}$ encrypted reports from hosts are forwarded to GTO by

Table 15.3 Crypto Operation Time

Crypto Operation	Operation Time
PailEncrypt	2.7 ms
PailDecrypt	2.1 ms
RSA Sign	0.2 μs
RSA Verify	0.013 μs
SHA-1	2.3 μs

Execution time of Paillier algorithms with different key lengths

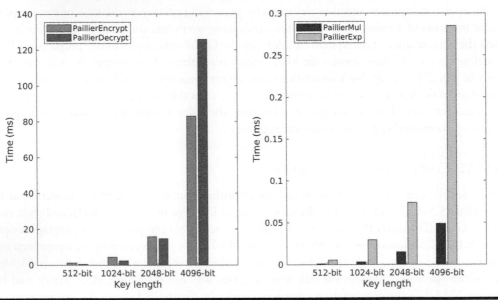

Figure 15.3 The execution time of the Paillier algorithms with different key lengths.

ISPs and should be decrypted by GTO before evaluating the trust of involved entities. Thus, the computation complexity of GTO is $(N_s \times N_{rs})$, where N_{rs} is the average number of reporting hosts regarding a suspicious source of unwanted traffic.

Table 15.4 summarizes the above analysis about the computation complexity of host, ISP, and GTO in the proposed system.

Figure 15.4 presents the aggregation time at ISP with different numbers of host reports and different security parameter sizes. As shown in the figure, aggregating 106 host reports only takes about 4.5 s with 512-bit Paillier key, which implies that the aggregation algorithm in the proposed system does not introduce a significant computation burden to ISP.

Figure 15.5 shows the execution time to calculate the cosine similarity of different numbers of messages. As we can see from the figure, the cosine similarity calculation is very efficient: calculating the cosine similarity of 100 messages (message length within 140 bytes) only takes 1.03 s.

In summary, all the above results show the practicality of our system from the perspective of computation cost, especially considering the strong computing power of ISPs and GTO.

Table 15.4   The Computation Complexity of Different Types of System Entities

System Entity	Algorithm	Operation	Computation Complexity
Host	PailEncrypt	$N_u \times (2 \text{ MODExp})$	$\mathcal{O}(N_u)$
ISP	PailMul, PailExp	$(N_m \times N_r) \times (1 \text{ MODMul} + 1 \text{ MODExp})$	$\mathcal{O}(N_m \times N_r)$
GTO	PailSetup	—	$\mathcal{O}(1)$
	PailDecrypt	$(N_s \times N_{rs}) \times (2 \text{ MODExp} + 1 \text{ MODMul})$	$\mathcal{O}(N_s \times N_{rs})$

MODExp, modular exponentiation; *MODMul*, modular multiplication.

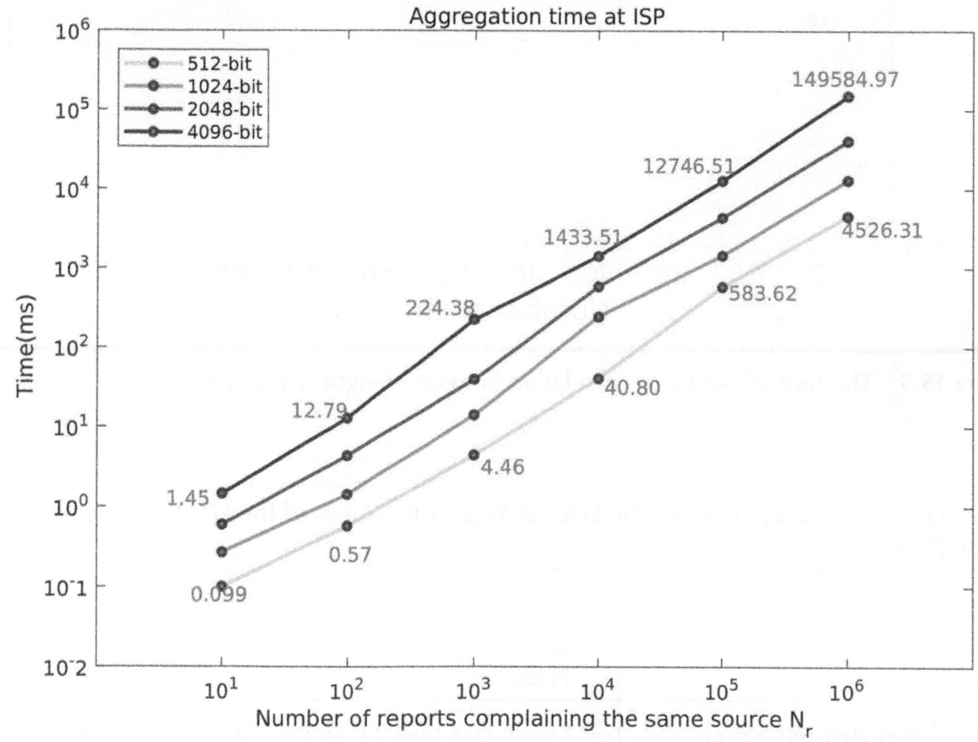

Figure 15.4   Aggregation time at ISP.

15.6.3.2 Communication Overhead

First of all, in the proposed scheme, public keys must be distributed when a new system entity is introduced. In contrast, no key needs to be shared in the original GTM system. However, such communication cost can be ignored since individual public-key size is small (451 bytes) (refer to Table 15.5) and the distribution is needed only when a new system entity is introduced or a key update is required.

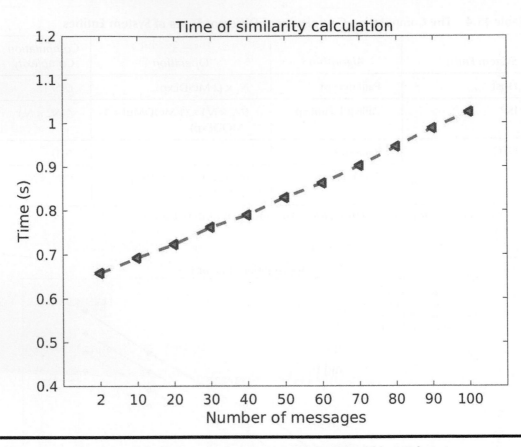

Figure 15.5 **The time of similarity calculation (message length within 140 bytes).**

Table 15.5 **The Comparison of the Sizes of Report Packages of the GTM System and That of the Proposed System**

GTM System		Proposed System	
Package	*Size (in Bytes)*	*Package*	*Size (in Bytes)*
$R(k) = \{gh(k), v_k^i(t), gh(k'), e_i^k, t\}$	$85 + L_r$	$R_{Enc}(k)$ (Refer to Section 4.2.1)	$85 + 2L_n + 256$
$R(n)\| R(k) = \{gh(n), sp_{k'}^n(t)\}$	$20 + L_{isp}$	$R_{isp}(n)\|R_{Enc}(k)$	$20 + L_{isp} + 256$

85: The total length of $gh(k), gh(k'), e_i^k$ and t if SHA-1 (20 bytes) is applied and the length of t is 25 bytes.
L_r: The length of plaintext host report $v_k^i(t)$.
20: The length in bytes of $gh(n)$ if SHA-1 is applied.
L_{isp}: The length of ISP monitoring report $sp_{k'}^n(t)$.
L_n: The size in bytes of security parameter n of the Paillier cryptosystem.
256: The signature size in bytes of 2048-bit RSA cryptosystem.

The main communication cost comes from the HE and appended signatures, and their size depends on the length of crypto security parameter (e.g., n in the Paillier cryptosystem). As mentioned before, the message expansion of the Paillier encryption scheme is only 2. Thus, the introduced communication cost from HE is not high and reasonable. Moreover, RSA signature size is small and can be practically appended without much influence on communication performance. Concretely, the sizes of packages $R_{Enc}(k)$ and $R_{isp}(n)|R_{Enc}(k)$ are shown in Table 15.5. We use $R_{isp}(n)|R_{Enc}(k) = \left\{ gh(n), sp_k^n(t) \right\}, Sign\left(h\left(R_{isp}(n) \right), SK_n \right)$ here to denote the ISP monitoring report package, where host report package $\left\{ R_{Enc}(k) \right\}$ is excluded for analysis convenience. As shown in Table 15.5, the introduced communication overhead of both packages is small, only 256 bytes for 2048-bit RSA signature and $2L_n$ for the Paillier encryption, where L_n is the selected length of security parameters and is normally 64, 128, or 256 in bytes.

In a word, the communication overhead introduced by privacy preservation in the proposed system is reasonable, acceptable, and thus practical.

15.6.3.3 Storage Consumption

Table 15.6 compares the storage consumption of GTM system and the proposed system at different types of system entity. From Table 15.6, we can see that the extra storage consumption in the proposed system is mainly caused by storing public keys and personal key pairs that do not appear in the original GTM system. Table 15.6 gives some example key sizes when using 2048-bit RSA cryptosystem and applying 1024-bit Paillier cryptosystem. Storing homomorphically encrypted reports instead of plaintext reports needs more storage space, but the extra cost is not high due to the low message expansion of the Paillier cryptosystem. Since ISP and GTO are deployed with servers full of storage space, we pay more attention to the extra storage introduced at the host side. Luckily, extra storage consumption in the proposed system at hosts comes only from the key pair of host (2130 bytes) and GTO's homomorphic public key (256 bytes), both of which are reasonably small. In addition, such extra storage cost at hosts does not scale with the number of system entities. Therefore, the extra storage consumption of our system is reasonable and acceptable in practice.

15.6.4 Comparing Our System Performance with GTM System

We further compared the time spent to find a source of unwanted traffic of the original GTM system to that of our proposed system. Since we consider more how the proposed system influences the GTM system in terms of time to find an unwanted content source, we assumed that hosts and ISPs would honestly report their detection and monitoring results, and would not frame good traffic as unwanted (i.e., $dt_k^t = 1$). The initial value of global trust is 1, i.e., $ut_{k'}^{t_p} = 1$. Table 15.7 presents the values of system parameters set for the following tests, except that they are explicitly specified. They were set mainly based on the simulation results achieved in [10] in order to ensure expected system performance for unwanted traffic detection.

According to Formulas (15.7) and (15.11), the similarity between traffic messages affects the value of $v_k^i(t)$ and $sp_{k'}^n$, which will then affect the decreasing rate of the global trust, thus the time to find the unwanted content source. Particularly, we examined the effect of message similarity on the efficiency of detecting an unwanted content source by fixing the value of $\varphi^k \times \tau_i$ and $\varphi_{sp}^k(t)$ as 1. We set $thr = thr0 = 0.4$ in this test. Figure 15.6 shows that the higher the similarity, the faster the system can detect an unwanted source. However, when the similarity is less than 0.4, the time

Table 15.6   The Storage Consumption of Each Kind of System Entity

System Entity	GTM System [10]		Proposed System	Size (Bytes)
Host	None		Own public-key cryptography (PKC) key pair	2130
			HE_PK	256
ISP	None		Own PKC key pair	2130
			HE_PK	256
			PKC public keys of hosts	$451N_h$
	Plaintext host reports	L_r	Encrypted host reports	$2L_n$
	Trust values of hosts		Trust values of hosts	
	Gray list		Gray list	
GTO	None		Own PKC key pair	2130
			Homomorphic key pair	512
			PKC public keys ISPs	$451N_l$
	ISP reports		ISP reports	
	Plaintext reports from hosts		Plaintext reports from hosts	
	Trust values of hosts and ISPs		Trust values of hosts and ISPs	
	Gray list		Gray list	

N_h: The total number of host in the system.
N_l: The total number of ISP in the system.
L_r: The total length of plaintext host reports.
L_n: The size in bytes of security parameter n of the Paillier cryptosystem.

Table 15.7   The Settings of System Parameters

Parameters	Values	Parameters	Values
thr	0.8	σ	30
thr0	0.7	τ	2
thr1	0.8	δ	0.05
thr2	0.1	μ	0.1
thr3	5	T	10
		$d_t^i - r_t^i$	1

tends to be infinite. This is because similarity less than 0.4 leads to the values of $v_k^i(t)$ to be lower than 0.4, resulting the receiving host not sending any report; thus, the unwanted content source will never be discovered.

We also observe from Figure 15.6 that the difference of the detection time under similarity from 0.6 to 1 is very small. The reason is that when the similarity is high (>0.6), the value deduction of *ut* of the complained host is equally quick to reach a value below *thr2*, which is the threshold to put a host into the gray list.

To get the time to find an unwanted traffic source, timing process starts when an unwanted message is sent at a host and ends when the unwanted message from the host is blocked by ISPs. In this test, we set one ISP in the system that has 501 hosts. One host is an unwanted traffic source that sends unwanted content to other 10, 100, and 500 good hosts. The unwanted content is randomly selected from the message database. Moreover, we fixed the value $v_k^i(t)$ and $sp_{k'}^n$ to be 1 in order to easily compare the proposed system with the original GTM system regarding unwanted traffic detection and control. Figure 15.7 shows the comparison result where 2048-bit RSA, SHA-1, and 512-bit Paillier cryptosystem are applied. As shown in the figure, the proposed system spent more time to find the unwanted content source than the original GTM system. The difference is only about 2 s that mainly resulted from RSA signature generation and verification as well as the Paillier crypto operations. Note that since all the system entities ran in the same machine, the network latency is ignored here. Although the proposed system introduces some extra costs in order to enhance privacy, this result is still acceptable in practice.

We also observed from Figure 15.7 that the time to find an unwanted content source did not increase according to the number of receivers as we were expecting. This is because upon receiving the first few reports, the GTO can already detect the spam source and put it into the gray list. However, in both the GTM system and the proposed system, ISP continues to monitor the suspicious host upon receiving reports that come after the source has already been put into the

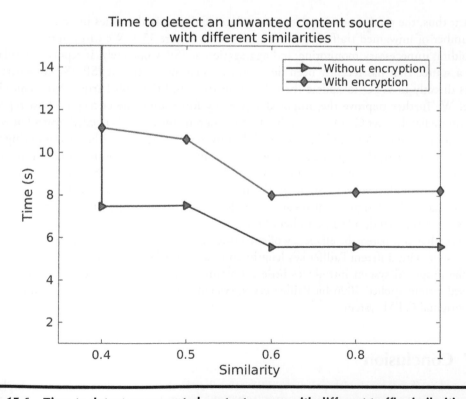

Figure 15.6   Time to detect an unwanted content source with different traffic similarities.

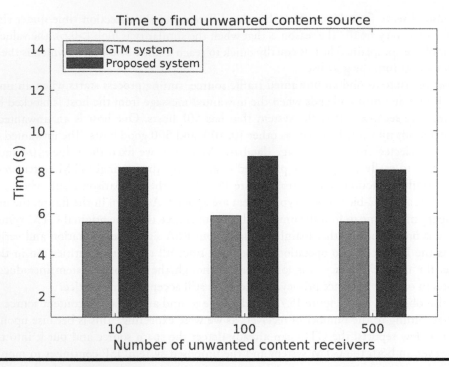

Figure 15.7   Time to find an unwanted traffic source.

gray list; thus, the total time to update trust values of all involved entities increases according to the number of unwanted traffic receivers, as shown in Figure 15.8. We can improve the system by avoiding unnecessary monitoring and aggregation at ISP. Concretely, if reports complaining about a source that has recently been detected as a spammer arrive at ISP, ISP forwards those reports directly to GTO to update their detection trust and the global trust of the complained source. We further improve the proposed system by forwarding the encrypted host reports to GTO immediately after GTO decides that further monitoring at ISP is needed instead of waiting for the monitoring result is available and send the host reports together with the monitoring report to GTO. In this way, the report decryption and ISP monitoring can be performed in parallel in order to improve the performance of the system. Figure 15.8 compares the time spent to update the trust value of all involved system entities in the original systems and the improved ones. We observed that such a design optimizes system performance significantly, especially in the situation where spammers intrude a large number of hosts.

We further compared the efficiency of detecting an unwanted traffic source between the proposed system with different Paillier key lengths and the original GTM system. As shown in Figure 15.9, the proposed system introduces little extra time to the original system. Even though the proposed system applied 4096-bit Paillier cryptosystem, only about 4 s of extra time was incurred to the original GTM system.

15.7 Conclusion

Unwanted traffic control with privacy preservation has become critical in order to comply with privacy laws and satisfy user demands. To fulfill such practical needs, we proposed in this chapter

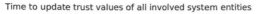

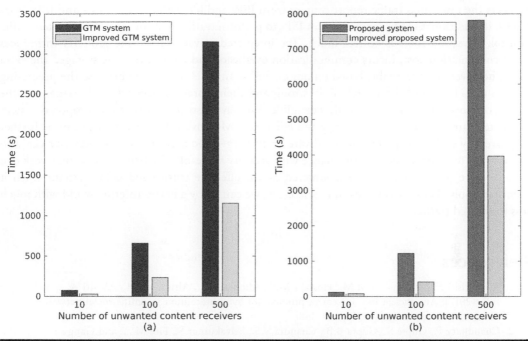

Figure 15.8   The comparison of time to update all the trust values of involved system entities: (a) GTM system and improved GTM system, and (b) proposed system and improved proposed system.

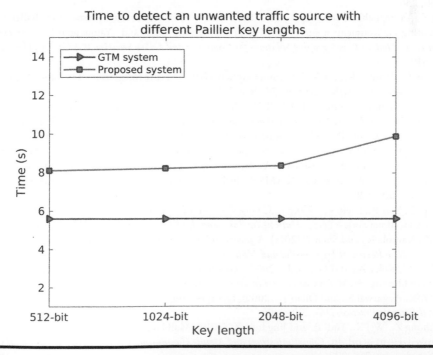

Figure 15.9   Time to detect an unwanted traffic source with different Paillier key lengths.

a trust-based unwanted traffic control system with privacy preservation. The proposed system protects the unwanted traffic report content from ISPs and hides the IDs of hosts and ISPs from GTO. In addition, GTO cooperates with ISPs to perform traffic monitoring and unwanted traffic control. However, there is no free lunch. The integrated privacy-preserving property introduces extra computation cost, incurs communication overhead, and consumes more storage. The extra costs, however, are acceptable based on our extensive analysis. Especially because the processing powers of GTO and ISPs are relatively strong and their storage spaces relatively large, and the extra costs over them are practically negligible. We have also proved that our proposed system can detect unwanted traffic effectively and efficiently. Moreover, the performance can be further improved by dedicated processing hardware or cryptographic accelerators. The key size can also be adjusted to achieve better performance with security trade-off. We believed that our work can help to solve the privacy issues encountered by the effective trust-based UTC systems when it comes to apply them into our real life. Therefore, we can enjoy a better Internet world with much less unwanted traffic.

References

1. Al-Qurishi M., Rahman S.M.M., Hossain M.S., Almogren A., Alrubaian M., Alamri A.,... and Gupta B.B. (2017). An efficient key agreement protocol for Sybil-precaution in online social networks. *Future Generation Computer Systems*, 84, 139–148.
2. Chaudhary P., Gupta S., Gupta B.B., Chandra V.S., Selvakumar S., Fire M.,... and Gangwar S. (2016). Auditing defense against XSS worms in online social network-based web applications. In: Gupta B., Agrawal D.P., and Yamaguchi S. (eds) *Handbook of Research on Modern Cryptographic Solutions for Computer and Cyber Security*, IGI Global, Hershey, PA, vol. 36, no. 5, pp. 216–245.
3. Livingstone S., and Haddon L. (2009). EU Kids Online. *Zeitschrift Für Psychologie/Journal of Psychology*, 217(4), 236.
4. Gou Z., Yamaguchi S., and Gupta B.B. (2016). Analysis of various security issues and challenges in cloud computing environment: a survey. In: Gupta B., Agrawal D.P., and Yamaguchi S. (eds) *Handbook of Research on Modern Cryptographic Solutions for Computer and Cyber Security*, IGI Global: Hershey, PA, pp. 393–419.
5. Stergiou C., Psannis K.E., Kim B.G., and Gupta B. (2016). Secure integration of IoT and cloud computing. *Future Generation Computer Systems*, 78, 964–975.
6. Zkik K., Orhanou G., and El Hajji S. (2017). Secure Mobile Multi Cloud Architecture for Authentication and Data Storage. *International Journal of Cloud Applications and Computing (IJCAC)*, 7(2), 62–76.
7. Tewari A., and Gupta B.B. (2017). A lightweight mutual authentication protocol based on elliptic curve cryptography for IoT devices. *International Journal of Advanced Intelligence Paradigms*, 9(2–3), 111–121.
8. Memos V.A., Psannis K.E., Ishibashi Y., Kim B.G., and Gupta B.B. (2017). An efficient algorithm for media-based surveillance system (EAMSuS) in IoT Smart City Framework. *Future Generation Computer Systems*, 83, 619–628.
9. Zhang Z., Sun R., Zhao C., Wang J., Chang C.K., and Gupta B.B. (2017). CyVOD: a novel trinity multimedia social network scheme. *Multimedia Tools and Applications*, 76(18), 18513–18529.
10. Yan Z., Kantola R., and Shen Y. (2014). A generic solution for unwanted traffic control through trust management. *New Review of Hypermedia and Multimedia*, 20(1), 25–51.
11. Zheleva E., Kolcz A., and Getoor L. (2008). Trusting spam reporters: A reporter-based reputation system for email filtering. *ACM Transactions on Information Systems (TOIS)*, 27(1), 3.
12. Liu W.W., Aggarwal S., and Duan Z. (2009). Incorporating accountability into internet e-mail. *Journal of Digital Forensic Practice*, 2(4), 209–220.
13. Jianzhong Z., Wei X., Yudi P., and Jingdong X. (2010). MailTrust: a mail reputation mechanism based on improved TrustGuard. In: *Communications and Mobile Computing (CMC), 2010 International Conference*, IEEE, vol. 1, pp. 218–222.

14. Sirivianos M., Kim K., and Yang X. (2011). Socialfilter: Introducing social trust to collaborative spam mitigation. In: *INFOCOM, 2011 Proceedings IEEE*, IEEE: Shanghai, China, pp. 2300–2308.

15. Hameed S., Fu X., Hui P., and Sastry N. (2011). LENS: Leveraging social networking and trust to prevent spam transmission. In Network Protocols (ICNP), In: *2011 19th IEEE International Conference*, IEEE: Vancouver, BC, pp. 13–18.

16. Li Z., and Shen H. (2011). Soap: A social network aided personalized and effective spam filter to clean your e-mail box. In: *INFOCOM, 2011 Proceedings IEEE*, IEEE: Shanghai, China, pp. 1835–1843.

17. Page L., Brin S., Motwani R., and Winograd T. (1999). The PageRank citation ranking: Bringing order to the web. Stanford InfoLab.

18. Gyöngyi Z., Garcia-Molina H., and Pedersen J. (2004). Combating web spam with trustrank. In: *Proceedings of the Thirtieth international conference on Very large data bases*, VLDB Endowment: Toronto, Canada, vol. 30, pp. 576–587.

19. Wu B., Goel V., and Davison B.D. (2006). Topical TrustRank: Using topicality to combat web spam. In: *Proceedings of the 15th international conference on World Wide Web*, ACM: Edinburgh, Scotland, pp. 63–72.

20. Krishnan V., and Raj R. (2006). Web spam detection with anti-trust rank. In: *AIRWeb*, Seattle, WA, vol. 6, pp. 37–40.

21. Wu B., Goel V., and Davison B.D. (2006). *Propagating Trust and Distrust to Demote Web Spam*, MTW: Edinburgh, Scotland, p. 190.

22. Liu X., Wang Y., Zhu S., and Lin H. (2013). Combating Web spam through trust–distrust propagation with confidence. *Pattern Recognition Letters*, 34(13), 1462–1469.

23. Zhang X., Wang Y., Mou N., and Liang W. (2014). Propagating both trust and distrust with target differentiation for combating link-based Web spam. *ACM Transactions on the Web (TWEB)*, 8(3), 15.

24. Wang W., Zeng G., and Tang D. (2010). Using evidence based content trust model for spam detection. *Expert Systems with Applications*, 37(8), 5599–5606.

25. Yan, Z. (Ed.). (2013). *Trust Management in Mobile Environments: Autonomic and Usable Models: Autonomic and Usable Models*. IGI Global.

26. Chen L., Yan Z., Zhang W., and Kantola R. (2015). TruSMS: a trustworthy SMS spam control system based on trust management. *Future Generation Computer Systems*, 49, 77–93.

27. Wang Y., Xiang Y., Zhang J., Zhou W., Wei G., and Yang L.T. (2014). Internet traffic classification using constrained clustering. *IEEE Transactions on Parallel and Distributed Systems*, 25(11), 2932–2943.

28. Zhang J., Chen C., Xiang Y., Zhou W., and Xiang Y. (2013). Internet traffic classification by aggregating correlated naive bayes predictions. *IEEE Transactions on Information Forensics and Security*, 8(1), 5–15.

29. Wang D., Irani D., and Pu C. (2013, October). A study on evolution of email spam over fifteen years. In: *Collaborative Computing: Networking, Applications and Worksharing (Collaboratecom)*, 2013 9th International Conference Conference, IEEE: Austin, TX, pp. 1–10.

30. Kargupta H., Datta S., Wang Q., and Sivakumar K. (2005). Random-data perturbation techniques and privacy-preserving data mining. *Knowledge and Information Systems*, 7(4), 387–414.

31. Ibtihal M., and Hassan N. (2017). Homomorphic Encryption as a Service for Outsourced Images in Mobile Cloud Computing Environment. *International Journal of Cloud Applications and Computing (IJCAC)*, 7(2), 27–40.

32. Yu C., Li J., Li X., Ren X., and Gupta B.B. (2017). Four-image encryption scheme based on quaternion Fresnel transform, chaos and computer generated hologram. *Multimedia Tools and Applications*, 77(4), 4585–4608.

33. Jararweh Y., Al-Sharqawi O., Abdulla N., Tawalbeh L.A., and Alhammouri M. (2014). High-Throughput Encryption for Cloud Computing Storage System. *International Journal of Cloud Applications and Computing (IJCAC)*, 4(2), 1–14.

34. Machanavajjhala A., Gehrke J., Kifer D., and Venkitasubramaniam M. (2006, April). l-diversity: Privacy beyond k-anonymity. In: *Data Engineering, 2006. ICDE'06. Proceedings of the 22nd International Conference*, IEEE, pp. 24–24.

35. Malina, L., Hajny, J., Fujdiak, R., and Hosek, J. (2016). On perspective of security and privacy-preserving solutions in the Internet of Things. *Computer Networks*, 102, 83–95.

36. Fontaine C., and Galand F. (2007). A survey of homomorphic encryption for nonspecialists. *EURASIP Journal on Information Security*, 2007(1), 013801.
37. Diffie W., and Hellman M. (1976). New directions in cryptography. *IEEE Transactions on Information Theory*, 22(6), 644–654.
38. Bellare M., Desai A., Pointcheval D., and Rogaway P. (1998). Relations among notions of security for public-key encryption schemes. In: *Advances in Cryptology—CRYPTO'98*, Springer: Berlin/Heidelberg, pp. 26–45.
39. Zhang L., Zheng Y., and Kantoa R. (2016). A Review of Homomorphic Encryption and its Applications. In: *Proceedings of the 9th EAI International Conference on Mobile Multimedia Communications*, ICST (Institute for Computer Sciences, Social-Informatics and Telecommunications Engineering): Xi'an, China, pp. 97–106.
40. Rivest R.L., Shamir A., and Adleman L. (1978). A method for obtaining digital signatures and public-key cryptosystems. *Communications of the ACM*, 21(2), 120–126.
41. Hwang M.S., Chang C.C., and Hwang K.F. (2002). An ElGamal-like cryptosystem for enciphering large messages. *IEEE Transactions on Knowledge and Data Engineering*, 14(2), 445–446.
42. Cramer R., Gennaro R., and Schoenmakers B. (1997). A secure and optimally efficient multi-authority election scheme. *Transactions on Emerging Telecommunications Technologies*, 8(5), 481–490.
43. Paillier P. (1999). Public-Key Cryptosystems Based on Composite Degree Residuosity Classes. In: Stern J. (ed) *Advances in Cryptology – EUROCRYPT '99*. Springer: Berlin, Heidelberg, pp. 223–238.
44. Gentry C. (2009). *A Fully Homomorphic Encryption Scheme*, Stanford University: Stanford.
45. Stehlé, D., and Steinfeld R. (2010). Faster fully homomorphic encryption. *Advances in Cryptology-ASIACRYPT*, 2010, 377–394.
46. Van Dijk M., Gentry C., Halevi S., and Vaikuntanathan V. (2010, May). Fully homomorphic encryption over the integers. In: *Annual International Conference on the Theory and Applications of Cryptographic Techniques*, Springer: Berlin Heidelberg.
47. Gentry C. (2009). Fully homomorphic encryption using ideal lattices. In: *STOC*, vol. 9, no. 2009, pp. 169–178).
48. Vaikuntanathan V. (2011). Computing blindfolded: New developments in fully homomorphic encryption. In: *Foundations of Computer Science (FOCS), 2011 IEEE 52nd Annual Symposium*, IEEE: Palm Springs, CA, pp. 5–16.
49. Gentry C., and Halevi S. (2011). Implementing Gentry's Fully-Homomorphic Encryption Scheme. In: Paterson K.G. (ed) *Advances in Cryptology – EUROCRYPT 2011*. Springer: Berlin, Heidelberg, pp. 129–148.
50. Coron J.S., Mandal A., Naccache D., and Tibouchi M. (2011). Fully Homomorphic Encryption over the Integers with Shorter Public Keys. In: Rogaway P. (ed) *Advances in Cryptology – CRYPTO 2011*. Springer: Berlin, Heidelberg, pp. 487–504.
51. Brakerski Z., and Vaikuntanathan V. (2014). Efficient fully homomorphic encryption from (standard) LWE. *SIAM Journal on Computing*, 43(2), 831–871.
52. Brakerski Z., Gentry C., and Vaikuntanathan V. (2014). (Leveled) fully homomorphic encryption without bootstrapping. *ACM Transactions on Computation Theory (TOCT)*, 6(3), 13.
53. Zhang L., Yan Z., and Kantola R. (2017). Privacy-preserving trust management for unwanted traffic control. *Future Generation Computer Systems*, 72, 305–318.

Chapter 16

DOM-Guard: Defeating DOM-Based Injection of XSS Worms in HTML5 Web Applications on Mobile-Based Cloud Platforms

Brij B. Gupta, Himanshu Soni, Pankaj Siwan, and Ankit Kumar
National Institute of Technology Kurukshetra

Shashank Gupta
Birla Institute of Technology and Science Pilani

Contents

16.1 Introduction

The evolution of mobile cloud computing exempted the industries and their consumers from handling the description of countless specifics, like loading resources and computation constraints. It is clearly highlighted in [1] that almost 91% of administrations in Europe and United States approved that drop in the cost is the main motivation for them to move to the platforms of cloud infrastructure. Slight investment, price deduction, and prompt implementation are some of the key aspects that motivate the enterprises to facilitate the services of mobile cloud infrastructure and permit them for putting the emphasis on essential industry worries and main concern, instead of dealing with nominal concerns. Though, such advantages turn out to be problematic for applications, which are latency-sensitive and that need nodes in the area to avail their suspension requests. Smartphones are getting largely utilized in the day-to-day routine lifecycle of the people. The existing cloud computing prototypes cannot satisfy their necessities of motion provision, position alertness, and low latency [2]. In addition, the virtual machines of cloud platforms cannot support endpoints with rich facilities, comprising the applications with small latency necessities. The reason behind such nonoptimal performance is that the virtual machines of cloud platforms perform the computation at the core of the network, which is very far away from ground level.

H5-XSS attack vectors are continuously posing a risk to contemporary web platforms of HTML5 in addition to Web 2.0, despite ample XSS defensive methodologies [3–6,40–43]. Recently, abundant H5-XSS attack vector solutions have been proposed for the mobile cloud-hosted web platforms. However, regardless of growing utilization of cloud computing, numerous issues are still unsettled due to in-built complications of cloud computing like untrustworthy latency, absence of movement provision, and position alertness [7–9]. Figure 16.1 explains one pattern of XSS attack.

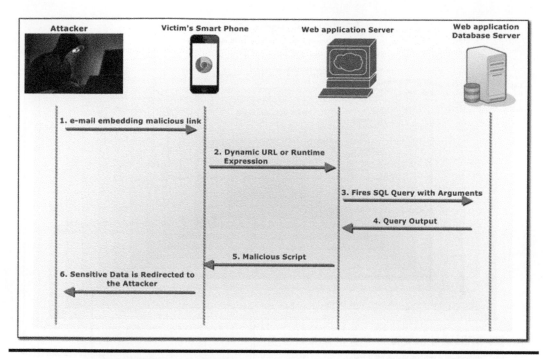

Figure 16.1   Exploitation of XSS attack.

The existing XSS filters [23–25] merely scan for such suspicious sequence of H5 strings. A popup message would blink on the screen with note "10". The recent H5-defensive models were regularly assessed by using conventional JS suspicious strings from single XSS cheat sheet. Though, four new attack vector sources of strings (that comprises H5-XSS attack scripts specially designed for vulnerable HTML5 web applications) are accessible on WWW. Hence, vigorous solutions ought to be tested by using suspicious sequence of attack strings from such sources too [10–11]. A maximum quantum of solutions were validated on static web platforms. However, none of them were analyzed on real virtual infrastructures of web platforms. Furthermore, sanitization of vulnerable sequence of script was well-thought-out to be the utmost vigorous practice. However, our recent work filters such suspicious scripts by defining their first-level hierarchy of background. They usually avoid finding out nested backgrounds of such illicit scripts. Without realizing the nested background of such suspicious strings of different script, sanitization mechanism of any defensive methodology is no longer considered to be effective. Figure 16.2 illustrates the abstract view of the procedure used to XSS attack on a vulnerable web application. The following are the chain of steps of exploiting the vulnerabilities of Document Object Model (DOM)-based XSS attacks:

■ The attacker creates a URL web address incorporating a malicious JavaScript string and transmits to the browser of the victim.
■ The victim is tricked by an attacker into requesting the URL address from the VWA.
■ The VWA accepts the HTTP request, although it does not incorporate the malicious injected JavaScript string in the HTTP response message.
■ The web browser of the victim runs the benign JavaScript code inside the HTTP response, resulting the malicious JavaScript to be injected into web page.

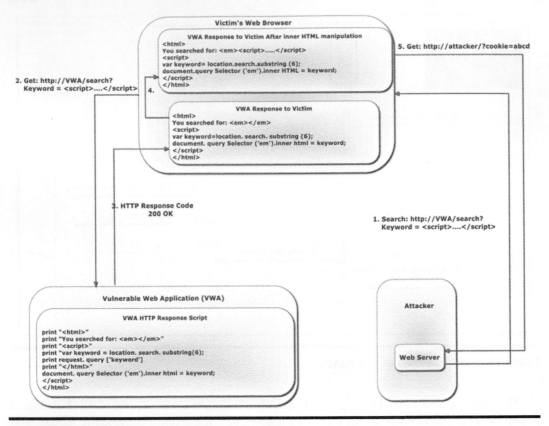

Figure 16.2   Exploitation of DOM-based XSS attack.

The web browser of the victim runs the malicious injected JavaScript, transferring the victim's credentials (e.g., cookies) to the web server of an attacker.

16.1.1 Existing Work

Galan et al. [31] proposed multi-agent system for the scanning of websites in an automated manner to discover the occurrence of XSS vulnerabilities exploitable by stored XSS attack. Likarish et al. [32] proposed a method that generates a robust database of scripts (including benign and malicious script code) and extracts the features of web page for classifying them vulnerable or non-vulnerable. The technique finally utilizes the classifiers that further utilize the extracted features and database to detect the infected web page.

Vogt et al. [33] proposed a technique that explores the tainted information and track this information whenever it is being retrieved by the malicious functions executed inside the browser. If such process triggers the information flow to untrusted third party, then it informs the user to execute defending actions like stop transfer, etc. Wang et al. [34] proposed a technique that utilizes static detection algorithm to identify vulnerabilities and use this information for program slicing to create slices of application that corresponds to stored XSS bugs in program. However, it is not compatible with the object-oriented features of PHP, and also the complex program will make slicing difficult. Vishnu et al. [35] designed a machine learning algorithm that initially collects the malicious and benign web pages and then, extracts URL and JavaScript-based features.

Acker et al. [36] designed a technique, FlashOver, to detect XSS susceptibilities in the Adobe Flash-based web platforms. The technique implements static analysis to identify vulnerable variables in the ActionScript (scripting language for Flash applications), which are initialized using the user input. These variables are then used by the dynamic analysis component to determine real vulnerability present in the web applications. Nunan et al. [37] present an automated classification technique using supervised machine learning algorithm that initially performs the obfuscation and de-obfuscation of untrusted JavaScript code. Hereafter, the process of feature classification gets initiated on the de-obfuscated code. These features are classified into three main sub-classes: obfuscation-based features, suspicious patterns, and HTML/JavaScript features. Finally, classification is executed, where it is used to predict whether the web page is vulnerable or not. Recently, numerous researchers designed background-familiar filtering of suspicious strings of scripts. Livshits [15] proposed a method of sanitizer assignment by examining the path of illicit data in the web application. Though, assignment of sanitizer is fixed and from time to time transforms to dynamic, anywhere essential. Samuel [16] designed a technique that could be operated with current templating language development platforms for executing background-familiar sanitization. Usually, web platform development background has limited feeling of contexts, and hence, the existing solutions [31–35] cannot offer correct and complete nested context-aware auto-sanitization mechanisms. In addition, they are unable to sense the nested backgrounds of suspicious sequence of susceptible scripts.

16.1.2 Existing Performance Issues

In view of the growing popularity of the XSS-Guard [12] and the limited use of the source code of web applications in their experiments of malicious script detection particularly aiming to look at online users endpoints, non-source code analysis in XSS attack prediction and False Positive Rate (FPR) assessment are gaining momentum, more specifically on the platforms of Online Social Network (OSN). In recent years, tremendous progresses have been made in web proxy-based monitoring systems [34–36] and are constantly omitting the designing and development of precise sanitizers and their appropriate placement in the source code of web applications. Recently, machine learning algorithms (Naïve Bayes, Support Vector Machine, and J48 Decision Tree) have emerged as a fast and cost-effective alternative technique for early assessment of malicious script attack vectors [13]. Commercial expert systems (like AppScan, N-Stalker, Zed Attack Proxy, WebInspect, and Acunetix) are constantly utilized by web developers in predicting the XSS attack vectors [17]. The drawback of these scanners is that they use regular expressions to detect the presence of dynamic content that results in low fidelity and banning of benign HTML content. Therefore, for many years, FPR of such techniques is still uncontrollable. Most of the recent XSS defensive techniques are platform-dependent, as different parsers have different ways of interpretation of script content and hence, web browsers have a variety of different parsing quirks. To solve this issue, a customized platform-independent HTML parser (i.e., BIXSAN) generates a parse tree at browser-side to reduce the irregular behavior of web browsers [38]. Later on, it was evaluated on several infrastructures of web browsers (such as Opera, Netscape, Internet Explorer (IE), Firefox, and Google Chrome) and found to be less adaptive, since it demands re-architecting the existing infrastructure of such web browsers. In addition, the infrastructure settings of such existing techniques are not scalable enough to be integrated effectively and evaluated for the web applications hosted on the virtual machines of cloud platforms. XSS exploitations are practiced in two forms: Stored and Reflected XSS, and malicious script code is usually introduced on the server-side.

Innumerable defensive solutions exist for the two classes of XSS worms. Despite the many solutions available, very few are up to the mark against the latest type of XSS attacks, for instance, one factor is introduction of HTML5, though HTML5 is helping to achieve high caliber for the web applications in terms of facilities, design, and evolving user instructiveness to a whole new different level and is also viewed as a substitute to the Adobe's Flash and Microsoft's Silverlight but also HTML5 hurled us with new security challenges and attack vulnerabilities which *Machine Learning for Computer and Cyber Security: Principles, Algorithms, and Practices* needs to be taken care of while developing web applications. HTML5 offers Cross-Origin Resource Sharing (CORS) which circumvent same origin policy, and hence, it increases the vulnerabilities to attacks such as XSS and CSRF. HTML5 offers many APIs like web worker, history, and properties including <video>, <source>, and <autofocus> tags, which are used for creating new XSS attack vectors like <video><source on error= "<script>alert("XSS ATTACK")</script>"></video>. Contemporary web browsers or available XSS attack filters are inefficient against these new HTML5 attack vectors. Furthermore, unlike another language, malicious functions are detected at the runtime [7]. Moreover, most of the web applications allow third-party JavaScript through <script> tag or link tag <a>, which is the main reason for such attacks; thus, the code is retrieved directly from the third-party source and processed immediately. So, this code is not controlled by the application at the host, not even at the web servers. Therefore, there is a requirement for a DOM-based XSS attack defensive solution that will ferret out the XSS attack vectors and diagnose them with an effective mechanism of sanitizing/filtering the HTML5 XSS attack vectors. Majority of the available techniques focused on methods of string matching, which were not able to recognize the skewed JavaScript attack vector injections. Moreover, the choice of parser also matters a lot as JSOUP Parser can sanitize the whitelist, so it can be a good choice. Sanitization/filtering of dangerous variables of JavaScript code without assessing their context is an ineffective sanitization technique in attenuating the effect of JavaScript attack vector.

16.1.3 Key Contributions

Based on such severe performance issues, this chapter presents a DOM-Guard, which detects and mitigates the DOM-based injection XSS attacks from the HTML5 web applications accessed through the mobile cloud computing platforms. DOM-Guard detects the injection of XSS worms in the DOM tree at runtime and performs the context-sensitive sanitization on the malicious variables embedded in such worms. The prototype of our DOM-Guard was developed in Java development framework and integrated its settings on the virtual machines of mobile cloud platforms. Experimental evaluation of our mobile cloud-based framework was done on the tested suite of real-world, mobile-based, HTML5-based web applications by referring the latest XSS attack vectors from the freely available XSS attack vector repositories [18–22]. Performance evaluation results revealed that our mobile cloud-based framework detects the injection of XSS worms in the runtime generation of DOM tree with a tolerable rate of false positives and false negatives and experienced acceptable performance overhead during the runtime sanitization of XSS worms. The rest of the chapter is organized as follows: in Section 16.2, we have introduced our work in detail. Implementation and evaluation of our work are discussed in Section 16.3. Finally, Section 16.4 concludes our work and discusses further scope of the work.

16.2 Proposed Framework: DOM-Guard

DOM-Guard detects the injection of XSS worms in the DOM tree of HTTP response and alleviates the effect of such worms by performing the context-aware sanitization on the malicious variables embedded in such worms. Our framework works for the contemporary mobile cloud-based HTML5 web applications. The novelty of our framework lies in the fact that it generates the DOM tree of the HTTP response at runtime and obstructs the execution of untrusted injected JavaScript code in this tree. In addition, it identifies those script nodes in which such malicious injection happens, and recognizes not only the context but also the nested context of embedded variables in such malicious worms. Such nested contexts are determined automatically for executing the process of context-aware sanitization on such malicious variables.

16.2.1 Abstract View

DOM-Guard is a runtime DOM tree generator and context-aware sanitization-based framework that scans for the DOM-based XSS vulnerabilities in the mobile cloud-based HTML5 web applications. Figure 16.3 highlights the abstract design view of our proposed mobile cloud-based framework. The OSN server deployed in the virtual machine of cloud platform initially extracts the HTTP request (HREQ) from the smartphone user. The OSN server generates the DOM tree at runtime corresponding to generated HTTP response (HRES) message. This tree is traversed and explored for the extraction of script nodes. The variable context finder will match the script content against the whitelist of scripts which is generated at the offline mode by referring the existing modules of web applications. Any variation observed in the script content will simply indicate the injection of XSS worms in the DOM tree. The injected script content will be transmitted to the automatic context-aware escaping tool component that determines the nested context of such variables. Based on the determined context of such variables, this component will perform the context-sensitive sanitization on such untrusted variables, and finally it generates and transmits a sanitized safe HTML document to the smartphone user.

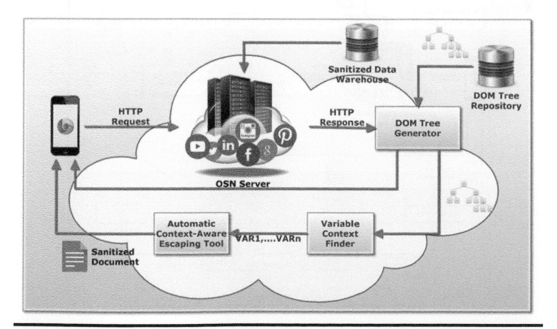

Figure 16.3 Overview of abstract view of DOM-Guard.

16.2.2 *Detailed Design Illustration*

DOM-Guard Executes in Two Modes: Offline and online modes. Figure 16.4 provides a detailed design view of our DOM-Guard. The training mode extracts all the benign JavaScript code by referring the script nodes of DOM tree and generates a whitelist of such script code. This whitelist will be further utilized for the detection of injected scripts in the DOM tree at the online

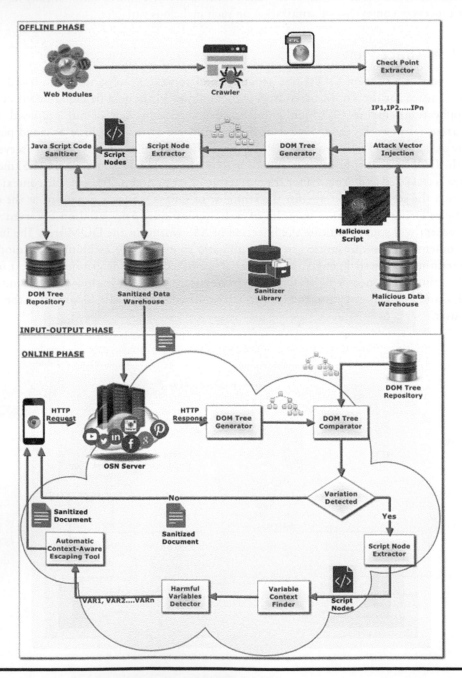

Figure 16.4   Detailed design overview of DOM-Guard.

mode. The detection mode performs the context-sensitive sanitization on the injected obfuscated JavaScript code embedded in the DOM tree generated during runtime. The following subsection discusses the detailed illustration of both these modes.

16.2.2.1 Offline Phase

This phase extracts and scans all the modules of the existing web applications by utilizing the web spider component. The mode extracts all the script content embedded in such modules by generating the static DOM tree. All the legitimate script content is saved in the whitelist of scripts.

- This phase starts with crawling of web pages in which the web modules are scanned and HTML pages, Style Sheets, and JavaScripts are produced and act as input to Check Point Extractor which is used for extracting check points.
- These check points are generally those fields that require interaction with users or the fields that are affected by the input provided by users for textboxes, email fields, etc.
- The attack vectors are the main input of training phase because the existing attack vectors add resistance to the crawled web pages and also prevent attack by related attack vectors. Malicious data warehouse is provided with the existing attack vectors which are injected through these check points extracted above.
- These attack vectors result in malicious pages from which DOM trees containing script nodes are generated, and these script nodes are sanitized with the help of data sanitization algorithms, and the outputs are passed to input/output phase.

Figure 16.5 provides a detailed illustration of offline phase of DOM-Guard. Extract all the web pages Wp from websites. Crawl all the web pages and generate HTML pages, style sheets, JavaScripts, etc. Extract all the injection points, and save them to IP_Log. Extract all the attack vectors from malicious data warehouse to AV_Log. Inject attack vectors on the crawled web pages. Generate DOM tree DT from malicious web pages. Extract the script nodes in DOM tree, and send them to JavaScript sanitizer and further to context-aware escaping tool.

16.2.2.2 Input/Output Phase

This phase handles storage units, i.e., repositories, warehouses, and libraries, that store the data transacted between other two phases. It provides input libraries for the functionality of modules and stores the output of phases for further use. All the transactions performed in each phase require some storage units like registers, repository to restore failed transactions for, e.g., storing multiple DOM trees which may be used in future, so the input/output phase is an important phase of the framework.

16.2.2.3 Online Phase

This phase detects the injection of XSS attack vectors in the DOM tree. The different context of malicious variables will be determined in this mode and accordingly perform the context-sensitive sanitization on such variables for alleviating the effect of DOM-based XSS vulnerabilities. Figure 16.6 describes the algorithm for online phase. Extract the parameters and URL links contained in the HTTP response. Generate DOM tree DT from the HTTP response. The DOM tree may contain malicious nodes, so compare DOM tree with the existing DOM trees in DOM tree

Algorithm: Offline Phase
Input: Modules of OSSN websites
Output: Sanitized Code and DOM Trees
Start
DOM_tree_Repo DR $\Leftarrow \phi$
San_code_Repo SR $\Leftarrow \phi$
AV_Log $\Leftarrow \phi$
IP_Log $\Leftarrow \phi$
Mod_Log $\Leftarrow \phi$
SN_Log $\Leftarrow \phi$
foreach Wp $\in$ WS
Mj $\Leftarrow$ retrieve_modules(Wp);   /*Extract web modules from web pages*/
Mod_Log $\Leftarrow$ Mj $\cup$ Mod_Log;
End
foreach Mj $\in$ Mod_Log
Cwp $\Leftarrow$ crawl_module(Mj);   /*Crawl to traverse internal links*/
foreach Cwp $\in$ Wp
IPj $\Leftarrow$ extract_injection_points(Cwp);
IP_Log $\Leftarrow$ IPj $\cup$ IP_Log;
End
foreach IPj $\in$ IP_Log
AV_Log $\Leftarrow$ extract_attack_vectors( );   /*Extract attack vectors for injection*/
Cwp $\Leftarrow$ Cwp $\cup$ perform_Attack(Cwp, IP_Log, AV_Log);
End
DT $\Leftarrow$ generate_DOM_tree(Cwp);
SN_Log $\Leftarrow$ SN_Log $\cup$ extract_script_nodes(DT);
San_code $\Leftarrow$ javascript_Sanitizer(SN_Log);   /*Sanitize the script nodes*/
DR.add_tree(DT);
SR.add_code(San_code);
End

Figure 16.5   Detailed algorithm of offline phase.

repository, i.e., DT is equal to DT_R or not. If they are equal, extract the sanitized code San_Code from sanitized data warehouse and generate a final response Fin_Res from H_{RES} and San_Code. If they are not equal, then process the DOM tree DT further to remove malicious content. Extract the script nodes SN in SN_Log from DT, and find the context of variables in each of the script nodes SN_J, and save the output in Var_Log. Extract harmful variables from Var_Log using harmful_Var(), and store the result in H_Var_Log. Sanitize the harmful variables VAR1, VAR2, ..., VARn using context escaping tool, and store the sanitized output in San_Code, and generate a final response Fin_Res from H_{RES} and San_Code. Return the Fin_Res to mobile browser. This phase starts with the extraction of parameters from HTTP requests that contain parameters and URL links and are sent to OSN server.

■ OSN server generates HTTP response, and the HTTP response is used to generate DOM trees, and DOM trees are stored in repository.

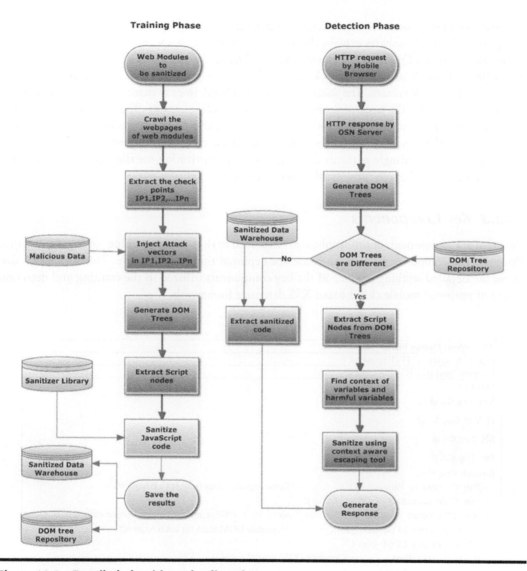

Figure 16.6 Detailed algorithm of online phase.

- These DOM trees are compared with the trees in DOM tree repository using comparator, and the degree of variation is calculated by observing the difference between the arrangements of nodes in trees.
- If variations are detected, the script nodes extractor extracts the script nodes from DOM trees to filter the malicious script nodes from the web pages.
- Variables that behave differently in different contexts are extracted using variable context finder and harmful variables VAR1, VAR2, ..., VARn are further sanitized using context-aware sanitization to generate a final sanitized document which is passed to mobile web browser.
- If variations are not detected in DOM trees, the sanitized document from sanitized data warehouse is passed to mobile web browser.

The working flow of both the offline and online modes of our proposed framework is illustrated in Figure 16.7. The flowcharts explain the working of the framework in offline and online modes. In the offline mode, DOM tree is generated according to the offline HTTP response embedded in sanitized HTML5-based XSS attack vectors. The context-aware sanitization is used for sanitization of such attack vectors. The variation between DOM trees is detected in the online mode by comparing the DOM trees of both the offline and online modes. The variation observed in the DOM tree of online mode will indicate the injection of XSS attack vector during the online mode. Finally, the context of variables is found in attack vectors, and harmful variables will be determined and accordingly perform the context-aware sanitization for the safe interpretation of HTTP response on the web browser of smartphone user.

16.2.3 Key Components

Note that the components of online phase are deployed in the virtual machines of cloud platforms. However, the components of offline phase are deployed on the server-side. This subsection discusses the detailed working of some of the key components utilized in the training and detection modes of proposed mobile cloud-based XSS defensive framework.

Algorithm: Online Phase
Input: A series of HTTP requests
Output: Sanitized HTTP Response

```
Start
Var_Log ⟸ φ
H_Var_Log ⟸ φ
SN_Log ⟸ φ
Par_Log ⟸ φ
foreach HJ ∈ HREQ
    ParJ ⟸ retrieve_Parameters(HJ);          /*Retrieve parameters from HTTP requests*/
    San_Code ⟸ extract_Sanitized_Code();
    HRES ⟸ generate_Response(HJ, ParJ, San_Code)       /*Generate response for requests*/
    DT ⟸ generate_DOM_tree(HRES);          /*Generate DOM trees for each request*/
    DTR ⟸ extract_DOM_tree();
    if (DT == DTR) then          /*Compare DOM trees*/
        │ Fin_HRES ⟸ HRES;
    End
    Else
        SN_Log ⟸ SN_Log ∪ extract_script_nodes(DT);
        foreach SNJ ∈ SN_Log
            │ Var_Log ⟸ Var_Log ∪ variable_Context(SNJ);    /*Find context of variables*/
        End
        H_Var_Log ⟸ harmful_Var(Var_Log);
        foreach VarJ ∈ H_Var_Log
            │ San_Code ⟸ San_Code ∪ context_escape(VarJ);   /*Escape harmful content using tools*/
        End
        Fin_HRES ⟸ generate_Response(HRES, San_Code);
    End
    return Fin_HRES;
end
```

Figure 16.7 Flowcharts of offline and online phase.

16.2.3.1 Web Module

A web module contains web components and static web content files, such as images, which are called web resources. A web module is a specific structure. The top-level directory of web module is the document root of the application. The document root is where PHP pages, client-side classes and archives, and static web resources, such as images, are stored.

16.2.3.2 Web Crawler

A web crawler browses the web pages for the purpose of extracting required data. Web crawlers can copy all the browsed pages and save them for later processing. Crawlers come into play when large collections of pages are accessed. It can validate hyperlinks and HTML code. The web crawler starts with a list of URLs to visit. The URLs are recursively visited according to a set of policies. If the crawling is performed on websites, it copies and saves the information in such a way that they can be viewed, read, and navigated as they were on the live web.

16.2.3.3 Check Point Extractor

The injection points on web pages are those places where there is possibility of an attack. These injection points can be input fields, dynamic content on web pages, etc. The check point extractor searches for vulnerable areas in crawled web pages to identify the injection points. All identified injection points may or may not be vulnerable to different kinds of attacks, so these points are further processed using the existing attack vectors to extract the vulnerable injection points. Figure 16.8 depicts a detailed algorithm of extraction of check points from the existing modules of web applications. For each web page W_P, crawl the web page to generate crawled web pages C_{WP}. Extract the malicious content from crawled web pages, and store them in Mal_Log. Extract URLs of crawled pages, and store them in URL_Log. Extract injection points using crawled pages C_{WP}, Mal_Log, URL_Log, and save them to IP_Log. Return the list of injection points in IP_Log.

Algorithm: Extraction of Check Points
Input: A series of web pages
Output: Set of Injection Points
Start
Mal_Log $\Leftarrow \phi$
URL_Log $\Leftarrow \phi$
IP_Log $\Leftarrow \phi$
foreach $W_P \in$ WP
$C_{WP} \Leftarrow$ crawl_Page(W_P);
Mal_Log $\Leftarrow$ Mal_Log $\cup$ malicious_content(W_P);
URL_Log $\Leftarrow$ URL_Log $\cup$ extract_url_addr(C_{WP});
$IP_J \Leftarrow$ extract_injection_points(C_{WP}, Mal_Log, URL_Log);
IP_Log $\Leftarrow$ IP_Log $\cup$ IP_J;
end
return IP_Log;

Figure 16.8 Algorithm of extraction of injection points.

16.2.3.4 DOM Tree Generator

The DOM is a convention for representing and interacting with objects in HTML and XML documents. The DOM is platform-independent, and nodes of every document are organized in a tree structure, and this type of tree representation of HTML and XML objects is called DOM Trees. The node in a DOM tree can have several child nodes, and these nodes are called siblings. The DOM trees can be generated using DOM Tree generator, and these trees can be compared to verify the addition of malicious scripts in web pages. Figure 16.9 displays a detailed algorithm of DOM tree generation.

For each web page, extract HTML tags and store them to new_Tag variable. Create a set of all HTML tags into a Tag_Log. Push first tag to a stack, and add it to first node of tree and root points to that node. Run a loop till stack is not empty, and every time extract a new tag, and store it to a temp variable. If the tag is opening tag, then retrieve size of stack in variable n, and insert temp to Tag_Log. Crawl the DOM tree to the position where node is to be inserted. Add temp to this position, and push temp to stack. If the tag is closing tag then, pop the node from stack.

Algorithm: DOM Tree Generator
Input: A series of crawled web pages
Output: Set of DOM Trees
Start
Stack s ⇐ φ
Tree t ⇐ φ
Tag_Log ⇐ φ
foreach Wp ∈ WP
new_Tag ⇐ extract_Tag(Wp);   /*Extract tags*/
Tag_Log ⇐ new_Tag ∪ Tag_Log;
s.push(new_Tag);   /*Add node to stack*/
t.add_node(new_Tag, null);   /*Add first node to tree*/
while stack is not empty **do**
temp ⇐ extract_Tag(Wp);
if opening_Tag(temp) **do**
n ⇐ s.size();
Tag_Log ⇐ temp ∪ Tag_Log;   /*Store all opening tags*/
p ⇐ crawl_DOM_tree(t, n);   /*Crawl tree to get pointer for new node*/
t.add_node(temp, p);
s.push(temp);
End
else closing_Tag(temp) **do**
s.pop();
End
End
End
return t;

Figure 16.9 Algorithm of DOM tree generation.

16.2.3.5 Attack Vector Injection

Attack vectors are the JavaScript codes which, if injected to injection points, may cause malicious behavior in web page. There are many attack vectors, and new attack vectors are introduced very frequently. The existing attack vectors are stored in malicious data warehouse, and these can be used wherever required. When injected to web page, the attack vectors cause malicious nature if the web page is not immune to these types of attacks, i.e., the attack vectors are not processed before using them as an input in web pages.

16.2.3.6 Script Nodes Extractor

Script nodes are the nodes in DOM trees which contain the JavaScript content and may also contain malicious data, so it needs to be sanitized. These script nodes are extracted from DOM trees generated in the previous step, and the extracted script nodes are further sanitized to remove malicious content.

16.2.3.7 JavaScript Code Sanitizer

Code sanitization is a process of removing harmful data from the input information so as to reduce the malicious nature of the information. In HTML pages, malicious data is in the form of JavaScript code which needs to be filtered before storing to database. Code sanitization can be of the following types:

- Removing complete tag with malicious content in the form of attributes,
- Processing only harmful attributes and leaving the rest,
- Escaping the special characters to inhibit the execution of code.

16.2.3.8 Sanitized Data Warehouse

Sanitized data warehouse stores the sanitized code which is stored as the output of the last step of training phase. This sanitized code is resistant against the existing attack vectors, and it can be used in detection phase if no new attack vector is inserted in the web page.

16.2.3.9 DOM Tree Repository

Every web page has a separate DOM tree, so to store a large number of DOM trees, repository is used. The DOM tree is tree representation of HTML objects where the objects are represented as nodes. The main concern is to filter the script nodes and compare one DOM tree with another. DOM tree repository stores the DOM tree which is stored as the output of the last step of training phase and further used for comparison in detection phase.

16.2.3.10 Sanitizer Library

The sanitizer library provides the input libraries required for code sanitization. It contains the required functions and classes which can be used with ease to perform sanitization process.

16.2.3.11 Malicious Data Repository

The malicious data repository stores the existing attack vectors and information regarding each attack vector. The attack vectors are used for injection on check points to identify the vulnerable check points.

16.2.3.12 Mobile Web Browser

A mobile browser is a web browser designed for use on a mobile device such as a mobile phone. Mobile browsers are optimized so as to display web content most effectively for small screens of portable devices. Parameters in HTTP requests from mobile browsers may contain malicious information which needs to be sanitized before final response is generated. The request from browser contains parameters and URL links, and the URL links are accessed to extract hidden JavaScript within the URL for proper sanitization. Figure 16.10 describes the algorithm of extraction related to parameter and URL values.

Extract parameters from each HTTP request H_J, and save them to Par_Log. For each parameter in Par_Log, extract internal links for processing. Request data contained in links, and extract JavaScript content from these links. Store the JavaScript code in JL_Log for processing the HTTP response.

16.2.3.13 OSN Server

OSN server is a server that provides services to OSSN (Open Source Social Networking) web application, e.g., Wordpress, HumHub, and Drupal. The work of server is to handle HTTP request and process the malicious parameters from it. It further generates HTTP response using

---

Algorithm: Parameter and URL Value Extraction
Input: A series of HTTP requests
Output: Extracted parameters and URLs
Start
JL_Log $\Leftarrow \phi$
Par_Log $\Leftarrow \phi$
foreach $H_J \in H_{REQ}$
$Par_J \Leftarrow$ retrieve_Parameters(H_J);
Par_Log $\Leftarrow$ Par_Log $\cup$ Par_J;
end
foreach $Par_J \in$ Par_Log
$L_J \Leftarrow$ extract_links(Par_J);
if ($\exists$ L_J) **then**
Request data contained in Links from server
$JS_L \Leftarrow$ extract_JS_links(L_J);
JL_Log $\Leftarrow$ JL_Log $\cup$ JS_J;
end
else
Transmit (H_J, Par_J) to server
end
end

Figure 16.10 Algorithm of parameter and URL value extraction.

parameters extracted from requests and sanitized code from repository which is further processed in online mode to detect malicious data. For each HTTP request, retrieve parameters and URL and store it in URL_J. Parse the URL form malicious content detection, and generate web pages from parsed URLs. Generate DOM trees according to HTTP response, and extract corresponding trees from repository. Compare the trees, and process the response further according to the result of comparator. Figure 16.11 illustrates the algorithm of detection of untrusted JavaScript code in the dynamically generated DOM tree at online phase.

16.2.3.14 Sanitized Code Extractor

Sanitized code extractor extracts the sanitized code generated in training phase, and if variation between DOM trees is not present, then this sanitized code is used for generating final HTTP response with sanitized code as input and sanitized document as output.

Algorithm: Processing HTTP Response
Input: A series of HTTP response
Output: Sanitized HTTP response
Start
Var_Log $\Leftarrow \phi$
H_Var_Log $\Leftarrow \phi$
SN_Log $\Leftarrow \phi$
Par_Log $\Leftarrow \phi$
foreach $H_J \in H_{RES}$
$URL_J \Leftarrow$ retrieve_URL(H_J);   /*Retrieve all URLs from HTTP requests*/
$P_{URL} \Leftarrow$ parse_URL(URL_J);
$W_P \Leftarrow$ generate_Webpage(P_{URL});   /*Generate web pages using URLs*/
foreach $W_J \in W_P$
DT $\Leftarrow$ generate_DOM_tree(H_{RES});   /*DOM tree from response*/
$DT_R \Leftarrow$ extract_DOM_tree();   /*DOM tree from repository*/
if (DT == DT_R) **then**
| Fin_$H_{RES} \Leftarrow H_{RES}$;
End
Else
SN_Log $\Leftarrow$ SN_Log $\cup$ extract_script_nodes(DT);
foreach $SN_J \in$ SN_Log
| Var_Log $\Leftarrow$ Var_Log $\cup$ variable_Context(SN_J);
End
H_Var_Log $\Leftarrow$ harmful_Var(Var_Log);   /*List of harmful variables*/
foreach $Var_J \in$ H_Var_Log
| San_Code $\Leftarrow$ San_Code $\cup$ context_escape(Var_J);   /*Escape harmful variables*/
End
Fin_$H_{RES} \Leftarrow$ generate_Response(H_{RES}, San_Code);   /*Generate response*/
End
return Fin_H_{RES};
End

Figure 16.11   Algorithm of processing of HTTP response.

16.2.3.15 DOM Tree Comparator

DOM tree comparator compares the DOM trees generated from training phase to the DOM tree generated from detection phase. The DOM tree generated from HTTP response may differ from DOM tree contained in DOM tree repository. The comparison of DOM trees is on the basis of arrangement of nodes within it. If new scripts are inserted in the web page, then the structure of DOM tree is altered, so point where new script is inserted can be identified by comparing every node from root to leaf. If there is variation between structures of DOM trees, then the DOM tree generated due to HTTP response is further filtered with the help of context-aware sanitization; otherwise, sanitized code from repository is extracted, and final HTTP response is generated.

For given HTTP response, generate DOM trees and store them in DT. Extract corresponding DOM trees from repository, and store them in DT_R. Compare the trees node by node, and if variation is found, return 0 otherwise return 1. The comparison is performed on the basis of arrangement of nodes in the trees, and if arrangement is not same, then some JavaScript code may have been injected. Figure 16.12 shows a detailed algorithm of detecting the variation in the values of script node in the DOM trees of both offline and online phases.

16.2.3.16 Variable Context Finder and Context-Aware Escaping

The dynamically generated variables may cause attack on websites as they behave differently in different contexts. Since variables behave differently, handling these types of variables becomes

```
Algorithm: DOM Tree Comparator
Input: Set of DOM trees from repository and HTTP response
Output: DOM trees are equal or not
Start
DT ⇐ φ

DTR ⇐ φ

Flag ⇐ φ

DT ⇐ generate_DOM_tree(HRES);
DTR ⇐ extract_DOM_tree();
P ⇐ DT
Q ⇐ DTR
while P or Q is not NULL
    flag ⇐ compare_tree(P,Q);      /*Compare trees from root*/
    if (flag==1) then        /*To check arrangement of nodes*/
        flag = flag + 1
    End
    Else
        break loop
    End
End
if (P != Q) then        /*nodes are different*/
    return 0
End
Else
    return 1
End
```

Figure 16.12 Algorithm of DOM tree comparator.

difficult. The variables are observed in different contexts with the help of variable context finder, and the malicious nature of variables is identified. A set of harmful variables are created, and then they are sanitized using automatic context-aware escaping tool.

16.3 Implementation and Experimental Evaluation

16.3.1 Implementation

The authors have developed their prototype model on the Java platform and integrated their settings into infrastructure settings of web browser in the form of an extension. This framework includes various networked devices as host systems for deploying the services of all components of online mode. Alternatively, the components of preprocessing mode are executed in self-training mode and adjusted their backgrounds on various desktop systems. The components referred for parsing and execution of feature estimation of script code was estimated in preprocessing approach. The setup backgrounds of all components were positioned on virtual desktop systems of VMware Terminal 7. This terminal was operated for changing the current setups of five virtual systems. The components referred to in preprocessing mode were adjusted on these structures with satisfactory response interval. Alternatively, the components in other host systems perform in virtual mode on the function of HTTP request. The authors consumed the setup of XAMPP server for acting as an online server. Furthermore, the setup of modules (like code instrumentation, context determination, etc.) was integrated on other online web servers. Web application's parsing was performed by consuming the proficiencies of Jsoup. It accelerates the offline web servers with fully functional APIs, which excerpt the DOM tree, giving the evidence on the subject related to susceptible inputs and an implanted HTML5 script strings in such locations.

16.3.2 Experimental Outcomes

We found selected verified platforms of web applications. Their setups are positioned on XAMPP server. Different tested freeware setups of web platforms were also hosted on desktop systems. Table 16.1 shows the outline of these infrastructures of web platforms. These web platforms have also undergone the procedure of parsing at preprocessing phase on different virtual desktop systems. The platforms involve different susceptible injection plugs surrounded with miscellaneous classes of scripting language.

Table 16.1   Summary of Configuration of Web Applications

Web Application	Version	Description	Quantity of Files	Lines of Code
Wackopicko [26]	2.0	Blogging board	13	17,884
BlogIt [27]	2.0	Blog application	16	767
Elgg [28]	1.8.16	Details available in CVE-2012–6561	27	114,735
Drupal [29]	7.23	Details available in CVE-2012–0826	12	43,835
Wordpress [30]	3.6.1	Details available in CVE-2013–5738	19	135,540

We have integrated the existing setup of such four web applications into XAMPP server configured on the Windows 10 on virtual desktop systems of our proposed technique. The related database of such web applications is saved in MySQL database as backend. During the assessment of XSS attack vector recognition proficiency, the proposed technique accesses the attack vectors and inserted them in vulnerable input locations. These suspicious vectors are effortlessly available via XSS Cheat Sheet [18], HTML5 attack vector repository [19], and @XSS Vector Twitter Account [22]. We injected all such attack vectors (accessed from such repositories) into the weak input fields accessed through online virtual desktop systems.

Table 16.2 focuses on few such groupings and their related illustration outlines. All such attack snippets are thrown on web server. Figure 16.13 highlights the XSS attack vector detection outcomes on these infrastructures of web applications. The technique inserted 127 suspicious patterns of scripting language encompassing each class of abovementioned attack snippets. The proposed technique throws these strings on the suspicious input locations. Furthermore, the proposed

Table 16.2   Category of XSS Attack Vectors and Their Example Patterns

S. No.	XSS Attack Vector Category	Description	Example Pattern
1.	HTML Malicious Event handler	Such code execute on the occurrence of some events (like click)	\<img src=asdf onerror=alert(document.cookie)>
2.	HTML Malicious Tags	Such scripts injected inside the web page that run on web browser instead of web server.	\<BODY BACKGROUND= "javascript:alert('XSS')">
3.	Non-obfuscated Code	Such code is injected in the injection points of web application in its clear form.	\<BR SIZE="&{alert('XSS')}">
4.	URL Attack Vectors	JavaScript code embedded in the URL.	\<A HREF="javascript:document.location='www.google.com/'">XSS\</A>
5.	Event Handlers	These are non-compulsory system commands in the form of scripts, which only execute when an alteration is observed in the service state.	1. \<body ONLOAD=alert(document.cookie)> 2. \<input onBlur = "alert('xss')" type="text">
6.	Obfuscated Code	This code is utilized for exemplifying a database of typescripts through certain encoding system.	<aonmouseover= "alert(document.cookie)">xxs link </a&# x3E;

methodology also inserted the features in the shape of remark statements in such suspicious locations of input fields.

Furthermore, the perceived rates of FPs and FNs are tolerable in every utilized infrastructure of websites. The proposed scheme also estimated the XSS attack payload recognition rate on diverse infrastructures of web applications. This rate is calculated by dividing the number of TPs to the number of illicit scripts injected. Figure 16.13 shows the recognition rate of proposed scheme on different infrastructures of web applications. The maximum suspicious XSS attack recognition rate is perceived for Joomla.

In addition, the observed rate of false positives and false negatives is acceptable in all the five platforms of web applications. We have also calculated the XSS attack payload detection rate of our framework on all five platforms of OSN-based web applications. This is done by dividing the number of TPs by the number of malicious scripts injected for each category of context of attack vectors. Figure 16.14 highlights the XSS worm detection rate of our framework on all the five

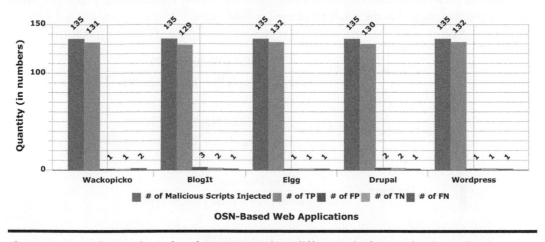

Figure 16.13 Observed results of DOM-Guard on different platforms of web applications.

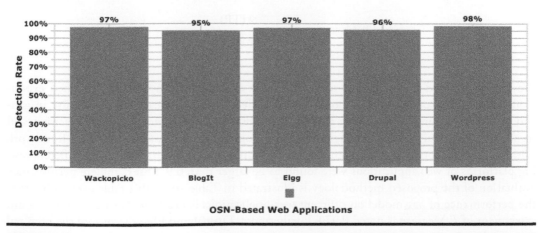

Figure 16.14 DOM-based XSS detection rate (in percentage) of DOM-Guard in all HTML5 web applications.

platforms of OSN-based web applications w.r.t. individual category of XSS attack vectors. It is clearly reflected from the figure that the highest overall DOM-based XSS worm detection rate is observed in Wordpress. In addition, the overall XSS worm detection rate falls in the range of 95–98% for all the platforms of HTML5 web applications.

16.3.3 Performance Analysis

A comprehensive validation as well as performance evaluation of our proposed framework is analyzed in this section by executing two statistical techniques, namely, *F*-Measure and *F*-Test Hypothesis.

16.3.3.1 Performance Analysis Using F-Measure

Precision and recall values are utilized for computations in binary classification. Harmonic mean values of precision as well as the recall are termed as *F*-Measure:

$$\text{False Positive Rate (FPR)} = \frac{\text{False Positives (FP)}}{\text{False Positives (FP)} + \text{True Negatives (TN)}}$$

$$\text{False Negative Rate (FNR)} = \frac{\text{False Negatives (FN)}}{\text{False Negatives} + \text{True Positives (TP)}}$$

$$\text{Precision} = \frac{\text{True Positives (TP)}}{\text{True Positives (TP)} + \text{False Positives (FP)}}$$

$$\text{Recall} = \frac{\text{True Positives (TP)}}{\text{True Positives (TP)} + \text{False Negatives (FN)}}$$

$$\text{F-Measure} = \frac{2\,(\text{TP})}{2\,(\text{TP}) + (\text{FP}) + (\text{FN})}$$

We have computed precision and recall to finally evaluate *F*-Measure for examined experimental outputs of our detection model on five different web applications. *F*-Measure in general analyzes system's performance through computing the harmonic mean of precision and recall. Experimental analysis highlights that our proposed detection and alleviation framework achieved high performance since computed *F*-Measure values of our framework on different testing platforms of web applications were found to be larger than 0.9. Our complete performance evaluation of the proposed methodology is illustrated in Table 16.3. This table exemplifies that the performance of our model on different web applications is nearly 97% since the maximum assessment of *F*-Measure is noted 0.970. Furthermore, Drupal and Elgg discovered the nominal rate of false negatives.

Table 16.3 Performance Analysis of our Mobile Cloud-Based Framework by Calculating *F*-Measure

Web Applications	Total	# of TP	# of FP	# of TN	# of FN	Precision	FPR	FNR	Recall	F-Measure
Wackopicko [26]	135	131	1	1	2	0.992	0.5	0.015	0.984	0.988
BlogIt [27]	135	129	3	2	1	0.977	0.6	0.007	0.992	0.984
Elgg [28]	135	132	1	1	1	0.992	0.5	0.007	0.992	0.992
Drupal [29]	135	130	2	2	1	0.984	0.5	0.007	0.992	0.988
Wordpress [30]	135	132	1	1	1	0.992	0.5	0.007	0.992	0.992

16.3.3.2 *Performance Analysis Using F-Test*

To verify that detected XSS count (True Positives (TP)) is lower than injected XSS attack vectors count, we have utilized the concept of *F*-Test Hypothesis. We have assumed two hypotheses defined as follows:

Null Hypothesis: H_0 = No. of detected XSS attack vectors count is greater than the injected one's ($S_1 > S_2$).

Alternate Hypothesis: H_1 = No. of detected XSS attack vectors count is lesser than the injected one's ($S_1 < S_2$).

# of H5-XSS Attack Vectors Injected
Observation # (N_1) = 4
Degree of Freedom (dof_1) = $N_1 - 1 = 3$
# of H5-XSS Attack Vectors Detected
Observation # (N_2) = 4
Degree of Freedom (dof_2) = $N_2 - 1 = 3$
Level of Significance $\alpha = 0.05$

$$F_{\text{CALC}} = S_1^2 / S_2^2 = 0.888$$

The tabulated value of *F*-Test at $\text{dof}_1 = 3$, $\text{dof}_2 = 3$, and $\alpha = 0.05$ is as follows:

$$F_{(\text{dof}_1, \text{dof}_2, 1-\alpha)} = F_{(4,4,0.95)} = 6.3882$$

We know that the Null Hypothesis would be discarded in case

$$F_{\text{CALC}} < F_{(\text{dof}_1, \text{dof}_2, 1-\alpha)}$$

The detailed analyses of statistics of the number of XSS attack vectors injected and detected are elucidated in Tables 16.4 and 16.5. Note that, here, we have injected different quantities of XSS attack vectors on different platforms of web application for validating the performance of our work by this hypothesis. Since $F_{\text{CALC}} < F_{(4,4,0.95)}$, we concur the alternate hypothesis (H_1) that standard

Table 16.4 Statistics of XSS Attack Vectors Applied

# of Malicious Scripts Injected (X_i)	$(X_i - \mu)$	$(X_i - \mu)^2$	Standard Deviation $S_1 = \sqrt{\sum_{i=1}^{N_1}(X_i - \mu)^2/(N_1 - 1)}$
130	0	0	
133	3	9	
129	−1	1	2.397
127	−3	9	
132	2	4	
Mean $(\mu) \sum X_i/N_1 = 130$		$\sum_{i=1}^{N_1}(X_i - \mu)^2 = 23$	

Table 16.5 Statistics of XSS Attack Vectors Detected

# of JS Malicious Scripts Detected (X_i)	$(X_i - \mu)$	$(X_i - \mu)^2$	Standard Deviation $S_2 = \sqrt{\sum_{i=1}^{N_1}(X_i - \mu)^2/(N_1 - 1)}$
127	0	0	
130	3	9	
126	−1	1	2.236
124	−3	9	
128	1	1	
Mean $(\mu) \sum X_i/N_2 = 127$		$\sum_{i=1}^{N_1}(X_i - \mu)^2 = 20$	

deviation 1 value (S_1) is greater than standard deviation 2 value (S_2). Therefore, it can be clearly stated that the detected XSS attack vector count is lower than injected XSS attack vector count; hence, it is 95% claimed assurance that the variations within standard deviations were caused by randomly occurred error.

# of Malicious Scripts Injected
# of Observation $(N_1) = 5$
Degree of Freedom dof $(\text{dof}_1) = N_1 - 1 = 4$.
# of Malicious Scripts Detected
# of Observation $(N_2) = 5$
Degree of Freedom dof $(\text{dof}_2) = N_2 - 1 = 4$.

$$F_{\text{CALC}} = S_1^2 / S_2^2 = 5.745609/4.999696 = 1.149$$

The tabulated value of *F*-Test at $\text{dof}_1 = 4$, $\text{dof}_2 = 4$ and $\alpha = 0.05$ is

$$F_{(\text{dof}_1, \text{dof}_2, 1-\alpha)} = F_{(4,4,0.95)} = 6.3882$$

We know that the hypothesis that the two variances are equal (Null Hypothesis) is rejected if

$$F_{\text{CALC}} < F_{(\text{dof}_1, \text{dof}_2, 1-\alpha)}$$

Since $F_{\text{CALC}} < F_{(4,4,0.95)}$, we accept the alternate hypothesis (H_1) that the first standard deviation (S_1) is less than the second standard deviation (S_2). Hence, it is clear that the number of XSS worms detected is less than the number of XSS attack vectors injected, and we are 95% confident that any difference in the sample standard deviation is due to random error.

16.3.4 Comparison

We have also performed the comparison of our framework with the other recent existing XSS defensive methodologies. Table 16.6 equates recent XSS defensive methodologies with our technique based on the following worthwhile performance constraints: AM – Analyzing Mechanism, MP – Monitoring Procedure, TOXH – Type of XSS Worm Handled, Ttrac – Taint Tracking, CRW – Code Rewriting, APPR – Automated Preprocessing Required, PSID – Partial Script Injection Detection, and SCM – Source Code Monitoring.

This is undoubtedly perceived from Table 16.6 that very rare current procedures had concentrated on two key classifications of XSS attacks concurrently (i.e., stored and reflected). Also, the existing related work does not focus on the tracking of tainted flow of the data. Also, acknowledgment of script functions is purely escaped by maximum methodologies. Additionally, a huge

Table 16.6 Summary of Comparison of the Existing XSS Defensive Methodologies with Our Work

Metrics Techniques	AM	MP	TOXH	Ttrac	CRW	APPR	PSID	SCM
Galan et al. [31]	Medium	No	No	Yes	Yes	Yes	Passive	No
Likarish et al. [32]	Low	No	No	Yes	Yes	No	Passive	Yes
Vogt et al. [33]	Medium	Yes	No	No	No	Yes	Active	No
Wang et al. [34]	Low	No	Yes	Yes	Yes	Yes	Passive	No
Vishnu et al. [35]	Medium	No	No	No	No	Yes	Passive	No
Van et al. [36]	Medium	No	No	Yes	Yes	No	Active	No
DOM-Guard (Our Work)	Acceptable	Yes	Yes	No	No	No	Active	Yes

percentage of initial processing is essential in the recent infrastructure of websites. Most of the existing work relies on the concept of exact JavaScript injection; however, they could not detect the partial injection of XSS worms.

Our framework simply isolates the untrusted JavaScript code from the actual data by executing the process of code rewriting, which is not handled by most of the existing XSS defensive techniques. In addition, the proposed framework executes the runtime monitoring on the JavaScript code for determining the dependency between the tainted source and sink functions in the program code. Moreover, the background of untrusted scripts inserted in such code is determined. Now, here, instead of performing context-sensitive sanitization on such variables, our framework performs the deep string analysis on such variables for tracking their tainted flow. The examination of tainted variables will be carried out in order to determine whether it may function as vulnerable point or not. The existing work executes the background-aware sanitization at these variables; however, such sanitization suffers from numerous complexity errors. Reliability of such sanitization routine is a serious concern due to constant modernizing nature of current browsers. Additionally, no automated method of injection of sanitizers has been introduced, and the information regarding sanitizers, source, and sinks needs to be known in advance. Therefore, a large proportion of initial processing is prerequisite in an existing defensive framework of XSS. Table 16.7 highlights the performance comparison of our framework with XSS-Auditor [39]. It can be clearly observed from the table that the value of *F*-Measure is decreasing in all the platforms of HTML5 web applications for XSS-Auditor in comparison to our work.

16.4 Conclusion and Future Work

This chapter presents DOM-Guard, a mobile cloud-based framework that alleviates the DOM-based XSS vulnerabilities from the contemporary platforms of mobile cloud-based HTML5 web applications. The framework executes in dual mode: offline and online. The former performs the sanitization on the HTML5-based XSS attack vectors in a context-sensitive manner and accordingly generates the DOM tree and stores it in a DOM tree repository for further reference in online mode. The online mode detects the injection of untrusted/malicious JavaScript code in the script nodes of dynamically generated DOM tree. This is done by detecting the variation in the DOM tree generated dynamically in the online mode with the offline mode. Any discrepancy observed in the values of script nodes of both these trees will simply indicate the injection of XSS worms into the DOM tree of online mode. Finally, context-sensitive sanitization is performed on such worms for the safe interpretation of modified HTTP response on the web browser of smartphone user.

Very low and acceptable rates of FPs and FNs were found during the DOM-based XSS detection phase of the attack vectors on the web servers incorporated on the cloud platforms. Performance validation results disclosed that complex computations performed during runtime by nested context-aware sanitization process on the cloud platforms suffer from satisfactory performance overhead. For our future work, we would prefer to analyze the response time of our framework by completely integrating its settings on the online edge servers of Fog computing infrastructure without the intervention of cloud data centres. In addition, we would also assess the attack detection capabilities of our work on the framework of Internet of Thing devices.

Table 16.7 Performance Comparison of XSS-Auditor with DOM-Guard

Web Application	# of TP		# of FP		# of TN		# of FN		Precision		Recall		F-Measure	
	XA	DG	XA	DG	XA	DG	XA	DG	XA	DG	XA	DG	XA	DG
Wackopicko [26]	102	131	8	1	11	1	5	2	0.772	0.992	0.739	0.984	0.726	0.988
BlogIt [27]	109	129	11	3	17	2	6	1	0.723	0.977	0.762	0.992	0.746	0.984
Elgg [28]	105	132	13	1	15	1	7	1	0.710	0.992	0.772	0.992	0.782	0.992
Drupal [29]	97	130	8	2	16	2	8	1	0.720	0.984	0.752	0.992	0.734	0.988
Wordpress [30]	101	132	14	1	17	1	11	1	0.748	0.992	0.771	0.992	0.745	0.992

References

1. Dinh H.T., C. Lee, D. Niyato, and P. Wang. A survey of mobile cloud computing: architecture, applications, and approaches. *Wireless Communications and Mobile Computing*, 13, no. 18, (2013), 1587–1611.
2. Modi C., et al. A survey on security issues and solutions at different layers of Cloud computing. *The Journal of Supercomputing*, 63, no. 2, (2013), 561–592.
3. Gupta S., and B.B. Gupta. JS-SAN: defense mechanism for HTML5-based web applications against javascript code injection vulnerabilities. *Security and Communication Networks*, 9, (2016).
4. Gupta S., and B.B. Gupta. XSS-SAFE: A server-side approach to detect and mitigate cross-site scripting (XSS) attacks in javascript code. *Arabian Journal for Science and Engineering*, 41, (2015), 1–24.
5. Gupta S., and B.B. Gupta. PHP-sensor: A prototype method to discover workflow violation and XSS vulnerabilities in PHP web applications. In: *Proceedings of the 12th ACM International Conference on Computing Frontiers*, ACM, Ischia, Italy, (2015), p. 59.
6. Gupta, B.B., S. Gupta, S. Gangwar, M. Kumar, and P.K. Meena. Cross-site scripting (XSS) abuse and defense: exploitation on several testing bed environments and its defense. *Journal of Information Privacy and Security*, 11, no. 2, (2015), 118–136.
7. Gupta S., and B.B. Gupta. BDS: browser dependent XSS sanitizer.In: *Book on Cloud-based Databases with Biometric Applications. IGI-Global's Advances in Information Security, Privacy, and Ethics (AISPE) Series*, IGI-Global: Hershey, (2014): pp. 174–191.
8. Gupta S, and B.B. Gupta. Cross-site scripting (XSS) attacks and defense mechanisms: classification and state-of-Art. *International Journal of System Assurance Engineering and Management*, 8, (2015), 512–530.
9. Gupta S., and B.B. Gupta. An infrastructure-based framework for the alleviation of JavaScript worms from OSN in mobile cloud platforms. In: *International Conference on Network and System Security*, Springer: Cham, (2016), pp. 98–109.
10. Gupta S., and B.B. Gupta. Detection, avoidance, and attack pattern mechanisms in modern web application vulnerabilities: present and future challenges. *International Journal of Cloud Applications and Computing (IJCAC)*, 7, no. 3, (2017), 1–43.
11. Gupta S., and B.B. Gupta. Automated discovery of javascript code injection attacks in PHP web applications. *Procedia Computer Science*, 78, (2016), 82–87.
12. Bisht P., and V.N. Venkatakrishnan. XSS-GUARD: Precise dynamic prevention of cross-site scripting attacks. In: *International Conference on Detection of Intrusions and Malware, and Vulnerability Assessment*, Springer: Berlin, Heidelberg, (2008), pp. 23–43.
13. Vishnu B.A., and K.P. Jevitha. Prediction of cross-site scripting attack using machine learning algorithms. In: *Proceedings of the 2014 International Conference on Interdisciplinary Advances in Applied Computing*, ACM, Amritapuri, India, (2014).
14. Bates D., A. Barth, and C. Jackson. Regular expressions considered harmful in client-side XSS filters. In: *Proceedings of the Conference on the World Wide Web*, (2010), pp. 91–100.
15. Livshits B., and S. Chong. Towards fully automatic placement of security sanitizers and declassifiers. *ACM SIGPLAN Notices*, 48, no. 1, (2013), 385–398.
16. Samuel M., P. Saxena, and D. Song. Context-sensitive auto-sanitization in web templating languages using type qualifiers. In: *Proceedings of the 18th ACM conference on Computer and communications security*, ACM, Chicago, IL, (2011).
17. Ceponis J., L. Ceponiene, A. Venckauskas, and D. Mockus. Evaluation of open source server-side XSS protection solutions. In: *International Conference on Information and Software Technologies*, Springer: Berlin, Heidelberg, (2013), pp. 345–356.
18. Rsnake. XSS Cheat Sheet. http://ha.ckers.org/xss.html, (2008).
19. HTML5 Security Cheat Sheet. Available at: http://html5sec.org/.
20. 523 XSS vectors. Available at: http://xss2.technomancie.net/vectors/.
21. Technical Attack Sheet for Cross Site Penetration Tests. Available at: www.vulnerability-lab.com/resources/documents/531.txt.
22. @XSS Vector Twitter Account. Available at: https://twitter.com/XSSVector.

23. Reith J., Internals of noXSS, October 2008. Retrieved from: www.noxss.org/wiki/Internals.
24. Ross D. IE 8 XSS filter architecture/implementation, August 2008. Retrieved from: http://blogs.technet.com/srd/archive/2008/08/18/ie-8-xss-filter-architecture-implementation.aspx.
25. Maone G., NoScript. Retrieved from: www.noscript.net.
26. Wackopicko. Retrieved from: https://github.com/adamdoupe/wackopicko.
27. Blogit. Retrieved from: www.blogit.com/Blogs/.
28. Elgg social networking engine. Available at: https://elgg.org.
29. Drupal social networking site. Available at: www.drupal.org/download.
30. WordPress. Available at: http://wordpress.org/.
31. Galán E., et al. A multi-agent scanner to detect stored-XSS vulnerabilities. In: *Internet Technology and Secured Transactions (ICITST), 2010 International Conference*, IEEE, London, UK, (2010).
32. Likarish P., E. Jung, and I. Jo. Obfuscated malicious javascript detection using classification techniques. *MALWARE*, (2009).
33. Vogt P., et al. Cross site scripting prevention with dynamic data tainting and static analysis. *NDSS*, 2007, (2007).
34. Wang Y., Z. Li, and T. Guo. Program slicing stored XSS bugs in web application. *Theoretical Aspects of Software Engineering (TASE), 2011 Fifth International Symposium*, IEEE, Xi'an, China, (2011).
35. Vishnu B.A., and K.P. Jevitha. Prediction of cross-site scripting attack using machine learning algorithms. *Proceedings of the 2014 International Conference on Interdisciplinary Advances in Applied Computing*, ACM, Amritapuri, India, (2014).
36. van Acker S., et al. "FlashOver: Automated discovery of cross-site scripting vulnerabilities in rich internet applications. *Proceedings of the 7th ACM Symposium on Information, Computer and Communications Security*, ACM, Seoul, Republic of Korea, (2012).
37. Nunan, A.E., et al. Automatic classification of cross-site scripting in web pages using document-based and URL-based features. *Computers and Communications (ISCC), 2012 IEEE Symposium*, IEEE, Cappadocia, Turkey, (2012).
38. Chandra V.S., and S. Selvakumar. BIXSAN: Browser independent XSS sanitizer for Prevention of XSS attacks. *ACM SIGSOFT Software Engineering Notes*, 36, no. 5, (2011), 1–7.
39. Bates D., A. Barth, and C. Jackson. Regular *expressions* considered harmful in client-side XSS filters. In: *Proceedings of the 19th International Conference on World Wide Web*, ACM, Raleigh, NC, (2010).
40. Gupta S., B.B. Gupta, and P. Chaudhary. Hunting for DOM-Based XSS vulnerabilities in mobile cloud-based online social network. *Future Generation Computer Systems*, 79, (2018), 319–336.
41. Gupta S., and B.B. Gupta. XSS-secure as a service for the platforms of online social network-based multimedia web applications in cloud. *Multimedia Tools and Applications*, 77, (2016), 1–33.
42. Gupta S., and B.B. Ghooshan. XSS-immune: a Google chrome extension-based XSS defensive framework for contemporary platforms of web applications. *Security and Communication Networks*, 9, no. 17, (2016), 3966–3986.
43. Gupta B.B., S. Gupta, and P. Chaudhary. Enhancing the browser-side context-aware sanitization of suspicious HTML5 Code for halting the DOM-based XSS vulnerabilities in cloud. *Application Development and Design: Concepts, Methodologies, Tools, and Applications: Concepts, Methodologies, Tools, and Applications*, 7, (2017), 216.

Bibliography

1. Lekies S., B. Stock, and M. Johns. *A Tale of the Weaknesses of Current Client-Side XSS Filtering*, BlackHat USA, (2014).
2. Lekies S., B. Stock, and M. Johns. 25 million flows later: Large-scale detection of DOM-based XSS." In: *Proceedings of the 2013 ACM SIGSAC Conference on Computer & Communications Security*, ACM, Berlin, Germany, pp. 1193–1204, (2013).
3. Stock B., S. Lekies, T. Mueller, P. Spiegel, and M. Johns. Precise Client-side Protection against DOM-based Cross-Site Scripting. In: *USENIX Security Symposium*, pp. 655–670, (2014).

4. Duchene F., S. Rawat, J.-L. Richier, and R. Groz. KameleonFuzz: Evolutionary fuzzing for black-box XSS detection. In: *Proceedings of the 4th ACM Conference on Data and Application Security and Privacy*, ACM, pp. 37–48, (2014).

5. Chaudhary P., B.B. Gupta, and S. Gupta. Defending the OSN-Based Web Applications from XSS Attacks Using Dynamic JavaScript Code and Content Isolation. In: *Quality, IT and Business Operations*, Springer: Singapore, (2018), pp. 107–119.

7. Yan R., X. Xiao, G. Hu, S. Peng, and Y. Jiang. New deep learning method to detect code injection attacks on hybrid applications. *Journal of Systems and Software*, 137, (2018), 67–77.

8. Mereani F.A., and J.M. Howe. Detecting Cross-Site Scripting Attacks Using Machine Learning. In: *International Conference on Advanced Machine Learning Technologies and Applications*, Springer: Cham, pp. 200–210, (2018).

9. Deka G.C. (ed.). *Handbook of Research on Securing Cloud-Based Databases with Biometric Applications*, IGI Global, 2014.

10. Gupta B., D.P. Agrawal, and S. Yamaguchi (eds). *Handbook of Research on Modern Cryptographic Solutions for Computer and Cyber Security*, IGI Global, (2016).

11. Benson V., J. McAlaney, and L.A. Frumkin. Emerging Threats for the Human Element and Countermeasures in Current Cyber Security Landscape. In: *Psychological and Behavioral Examinations in Cyber Security*, IGI Global, pp. 266–271, (2018).

12. Rajeyyagari S., and A.S. Alotaibi. A study on cyber-crimes, threats, security and its emerging trends on latest technologies: influence on the Kingdom of Saudi Arabia. *International Journal of Engineering & Technology*, 7, no. 2–3, (2018), 54–58.

13. Choo K.-K.R., and A. Dehghantanha. Introduction to the minitrack on cyber threat intelligence and analytics. In: *Proceedings of the 51st Hawaii International Conference on System Sciences*, Hawaii, USA, (2018).

14. Sani A.S., D. Yuan, J. Jin, L. Gao, S. Yu, and Z.Y. Dang. Cyber security framework for internet of things-based energy internet. *Future Generation Computer Systems*, (2018).

15. Jakóbik A., F. Palmieri, and J. Kołodziej. Stackelberg games for modeling defense scenarios against cloud security threats. *Journal of Network and Computer Applications*, 110, (2018), 99–107.

Chapter 17

Secure and Fault-Tolerant Computing in Mobile Ad Hoc Networks

Parmeet Kaur
Jaypee Institute of Information Technology

Awadhesh Kumar Singh
National Institute of Technology

Contents

17.1 Introduction

The rapid technological advances in mobile computing along with the increasing requirements of users have resulted in the development of a variety of mobile applications. There exist mobile applications for diverse domains such as web search, social networks and social media, e-commerce transactions, gaming, health care, and education. Each mobile application may be comprised of multiple services or computations involving processing and managing of large and complex data of varied types, such as text, audio, and video [1]. Moreover, mobile devices such as laptops, smart phones, and tablets of each generation possess better features, resources, and are computationally more powerful than the earlier generations. However, in many instances, an isolated mobile device does not possess sufficient resources to handle the complexity and volumes of the underlying data and computations. A key challenge to distributed execution of applications solely on mobile devices is due to the high requirement of computing or processing power besides the communication capability of wireless networks. One effective method for satisfying these requirements involves organization of mobile devices situated in vicinity into an ad hoc network such that their computing and storage capabilities can be used collectively to execute any modern application. This alleviates the need for any external or static infrastructure and resources for execution of applications on mobile devices alone. A mobile ad hoc network (MANET) provides an on-demand access to a shared pool of computing resources so that high performance may be achieved with respect to collecting, storing, processing, and accessing voluminous data. Humungous amounts of data can be collected by mobile devices and processed to support complex services on mobile devices.

However, MANETs are characterized by heterogeneity and dynamicity of resources. Though there is a high interest in developing suitable applications as well as architectures, security is a principal concern. This is due to the fact that MANETs are, in general, open networks and allow nodes to freely join or leave the network. A malicious or selfish node in the network can act as an impediment to the progress of application execution. Security challenges seek attention before MANETs can be effectively used for computing and running applications through collaborative actions at various nodes in the network. It is required to integrate security solutions in a MANET in a way that efficiency or accuracy is not compromised. This is possible if the implementation of the security scheme does not add substantial overhead to the network operations. The following need to be reduced or avoided by a security scheme since they cause unnecessary overheads:

- *Message or Packet Overhead*: A low number of messages should be generated by a security scheme. Nodes in MANETs share wireless bandwidth, and a high number of security-related messages can hinder transmission of application messages by causing congestion, collision, or packet drops. This subsequently leads to retransmissions and wastes network resources.
- *Time for Processing*: MANETs are characterized by dynamic topology, i.e., frequent link creations and disruptions due to node mobility and disconnections. The security approach should be able to detect and eliminate malicious nodes within a short time by processing security information as fast as possible. This will avoid the need to reroute messages to new locations of nodes.

■ *Energy Consumption*: Nodes in a MANET have limited battery life. It is necessary to optimize the energy consumption of nodes to increase a network's lifetime. In such a scenario, security approaches should not add to energy expenditure of nodes in a MANET.

The design of a security approach must consider these parameters for efficiency of network resources. If security mechanism can be combined with some other existing approaches in the network, it will lead to improvement in the network performance. This chapter presents the implementation of a two-tier security scheme in a MANET that is incorporated into a checkpointing and rollback recovery protocol used for fault tolerance. A fault tolerance mechanism will generally be in place in a MANET for successful application execution. An integration of security and fault tolerance schemes is challenging, but we postulate that it will deal with the major concerns of using mobile devices for computations while minimizing the overheads. An erasure coding [2] based checkpointing scheme is developed. This involves dividing the checkpoint data into k blocks and encoding it into n $(n > k)$ copies, distributed among n other nodes, subsequently referred to as the checkpoint storage nodes (CSNs). At the time of recovery, the survival of any k out of n copies can ensure the successful recovery of the node. This scheme offers a two-fold benefit. First, erasure coding the checkpoint data results in a higher degree of fault tolerance in comparison to storing a single copy of the checkpoint as it introduces redundancy. Moreover, it provides this redundancy by employing a lower storage overhead as compared to complete replication of checkpoints at multiple nodes for obtaining the same level of reliability [2]. Second, successful recovery is possible if any k out of n checkpoint chunks can be retrieved. Thus, erasure coding-based checkpointing allows secure recovery by handling up to $n − k$ malicious nodes or failures. An additional level of security is provided by maintaining a trust value [3] for the CSNs. Only the nodes with high trust value are entrusted the task of storing the checkpoints of the nodes executing an application. The efficacy of the proposed scheme has been verified by the simulation results. The main contributions of this work are as follows:

■ An insight is presented into the issues and concepts of security and fault tolerance in MANETs.
■ The existing approaches and challenges are discussed.
■ A novel fault tolerance scheme integrated with security mechanisms is presented. Though there exists fault tolerance as well as security schemes for MANETs, this is an attempt at addressing both concerns with a single protocol.
■ The proposed checkpointing protocol is based on erasure coding to provide the first layer of security. Further, the CSNs are selected based on a trust value computed for these nodes by their neighboring nodes for providing the second layer of security.
■ The scheme significantly lowers the storage overhead for mobile nodes as compared to replication while providing a higher degree of redundancy.
■ Opportunistic contacts among the mobile nodes are used to propagate the trust values maintained by a node in the system. This avoids the use of control messages for the update of trust values.

17.2 Mobile Ad Hoc Networks

Mobile computing is a logical extension to the distributed computing paradigm which allows distributed computations on mobile devices. The remarkable developments in mobile technology, along with the widespread availability of sophisticated mobile devices, have facilitated the conduct of communication and computing tasks on the move. Each generation of mobile devices such as laptops, smartphones, and tablets is more powerful than the preceding generations. These devices are equipped with increased computing capability, improved battery lives, and high networking speeds. Consequently, the applications being run on mobile devices involve complicated operations on varied data types, for instance video processing on mobile phones, object tracking or recognition on mobile sensors, and event detection in surveillance big data [1].

However, there still exists a difference between the need for executing complex jobs and the availability of resources. In order to achieve high performance, the computing potential of the mobile devices located in proximity can be utilized by organizing the devices into a MANET, as depicted in Figure 17.1 [4]. MANETs are autonomous networks of mobile nodes which do not require static infrastructure, like base stations, routers, etc. [5]. Each node itself acts both as a host and as a router for communication with other nodes in the network. These networks permit the devices to perform computing tasks irrespective of their physical location. These systems may be used on stand-alone basis or in tandem with the existing cellular networks or the Internet. They offer the convenience of mobility along with computing power and facilitate a variety of applications on mobile devices in an anytime, anyplace manner. However, mobile devices are still prone to failures due to the unpredictability or limitation of battery power, stable storage, and wireless connectivity. Therefore, applications designed to execute on these networks require being secure and faulting tolerant.

17.3 Security in MANETs

MANETs are inherently susceptible to security concerns due to their infrastructure-less architecture. There are no secure boundaries for a MANET. This is in contrast to the wired networks where attackers require physically accessing the network or crossing security mechanisms at network boundaries such as firewalls and gateways. Moreover, there is no centralized mechanism for network management, which makes it difficult to check, control, or detect network attacks. The communication medium is completely wireless, and therefore, a node receives all messages in its communication range even if these are not destined for this node itself. As a result, it is possible for a node to access other nodes' messages or inject malicious packets or drop other nodes' messages. Apart from malicious nodes, some nodes may exhibit selfish behavior and may behave improperly to conserve their battery life or other resources. Such nodes do not forward other nodes' messages, while they use other nodes to route their own messages. It is also challenging to diffuse the information obtained about any malicious or suspicious nodes in the network.

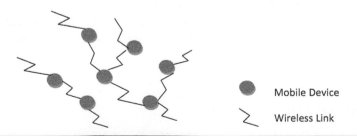

Figure 17.1   Mobile ad hoc network.

17.3.1 Types of Security Attacks in MANETs

Common categories of network attacks are listed in the following [6,7].

17.3.1.1 Active

These attacks are performed by malicious nodes by either modifying the information being carried by a message or creating some false information. The following attacks are examples of active attacks:

- *Sink Holes*: A malicious node tries to become a part of routing path of messages in the network by, e.g., minimizing the hop count on the message. Subsequently, it does not forward the message to its destination. Such an attack is common in MANETs.
- *Denial of Service Attacks*: Attempting to exhaust the processing power of a target node and thus, making its service unavailable to the network. This attack is performed by flooding network traffic to the target.
- *Wormhole Attack*: An attacker redirects traffic to a location different from where it was intended for.
- *Modification*: Attack on data integrity of data by altering the packet itself.
- *Fabrication*: Generation of false routing information. For instance, an attacker may claim that its neighbor can no longer be contacted.
- *Spoofing or Man-in-the-Middle Attack*: When an attacker pretends to be some other node.
- *Sybil Attack*: A related attack where a node may assume multiple identities; either simultaneously or non-simultaneously.

17.3.1.2 Passive

In passive attacks, instead of affecting the routing protocol of the network, attackers try to gain information about structure or topology of the network. These are difficult to identify as they do not involve any modification of data. The following are some common passive attacks:

- *Eavesdropping*: An eavesdropping attack aims to intercept or gain access to a private communication to which the attacker is not authorized to. This is done with the aim of acquiring confidential information such as keys (public or private) and passwords that are passed during communication.
- *Monitoring of Nodes and Analysis of Traffic*: Traffic analysis is a kind of deduction attack that observes or monitors the pattern of communication between nodes in networks like MANETs. In this attack, messages are intercepted and examined to figure out information from communication patterns. The strength of this attack is that it can be performed over encrypted messages and also when decryption is not possible for attacker. The attacker analyzes which node is communicating with which other nodes, for what duration, and with what size of messages. Therefore, the attacker node is able to infer more if it observes a high number of messages. However, the messages or their content is not modified.

In this environment, it is necessary that nodes cooperate with each other in detecting malicious attackers and prevent them from interrupting network operations.

460 ■ *Computer and Cyber Security*

17.3.2 Existing Approaches to Security in MANETs

Though security is a prime concern for wired as well as wireless networks, its solutions are more complicated for wireless networks owing to the features of communication medium and mobility of users. The absence of fixed links and dynamic topology makes it difficult to locate or hinder a malicious user [8,9]. As for other networks, the following are also the objectives of a security mechanism for MANETs [3,10]:

■ *Availability*: The designated services of a node are always available. It aims to secure itself from attacks on its service capability.
■ *Integrity*: Maintaining and guaranteeing that data or information is correct, accurate, and trustworthy
■ *Confidentiality*: Information is accessible to only those who are authorized to access it. Unauthorized processes or nodes should not be able to access confidential information.
■ *Authenticity*: Checking that a node is not impersonating, i.e., faking its identity. The identities of the constituent nodes should be secured so that only the intended nodes can access confidential information resources.
■ *Non-repudiation*: Ensuring that the sending or receiving of a message cannot be later denied or refuted by the sender or receiver, respectively.
■ *Authorization*: Determining if a node has the required permissions to use a message or information. These permissions may be granted to the users by the owner of a resource or a centralized and appropriate authority.
■ *Anonymity*: The need to keep a user or a node's identity secret or confidential. This may be done to maintain privacy or for protection against malicious nodes.

The most prominent techniques of security in MANETs follow the approaches of either prevention or intrusion detection. In order to prevent attacks on nodes from outside the network, a variety of key and trust management techniques have been developed. On the other hand, security is incorporated into the routing protocols for preventing attacks from the constituent nodes of the network. The focus of the intrusion detection methods is mainly on monitoring of the network for any possible violations or attacks. An effective security method can be designed by using prevention as well as detection techniques. Once a node is detected for malicious behavior, the network responds in a manner to avoid or limit the damage.

A common prevention approach employed for ensuring security is that of detecting malicious nodes by establishing trust among the nodes. Trust has been defined as the belief that an entity is capable of acting reliably, dependably, and securely in a particular case [3]. Trust acts as a technique for ensuring the cooperation of all nodes for the successful network operation.

However, the implementation is made difficult due to their constraints of limited computing and communication resources and a dynamic topology. The security solutions based on encryption are not feasible in MANETs as these cannot prevent packet dropping attacks by malicious nodes.

Similarly, the cryptographic primitives of authentication and key distribution services (e.g., the Pretty Good Privacy (PGP)6 or X.5097 certificate systems), which implicitly use the concept of trust-management, are not possible in MANETs due to the lack of trusted certificate-issuing authorities. In general, distributed trust or reputation models have been used for MANETs to mitigate the selfish or malicious behavior of nodes in a MANET. A node's trust on another node is determined by its own evaluation of the node's activities and also that of the other network nodes.

A protocol, called CONFIDANT, was proposed by Buchegger and Boudec [11] with the objective of preventing node misbehavior. The misbehaving nodes are detected and subsequently isolated from the network, thus ensuring cooperation among the nodes. A node evaluates the behavior of other nodes within its transmission range by sensing the packets transmitted. The protocol also uses a reputation system which maintains the ratings of all nodes and a trust manager which broadcasts a message in the network on detection of a malicious node. However, the computation of reputation values is not discussed in detail.

A watchdog and pathrater method has been presented by Marti et al. in [12]. The watchdog component monitors the packet transmission of its neighbors and detects the malicious or misbehaving nodes. The pathrater component aims to prevent the routing paths which comprise the detected malicious nodes. This method has the obvious limitation that selfish nodes benefit by being detected as misbehaving nodes as they are excluded from routing paths, but they continue to be provided service. Another system, called the Collaborative Reputation Mechanism or CORE [13], is a generic method to promote cooperation among the nodes of a MANET. Each node monitors the other nodes' behavior and distributes its local observations in the network. The observations from nodes are combined and distributed to calculate a reputation value for each node. The participation or exclusion of a node from the network is based on its reputation. The CORE uses the method of Marti [12] for the actual detection of misbehaving nodes. The work presented in [9] discusses ad hoc networks and their computing models that require secure protocols. A classification of threats and attacks common in MANETs is provided along with a discussion regarding available tools for analyzing the performance of a given security protocol.

A few other security methods for MANETs have relied on intrusion detection techniques in the MANETs, such as Zhang et al. [14]. The authors have presented a distributed and cooperative intrusion detection framework for MANET. The distributed intrusion detection system (IDS) is discussed in [14], which consists of the local components for data collection, anomaly detection and response, and of the global components for cooperative detection and a global response. The authors have pointed out that the trace analysis and anomaly detection should be performed locally at each node and also globally through cooperation with all nodes in the network. The intrusion detection method should be integrated with the networking layers. A survey of intrusion detection methods can be found in [15].

Recently, there has been a surge in the use of cloud computing by mobile devices. The mobile devices can expand their computation and storage capabilities by migrating tasks to powerful and flexible cloud servers. However, the use of cloud computing increases security risks for mobile devices since these need to connect to the Internet for using cloud resources. The authors of [16] have proposed a homomorphic encryption-based authentication and confidentiality scheme. They claim that the scheme provides secure access to cloud servers by mobile devices. The efficiency of the scheme has been verified by an implementation of the scheme.

17.4 Fault Tolerance in MANETs

The MANETs are expected to play a dominant role in pervasive computing environments that support users in processing information and communicating in the anytime, anywhere manner. However, due to the constraints in their capabilities, like computation power, battery backup, stable storage, etc., the mobile nodes are susceptible to different types of transient and permanent failures. The occurrence of any such failure may lead to loss of data and computation time. Therefore, the applications designed to execute in MANETs should be fault tolerant so that they can accomplish the assigned task independently. The fault tolerance is a property that enables a system to continue operating properly in the event of failure of some component(s).

There exist several approaches for achieving fault tolerance in distributed systems, e.g., checkpointing and rollback recovery, consensus algorithms, replication, and self-stabilization [17]. Among these approaches, checkpointing and rollback recovery is used to restore a useful state in a distributed system after the failure of some process(s). It prevents the loss of progress in application execution, especially in systems that involve extensive computations or voluminous data.

17.4.1 Checkpointing and Rollback Recovery

Checkpointing and recovery is an established and popular technique to provide fault tolerance in static distributed systems [18]. The technique renders fault tolerance by saving the error-free process states on the stable storage periodically during failure-free execution. A process state saved on the stable storage is called its checkpoint. A global state of the system is formed as a set of checkpoints, one from each process in the system. At the time of recovery, the failed process retrieves its latest checkpoint from stable storage and resumes computation from that state. This is termed as rollback recovery. However, an earlier saved local checkpoint of a failed process may not always be consistent with the current system state. This is because exchange of messages between the nodes during the failure-free execution of an application may result in the creation of dependencies among the checkpoints of processes. Due to this, the failure and subsequent rollback of a node may cause the creation of orphan messages in the system. An orphan message is a message whose send event is undone due to the rollback of the failed process but which has been recorded as received at some other process. The recipient of such a message also needs to roll back to a state previous to the receipt of the message in order to maintain a consistent state in the system. A system state is thus defined to be consistent if it does not include any orphan messages.

Consider a three-process system as shown in Figure 17.2. If the process q fails after sending the message m2 to process r, the message will be rendered orphan in the global state formed by a set of checkpoints, $G_1 = \{C_{p,j+1}, C_{q,k}, C_{r,j+1}\}$. Hence, the process r will have to roll back to its checkpoint $C_{r,j}$ in order to construct a consistent global state, $G_2 = \{C_{p,j+1}, C_{q,k}, C_{r,j}\}$.

Involving multiple processes, such as q as well as r in the example of Figure 17.2, in the recovery of a failed node, q incurs a high overhead. Therefore, in order to accomplish the recovery of a failed node independently or asynchronously, a node additionally maintains a log of the messages it receives from other nodes. In case a node fails, it restarts execution from the saved state, i.e., its latest checkpoint and re-executes the received messages from the log to recreate its exact pre-failure state. This prevents the formation of orphans, and further, the rollback of a node does not involve the rollback of any other node in the system.

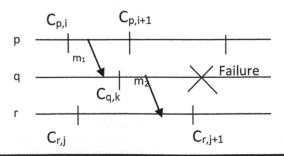

Figure 17.2   Orphan messages.

17.4.2 Classification of Rollback Recovery Techniques

The approaches to rollback recovery can be classified into checkpoint-based recovery and log-based recovery. The checkpoint-based approach to rollback recovery relies only on checkpoints to achieve fault tolerance [18]. Recovery restores the system to an earlier consistent state which may or may not have actually existed earlier; this state could be a possible consistent state during the error-free execution. The recovery process could involve the rollback of multiple processes, some of which may not have failed. An alternative approach to rollback recovery allows asynchronous recovery of a failed process by combining checkpointing with message logging at the processes in the system. In this log-based rollback recovery, the determinants of messages are logged into the stable storage during failure-free operation [18]. At the time of recovery, a process uses its checkpoint and logged determinants to reconstruct the process's pre-failure state exactly, i.e., beyond the latest checkpoint.

17.4.2.1 Checkpoint-Based Rollback Recovery

Checkpoint-based rollback recovery relies only on checkpoints to achieve fault tolerance. If a failure occurs, checkpoint-based rollback recovery restores the system state to the most recent consistent set of checkpoints, known as the recovery line. The system may not have actually encountered this state earlier; this state could be a possible consistent state during the error-free execution. This approach does not detect or log the nondeterministic events in the system, and hence, there is no guarantee that the pre-failure execution can be deterministically regenerated subsequent to a rollback. Recovery may involve the rollback of multiple processes, some of which may not have failed, to restore the system to an earlier consistent state. The rollback propagation may, in the worst case, even lead to the domino effect, in which all processes roll back to the initial state of computation.

Three types of checkpointing protocols have been proposed in the literature based on the coordination required among the processes in the distributed system at the time of checkpointing [18]. The synchronous or coordinated checkpointing requires each process in the system to take its checkpoint simultaneously with every other process. The uncoordinated or asynchronous checkpointing allows each process to checkpoint independently in the system. The communication-induced checkpointing (CIC) requires the communication history to be piggybacked on each message, and each process takes some checkpoints independently while others are forced based on the received information. The characteristics of each of these techniques are discussed next.

17.4.2.1.1 Coordinated Checkpointing

Coordinated checkpointing requires processes to coordinate or synchronize their checkpoints so that a set of local checkpoints, one from each process, always forms a consistent global state. Coordinated checkpointing simplifies recovery as each global checkpoint is a consistent checkpoint. In case a process fails, all the processes roll back to their latest checkpoint. Since the rollback at the time of recovery is limited to the latest checkpoint, recovery procedure is domino-free. Moreover, each process is required to maintain only one checkpoint on the stable storage, thereby reducing the storage overhead. This also eliminates the need for garbage collection by the coordinated checkpointing protocols [17].

The limitation of this method arises from the need of synchronization among processes at each checkpointing procedure. Synchronization leads to the exchange of multiple messages between processes, causing a high communication overhead in wireless systems. The failure of a single process causes the rollback of all processes to their last checkpoints. Further, the message passing between processes during the checkpointing procedure may result in the construction of an inconsistent global checkpoint. Therefore, coordinated checkpointing either requires the blocking of computation at processes during checkpointing or prevents the processes from receiving application messages that could make the checkpoint inconsistent. Non-blocking coordinated checkpointing protocols work by either piggybacking application messages with the checkpoint sequence numbers or sending out special control messages.

The coordinated checkpointing is not scalable as it requires all processes to participate in every checkpointing procedure. This leads to simultaneous contention for shared resources, such as stable storage and communication channels, by the processes at the time of checkpointing. Therefore, it is desirable that the number of processes involved in a coordinated checkpointing session be reduced. This is possible only if the processes that have communicated with the checkpoint initiator, either directly or indirectly since the last checkpoint take new checkpoints.

17.4.2.1.2 Uncoordinated Checkpointing

The uncoordinated checkpointing technique allows each process in the system to take its checkpoint independently in the system. Since coordination is not required at the time of checkpointing, this method does not impose synchronization overhead at the time of checkpointing. However, as the checkpoints at processes are taken independently, there is no guarantee that a given set of local checkpoints will be consistent. Moreover, a process may take a useless checkpoint which can never belong to any global consistent state [19]. The recovery algorithm must search for the most recent consistent set of checkpoints at the time of recovery. Therefore, the processes keep a record of the dependencies among their checkpoints caused by message passing during normal execution. The recovery of a failed process may cause the rollback of the processes which may not have failed. This rollback propagation may, in the worst case, even lead to the domino effect [20], in which all processes roll back to the initial state of computation. Since processes may need to roll back to an earlier checkpoint due to the failure at any process in the system, they are required to maintain multiple checkpoints. If processes p, q, and r, in Figure 17.3, take checkpoints independently, the checkpoints $C_{p,i}$ and $C_{r,j}$, both, cannot be part of the same global checkpoint.

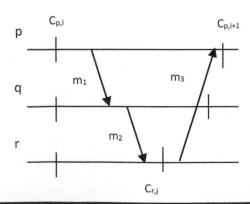

Figure 17.3   Uncoordinated checkpointing.

17.4.2.1.3 Communication-Induced Checkpointing

CIC is a technique that allows processes to take some checkpoints independently, although the processes are required to take some additional checkpoints to ensure the eventual progress of the recovery line. The additional checkpoints, i.e., those forced by the checkpointing procedure, prevent useless checkpoints at processes. This technique does not involve any kind of control messages related to the checkpointing procedure. The application messages exchanged between the processes are appended with protocol-related information. On receipt of an application message, a process uses the piggybacked information to determine if it needs to take a forced checkpoint for the progress of the global recovery line. The receiver process needs to take the forced checkpoint before processing the application message, resulting in overhead and possible latency. Therefore, it is desired that the number of forced checkpoints be minimized.

17.4.2.2 Log-Based Rollback Recovery

The independent recovery of a process, such that the system remains in a consistent state, can be accomplished by combining message logging with checkpointing. This approach models the execution of a process as a sequence of deterministic state intervals, where each interval starts with the execution of a nondeterministic event. A nondeterministic event can either be an event internal to the process or the receipt of a message from another process in the system. The event of sending a message is not a nondeterministic event. The concept of piecewise deterministic (PWD) assumption related to the state interval is presumed. This implies that the same output will be produced each time a process starts from the same state and the same nondeterministic events happen at the same locations within the execution [18]. This approach postulates that all nondeterministic events that a process executes can be identified and the information necessary to replay each event during recovery can be logged. Further, if all the nondeterministic events are logged and replayed in their exact original order, a process can deterministically recreate its pre-failure state beyond the latest, even if this state has not been checkpointed.

Therefore, when a process recovers, it first restores its latest saved checkpoint. Subsequently, it retrieves the messages it had received after the last checkpoint and before the failure from the log, and replays these messages. In this manner, log-based recovery moves the recovery line beyond the latest checkpoint of a process. Further, there will be no process whose state is dependent on a nondeterministic event that cannot be reproduced during recovery. Based on how the determinants are logged, the message logging protocols can be classified as pessimistic, optimistic, or causal.

17.4.3 Existing Approaches to Fault Tolerance in MANETs

Extensive work has been performed in the field of checkpointing and rollback recovery for static and cellular mobile systems [18,21–24]. The algorithms for cellular mobile systems assume the existence of static infrastructure such as base stations. The recovery algorithms, in general, delegate the responsibility of storing the checkpoint data and handling the recovery requests to these base stations. However, the existing algorithms are insufficient in dealing with the challenges posed by the ad hoc environment [4] since these assume the availability of resources such as stable storage (either at the fixed hosts or at base stations in cellular mobile systems) and high bandwidth links. In contrast, nodes in the ad hoc environment need to cooperate with each other to handle the absence of static infrastructure in the network. A node uses stable storage available at its neighboring nodes to save its recovery-related data.

Recently, there have been attempts at utilizing the development of techniques adapted to the challenges of MANETs. The implementation of an effective fault tolerance scheme allows MANETs to be used as a viable computational platform. A Quality of Service (QoS)-aware checkpointing arrangement has been presented by Darby et al. in [21]. A mobile node selects another node in the network, according to a reliability metric, to save its checkpoint. Similarly, the node itself acts as checkpoint storage for another node in the network. However, successful recovery is possible if the node recovers at a location neighboring its CSN. Another recovery protocol for mobile hosts employing proxies on static hosts has been presented in [25]. A protocol for allowing successful recovery in a purely mobile environment has been presented in [4]. The protocol employs movement-based checkpointing in a clustered MANET. A mobile node saves its checkpoint and message log data at the Cluster Heads with which it affiliates. A node may recover at any location, and the recovery of a node is completely asynchronous.

Since the checkpointing protocols for MANETs involve the cooperation of constituent nodes, security of the checkpoint data becomes an important issue. Nodes are required to cooperate for the operation of the network, while there is no centralized administration that may enforce a security policy for the network. The dynamic and open nature of MANETs makes these networks vulnerable to security threats as the networks are constituted of hosts which may never have previously interacted with each other [3]. Moreover, MANETs allow nodes to join or leave the network and freely move within the network. As a result, there is no network boundary at which some security measure may be implemented. In such a scenario, a node may act selfishly by using the resources of other nodes for its own communication or computation purposes. However, it may not offer its own resources to the other nodes in the network. Further, if a node exhibits corrupt or malicious behavior, it may cause more damage to the application execution by damaging, modifying, or dropping the network data. Since a node may keep changing its location, it is difficult to track the malicious node. Thus, security is an important concern if MANETs have to be utilized for application execution. Also, the infrastructure-less nature of MANETs and the resource limitation of mobile devices necessitate that the security solutions for MANETS are lightweight, decentralized, and fault tolerant.

The issue of security in the context of checkpointing and rollback recovery has been explored in [26]. The paper proposes an incremental checkpointing and encryption technique that saves in stable storage only the data that has been modified since the last checkpoint. A secure checkpointing protocol for MANETs has been presented in [27]. The protocol combines the technique of encryption with the application of a trust model. The checkpoint-related data is stored in the stable storage of a neighboring node, and if this neighboring node is not a trusted node, the checkpoint is encrypted before being sent. However, encryption may result in a significant overhead to the system.

The current chapter presents a secure rollback recovery protocol that utilizes erasure coding-based checkpointing technique. To the best of our knowledge, this is the first attempt to apply erasure coding for checkpoint data. This technique has multiple benefits since it provides security and higher system reliability as compared to keeping a single checkpoint copy while taking up less storage than a replication-based scheme. Further, a trust mechanism mitigates the problems caused due to the presence of malicious or selfish nodes in the system.

17.5 Open Research Issues in MANETs

MANETs have significant use in multiple domains such as military, recovery in times of disaster, monitoring and surveillance, and conferencing. However, the design of a reliable MANET involves problems like routing, security, fault tolerance, scalability, and many other related problems. There has been significant research in a few fields like MANET routing and clustering; yet problems like security and fault tolerance are still open to efficient solutions.

There exist multiple issues open to research contributions in the two significant challenges in MANETs, i.e., security and fault tolerance. The security issues pertaining to the various layers of network architecture are as follows:

- Detection and prevention of malicious code, viruses, etc. in the application layer;
- Authentication and security of communication using methods as encryption in the transport layer;
- Security of routing and forwarding protocols in network layer;
- Provision of security in Link layer;
- Prevention of denial-of-service attacks in physical layer.

Trust management is another crucial aspect of security since a solution may incorrectly suspect a benign or correct node as malicious. Another related field open to research is key distribution and management.

Securing MANETs is a challenge encompassing a number of open problems of research that seek attention from researchers. The existing security solutions in MANETs address mainly the attacks by and misbehavior of malicious nodes, as discussed in previous sections. However, there is still ample scope for improving the solutions with respect to the following dimensions:

- *Reduction in Overheads Caused to Normal Execution*: Overheads may be decreased by integrating security mechanisms with other existing protocols. Another direction for research may be aimed at reducing the processing time and overhead for complex operations as encryption. Limiting redundancy due to duplicate packets will also reduce resource overheads.
- *Requirement of Decentralized Solution Approaches*: A centralized system is not feasible in a self-organizing and infrastructure-less network as MANET. Research efforts can be placed for finding distributed solutions apt for MANETs.
- *Cooperation of Nodes*: Nodes are required to cooperate with each other in a MANET for routing of messages, and a similar behavior is required for maintaining security and trust in the network. Solutions based on cooperative or collaborative behavior are the need for MANETs.
- *Scalability*: One area related to MANETs that requires research attention is scalability of protocols for large-area MANETs. Generally, these networks have been envisaged as networks confined to small areas. However, they are increasingly finding applications in the context of heterogeneous networks and mobile cloud computing [23,28–30], and therefore, scalable solutions should be looked into. Clustering the nodes is an effective solution for scalability where a special node is designated as the Cluster Head and is responsible for coordinating the nodes in its cluster. As an instance, the Cluster Head can be made responsible for maintaining the trust values for nodes in its cluster. Cluster maintenance is challenging due to dynamic topology of MANETs.
- *Proactive Approach to Security*: The existing proposals, in general, first identify a security threat and subsequently, propose a solution to address this threat. Therefore, this solution fails if an unexpected or unforeseen attack occurs. It will be of utmost importance if a security solution acts against multiple threats, both known and unknown.

Apart from security, another area open to novel solutions is that of fault tolerance in MANETs. Nodes in a MANET are particularly prone to failures due to their mobility, limited battery lives, and constrained resources. Therefore, an effective utilization of MANETs for computing or communication requires a fault tolerance mechanism. This problem has garnered attention of researchers, and solutions have been proposed for the same. The solutions can be improved by optimizing with respect to the following directions:

- *Reduction in Overhead Caused to Error-Free Execution*: The system may make use of underlying network topology and routing mechanism to avoid extra control messages. These may be piggybacked on redundant copies of application messages, wherever possible [16]. Research can explore construction of virtual backbones for network topology in order to reduce the communication overheads. These will also allow scalability of protocols as the number of nodes in the network increases.
- *Network Partition Tolerance*: Another issue that remains to be effectively addressed is handling of network partitions. The fault tolerance mechanisms for MANETs generally assume dynamic topology without partitions. However, occurrence of network partitions is highly probable, especially as the network size grows.
- *Consideration for Heterogeneity in Devices*: Any protocol should take into account device heterogeneity. A device may face unique constraints related to availability of resources, cost of security or fault tolerance mechanism deployment, or concerns with respect to complexity.
- *Evaluation of Protocols*: New avenues of research are made available by evaluation of protocols and their suitability to MANETs. The effectiveness of each protocol should be evaluated through analysis, measurements, and simulations. It has been observed that there is a lack of effective tools for evaluation which take into account trade-offs between strength, overhead, complexity, scalability, etc.

17.6 Proposed Security and Fault Tolerance Algorithm

A MANET consists of mobile nodes with varied processing power, limited stable storage, and random movement patterns which communicate with each other over wireless connections. These networks are characterized by the absence of any centralized or static infrastructure or control mechanism. Therefore, the nodes in such a network require collaborating with each other for distributed application execution, network operations such as packet routing. In the context of the current problem, if a mobile node does not possess adequate stable storage to save its own checkpoint, it utilizes the stable storage present at other capable nodes in the network for the same. A node can declare itself as a potential CSN if it has sufficient stable storage and battery power. Other nodes use the storage at the CSNs for saving their checkpoints.

Since the lifetime and location of nodes in a MANET is unpredictable and nodes may exhibit undesirable behavior, storing the complete checkpoint and message log of a node at a single other node lowers the probability of successful recovery. This node may fail, disconnect, selfishly or maliciously refuse to reply to a recovery request. The introduction of redundancy to the system by utilizing the available resources, which would remain idle otherwise, can significantly improve the reliability of the system by increasing the likelihood of recovery. The presented protocol employs redundancy in the form of erasure coding to offset the effect of dynamic topology and unpredictable lifetime of nodes on system reliability. Refer to Table 17.1 for description of pneumonics used in the algorithm and their descriptions.

Table 17.1　List of Pneumonics and Their Meanings

Pneumonic	Meaning
AN_p	Application node
CSN_i	Checkpoint Storage Node
$TRUST\_LIST_p$	List of trust values at AN_p for the CSNs it has knowledge about
$Trust_i$	The trust value of a CSN_i that lies between 0 and 1
ts_i	Last time of direct contact with the CSN_i when the value of $Trust_i$ was updated
$Trust\_own(p,i)$	AN_p's own evaluation of CSN_i's behavior
$Trust\_rec(p,i)$	average value of the recommendations about CSN_i received by AN_p from other nodes
α	Weight with value between 0 and 1, used for trust calculation
$Neighbor_p$	List of CSN neighbors of AN_p
rec_req_i	Number of recovery requests received by CSN_i in a time interval
rec_rep_i	Number of replies to received recovery requests sent by CSN_i in a time interval
ERA_List_p	List of ids of the nodes holding erasure coded chunks of the checkpoint data of the node p
$Chkpt\_sno_p$	Current checkpoint sequence number
τ	Time period after which the trust value is updated
CHK_List_j	List of ids of the nodes for which the node j is the CSN

Erasure coding is a well-established approach for the design of stable storage in resource-constrained systems [2]. Using this technique, data can be encoded by adding some redundancy. Subsequently, the original data can be retrieved from the encoded data even if some parts are not available. An erasure coding scheme is used in this work for encoding the checkpoints before sending them to the CSNs. A node erasure codes its checkpoint, i.e., divides the data into k blocks and encodes into n ($n > k$) copies, before distributing these among n CSNs (as depicted in Figure 17.4). The node logs the received messages in its own stable storage. At the time of recovery, the survival of any k out of n copies of the checkpoint data ensures the successful recovery of the node. Thus, reliability improves by a factor dependent on the value of $n - k$.

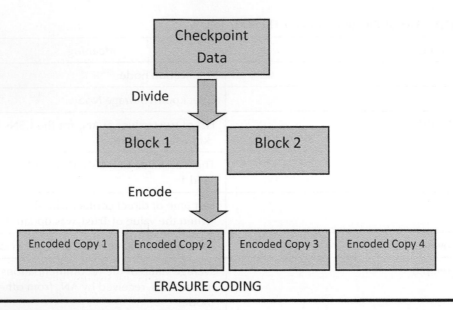

Figure 17.4 Erasure coding of checkpoint data.

It may be pointed out that the complete replication of checkpoint and message log on multiple nodes can further increase the reliability of the network. However, this may not be always feasible, considering the limited availability of storage in a MANET. It has been pointed out by studies that though erasure coding requires computational overhead, it results in a decrease in stable storage requirement as compared to replication while providing the same level of availability and reliability [2]. Therefore, it is advantageous to be used in scenarios where storage and reliability are the concerns, but the computational resources are available. Erasure coding helps to meet the orthogonal requirements of redundancy and dealing with limited storage capability of the ad hoc environment. Moreover, the requirement of k out of n copies for recovery provides the first level of security by the erasure coding-based checkpointing, since successful recovery is possible in the presence of up to $n - k$ malicious nodes or failures.

The second level of security is provided by maintaining a trust value for the CSNs. Each node, p, executing an application maintains a list; TRUST_LIST<CSN_i, $Trust_i$, ts_i> to hold the trust value at time, ts_i, for the CSNs it has knowledge about. The trust value of a CSN is formed from two components: Trust_own(p,i) that denotes the node p's own evaluation of CSN_i's behavior and Trust_rec(p,i) that is the average value of the recommendation received from other nodes about CSN_i. The complete trust value for a CSN lies between 0 and 1, representing complete distrust and complete trust.

The node p can evaluate CSN_i by itself when CSN_i lies within its transmission range. It operates in a promiscuous mode to overhear the recovery requests sent to the CSN_i and the replies sent back by CSN_i. Subsequently, in a given time interval, the node p estimates the CSN_i's trust value as follows:

$$\text{Trust\_own}(p,i) = \left(\text{rec\_rep}_i\right)/\left(\text{rec\_req}_i\right) \tag{17.1}$$

When the node AN_p comes in contact with node AN_q, it exchanges its TRUST_LIST with the node AN_q. Thus, the trust values are propagated in the system as a result of the opportunistic contacts between the nodes, rather than by an all-to-all broadcast. Each node appends the tuple corresponding to the CSN for which it has no previous information in its TRUST_LIST. For the CSNs whose trust value exists in both the lists, the CSN_i's trust value is updated using the latest value. For instance, if TRUST_LIST(q).ts$_i$ is greater than TRUST_LIST(p).ts$_i$, then the node p updates its Trust_rec(p,i) value based on q's recommendation. This ensures that a CSN's trust value is not updated based on an obsolete experience. The complete trust of a node p on a CSN_i is computed as follows:

$$TRUST\_LIST(p).Trust_i = \alpha\ Trust\_own(p,i) + (1-\alpha)Trust\_rec(p,i) \qquad (17.2)$$

The value of the weight, α, is dependent on the timestamp of Trust_own(p,i) and Trust_rec(p,i). If CSN_i is within the transmission range of p, α can be set to 1 and the node p may not update based on recommendations. However, if CSN_i is not in its transmission range, α can be set to 0.5 to give credit to both the recommendations an own evaluation. However, if p has never been in contact with CSN_i, α can be set to 0 to base the trust on the recommendations alone. The trust value of a CSN is used by the erasure coding module for the selection of CSNs for storing the encoded checkpoint data. If more than n number of CSNs is available for storing the k chunks of data, the n CSNs with the highest trust values may be sent the checkpoint data blocks.

It may be observed that the two tiers of security complement each other by mitigating the other's limitations. For instance, a malicious node may declare itself as the CSN to cause data loss in the system or the limitation of space may cause a selfish node to delete another node's recovery-related data. In this case, the trust value of the CSN will be decreased by its neighboring nodes, and therefore, the misbehaving node will be detected. Similarly, a malicious node may propagate a low trust value for a properly functioning CSN. However, it will not be able to prevent successful recovery since the checkpoint and message log data is available at $n-1$ other nodes also and can be reconstructed till the number of misbehaving nodes is limited by $n-k$.

17.6.1 Checkpointing Algorithm

Actions at each node p operating in a promiscuous or overhearing mode
  $\forall\ CSN_i \in$ Neighbor$_p$:

■ If a recovery request received by a CSN_i,

Neighbor$_p$.rec_req$_i$+ = 1

■ If a reply is sent back by a CSN_i,

Neighbor$_p$.rec_rep$_i$+ = 1
Actions by each node p at time period τ

■ Append Neighbor$_p$ list with periodic beacon messages and exchange list with neighbors
■ $\forall\ CSN_i \in$ Neighbor$_p$: Update Trust value as

1. For the previous interval
   i. Trust_prev$_i$ = (rec_rep$_i$)/(rec_req$_i$)
   ii. Trust_own(p,i) = average(TRUST_LIST$_p$.Trust$_i$, Trust_prev$_i$)

2. $\forall\ q \in$ Neighbor$_p$: TRUST_LIST$_q$.ts$_i$ > TRUST_LIST$_p$.ts$_i$

   Trust_recommendation$_i$ = average(TRUST_LIST(q).Trust$_i$)

3. TRUST_LIST(p).Trust$_i$ = α Trust_own(p,i)+ (1 − α) Trust_rec(p,i)

When it is time to checkpoint, actions performed by the application node, AN$_p$

- Broadcast a *chkpt<p, n>* message
- On receiving replies from the CSN nodes, select the *n* nodes with the highest trust values among them to act as its CSNs
- Chkpt_sno$_p$+ = 1
- Take checkpoint C numbered Chkpt_sno$_p$
- Erasure code the checkpoint C and send the *n* chunks to each of the CSNs
- Append the id of each CSN to Era_List$_p$

On receipt of checkpoint C at CSN$_i$

- If AN$_p$ ∈ CHK_List$_i$
- Delete previous checkpoint and message log of AN$_p$
- *Else* Append AN$_p$ to CHK_List$_i$
- Save C onto disc

On receipt of message M by AN$_p$

- Save <M, ts> in own stable log
- If memory not available, take a new checkpoint and erase the message log

17.6.2 Handling Mobility of Nodes

Messages Used by the Algorithm
   <move, p>: Sent by AN$_p$ to its neighbors when it starts moving
   <stop, p>: Sent by AN$_p$ to its neighbors when it stops moving
   <del_chkpt, p>: Sent by AN$_p$ to request deletion of its previous checkpoint data
   When AN$_p$ starts to move

- Append <move, p> with beacon messages

   On receipt of <move, p>, Action by CSN$_i$
   While beacon messages received from node AN$_p${

- On receipt of <stop, p> appended with beacon messages received from node p, exit
- If <del_chkpt, p> is received from node p

{Delete checkpoint and message log of p from disc
   Remove AN$_p$ from CHK_List$_i$}
   }

When AN_p stops moving

- Append <stop, p> with beacon messages
- Send <del_chkpt, p> message to previous CSN
- Chkpt_sno$_p$+ = 1
- Take checkpoint C numbered Chkpt_sno$_i$

17.6.3 Asynchronous Recovery of a Mobile Host

The presented recovery procedure of a failed mobile node is completely asynchronous since it does not require any other node to roll back. A failed node can recover successfully if it is able to retrieve its latest checkpoint data from at least k CSN nodes. If the k chunks of the checkpoint data have been encoded into n copies, the failure of up to $n-k$ copies can be tolerated. In case, more than $n-k$ nodes fail, recovery will not be possible. We use a metric, *Recoverability of the network*, to analyze the performance of the recovery algorithm. It is defined as follows:

Recoverability = (Number of times checkpoint and message log reaches the recovering node in a given time interval)/(Total number of recovery procedures executed by nodes in the network over a time period)

When a node (or a replacement node) recovers after failure, it requires retrieving its checkpoint data. Since a node may recover at a location different from where it failed, it needs to locate the CSNs in the network. The retrieval of any k out of n copies of the encoded checkpoint will ensure successful recovery. Therefore, a recovering node broadcasts a *recover*<node_id, chkpt_sno> message. On receiving the *recover* message from some node, say i, a node j checks if CHK_List$_j$ contains node i. If it does, the node j sends the checkpoint data to the node i. Each node in a MANET may overhear transmission of its neighboring nodes. Therefore, a node broadcasts the *recover* message further if it does not hear the broadcast of the *recover* message by any other node. However, it waits for a random time before broadcasting the *recover* message, so that if it overhears the broadcast by some other node, it suppresses its own broadcast. On obtaining the required data, the recovering node rolls back to the saved checkpoint and replays the messages from its own log to recover to its correct pre-failure state.

17.7 Performance Analysis

MANETs are finding important applications in the areas of emergency situations as disaster relief, environment monitoring, intelligent transportation systems, and battlefields. They are offering a way to expand the computing capability of mobile networks by combining with the infrastructure-based cellular mobile networks in the form of heterogeneous networks. More importantly, they are being used for mobile computing grids and mobile cloud computing where intensive computations involving complex data are executed on nodes. Consequently, security and fault tolerance are required for successful execution of applications in MANETs in order to deal with the fragile nature of these networks.

The performance of the presented scheme is evaluated by analyzing the recoverability of a node with the application of the secure checkpointing scheme. A node is able to recover successfully if it can retrieve its checkpoint data from the system during its recovery. The general term "failure" is used to describe the case of a transient or crash failure of a node. A failed node will be unable to recover if its checkpoint data is stored with a selfish or malicious node. We assume an exponential failure distribution for the network, taking a constant failure rate for the mobile nodes, λ. The exponential distribution provides a good model for the current problem since a mobile node may fail at any instant of time.

Case I: A node's complete checkpoint data is stored in the stable storage of another node:

For a given failure rate, $h(t) = \lambda$.

The recoverability of the system is the probability that the checkpoint will survive from time 0 (i.e., when it was stored) to time t (i.e., the time of recovery)

$$\text{Recover}(t) = P(T > t) \text{ where } t >= 0$$

$$= 1 - F(t) = e^{-\lambda t}$$

(17.3)

where $F(t)$ is the probability that the checkpoint data will not survive by time t.

Case II: A node's checkpoint data is replicated:

Assuming k replicas of the checkpoint data, the system can be modeled as a parallel system.

$$\text{Recover}(t) = 1 - P(\text{checkpoint is unavailable})$$

$$= 1 - P(\text{none of the } k \text{ replicas is available})$$

$$= 1 - P(\text{one replica is unavailable})^k$$

(17.4)

$$= 1 - \left(1 - e^{-\lambda t}\right)^k$$

Case III: A node's checkpoint data is erasure coded:

Assuming that the checkpoint data of a node is divided into k parts and encoded into n chunks, the system can be modeled as a k out of n system. In this case, the successful recovery of a node is possible if any k nodes storing the erasure coded data are surviving, i.e., have not failed and are not exhibiting selfish or malicious behavior.

If the probability of availability of each node i, having a copy of the checkpoint data chunk of node j, at the time of node j's recovery is assumed identical and as $R(t)$

Recover(t) = Probability of availability of any k out of n copies at t

$$\langle I \rangle \text{Recover}_{k\text{-of-}n}(t) = \sum_{i=0}^{n-k} \binom{n}{i} (1 - R(t))^i R(t)^{n-i} \langle /I \rangle$$

$$\langle I \rangle = \sum_{i=m}^{n} \binom{n}{i} R(t)^i (1 - R(t))^{n-i} \langle /I \rangle$$

(17.5)

where

$$\langle I \rangle \binom{n}{i} = \frac{n!}{i!(n-i)!} \langle /I \rangle$$

The proposed scheme has been simulated for a network with 100 mobile nodes using the network simulator, ns2. We compare the recoverability obtained by the proposed scheme with a scheme employing a single-copy replication of the checkpoint data. The percentage of malicious nodes is

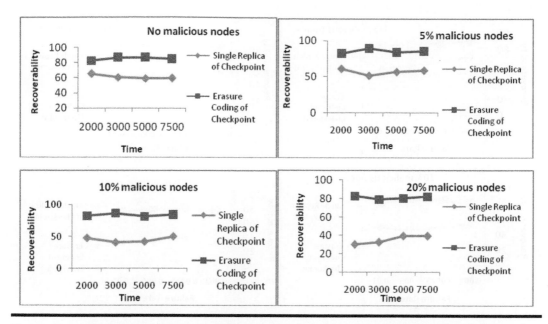

Figure 17.5 Comparison of recoverability of the network under replication and erasure coding with varying percentage of malicious nodes.

varied in different simulation experiments, and the results are presented for an erasure coding and trust-based scheme along with the replication-based scheme which does not employ trust values. The failure rate of a MH follows an exponential distribution with a rate λ_f and on the failure; the MH instantly performs the proper action for the recovery.

Figure 17.5 presents the results of comparison of recoverability of the network under replication and erasure coding (with trust values) with a varying percentage of malicious nodes. It can be observed that the erasure coding-based scheme provides a higher recoverability in all cases. In addition, the benefit of the proposed scheme is more evident as the percentage of malicious nodes increases in the network. This fact is due to the reason that a single replica of the checkpoint is more vulnerable to the malicious behavior as compared to the case of erasure coding where successful recovery is possible if any k out of n checkpoint chunks can be retrieved. Therefore, erasure coding-based checkpointing allows secure recovery in the presence of up to $n-k$ malicious nodes.

The recovery procedure involves locating the k out of n checkpoint chunks in the network. Hence, the proposed scheme will involve a higher message overhead as compared to a single-checkpoint replica-based scheme at the time of recovery. However, this overhead is offset by the dual benefits of security as well as fault tolerance provided by the proposed scheme. Even if the percentage of malicious nodes or the failure rate of mobile nodes increases, the recoverability of the network remains high.

Figure 17.6 presents a comparison of performance of the considered schemes under varying failure rates. The proposed erasure coding-based checkpointing scheme consistently exhibits a higher recoverability than a single replica-based scheme. It can be observed that even at higher failure rates, the recoverability due to the proposed scheme exceeds that of the scheme not employing erasure coding. Further, an increase in the percentage of malicious nodes does not deteriorate the performance of the proposed scheme.

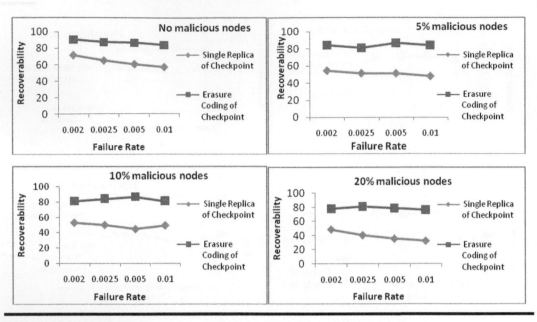

Figure 17.6   Comparison of recoverability of the network under replication and erasure coding with a varying percentage of malicious nodes and varying failure rates.

17.8 Conclusion and Future Directions

The work presented in the chapter addresses two important requirements for utilizing the MANETs as a computational platform, i.e., security and fault tolerance. The existence in abundance of mobile devices gives an impetus to harness the computing power of these devices. Considering that utilizing these devices can provide immense benefits, it is imperative to handle the limitations and challenges of a mobile computing environment. Therefore, the chapter has presented a protocol that handles the two most important issues of a MANET: fault tolerance and security. The proposed checkpointing protocol allows asynchronous recovery of a failed node without causing the rollback of any other node. Erasure coding the checkpoints, instead of saving only a single copy of the checkpoint, ensures the optimal use of stable storage while providing higher system reliability. It also provides security as the complete checkpoint of a node is not available to any other node. The trust values maintained for the CSNs provide the second tier of security in a MANET.

The proposed solution is extensible to a system where the MANET can be used in tandem with a cloud computing platform. In case of resource constraints in the MANET due to volume of multimedia data or complexity of computations, the mobile devices can offload computation tasks of an application to more powerful cloud servers [31]. On the one hand, it will avoid the time and bandwidth required for offloading and migration till the mobile devices in the MANET can satisfy the computational requirements of an application. On the other, this will allow the scalability and flexibility of resources using the cloud and thus, overcome the constraints of MANETs.

References

1. Tous R., Torres J. and Ayguadé E., Multimedia big data computing for in-depth event analysis. *2015 IEEE International Conference on Multimedia Big Data (BigMM)*, Beijing, 2015, pp. 144–147.

2. Weatherspoon H. and Kubiatowicz J. D., Erasure coding vs. replication: A quantitative comparison. In: *International Workshop on Peer-to-Peer Systems*. Springer, Berlin, Heidelberg, 2002.

3. Li H. and Singhal M., Trust management in distributed systems. *Computer*, 40, no. 2, 2007, 45–53.

4. Jaggi P.K. and Singh A.K., Movement-based checkpointing and message logging for recovery in MANETs. *Wireless Personal Communications*, 83, no. 3, 2015, 1971–1993.

5. Basagni S., Conti M., Giordano S. and Stojmenovic I. (eds), *Mobile Ad Hoc Networking*, Wiley, Vol. 35, 2004.

6. Yang H., Luo H., Ye F., Lu S. and Zhang L., Security in mobile ad hoc networks: Challenges and solutions. *IEEE Wireless Communications*, 11, no. 1, 2004, 38–47.

7. Qiu T., Chen N., Li K., Qiao D. and Fu Z., Heterogeneous ad hoc networks. *Ad Hoc Networks*, 55, 2017, 143–152.

8. Prakash A. and Agarwal D.P., Data security in wired and wireless systems, *Handbook of Research on Modern Cryptographic Solutions for Computer and Cyber Security*, IGI Global, 2016, 1–27.

9. Saini P. and Singh A.K., Security in ad hoc network and computing paradigms, *Handbook of Research on Modern Cryptographic Solutions for Computer and Cyber Security*, IGI Global, 2016, 30, 96–125.

10. Badonnel R., State R., Festor O., Management of mobile ad-hoc networks: Evaluating the network behavior. *Integrated Network Management*, 17, no. 30, 2005, 15–19; IM 2005. *2005 9th IFIP/IEEE International Symposium*.

11. Buchegger S. and Boudec J.-Y. L., Performance Analysis of the CONFIDANT Protocol: Cooperation Of Nodes – Fairnessin Distributed Ad-hoc Networks, *Presented at IEEE/ACM Workshop on Mobile Ad Hoc Networking and Computing (MobiHOC)*, Lausanne, 2002.

12. Marti S., Giuli T.J., Lai K. and Baker M., Mitigating routing misbehaviour in mobile ad hoc networks. *Proceedings of the 6th annual international conference on Mobile computing and networking*, ACM, 2000, 255–265.

13. Michiardi P. and Molva R., CORE: A collaborative reputation mechanism to enforce node cooperation in mobile ad hoc networks. *Presented at Communication and Multimedia Security*, Portoroz, Slovenia, 2002.

14. Zhang Y., Lee W. and Huang Y., Intrusion detection techniques for mobile wireless networks. *ACM/Kluwer Wireless Networks Journal(ACM WINET)*, 9, no. 5, 2003, 545–556.

15. Anantvalee T. and Wu J., A Survey on Intrusion Detection in Mobile Ad Hoc Networks. In: Wireless/Mobile Security, Springer-Verlag: New York, 2008.

16. Zkik K., Orhanou G., and Hajji S.E., Secure mobile multi cloud architecture for authentication and data storage. *International Journal of Cloud Applications and Computing*, 7, 2017, no. 2, 62–76.

17. Kshemkalyani A.D. and Singhal M., *Distributed Computing: Principles, Algorithms and Systems*, Cambridge University Press, 2011.

18. Elnozahy E.N., Alvisi L., Wang Y.M., Johnson D.B., A survey of rollback-recovery protocols in message-passing systems. *ACM Computing Surveys (CSUR)*, 34, no. 3, 2002, 375–408.

19. Netzer R.H.B. and Xu J., Necessary and Sufficient Conditions for Consistent Global Snapshots, *IEEE Transactions on Parallel and Distributed Systems*, 6, no. 2, 1995, pp. 165–169.

20. Randell, B., System structure for software fault tolerance, *IEEE Transactions on Software Engineering*, 1, no. 2, 1975, pp. 220–232.

21. Darby P.J., Tzeng N.-F., Decentralized QoS-Aware Checkpointing Arrangement in Mobile Grid Computing. IEEE Transactions on Mobile Computing, 9, no. 8, 2010, 1173–1186.

22. Basagni S., Conti M., Giordano S. and Stojmenovic I. (eds), *Mobile Ad Hoc Networking*, Wiley, 2004.

23. Lalouani W., Younis M., Badache N., Optimized repair of a partitioned network topology. *Computer Networks*, 128, 2017, 63–77.

24. Jaggi P.K., Singh A.K., Rollback recovery with low overhead for fault tolerance in mobile ad hoc networks. *Journal of King Saud University - Computer and Information Sciences*, 27, no. 4, 2015, 402–415.

25. Rao I., Imran N., Woo Lee P., Huh E. and Chung T., A proxy based efficient checkpointing scheme for fault recovery in mobile grid system. In: *Proceedings of the 13th international conference on High Performance Computing (HiPC'06)*, 2006, pp. 448–459.

26. Nam H., Kim J., Hong S.J. and Lee S., Secure checkpointing. *Journal of Systems Architecture*, 48, no. 8–10, 2003, 237–254.

27. Biswas S., Dey P. and Neogy S., Secure checkpointing-recovery using trusted nodes in MANET, Computer and Communication Technology (ICCCT), *2013 4th International Conference on. IEEE*, vol. 174–180, 2013, pp. 20–22.

28. Jaggi P.K. and Singh A.K., Message efficient checkpointing and rollback recovery in heterogeneous mobile networks, *Journal of The Institution of Engineers (India): Series B*, 97, no. 2, 2016, 155–165.

29. Qiu T., Chen N., Li K., Qiao D., Fu Z., Heterogeneous ad hoc networks: Architectures, advances and challenges. *Ad Hoc Networks*, 55, 2017, 143–152.

30. Zhou J., Zhang Z., Tang S., Huang X., Mo Y. and Du D.Z., Fault-tolerant virtual backbone in heterogeneous wireless sensor network. *IEEE/ACM Transactions on Networking*, 99, 2017, 1–13.

31. Deng S., Huang L., Taheri J. and Zomaya A.Y., Computation offloading for service workflow in mobile cloud computing. In: *IEEE Transactions on Parallel and Distributed Systems*, vol. 26, no. 12, 2015, pp. 3317–3329 (condition).

## Chapter 18

Applications of Digital Signatures in Cryptography

Sarvesh Tanwar and Anil Kumar Verma

Department of Computer Science & Engineering
Mody University of Science & Technology

Contents

18.1 Background

Before proceeding to the applications of digital signature, we must understand about background of digital signatures and role of trusted parties. The concept of public key cryptography is introduced by Diffie and Hellman. In 1976, they published the paper "New directions in cryptography," which introduced public key cryptography and claimed to solve the key management problem, by introducing the public file. The public file contains entries such as number, name, and public key. According to the public key cryptography, the public key needs not to be kept secret. The receiver who has corresponding private key can decrypt the message. Now, the key management problem was solved, but a new problem was introduced, e.g., name management and problem of naming.

Kohnfelder proposed the concept of signed data structure to convey the public key to relying parties in 1978. Kohnfelder proposed to take name and public key in the public document and digitally sign them. He authored the expression "*certificate*" for this digitally signed form of the entries in the public file. In the past two decades, authentications are perceived as adaptable and secure strategy for the conveyance of the public keys to the other parties. In the 1980s, ITU begun to work about building a directory like the one proposed by Diffie and Hellman. The public key directory assembles all the data in one place about individuals and devices. The X.500 standard defines all the characteristics of a public key directory. A common standard, X.509 format, was introduced for the authentication purpose so that no one could change an entry in the directory. A trusted party referred as *Certificate Authority* is responsible to sign the certificates. Certification Authority (CA) is a reliable authority with its very own public key, publically accessible, which would digitally sign the X.509 certificates.

18.1.1 Loss Due to Cyberattacks

There are various cases where attackers can break the entire system by attacking the certificate issuing authority. Attack on security is vulnerable against various types of malicious behavior, e.g., Denial of service (DoS), phishing and spoofing attack, replay, and man-in-the-middle (MITM) attack. Phishing attack of online banking accounts and cloning of ATM cards are regular events where gatecrashers send spam mail to demand to approve or share Internet banking usernames and passwords. Due to cyberattacks on CAs and Private Key Generator (PKG), there is huge loss in terms of money, reputational damage, disclosure of privacy, and employee morale (Figure 18.1).

From Figure 18.2, we can see the impact of cyberattacks on the employees, their morale, financial, and society.

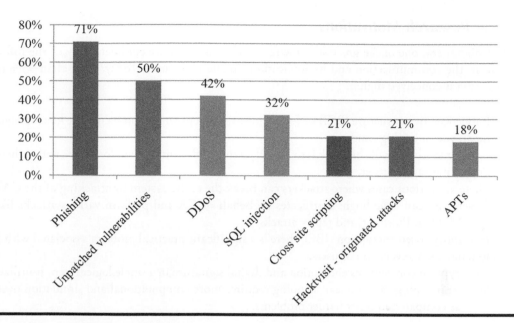

Figure 18.1   Different cyberattacks.

Source: Dan Lohrmann, hacking critical infrastructure is accelerating and more destructive, cyber security and infrastructure, April 11, 2015.

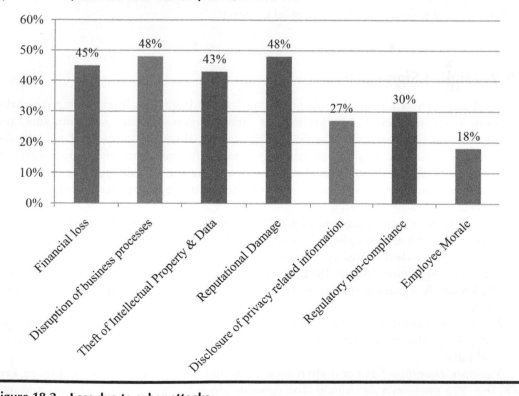

Figure 18.2   Loss due to cyber attacks.

Source: www.pcquest.com/financial-sector-most-vulnerable-to-cybercrime/.

18.1.2 Research Motivations

In this digital era, one of the greatest challenging issues is to ensure confidentiality of the information in the communication and its applications in the real world. Today, more than 93% of information is conceived digital.

1. Public Key Infrastructure (PKI) suffers from various deployment problems like key management, which is a big issue.
2. A major motivation of this work is to identify a more efficient method for secure and authenticated message transfer.
3. There are various cases where attackers can break the entire system by attacking of the CAs. Adversaries can issue bogus certificates on behalf of CA and perform various attacks like MITM, DoS, Phishing, and replay attacks.
4. In identity based encryption (IBE), there is a significant practical problem associated with it to handle key revocation of users.
5. Signcryption consolidates encryption and digital signature in a single logical step. It utilizes bilinear mapping. But bilinear mapping requires more computational and simulation overhead as compared to other harder problems.

We are motivated to work in the sphere of security because of different security issues related to CAs, ID-based signature, and signcryption schemes which leads to lots of financial loss on the government and the society. But security is a wide area, so we specifically find out to work in the field of signature to reduce this loss with novel proposal.

18.2 Digital Signature

A digital signature is a cryptographic primitive that minimally produces the same security functions as a conventional signature such as authentication, integrity, confidentiality, and non-repudiation. It ensures that the document was not altered in course and nobody else can read the document. Digital signature serves to verify that signer of the document has created and signed that document and that document has not been tampered with. It is utilized for non-renouncement, validation, and information integrity, produced using public key cryptography.

If two parties are exchanging some digital document, it may be important to protect that data so that the recipient knows that the document has not been altered since it was sent and that document received was indeed created by the sender.

Definition (Signature Scheme): The first signature scheme was proposed by Rivest, Shamir, and Adleman. A signature scheme is composed of the following three polynomial time algorithms.

Key generation algorithm, KeyGe(K): On input 1^k, where k is the security parameters, the algorithm *KeyGen* produces a key pair (PK, SK) of public and private (secret) keys. Algorithm *KeyGen* is probabilistic.

Signature algorithm, Sig: For a given message m and a key pair of public and secret keys (PK, SK), *Sign* produces a signature σ. The signature algorithm might be probabilistic and may receive some other inputs such as identity of sender and receiver.

Verification algorithm, Ver: Given a signature σ on a message *m* and a public key *PK*, *Ver* algorithm tests if σ is a valid signature of *m* with respect to public key *PK*. The output of this algorithm is 1 for accept or 0 for reject.

A signature scheme is correct if it satisfies the following condition: if *KeyGen K = SK,PK* and *Sig(m,SK)* = 0, then *Ver(m,σ,PK)* = *true* and we say that *(m,σ)* is a valid message signature pair.

Different public key cryptography techniques have been used to implement digital signature. For example,

- Rivest Shamir Adleman (RSA),
- Digital Signature Algorithm (DSA),
- ElGamal scheme,
- Elliptic Curve Digital Signature Algorithm.

Digital signatures guarantee the following information security properties:

Authenticity: The importance of authentication, verifying the identity of users and machines, becomes crucial when an organization opens its doors to the Internet. Robust authentication components guarantee that people and machines are the entities they claim to be.

Integrity: Hash functions used to maintain the integrity level of messages, which can be used to prove that data has not been tampered or altered within transit.

Non-repudiation: Non-repudiation provides a proof-of-participation in an action or transaction by establishing that a user's private key was used to digitally sign an electronic business transaction. This proves that a specific user performs the particular task at a given time.

Credibility: Receiver can verify that the received signature is indeed signed by a legitimate signer.

Unforgeability: Digital signature generation process is a trained reflex which is not subject to conscious muscular control. That is why it is hard to forge. Only sender can generate and sign his own signature as he knows his private key.

Non-reusable: Digital signature could be an operation of the file which cannot be converted into another file. It is not reusable. Other persons cannot cut and paste the signature to different documents.

Unalterable: The signed documents are unalterable. The signature on a document guarantees the origin and integrity of the document that bears signature.

18.2.1 Applications

The applications are as follows:

- Secure email login;
- Credit card transaction over the Internet;
- Internet banking;
- Mobile banking;
- Stock trading;
- Secure electronic transaction (SET);
- Tax and insurance;
- For signing documents like MSWord, MSExcel, and PDFs;
- Web-based transactions.

18.2.2 Digital Signature Schemes

18.2.2.1 Single Key Signature

Although a conventional cryptography provides authentication as long as the key remains private between both parties, it cannot establish integrity and non-repudiation without an arbitrated protocol. Therefore, it required a trusted third party.

Let,

TP = Trusted third party
P = Plaintext
S_k = Private key shared between Sender and TP
R_k = Private key shared Receiver and TP
C_{ST} = Cipher text sent from S to TP
C_{TR} = Cipher text sent from TP to R

Then,

$C_{ST} = E(S_k, P)$
$P = D(C_{ST}, S_k)$
$C_{TR} = E(R_k(S, P, E(S_k, P)))$
$S + P + E(S_k, P) = D(R_k, C_{TR})$

This scheme provides security features, but it increases considerable overhead and requires that significant trust can be placed in hands of TP. Sender encrypts P using a key *sk* that is shared between sender and the TP. TP can decrypt P and establishes that P is from sender only.

After that TP encrypts everything with R_k and sends it to receiver. Receiver decrypts it using R_k. Both sender and receiver trust on TP and authenticate each other. Receiver must store P, and (S_k, P) protects against dispute in future. Receiver is not able to decrypt (S_k, P); only TP can recover this and settle out dispute.

But this approach is not scalable. It would require a separate key for each TP. Although it can be used for authentication in private network, but it is not suitable for digital signature.

18.2.2.2 Public Key Signatures

Using public key cryptography, sender's private key can be used for encryption as well as for decryption. At the receiver side, sender's public key can be used for decryption as well as for encryption. It is used with hashing functions.

Let,

P = Plaintext
S_{pr} = Sender's private key
S_{pub} = Sender's public key
H = Harshing function
CA_{sign} = Sender's digital signature

Then:

$$CA_{sign} = E(H(P), S_{pr})$$
$$CT = P + CA_{sign}$$
$$P = D(CA_{sign}, S_{pup})$$
Compute $H'(P)$
$$H(P) = H'(P)$$

Receiver can verify the signature utilizing sender's public key. Receiver can then compute digest on plain text extracted from signature $H'(P)$ and compute it with $H(P)$. Public key signatures are giving integrity, authentication, and non-repudiation without the aid of TP. For the functionality of confidentiality, receiver public key can be used. Key management is not trivial; it is much easier to manage than single shared key.

In any case, how beneficiary can trust on sender and vice versa. How does receiver protect himself from the possibility that an unscrupulous user might fraudulently post a public key and represent it as sender's public key?

■ Does public key have a place with that individual?
■ Is public key substantial?
■ If private key is compromised, how public key is renounced?

18.2.3 How Digital Signature Works

If A want to send a signed message to B, then the digital signature is as follows:

■ On plaintext a unique fingerprint is calculated with the help of a one-way hash function-(p).
■ The result of the computation is signed with A's private key PR_a. In this manner, the digital signature now comprises $(PR_a, H(p))$.
■ A sends plaintext along with his signature $(PR_a, H(p))$ to B.

B will take the following steps after receiving the message (Figure 18.3):

■ On plaintext, he will compute the unique fingerprint with the help of same hash algorithm as applied by A.
■ He at that point will decrypt the encoded hash or signature with the assistance of the public key of A, e.g., PU_a.
■ B then compares the values of decrypted signature and hash computed by B. If the two match, then the message has been signed by A and the message is unaltered. B will accept that.

18.2.4 Digital Signatures Can Be Classified into Two Categories

18.2.4.1 Single Signature

According to the Information Technology Act 2000, use of digital signatures on the documents submitted in electronic form in order to ensure the security and authenticity of the documents filed electronically. A digital signature is created by first computing a hash of the biological information provided by the entities, encrypting the hash with the private key of the sender or public

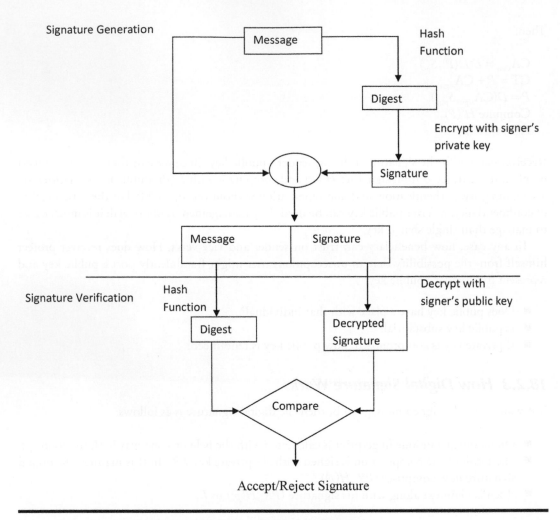

Signature Generation

Hash Function

Message

Digest

Encrypt with signer's private key

Signature

Message | Signature

Signature Verification

Hash Function

Decrypt with signer's public key

Digest

Decrypted Signature

Compare

Accept/Reject Signature

Figure 18.3   Generation and verification of digital signature.

key of the receiver, and affixing the encrypted hash to the information. A copy of the signer's certificate is generally included with the signed information.

18.2.4.2 Multiple Signatures

Multiple signatures are digital signature where a group of people sign a document or a certificate in such a way that the signature is valid if and only if it is determined by signature of every member of the group:

- In multiple signature, n random secret keys k_1, k_2,k_n and a t public key t is generated such that

$$(k_1 + k_2 + \cdots + k_n)t = 1 \bmod \varphi(n)$$

- Each signor takes the message M and signs it by

$$S_1 = M^{k_1} \bmod n$$

■ N signed are then multiplied by CA to form signature S

$$S = S_1 \times S_2 \times S_n \bmod n$$

■ This signature S is sent to the recipient. The recipient can verify the signature using t

$$M = S^t \bmod n$$

■ Original message can be verified by any member by using the public key t.

Types of multiple signatures are as follows:

1. Sequential Multiple Signature

    In this scheme, the first signer signs the contents and the second signer signs on the content and the first signer's signature. The form is considered signed when all signers sign the form and the last signature is appended on it. It can be distinguished as follows:
    - *Independent Sequential Multiple Signatures*: In this scheme, the sequence of signing is not important; the signer only signs the content.
    - *Dependent Sequential Multiple Signatures*: In this scheme, sequence is important. The last signer signs on the content and signature.

$$S_1 = C^{\mathrm{pr}} \bmod n$$

$$S_2 = S_1^{\mathrm{ps}} \bmod n$$

2. Parallel Multiple Signature

    In this scheme, the signer signs on the content of the form but not on the signature of other signers.

18.3 Application of Digital Signature

Digital signature is one of the basic primitives of cryptography. It provides authentication, integrity, and non-repudiation. There are various applications where digital signatures are used, such as

■ PKI,
■ ID-based cryptography,
■ Signcryption,
■ Certificate-less signature.

Many researchers have proposed different approaches related to PKI, ID-based cryptography, signcryption, and certificate-less signature schemes. Various schemes related to work are highlighted in this section.

Wang et al. (2015) proposed multiple signature on a certificate. A compromised single CA can break the whole PKI framework and can issue bogus certificate for any domains without the consent of the domain owners. Bogus certificate might be used in MITM attacks. They proposed multiple signature approach on a server's certificate as the probability of breaking multiple CAs in a short period of time is reduced significantly. They modify the current X.509 V3 certificate to impose multiple signatures.

Jain et al. (2015) portrayed digital signature (DS) structure to recognize signing of transactions for e-Govt. and non e-Govt. applications. They talked about a cloud-based DS initiative taken for empowering e-verification and security in the exchange period of e-Government in India. After validation of incoming request, forwards the Aadhaar authentication data to e-Sign KYC service, which whenever effective or unsuccessful is returned to the e-Sign authority. On successful e-KYC, e-Sign provider generates a key pair and certificate signing request, and creates a DS with a message digest of 160 bits.

Nia et al. (2014) looked at different sorts of DS schemes in light of efficiency, security level, and complexity. They explained different types of DS schemes and procedures such as batch scheme, forward secure scheme, blind scheme, and proxy scheme.

Szalachowski et al. (2014) said fraudulent transport layers certificate have been issued for many sites by compromised CAs. Adversaries impersonate domains to clients by performing active MITM attacks and intercept secure communication by stealing potentially sensitive information. To address inefficiencies in certificate transparency, they designed and proposed PoliCert, a log-based proposal that defines Subject Certificate Policies (SCPs). They also proposed multi-signature certificate which allowed multiple CA signatures on a certificate and serve as format for encoding SCPs. This technique provides stronger authentication and resilience to CA compromise. The public key logs maintain Merkle Hash Trees to store, generate, and revoke certificate and policies. This avoids forging fake certificate or policies and prevents adversaries from suppressing valid information.

Tanwar et al. (2016) have worked on digital signature and multiple signatures to handle MITM attack on certificate authority. The proposed approach was based on Aadhaar number, and the information is stored in blob form in database.

Moussa et al. (2003) reviewed the digital signature and multiple signatures. Digital signatures are of two types—single signature and multiple signatures. In single signature, one party signs on the document, whereas in multiple signatures, more than one party signs a single document.

Tianhuang et al. (2010) focused on DSA digital signature technology in e-commerce security issues and proposed algorithm for the improvement of DSA. They simulate signatures to solve e-commerce security issues. They said digital signature technology needs further improvement and efforts to improve security of it.

Wu et al. (2016) proposed a practical RIBE scheme. The authors have not addressed the critical issue of key escrow issue.

Yang et al. (2015) proposed Hierarchical Identity-Based Signature (HIBS) protocol for cloud computing. In this protocol, PKG is distributed in tree structure. The root PKG generated private key for its lower-layer PKG or users. This protocol has resolved the problem of overburdened PKG.

Fuw-Yi Yang et al. (2013) proposed improved multi-signature scheme based on Shamir [SHA, 84]. Instead of broadcasting $(r_{j,i})$, they broadcast encrypted value $t_j = (r_j)^e$ mod n to all signers which is difficult to find value of t_j to avoid type-1 attacks.

Tan et al. (2009) proposed an improved identity-based group signature scheme which was secured under the Computational Diffie-Hellman Problem (CDHP). The proposed protocol has six phases—setup, extract, join, sign, verify, and open. In setup phase, key generator centre (KGC) picked a generator P of G_1 and an arbitrary number $s \in \mathbb{Z}$, and computed $P_{pub} = sP$.

KGC computes private key $S_{\text{ID}} = sH_2(\text{ID}\|rP)$ and associated public key $Q_{\text{ID}} = H_2(\text{ID}\|rP)$. In enhanced scheme, a member cannot impersonate other group members to sign the message. The authors have presented proof for unforgeability, traceability, anonymity, and collision resistance for the generation of a valid signature.

Harn et al. (2008) surveyed Shamir's signature and proposed their ID-based multi-signature which was secure against adaptive chosen-ID attack, forger ability, and multi-signer collusion attack. The signer got secret key from PKG by signing message digest of id_i. Secret key $g_j = id_j$ mod n. Select an arbitrary number r_j, and then compute $t_j = r_j^e$ mod n. Each signer computes

$$t = \prod_{j}^{l} r_j \bmod n, \text{ and signature is } s = \prod_{j=1}^{l} s_j \text{ where } s_j = g_j r_j^{H(t,m)} \bmod n.$$

Gangishetti et al. (2006) proposed ID-based serial and parallel multiple signatures utilizing bilinear pairing. The proposed ID-based multiple signatures constrained verification and intermediate level to abstain from overlooking of predecessor's signature. These signatures are secure against chosen message and existential forgery attack. For a signer with ID_i, public key is (ID_i) and the private key is generated by PKG as $S_{ID_i} = s0_{Q_{ID_i}}$. The last nth signer verifies the signature received from $(n-1)$th signer by computing

$$r_{n-1} = e\left(u_{n-1}, p\right) e\left(\sum_{j=1}^{n-1} c_j Q_{ID_j}, -P_{\text{pub}}\right)$$

The receiver verifies the signature by computing

$$r_n = e\left(u_n, p\right) e\left(\sum_{i=1}^{n-1} c_i Q_{ID_i}, -P_{\text{pub}}\right)$$

In multiple signature, each signer selects a random integer $k_i \in Z_r^*$, computes $r_i = e(p,p)^{k_i}$, and broadcasts r_i to the remaining $(n-1)$ signers. The signature is generated in the following manner:

$$r = \prod_{i=1}^{n} r_i, c = h(m,r), c_i = h(m,r_i), u_i = cS_{ID_i} + k_i P \text{ the partial signature is } (U,c).$$

The clerk finally verifies each signature and computes $U = \sum_{i=1}^{n} U_i$.

Youngblood et al. (2005) compared ID-based cryptography with PKI. According to him, Alice got public–private key pair generated by PKG-trusted third party. Alice generates signature σ for message M utilizing her private key $\left(pk_{\text{pkg}}, sk_{\text{ID Alice}}\right)$ and transmits it to Bob. Bob $\left(sk_{\text{ID Alice}}\right)$ confirms signature σ using ID_{Alice} and pk_{pkg}.

Hafizul Islam, S. K., et al. (2017) proposed CL digital multi-signature scheme which seems to be more secure and efficient. They designed CL-DMS without bilinear pairing and MTS hash function. They demonstrated that proposed approach is reliable against adaptive chosen message attack.

Kar et al. (2017) outlined an ID-based signcryption scheme which was provably secure in the random oracle model. They also presented formal proofs of security for signcryption. The scheme was secure against side channel, chosen message, chosen cipher, and fault-tolerant attack.

Pang et al. (2016) proposed completely anonymity-based multi-receiver scheme. At the same time, anonymity of the sender is also maintained. It runs three algorithms: key extract query, anony-signcrypt query, and de-signcrypt query. Anony-signcrypt algorithm maintains a list of receivers with $ID_1, ID_2,...,ID_n$. It was secured against outsider and insider security attacks.

Wei et al. (2016) demonstrated that Sue et al.'s ePASS attribute-based signature scheme failed to satisfy attribute signer privacy.

Braeken et al. (2015) extended pairing-free signcryption with multiple users. Signcryption is used to share the key between the sink and network node. It satisfies forward secrecy, public verification with security principles.

Devi et al. (2015) have proposed an efficient digital multiple signature scheme that is vulnerable to inside and forgery attack, as receiver can verify signer's identity by comparing the received one with the actual identities.

Ch, Shehzad Ashraf et al. (2015) designed lightweight signcryption scheme which was based on HECC to satisfy security requirements to reduce communication, computation cost, and message size.

Swapna et al. (2014) proposed ID-based multiple signcryption schemes with presumptions that the CBDH and CDH problems are hard to solve. The proposed scheme provides the functionalities of both multiple signature and secure encryption for multiple senders. The scheme met the security requirements [Beak, 2002] such that confidentiality, unforgeability, and public verification with four phases—setup, key extract, multi-signcryption, and unsigncryption algorithms.

Lu Yang and Jiguo Li (2014) presented a scheme to upgrade the security of certificate-based signcryption. The proposed scheme accomplished both insider security and secured against public key replacement attack. It used five algorithms:

Setup(k),
UserkeyGen(params),
CertGen(params,m_{sk},ID_U,PK_U),
Signcrypt(params,M,ID_S,$ID_R PK_S$,SK_S,$Cert_S$,PK_R),
DeSigncrypt(params,σ,ID_S,$ID_R PK_S$,SK_S,$Cert_S$,PK_R).

The proposed scheme did not use bilinear pairing. It was secured against public key replacement and insider attack attacks. Security of this model could be achieved only on random oracle model and did not work without random oracles.

Zhang, Zhenfeng et al. (2006) designed a CL signature scheme based on CDHP which was secured against public key replacement attack in the random oracle model (Table 18.1).

18.3.1 Public Key Infrastructure

To address all these issues, PKI came into existence. With a specific end goal to guarantee the legitimacy of the public keys and to exchange trust dependably should be set up. How does receiver protect himself from plausibility that a corrupt client may deceitfully post a public key and speak to as sender's public key? If confidentiality of private key is compromised, how to repudiate public key? A digital certificate was first proposed by Loren Kohnfelder in 1978 to securely guarantee the legitimacy of the public keys.

Organizations require upgraded security for information and robust credentials for identity management. For this, certificates play an important role to map between the user identities and the public key. Digital certificates are used for secure data and proper authentication from users and computers both within and outside the organization. A certificate includes identity (common name), associated public key, valid from and valid to dates, and unique identifier of signature authority.

Table 18.1   Summary of Literature Review

Authors	Year	Contribution
PKI		
Yang et al.	2015	Addressed challenges in VSN such as information discrimination, resource-aware information, and algorithm to compute indirect trust.
Ray et al.	2014	Proposed medical centre server that should be installed at each hospital for securing handling of protected health information.
Jøsang et al.	2013	Took a closer look at the most important and mostly used PKI trust models and related semantic issues.
Janabi et al.	2012	Aimed to design and implement a CA to create and assign public key certificates for web application.
Reddy et al.	2011	Demonstrated simple application of PKI, CA, and certificate repository using openSSL.
Zhang et al.	2010	Proposed a novel AC-PKI framework for ad hoc networks which empower public key services with certificate less (CL) public keys so that the complications regarding certificate management can be avoided which are inevitable in conventional certificate-based solutions.
Huston et al.	2009	Presented PKI to take care of the issue of security in WSN by the utilization of PKC as a tool for guaranteeing authenticity of the base station.
Toorani et al.	2008	Acquainted lightweight public key infrastructure to remove computational expenses required for validations for mobile environments.
Jachtoma et al.	2006	Provided tutors with the possibility of assigning grades and generating a report. The tutor creating the report is to be authenticated by means of DS.
Jancic et al.	2004	Most of the countries inside the European Union have their own national PKIs, but the main challenge of the EU is to overcome issues of interoperability between vendors, and to make a global interoperable PKI.
Weise et al.	2001	The implementation of a PKI is intended to provide mechanisms to ensure trusted relationships are established and maintained.
Smart et al.	2000	Proposed wearable public key infrastructure for small communication to provide balanced and low computational overhead on both the customer and server.
Desind et al.	1997	Deployed PKI in U.S. Department of Energy's Nuclear Weapons.

(Continued)

Table 18.1 (*Continued*)   Summary of Literature Review

Authors	Year	Contribution
Multiple Digital Signatures		
Wang et al.	2015	Proposed multiple signature approach on a server's certificate as the probability of breaking multiple CAs in a short period of time is reduced significantly.
Jain et al.	2015	Described DS framework to realize digital signing of transactions for e-Govt. and non-e-Govt. applications.
Nandhini et al.	2015	Proposed a solution for the DoS attacks in PKI for different application. They simulated the proposed mechanism on NS2 simulator. The solution has only analytical proof without empirical study.
Dongoh Park	2015	Described various applications of PKI such as email, payment security digital document security, and server identification.
Albarqi et al.	2015	Explained the demand for securing communications is increasing dramatically day by day.
Martínez et al.	2015	Implemented multi-signature scheme using JAVA based on the DLP.
Szalachowski et al.	2014	To address inefficiencies in certificate transparency, they designed and proposed PoliCert, a log-based proposal that defines SCPs to specify parameters such as trusted CAs, update certificates, error handling in certificate, and loss of private key.
Rolf	2014	Explained attacks against CAs.
Domiguez et al.	2011	Implementation of RSA-based efficient ID-based multi-signature scheme.
Durán Díaz, Raúl, et al.	2010	Reviewed multiple signatures with their pros and cons.
Giri et al.	2007	Proposed a scheme that is improved over Rahul et al.'s scheme.
Lio et al.	2007	Showed Chen et al.'s scheme is insecure and vulnerable to substitution and public key replacement attack.
Song et al.	2004	Proposed new certificate architecture and DS that permits certificate path whose length is 1 regardless of the distance between the client and the RCA.
Rahul et al.	2004	Presented DMS scheme for authentication in group communication. For this, server used single group signed acknowledgment from group members for a message.
Moussa et al.	2003	Reviewed the DS and multiple signatures.
Levi et al.	1998	Purposed multiple signature schemes and introduced classification of cases that need multiple signatures.

(Continued)

Table 18.1 (*Continued*)   Summary of Literature Review

Authors	Year	Contribution
ID-Based Digital Signature		
Wu et al.	2016	Presented revocable ID-based model for PKC.
Yang et al.	2013	Showed Shamir and Harn's IBS schemes are not secure. Shortcomings are found in both that prompted an absence of security around the signer's secret key. They proposed an enhanced scheme to solve the problem of attacker's knowledge of the signer's secret key.
Fagen et al.	2011	Constructed a more flexible scheme which allows ID and message of arbitrary length, collision resistance hash function, and used a secure one-time symmetric key encryption scheme.
Sharmila deva	2010	Described an ID-based cryptosystem that serves as an efficient alternative to PKI.
Tan et al.	2009	An improved identity-based group signature scheme.
Harn et al.	2008	Proposed efficient identity-based multi-signatures. The proposed idea is safe against adaptive chosen-ID attack, forgeability and collusion attack.
Gangishetti et al.	2006	Proposed ID-based multiple signatures that provide forced verification and intermediate level to avoid overlooking of predecessor's signature.
Young blodd et.al	2005	Compared IDC with PKI-based approaches.
Lee et al.	2004	Described the key escrow issue against dishonest PKG. Secure key is issued by PKG with cooperation of KPAs.
Shamir	1984	Identity-based signature but against MITM attack.
Signcryption and Certificate-less Digital Signature		
Hafizul Islam, S. K., et al.	2017	CL DMS without bilinear paring.
Kar et al.	2017	Presented formal proofs of security for signcryption which were secure against side channel, chosen message, chosen cipher, and fault-tolerant attack.
Pang et al.	2016	Proposed completely anonymity-based multi-receiver scheme.
Braeken et al.	2015	Extended pairing-free signcryption with multiple users.
Bolong Yang et al.	2015	HIBS protocol for cloud computing.
Swapna et al.	2014	Proposed ID-based multiple signcryption scheme which provides confidentiality, unforgeability, and public verification.

(*Continued*)

Table 18.1 (*Continued*) Summary of Literature Review

Authors	Year	Contribution
Hassouna et al.	2013	Examined the shortcoming of the current mobile banking schemes based on PKI and IDC, and proposed a web-based mobile banking scheme based on CL cryptography.
Laura	2012	Represented a signcryption framework which was based on Schnorr DS algorithm.
Xie et al.	2010	Presented pairing-free CL signcryption scheme.
Zhang et al.	2010	Proposed a novel AC-PKI for ad hoc networks which enable public key services with certificate-less public keys, and so the complications regarding certificate management can be avoided which are inevitable in conventional certificate-based solutions.
Duan	2008	Presented the first CL undeniable signature scheme which was secure against unforgeability and adaptive chosen message attack.
Zhenfeng et al.	2006	Examined Yap et al.'s CL scheme and showed it is vulnerable to key replacement attack. An attacker can forge signature without the knowledge of signer's private key.
Shi et al.	2005	Presented CL-PKE based on weil pairing. Proposed scheme is secure for computation of public key information.

PKI empowers secure communications and business exchanges by the exchange of digital certificates between authenticated users and trusted resources. It is the combination of programming, encryption innovations, and administrations for actualizing validation utilizing public key cryptography to ensure the security of their interchanges and business exchanges on the Internet. Thus, the idea of PKI incorporates public key cryptography and certificates trusted third party called CA into network security architecture. It offers validation and secure exchange of sensitive information over unsecure channels by means of computerized authentications, which are signed by CA. It enables its clients to maintain a level of trust by providing security services like authentication, confidentiality, integrity or validation, and non-repudiation.

Thus, PKI accommodates an advanced authentication that can distinguish an individual or an association and directory services that can store and repudiate the certificates according to the needs of the user. A PKI is likewise called a chain of trust.

Public keys are accessible in the public key directories. Before using one's public key, we must ensure its legitimacy by checking certificate revocation list (CRL). Status of certificate can be checked online using Online Certificate Status Protocol (OCSP). Management of trust is the most difficult issue when using such certificates.

18.3.1.1 PKI Components

A PKI consists of different CAs (Figure 18.4):

■ MTNL CA,
■ TCS,

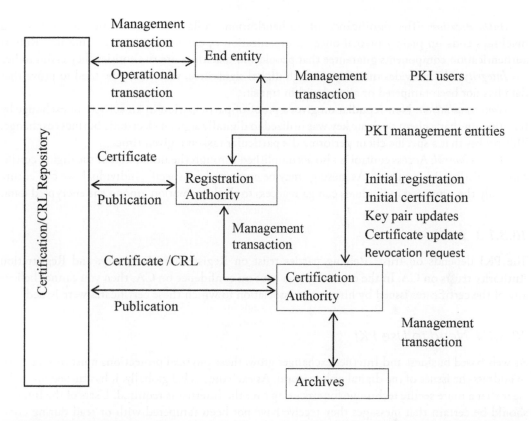

Figure 18.4   PKI components.

- IDBRT,
- SAFESCRYPT(SATYAM),
- *n*CODE Solutions,
- NIC,
- Central Excise and Customs,
- e-Mudhra.

Every CA has a certificate to prove its identity, issued by trusted CA. If it is Root CA, it has a self-signed certificate. Examples of CA's are VeriSign, GoDaddy, Entrust, and Thawte. CA is responsible for

- Issuing certificates,
- Revoking certificates,
- Formulating a certificate policy
- Implementing the Certificate Practice Statement.

18.3.1.2 What Does PKI Offer?

Confidentiality: The public key inside the digital certificate is employed to encrypt data to make sure that only the supposed recipient will decrypt it with associated private key and browse it.

Authentication: The significance of authentication, collateral the identity of clients and machines ends up plainly pivotal once an organization opens its doors to the Internet. Robust authentication components guarantee that people and machines are the entities they claim to be.

Integrity: PKI provides integrity through digital signatures, which may be used to prove that data has not been tampered or altered within transit.

Non-repudiation: Non-repudiation gives a proof-of-participation in an activity or exchange by building up that a client's private key was utilized to digitally sign an electronic business exchange. This proves that a specific client performs the particular task at a given time.

Access Control: Access control is also accomplished through the utilization of the digital certificate for distinguishing proof. As message may be encrypted for specific individual, we can ensure that only the supposed individuals can gain access to the information among the encrypted data.

18.3.1.3 Trust

The PKI depends on trust. Relying parties trust on Registration Authority, and Registration Authority trusts on CA. In the event that you have no confidence on CA, then you cannot believe any of the certificates issued by him or the association to which these certificates were issued.

18.3.1.4 Need to Use PKI

As web-based business and Internet exchanges grow, these physical protections must be replicated to address the issues of the digital online world. As exchange is led globally, it has turned out to be clear that a more secure technique for executing over the Internet is required. Users of the Internet should be certain that messages they receive have not been tampered with or read during communication. Further, they should be agreeable that the guaranteed initiator of the exchange has really sent the message.

18.3.1.5 Applications of PKI

A PKI does not serve a specific business exchange; rather, a PKI provides a foundation to different security services. The essential function of a PKI is to permit the circulation and utilization of public keys and authentications with security and respectability. A PKI is an establishment on which different applications and system security segments are fabricated. Frameworks that regularly require PKI-based security components incorporate email, different chip card applications, value exchange with e-commerce (e.g., debit and credit cards), home banking, and electronic postal systems. PKI can be viewed as critical not only to the commercial sector but also to the government sector. PKI can be applied in many applications for achieving security features like

- ■ Authentication
  Web applications
    - Portals
    - Student information systems
    - Library online journals
  Network appliances
    - VPN concentrators
    - Firewalls
    - Wireless access points

- Encryption
- Digital signatures.

18.3.2 Identity-Based Cryptography

PKI is based on certificate. Certificates are playing an important role to map between the user identities and the public key. A certificate includes identity (common name), associated public key, valid from and valid to dates, and unique identifier of signature authority. Public keys are accessible in the public key directories. Before using one's public key, we must ensure its legitimacy by checking CRL. Status of certificate can be checked online using OCSP. Management of trust is the most difficult issue when using such certificates. Who will assure to trust on certificate holder? This issue is explained in hierarchical organization. The appropriate answer of this question is extremely sensitive.

In 1984, Adi Shamir presented the notation of ID-based cryptography to tackle the issues of certificate-based cryptography. It is a public key system where public key can be represented by an arbitrary string such as name, contact number, email address, network, or IP address and SSN. Rather than generating random private/public key, Shamir proposed mathematically generating recipient public key from receiver's identity information such as name, IP address, email address, SSN, or contact number as a public key, and the PKG generates mathematics-related private key using private component. The main motivation to propose this approach is to eliminate the need of the certificate and issues related to them such as whether certificate is valid or not, key/certificate revocation, trust on CA, and maintenance of public key directory. As the public key is derived from the publically accessible information, then there is no requirement for public key directory and certificate management.

18.3.2.1 Algorithm

Ge(1,k): On input security parameter k, this algorithm outputs the public parameter param and m_{sk} for the PKG.

ExtractUse(ID): This algorithm interacts with the user and PKG. Upon successful execution of protocol, the user obtains secret key D_{ID} with respect to identity ID.

getstatus(ID): This allows the public to determine that PKG has generated signature on behalf of an honest user. It returns 1 if Aadhaar number and email id match or else returns to 0.

Sig(m,ID,D_{ID}): It outputs a signature σ on message m with respect to identity ID.

Verif(m,ID,D_{ID}): It verifies signature σ on message m with respect to identity ID.

18.3.2.2 Applications of ID-Based Cryptography

ID-based cryptography is used in Mobile Ad Hoc Network (MANET) and Vehicular Ad Hoc Network (VANET) for node authentication. Today, it attracts more attention from researchers in the field of e-voting with four phases: registration, authentication, voting, and counting which meets the properties of the voter privacy and robustness. Thus, applications of ID-based cryptography are as follows:

- MANET,
- VANET,
- Distributed Social Network,
- Wireless Sensor Network,
- E-Voting.

Table 18.2 Key Differences between a Certificate-Based PKI and an ID-Based Approach

Basis	PKI	ID-Based Approach
Private key generation	Either CA or Client itself	PKG
Public key generation	Either CA or Client itself	PKG
Key distribution	Yes	No
Certification	Yes	No
Public key extraction	Yes	No
Key escrow problem	No	Yes
Key recovery	Must maintain key database	No key database is required
Scalability	Operational complexity	Yes
Server certificate	Yes	No server certificate requirement
Key Revocation	OCSP, CRL	No key revocation protocols required
Expensive	Expensive to deploy and run	No

18.3.2.3 PKI versus ID-Based Approach

This section describes the key differences between IDC and PKI (Table 18.2).

18.3.3 Signcryption

Authentication, integrity, confidentiality, and non-revocation are critical cryptographic primitives in data security. In security, sender should guarantee that message can only be read by intended authorized receiver, whereas the receiver needs to ensure about the origin and content of the message. Both of the requirements are achieved by signcryption scheme. In 1997, signcryption was discovered by Yuliang Zheng from Monash University, Australia. Signcryption gives the functionalities of digital signature and public key encoding in the meantime at a lower computational and communication overhead than conventional signature-then-encryption technique (STE). The most vital elements of cryptography are to supply information secrecy and integrity. Confidentiality is accomplished by utilizing encryption algorithms, though integrity will be given by utilization of hash functions and authentication methods. Encryption techniques are of two types—private key encryption and public key encryption. Likewise, authentication can be classified by private key (shared) authentication algorithm and digital signature (public key encryption along with hash function). Signcryption, moreover, verifies the sender while not perusing the content of the message by the third party. Signcryption cost is 58% less in average calculation time and 70% less in message extension because of discrete logarithm problem (DLP). That is why it is generally utilized as a part of numerous applications because of ease and effectiveness.

In this scheme, sender creates a one-time secret key utilizing the recipient's public key for symmetric key encryption. Sender at that point sends the ciphertext to the receiver. After receiving ciphertext, receiver derives the same secret key using his private key. It is used in many applications like key management, routing protocol, mobile agent protocol, and electronic transaction protocols. It should be possible to achieve:

$$\text{Cost(Signature \& Encryption)} \ll \text{Cost(Signature)} + \text{Cost(Encryption)}$$

In traditional signcryption scheme, public key of user is based on a random element chosen from a group. It does not provide the authentication of users as group element cannot be defined as user's identity. This problem was solved by certificate-based signcryption, in which public key with respective identities are binds in it and signed by CA. This infrastructure is known as PKI. But PKI suffers the limitation of certificate storage, distribution, and key management problems. Shamir reduces key management problem by introducing the concept of ID-based cryptosystem. In this scheme, users communicate securely without the need of certificates, and there is no need to store public keys in public key directory. Malone-Lee first introduced ID-based signcryption. Various signcryption schemes are available based on public key cryptosystem and ID-based public key cryptosystems.

In ID-based signcryption, user's identity like name, email address, mobile number, IP address, and Aadhaar number is used as public key. Lots of work has been wiped out the sphere of identity-based signcryption.

18.3.3.1 Signature-Then-Encryption

It is a traditional method of providing both confidentiality and authenticity by using two serial algorithms:

- At the sender's side, the first message is encrypted using his private key for authentication and then encrypted using the public key of the receiver.
- Now the message and signature pair is sent to the recipient where receiver confirms the signature and then decrypts the message. This technique is known as STE. Figure 18.5 shows the process of STE:

Disadvantages of STE Approach: This process takes lots of machine cycles that increase its computation time and communication overheads. It is not appropriate where quick reactions are required.

Signcryption: Signcryption effectively performs encryption and signature process in a single logical step to acquire privacy, non-repudiation at a lower computational expenses and communication overhead when compared with traditional STE scheme (Figure 18.6).

In some applications, multiple senders authenticate a message or document without revealing it by applying multiple signatures on it. It is not efficient to perform signcryption by each signer individually as unsigncryption cost is high. An alternative to reduce cost is multi-signcryption. Many researchers have given signcryption schemes to accomplish security objective, for example confidentiality, non-repudiation, integrity, unforgeability, forward secrecy, and public verification. But none has provided solution to private key exposure. The biggest threat to the security is private key exposure. With the increasing number of users, the threat is increasing on the low computation devices such as mobile phones, which require private key for signature. Public key is derived from the identity of the user, if anyone comes to know corresponding private key can store the message and perform replay attack.

18.3.3.2 Applications of Signcryption

Today, signcryption is seen in various applications with less computational and communicational costs such as

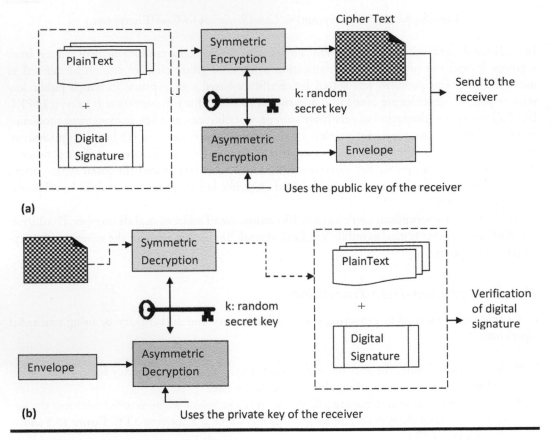

Figure 18.5 Signature-then-encryption.

- Secure routing in MANET,
- Secure message transmission by proxy,
- Encrypted email authentication by firewalls,
- Authenticated key recovery,
- Secure ATM networks,
- Secure multicasting,
- Electronic payment,
- E toll collection,
- Authenticated and secured transactions with smart cards.

18.3.3.3 Properties of Signcryption

1. Correct and Consistent

    The scheme should be correct and consistent.

2. Confidentiality

    For making information secure, it must be hidden from the unauthorized access. An attacker Eve wants to derive d_i from d_iP which is infeasible to solve ECDLP.

    Suppose he is able to get (m) and knows the seed value of curve, which is public to all still it is quiet infeasible to solve it.

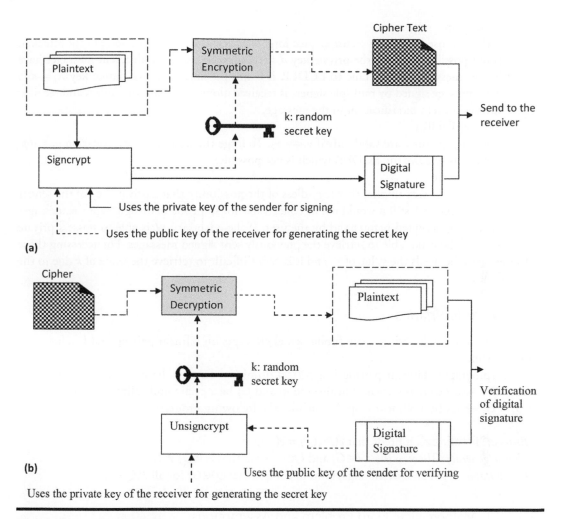

Figure 18.6 Signcryption.

3. Authentication

Authentication ensures that message received by the user is exactly the same sent by the sender and verifies the participants are really whom they claim to be. In this, identities of both the parties are verified by verifying the checksum $h = (\text{ID}_i \| U)$.

4. Integrity

In the proposed scheme, the receiver can verify whether the message is sent by the sender or not. If the attacker changes the cipher text s to s', it is infeasible to obtain the same digest for the two messages.

5. Unforgeability

It is difficult to forge the signature (s, Y) for a message. In ECC, an attacker selects random number k and prove multiple signatures $(k + ed)p = Y + eX$.

6. Non-repudiation

The target of non-repudiation is to prevent the sender from denying the signature he has made. Unforgeability implies non-repudiation.

7. Secure against forgery

The proposed scheme is secure against forgery attack as scheme does not. For the attacker, it is not possible to derive the private key $d_i = (ID_i\|r)$. Because two different messages have different message digests. Due to ECDLP, it is not possible to derive public key $X_i = d_iP$. When message signed by multiple signers is received along with hash of senders and receiver identities prevent modification in the message.

8. Public verifiability

Multi-signatures are valid only if $v_1 == v_2$. To forge the signature with equation $v_1 = shp$, attacker has to solve the ECDLP, which is not possible.

9. Forward secrecy

Forward secrecy implies that regardless of the possibility that a private key of the sender gets compromised, still it would not be conceivable for someone to unsigncrypt the messages that were signcrypted beforehand by the user. If the adversary $\mathscr{A}$ is able to possess private key d, still he is not able to retrieve the previously sent signed messages. For accessing those messages, he needs the value of r_i, and it is very difficult to retrieve the value of k due to the ECDLP.

18.3.3.4 Preliminaries

In this section, we will outline some fundamental concepts on bilinear pairing and fundamental hard problems.

In cryptography, bilinear pairing is a critical primitive. Let $G_{1,2}$ be two groups of the same order q. We assume G_1 as a cyclic additive group and G_2 be a cyclic multiplicative group. A map $\hat{e} = G_1 \times G_1 \rightarrow G_2$ be a bilinear map if it satisfies the following properties:

Bilinear: for all, $\in Z_r$, it holds that $\hat{e}(P^a, Q^b) = \hat{e}(P,Q)^{ab}$.
Non-degeneracy: There exists a $P \in G_1$ and $Q \in G_2$ such that $\hat{e}(P,Q) \neq 1$.
Computable: Used an efficient algorithm to compute $(P,Q) \in G_2$ for all $P, Q \in G_1$.

18.3.3.4.1 Mathematical Hard Problem and Assumptions

The security of ECC depends on the difficulty of solving the elliptic curve logarithm problem:

- *Computational Diffie-Hellman Problem (CDHP):* Given $P, P, bP \in G_1$ for some $a, b, c \in Z_q^*$ and $\in G_1$, the CDHP problem is to compute $abP \in G_1$.
- *Computational Bilinear Diffie-Hellman Problem (CBDHP):* Given $P, P, bP, cP \in G_1$ for some $a, b, c \in Z_q^*$ and $\in G_1$, the CBDHP problem is to compute $\hat{e}(P,P)^{abc} \in G_2$.

18.3.3.5 Signcryption Algorithm

A signcryption consists of following algorithms:

Setup (k): PKG randomly chooses a secret value k, generates master secret key m_{sk}, and outputs public parameters params of system required by signcryption schemes.

Key extract (ID): PKG computes corresponding public key, for a given identity $Q_{ID} = H(ID)$ and private key S_{ID} for sender and R_{ID} for receiver, and transmits to the corresponding user through a secure channel.

Signcrypt $(m, ID_A, S_{ID}, I_{DB})$: This is a probabilistic algorithm which a sender runs to generate signcryption σ with identity ID_A and private key S_{ID} to send a message m to receiver with identity ID_B.

Unsigncrypt $(\sigma, ID_A, ID_B, R_{ID})$: After receiving cipher text σ from sender with identity ID_A, receiver with identity ID_B and private key R_{ID} runs the deterministic algorithm to obtain whether the message m is valid signcryption of m or message m is invalid with respect to the validity of signature σ.

18.3.3.6 Shorten Digital Signature Standard

p: A large prime number, public to all
q: A large prime factor of $p - 1$, public to all
g: An integer $0 < g < p$ with order q modulo p, public to all
hash: One-way hash function
x_a: Secret key
y_a: Public key

$$y_a = g^{x_a} \bmod p$$

$$r = (g^x \bmod p) \bmod q$$

Method 1:

$k = g^x \bmod p$ where $x \in_R \{1, \ldots, q - 1\}$
$r = hash\ (k, m)$

$$s = \frac{x}{r + x_a} \bmod q$$

Output: (m, r, s)

Method 2:

$k = g^x \bmod p$ where $x \in_R \{1, \ldots, -1\}$
$r = hash(k, m)$

$$s = \frac{x}{r + x_a r} \bmod q$$

Output: (m, r, s)

Signcryption schemes are based on

1. Elgamal signcryption,
2. RSA signcryption,
3. Elliptic curve signcryption.

18.3.3.7 Zheng and Imai Signcryption Scheme

Zheng has proposed the most popular scheme of signcryption. Signcryption and unsigncryption phases are as follows.

18.3.3.7.1 Signcryption Phase

1. Alice randomly selects a number, where $v \leq n - 1$.
2. Computes $(k_1, k_2) = \text{hash}(vPb)$
3. Computes $c = Ek_1(M)$
4. Computes $r = \text{KH}k_2(M)$, where KH is the keyed hash function.

5. $s = \dfrac{v}{r + v_a} \bmod n$

6. Sends (c, r, s) to Bob.

18.3.3.7.2 Unsigncryption Phase

Bob runs unsigncryption algorithm on $\langle c, r, s \rangle$

1. $u = sv_b \bmod q$
2. $(k_{1,2}) = \text{hash}(uP_a + urG)$
3. $m = Dk_1(c)$
4. Bob accepts message only if $\text{KH}k_2\, M = r$

18.3.3.8 Dutta's (2012)

18.3.3.8.1 Signcryption Phase

Assume Alice and Bob are two users who want to communicate. Alice generates digital signature T, S on message M and uses symmetric encryption algorithm, e.g., AES and secret key K to encrypt message M. Alice follows the following steps to generate signcrypted text (C, T, S):

1. From digital certificate, Alice verifies Bob's public key P_b.
2. Randomly selects an integer v_a as her private key, where $v \leq n - 1$. She computes her public key $P_a = v_a G$.
3. Computes $k_1 = \text{hash}(vG)$ and $k_2, k_3 = \text{hash}(vP_b)$.
4. Generates cipher text using symmetric encryption algorithm

$$C = E_{k_2}(M).$$

5. Computes one-way keyed hash function to generate

$$r = kH_{k_3}\left(C \| k_1 \| ID_A\, ID_B\right).$$

6. Computes $s = \dfrac{v}{r + v_a} \bmod n$.
7. Computes $T = rG$.
8. Sends C, T, S to Bob.

18.3.3.8.2 Unsigncryption Phase

Bob decrypts cipher text C by performing symmetric decryption algorithm with secret key k. He verifies signature and gets original message. He also selects a random integer v_b as his private key and computes his public key $P_b = v_b G$.

1. Gets Alice's public key P_a from her certificate.
2. Computes $k_1 = \text{hash}(sT + sP_a)$.
3. Computes $k_2, k_3 = \text{hash}(vb_sT + vb_sP_a)$.
4. Computes one-way hash function, and generates $r = \text{KH}k_3\left(C\|k_1\|\text{ID}_A\text{ID}_B\right)$.
5. Performs symmetric decryption algorithm to get original message $m = Dk_2(C)$.
6. If $rG = T$, Bob accepts the message, otherwise rejects.

18.3.3.8.3 Verification Phase

Signature can be verified by anyone by performing the following steps:

1. Computes $k_1 = \text{hash}(sT + sP_a)$,
2. Computes $r = \text{KH}k_3\left(\|k_1\|\text{ID}_A\text{ID}_B\right)$.

If $rG = T$, message is sent by Alice, otherwise not.

18.3.4 Certificate-Less Signature

IBE removes the need for a PKI, by replacing it with a PKG that computes user's private key. IBE is more efficient, but it suffers from key escrow problem. Key escrow means that PKG who is a trusted third party computes the private keys for the users; it means PKG can read the messages of users in the system. In IBE, a significant practical problem associated with it is to handle key revocation of users. A new type of public key encryption scheme known as Certificate-less Public Key Encryption (CL-PKE) was presented by Al-Riyami and Paterson, which avoids the drawbacks of both public key encryption and IBE in order to resolve the key escrow problem. The main purpose of using CL-PKE is to resolve key escrow problem inherited from IBE without the use of certificates as in PKI. It provides some benefits over ID-based signature. There are many proposals on CL-DS.

In this scheme, PKG computes a partial private key d for each user using his master private key ms. The user combines this partial key with some user-selected secret information to generate a complete private key. Thus, PKG has no knowledge of user's private key. The private/public key of user is computed from user's private key and PKG's public parameters params. The public key is made available by transmitting it with the message. Thus, public key does not require any authentication mechanism. So, it is better than certificate-based signature because public key cannot be computed from user's identity alone.

18.3.4.1 Preliminaries

- *Setup (k)*: PKG randomly arbitrarily picks a secret value k, generates master secret key m_{sk}, and generates public parameters params of system required by signature schemes.
- *Set Secret Key*: Given user with identity ID_i as input and select $x_i \in RZ_q^*$ as user's secret key, PKG computes corresponding public key $P_i = x_i$.
- *Partial Private Key*: User with identity ID_i sends (ID_i, P_i) to PKG. PKG executes this algorithm on $(\text{ID}_i, P_i, \text{params}, m_{sk})$ to generate partial private key d_i.
- *Set Private Key*: For given $(\text{ID}_i, \text{params})$, returns complete private key as $sk_i = (d_i, x_i)$.
- *Set Public Key*: For given $(\text{ID}_i, \text{params})$, returns complete public key as $pk_i = (Q_i, P_i)$.

- *Certificate-less Digital Multi Signature*: For given $(\text{ID}_i, \text{params}, sk_i, m, \text{PK}_R, L_1 = \text{ID}_{R1}, \text{ID}_{R2}, \ldots \text{ID}_{Rn})$, outputs signature σ. Authenticated designated clerk with ID_n combines and computes final multi-signature σ on message m.
- *Certificate-less Digital Multi-signature Verification*: For given $(\text{ID}_i, \text{params}, p_i, \text{SK}_R, L_1, \sigma)$, returns *true* if the signature σ is valid, otherwise returns *false*.

18.4 Conclusion

In this chapter, we have presented digital signature with their applications. Today, over 93% of data is conceived digital, approximately 1 ZB of information annually added to the digital universe like images, journals, research publications, and database and government reports. So, there is requirement for securing these information and applications. In this digital era, data security is one of the basic components for an organization to keep the information secure from unauthorized persons or attackers and ensure the integrity and privacy of the information.

People are doing banking on their mobile phones such as Internet banking, Airtel money, Paytm, and JioMoney. In 2013, almost one out of five users was using mobile banking; however, in 2017, the number of users was increasing rapidly over a billion. Cyber criminals are expected cybercrimes to ramp up attack and make two stage verification, e.g., mobile pin and OTP in effective.

After the study of the different types of public key cryptographic primitives, we can say that trust management certificates in PKI are getting more consideration, but in case of authentication, it can be replaced with ID-based cryptography. To save bandwidth and communication overhead, signcryption and certificate-less signcryption are getting more attention from the researchers.

Bibliography

1. Zkik, K., Orhanou, G., and El Hajji, S. Secure mobile multi cloud architecture for authentication and data storage, *International Journal of Cloud Applications and Computing (IJCAC)*, vol. 7(2), pp. 62–76, 2017.
2. Hafizul Islam, S.K., Sabzinejad Farash, M., Biswas, G.P., Khurram Khan, M., and Obaidat, M.S. A pairing-free certificateless digital multisignature scheme using elliptic curve cryptography, *International Journal of Computer Mathematics*, vol. 94(1), pp. 39–55, 2017.
3. Kar, J., and Naik, K. Security analysis and implementation issues of signcryption scheme for smart card, *A Journal of the Academy of Business and Retail Management (ABRM)*, vol. 1(2), pp. 24–36, 2017.
4. Tanwar, S., and Kumar, A. Identity based cryptography, *Indian Journal of Computer Science (IJCS)*, vol. 2(4), pp. 7–13, 2017.
5. Le, M.H., and Hwang, S.O. Certificate-based signcryption scheme without pairing: Directly verifying signcrypted messages using a public key, *ETRI Journal*, vol. 38(4), pp. 724–734, 2016.
6. Gupta, B., Agrawal, D.P., and Yamaguchi, S. *Handbook of Research on Modern Cryptographic Solutions for Computer and Cyber Security, Advances in Information Security*, IGI Global, Hershey, PA, 2016.
7. Zhang, Z., and Gupta, B.B. Social media security and trustworthiness: Overview and new direction, *Future Generation Computer Systems*, vol. 86, pp. 914–925, 2016.
8. Gupta, S., and Gupta, B.B. XSS-secure as a service for the platforms of online social network-based multimedia web applications in cloud, *Multimedia Tools and Applications*, vol. 7, pp. 1–33, 2016.
9. Pang, L., Yan, X., Zhao, H., Hu, Y., and Li, H. A novel multi-receiver signcryption scheme with complete anonymity, *PLoS One*, vol. 11(11), pp. 1–18, 2016.
10. Wei, J., Liu, W., and Hu, H. Security pitfalls of ePASS, *Journal of Information Security and Applications*, vol. 30(C), pp. 40–45, 2016.

11. Tanwar, S., and Kumar, A. A proposed scheme for remedy of man-in-the-middle attack on certificate authority, *International Journal of Information Security and Privacy (IJISP)*, vol. 11(3), 2016, doi: 10.4018/IJISP.

12. Wu, T.Y., Lin, J.C.W., Chen, C.M., Tseng, Y.M., Frnda, J., Sevcik, L., and Miroslav, V. A brief review of revocable ID-based public key cryptosystem, *Perspectives in Science*, vol. 7, pp. 81–86, 2016.

13. Sayid, J., Sayid, I., and Kar, J. Certificateless public key cryptography: A research survey, *International Journal of Security and Its Applications*, vol. 10(7), pp. 103–118, 2016.

14. Tanwar, S., and Prema K.V. Design and Implementation of a Secure Hierarchical Trust Model for PKI. In: *International Conference – CSI -50th Golden Jubilee Annual Convention*, Springer under AISC Series, Delhi, India, 2015.

15. Jain, V., Kumar, J., and Saquib, Z. An Approach towards Digital Signatures for e-Governance in India. In: *Proceedings of the 2015 2nd International Conference on Electronic Governance and Open Society: Challenges in Eurasia*, ACM, St. Petersburg, Russian Federation, pp. 82–88, 2015.

16. Wang, X., Bai, Y., and Lihui, H. Certification with Multiple Signatures. In: *Proceedings of the 4th Annual ACM Conference on Research in Information Technology*, ACM, Chicago, IL, pp. 13–18, 2015.

17. Swapna, G. Efficient identity based multi-signcryption scheme with public verifiability, *Journal of Discrete Mathematical Sciences & cryptography*, vol. 17(2), pp. 181–192, 2014.

18. Jøsang, A. PKI trust models. *Theory and Practice of Cryptography Solutions for Secure Information Systems*, Scopus, IGI Global, USA, pp. 279–301, 2013.

19. Dutta, M., Singh, A.K., and Kumar, A. An Efficient Signcryption Scheme Based on ECC with Forward Secrecy and Encrypted Message Authentication. In: *Advance Computing Conference (IACC), IEEE 3rd International*, 2013.

20. Savu, L. Signcryption Scheme Based on Schnorr Digital Signature, *arXiv preprint arXiv:1202.1663*, 2012.

21. Vatră, N. Interoperability of digital signatures in public administration, *World of Computer Science and Information Technology Journal (WCSIT)*, vol. 1(6), pp. 264–268, 2011.

22. Tianhuang, C., and Xiaoguang, X. Digital Signature in the Application of e-Commerce Security, E-Health Networking. In: *Digital Ecosystems and Technologies (EDT), IEEE, International Conference on*. Vol. 1, 2010.

23. Duran Diaz, R., Hernandez Alvarez, F., Hernandez Encinas, L., Queiruga Dios, A. A Review of Multisignatures Based on RSA. *DIGITAL.CSIC*, pp. 1–7, 2010.

24. Joux, A. Introduction to Identity-Based Cryptography. *Cryptology and Information Security Series-Identity-Based Cryptography*, ebooks.iospress.nl, vol. 2, pp. 1–12, 2009.

25. Subramanya, S.R., and Yi, B.K. Digital signatures, *IEEE Potentials*, vol. 25(2), pp. 5–8, 2006.

26. Wilson, S. The importance of PKI today, *China Communications*, p. 15, 2005.

27. Youngblood, C. An Introduction to Identity-Based Cryptography, *CSEP 590TU*, 2005.

28. Moussa, C. Digital Signature and Multiple Signature: Different Cases for Different Purposes, *GSEC Practical Assignment, Version 1*, pp. 1–11, 2003.

29. Choudhury, S., Bhatnagar, K., and Haque, W. *Public Key Infrastructure Implementation and Design*, M&T Books, New York, NY, 2002.

30. Zhou, J., and Deng, R. On the validity of digital signatures, *ACM SIGCOMM Computer Communication Review*, vol. 30(2), pp. 29–34, 2000.

31. Gaya, C. *Public Key Infrastructure-A Brief Overview*, SANS Institute, 2000.

32. Zheng, Y., and Imai, H. How to construct efficient signcryption schemes on elliptic curves, *Information Processing Letters*, vol. 68(5), pp. 227–233, 1998.

33. Schnorr, C.P. Efficient signature generation for smart cards, *Journal of Cryptology*, vol. 4, pp. 161–174, 1991.

34. Goldwasser, S., Micali, S., and Rivest, R. A digital signature scheme secure against chosen message attacks, *SIAM Journal of Computing*, vol. 17(2), pp. 281–308, 1988.

35. Shamir, A. Identity-based Cryptosystems and Signature Schemes. In: *Workshop on the Theory and Application of Cryptographic Techniques*, Springer: Berlin, Heidelberg, 1984.

36. Diffie, W., and Hellman, M. New directions in cryptography, *IEEE transactions on Information Theory*, vol. 22(6), pp. 644–654, 1976.

Chapter 19

Credit Scoring Using Birds Swarm Optimization

Damodar Reddy Edla, Pedunayak G, Tejaswini K, and Hareesh K
National Institute of Technology Goa

Ramalingaswamy Cheruku
Mahindra Ecole Centrale College of Engineering

Contents

19.1 Introduction

Credit scoring is a method of defining a person's chances to gain or lose credit from financial institutions. This credit score is predicted using customer's historical data. All over the world, banks profit from granting loans to customers and collecting them with interests in return. So, it is important for banks to identify those customers who can repay the loans. For this purpose, credit scoring came into existence. Customer data is mainly collected from multiple sources of past borrowing and repaying records. Generally, credit scoring is a binary or multi-class classification problem. Therefore, classifiers are introduced to develop decision support systems. These systems assist banks in granting or rejecting loans to applicants. The credit scoring can be applied with two predictive model groups [1].

1. Statistical methodology,
2. Artificial intelligence.

A number of algorithms have been proposed to enhance the credit scoring accuracy. Statistical methodology includes linear discriminate analysis (LDA) and logistic regression (LR). Artificial intelligence consists of methods like artificial neural network (ANN), support vector machines (SVMs), and decision trees. Datasets obtained from different banks have different properties in data and predictive variables like the number of features. The main aim of implementing these methodologies is to improve the credit scoring accuracy. Fractional improvement of credit scoring can lead to high savings in future. Multilayered perceptron (MLP) is the most widely used neural network architecture. In order to improve scoring accuracy, one should implement methodologies beyond the traditional MLP. In this work, a bio-inspired algorithm is implemented to optimize the neural network weights. The accuracy is compared with various neural network architectures, and the results are drawn.

19.1.1 Types of Credit Scores

There are more than 60 types of credit scores in usage. The reason for the existence of many credit scores is that they are collected from different sources. Each credit bureau maintains its own records about applicants' profiles. Generally, these records vary from bureau to bureau. The agencies use different systems to calculate credit scores of the customers. Although the collected applicant data is the same for all bureaus, the ways they weigh this information is different. We mention below few famous credit scores used by different bureaus [2]:

1. *Application Scoring*: Application scores are one type of credit score where the decision of approving or rejecting the loan of the customer is purely based on the submitted application. The information present in the application includes name of the customer, residence

address, contact number, gender of the customer, date of birth, occupation, monthly income, sorting codes, account number, account holder name, loan requirements, and so on. Application score does not take the customers' credit report into consideration for credit approval. Studies indicate that application scores are highly accurate in selecting the worthy applicants. The method is efficient when granting loan decision is based on subjective analysis.

2. *Behavioral Scoring*: Behavior scoring involves assigning point values to internally derived information such as payment behavior, usage pattern, and delinquency history. Behavior scores are intended to embody the cardholders' history with the bank. Their usage assists management in evaluating credit risk and correspondingly making account management decisions for the existing accounts. As with credit bureau scores, there are a number of scorecards from which behavior scores are calculated. These scorecards are designed to capture unique characteristics of products such as private label, affinity, and co-branded cards. Behavioral scoring is based on the derived information of the customer such as payment behavior, credit usage, and history of all transactions. This scoring merges the customers' history with the bank. This can be used to evaluate credit risk and eventually take accurate decisions. Behavioral scoring is commonly implemented by adaptive controlling systems. This adaptive controlling evaluates customer behavior and other necessary information for decision-making. The main motive is to reduce credit loss. Adaptive controlling systems consist of software packages for evaluating the customer behavior. These systems are constructed based on some optimization algorithms.

3. *Collection Scoring*: The goal of collection scoring is to develop a cost-efficient strategy in the financial institution. Collection scoring gives the probability of recovering all those outstanding balances of all the customer accounts available in the collection. Collection scoring helps in the development of robust delinquency management strategy. This scoring systems rank the customer accounts for taking debt management decisions. Some of the applications of collection scoring are mentioned below:
   a. Minimize write-offs,
   b. Maximize profits in collections,
   c. Employing cost-efficient debt management decisions,
   d. Minimize collection expenses.

4. *Fraud Scoring*: Fraud scoring consists of models to identify those customer accounts with fraudulent motto. These models are helpful in the identification of high-risk transactions. Modern scoring models use software techniques to identify the fraud patterns and distinguish them from legitimate transactions. These models help in minimizing losses to the financial institutions [3].

5. *Fair Isaac Corporation (FICO) Score*: This score is accepted by different financial services in the United States with multiple lending requirements. FICO is the largest used credit score. The range of this score fluctuates between 350 and 850. The upper limit 850 is considered a perfect credit score of the applicant. This FICO score is calculated based on five factors:
   a. Payment history,
   b. Credit usage,
   c. Age of accounts,
   d. New credit.

Based on these factors' weightage, credit scores are calculated. The weightage is highest for payment history. There are many versions of this FICO score and FICO-9 being the most used version. The choice of FICO score depends on the type of loan applied by the customer.

6. *Vantage Score*: This Vantage credit score competes with FICO score. There are more than 2000 lenders in United States using this score. Every six out of ten banks in the United States use Vantage Score. Initially, the range of Vantage Score varies between 501 and 990, but a new version, Vantage Score 3.0, uses a scale of 300–850. Vantage Score uses a different factors for calculation [4]:
   a. Payment history,
   b. Credit utilization,
   c. Balances,
   d. Depth of credit,
   e. Recent credit,
   f. Available credit.

The advantage of Vantage Score is that six months' data is sufficient to calculate the score, whereas at least one year's data is required for FICO score. In six credit scoring using Birds Swarm Optimization (BSO), in addition to the above two types of credit scoring, there are various other types like Experian, Equifax, TransUnion, and so on. Each type has its own score range determining weightage factors.

19.1.2 Applications of Credit Scoring Models

Credit scoring models, commonly referred to as scorecards in banking industry, have many applications. Few of them are mentioned below:

1. Management of credit loss,
2. Implementing modern loan programmers,
3. Minimizing the loan-approving process times,
4. Maximizing profits for the organization,
5. Redefining solicitation leading to the minimization of acquisition costs.

19.2 Related Work

In spite of all the criticisms, it has been believed that credit card scoring could really help us in answering many of the key questions. An argument has been made by Al Amari that most of the important questions have not been answered, though lot of these scoring models are being used. What would be the optimal method for evaluating customers? What are the variables a credit analyst needs to include in order to assess the applications of customers? What kind of information would be needed for improvising and facilitating the process of decision-making? What would be considered as the best measure for predicting the loan quality? To what extent a customer can be classified to be good or bad? Besides his questions, the following could also be added: The best statistical technique based on low misclassification cost or the highest rate of average correct classification. The possibility to identify the key factors that have strong influence on loan quality [5].

The role of efficient management of various financial and credit risks has become very much important for bankers specially, who realized that the banking operations are affecting and are being affected by the social environmental risks they face; thus, the banks have a crucial role in helping to raise the requirements of banking environment. Though the significant risks are being presented by environment to banks, particularly the environment credit risk, it also possibly gives us beneficial opportunities [6]. The management risk plays a significant role in the banking sector over the world. One among the various components of management is the risks associated with the personal credit decisions. In fact, it is the most critical decision to be made by bank, requiring a differentiation between the customers having good credits and bad credits. In predicting the behavior of new applicants, the behavior of previous and present customers can give us a beneficial dataset [7].

Credit scoring has been considered as a critical tool and much important technique in banks in recent years. Because of rapid growth of the industry and management of huge loans. These models are being used widely by many financial institutions and banks to distinguish the good and bad credits and also in assigning the credit to better applicants. Credit scoring can be used for reducing the cost of this credit process and the risk that is associated with the bad loans, improvising the credit decisions, and efforts and time saving [8,9]. The judgmental techniques and credit scoring models support decision-making which involves accepting or rejecting the client's credit. The judgmental techniques usually rely on the knowledge and also the previous and current experiences of analysts where evaluation consists of capability to repay and the character of the client [10].

Previously many classification techniques were applied to credit scoring. Xu et al. [11] and Shi et al. [12] worked on the types of classification methods. Garcia et al. [13] proposed a short format framework for comparing four credit scoring methods. Lessmann et al. [14] worked on many classifications methodologies. Still many methods can be employed on binary classification. Lessmann's methodologies did not contain genetic and fuzzy algorithms. In modern research, Lee et al. [15] introduced a discriminant neural model to perform credit rating, and Gestel et al. [16] proposed an SVM model within a Bayesian evidence framework. Hoffmann et al. [17] proposed a genetic fuzzy model, and Hsieh and Hung [18] proposed a combined methodology covering neural networks, SVM, and Bayesian networks. A comparative study was carried out by West [19] with the traditional techniques. The results show that the neural networks can improve the credit scoring accuracy significantly [20]. Baesens et al. [21] performed a comparative analysis on discriminant analysis, logic programming, SVMs, neural networks architectures, Bayesian networks, decision trees and k-nearest neighbor, and LR. Dryver and Sukkasem [22] worked on performance measures in classification. Damodar Reddy et al. [23] have proposed hybrid credit scoring model based on ensemble framework.

19.3 Motivation and Problem Statement

19.3.1 Motivation

There is a significant growth in credit industries over the past two decades. Different credit scoring models have been employed by financial institutions to increase cash flows and profits from customers. These credit scoring models reduce the cost of credit analysis regarding customers' accounts. These models often increase the speed of credit decisions and are also helpful in close observation of the existing customer accounts. Today, 97% of the banks employed credit scoring models. Today, corporations like Federal Home Loan Mortgage Corporation and Federal National Mortgage Corporation consistently encourage the usage of credit scoring [24]. With respect to growth in financial services, there have been significant losses also. For example, in 1991, $1 billion of a chemical bank's $6.7 billion in real estate loans were delinquent, and the bank held $544 million in foreclosed property [25]. Consider the situation in 1991 where a chemical bank's $1 billion in real estate loans were delinquent out of $6.7 billion, and the respective bank put a $544 million in foreclosed property. Another situation is where an organization named Manufacturers Hanover was burdened with $385 million out of $3.5 billion commercial property portfolio in nonperforming loans. The above examples show the significant need for credit scoring models. In response to these situations, organizations from around the world showed interest toward developing models for credit decision.

19.3.2 Problem Statement

Banking and financial institutions spend considerable expenditure toward credit risk management. This situation drew the interest of statistical researchers in developing efficient credit scoring models. In the banking industry, credit risk has been the leading source of problems above all. There is a significant need to improve the credit scoring accuracy.

19.4 Proposed Method

19.4.1 Artificial Neural Network

ANN classifiers contain different sets of neurons and layers. There is an input layer consisting of all the input neurons. All the neurons in input layer are connected to the hidden layer's neurons by using arcs, where each of them has a particular weight. Each of the weights in the connections represents the contribution of corresponding inputs in prediction [26]. Every neuron in each of the hidden layers is connected to all the neurons in the next hidden layer of it, and all the last hidden layer's units are connected to output units with the corresponding weights. The two kinds of information flow in ANNs are back propagation and feed-forward. In feed-forward process, an instance is actually introduced to the input layer where all its attribute values are known. The input neurons pass data into hidden units, layer by layer till it reaches the final layer called output layer. The result of the output layer is output of the network for the corresponding instance, and the result we have obtained is compared by the target value (desired value) using error functions such as mean squared error (MSE) and root mean squared error (RMSE). The objective is to minimize the error function and during the process of back propagation, all weights are adjusted in accordance with gradient descent algorithm. So, this forward and backward process is normally continued till an acceptable value of error is obtained (Figure 19.1).

19.4.2 Bio-inspired Algorithms

Bio-inspired algorithms are commonly referred in the subsection of artificial intelligence as the concepts are closely related to machine learning. Bio-inspired algorithms mainly rely on the fields of biological science, computer science, and mathematics. Over the time, these algorithms have gained much importance. In this digital era, there has been significant increase in data. This led to the data extraction challenges. Standard algorithms have been brought into existence due to the increasing complexity of analysis. Obtaining the best solution has always been difficult due to the complexity in computations. Therefore, there is a great need for intelligent approaches to obtain the best solutions.

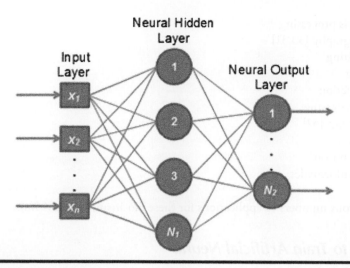

Figure 19.1   Artificial neural network.

Bio-inspired algorithms being intelligent are the perfect choice for these types of problems. These algorithms are often referred as meta-heuristic as they can be applied irrespective of the problem type. Bio-inspired algorithms can be broadly classified into following sections [27]:

Evolution algorithms
Swarm-based algorithms
Ecology algorithms

The present work includes a newly proposed bio-inspired algorithm called the Birds Swarm Optimization inspired from swarm intelligence. Here are few examples of bio-inspired algorithms:

Ant colony optimization algorithm (ACO)
Artificial immune systems (AIS)
Genetic algorithm (GA)
Particle swarm optimization (PSO)
Lion optimization algorithm (LOA)
Water wave optimization algorithm (WOA)
Social spider algorithm (SSA), and so on.

Researchers work on multiple domains using bio-inspired algorithms. Their nature to adapt to any problem shows their priority. Some of the fields in which bio-inspired algorithms were applied are mentioned below [28]:

Clustering and classification
Image analysis
Computer vision
Cloud computing [29]
Job/task-scheduling

Speech analysis processing
Visual cryptography [30,31]
Machine learning
Path planning
Pressure prediction
Document processing
Internet of things [32]
Software testing
Gesture recognition
Fields of bio-informatics

There are numerous numbers of applications for these bio-inspired algorithms.

19.4.3 BSO to Train Artificial Neural

19.4.3.1 Network

Swarm intelligence mainly focuses on the collective behavior of the individuals with each other and with their environment. Examples of swarm intelligence are colonies of ants, school of fish, flock of birds, and herd of land animals. Properties of swarm intelligence are as follows:

Scalability: Swarm can maintain its function while increasing its size with cooperation.
Parallel activity: Individuals inside the swarm can perform different actions in different places at the same time complexity [33].
Fault tolerance: Failing individual can be easily removed and substituted by another individual that is correctly functioning.

In this chapter, the methodology is inspired from birds' swarm behavior. Birds travel in flocks in V shape. They communicate with each other in the group. Each bird communicates with the neighboring birds, and so the process goes till the tail of the flock. The communication takes much time to traverse the information from head to the tail of the flock. So for the sake of convenience, the flock is partitioned into *n* blocks. Now, the optimization algorithm is applied to individual blocks simultaneously. All the individual birds are considered as solutions (weights). This parallel activity is helpful in the reducing the time complexity. The approach eliminates the method of applying optimization algorithm to the whole set of birds. In this project, we compare the proposed approach with the different neural network architectures. The results show better performance using the proposed approach.

19.4.4 Objective Function

The objective function used in this methodology is the traditional MSE. Through the continuous iterations, the optimal solution is finally achieved, which is regarded as the solution set (weights) of the neural network. The mathematical representation is given as

$$\text{MSE} = \frac{1}{n}\sum_{i=1}^{n}\left(\hat{Y}_i - Y_i\right)^2$$

where $\left(\hat{Y}_i - Y_i\right)$ is (actual − computed) [34].

19.4.5 *Optimization of Weights by BSO*

This BSO algorithm is a neighborhood weight optimization. The procedure is as follows:

Initialize the parameters of solution size S_i.
Generate the number of solutions S_i.
Apply BSO to these solutions.
The objective function which is taken into consideration is MSE.
The error is minimized and the process is repeated till we obtain the least error, and the accuracy is noted.
If least error is obtained, then the best solution set is obtained else go to step 2.

The main idea of the algorithm is given as follows:

Compare s_0 < - initial solution in S
Compare s_{BSF} < -s_0 (Best solution so far)
Insert s_0 in the best solution set.
For (i=0 to I-1)
    Generating a set V of neighborhood solutions.
    Select the best solution s' in V which is not in the set.
    If s_{i+1} < -s then
    Insert s_{i+1} in the Best solution set.
    If $f(s_{i+1})$ <=$f(s_{BSF})$ then
    Return s_{BSF}.
    else
    Return s_{i+1}
    End-if
End-For

The above algorithm is a neighborhood search technique. The main advantage of this algorithm is its flexibility. In the process of searching individuals in a group, this algorithm avoids circuit search. Once an individual is searched, the algorithm does not roll back to the searched individual ever again. The process includes comparing the error with neighborhood solutions and obtaining the best solution set.

19.5 Results

The performance of the proposed approach is evaluated by a series of simulations using MATLAB 2015Ra and Python with many machine learning libraries.

19.5.1 *Dataset Description*

In this chapter, a real-world credit card dataset is used for experiments. This real-world dataset is obtained from the UCI Machine Learning Repository [35]. The financial institution mentioned in the repository is kept hidden in order to protect sensitive customer data. The dataset extracted is "German credit dataset." This real-world dataset contains a total of 1,000 cases out of which 700 applicants are marked as credit worthy and the remaining 300 are considered non-credit worthy. This dataset contains 25 numerical variables in total. However, 24 input variables and 1 output variable are in the dataset. This output variable takes care of the status of the credit applicant.

Analysis is conducted on the dataset with different neural networks, and the bio-inspired algorithm is applied on all the neural network structures for comparison purpose. This simulation has gone through three steps:

1. Preprocessing,
2. Feature extraction using principle component analysis (PCA),
3. Classification.

Preprocessing includes removing empty or null transaction in the dataset which are generated while checking account balance. Those are of no use to our classification problem. Training high-dimensional data takes a lot of time to train the model. So, we have applied feature extraction technique (PCA) to the dataset to reduce the dimensionality of data which helps in reducing training time. PCA uses linear projection method to reduce the number of parameters. Feature extraction methods are used to identify and remove attributes which are irrelevant (e.g., gender) and redundant from data that does not contribute for classification of data.

We have extracted around 15 features among 24 attributes by applying feature extraction technique. Then, we have applied association rule mining (ARM) and different neural networks to train the model. First, we have divided the dataset into training data and testing data.

19.5.2 Classification Techniques

ARM, an association rule, can be seen as an implication of the form $X \Rightarrow Y$. Let $A = \{a_1, a_2, \ldots, a_n\}$ be a set of n attributes called items. Let $D = \{t_1, t_2, \ldots, t_m\}$ be a set of transactions in a database. Every transaction has an ID which is unique and contains a subset of items in A. Then, the rule is defined as implication of the form

$$X \Rightarrow Y$$

Where X is called antecedent or LHS, and Y is called consequent or RHS. $X, Y \subseteq I$ and $X \cap Y = \emptyset$. It represents the presence of items X, Y in transactions of dataset D. To select interesting rules from a set of all possible rules, we impose constraints on various measures of significance, i.e., the intensity of an association rule is measured by support and confidence.

$$\text{Supp}(X \Rightarrow Y) = \text{Supp}(X \cup Y)$$

$$\text{conf}(X \Rightarrow Y) = \text{Supp}(X \cup Y)/\text{Supp}(X)$$

First, we have used ARM for classification. ARM uses Apriori algorithm to generate frequent patterns and generate rules [36]. From the above Apriori algorithm, we get two sets of rules (for class 1 and class 2). The accuracy of this model is very less which is around 57%. Most of the rules generated in ARM are redundant which leads to less prediction accuracy (Figure 19.2).

Back Propagation: After ARM, we have applied simple Back Propagation algorithm to train the model which has one input layer, one hidden layer, and one output layer [37]. Activation function used in this neural network is sigmoid function. Objective function used here is MSE. While

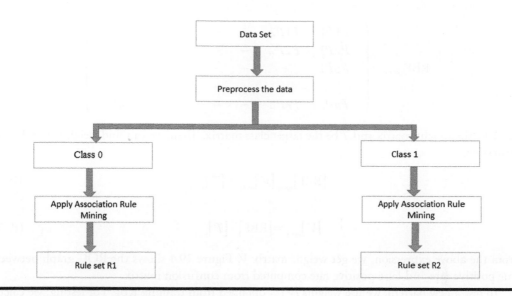

Figure 19.2   Rules generation process.

testing the accuracy of this model is 71%, which is better than ARM, Figure 19.3 shows the ROC graph where *X*-axis shows true positive rate and *Y*-axis shows false negative rate.

Radial Basis Function: Radial basis function (RBF) neural networks typically have three layers: an input layer, a hidden layer with a nonlinear RBF activation function, and output layer. RBF uses Euclidean distance to classify the data. Activation function used in RBF neural network is sigmoid function. In RBF, we usually find Euclidean distance between each pattern in the given dataset. It forms an RBF matrix. Let P1P2 be the distance between pattern 1 and pattern 2 [38].

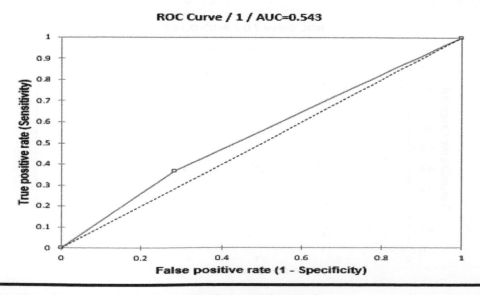

Figure 19.3   ROC curve for back propagation neural network.

$$\text{RBF}_{\text{Matrix}} = \begin{pmatrix} P1P1 & P1P2 & - & - & - & - & P1Pn \\ P2P1 & P2P2 & - & - & - & - & - \\ P3P1 & - & - & - & - & - & - \\ - & - & - & - & - & - & - \\ PnP1 & PnP2 & - & - & - & - & PnPn \end{pmatrix}$$

Let V be the weight matrix and T be the target class matrix. Then, we can find weights from below expression:

$$[\text{RBF}]_{n \times m} [V]_{m \times 1} = [T]_{n \times 1} \tag{19.1}$$

$$[V]_{m \times 1} = [\text{RBF}]^{-1} [T]_{n \times 1} \tag{19.2}$$

From the above expression, we get weight matrix V. Figure 19.4 shows the ROC graph between true positive rate and false positive rate computed from confusion matrix.

To test a new pattern, we use weights $[V]_{n \times 1}$ obtained from training RBF. For testing, we calculated the distance between new pattern and all previous trained patterns. Then, we get $[W]_{I \times n}$ matrix:

$$\text{ClassLabel} = [W]_{1 \times n} [V]_{n \times 1} \tag{19.3}$$

From the above multiplication between two matrices $[W]$ and $[V]$, we get class label of that particular corresponding pattern. The testing accuracy of RBFN is 69%.

19.5.2.1 Convolutional Neural Network

Convolutional neural network (CNN) takes patterns as images or matrices of $n \times m$ and trains the model [39]. We have coded this CNN model using python programming language which has default neural network libraries.

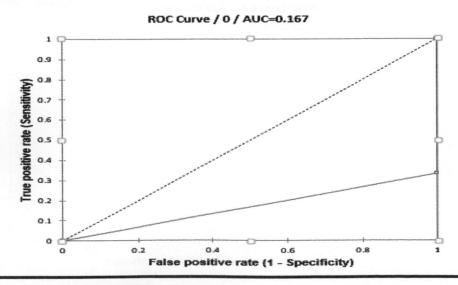

Figure 19.4 ROC curve of RBFN.

```
900/900 [==============================] - 1s - loss: 0.1391 - acc: 0.9489
Epoch 294/300
900/900 [==============================] - 1s - loss: 0.1501 - acc: 0.9322
Epoch 295/300
   2/900 [..............................] - ETA: 1s - loss: 1.0903e-04 - acc: 1.0
  10/900 [..............................] - ETA: 1s - loss: 0.0830 - acc: 1.0000
900/900 [==============================] - 1s - loss: 0.1412 - acc: 0.9389
Epoch 296/300
900/900 [==============================] - 1s - loss: 0.1429 - acc: 0.9422
Epoch 297/300
900/900 [==============================] - 1s - loss: 0.1368 - acc: 0.9478
Epoch 298/300
900/900 [==============================] - 1s - loss: 0.1485 - acc: 0.9389
Epoch 299/300
   2/900 [..............................] - ETA: 1s - loss: 6.9742e-05 - acc: 1.0
   8/900 [..............................] - ETA: 1s - loss: 0.2407 - acc: 0.8750
900/900 [==============================] - 1s - loss: 0.1425 - acc: 0.9456
Epoch 300/300
900/900 [==============================] - 1s - loss: 0.1436 - acc: 0.9378
100/100 [==============================] - 0s
Baseline: 72.90% (5.09%)
lab1@lab1-OptiPlex-3010:~/Desktop/code/new$ []
```

Figure 19.5   Accuracy of CNN.

The accuracy of the model while training using CNN is around 72.9%, which is way better than ARM, but still it needs to be improved.

19.5.2.2 BSO-Trained Back Propagation

Previously, we have implemented a simple Back Propagation Neural Network. Now, we have used BSO to optimize weights in Back Propagation algorithm which reduces the over-fitting while training the model. It uses sigmoid function as activation function and MSE as objective function or fitness function. BSO uses simple birds swarm behavior to optimize weights as shown in the algorithm in proposed method.

While training, the error decreases. While optimization, the population weights are updated at every iteration using global best and local best solutions. Figure 19.5 shows the decrease in error at every iteration [40].

The error in the error graph converges at epoch number 150, i.e., it almost reaches 0. The accuracy of this model is 79.4%, which is better than all the above neural networks classification accuracy. Figure 19.6 shows the graph between actual targets and predicted targets.

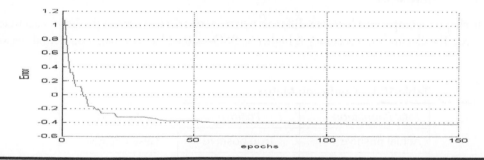

Figure 19.6   Graph showing error decrease at every epoch.

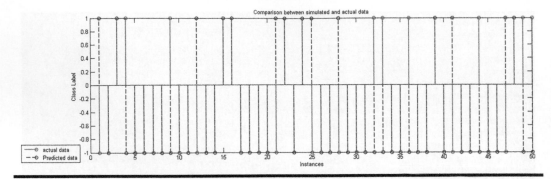

Figure 19.7 Graph between actual and predicted classes.

Class labels are normalized to 1 or −1. In Figure 19.7 (Stem plot), testing instances are along *X*-axis and class labels are on *Y*-axis. Doted line gives predicted class label, and red line shows actual class label. Overlapping of red line and dotted blue line shows the correct prediction (true positive or true negative).

19.5.3 Comparison and Discussion

BSO-trained multilayer perceptron neural network gives better prediction accuracy than all the other models. The prediction accuracy of all the models is listed in Table 1.1. From confusion matrix,

$$\text{Accuracy} = \frac{\text{TP} + \text{TN}}{N} \tag{19.4}$$

For *n* given training instances, RBFN is a one-pass algorithm. It is not iterative. ARM is just brute force which computes all possible combinations of attributes to generate rules, and still the accuracy is very low because the rules generated are redundant. The accuracy of RBFN is less than Back Propagation, which is a rare case. CNN gives better results compared to previous ARM, BP, and RBFN. BSO-trained back propagation gives better results since all solutions try to get the global minimum solution where the error is very less or near to zero.

19.6 Conclusion and Future Work

19.6.1 Conclusion

In this chapter, comparison between different neural networks in terms of prediction accuracy is discussed. The classification accuracy is higher in BSO-trained back propagation neural network,

Table 19.1 Confusion Matrix

Total Population	Positive	Negative
Actual positive	True positive	False negative
Actual negative	False positive	True positive

Table 19.2   Accuracy of All Models

Model	Accuracy (%)
ARM	57
RBFN	69
BP(MLP)	71.43
CNN	73
BSO·BP	79

i.e., with 79.4%. From the comparison of experimental results, it is evident that bio-inspired algorithms play a vital role in credit scoring models.

19.6.2 Future Work

For financial sectors, credit scoring has been a critical area. For these financial sectors to survive, good credit scoring techniques are essential. It is indeed an interesting area with a lot of research going on in it. Models and algorithms that attain higher prediction rates are often researched and improved further. Particularly in the field of machine learning, there is a great scope for bio-inspired algorithms as they provide great computational results. The field of bio-inspired algorithms is gaining its importance over the years and certainly useful in many real-life applications. Moreover, future research in the subfields of bio-inspired algorithms can lead to solving complex problems in real-life applications.

References

1. Quinlan JR. (1997). Simplifying decision trees. *International Journal of Man-Machine Studies*, 27, 221–34.
2. Lacher RC, Coats PK, Sharma S, & Fant LF. (1995). A neural network for classifying the financial health of a firm. *European Journal of Operational Research*, 85, 53–65.
3. Desai VS, Crook JN, & Overstreet GA. (1996). A comparison of neural networks and linear scoring models in the credit union environment. *European Journal of Osperational Research*, 95, 24–37.
4. Altman EI. (1994). Corporate distress diagnosis: comparisons using linear discriminant analysis and neural networks (the Italian experience). *Journal of Banking and Finance*, 18, 505–29.
5. Abdou, H & Pointon, J. (2011). Credit scoring, statistical techniques and evaluation criteria: a review of the literature, *Intelligent Systems in Accounting, Finance Management*, 18(2), 59–88.
6. Casu B & Girardone C. (2006). Bank competition, concentration and efficiency in the single European market. *The Manchester School*, 74(4), 441–468.
7. Yang XS. (2010). Firefly algorithm, stochastic test functions and design optimization. *International Journal of Bioinspired Computation*, 2(2), 78–84.
8. Lee T-S, et al. (2002). Credit scoring using the hybrid neural discriminant technique. *Expert Systems with Applications*, 23(3), 245–254.
9. Ong C-S, Jih-Jeng H & Gwo-Hshiung T. (2005). Building credit scoring models using genetic programming. *Expert Systems with Applications*, 29(1), 41–47.
10. Sarlija N, Beni M & Bohaek Z. (2004). Multinomial model in consumer credit scoring. *10th International Conference on Operational Research*, Trogir, Hrvatska.

11. Xu X, Zhou C & Wang Z. (2009). Credit scoring algorithm based on link analysis ranking with support vector machine. *Expert Systems with Applications*, 36(2), 2625–2632.

12. Shi Y et al. (2005). Classifying credit card accounts for business intelligence and decision making: A multiple-criteria quadratic programming approach. *International Journal of Information Technology & Decision Making*, 4(04), 581–599.

13. Garca-Teruel PJ, Martnez-Solano P & Snchez-Ballesta JP. (2014). The role of accruals quality in the access to bank debt. *Journal of Banking & Finance*, 38, 186–193.

14. Lessmann S et al. (2015). Benchmarking state-of-the-art classification algorithms for credit scoring: An update of research. *European Journal of Operational Research*, 247(1), 124–136.

15. Lee T-S et al. (2002). Credit scoring using the hybrid neural discriminant technique.Expert Systems with applications, 23(3), 245–254.

16. Van Gestel T et al. (2001). Financial time series prediction using least squares support vector machines within the evidence framework. *IEEE Transactions on Neural Networks*, 12(4), 809–821.

17. Hoffmann F et al. (2007). Inferring descriptive and approximate fuzzy rules for credit scoring using evolutionary algorithms. *European Journal of Operational Research*, 177(1), 540–555.

18. Hsieh N-C & Hung L-P. (2010). A data driven ensemble classifier for credit scoring analysis. *Expert systems with Applications*, 37(1), 534–545.

19. West D. (2000). Neural network credit scoring models. *Computers & Operations Research*, 27(11), 1131–1152.

20. Gee AH & Prager RW. (1995). Limitations of neural networks for solving traveling salesman problems, *IEEE Transactions on Neural Networks*, 6(1), 280–282.

21. Baesens B et al. (2003). Benchmarking state-of-the-art classification algorithms for credit scoring. *Journal of the Operational Research Society*, 54(6), 627–635.

22. Dryver AL & Sukkasem J. (2009). Validating risk models with a focus on credit scoring models. *Journal of Statistical Computation and Simulation*, 79(2), 181–193.

23. Damodar Reddy E, Tripathi D, Cheruku R & Kuppili V. (2017). An efficient multilayer ensemble framework with BPSOGSA-Based feature selection for credit scoring data analysis. *Arabian Journal for Science and Engineering*, 1–20.

24. Kamger-Parsi B. (1997). An efficient model of neural networks for optimization. In: *Proceedings IEEE International Conference on Neural Networks*, Nagoya, Japan, 785–790.

25. Eberhart RC & Kennedy J. (1995). A new optimizer using particle swarm theory. In: *Proceedings of the Sixth International Symposium on Micro-Machine and Human Science*, 39–43.

26. Kennedy J & Eberhart R. (1995). Particle swarm optimization. In: *Proceedings IEEE International Conference on Neural Networks*, Perth, Australia, 1942–1948.

27. Krishnanand KN & Ghose D. (2009). Glowworm swarm optimisation: a new method for optimising multi-modal functions. *International Journal of Computational Intelligence Studies*, 1(1), 93–119.

28. Hedayatzadeh R, Salmassi FA, Keshtgari M, Akbari R & Ziarati K. (2010). Termite colony optimization: A novel approach for optimizing continuous problems. In: *18th Iranian Conference on Electrical Engineering (ICEE)*, Isfahan, Iran, 553–558.

29. Stergiou C et al. (2016). Secure integration of IoT and cloud computing. *Future Generation Computer Systems*, 78(3), 964–975.

30. Gupta B, Agrawal DP & Yamaguchi S (eds). (2016). *Handbook of Research on Modern Cryptographic Solutions for Computer and Cyber Security*, IGI Global, Hersey, PA.

31. Muhammad A-Q et al. (2017). An efficient key agreement protocol for Sybilprecaution in online social networks. *Future Generation Computer Systems*, 84, 139–148.

32. Tewari A & Gupta BB. (2017). A lightweight mutual authentication protocol based on elliptic curve cryptography for IoT devices. *International Journal of Advanced Intelligence Paradigms*, 9(3), 111–121.

33. Eusuff MM & Lansey KE. (2003). Optimization of water distribution network design using the shuffled frog leaping algorithm. *Journal of Water Resources Planning and Management*, 129(3), 210–225.

34. Karaboga D & Basturk B. (2007). A powerful and efficient algorithm for numerical function optimization: artificial bee colony (abc) algorithm. *Journal of Global Optimization*, 39(3), 459–471.

35. http://archive.ics.uci.edu/ml/.

36. Martens D et al. (2007). Comprehensible credit scoring models using rule extraction from support vector machines. *European Journal of Operational Research*, 183(3), 1466–1476.
37. Hagan MT & Menhaj MB. (1994). Training feedforward networks with the Marquardt algorithm, IEEE Trans. *Neural Networks*, 5(6), 989–993.
38. Thandar AM & Khaing MK. (2012). Radial Basis Function (RBF) neural network classification based on consistency evaluation measure. *International Journal of Computer Applications*, 54(15), 20–23.
39. Krizhevsky A, Sutskever I & Hinton GE. (2012). Image net classification with deep convolutional neural networks. In: *Advances in Neural Information Processing Systems*, Lake Tahoe, NV, pp. 1097–1105.
40. Nan-Chen H. (2005). Hybrid mining approach in the design of credit scoring models. *Expert Systems with Applications*, 28(4), 655–665.

Chapter 20

A Review of Cryptographic Properties of 4-Bit S-Boxes with Generation and Analysis of Crypto Secure S-Boxes

Sankhanil Dey and Ranjan Ghosh

Institute of Radio Physics and Electronics and University of Calcutta

Contents

20.1 Introduction

Substitution box or S-box in block ciphers is of utmost importance in public key cryptography from the initial days. A 4-bit S-box has been defined as a box of (2^4 =) 16 elements varies from 0 to F in hex, arranged in a random manner as used in Data Encryption Standard or DES [1–4]. Similarly for 8-bit S-box, the number of elements is 2^8 or 256 which varies from 0 to 255 as used in Advance Encryption Standard or AES [5,6]. Hence, the construction of S-boxes is a major issue in cryptology from initial days. Use of irreducible polynomials (IPs) to construct S-boxes had already been adopted by crypto-community. But the study of IPs has been limited to almost binary Galois field GF(2^q) as used in AES S-boxes [5,6]. So, it is important to study 4-bit BFs, 8-bit BFs, and polynomials over Galois field GF(p^q), where $p > 2$ in public key cryptography. A brief literature study on security in cryptography and polynomials has been elaborated in Section 20.2.

A 4-bit Boolean Function (BF) gives 1-bit output for four input bits [1] represented in the form of a 16-bit output (column) vector. The Truth Table of a 4-bit BF has been represented by a 16-bit output vector, each of whose bit is an output bit corresponding to 16 possibilities of 4-bit sequential inputs from '0000' to '1111.' The 16 rows of the 4-bit sequential inputs, each bit at the same column position comprises 16 bits and thereby four 16-bit columns provide four 4-bit input vectors (IPVs), which are common for all 4-bit BFs. Since there are 16 output bits, there are 2^{16} (= 65,536) different possibilities whose decimal equivalents vary between 0 and 65,535 [1]. Hence, 4-bit BFs have four 16-bit IPVs (IPVs) and 65,536 possible 16-bit output vectors. Where an 8-bit BF gives 1-bit output for eight input bits [5] represented in the form of a 256-bit output (column) vector. The Truth Table of a 8-bit BF is represented by a 256-bit output vector, each of whose bit is an output bit corresponding to 256 possibilities of 8-bit sequential inputs from '00000000' to '11111111.' The 256 rows of the 8-bit sequential inputs, each bit at the same column position comprises 256 bits and thereby eight 256-bit columns provide eight 8-bit IPVs, which are common for all 8-bit BFs. Since there are 256 output bits, there are 2^{256} different possibilities whose decimal equivalents vary between 0 and $2^{256} - 1$ [6]. Hence, 8-bit BFs have eight 256-bit-long 8-bit IPVs and 2^{256} possible 256-bit output vectors. Hence, for generation and security analysis of 4- or 8-bit S-boxes, it is an urgent need to study cryptographic properties of S-boxes as well as security of S-boxes with 4- or 8-bit BFs. In other words, a 4-bit S-box can be represented by a four-valued 4-bit BF. If the 1st bit of the four output bits is taken sequentially for each element of the 16 elements of an S-box, one gets the 1st BF; 2nd sequence of output bit, the 2nd BF; 3rd sequence of output bit, the 3rd BF; and 4th sequence of output bit, the 4th BF [1], respectively. Some cryptographic properties and security analysis of 4-bit S-boxes such as Output Bit Independence Criterion (BIC) of 4-bit S-boxes, SAC of 4-bit S-boxes, Higher-Order Strict Avalanche Criterion (HO-SAC) of 4-bit S-boxes, Extended SAC of 4-bit S-boxes, Linear Cryptanalysis of 4-bit S-boxes, Differential Cryptanalysis of 4-bit S-boxes, and Differential Cryptanalysis with 4-bit BFs of 4-bit S-boxes as well as Linear Approximation Analysis of 4-bit S-boxes have been reported below in brief.

A 4-bit S-box consists of four 4-bit BFs. In Output BIC, the difference or xored BFs of all two possible 4-bit BFs of the concerned S-box have been taken under consideration. If all six difference 4-bit BFs have been balanced, then the criterion has been satisfied for the concerned S-box. Since all six difference 4-bit BFs have been balanced, the prediction of a bit value to be one or zero is in at most uncertainty [1].

In SAC, four IPVs of a 4-bit BF have been complemented one at a time. If in complemented four 4-bit BFs, 8-bit values have been changed and 8-bit values remain the same, then the 4-bit BF has been said to satisfy SAC of 4-bit BFs [1,7]. Complementing 4th IPV means interchanging each distinct 8-bit halves of a 4-bit output BF (OPBF), whereas complementing 3rd IPV means interchanging each distinct 4-bit halves of each distinct 8-bit halves, whereas complementing 2nd IPV means interchanging each distinct 2-bit halves of each distinct 4-bit halves of each distinct 8-bit halves and complementing 1st IPV means interchanging each bit of all distinct 2-bit halves of a 16-bit-long 4-bit BF. In this chapter, this shifting property has been used to construct an algorithm of SAC of 4-bit BFs. Another new algorithm with flip of index bits has also been introduced in this chapter. If all four 4-bit BFs of a 4-bit S-box satisfy SAC for 4-bit BFs, then the concerned S-box has been said to satisfy SAC of 4-bit S-boxes [1,7].

In HO-SAC of 4-bit BFs, four IPVs of a 4-bit S-box have been complemented two or three at a time [8]. If in complemented ten 4-bit BFs, 8 bit values have been changed and 8-bit values remain the same, then the 4-bit BF has been said to satisfy HO-SAC of 4-bit BFs. A detailed review of old as well as two new algorithms with previous shift method and flip of index bits method has been introduced in this chapter in Section 20.3.3. In this chapter, a detailed review of a new algorithm entitled Extended HO-SAC has been introduced in which four IPVs have been complemented at a time.

In Differential Cryptanalysis of 4-bit crypto S-boxes, the 16 distant input S-boxes have been obtained by xor operation with each of 16 input differences varies from 0 to F in hex to all 16 elements of input S-box one at a time. The 16 distant S-boxes have been obtained by shuffling the elements of the original S-box in a certain order in which the elements of the input S-boxes have been shuffled in concerned distant input S-boxes. The 16 elements of each S-box and the elements in corresponding position of corresponding distant S-box have been xored to obtain the Difference S-box. The Difference S-box may or may not be a Crypto S-box since it may not have all unique and distinct elements in it. The count of each element from 0 to F in Difference S-box has been noted and put in Difference Distribution Table (DDT) for security analysis of the S-box [9,10].

In this chapter, a review of the new algorithm using 4-bit BFs for Differential Cryptanalysis of 4-bit crypto S-boxes has been presented. An input S-box can be decomposed into four 4-bit IPVs with decimal equivalents 255 for 4th IPV, 3,855 for 3rd IPV, 13,107 for 2nd IPV, and 21,845 for 1st IPV. Now, we complement all IPVs one, two, three, and four at a time to obtain 16 4-bit distant input S-boxes. Each of the four OPBFs is shifted according to the shift of four IPVs of input S-boxes to form four IPVs of distant input S-boxes to obtain distant S-boxes. The four 4-bit OPBFs of S-boxes are xored bitwise with four 4-bit BFs of distant S-boxes to obtain four 4-bit difference BFs. For 16 distant output S-boxes, there are 64 difference BFs. Difference BFs are checked for balanced-ness, i.e., for at most uncertainty. The table in which the balanced-nesses of 64 difference BFs have been noted has been called as Differential Analysis Table (DAT).

In Linear Cryptanalysis of 4-bit crypto S-boxes, every 4-bit linear relations have been tested for a particular 4-bit crypto S-box. The presence of each 4-bit unique linear relation is checked by satisfaction of each of them for all 16 4-bit unique input bit patterns and corresponding 4-bit output bit patterns, generated from the index of each element and each element, respectively, of that particular crypto S-box. If they are satisfied eight times out of 16 operations for all 4-bit unique input bit patterns and corresponding 4-bit output bit patterns, then the existence of the 4-bit linear equation is at a stake. The probability of the presence and absence of a 4-bit linear relation both is (= 8/16) 1/2. If a 4-bit linear equation is satisfied 0 times, then it can be concluded that the given 4-bit linear relation is absent for that particular 4-bit crypto S-box. If a 4-bit linear equation is satisfied 16 times, then it can also be concluded that the given 4-bit linear relation is present for that particular 4-bit crypto S-box. In both the cases, full information is adverted to the cryptanalysts. The concept of probability bias was introduced to predict the randomization ability of that 4-bit S-box from the probability of the presence or absence of unique 4-bit linear relations. The result is better for cryptanalysts if the probability of the presence or absence of unique 4-bit linear equations is far away from 1/2 or near to 0 or 1. If the probabilities of the presence or absence of all unique 4-bit linear relations are 1/2 or close to 1/2, then the 4-bit crypto S-box has been said to be linear cryptanalysis immune, since the existence of maximum 4-bit linear relations for that 4-bit crypto S-box is hard to predict [9,10]. Heys also introduced the concept of Linear Approximation Table (LAT) in which the numbers of times each 4-bit unique linear relation has been satisfied for all 16 unique 4-bit input bit patterns and corresponding 4-bit output bit patterns of a crypto S-box have been noted. The result is better for a cryptanalysts if the numbers of 8s in the table are less. If numbers of 8s are much more than the other numbers in the table, then the 4-bit crypto S-box has been said to be more linear cryptanalysis immune [9,10].

In another look, an input S-box can be decomposed into four 4-bit IPVs with decimal equivalents 255 for 4th IPV, 3,855 for 3rd IPV, 13,107 for 2nd IPV, and 21,845 for 1st IPV. The S-box can also be decomposed into four 4-bit OPBFs. Each IPV can be denoted as an input variable of a linear relation and OPBF as an output variable (OPV) and '+' as xor operation. Linear relations have been checked for satisfaction, and 16-bit OPVs due to linear relations have been checked for balanced-ness. Balanced OPVs indicate that out of 16 bits of IPVs and OPBFs, 8 bits satisfy the linear relation and 8 bits are out of satisfaction, i.e., the best uncertainty. A total of 256 4-bit linear relations have been operated on four 16-bit IPVs and four 16-bit OPBFs, and 256 OPVs have been generated. The count of 1s in OPVs has been entered in LAT. Better the number of 8s in LAT, better the S-box security [9,10].

In this chapter, a detailed review of a new technique to find the existing linear relations or linear approximations for a particular 4-bit S-box has been presented. If the nonlinear part of the ANF equation of a 4-bit OPBF is absent or calculated to be 0, then the equation is termed as a linear relation or approximation. Searching for the number of existing linear relations through this method is ended up with the number of existing linear relations, i.e., the goal to conclude the security of a 4-bit crypto S-box has been attended in a very lucid manner by this method.

Polynomials over finite field or Galois field $GF(p^q)$ have been of utmost importance in public key cryptography [8]. The polynomials over Galois field $GF(p^q)$ with degree q have been termed as basic polynomials or BPs over Galois field $GF(p^q)$, and polynomials with degree $<q$ have been termed as elemental polynomials or EPs over Galois field $GF(p^q)$ [11]. The EPs over Galois field $GF(p^q)$ with only constant terms have been termed as constant polynomials or CPs over Galois field $GF(p^q)$. The BPs over finite field or Galois field $GF(p^q)$ that cannot be factored into at least

two nonconstant EPs have been termed as IPs over finite field or Galois field GF(p^q), and the rest have been termed as reducible polynomials or RPs over finite field or Galois field GF(p^q) [11]. The polynomials over Galois field GF(p^q) with coefficient of the highest degree term as 1 have been termed as monic polynomials over Galois field GF(p^q), and the rest have been termed as non-monic polynomials over Galois field GF(p^q) [11].

q-bit crypto substitution box or S-box has 2^q elements in an array where each element is unique and distinct and arranged in a random fashion varies from 0 to 2^q. Polynomials over Galois field GF(p^q) have been termed as binary polynomials if $p = 2$. The binary number that has been constructed with binary coefficients of all q values with $q = 0$ at LSB and $q = q$ at MSB has been termed as binary coefficient number or Binary Coded Number (BCN) of $q + 1$ bits. The BCN over Galois field GF(p^q) has been similar to $\log_2^{q+1}$ bit BFs. The $\log_2^{q+1}$ bit S-boxes have been generated using $\log_2^{q+1}$ bit BCNs. In this chapter, crypto 4- and 8-bit S-boxes have been generated using BCNs, and the procedure has been continued as a future scope to generate 16- and 32-bit S-boxes. The non-repeated coefficients of BPs over Galois field GF(p^q), where $p = 2^{\left(\log_2^{q+1}\right)}$ and $q = p - 1$, have been used to generate $\log_2^{q+1}$ bit S-boxes. In this chapter, proper 4- and 8-bit S-boxes have been generated using BCNs, and the procedure has been continued as a future scope to generate 16- and 32-bit S-boxes. In this chapter, polynomials over Galois field GF(p^q) and the roll of IPs to construct S-boxes have been reviewed in Section 20.3.1. The generation of 4- and 8-bit S-boxes using BCNs has been elaborated in Section 20.3.2. The generation of 4- and 8-bit S-boxes with coefficients of nonbinary Galois field polynomials has been depicted in Section 20.3.3. A cryptographic and security analysis of 32 DES 4-bit S-boxes has been given in Section 20.3.4. A detailed cryptographic and security analysis of generated ten 4-bit S-boxes with discussed crypto-related cryptographic properties and security criterion has also been given in Section 20.3.4. Results have been discussed in Section 20.3.5. Conclusions are provided in Section 20.4. Acknowledgment and references are given in later sections.

20.2 Literature Survey

In this section, an exhaustive relevant literature survey with their specific references has been introduced to crypto literature. In Section 20.2.1, the relevant topic has been cryptography and cryptology; in Section 20.2.2, the topic has been linear cryptanalysis; in Section 20.2.3, the topic has been differential cryptanalysis; in Section 20.2.4, the topic has been cryptanalysis of stream ciphers; and in Section 20.2.5, the relevant topic has been SAC of S-boxes. At last, a literature study on IPs and primitive polynomials has been given in Section 20.2.6.

20.2.1 Cryptography and Cryptology

In the end of the twentieth century, a bible of cryptography had been introduced [12]. The various concepts involved in cryptography and also some information on cryptanalysis had been provided to crypto-community in the late 1990s [8]. A simplified version of DES that has the architecture of DES but has much lesser rounds and much lesser bits had also been proposed at the same time. The cipher has also been better for educational purposes [13]. Later in the early twenty-first century, an organized pathway toward learning how to cryptanalyze had been charted [14]. Almost at the same time, a new cipher as a candidate for the new AES, main concepts and issues involve in block cipher design and cryptanalysis had also been proposed [15] that is also a measure of cipher strength. A vital preliminary introduction to cryptanalysis has also been introduced to cryptanalysts [16]. At the same time, somewhat similar notion as [16] but uses a more descriptive approach and focused on linear cryptanalysis and differential cryptanalysis of a given SPN cipher had been elaborated [17]. Particularly, it discusses DES-like ciphers that had been extended with it [18]. Comparison of modes of operations such as CBC, CFB, OFB, and ECB had also been elaborated [19]. A new cipher called Camelia had been introduced with its cryptanalysis technique to demonstrate the strength of the cipher [20]. History of commercial computer cryptography and classical ciphers and the effect of cryptography on society had also been introduced in this queue [21]. The requirements of a good cryptosystem and cryptanalysis had also been demonstrated later [22]. Description of the new AES by Rijndael, which provides good insight into many creative cryptographic techniques that increases cipher strength, had been included in literature. A bit later a highly mathematical path to explain cryptologic concepts had also been introduced [23]. Investigation of the security of Ron Rivest's DESX construction, a cheaper alternative to triple DES had been elaborated [24]. A nice provision to an encyclopedic look at the design, analysis, and applications of cryptographic techniques had been depicted later [25], and last but not the least a good explanation on why cryptography has been hard and the issues which cryptographers have to consider in designing ciphers had been elaborated [26]. Simplified Data Encryption Standard or S-DES is an educational algorithm similar to DES but with much smaller parameters [27,28]. The technique to analyze S-DES using linear cryptanalysis and differential cryptanalysis had been the interest of crypto-community later [27,28]. The encryption and decryption algorithm or cipher of twofish algorithm had been introduced to crypto-community, and a cryptanalysis of the said cipher had also been elaborated in subject to be a part of Advance Encryption Algorithm proposals [29].

20.2.2 Some Old and Recent References on Linear Cryptanalysis

The cryptanalysis technique to 4-bit crypto S-boxes using linear relations among four 4-bit IPVs and four output 4-bit BF(OPBFs) of a 4-bit S-box have been termed as linear cryptanalysis of 4-bit crypto S-boxes [9,10]. Another technique to analyze the security of a 4-bit crypto S-box using all possible differences had also been termed as differential cryptanalysis of 4-bit crypto S-boxes [9,10]. The search for the best characteristic in linear cryptanalysis and the maximal weight path in a directed graph and correspondence between them had also been elaborated with a proper example [30]. It had also proposed the use of correlation matrix as a natural representation to understand and describe the mechanism of linear cryptanalysis [31]. It was also formalized that the method described in [32] showed that at the structural level, linear cryptanalysis has been very similar to differential cryptanalysis. It was also used for further exploration into linear cryptanalysis [33]. It had also been provided with a generalization of linear cryptanalysis and suggested that IDEA and SAFER K-64 have been secure against such generalization [34]. It had been surveyed to the use of multiple linear approximations in cryptanalysis to improve efficiency and to reduce the amount of data required for cryptanalysis in certain circumstances [35]. Cryptanalysis of DES cipher with linear relations [32] and the improved version of the said cryptanalysis [32] with 12 computers had also been reported later [36]. The description of an implementation of Matsui's linear cryptanalysis of DES with strong emphasis on efficiency had also been reported [37]. In early decades of this century, the cryptanalytic attack based on multiple linear approximations to AES candidate Serpent had also been reported [38]. Later, a technique to prove security bounds against linear and differential cryptanalytic attacks using Mixed-Integer Linear Programming (MILP) had also been elaborated [39]. Later to this on the strength of two variants of reduced round lightweight block cipher SIMON-32 and SIMON-48 had been tested against linear cryptanalysis and had been presented the optimum possible results [40]. Almost at the same time, the strength of another light-weight block ciphers SIMECK had been tested against linear cryptanalysis [41]. The fault analysis of light-weight block cipher SPECK and linear cryptanalysis with zero statistical correlation among plaintext and respective cipher text of reduced round lightweight block cipher SIMON to test its strength had also been introduced in recent past [42].

20.2.3 Some Old and Recent References on Differential Cryptanalysis

The design of a Feistel cipher with at least five rounds that has been resistant to differential cryptanalysis had been reported to crypto-community [43]. The exploration of the possibility of defeating differential cryptanalysis by designing S-boxes with equiprobable output XORs using bent functions had been reported once [44]. The description of some design criteria for creating good S-boxes that are immune to differential cryptanalysis and these criteria are based on information theoretic concepts had been reported later [45]. It had been introduced that the differential cryptanalysis on a reduced round variant of DES [46] and broke a variety of ciphers, the fastest break being of two-pass Snefru [47] and also described the cryptanalysis of the full 16-round DES using an improved version [46,48]. It had been shown that there have been DES-like iterated ciphers that do not yield to differential cryptanalysis [49] and also introduced the concept of Markov ciphers and explained its significance in differential cryptanalysis. It had also been investigated that the security of iterated block ciphers shows how to and when an r-round cipher is not vulnerable to attacks [50]. It had also been proposed that eight-round twofish can be attacked and investigated the role of key-dependent S-boxes in differential cryptanalysis [51]. It had been on the same line with [44] but proposed that the input variables be increased and that the S-box be balanced to increase resistance toward both differential and linear cryptanalyses [52]. In the previous decade of this century, estimation of probability of block ciphers against linear and differential cryptanalytic attacks had been reported. Later, a new algebraic and statistical technique of cryptanalysis against block cipher PRESENT-128 had been reported [53]. Almost three years later, a new technique entitled Impossible Differential Cryptanalysis had also been reported [54]. A detailed comparative study of DES based on the strength of DES against linear and differential cryptanalyses had been reported later [55]. At last, constraints of Programming Models of Chosen Key Differential Cryptanalysis had been reported to crypto-community [56].

20.2.4 Linear and Differential Cryptanalyses of Stream Ciphers

In the late twentieth century, a stepping stone of the differential–linear cryptanalysis method that is a very efficient method against DES had also been grounded [57]. The relationship between linear and differential cryptanalyses and present classes of ciphers which are resistant toward these attacks had also been elaborated [6]. It was described that the description of statistical cryptanalysis of DES, a combination and improvement of both linear and differential cryptanalysis with suggestion of the linearity of S-boxes was not been very important [58]. Later in the twenty-first century, description of analysis with multiple expressions and differential–linear cryptanalyses with experimental results of an implementation of differential–linear cryptanalyses with multiple expressions applied to DES variants had also been proposed [59]. At the same time, the attack on seven- and eight-round Rijndael using the Square method with a related-key attack that can break nine-round Rijndael with 256-bit keys had been described [60]. In the late or almost end of the twentieth century, the strength of stream ciphers has been tested against differential cryptanalytic attack [61]. Later, their strength had also been tested against linear cryptanalytic attack [62]. A separate method of linear cryptanalytic attack had been reported once [63]. At least six years later, the strength of stream cipher helix had been tested against differential cryptanalytic attack [64]. Later, the strength of stream ciphers Py, Py6, and Pypy had also been tested against differential cryptanalytic attack [65]. Recently, the test of strength of stream cipher ZUC against differential cryptanalytic attack had also been reported to crypto-community [66].

20.2.5 SAC of S-Boxes

In the beginning, SAC of 4-bit BFs and BIC of 4-bit S-boxes had been introduced [67], and design of good S-boxes based on these criteria had also been reported later [7]. In end of the twentieth century, the construction of secured S-boxes to satisfy SAC of S-boxes had been reported with ease [68]. The test of 4-bit BFs to satisfy HO-SAC had also been illustrated [69]. In the early twenty-first century, the analysis methods of SAC had been reported. A new approach to test degree of suitability of S-boxes in modern block ciphers had been introduced to crypto-community [70]. A total of 16! 4-bit S-boxes had also been tested for optimum linear equivalent classes later [71]. The strength of several block ciphers against several cryptanalytic attacks had been tested and reported later [72]. Recently, the key-dependent S-boxes and simple algorithms to generate key-dependent S-boxes had been reported [73]. An efficient cryptographic S-box design using soft computing algorithms had also been reported [74]. In recent past, the cellular automata had been used to construct good S-boxes [75].

20.2.6 Polynomials

In the early twentieth century, Radolf Church initiated the search for IPs over Galois field GF(p^q) for p = 2, 3, 5, and 7 and for p = 2, q = 1 through 11, for p =3, q = 1 through 7, for p = 5, q = 1 through 4 and for p = 7, q = 1 through 3. A manual polynomial multiplication among respected EPs gives RPs in the said Galois field. All RPs have been canceled from the list of BPs to give IPs over the said Galois field GF(p^q) [76]. Later, the necessary condition for a BP to be an IPs had been generalized to even two characteristics. It had also been applied to RPs and gave irreducible factors mode 2 [77]. Next to it, elementary techniques to compute over finite fields or Galois field GF(p^q) had been described with proper modifications [78]. Next, the factorization of polynomials over Galois field GF(p^q) had been elaborated [79]. Later, appropriate coding techniques of polynomials over Galois field GF(p^q) had been illustrated with examples [80]. The previous idea of factorizing polynomials over Galois field GF(p^q) [79] had also been extended to large value of P or large finite fields [81]. Later, few probabilistic algorithms to find IPs over Galois field GF(p^q) for degree q had been elaborated with examples [82]. Later, factorization of multivariate polynomials over Galois fields GF(p) had also been introduced to mathematics community [83]. With that the separation of irreducible factors of BPs [79] had also been introduced later [84]. Next to it, the factorization of BPs with Generalized Reimann Hypothesis (GRH) had also been elaborated [85]. Later, a probabilistic algorithm to find irreducible factors of basic bivariate polynomials over Galois field GF(p^q) had also been illustrated [86]. Later, the conjectural deterministic algorithm to find primitive elements and relevant primitive polynomials over binary Galois field GF(2) had been introduced [87]. Some new algorithms to find IPs over Galois field GF(p) had also been introduced at the same time [88]. Another use of GRH to determine irreducible factors in a deterministic manner and also for multiplicative subgroups had been introduced later [89]. The table binary equivalents of binary primitive polynomials had been illustrated in literature [90]. The method to find roots of primitive polynomials over binary Galois field GF(2) had been introduced to mathematical community [91]. A method to search for IPs in a random manner and factorization of BPs or to find irreducible factors of BPs in a random fashion had been introduced later [92]. After that, a new variant of Rabin's algorithm [82] had been introduced with probabilistic analysis of BPs with no irreducible factors [93]. Later, a factorization of univariate polynomials over Galois field GF(p) in sub-quadratic execution time had also been notified [94]. Later, a deterministic algorithm to factorize IPs over one variable had also been introduced [95]. An algorithm to factorize bivariate polynomials over Galois field GF(p) with Hensel lifting had also been notified [96]. Next to it, an algorithm had also been introduced to find factor of irreducible and almost primitive polynomials over Galois field GF(2) [97]. Later, a deterministic algorithm to factorize polynomials over Galois field GF(p) to distinct degree factors had also been notified [98]. A detailed study of multiples and products of univariate primitive polynomials over binary Galois field GF(2) had also been done [99]. Later, algorithm to find optimal IPs over extended binary Galois field GF(2^m) [100] and a deterministic algorithm to determine Pascal polynomials over Galois field GF(2) [101] had been added to literature. Later, the search of IPs and primitive polynomials over binary Galois field GF(2) had also been done successfully [102]. At the same time, the square-free polynomials had also been factorized [103] where a work on divisibility of trinomials by IPs over binary Galois field GF(2) [104] had also been notified. Later, a probabilistic algorithm to factor polynomials over finite fields had been introduced [105]. An explicit factorization to obtain irreducible factors to obtain for cyclotomic polynomials over Galois field GF(p^q) had also been reported later [106]. A fast randomized algorithm to obtain IPs over a certain Galois field GF(p^q) had been notified [107]. A deterministic algorithm to obtain factors of a polynomial over Galois field GF(p^q) had also been notified at the same time [108]. A review of construction of IPs over finite fields and algorithms to factor polynomials over finite fields had been reported to literature [109,110]. An algorithm to search for primitive polynomials had also been notified at the same time [111]. The residue of division of BPs by IPs must be 1, and this is reported to literature a bit later [11]. The IPs with several coefficients of different categories had been illustrated in literature a bit later [112]. The use of zeta function to factor polynomials over finite fields had been notified later on [113]. At last, integer polynomials had also been described with examples [114].

20.3 S-Box Generation

In this section, polynomials over Galois field GF(p^q) and the roll of IPs to construct S-boxes have been reviewed in Section 20.3.1. The generation of 4- and 8-bit S-boxes using BCNs has been elaborated in Section 20.3.2 20.3. The generation of 4- and 8-bit S-boxes with coefficients of nonbinary Galois field polynomials has been depicted in Section 20.3.3. A cryptographic and security analysis of 32 DES 4-bit S-boxes has been given in Section 20.3.4. A detailed cryptographic and security analysis of generated ten 4-bit crypto S-boxes with discussed crypto-related cryptographic properties and security criterion has also been given in Section 20.3.4. Results have been discussed in Section 20.3.5.

20.3.1 *Polynomials Over Galois Field GF(p^q) and* $\log_2^{q+1}$ *Bit S-Boxes*

Section 20.3.1.1 has been devoted to a small review of polynomials. Section 20.3.1.2 has been of utmost importance since in it a 4-bit crypto or proper S-box has been defined in brief. At last, in Section 20.3.1.3, the equation among 2^{15} Galois field polynomials and a 4-bit crypto S-box has been elaborated in detail.

20.3.1.1 Polynomials Over Galois Field GF(p^q)

Polynomials over Galois field GF(p^q) have been of utmost importance in cryptographic applications. Polynomials with degree q have been termed as BPs over Galois field GF(p^q), and polynomials with degree less than q have been termed as EPs over Galois field GF(p^q). Polynomials with leading coefficient as 1 have been termed as monic polynomials irrespective of BPs and EPs over Galois field GF(p^q). An example of the said criteria has been described as follows: an example of BP over Galois field GF(p^q) is given below:

$$BP(x) = co_q x^q + co_{q-1} x^{q-1} + co_{q-1} x^{q-2} + \ldots + co_2 x^2 + co_1 x^1 + a_0 \ldots \tag{20.1}$$

In Equation (20.1), BP(x) has been represented as BP over Galois field GF(p^q) since the highest degree term of the said polynomial over Galois field GF(p^q) has been q. The BP has been called as a monic BP over Galois field GF(p^q) if $co_q = 1$. The number of terms in a BP over Galois field GF(p^q) has been ($q + 1$). The number of possible values of a particular coefficient co_q, where $0 \le p \le q$, has been from 0 to p, i.e., ($p + 1$). If the value of q has been <q, then the polynomial over Galois field GF(p^q) has been termed as EPs over Galois field GF(p^q). If a BP or EP contains only constant term, then the polynomial has been termed as CP over Galois field GF(p^q). If a BP over Galois field GF(p^q) can be factored into two nonconstant Eps, then the BP can be termed as RPs over Galois field GF(p^q). If the two factors of a BP over Galois field GF(p^q) have been the BP itself and a CP, then the BP has been said as an IP over Galois field GF(p^q).

20.3.1.2 4-Bit Crypto S-Boxes

A 4-bit crypto S-box can be written as follows: where each element of the 1st row of Table 20.1, entitled as index, is the position of each element of the S-box within the given S-box and the elements of the 2nd row, entitled as S-box, are the elements of the given S-box. It can be concluded that the 1st row is fixed for all possible crypto S-boxes. The values of each element of the 1st row are distinct, unique, and vary between 0 and F. The values of the each element of the 2nd row of a crypto S-box have also been distinct, unique, and also vary between 0 and F. The values of the elements of the fixed 1st row are sequential and monotonically increasing where for the 2nd row they can be sequential or partly sequential or nonsequential. Here, the given S-box is the 1st 4-bit S-box of the 1st S-box out of eight of DES [1,3,4].

20.3.1.3 Relation between 4-Bit S-Boxes and Polynomials over Galois Field GF (2^15)

Index of each element of a 4-bit crypto S-box and the element itself is a hexadecimal number and that can be converted into a 4-bit bit sequence. From row 2 through 5 and row 7 through A of each column from 1 through G of Table 20.2 shows the 4-bit bit sequences of the corresponding

Table 20.1   4-Bit Crypto S-Box

Row	Column	1	2	3	4	5	6	7	8	9	A	B	C	D	E	F	G
1	Index	0	1	2	3	4	5	6	7	8	9	A	B	C	D	E	F
2	S-Box	E	4	D	1	2	F	B	8	3	A	6	C	5	9	0	7

Table 20.2 Input and Output BCNs of the S-Box

Row	Column	1	2	3	4	5	6	7	8	9	A	B	C	D	E	F	G	H. Decimal Equivalent
1	Index	0	1	2	3	4	5	6	7	8	9	A	B	C	D	E	F	Equivalent
2	IGFP4	0	0	0	0	0	0	0	0	1	1	1	1	1	1	1	1	00,255
3	IGFP3	0	0	0	0	1	1	1	1	0	0	0	0	1	1	1	1	03,855
4	IGFP2	0	0	1	1	0	0	1	1	0	0	1	1	0	0	1	1	13,107
5	IGFP1	0	1	0	1	0	1	0	1	0	1	0	1	0	1	0	1	21,845
6	S-Box	E	4	D	1	2	F	B	8	3	A	6	C	5	9	0	7	
7	OGFP4	1	0	1	0	0	1	1	1	0	1	0	1	0	1	0	0	42,836
8	OGFP3	1	1	1	0	0	1	0	0	0	0	1	1	1	0	0	1	58,425
9	OGFP2	1	0	0	0	1	1	1	0	1	1	1	0	0	0	0	1	36,577
A	OGFP1	0	0	1	1	0	1	1	0	1	0	0	0	1	1	0	1	13,965

hexadecimal numbers of the index of each element of the given S-box and each element of the S-box itself. Each row from 2 through 5 and 7 through A from column 1 through G constitutes a 16 bit bit sequence that is a BP over Galois field GF(2^{15}). Column 1 through G of row 2 has been termed as 4th IGFP, row 3 has been termed as 3rd IGFP, row 4 has been termed as 2nd IGFP, and row 5 has been termed as IGFP, whereas column 1 through G of row 7 has been termed as 4th OGFP, row 8 has been termed as 3rd OGFP, row 9 has been termed as 2nd OGFP, and row A has been termed as 1st OGFP. The decimal equivalents of each IGFP and OGFP have been noted at column H of respective rows. Here, IGFP stands for Input Galois Field Polynomial and OGFP stands for Output Galois Field Polynomial. The respective polynomials have been shown in row 1 through 8 of column 3 of Table 20.3.

Table 20.3 Respective Polynomials of IGFP4 through IGFP1 and OGFP4 through OGFP1

Col.	1	2	3
Row	Index	DCM Eqv.	Polynomials over Galois Field GF(2^{15})
1	IGFP4	00,255	$BP(x) = x^7 + x^6 + x^5 + x^4 + x^3 + x^2 + x^1 + 1$
2	IGFP3	03,855	$BP(x) = x^{11} + x^{10} + x^9 + x^8 + x^3 + x^2 + x^1 + 1$
3	IGFP2	13,107	$BP(x) = x^{13} + x^{12} + x^9 + x^8 + x^5 + x^4 + x^1 + 1$
4	IGFP1	21,845	$BP(x) = x^{14} + x^{12} + x^{10} + x^8 + x^6 + x^4 + x^2 + 1$
5	OGFP4	42,836	$BP(x) = x^{15} + x^{13} + x^{10} + x^9 + x^8 + x^6 + x^4 + x^2$
6	OGFP3	58,425	$BP(x) = x^{15} + x^{14} + x^{13} + x^{10} + x^5 + x^4 + x^3 + 1$
7	OGFP2	36,577	$BP(x) = x^{15} + x^{11} + x^{10} + x^9 + x^7 + x^6 + x^5 + 1$
8	OGFP1	13,965	$BP(x) = x^{13} + x^{12} + x^{10} + x^9 + x^7 + x^3 + x^2 + 1$

20.3.2 4- and 8-Bit S-Box Generation by Respective BCNs Over Binary Galois Field GF(2^q) Where q €(15 and 255)

In this chapter, 4- and 8-bit identity S-boxes have been taken, for example, for generation of 4- and 8-bit S-boxes over binary Galois fields GF(2^q) where q €(15 and 255), respectively. The generation of identity 4-bit S-box from four BCNs over binary Galois field GF(2^{15}) has been elaborated in Section 20.3.2.1, and the generation of identity 8-bit S-box from eight BCNs over binary Galois field GF(2^{255}) has been elaborated in Section 20.3.2.2. The algorithm for generation of $\log_2^{q+1}$ bit S-boxes over binary Galois field GF(2^q) has been depicted with time complexity of the algorithm in Section 20.3.2.3.

20.3.2.1 Generation of 4-Bit Identity Crypto S-Box from Four Polynomials Over Binary Galois Field GF(2^{15})

The concerned 4-bit identity S-box has been shown in Table 20.4 where each element of the 1st row of Table 20.4, entitled as index, has been the position of each element of the S-box within the given S-box, and the elements of the 2nd row, entitled as S-box, are the elements of the given identity S-box. It can be concluded that the 1st row has been fixed for all possible crypto S-boxes. The values of each element of the 1st row are distinct, unique, and vary between 0 and F. The values of the each element of the 2nd row of the identity crypto S-box have also been distinct, unique, and also vary between 0 and F. The values of the elements of the fixed 1st row are sequential and monotonically increasing, whereas for the 2nd row, they are also sequential and monotonically increasing for this identity S-box. Here, the given S-box is the 4-bit identity crypto S-box.

Index of each element of a 4-bit crypto S-box and the element itself is a hexadecimal number and that can be converted into a 4-bit bit sequence. From row 2 through 5 and row 7 through A of each column from 1 through G of Table 20.5 shows the 4-bit bit sequences of the corresponding hexadecimal numbers of the index of each element of the given S-box and each element of the S-box itself. Each row from 2 through 5 and 7 through A from column 1 through G constitutes a 16 bit bit sequence that is a BP over Galois field GF(2^{15}). Column 1 through G of row 2 has been termed as 4th IGFP, row 3 has been termed as 3rd IGFP, row 4 has been termed as 2nd IGFP, and row 5 has been termed as IGFP, whereas column 1 through G of row 7 has been termed as 4th OGFP, row 8 has been termed as 3rd OGFP, row 9 has been termed as 2nd OGFP, and row A has been termed as 1st OGFP. The decimal equivalents of each IGFP and OGFP have been noted at column H of respective rows, where IGFP stands for Input Galois Field Polynomial and OGFP stands for Output Galois Field Polynomial. The respective polynomials have been shown in row 1 through 8 of column 3 of Table 20.6.

Table 20.4   4-Bit Identity Crypto S-Box

Row	Column	1	2	3	4	5	6	7	8	9	A	B	C	D	E	F	G
1	Index	0	1	2	3	4	5	6	7	8	9	A	B	C	D	E	F
2	S-Box	0	1	2	3	4	5	6	7	8	9	A	B	C	D	E	F

Table 20.5 Input and Output BCNs of the Identity S-Box

Row	Column	1	2	3	4	5	6	7	8	9	A	B	C	D	E	F	G	H. Decimal Equivalent
1	Index	0	1	2	3	4	5	6	7	8	9	A	B	C	D	E	F	
2	IBCN4	0	0	0	0	0	0	0	0	1	1	1	1	1	1	1	1	00,255
3	IBCN3	0	0	0	0	1	1	1	1	0	0	0	0	1	1	1	1	03,855
4	IBCN2	0	0	1	1	0	0	1	1	0	0	1	1	0	0	1	1	13,107
5	IBCN1	0	1	0	1	0	1	0	1	0	1	0	1	0	1	0	1	21,845
6	S-Box	0	1	2	3	4	5	6	7	8	9	A	B	C	D	E	F	
7	OBCN4	0	0	0	0	0	0	0	0	1	1	1	1	1	1	1	1	00,255
8	OBCN3	0	0	0	0	1	1	1	1	0	0	0	0	1	1	1	1	03,855
9	OBCN2	0	0	1	1	0	0	1	1	0	0	1	1	0	0	1	1	13,107
A	OBCN1	0	1	0	1	0	1	0	1	0	1	0	1	0	1	0	1	21,845

Table 20.6 Respective Polynomials of IGFP4 through IGFP1 and OGFP4 through OGFP1

Col.	1	2	3
Row	Index	DCM Eqv.	Polynomials over Galois Field GF(2^{15})
1	IGFP4	00,255	$BP(x) = x^7 + x^6 + x^5 + x^4 + x^3 + x^2 + x^1 + 1$
2	IGFP3	03,855	$BP(x) = x^{11} + x^{10} + x^9 + x^8 + x^3 + x^2 + x^1 + 1$
3	IGFP2	13,107	$BP(x) = x^{13} + x^{12} + x^9 + x^8 + x^5 + x^4 + x^1 + 1$
4	IGFP1	21,845	$BP(x) = x^{14} + x^{12} + x^{10} + x^8 + x^6 + x^4 + x^2 + 1$
5	OGFP4	00,255	$BP(x) = x^7 + x^6 + x^5 + x^4 + x^3 + x^2 + x^1 + 1$
6	OGFP3	03,855	$BP(x) = x^{11} + x^{10} + x^9 + x^8 + x^3 + x^2 + x^1 + 1$
7	OGFP2	13,107	$BP(x) = x^{13} + x^{12} + x^9 + x^8 + x^5 + x^4 + x^1 + 1$
8	OGFP1	21,845	$BP(x) = x^{14} + x^{12} + x^{10} + x^8 + x^6 + x^4 + x^2 + 1$

20.3.2.2 Generation of 8-Bit Identity Crypto S-Box from Eight Polynomials Over Binary Galois Field GF(2^{255})

The concerned 8-bit identity S-box has been shown in Table 20.7, where each element of the 1st row of Table 20.7, entitled as index, is the position of each element of the S-box within the given S-box and the elements of the column 1 through G of 2nd to 17th row, entitled as S-box, have been the elements of the given 8-bit identity S-box sequentially. It can be concluded that the 1st row is fixed for all possible 8-bit bijective crypto S-boxes. The values of each element of the 1st row are distinct, unique, and vary between 0 and F. The values of the each element of the column 1 through G of 2nd row to 17th row of the 8-bit identity crypto S-box are also distinct, unique, and

Table 20.7 8-Bit Identity Crypto S-Box

Row	Column	1	2	3	4	5	6	7	8	9	A	B	C	D	E	F	G
1	Index	0	1	2	3	4	5	6	7	8	9	A	B	C	D	E	F
2	S-Box	0	1	2	3	4	5	6	7	8	9	10	11	12	13	14	15
3		16	17	18	19	20	21	22	23	24	25	26	27	28	29	30	31
4		32	33	34	35	36	37	38	39	40	41	42	43	44	45	46	47
5		48	49	50	51	52	53	54	55	56	57	58	59	60	61	62	63
6		64	65	66	67	68	69	70	71	72	73	74	75	76	77	78	79
7		80	81	82	83	84	85	86	87	88	89	90	91	92	93	94	95
8		96	97	98	99	100	101	102	103	104	105	106	107	108	109	110	111
9		112	113	114	115	116	117	118	119	120	121	122	123	124	125	126	127
10		128	129	130	131	132	133	134	135	136	137	138	139	140	141	142	143
11		144	145	146	147	148	149	150	151	152	153	154	155	156	157	158	159
12		160	161	162	163	164	165	166	167	168	169	170	171	172	173	174	175
13		176	177	178	179	180	181	182	183	184	185	186	187	188	189	190	191
14		192	193	194	195	196	197	198	199	200	201	202	203	204	205	206	207
15		208	209	210	211	212	213	214	215	216	217	218	219	220	221	222	223
16		224	225	226	227	228	229	230	231	232	233	234	235	236	237	238	239
17		240	241	242	243	244	245	246	247	248	249	250	251	252	253	254	255

vary between 0 and 256. The values of the elements of the fixed 1st row are sequential and monotonically increasing, whereas for the 2nd to 17th row, they can be sequential or partly sequential or nonsequential, and for this case, elements are sequential and monotonically increasing. Here, the given S-box has been the 8-bit identity crypto S-box.

Index of each element of an 8-bit crypto S-box and the element itself is a hexadecimal number and that can be converted into a 256-bit long 8-bit bit sequence. From row 2 through 9 and row A through H of column 2 of Table 20.8 shows the 8-bit bit sequences of the corresponding hexadecimal numbers of the index of each element of the given S-box and each element of the S-box itself. Each row from 2 through 9 and A through H of column 2 constitutes a 256 bit bit sequence that is a BP over Galois field GF(2^{255}). Column 2 of row 2 has been termed as 8th IGFP, row 3 has been termed as 7th IGFP, row 4 has been termed as 6th IGFP, row 5 has been termed as 5th IGFP,

Table 20.8   BCNs for 8 IGFPs and OGFPs

Row	Col.	
1	1	**MSB Polynomials (BCNs)[col.2] LSB**
2	IGFP 8	0000000000000000000000000000000000000000000000000000000000000000 0000000000000000000000000000000000000000000000000000000000000000 1111111111111111111111111111111111111111111111111111111111111111 1111111111111111111111111111111111111111111111111111111111111111
3	IGFP 7	0000000000000000000000000000000000000000000000000000000000000000 1111111111111111111111111111111111111111111111111111111111111111 0000000000000000000000000000000000000000000000000000000000000000 1111111111111111111111111111111111111111111111111111111111111111
4	IGFP 6	0000000000000000000000000000000011111111111111111111111111111111 0000000000000000000000000000000011111111111111111111111111111111 0000000000000000000000000000000011111111111111111111111111111111 0000000000000000000000000000000011111111111111111111111111111111
5	IGFP 5	0000000000000000111111111111111100000000000000001111111111111111 0000000000000000111111111111111100000000000000001111111111111111 0000000000000000111111111111111100000000000000001111111111111111 0000000000000000111111111111111100000000000000001111111111111111
6	IGFP 4	0000000011111111000000001111111100000000111111110000000011111111 0000000011111111000000001111111100000000111111110000000011111111 0000000011111111000000001111111100000000111111110000000011111111 0000000011111111000000001111111100000000111111110000000011111111
7	IGFP 3	0000111100001111000011110000111100001111000011110000111100001111 0000111100001111000011110000111100001111000011110000111100001111 0000111100001111000011110000111100001111000011110000111100001111 0000111100001111000011110000111100001111000011110000111100001111
8	IGFP 2	0011001100110011001100110011001100110011001100110011001100110011 0011001100110011001100110011001100110011001100110011001100110011 0011001100110011001100110011001100110011001100110011001100110011 0011001100110011001100110011001100110011001100110011001100110011

(Contiuned)

Table 20.8 (*Continued*) BCNs for 8 IGFPs and OGFPs

Row	Col.	MSB Polynomials (BCNs)[col.2] LSB
9	IGFP 1	0101010101010101010101010101010101010101010101010101010101010101 0101010101010101010101010101010101010101010101010101010101010101 0101010101010101010101010101010101010101010101010101010101010101 0101010101010101010101010101010101010101010101010101010101010101
A	OGFP8	0000000000000000000000000000000000000000000000000000000000000000 0000000000000000000000000000000000000000000000000000000000000000 1111111111111111111111111111111111111111111111111111111111111111 1111111111111111111111111111111111111111111111111111111111111111
B	OGFP 7	0000000000000000000000000000000000000000000000000000000000000000 1111111111111111111111111111111111111111111111111111111111111111 0000000000000000000000000000000000000000000000000000000000000000 1111111111111111111111111111111111111111111111111111111111111111
C	OGFP 6	0000000000000000000000000000000111111111111111111111111111111111 0000000000000000000000000000000111111111111111111111111111111111 0000000000000000000000000000000111111111111111111111111111111111 0000000000000000000000000000000111111111111111111111111111111111
D	OGFP 5	0000000000000000111111111111111100000000000000001111111111111111 0000000000000000111111111111111100000000000000001111111111111111 0000000000000000111111111111111100000000000000001111111111111111 0000000000000000111111111111111100000000000000001111111111111111
E	OGFP 4	0000000011111111000000001111111100000000111111110000000011111111 0000000011111111000000001111111100000000111111110000000011111111 0000000011111111000000001111111100000000111111110000000011111111 0000000011111111000000001111111100000000111111110000000011111111
F	OGFP 3	0000111100001111000011110000111100001111000011110000111100001111 0000111100001111000011110000111100001111000011110000111100001111 0000111100001111000011110000111100001111000011110000111100001111 0000111100001111000011110000111100001111000011110000111100001111
G	OGFP 2	0011001100110011001100110011001100110011001100110011001100110011 0011001100110011001100110011001100110011001100110011001100110011 0011001100110011001100110011001100110011001100110011001100110011 0011001100110011001100110011001100110011001100110011001100110011
H	OGFP 1	0101010101010101010101010101010101010101010101010101010101010101 0101010101010101010101010101010101010101010101010101010101010101 0101010101010101010101010101010101010101010101010101010101010101 0101010101010101010101010101010101010101010101010101010101010101

row 6 has been termed as 4th IGFP, row 7 has been termed as 3rd IGFP, row 8 has been termed as 2nd IGFP, and row 9 has been termed as 1st IGFP, whereas column 2 of row A has been termed as 8th OGFP, row B has been termed as 7th OGFP, row C has been termed as 6th OGFP, row D has been termed as 5th OGFP, row E has been termed as 4th OGFP, row *F* has been termed as 3rd OGFP, row G has been termed as 2nd OGFP, and row H has been termed as 1st IGFP. The BCN

Table 20.9   Respective Polynomial of IGFP8 and OGFP8 of the Given 8-Bit S-Box

BCNs of	Polynomial
IGFP8 & OGFP8	$x^{127} + x^{126} + x^{125} + x^{124} + x^{123} + x^{122} + x^{121} + x^{120} + x^{119} + x^{118} + x^{117} + x^{116} + x^{115} + x^{114} + x^{113} + x^{112} + x^{111} + x^{110} + x^{109} + x^{108} + x^{107} + x^{106} + x^{105} + x^{104} + x^{103} + x^{102} + x^{101} + x^{100} + x^{99} + x^{98} + x^{97} + x^{96} + x^{95} + x^{94} + x^{93} + x^{92} + x^{91} + x^{90} + x^{89} + x^{88} + x^{87} + x^{86} + x^{85} + x^{84} + x^{83} + x^{82} + x^{81} + x^{80} + x^{79} + x^{78} + x^{77} + x^{76} + x^{75} + x^{74} + x^{73} + x^{72} + x^{71} + x^{70} + x^{69} + x^{68} + x^{67} + x^{66} + x^{65} + x^{64} + x^{63} + x^{62} + x^{61} + x^{60} + x^{59} + x^{58} + x^{57} + x^{56} + x^{55} + x^{54} + x^{53} + x^{52} + x^{51} + x^{50} + x^{49} + x^{48} + x^{47} + x^{46} + x^{45} + x^{44} + x^{43} + x^{42} + x^{41} + x^{40} + x^{39} + x^{38} + x^{37} + x^{36} + x^{35} + x^{34} + x^{33} + x^{32} + x^{31} + x^{30} + x^{29} + x^{28} + x^{27} + x^{26} + x^{25} + x^{24} + x^{23} + x^{22} + x^{21} + x^{20} + x^{19} + x^{18} + x^{17} + x^{16} + x^{15} + x^{14} + x^{13} + x^{12} + x^{11} + x^{10} + x^9 + x^8 + x^7 + x^6 + x^5 + x^4 + x^3 + x^2 + x + 1$

of each IGFP and OGFP from MSB [256th bit] to LSB [0th bit] has been given in corresponding rows of each IGFP and OGFP, where IGFP stands for Input Galois Field Polynomial and OGFP for Output Galois Field Polynomial. The respective polynomial for IGFP8 and OGFP8 has been shown in Table 20.9.

20.3.2.3 Algorithm to Generate S-Box from Polynomials Over Galois field GF(2^{15}) or GF(2^{255})

START

  Step OA: Choose 4 Galois field polynomials over Galois field GF(2^{15}) or 8 Galois field polynomials over Galois field GF(2^{255}).

  Step 01: If the number of terms in BCNs is half of the number of total terms, then Step 02. Else Step 0A.

  Step 02: Convert to decimal the 4- or 8-bit binary number generated by bits in the same position of 4 BCNs for Galois field polynomials over Galois field GF(2^{15}) or 8 Galois field polynomials over Galois field GF(2^{255}).

  STOP

  Time Complexity of the given Algorithm O(n).

20.3.3 4- and 8-Bit S-Box Generation by Respective BCNs Over Nonbinary Galois Field GF(16^{15}) and Galois Field GF(256^{255})

The coefficients of each polynomial over nonbinary Galois field GF(16^{15}) form a 4-bit S-box. The coefficient of the highest or lowest degree term must be the 1st element in 4-bit S-box, and the value of other elements is the value of coefficients with immediate degree less or greater than the previous one. Let the polynomial be

$$BP(x) = 0x^{15} + 1x^{14} + 2x^{13} + 3x^{12} + 4x^{11} + 5x^{10}$$

$$+ 6x^9 + 7x^8 + 8x^7 + 9x^6 + 10x^5 + 11x^4$$

$$+ 12x^3 + 13x^2 + 14x + 15 \ldots \tag{20.2}$$

For the above polynomial, the constituted 4-bit S-box has been given in Table 20.10.

  The polynomial with coefficients in reverse order:

Table 20.10 Constituted 4-Bit Crypto S-Box

Row	Column	1	2	3	4	5	6	7	8	9	A	B	C	D	E	F	G
1	Index	0	1	2	3	4	5	6	7	8	9	A	B	C	D	E	F
2	S-box	0	1	2	3	4	5	6	7	8	9	A	B	C	D	E	F

Table 20.11 Constituted 4-Bit Crypto S-Box

Row	Column	1	2	3	4	5	6	7	8	9	A	B	C	D	E	F	G
1	Index	0	1	2	3	4	5	6	7	8	9	A	B	C	D	E	F
2	S-box	15	14	13	12	11	10	9	8	7	6	5	4	3	2	1	0

$$BP(x) = 15x^{15} + 14x^{14} + 13x^{13} + 12x^{12} + 11x^{11}$$

$$+ 10x^{10} + 9x^9 + 8x^8 + 7x^7 + 6x^6 + 5x^5 \tag{20.3}$$

$$+ 4x^4 + 3x^3 + 2x^2 + 1x + 0 \ldots$$

For the above polynomial, the constituted 4-bit S-box has been given in Table 20.11.

The coefficients of each polynomial over nonbinary Galois field GF(256^{255}) form an 8-bit S-box. The coefficient of the highest or lowest degree term must be the 1st element in 4-bit S-box, and the value of other elements is the value of coefficients with immediate degree less or greater than the previous one. Let the polynomial be the one given in Table 20.12.

For the above polynomial, the constituted 8-bit S-box has been given in Table 20.13.

Note: The 32-bit S-boxes can be constituted by polynomials over Galois field $\text{GF}\left[(232)^{\left(2^{32}-1\right)}\right]$, and the 64-bit S-boxes can be constituted by polynomials over Galois field $\text{GF}\left[(264)^{2^{64}-1}\right]$.

20.3.4 Cryptographic Analysis of 32 DES 4-Bit S-Boxes and 10 Better 4-Bit S-Boxes with Relevant Cryptographic Properties of 4-Bit Crypto S-Boxes

In Section 20.3.4.1., the cryptographic analysis procedures of the said cryptographic properties have been described. The cryptographic analysis of 32 DES 4-bit S-boxes has been evaluated in Section 20.3.4.2. Cryptographic analysis of ten generated better S-boxes has been described in Section 20.3.4.3.

20.3.4.1 Analysis Procedure

For SAC, HO-SAC, and Extended SAC of 4-bit S-boxes as the numbers of satisfied COPBFs have been increased, it will give better security and optimum value given at most security.

In DDT, there have been 256 cells, i.e., 16 rows and 16 columns. Each row has been for each input difference that varies from 0 to *F*. Each column in each row represents each output difference varies from 0 to *F* for each input difference. 0 in any cell indicates the absence of that output

Table 20.12 Polynomial to Construct 8-Bit Identity S-Box

Polynomial BP(x) =

$0x^{255} + 1x^{254} + 2x^{253} + 3x^{252} + 4x^{251} + 5x^{250} + 6x^{249} + 7x^{248} + 8x^{247} + 9x^{246} + 10x^{245} + 11x^{244} + 12x^{243} +$
$13x^{242} + 14x^{241} + 15x^{240} + 16x^{239} + 17x^{238} + 18x^{237} + 19x^{236} + 20x^{235} + 21x^{234} + 22x^{233} + 23x^{232} + 24x^{231} +$
$25x^{230} + 26x^{229} + 27x^{228} + 28x^{227} + 29x^{226} + 30x^{225} + 31x^{224} + 32x^{223} + 33x^{222} + 34x^{221} + 35x^{220} + 36x^{219} +$
$37x^{218} + 38x^{217} + 39x^{216} + 40x^{215} + 41x^{214} + 42x^{213} + 43x^{212} + 44x^{211} + 45x^{210} + 46x^{209} + 47x^{208} + 48x^{207} +$
$49x^{206} + 50x^{205} + 51x^{204} + 52x^{203} + 53x^{202} + 54x^{201} + 55x^{200} + 56x^{199} + 57x^{198} + 58x^{197} + 59x^{196} + 60x^{195} +$
$61x^{194} + 62x^{193} + 63x^{192} + 64x^{191} + 65x^{190} + 66x^{189} + 67x^{188} + 68x^{187} + 69x^{186} + 70x^{185} + 71x^{184} + 72x^{183} +$
$73x^{182} + 74x^{181} + 75x^{180} + 76x^{179} + 77x^{178} + 78x^{177} + 79x^{176} + 80x^{175} + 81x^{174} + 82x^{173} + 83x^{172} + 84x^{171} +$
$85x^{170} + 86x^{169} + 87x^{168} + 88x^{167} + 89x^{166} + 90x^{165} + 91x^{164} + 92x^{163} + 93x^{162} + 94x^{161} + 95x^{160} + 96x^{159} +$
$97x^{158} + 98x^{157} + 99x^{156} + 100x^{155} + 101x^{154} + 102x^{153} + 103x^{152} + 104x^{151} + 105x^{150} + 106x^{149} + 107x^{148} +$
$108x^{147} + 109x^{146} + 110x^{145} + 111x^{144} + 112x^{143} + 113x^{142} + 114x^{141} + 115x^{140} + 116x^{139} + 117x^{138} +$
$118x^{137} + 119x^{136} + 120x^{135} + 121x^{134} + 122x^{133} + 123x^{132} + 124x^{131} + 125x^{130} + 126x^{129} + 127x^{128} +$
$128x^{127} + 129x^{126} + 130x^{125} + 131x^{124} + 132x^{123} + 133x^{122} + 134x^{121} + 135x^{120} + 136x^{119} + 137x^{118} +$
$138x^{117} + 139x^{116} + 140x^{115} + 141x^{114} + 142x^{113} + 143x^{112} + 144x^{111} + 145x^{110} + 146x^{109} + 147x^{108} +$
$148x^{107} + 149x^{106} + 150x^{105} + 151x^{104} + 152x^{103} + 153x^{102} + 154x^{101} + 155x^{100} + 156x^{99} + 157x^{98} + 158x^{97} +$
$159x^{96} + 160x^{95} + 161x^{94} + 162x^{93} + 163x^{92} + 164x^{91} + 165x^{90} + 166x^{89} + 167x^{88} + 168x^{87} + 169x^{86} +$
$170x^{85} + 171x^{84} + 172x^{83} + 173x^{82} + 174x^{81} + 175x^{80} + 176x^{79} + 177x^{78} + 178x^{77} + 179x^{76} + 180x^{75} +$
$181x^{74} + 182x^{73} + 183x^{72} + 184x^{71} + 185x^{70} + 186x^{69} + 187x^{68} + 188x^{67} + 189x^{66} + 190x^{65} + 191x^{64} +$
$192x^{63} + 193x^{62} + 194x^{61} + 195x^{60} + 196x^{59} + 197x^{58} + 198x^{57} + 199x^{56} + 200x^{55} + 201x^{54} + 202x^{53} +$
$203x^{52} + 204x^{51} + 205x^{50} + 206x^{49} + 207x^{48} + 208x^{47} + 209x^{46} + 210x^{45} + 211x^{44} + 212x^{43} + 213x^{42} +$
$214x^{41} + 215x^{40} + 216x^{39} + 217x^{38} + 218x^{37} + 219x^{36} + 220x^{35} + 221x^{34} + 222x^{33} + 223x^{32} + 224x^{31} +$
$225x^{30} + 226x^{29} + 227x^{28} + 228x^{27} + 229x^{26} + 230x^{25} + 231x^{24} + 232x^{23} + 233x^{22} + 234x^{21} + 235x^{20} +$
$236x^{19} + 237x^{18} + 238x^{17} + 239x^{16} + 240x^{15} + 241x^{14} + 242x^{13} + 243x^{12} + 244x^{11} + 245x^{10} + 246x^{9} +$
$247x^{8} + 248x^{7} + 249x^{6} + 250x^{5} + 251x^{4} + 252x^{3} + 253x^{2} + 254x + 255$

difference for subsequent input difference. Such as 0 in 2nd cell of Table 20.7 of relevant DDT means for input difference 0 the corresponding output difference 0 has been absent. If the number of 0s is too low or too high, it supplies more information regarding concerned output difference. So an S-box is said to be immune to this cryptanalytic attack if the number of 0s in DDT is close to 128 or half of total cells or 256. In the said example of 1st DES 4-bit S-box, total numbers of 0s in DDT are 168. That is close to 128. So, the S-box has been said to be almost secure from this attack.

As the total number of balanced 4-bit BFs increases in Difference Analysis Table or DAT, the security of S-box increases since balanced 4-bit BFs supplies at most uncertainty. Since number of 0s and 1s in balanced 4-bit BFs are equal, i.e., they are same in number! that means determination of each bit is at most uncertainty. In the said example of 1st DES 4-bit S-box, the total number of 8s in DAT is 36. That is close to 32 half of total 64 cells. So, the S-box has been said to be almost less secure from this attack.

In Linear Analysis Table or LAT, there are 256 cells for 256 possible 4-bit linear relations. The count of 16 4-bit binary conditions to satisfy for any given linear relation has been put into the concerned cell. Eight in a cell indicates that the particular linear relation has been satisfied for eight 4-bit binary conditions and remains unsatisfied for eight 4-bit binary conditions. That is at most uncertainty. In the said example of 1st DES 4-bit S-box, the total number of 8s in LAT has been 143. That is close to 128. So, the S-box has been said to be less secure from this attack.

Table 20.13 Constituted Identity 8-Bit S-Box

Row	Column	1	2	3	4	5	6	7	8	9	A	B	C	D	E	F	G
1	Index	0	1	2	3	4	5	6	7	8	9	A	B	C	D	E	F
2	S-box	0	1	2	3	4	5	6	7	8	9	10	11	12	13	14	15
3		16	17	18	19	20	21	22	23	24	25	26	27	28	29	30	31
4		32	33	34	35	36	37	38	39	40	41	42	43	44	45	46	47
5		48	49	50	51	52	53	54	55	56	57	58	59	60	61	62	63
6		64	65	66	67	68	69	70	71	72	73	74	75	76	77	78	79
7		80	81	82	83	84	85	86	87	88	89	90	91	92	93	94	95
8		96	97	98	99	100	101	102	103	104	105	106	107	108	109	110	111
9		112	113	114	115	116	117	118	119	120	121	122	123	124	125	126	127
10		128	129	130	131	132	133	134	135	136	137	138	139	140	141	142	143
11		144	145	146	147	148	149	150	151	152	153	154	155	156	157	158	159
12		160	161	162	163	164	165	166	167	168	169	170	171	172	173	174	175
13		176	177	178	179	180	181	182	183	184	185	186	187	188	189	190	191
14		192	193	194	195	196	197	198	199	200	201	202	203	204	205	206	207
15		208	209	210	211	212	213	214	215	216	217	218	219	220	221	222	223
16		224	225	226	227	228	229	230	231	232	233	234	235	236	237	238	239
17		240	241	242	243	244	245	246	247	248	249	250	251	252	253	254	255

The value of ^nC_r has been the maximum when the value of r is 1/2 of the value of n (when n is even). Here, the maximum number of linear approximations is 64. So if the total satisfaction of linear equation is 32 out of 64, then the number of possible sets of 32 linear equations has been the largest. Means if the total satisfaction is 32 out of 64, then the number of possible sets of 32 possible linear equations is $^{64}C_{32}$. That is the maximum number of possible sets of linear equations. If the value of the total number of linear approximations is closed to 32, then it is more cryptanalysis immune. The number of possible sets of linear equations is too large to calculate. As the value goes close to 0 or 64, it reduces the sets of possible linear equations to search, that reduces the effort to search for the linear equations present in a particular 4-bit S-box. In this example, total satisfaction is 21 out of 64, which means the given 4-bit S-box is not a good 4-bit S-box or not a good crypt analytically immune S-box.

If the values of the total number of existing linear equations for a 4-bit S-box are 24–32, then the lowest numbers of sets of linear equations are 250649105469666120. This is a very large number to investigate. So, the 4-bit S-box is declared as a good 4-bit S-box or 4-bit S-box with good security. If it is between 16 and 23, then the lowest numbers of sets of linear equations are 488526937079580. This not a small number to investigate in today's computing scenario, so the S-Boxes are declared as medium S-box or S-box with medium security. The 4-bit S-boxes having the existing linear equations less than 16 are declared as poor 4-bit S-box or vulnerable to cryptanalytic attack.

20.3.4.2 Cryptographic Analysis of 32 DES 4-Bit S-Boxes

The cryptographic analysis of 32 DES 4-bit S-boxes with the said relevant cryptographic properties of 4-bit BFs has been given in Table 20.14. Here in the table, column heading 'noelr' gives numbers of existing linear relations in a particular 4-bit crypto S-box. Column heading 'nobal' gives numbers of balanced DBFs in linear cryptanalysis. 'n0dif' gives numbers of 0s in DDT, and 'nodif' gives numbers of 8s in DAT. 'nosac' gives numbers of COPBFs that satisfy SAC of 4-bit

Table 20.14 Cryptographic Analysis of 32 DES S-Boxes

S-Box	noelr	nobal	n0dif	nodif	nosac	n2sac	n3sac	nalsac
e4d12fb83a6c5907	21	143	168	36	7	15	11	36
0f74e2d1a6cb9538	29	143	168	36	7	17	9	36
41e8d62bfc973a50	23	138	168	36	8	15	11	36
fc8249175b3ea06d	25	154	166	42	10	20	12	42
f18e6b34972dc05a	24	132	162	30	6	12	9	30
3d47f28ec01a69b5	21	143	166	30	8	12	7	30
0e7ba4d158c6932f	31	143	166	21	4	10	6	21
d8a13f42b67c05e9	20	126	168	36	8	12	12	36
a09e63f51dc7b428	17	133	162	30	7	12	8	30

(Continued)

Table 20.14 (*Continued*) Cryptographic Analysis of 32 DES S-Boxes

S-Box	noelr	nobal	n0dif	nodif	nosac	n2sac	n3sac	nalsac
d709346a285ecbf1	22	133	168	30	7	13	8	30
d6498f30b12c5ae7	23	151	166	21	6	9	4	21
1ad069874fe3b52c	28	158	174	30	6	11	10	30
7de3069a1285bc4f	22	136	168	36	8	16	10	36
d8b56f03472c1ae9	22	136	168	36	8	16	10	36
a690cb7df13e5284	20	136	168	36	8	16	10	36
3f06a1d8945bc72e	22	136	168	36	8	16	10	36
2c417ab6853fd0e9	25	137	162	30	6	14	8	30
eb2c47d150fa3986	20	143	166	36	8	16	9	36
421bad78f9c5630e	30	130	160	27	6	11	7	27
b8c71e2d6f09a453	21	134	166	18	3	7	6	18
c1af92680d34e75b	30	141	159	36	8	16	10	36
af427c9561de0b38	29	127	164	36	7	15	11	36
9ef528c3704a1db6	24	127	168	18	5	7	5	18
432c95fabe17608d	24	130	162	30	6	12	9	30
4b2ef08d3c975a61	26	134	168	30	7	13	8	30
d0b7491ae35c2f86	27	145	166	30	7	14	7	30
14bdc37eaf680592	28	137	168	36	8	16	10	36
6bd814a7950fe23c	25	135	173	0	0	0	0	0
d2846fb1a93e50c7	23	144	161	30	8	14	7	30
1fd8a374c56b0e92	20	147	174	27	9	12	4	27
7b419ce206adf358	27	132	166	18	5	7	5	18
21e74a8dfc90356b	28	138	168	39	8	16	12	39

BFs, and 'n3sac,' 'n3sac,' and 'nalsac' give numbers of COPBFs that satisfy 2nd-order SAC of 4-bit BFs, 3rd-order SAC of 4-bit BFs, and Extended SAC of 4-bit BFs, respectively.

20.3.4.3 Cryptographic Analysis of Ten Generated Better 4-Bit S-Boxes

The cryptographic analysis of ten generated better 4-bit S-boxes with the said relevant cryptographic properties of 4-bit BFs has been given in Table 20.15. Here in the table, column heading 'noelr' gives numbers of existing linear relations in a particular 4-bit crypto S-box. Column

Table 20.15 Cryptographic Analysis of ten Generated Better 4-Bit S-Boxes

S-Box	noelr	nobal	n0dif	nodif	nosac	n2sac	n3sac	nalsac
01235b8694ca7def	33	162	189	39	16	7	16	39
01235b86a4f97edc	33	200	206	45	16	13	16	45
10324a967b8fced5	27	156	175	39	16	11	8	39
103268957abcfde4	31	147	167	42	16	12	11	42
0132c5794a86fbed	26	164	189	39	16	7	16	39
1032c5684a97ebfd	28	162	189	39	16	7	16	39
1032c56879a4dbfe	27	196	206	39	16	7	16	39
1023c46a5b87e9fd	35	148	182	42	16	9	16	42
0123c7495b86eadf	23	149	170	42	16	11	13	42
103249adc65be87f	30	134	166	39	16	8	13	39

heading 'nobal' gives numbers of balanced DBFs in linear cryptanalysis. 'n0dif' gives numbers of 0s in DDT, and 'nodif' gives numbers of 8s in DAT. 'nosac' gives numbers of COPBFs that satisfy SAC of 4-bit BFs, and 'n3sac,''n3sac,' and 'nalsac' give numbers of COPBFs that satisfy 2nd-order SAC of 4-bit BFs, 3rd-order SAC of 4-bit BFs, and Extended SAC of 4-bit BFs, respectively.

20.3.5 Results and Discussion

In Table 20.14, out of 32 DES S-boxes, 1 have 17, 3 have 21, 4 have 22, 1 have 23, 3 have 24, 3 have 25, 1 have 26, 2 have 27, 3 have 28, 2 have 29, 2 have 30, and 1 have 31 existing linear relations, i.e., 24 S-boxes out of 32 have been less secure from this attack and 8 out of 32 have been immune to this attack. Again out of 32 DES S-boxes, 1 have 126, 2 have 127, 2 have 130, 1 have 132, 2 have 133, 2 have 134, 1 have 135, 4 have 136, 2 have 137, 2 have 138, 1 have 141, 5 have 143, 1 have 144, 1 have 145, 1 have 147, 1 have 151, 1 have 154, and 1 have 158 8s in LAT. That is all S-boxes are less immune to this attack. Again out of 32 DES S-boxes, 1 have 159, 1 have 160, 1 have 161, 4 have 162, 1 have 164, 8 have 166, 13 have 168, 1 have 173, and 2 have 174 0s in DDT. That is all S-boxes have been secured from this attack. At last out of 32 DES S-boxes, 1 have 0, 3 have 18, 2 have 21, 2 have 27, 10 have 30, 12 have 36, 1 have 39, and 1 have 42 8s in DAT, i.e., they have been less secure to this attack. The comparative analysis has proved that linear approximation analysis has been the most time-efficient cryptanalytic algorithm for 4-bit S-boxes. In 'nosac,' the lowest value is 0 and the maximum value is 10, whereas in 'n2sac,' 'n3sac,' and 'nalsac', the lowest values are 0, 0, and 0 and the maximum values are 16, 12, and 39, respectively. But numbers of optimum as well as better result, i.e., 16 for 'nosac' is absent, close to 24 for 'n2sac', close to 16 for 'n3sac,' and close to 64 for 'nalsac', have been very less. So, the 32 DES 4-bit S-boxes have been observed to be less secure.

But in Table 20.15, out of ten generated better 4-bit S-boxes the range of 'noelr' has been 27– 33, so it can be concluded that these S-boxes have been more immune to this attack. Now, the range of 'nobal' has been 134–200, i.e., very secure to linear cryptanalysis since the number of 8s in LAT is very large. Again, the range of 'n0dif' has been 166–206, i.e., the result is very similar to

32 DES 4-bit S-boxes. Now, in all ten 4-bit S-boxes, the 'nosac' have been 16, i.e., they satisfy SAC of 4-bit S-boxes. Again, the ranges of 'n2sac,' 'n3sac,' 'nalsac' have been 7–13, 13–16, and 39–45, respectively, i.e., most of them satisfies 3rd-order SAC of 4-bit S-boxes, and for 2nd-order SAC of 4-bit S-boxes, the results have been very similar to DES 4-bit S-boxes. In the case of 'nalsac' or Extended SAC, the results are better than DES 32 4-bit S-boxes.

Now, it is to be noted that all non-crypto S-boxes and 16! Crypto S-boxes can be generated by these two procedures by IPs over Galois field GF(p^q). The crypto S-boxes have then be chosen through the analysis of relevant cryptographic properties of 4-bit S-boxes. The procedure is the same for 8-, 16-, 32-, and 64-bit S-boxes. The generated 8-, 16-, 32-, or 64-bit S-boxes can be chosen like the way the 4-bit S-boxes have been chosen in this chapter.

20.4 Conclusion

From results and discussion, it can be concluded that generated and analyzed 4-bit S-boxes are better S-boxes than the 32 4-bit DES S-boxes. All algorithms of cryptographic properties and S-box generation have been given in the chapter. The reviews and algorithms have been presented in a very lucid manner in the chapter for convenient understanding of readers. The generation of 4- and 8-bit S-boxes has been very easy and lucid, and the chosen generated 4-bit S-boxes can be claimed to be the best 4- and 8-bit S-boxes.

Acknowledgment

For this exhaustive work, I would like to acknowledge my supervisors Dr. Ranjan Ghosh, Associate Professor, Institute of Radio Physics and Electronics, University of Calcutta and Prof. (Dr.) Amlan Chakrabarti Dean, Faculty Council of Postgraduate Studies in Engineering and Technology, University of Calcutta for their continuous encouragement and help. I would also like to acknowledge Prof. (Dr.) Debatosh Guha Head Dept. Institute of Radio Physics and Electronics, University of Calcutta for providing me with the nice infrastructure.

Key Terminology and Definitions

Substitution box (S-box): S-boxes have often been used in encryption and decryption algorithms or ciphers of public key cryptography. It consists of values from 0 to F for 4-bit S-boxes arranged in a random manner. It has been used for nonlinear substitution of plaintext or cipher-text bit stream.

Irreducible Polynomials (IPs): BPs with factors of CP and BP itself have been termed as IPs.

Finite Fields or Galois Field GF(p^q): A field with a finite number of elements has been termed as finite fields. P has been termed as prime modulus of the field, and q has been termed as extension of the field.

References

1. Adams C., Tavares S. (1990), The structured design of cryptographically good S-boxes, *Journal of Cryptology*, 344(3), 27–41.

2. Feistel H. (1971), *Block Cipher Cryptographic System*, US Patent 3798359.
3. Data Encryption Standard, Federal Information Processing Standards Publication (FIPS PUB) 46, National Bureau of Standards, Washington, DC (1977).
4. Data Encryption Standard (DES), Federal Information Processing Standards Publication (FIPS PUB) 46-3, National Institute of Standards and Technology, Gaithersburg, MD (1999).
5. Joan Daemen,Vincent Rijmen (2000), AES Proposal:Rijndael, http://csrc.nist.gov/encryption/aes/ Last Visited: February 7, 2001.
6. Vaudenay S., Moriai S. (1994), Comparison of the randomness provided by some AES candidates, *Eurocrypt*, Springer Verlag, no. 950, 386–397.
7. Adams C., Tavares S. (1990), *Journal of Cryptology*, 3, 27. doi: 10.1007/BF00203967.
8. Schneier B. (1996), *Applied Cryptography*, 2nd edn John Wiley and Sons: New York.
9. Heys H.M. (2002), A tutorial on linear and differential cryptanlysis, *Cryptologia*, 26, 189–221.
10. Heys H.M., Tavares S.E. (1996), Substitution-permutation networks resistant to differential and linear cryptanalysis. *Journal of Cryptology*, 9, 1–19.
11. Wang J., Zheng D. (2014, March 4), Simple method to find primitive polynomials of degree n over $GF(2)$ where $2^{\{n\}}-1$ is a Mersenne prime[OL]. http://www.paper.edu.cn/lwzx/en_releasepaper/content/4587059.
12. Menezes A., van Oorschot P., Vanstone S. (1996), *Handbook of Applied Cryptography*, CRC Press: Boca Raton, FL.
13. Schaefer E. (1996), A simplified data encryption standard algorithm, *Cryptologia*, 20, 77–84.
14. Schneier B. (2000), *A Self-Study Course in Block-Cipher Cryptanalysis*, Counterpane Internet Security: San Jose, CA.
15. Schneier B. et al. (1999), *The Twofish Encryption Algorithm*, John Wiley and Sons: New York.
16. Mirzan F. (2000), *Block Ciphers and Cryptanalysis*, Department of Mathematics, Royal Holloway University of London.
17. Heys H.M. (2000), *A Tutorial on Linear and Differential Cryptanalysis*, Memorial University of Newfoundland: Canada.
18. Schulzrinne H. (2000), *Network Security: Secret Key Cryptograph*, Columbia University: New York.
19. Pierson L.G. (2000), *Comparing Cryptographic Modes of Operation using Flow Diagrams*, Sandia National Labarotaries: USA.
20. Aoki K. et al. (2000), *Camellia: A 128-Bit Block Cipher Suitable for Multiple Platforms*, NTT Coporation and Mitsubishi Electric Corporation: Tokyo.
21. Singh S. (2000), *The Science of Secrecy*, Fourth Estate Limited.
22. Landau S. (2000), *Standing the Test of Time: The Data Encryption Standard*, Sun Microsystems: Palo Alto, CA.
23. Garrett P. (2001), *Making, Breaking Codes*, Prentice Hall, U.S.A.
24. Kilian J., Rogaway P. (2000), *How to Protect DES Against Exhaustive Key Search*, NEC Research Institute: USA.
25. Yeun Design C.Y. (2000), *Analysis and Applications of Cryptographic Techniques*, Department of Mathematics, Royal Holloway University of London: London.
26. Schneier B. (2001), *Why Cryptography Is Harder Than It Looks*, Counterpane Internet Security: San Francisco, CA.
27. Ooi K.S., Vito B.C. (2002), *Cryptanalysis of S-DES*, University of Sheffield Center, Taylor College, UK.
28. Schaefer E. (1996), A simplified data encryption standard algorithm, *Cryptologia*, 20, 77–84.
29. Schneier B. et al. (1999), *The Twofish Encryption Algorithm*, John Wiley and Sons: New York.
30. Buttayan L., Vajda I. (1995). Searching for best linear approximation on DES-like cryptosystems. *Electronics Letters*, 31(11), 873–874.
31. Daemen J.,Govaerts R., van de Walle J. (1995). Correlation Matrices. In: *Fast Software Encryption, Lecture Notes in Computer Science (LNCS) 1008*, Springer-Verlag: Berlin, Heidelburg, pp. 2–21.
32. Matsui M. (1994), Linear Cryptanalysis Method for DES Cipher. In: Helleseth T. (ed.) *Advances in Cryptology—EUROCRYPT '93. EUROCRYPT 1993. Lecture Notes in Computer Science*, Springer: Berlin, Heidelberg, vol. 765.
33. Biham E. (1994), *On Matsui's Linear Cryptnalysis*. Technion, Israel Institute of Technology: Israel.

34. Harpes C., Kramer G., Massey J. (1995), A generation of linear cryptanalysis and the applicability of Matsui's pilling-up lemma. *Advances in Cryptology–Eurocrypt*, 95, 24–38.
35. Kaliski B., Robshaw M. (1994), Linear cryptanalysis using multiple approximations. *Advances in Cryptology-CRYPTO*, 94, 26–39.
36. Matsui M. (1994), The first experimental cryptanalysis of data encryption standard. *Advances in Cryptology-CRYPTO*, 94, 1–11.
37. Junod P.A. (1998), *Linear Cryptanalysis of DES*, Eidgenssische Tenhcische Hochsschule: Zurich.
38. Collard B., Standaert F.X., Quisquater J.J. (2008), Experiments on the multiple linear cryptanalysis of reduced round serpent. In: Nyberg K. (ed), *Fast Software Encryption. FSE 2008. Lecture Notes in Computer Science*, Springer: Berlin, Heidelberg, vol. 5086.
39. Mouha N., Wang Q., Gu D., Preneel B. (2012), Differential and linear cryptanalysis using mixed-integer linear programming. In: Wu C.K., Yung M., Lin D. (eds), *Information Security and Cryptology. Inscrypt 2011. Lecture Notes in Computer Science*, Springer: Berlin, Heidelberg, vol. 7537.
40. Abdelraheem M.A., Alizadeh J., AlKhzaimi H., Reza Aref M., Bagheri N., Gauravaram P. (2015), Improved Linear Cryptanalysis of Reduced-Round SIMON-32 and SIMON-48, Cryptology e-print Archive, Report – 2015/988.
41. Bagheri N. (2015), Linear cryptanalysis of reduced-round SIMECK variants. In: Biryukov A., Goyal V. (eds), *Progress in Cryptology – INDOCRYPT 2015. Lecture Notes in Computer Science*, vol. 9462, Springer: Cham.
42. Yu X.L., Wu W.L., Shi Z.Q. et al. (2015), *Journal of Computer Science and Technology*, 30, 1358. doi: 10.1007/s11390-015-1603-5.
43. Canteaut A. (1997), *Differential Cryptanalysis of Fesitel Ciphers and Differentially d-Uniform Mappings*, Domaine de Voluceau: France.
44. Adams C. (1992), On immunity against Biham and Shamir's differential cryptanalysis. *Information Processing Letters*, 41, 77–80.
45. Dawson M., Tavares S. (1991), An expanded set of S-box design criteria based on information theory and its relation to differential-like attacks. *Advances in Cryptology – Eurocrypt*, 91, 353–367.
46. Biham E., Shamir A. (1990), Differential cryptanalysis of DES-like cryptosystems. *Advances in Cryptology – CRYPTO*, Springer-Verlag, 90, 2–21.
47. Biham E., Shamir A. (1991), Differential cryptanalysis of Snefru, Khafre, REDOC-II, LOKI and Lucifer. *Advances in Cryptology – CRYPTO*, Springer-Verlag, 91, 156–171.
48. Biham E., Shamir A. (1992), Differential cryptanalysis of the full 16-round DES. *Advances in Cryptology –CRYPTO*, Springer-Verlag, 92, 487–496.
49. Nyberg, K. 1991. Perfect nonlinear S-boxes. *Advances in Cryptology – Eurocrypt*, 91, 378386.
50. Lai X., Massey J.L. (1991), *Markov Ciphers and Differential Cryptanalysis*, Swiss Federal Institude of Technology, Royal Holloway University of London: London.
51. Murphy S., Robshaw M.J.B. (2002), Key-dependent S-boxes and differential cryptanalysis, *Designs, Codes and Cryptography*, 27, 229–255.
52. Youssef A., Tavares S. (1995), Resistance of balanced S-boxes to linear and differential cryptanalysis. *Information Processing Letters*, 56, 249–252.
53. Albrecht M., Cid C. (2009), Algebraic techniques in differential cryptanalysis. In: Dunkelman O. (eds), *Fast Software Encryption. Lecture Notes in Computer Science*, Springer: Berlin, Heidelberg, vol. 5665.
54. Bouillaguet C., Dunkelman O., Fouque P.A., Leurent G. (2012), New insights on impossible differential cryptanalysis. In: Miri A., Vaudenay S. (eds), *Selected Areas in Cryptography. SAC 2011. Lecture Notes in Computer Science*, Springer: Berlin, Heidelberg, vol. 7118.
55. Rajashekarappa, Sunjiv Soyjaudah K.M., Sumithra Devi K.A. (2013), Comparative study on data encryption standard using differential cryptanalysis and linear cryptanalysis, *International Journal of Advances in Engineering & Technology*, 6(1), 158–164.
56. Gerault D., Minier M., Solnon C. (2016), Constraint programming models for chosen key differential cryptanalysis. In: Rueher M. (ed), *Principles and Practice of Constraint Programming. CP 2016. Lecture Notes in Computer Science*, Springer: Cham, vol. 9892.
57. Hellman M., Langford S. (1994), Differential-linear cryptanalysis, *Crypto*, 94(839), 26–39.

58. Vaudenay S. (1995), *An Experiment on DES Statistical Cryptanalysis*. Ecole Normale Supérieure: France.
59. Gorska A. et al. (2000), *New Experimental Results in Differential-Linear Cryptanalysis of Reduced Variant of DES*, Polish Academy of Sciences: Poland.
60. Ferguson N. et al. (2001), *Improved Cryptanalysis of Rijndael*, Counterpane Internet Security: USA.
61. Ding (1993), The Differential Cryptanalysis and Design of Natural Stream Ciphers, In: *Fast Software Encryption*, Cambridge Security Workshop, LNCS 809.
62. Golic (1994), Linear Cryptanalysis of Stream Ciphers. In: *Fast Software Encryption*, Second International Workshop, LNCS 1008.
63. Tanaka M., Hamaide T., Hisamatsu K., Kaneko T. (1998), Linear cryptanalysis by linear sieve method, *IECE Transactions on Fundamentals of Electronics, Communications and Computer Science*, E81-A(1), 82–87.
64. Muller F. (2004), Differential attacks against the Helix stream cipher. In: Roy B., Meier W. (eds), *Fast Software Encryption. FSE 2004. Lecture Notes in Computer Science*, Springer, Berlin, Heidelberg, vol. 3017.
65. Wu H., Preneel B. (2007), Differential cryptanalysis of the stream ciphers Py, Py6 and Pypy. In: Naor M. (eds), *Advances in Cryptology - EUROCRYPT 2007. EUROCRYPT 2007. Lecture Notes in Computer Science*, Springer: Berlin, Heidelberg, vol. 4515.
66. Wu H., Huang T., Nguyen P.H., Wang H., Ling S. (2012), Differential attacks against stream cipher ZUC. In: Wang X., Sako K. (eds), *Advances in Cryptology – ASIACRYPT 2012. ASIACRYPT 2012. Lecture Notes in Computer Science*, Springer: Berlin, Heidelberg, vol. 7658.
67. Webster A.F., Tavares S.E. (1986), On the design of S-boxes. In: Williams H.C. (eds), *Advances in Cryptology – CRYPTO'85, Proceedings. CRYPTO 1985. Lecture Notes in Computer Science*, Springer: Berlin, Heidelberg, vol. 218.
68. Kim K., Matsumoto T., Imai H. (1991), A recursive construction method of S-boxes satisfying strict avalanche criterion. In: Menezes A.J., Vanstone S.A. (eds), *Advances in Cryptology-CRYPTO'90. CRYPTO 1990. Lecture Notes in Computer Science*. Springer: Berlin, Heidelberg, vol. 537.
69. Cusick T.W. (1994), Boolean functions satisfying a higher order strict avalanche criterion. In: Helleseth T. (eds), *Advances in Cryptology – EUROCRYPT'93. EUROCRYPT 1993. Lecture Notes in Computer Science*. Springer: Berlin, Heidelberg, vol. 765.
70. Lisiskaya I.V., Melnychuk E.D., Lisitskiy K.E. (2012), Importance of S-blocks in modern block Ciphers, *IJCN&IS*, 10, 1–12.
71. Saarinen M.J.O. (2012), Cryptographic analysis of all 4×4-bit S-boxes. In: Miri A., Vaudenay S. (eds), *Selected Areas in Cryptography. SAC 2011. Lecture Notes in Computer Science*, Springer, Berlin, Heidelberg, vol. 7118.
72. Alkhzaimi H.A., Knudsen L.R. (2016), Cryptanalysis of Selected Block Ciphers. Kgs. Lyngby: Technical University of Denmark (DTU). (DTU Compute PHD; No.360).
73. Kazlauskas K., Smailiukas R., Vaicekaus G. (2016), A novel method to design S-boxes based on key-dependent permutation schemes and its quality analysis, IJACSA, 7(4), 93–99.
74. Ahmad M., Mittal N., Garg P., Maftab Khan M. (2016), Efficient cryptographic substitution box design using travelling salesman problem and chaos. *Perspectives in Science*, 8, 465–468, (online publication date: September 1, 2016).
75. Mazurkov M.I., Sokolov A.V., (2016), *Radioelectronics and Communications Systems*, 59, 212. doi: 10.3103/S0735272716050034.
76. Church R. (1935), Tables of irreducible polynomials for the first four prime moduli, *The Annals of Maths*, 2nd Series, 36(1), 198–209. www.jstor.org/stable/1968675.
77. Swan R.G. (1962), Factorization of polynomials over finite fields. *Pacific Journal of Mathematics*, 12(3), 1099–1106. https://projecteuclid.org/euclid.pjm/1103036322.
78. Bartee T.C., Schneider D.I. (1963), Computation with finite fields, *Information and Control*, 6(2), 79–98, doi: 10.1016/S0019-9958(63)90129-3.
79. Berlekamp E.R., Factoring polynomials over finite fields, *Bell System Technical Journal* (Blackwell Publishing Ltd), 46(8) 1853–1859, doi: 10.1002/j.1538-7305.1967.tb03174.x, 10.1109/TIT.1968.1054226.

80. Kasami T., Lin S.H., Peterson W., (1968), Polynomial codes, *IEEE Transactions on Information Theory*, 14(6), 807–814.

81. Berlekamp E.R. (1970), Factoring polynomials over large finite fields, *Mathematics of Computation*, 24, 713–735, doi: 10.1090/S0025-5718-1970-0276200-X.

82. Rabin M.O., (1980), Probabilistic algorithms in finite fields, *SIAM Journal on Computing*, 9(2), 273–280, doi: 10.1137/0209024.

83. Lenstra A.K., (1985), Factoring multivariate polynomials over finite fields, *Journal of Computer and System Sciences*, 30(2), 235–248, doi: 10.1016/0022-0000(85)90016-9.

84. McEliece R.J. (1987), Factoring polynomials over finite fields. In: *Finite Fields for Computer Scientists and Engineers*, pp. 75–96, doi: 10.1007/978-1-4613-1983-2_7.

85. Rónyai L. (1988), Factoring polynomials over finite fields, *Journal of Algorithms*, 9(3), 391–400, doi: 10.1016/0196-6774(88)90029-6.

86. Wan D.Q. (1990), Factoring multivariate polynomials over large finite fields, *Mathematics of Computation*, 54, 755–770, doi: 10.1090/S0025-5718-1990-1011448-0.

87. Rybowicz M. (1990), Search of primitive polynomials over finite fields, *Journal of Pure and Applied Algebra*, 65(2), 139–151, doi: 10.1016/0022-4049(90)90115-X.

88. Shoup V. (1990), New algorithms for finding irreducible polynomials over finite fields, *Mathematics and Computation*, 54(189), 435–447.

89. Rónyai L. (1992), Galois groups and factoring polynomials over finite fields, *SIAM Journal on Discrete Mathematics*, 5(3), doi: 10.1137/0405026.

90. Zivkovic M. (1994), Table of primitive binary polynomials. *Mathematics of Computation*, 63(207), 301, doi: 10.1090/S0025-5718-1994-1240662-8.

91. Shparlinski I., (1996), On finding primitive roots in finite fields, *Theoretical Computer Science*, 157(2), 273–275, doi: 10.1016/0304-3975(95)00164-6.

92. Flajolet P., Gourdon X., Panario D. (1996), Random polynomials and polynomial factorization. In: *Lecture Notes in Computer Science*, Springer-Verlag: New York/Berlin, vol. 1099, pp. 232–243.

93. Gao S., Panario D. (1997), Tests and constructions of irreducible polynomials over finite fields. In: Cucker F., Shub M. (eds), *Foundations of Computational Mathematics*, Springer: Berlin, Heidelberg.

94. Kaltofen E., Shoup V., (1998), Subquadratic-time factoring of polynomials over finite fields, *Mathematics of Computation of the American Mathematical Society*, 67(223), 1179–1197.

95. Bach E., von zur Gathen J., Lenstra H.W. Jr. (2001), Factoring polynomials over special finite fields. In: *Finite Fields and Their Applications*, vol. 7, no. 1, pp. 5–28, doi: 10.1006/ffta.2000.0306.

96. Gao, S., Lauder, A.G.B. (2002), Hensel lifting and bivariate polynomial factorisation over finite fields. *Mathematics of Computation*, 71, 1663–1676.

97. Brent R.P., Zimmermann P. (2003), Algorithms for Finding Almost Irreducible and Almost Primitive Trinomials. In: *Proceedings of Brent*, Algorithms FF.

98. Gao S., Kaltofen E., Alan G.B.L. (2004), Deterministic distinct-degree factorization of polynomials over finite fields, *Journal of Symbolic Computation*, 38(6), 1461–1470, doi: 10.1016/j.jsc.2004.05.004.

99. Maitraa S., Gupta K.C., Venkateswar A. (2005), Results on multiples of primitive polynomials and their products over GF(2), *Theoretical Computer Science*, 341(1–3), 311–343, doi: 10.1016/j.tcs.2005.04.011.

100. Scott M. (2007), Optimal Irreducible Polynomials for GF(2^m) Arithmetic, Published 2007 in IACR Cryptology ePrint Archive.

101. Fernandez C.K. (2008), Pascal Polynomials Over GF(2), *Master's thesis*, Naval Postgraduate School Monterey CA Dept. of Mathematics, Accession Number: ADA483773.

102. Ahmed A., Lbekkouri A. (2009), Determination of irreducible and primitive polynomials over a binary finite field, In: *Workshop sur les Technologies de l'Information et de la Communication*, Agadir, Maroc, p. 94.

103. Richards C. (2009), Algorithms for Factoring Square-Free Polynomials over Finite Fields.

104. Kim R., Koepf W. (2009), Divisibility of Trinomials by Irreducible Polynomials over F2, *International Journal of Algebra*, 3(4), 189–197.

105. Hanif S., Imran M., (2011), *Factorization Algorithms for Polynomials over Finite Fields*, Degree Project, School of Computer Science, Physics and Mathematics, Linnaeus University: Sweden.

106. Wang L., Wang Q. (2012), On explicit factors of cyclotomic polynomials over finite fields, *Designs, Codes and Cryptography*, 63, 87. doi: 10.1007/s10623-011-9537-6.
107. Couveignes J.M., Lercier R. (2013), Fast construction of irreducible polynomials over finite fields, *Israel Journal of Mathematics*, 194, 77. doi: 10.1007/s11856-012-0070-8.
108. Marquis D. (2014), Deterministic factorization of polynomials over finite fields, *MS in Pur Mathematics*, Carleton University: Ottawa, Canada.
109. Hammarhjelm G. (2014), Construction of Irreducible Polynomials over Finite Fields, Uppasala Universitet, vol. 17, U.U.D.M Project Report 2014.
110. Cavanna N. (2014), Polynomial Factoring Algorithms and their Computational Complexity. *Honors Scholar Theses*, 384. http://digitalcommons.uconn.edu/srhonors_theses/384.
111. Sadique J.K.M., Zaman U., Dey S., Ghosh R. (2015), An algorithm to find the irreducible polynomials over Galois Field GF(p^m), *International Journal of Computer Applications*, 109(15), 24–29, doi: 10.5120/19266-1012.
112. Ha J. (2016), Irreducible polynomials with several prescribed coefficients, *Finite Fields and Their Applications*, 40, 10–25, doi: 10.1016/j.ffa.2016.02.006.
113. Poonen B. (2017), Using zeta functions to factor polynomials over finite fields, *arXiv:1710.00970*.
114. Feng J., Chen H., Gao S., Fan L., Feng D. (2016), Improved Fault Analysis on the Block Cipher SPECK by Injecting Faults in the Same Round, In: *Proceedings of the 19th International Conference on Information Security and Cryptology*, November 30–December 02, 2016.

Chapter 21

Role of Software-Defined Networking (SDN) in Internet of Things (IoT) Security: Attacks and Countermeasures

Megha Quamara and Brij B. Gupta

National Institute of Technology Kurukshetra

Contents

21.1 Introduction

Increasing popularity of Internet of Things (IoT) has led to the development of large-scale IoT sub-networks that offer multiple heterogeneous and ubiquitous access solutions, such as Wi-Fi, cellular networks, ad hoc networks, Bluetooth, GPRS, and ZigBee and allows coexistence of different routing protocols. These networking technologies are responsible for the transmission of data from the sensory units to the processing units. As a result, there is an exponential growth in the development of smart devices that are used by the users to access numerous online services and new IoT applications.

In order to support heterogeneous data over homogeneous network entities and to provide flexibility of dynamically joining or leaving the network to users and devices, it is desired to integrate these networking technologies in an effective manner. However, with rapidly changing trends of user requirements and with the introduction of a diverse set of applications in the field, it is challenging to manage these distributed network frameworks or infrastructures collaboratively. These challenges may be associated with the real-time data collection, monitoring of network traffic, efficient utilization of traffic paths, locating and identifying the target objects, sharing of network resources, uncoordinated development and deployment of applications, and so on (Figure 21.1). It

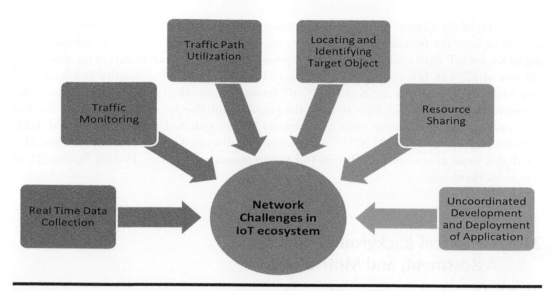

Figure 21.1 Network-related challenges in IoT environment.

is required to develop an infrastructure that is flexible enough to transmit the information in the network though IoT devices, such as switches, routers, and other access points in order to provide end services including Voice over IP (VoIP), Quality of Service (QoS), and sensor virtualization to the users. At the same time, it must ensure high security, availability, stability, and performance efficiency. To establish intelligent connectivity between the network entities, some efforts have been made including IoT frameworks proposed by Cisco [1], International Telecommunication Union (ITU) [2], European Telecommunication Standards Institute (ETSI) [3], etc. However, none of them are capable of handling the discussed challenges and meeting the requirements altogether.

To handle these challenges, concept of network device (re)-programmability termed as Software-Defined Networking (SDN) came into existence. It is a rapidly evolving solution with applications lying in a diverse set of domains, including cloud computing, Wireless Sensor Networks, virtualization technologies, and IoT. It has introduced the concept of separating the control plane from the forwarding devices of the network, so that the network devices can be configured depending upon the type of application, thereby providing more flexibility, enhanced control and decision-making, and improved network response.

Undoubtedly, merging the idea of SDN with IoT would resolve issues related to network management. However, full-scale implementation of SDN over network level also introduces a number of challenges among which security issues demand for greater attention. A number of solutions have been proposed in the literature to mitigate the security vulnerabilities and attacks, and to exploit the idea of SDN in order to enhance the security of the IoT networks. To get acquainted with these challenges and countermeasures, there is a need to understand the integrated framework for IoT and SDN, and how the associated entities would play their role in the heterogeneous IoT environment. In this chapter, the main focus is to highlight and analyze the possible security threats in an SDN-based IoT environment and the role of SDN in improving the security of the information system through emerging solutions.

The rest of the chapter is organized as follows. Section 21.2 deals with the historical background of both the technological paradigms, related statistics, and motivation behind adopting SDN for IoT environment. Section 21.3 presents an integrated architecture for describing the role of SDN in IoT environment. Sections 21.4 and 21.5 describe security attacks associated with each layer of the combined SDN-IoT framework and their existing countermeasures, respectively. Section 21.6 outlines some of the protocols suitable for this environment. Section 21.7 covers some open source tools and datasets for research and development in the field. Different applications of SDN in IoT environment are discussed in Section 21.8. Section 21.9 highlights some of the open challenges and future research directions. Finally, Section 21.10 concludes the chapter.

21.2 Historical Background, Statistical Assessment, and Motivation

21.2.1 Historical Background

IoT and SDN are two popular and rapidly emerging network trends. To understand their current state of importance, it would be useful to look into the past events associated with them. Table 21.1 summarizes the major events related to the evolution of these two technologies.

21.2.2 Statistical Assessment

IoT is influencing the consumer's behavior and transforming business and industries. According to Gartner, Inc. forecasts [4], there will be an increase in Internet-connected devices in use from 8.4 billion in the year 2017 to 20.4 billion by the year 2020. Consumer is the largest user segment of Internet-connected things with 5.2 billion devices in the year 2017, which is 63% of the total. This number will increase at a high rate, and consumers will purchase more devices. Due to this, businesses are also spending more (Figure 21.2). In the year 2017, it was estimated that the use of Internet-connected things in terms of hardware spending would drive $964 billion. Consumer-related applications will cost $725 billion in the year 2017, and hardware spending for both the segments will reach around $3 trillion by the year 2020.

According to Tayyaba et al. [5], an increase of 87% has been noted in SDN-based data center applications and a revenue of $960 million was generated in the year 2015. It is also expected that the revenue will increase to $8 billion by the year 2018, which is a rise of 734%. According to a survey conducted by International Data Corporation (IDC) and Statista estimates [6], Figure 21.3 shows the SDN worldwide market size from the year 2013 to 2021. In the year 2017, it was expected to reach 6.6 billion U.S. dollars, while in the year 2021, it is expected to increase up to 13.8 billion U.S. dollars. Similarly, Figure 21.4 shows the SDN worldwide market revenue from the year 2016 to 2022. It is expected to increase from 2.7 billion U.S. dollars in 2016 to 30.8 billion U.S. dollars in 2022.

21.2.3 Motivation

Deployment of SDN in resource-constrained environment will enable efficient and reliable network resource sharing among IoT devices and will reduce the investment in hardware domain.

Table 21.1   Evolution of IoT and SDN

Year	Events
1998	Former Sun Microsystems engineer Mark Medovich, launched a soft-switch startup "WebSprocket" to produce an object-oriented OS.
1999	The term "Internet of Things" was coined by Kevin Ashton.
2000	Gartner[a] introduced the term "Supranet" to describe aggregation of physical and digital world.
2001	Ohio State University and Ohio Academic Resources Network (OARnet) conducted the first SDN test and developed the first practical SDN use case for Internet2; Ericsson's soft-switch development program was terminated.
2003	Content delivery control network patent application was developed by Bob Burke and Zac Carman.
2004	Routing Control Platform was proposed to have a separate centralized platform for route selection.
2005	4D architecture was proposed for network control and management.
2006	Stanford University PhD student Martin Casado developed Ethane.
2007	"Nicira", a startup for SDN technology was founded by Martin Casado, Nick McKeown and Scott Shenker.
2008	OpenFlow Switching Consortium was created; NOS NOX entered the research community; Number of Internet-connected devices exceeded the number of users.
2009	Stanford published OpenFlow 1.0 specification.
2010	The term SDN was coined by MIT Technology Review when Casado and McKeown's work at Stanford University was featured in the TR10 in 2009.
2011	ONF was formed to promote SDN and to standardize OpenFlow protocol; Version 1.1 of OpenFlow protocol was released.
2012	"Floodlight," an open source SDN controller was released.
2013	NEC as the first OpenFlow certified wired company.
2014	Meru Networks announced the first OpenFlow conformant Wireless LAN (WLAN) controller.
2015	IoT Security Foundation (IoTSF) was formed.
2016	Floodlight v1.2 was released.
2017	Colt Technology Services[b] launched SDN based on Demand Services in Japan; Du[c] underwent a successful trial of Nokia's SDN technology to build smarter networks.

[a] Gartner, Inc. is an American research and advisory firm which provides IT related forecasts.

[b] Colt Technology Services is a UK-based multinational telecommunications and data center services company.

[c] Du, also known as Emirates Integrated Telecommunication Company (EITC), is one of the two telecommunication service providers in United Arab Emirates, the other one being Etisalat.

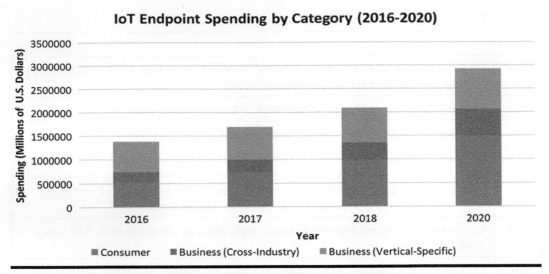

Figure 21.2   Overall IoT endpoint spending by category (2016–2020).

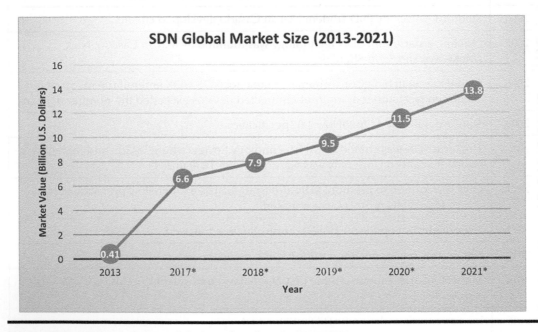

Figure 21.3   Estimated SDN global market size (2013–2021).

It is also suitable for the improvement of vendor's Service-Level Agreements. A number of other possibilities are also emerging. SDN is in the early stages of its deployment, and its full integration with the IoT still requires few more years. To get an insight of how both the technologies will work together, it is required to understand them in detail and what are the possible challenges that can hinder their integration, and possible countermeasures. Although their collaboration seems a distant future, service providers and vendors are actively involved today.

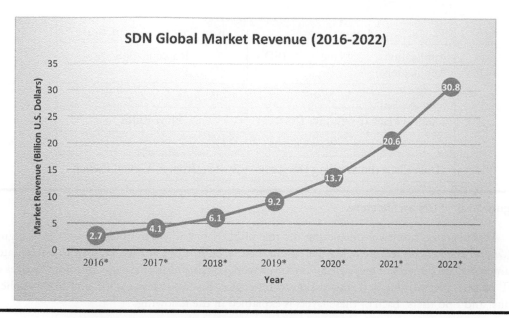

Figure 21.4   Estimated SDN global market revenue (2016–2022).

21.3 Integrated Architecture for SDN and IoT

IoT and SDN represent two entirely different concepts. IoT mainly deals with heterogeneous technologies engaged in sensing, identification, and communication of the information (Figure 21.5), while SDN deals with separation of way of transmission of information from the decision rules (Figure 21.6). To support a diverse set of tasks by establishing coordination among different devices through the existing technologies and optimal utilization of resources is challenging in an IoT environment. However, an integrated framework can be developed that can leverage the benefits from SDN in a heterogeneous IoT setting and can handle the existing issues.

IoT Layer	Main Functionality	Technologies Involved or Examples
End Users	Access Information and Services, Perform Data Manipulation	Home Users, Corporate Users, Government Sector Employees
Application Layer	Application Support (P2P Client-Server Exchange, Opportunistic Exchange, Monitoring)	Smart Homes, Smart Health-care Systems, Intelligent Transportation
Service Layer	Service Division, Service Integration, Service Implementation, Service Support, Smart Computations	Cloud, QoS, Access Control
Network or Transmission Layer	Network Infrastructure and Connectivity Establishment, Information Transmission	Internet, Mobile Network, WLAN, Satellite Network, Ad hoc Network
Physical or Perception layer	Sensing, Identification, Interaction, Computation, Communication, Actuation	RFID Readers, Sensors, ZigBee Nodes, Bluetooth Devices, Actuators
Physical Security, Information Security, Network Management, Trust Management		

Figure 21.5   A typical IoT framework.

Layers	Key Entities or Functions
Application Plane (SDN Applications)	Routing, QoS
Northbound API or Interface	
Control Plane (Controller Devices)	Flow Rules
Southbound API or Interface	
Data Plane (Forwarding Devices)	Switch, Router, Virtual Switch

Figure 21.6   SDN architecture.

An integrated framework depicting the role of SDN in IoT environment is shown in Figure 21.7, and the general requirements that are needed to be fulfilled at each layer of this integrated framework are shown in Figure 21.8. The framework consists of five layers—Terminal devices or IoT objects, Networking or Transmission technologies, Business services, IoT and SDN applications, and End users. Each of these layers is explained in the following.

21.3.1 Terminal Devices or IoT Objects

Terminal devices are the resources or assets that are responsible for gathering the data from the surroundings and its preprocessing. They identify the real world, as well as monitor and sense the environmental conditions. They directly interact with the data and map the information collected into digitized form. These devices include RFID readers, different kinds of sensors (such as ZigBee), actuators, and other such equipment. This layer is characterized by the constrained resources with varying properties and specifications. These are generally deployed in diverse environmental conditions in clustered or semi-clustered manner and deal with different data formats.

Layers of SDN-IoT Architecture				Examples			
5. End Users				Home and Industrial Users, Business Analysts			
4. IoT and SDN Applications				Power Grid	Smart Homes	Intelligent Transportation	Energy Harvesting
3. Business Services	Task 1	Task 2 ...	Task m	Load Balancing, Traffic & Security Monitoring			
Northbound Interface (Python, Java, REST, JSON, XML)							
2. Networking or Transmission Technologies	SDN Controllers (Control Layer)	Flow		NOX, Floodlight, Beacon, OpenDaylight, Open vSwitch			
		Security					
		General Purpose					
	Southbound Interface (OF, OVSDB, PCEP, I2RS, BGP-LS, NETCONF)						
	Infrastructure or Forwarding Devices (Data Layer)			Routers, Switches, Virtual Switches			
1. Terminal Devices or IoT Objects	Resource 1	Resource 2 ...	Resource n	RFID Readers, Sensors, ZigBee Nodes, Bluetooth Devices, Actuators			

Figure 21.7   Integrated framework for SDN and IoT.

Per-Layer Requirements
5. End User Requirements
4. Application Constraints
3. Policies and Task Requirements
2. Mapping Rules Constraints
1. Resource Characteristics and Constraints

Figure 21.8 Layer-wise constraints or requirements in SDN-based IoT environment.

21.3.2 Transmission Technologies

In an SDN-based IoT environment, network layer can be divided into two components—SDN controllers and forwarding devices. SDN controllers constitute the control layer and are responsible for global policy enforcement and for the abstraction of control decisions from the underlying terminal devices. Controllers can be designed for different purposes, such as to determine the flow rules, to define the security policies for the network, and to perform other general tasks. There are a variety of SDN controllers, such as Floodlight, NOX, and Maestro. In a multi-controller environment, interaction among the controllers takes place through east–west interface. Forwarding devices constitute the infrastructure or data layer, and these are responsible for performing some basic operations. These include hardware- or software-based networking equipment, such as routers, physical switches, and virtual switches connected to each other through wired or wireless links. Interaction between the controllers and forwarding devices occurs via southbound interface through the implementation of southbound protocols. The controller sends flow rules or instructions to the forwarding devices in order to manage the flow of network traffic. Depending upon the rule specification, the forwarding devices take appropriate actions on the incoming traffic, such as forwarding the traffic to a particular port, or dropping the packets. Mapping rules are defined at this stage that determine the resources that are needed to be allocated for the appropriate tasks.

21.3.3 Business Services

Business services can be broken down into tasks, such as load balancing, traffic monitoring, firewalls, routing, QoS, and security monitoring. These tasks may be associated with one or more application types depending upon the nature of application and the type of its usage, and have different resource requirements. Different services communicate with the controller through Application Program Interface (API) or northbound interface. Specific policies are defined for the execution of these services. These services range from value-added services, such as real-time streaming, mobile advertisements, and location-based services to inter- or cross-domain services, such as cloud and Wide Area Networks (WANs); from mission critical services, such as tele-medical applications and financial applications to Machine-to-Machine (M2M) services, such as logistics and management services [7, 8].

21.3.4 IoT and SDN Applications

These include real-time applications that utilize the high-quality services offered by the network to meet the user's requirements. These may include smart homes networks, cellular networks,

Bluetooth, Wi-Fi, and ZigBee-based wireless access networks, data centers, enterprise networks, smart homes, industrial automation, and optical networks. These applications provide users the capability of accessing the stored data as well as to operate on the retrieved data. Different applications have different constraints and resource requirements.

21.3.5 End Users

End users utilize the applications in order to access the services and to complete the specific tasks in an intelligent manner. They make use of hand-held devices, mobile devices, and terminals to run the applications. End users may belong to different sectors and include home users, company employees, market specialists, and so on. They may have a diverse set of requirements that are to be satisfied through different capabilities of the network. In order to enhance the user's experience and quality of living, innovative services are developed.

21.4 Taxonomy of Security Challenges in SDN-Based IoT Environment

Based on the number of controllers, architecture of SDN-based IoT environment can be broken down into two categories—Centralized and Distributed (Figure 21.9). Centralized architecture involves a single controller being responsible for mapping the application requirements to appropriate decisions over the traffic flow and for global policy enforcement. On the other hand, distributed

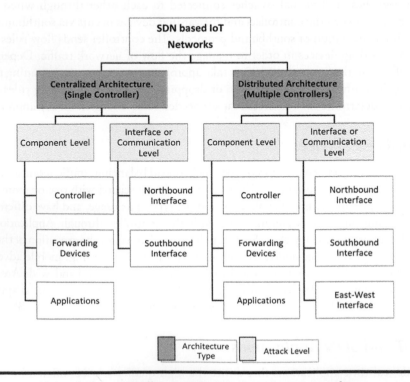

Figure 21.9 Attack levels for controller-centric SDN-based IoT networks.

architecture involves a set of controllers working in parallel and cooperative manner in order to establish flow rules in the network and serving the applications. In a centralized architecture, security attacks can be carried out at the component level which includes various applications, controller device, and forwarding devices, as well as on the communication interfaces—northbound and southbound interfaces. However, security attacks in a distributed architecture can be carried out on east–west interface through which different controllers communicate with each other.

Table 21.2 summarizes the attack types on different layers (or component level) of integrated SDN-IoT framework, and Table 21.3 outlines some of the possible attacks at the interface level through which the two layers can communicate.

Table 21.2 Security Attacks at Component Level of Integrated SDN-IoT Architecture

Layer	Target Entity	Vulnerabilities	Attacks
Layer 4—IoT & SDN applications	Applications	Application manipulation	Introduction of vulnerabilities in the network and compromised network
		Malicious application	
		Unauthenticated application	
		Lack of application isolation	Inconsistent flow rules and network updates
		Northbound API exploitation or vulnerable API	Compromised controller and network, fraudulent policy enforcement
	Flow rules	Absence of appropriate policy enforcement	Inappropriate resource consumption
		Fraudulent rule insertion	
		Illegal and inconsistent policies	
Layer 2—Networking or transmission technologies (control layer)	Controller devices	Parsing errors in encoding languages (XML, JSON)	Buffer overflow and compromised controller
		Unauthorized controller access	Controller hijacking
		Rogue controllers or controller hijacking	False entries in the flow table and compromised network
		Bad controller logic	DoS and flooding attacks
		Spoofed packets (handshake, or hello)	

(Continued)

Table 21.2 (*Continued*)   Security Attacks at Component Level of Integrated SDN-IoT Architecture

Layer	Target Entity	Vulnerabilities	Attacks
		Single point of failure	
		Centralized controller	
		ARP spoofing	Cache poisoning
	Flow rules	Flow rule modification	Flow of malicious traffic across the network
		Flow table limitation	Flooding attack
		Fraudulent rule insertion	Traffic manipulation
		Flooding attack	Network breakdown
		Open programmability	Lack of trust and weak authentication
		Southbound API exploitation	MITM and spoofing attacks
Layer 2—Networking or transmission technologies (data layer)	Forwarding devices	Switch Listener Mode activated	Connection establishment between controller and switch without default authentication and access control
		Flooding attack (massive flow rules)	DoS attack
		Device misconfigurations due to agent installed on the switch	Buffer overflow or DoS attacks
		Lack of trust or weak authentication	Spoofing attack
	Traffic	Side channel attacks	Information disclosure
		Traffic deviation	Information loss
		Forgery of traffic flow	Malicious attempts
		Traffic manipulation	
	Flow rules	Forwarding rule discovery	Malicious interruptions
		Forwarding rule modification	Packet modification
		Inconsistent flow rules	Network unavailability and instability
		Fraudulent rule insertion	

Table 21.3   Security Attacks on Interface in Integrated SDN-IoT Architecture

Interface/Communication Level	Vulnerabilities	Attacks
Northbound interface (service-controller)	Fraudulent rule insertion	Interface exploitation
	Absence of trust or weak authentication	Spoofing attack
	Inappropriate authorization	Malicious access on applications
Southbound interface (controller-forwarding devices)	Flooding attack	Unavailability of the communication interface
	Inappropriate authorization	Unauthorized access
	Controller hijacking	Modification of flow rules
	Flow rule manipulation	Malicious attempts
	Unauthorized controller access	Control decision manipulation and MITM attack
	Unencrypted traffic	Eavesdropping and spoofing attacks
	Absence of trust or lack of authentication	MITM or spoofing attacks
	Open programmability	Unauthenticated connections
East–west interface (controller-controller)	Auditing issues (absence of logs and audit trials)	Absence of control over the network due to malicious attempts

Apart from attacks mentioned in Tables 21.2 and 21.3, some other attacks that can impact all the layers and communication levels include operating system (OS) manipulation and software framework alteration (middleware) that can affect the application management functionalities; software or hardware failures that can affect all the functionalities across the network; configuration data alteration or extraction that can affect the resource, application, and data management; and unauthorized access to SDN services by authorized entities that do not have appropriate access level for those services.

21.5   Taxonomy of Existing Countermeasures

A number of techniques have been proposed in order to detect and prevent the attacks associated with SDN-based IoT environment in order to ensure confidentiality, integrity, availability, authentication, and non-repudiation of network devices, data, and communication interfaces. To identify the root cause behind the attacks, the chain of events needs to be reconstructed. This section presents a generic security model for the mitigation of security attacks in the network and also outlines some of the effective countermeasures against these attacks.

21.5.1 Security Model for SDN-Based IoT Environment

Figure 21.10 shows a hybrid (proactive and reactive) approach toward attack mitigation in SDN-based IoT environment. This approach consists of three modules—network monitoring, data analysis, and response generation. Network monitoring involves keeping track of the events occurring in the network and constantly collecting the security-related data of the traffic, and this is done through network traffic analyzers. In case of any unexpected event, anomaly detectors collect the event-related data. This collected data is then transferred to the controller. The applications running on the controller analyze and correlate the collected data in order to generate inferences. Based on these inferences, the controller defines or updates the flow rules that are distributed across the forwarding devices in the network.

21.5.2 Existing Countermeasures

21.5.2.1 Countermeasures for Device-Level Attacks

In order to prevent attacks such as single point of failures, a number of controller replication schemes have been proposed. A fault-tolerant scheme based on maintaining back-up controllers is given by Botelho et al. [9] in which a primary controller is responsible for defining the flow rules, and in case of failure of the primary controller, control switches to backup controllers. The controllers maintain a shared data store that stores the state of the network. It requires adoption of appropriate fault detection and leader election algorithms. To prevent spoofing attacks, Mattos et al. [10] proposed an authentication and access control mechanism, AuthFlow, which is based on credentials of the host. Authentication mechanism is employed above the Medium Access Control layer to ensure

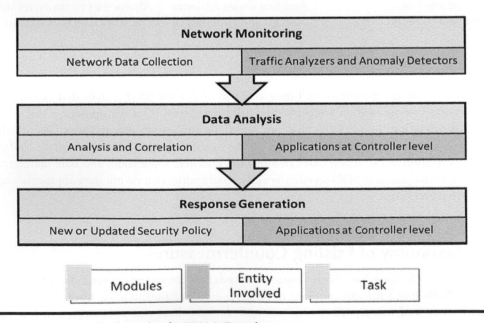

Figure 21.10 Anomaly detection in SDN-IoT environment.

low overhead and fine-grained access control according to the host privilege level which is mapped to a set of flow rules applicable to the host. Kim et al. [11] proposed an idea of Security as a Service (SaaS) for authentication in SDN environment which also guarantees physical security, security of the procedures, and a restoration strategy. Klaedtke et al. [12] proposed a permission-based access control schemes for SDN controllers. The scheme is suitable for heterogeneous resource environment having multiple security requirements and that may involve conflicts while reconfiguring network components (Table 21.4).

Shin et al. [13] proposed a framework called AVANT-GUARD that uses the concept of connection migration to protect the controller devices from saturation attacks, and actuating triggers to make the network more responsive toward attacks by enabling the forwarding devices to report the network status and payload information to the controllers. In [14], concept of entropy has been used for early detection of Distributed Denial of Service Attacks (DDoS) attacks on controller devices. The solution involves measuring the randomness of the incoming packets, termed as entropy, in the early stages to detect the presence of the attack. It is a light-weight solution that can avoid the use of excessive processing power; therefore, it is suitable for IoT environment. In [15], the authors highlighted the importance of diversity in host devices in order to enhance the robustness of systems and to prevent attacks that target a common set of vulnerabilities among host devices. Diversity can be achieved in system software, such as OS. Application software and management software can be made to run on controller or forwarding devices based on different system software which would limit the impact of attacks on similar vulnerabilities. To prevent discovery and scanning attacks against devices due to static configurations of the devices, a proactive approach of assigning random virtual IP to the mobile hosts can be adopted. Jafarian et al. [16] proposed a technique OpenFlow Random Host Mutation (OF-RHM), based on the same concept. It is a Moving Target Defense (MTD) framework in which IP mutation of the end-hosts is done frequently and unpredictably in order to distort the attacker's knowledge regarding the network.

To prevent intra-switch misconfigurations, Al-Shaer et al. [17] proposed a tool FlowChecker, in order to identify inconsistencies within a single flow table. The tool utilizes binary decision diagrams for encoding configuration of the flow table and then uses model checker technique for creating a model of the network of interconnected OpenFlow switches. In order to prevent device misconfigurations, design of the components should be made robust and secured keeping into account the performance efficiency. Kreutz et al. [18] highlight the importance of secure components for building reliable and secure systems in order to ensure security properties, such as confidentiality and integrity.

21.5.2.2 Countermeasures for Attacks over Policies

In [19], a network management approach EnforSDN is given which utilizes SDN principles to separate policy enforcement layer from policy resolution layer in the network plane without compromising the functionality of the network. Since policies in SDN-based IoT sub-networks are specified and controlled in a distributed fashion, so concurrency issues, such as concurrent policy update conflicts may arise. In order to deal with these issues, Canini et al. [20] proposed a policy composition abstraction, which is based on a transactional interface with all-or-nothing semantics. In this model, an update is either committed and the policy is enforced over the entire network consistently and complete updates are installed, or update is aborted, thereby preventing error-prone coordination tasks. It is a light-weight solution which requires low-level, per-switch port conflict resolution.

Table 21.4 Countermeasures for Security Attacks

Attack Category	Examples	Countermeasures
Attacks over devices	Single point of failures	Controller replication schemes through policy conflict resolution
	Spoofing attacks	Access control and authentication mechanisms
	Buffer overflow and DoS attacks	Language-based security
	Exploitation of a common set of vulnerabilities	Diversity
	Device misconfigurations	Secure components
	Scanning attacks	Random virtual IP addresses
	DDoS attacks	Monitoring systems
	Unauthorized access to network devices	Dynamic access control
	Intra-switch misconfigurations	Binary decision diagrams
Attacks over policies	Absence of suitable policies	Policy enforcement layer
	Inconsistencies in policies	Model checking
Attacks over applications	Application manipulation	Symbolic execution
	Malicious applications	Permission-based access
	Lack of application isolation	Application replication
	Unauthenticated applications	Customized information ·
Attacks over traffic	Traffic manipulation	To monitor the traffic between controller and the switch, introducing an abstraction layer between control and data plane
	Abnormal flows and flooding attacks	SOM
	Unencrypted traffic and DoS attacks	Transport Layer Security (TLS) between controller and switches
	Forgery of traffic flow	Network Intrusion Prevention System (NIPS), NIDS
	Traffic deviation	Tracking mechanism

21.5.2.3 Countermeasures for Attacks over Applications

To check the trustworthiness of an application accessing the controller operations and information regarding the network state through northbound interface, Scott-Hayward et al. [21] proposed a permission-based system, OperationCheckpoint, to ensure that only trusted applications should be able to use controller operations. The system provides security to the application–controller interface by defining a set of permissions that are subscribed by the application during the setup phase with the controller. In the later phase, permissions are checked in order to authorize the application commands.

To provide application isolation, an abstraction approach called LegoSDN has been proposed by Chandrasekaran et al. [22]. It is a fault-tolerant controller architecture which ensures application recovery from deterministic as well as nondeterministic failures. It provides application isolation by running the same in a sandbox environment; thus, any application failure is limited to this environment only. To enhance application security, a number of application classification techniques have been proposed based on the QoS marking on the IP header, port number, and Deep Packet Inspection (DPI). However, all these techniques have drawbacks related to lack of trust, execution on dynamic ports, and higher computation costs. A framework Atlas has been proposed for application identification and classification based on the network traffic [23]. It is based on the concept of machine learning and uses crowd-sourcing approach in which software for device management are deployed over the devices that collect information related to network state associated with each application running over the device. This framework is suitable for mobile application detection and leverages OpenFlow protocol.

To prevent application manipulation attacks, concept of symbolic execution over code model can be adopted which involves exploring all possible paths within the model. Stoenescu et al. [24] proposed a static analysis tool for the network, SymNet, based on the same concept. It works by injecting symbolic packets through the network and tracks their reachability. In order to authenticate an application, such as a website, trust certificates and cookie-based verification mechanisms can be used. Gasparini et al. [25] proposed a system for authenticating a website over the Internet based on the customized information, which is known to the user. If the website provides the already-known customization information to the user, then it is considered as an authentic website. In [26], a unique authentication code is used in order to authenticate a web application.

21.5.2.4 Countermeasures for Attacks over Traffic

To prevent traffic manipulation attacks, Hartung et al. [27] proposed a network-monitoring tool, SOFTmon, which stands for SDN monitoring and is compatible to work with OpenFlow controllers. It provides the controllers with statistics and utilization charts related to switches, port and flow level to extend controller's monitoring capabilities. Yu et al. [28] proposed a distributed model for traffic monitoring, named Distributed and Collaborative Monitoring (DCM) system, which enables switches to perform flow monitoring tasks in a collaborative manner in order to balance measurement load.

To check for abnormal flows and flooding attacks, Self-Organizing Maps (SOM)-based techniques can be used. Phan et al. [29] proposed a technique based on SOM for large-sized SDN in which security modules are implemented over distributed OpenFlow switches instead of controller or application layer, thereby resolving the bottleneck problem. A distributed controller is responsible to control the execution of security modules. PERM-GUARD [30], another scheme for flow rules authentication, implements a permission-based authentication model and utilizes identity-based signature scheme to check for the validity of flow rules.

To monitor the network traffic, Intrusion Prevention System (IPS)- and Intrusion Detection System (IDS)-based approaches have been widely used in conventional networks. However, single-point IPS and IDS only monitor the network traffic passing through them and cannot discover coordinated and distributed intrusions. In [31], the authors proposed a Collaborative Intrusion Prevention Architecture (CIPA) for SDN environment based on the concept of Artificial Neural Networks (ANNs) in which network monitoring functions are distributed over programmable switches or routers in order to achieve a global view of the network status. Jia et al. [32] proposed a Distributed Flexible Intrusion Prevention System (DFIPS) for SDN. It consists of three modules—a classifier which is responsible for traffic slicing, a detector pool which creates a number of detector nodes for detection, and a control agent which interacts with the classifier and detector pool. DFIPS can be flexibly deployed over SDN controllers as an application and can capture global view of the network.

To prevent traffic deviation attacks, flow-tracking mechanisms can be adopted. In [33], an extended SDN framework FlowTags has been proposed with flow tracking capability and enables routing control over the tagged packets with pre-defined network policies.

21.5.3 Countermeasures for Other Attacks

To prevent OS and software framework alteration, trusted computing can be adopted. To prevent unauthorized access to SDN services, secure administration modules can be deployed. High assurance can be established to prevent the impact of software and hardware failures.

21.6 Protocol Suite

Open Networking Foundation (ONF) defined OpenFlow as the first standardized communication interface between the controller and the data plane of SDN framework, still issues related to scalability and security exists that are among the dominant factors for IoT applications. Hence, there is a need for alternate communication means and specialized hardware while designing SDN-based IoT architecture that also includes conventional networking protocols in order to handle the requirements of IoT environment. Deployment of a protocol also depends upon the type of application. Table 21.5 summarizes a brief description of these protocols along with their security aspects [34].

21.7 Open Source Tools and Datasets

21.7.1 Open Source Tools for the Development of SDN-Based IoT Environment

Researchers and learners from academia and industries are utilizing a number of open source tools for experimentation purposes in order to facilitate the design of preliminary networks, to develop highly efficient SDN-based applications for IoT environment and to test the same in order to evaluate

Table 21.5 Protocols for SDN-Based IoT Environment

Protocol	Description	Specification	Security
OpenFlow	• Developed by ONF • Enables SDN controller to interact and remotely control the forwarding tables in a switch (southbound interface)	• Compatible with network layer switches • Layered on top of TCP—Port 6653 • Recommends use of TLS • Latest version—1.4	• Susceptible to MITM attacks • Single point of failures • Programming and communication channel issues • Tampering of data flow and information disclosure • Spoofing
Network Configuration Protocol (NETCONF)	• Developed by IETF • Allows configuration of network devices such as routers, switches, firewalls etc.	• Transport layer protocol • Installs, manipulates, and deletes configuration of network devices • Based on Remote Procedural Call • Uses Extensive Markup Language (XML) based data encoding	• Inherent access control • Uses Secure Shell (SSH) protocol for session creation
OpenFlow Configuration and Management Protocol (OF-Config)	• Developed by ONF • Protocol for remote device configuration in an OpenFlow network	• Communication between switch and configuration point • Configuration of authentication certificates	• Vulnerable to DoS attacks over data flows • Use of SSH or TLS to prevent repudiation and spoofing
Extensible Messaging and Presence Protocol (XMPP)	• Developed by Jabbar open source community • Open XML protocol based on client-server model	• Alternative to OpenFlow • Based on XML • Used for voice or video calls, online presence detection, multiparty chat, instant messaging	• Server isolation from public network • Security using TLS
OpFlex	• A southbound protocol for facilitating communication between SDN controller and forwarding devices	• Alternative to OpenFlow • Emphasis is on policies (centralized control)	SSL and TLS security

(*Continued*)

Table 21.5 (*Continued*)   Protocols for SDN-Based IoT Environment

Protocol	Description	Specification	Security
Border Gateway Protocol (BGP)	• Gateway protocol designed for exchanging routing or network reachability information among gateway hosts or autonomous systems in a network	• Supports Classless Inter-Domain Routing • Uses TCP as its transport protocol— Port 179 • Latest Version—BGP4	• Vulnerable to malicious disruptions • Replay attacks • Spoofed BGP messages
Open vSwitch Database Management Protocol (OVSDB)	• OpenFlow configuration protocol for managing Open vSwitch implementations	• Supports distribution across multiple physical servers	• Vulnerable to DoS attacks, information disclosure, and tampering over data flows • Spoofing and repudiation
Multiprotocol Label Switching— Transport Profile (MPLS-TP)	• Developed by IETF • Directs data from one node to other	• Network layer protocol • Used in packet-switched data networks	• Insertion of false labels • DoS attacks
Locator/ Identifier Separation Protocol (LISP)	• Developed by IETF • Protocol for separating routing locators (gateways) and identifiers (client)	• Network layer protocol • Enables network virtualization • Offers mobility benefits	• Allows different mapping database systems • No mechanism for automated key management related to message authentication
Path Computation Element (PCE) Communication Protocol (PCEP)	• Developed by IETF • Protocol for establishing communication between PCE and Path Computation Client (PCC)	• Uses TCP as its transport protocol— Port 4189 • Session oriented • Reliable message and flow control	• Vulnerable to spoofing and snooping attacks • DoS attack • Falsification attack • Encryption to ensure privacy

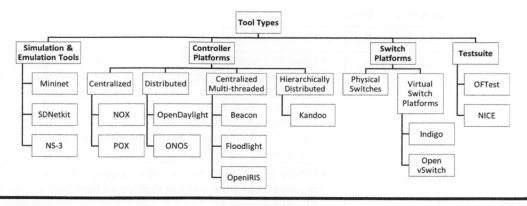

Figure 21.11 Open source tools.

the performance aspects. Figure 21.11 highlights different categories of some of the commonly used development tools with few examples of each, and Table 21.6 contains their brief description.

21.7.1.1 Simulation and Emulation Tools

These tools allow new applications, protocols, and services to be developed and tested on a predictable deployment environment prior to their release on the actual hardware or physical devices, thereby simplifying the process of real-time development and deployment. Table 21.6 provides a brief description of some of the common simulators and emulators—Mininet, SDNetkit, and Network Simulator-3 (NS-3).

Mininet is a network emulator used for prototyping of large-scale networks over a single host machine and for instantly creating virtual networks with controllers, switches, routers, and links. Unlike Mininet, SDNetkit can work with networks that simultaneously run both OpenFlow and conventional distributed routing protocols, such as Open Short Path First. NS-3 provides simulation and emulation environment for network topology creation, and analysis of the network traffic and currently supports OpenFlow module 1.3.

21.7.1.2 Controller Platforms

A diverse set of controller platforms with different designs and architectural adoption are available. On the basis of architecture, controller platforms can be categorized into centralized, distributed, centralized multi-threaded, and hierarchically distributed. In a centralized platform, a single entity is responsible for managing all the forwarding devices, while a distributed controller environment involves a centralized cluster of nodes or a distributed set of elements. Hierarchical controllers improve scalability by organizing a group of controllers in a hierarchy with each level having one or more interlinked controllers. In centralized multi-threaded controllers, component execution is parallelized with each component being executing on a thread and a single controller is responsible for coordinating the simultaneous executions. Table 21.6 provides description of few examples of each type.

21.7.1.3 Switch Platforms

A number of SDN-based software switches are available for developing SDN-based services and executing an SDN testbed. Similarly, OpenFlow-enabled commodity network hardware is also

Table 21.6 Open Source Tools

Tool Types	Examples	Description
Network simulation and emulation tools	Mininet [35]	• Used for creating realistic virtual networks capable of running real kernel, controllers, and switches along with application code over a single machine which can be a VM or cloud • Provides network testbed for the development of OpenFlow applications, and Python API for network creation and experimentation
	SDNetkit [36]	• Enhanced release of Netkit network emulator that can be used to develop and run topologies based on OpenFlow devices • Can be used for the networks that allow both OpenFlow and standard distributed routing protocols to run simultaneously
	NS-3 [37]	• Discrete event-based network simulation platform that contains in-built modules and libraries to analyze network performance • Works with both scalable and controllable SDN environment
Controller platform	NOX [38]	• A centralized OpenFlow controller platform to develop control applications • Provides modules for topology discovery, learning and network-wide switch
	POX [39]	• Python-based centralized SDN controller which provides a framework for establishing communication with SDN switches through OpenFlow or OVSDB
	OpenDaylight [40]	• A distributed multi-protocol controller and model-driven service abstraction framework • Used to develop applications to work with hardware and south-bound protocols
	Open Network Operating System (ONOS) [41]	• Java-based distributed controller platform that supports high availability through distributed state management and clustering • Provides Representational State Transfer API for Northbound abstractions and Command Line Interface (CLI) commands
	Beacon [42]	• Java-based centralized multi-threaded OpenFlow controller with a set of default applications to implement control plane functionality • Utilizes off-the-shelf libraries to promote code use
	Floodlight [43]	• Java-based centralized multi-threaded SDN controller that works with both physical and virtual switches that are based on OpenFlow protocol • Supports module loading system for extension and enhancement

(Continued)

Table 21.6 (*Continued*)   Open Source Tools

Tool Types	Examples	Description
	OpenIRIS [44]	• Java-based recursive SDN controller that supports OpenFlow • Provides learning mac, topology management, link discovery, forwarding, firewall, and other such modules
	Kandoo [45]	• A hierarchical SDN controller platform; provides local controllers that execute local applications and global controllers that run global applications • Restricts messages between global and local controllers
Virtual switches	Indigo [46]	• Provides OpenFlow access on physical as well as hypervisor switches • Includes core libraries and an abstraction layer to support OpenFlow in hybrid mode of the switch
	Open vSwitch [47]	• Multilayer virtual switch that enables network automation through program extension • Supports standard protocols and management interfaces such as Virtual LAN (VLAN), 802.1ag, NetFlow, and CLI
Physical switches	IBM, HP, Brocade, Pica8, Juniper, Pronto	Develop switches compliant with OpenFlow standard
Test suite	OFTest [48]	• Python-based framework to test OpenFlow 1.0, 1.1 specification compliance • Performs standards-based compliance testing
	NICE [49]	• Testing tool that applies model checking to test OpenFlow applications • Designed for NOX controller platform • Performs symbolic execution

available from a number of vendors including HP, IBM, Juniper, Pica8, Brocade, and Pronto. Hardware switches have fixed functionality and cannot accommodate new features, while software switches are flexible in the sense that they can be easily upgraded. Some of the SDN switch platforms are described in Table 21.6.

21.7.1.4 Test Suite

These include tools for software verification and debugging in order to test and verify the network behavior for the successful deployment of portable network applications. OFTest is a python-based test suite to check switch compliance to OpenFlow specification 1.0 and 1.1, while support for 1.2 is under development. On the other hand, NICE is used to test and debug OpenFlow controller applications.

21.7.2 Datasets

Many open source datasets that are freely available over the Internet are used by the researchers and learners for experimentation purposes. Some dataset sources, their type along with a brief description of the dataset, and the number of instances are summarized in Table 21.7. These datasets enable testers to test the functionality of the models developed so far in order to improve the efficiency.

21.8 Application Areas

SDN provides the capability to reconfigure the working behavior of the network based on the user requirements. It provides flexibility to enhance the network management and enables customized control, which is one of the basic needs in an IoT environment to develop and deploy novel

Table 21.7 Datasets Description

Source	Type	Datasets	Description	Number of Instances
Statistical analysis of network data [50]	Multi-dataset repository	Abilene	Aggregate flow volume data based on measurements of origin–destination flow on the Abeline network	For $12 \times 24 \times 7 =$ 2016 consecutive 5-minute time intervals over the week, across $11 \times 11 = 121$ origin–destination pairs (including self-loops) in an 11 node network.
Knowledge-defined networking training datasets—A deep-reinforcement learning (DRL) approach for SDN routing optimization [51]	Multi-dataset repository	Train	Evolution of DRL agent's performance during training, measured in average network delay	7,001 training instances with four attributes—delay, training step, traffic intensity, and tm
		Benchmark	Performance benchmark measured in average network delay	1,000,000 routings times 1,000 traffic matrices generated randomly
		Traffic	Traffic configurations varying on the basis of total volume of traffic and its distribution	1,000 test traffic matrixes (100 per each traffic intensity)
		100k	Dataset containing configurations for test routing	100,000 test routing configurations

protocols and services. This section describes some of the key application areas of IoT where SDN can be utilized in an efficient manner.

21.8.1 Transmission Security

In an IoT environment comprising of heterogeneous hosts, security of the entire system cannot rely upon hosts only. A host once compromised can leave the entire system susceptible to attacks. Moreover, in enterprise networks where most of the devices are temporarily connected to the network under the control of a third party, security becomes an important concern. So, transmission security comes into picture. However, varying data formats and different level of sensitivity of the applications make it difficult to secure the transmission flow. SDN plays a key role in such applications as it provides a framework to separate the flow rules from the actual transmission. It can be utilized to enforce or update network policies, to monitor the network activity, and to synchronize the network performance.

In [52], a user-centric architecture has been proposed which ensures data transmission in a secure manner and allows for the dynamic enhancement of transmission security based on the user's requests. While in [53], a gateway-centric approach has been given in which the traffic flow generated from and directed to the IoT devices is monitored by an SDN gateway which can detect an odd behavior, as well as can block or forward the traffic. The gateway is also capable of detecting and blocking flooding attacks based on Transmission Control Protocol (TCP) and Internet Control Message Protocol (ICMP) packets.

21.8.2 Smart Home Networks

In a smart home network where multiple low-cost devices and users are connected to the same access point, it is challenging to manage the users, to allocate the resources, and to design an efficient smart home management platform in order to manage and integrate the heterogeneous network resources. However, a number of SDN-based solutions have been proposed to coordinate the low-level configurations specified by the vendors with the high-level network policies in a smart home network.

In [54], a controller-centric framework Software-Defined Smart Home (SDSH) has been proposed in which controller, smart devices, and third-party services have been described as separate domains, and user requirements help in managing the resources. In [55], the authors have presented a management framework that defines policies for smart homes, which utilize access control for the user based on date or time of access, amount of data used, privileges or groups defined for users, and nature of the traffic flow.

21.8.3 Link Recovery

In conventional networks, automated recovery from a link failure is a difficult problem due to the unavailability of sufficient node information to re-establish the route. In such cases, human intervention is required to set up the path, again which is accompanied by huge delays. In such scenarios, SDN-based solutions provide customization of the existing link recovery algorithms.

In [56], a highly scalable, efficient, and proactive model named pro-VLAN for recovery from single link failure has been proposed in which a backup path is calculated for each link of the network and group tables are used to automatically switch to the backup path associated with the link in case of a link failure. In [57], a pipeline scheme named SPIDER, similar to OpenFlow, has been proposed which can detect the link failure by using periodic link probing mechanism of the switch and can reroute the traffic in case of distant failures regardless of the availability of the controller.

21.8.4 Mobile Networking

With the large-scale deployment of wireless infrastructure, smart devices are proliferating at a faster rate accompanied by tremendous increase in mobile traffic. Conventional centralized networks, in which all the traffic is managed at the central gateways, are not capable of handling such high traffic applications which gives rise to scalability issues. SDN provides efficient and flexible solutions for such scenarios.

In [58], two SDN-based models for mobile networking have been proposed—single controller and hierarchical controller model. Former is suitable for small-scale networks in which the controller does not interact with other controllers and is responsible for managing mobility of resource and monitor network states. In contrast, the latter is an advanced approach and is suitable for large-scale networks and involves two controllers—local and global. Local controller is responsible for policy enforcement in localized domains, and global controller collectively manages all the domains.

21.8.5 Real-Time Streaming

With the increasing access to broadband networks and ubiquitous availability of public cloud, streaming-based applications are gaining popularity. Real-time streaming-based applications demand for high efficiency, QoS, and availability of the network services. From the past few years, the concept of Quality of Experience (QoE) is becoming popular which gives emphasis on user's acceptance level for a particular service. However, concept of virtualization introduces new challenges such as end-to-end delays, due to which it becomes challenging to achieve high level of client satisfaction.

In [59], an adaptive SDN-based architecture for Cloud Mobile Media services has been proposed. In this model, user's experience is counted in terms of Mean Opinion Score (MOS) using a statistical technique based on Factor Analysis. Based on MOS, the controller schedules different tasks.

21.8.6 Network Virtualization

Concept of network virtualization is similar to the concept of virtualization in storage, OS, and processing. Network virtualization involves multiple virtual networks operating on a single infrastructure, with each having its own topology and routing characteristics, enabling different users to share different network resources. In conventional networks, network administrator is responsible for separating and managing these virtual networks with limited parameters and flexibility. However, SDN promises the development of advance virtual networks through the separation of control and data plane, thus offering greater flexibility [60].

For example, NetVM [61] provides a virtualization platform in which high-bandwidth network functions are mapped to multiple virtual machines (VMs) through inter-VM communication which simplifies allocation of resources and improves performance. In [62], an architecture has been proposed to leverage the benefits of Network Functions Virtualization in integration with SDN for IoT functionalities in customer premises. It includes user-friendly operations and security updates without any service disruption.

21.8.7 Data Centers

To meet rapidly changing demands of users in the field of computing technology, data centers are also evolving at a tremendous rate. Operations being performed at large scales require efficient traffic management along with strict policy enforcement in order to prevent massive financial and productivity losses due to delays or service disruptions. Building large-scale networks, dynamic adaptation toward application requirements, and energy management is quite challenging.

In [63], a power management system named ElasticTree is proposed which is capable of dynamically adjusting the active network elements including switches and links in order to satisfy the changing energy consumption of data-centric traffic. This system is capable of saving up to 50% of the network energy and can handle traffic surges. A real-time implementation of SDN-based framework in data centers is B4, which is a private WAN connecting data centers of Google across the globe [64]. Its centralized traffic engineering services lead to nearly 100% utilization of links, and partitions application flows across different paths in order to balance the capacity according to the application's demands.

Other IoT applications where SDN-based frameworks are currently being deployed include infrastructure-based WANs [65] (e.g. Wi-Fi and cellular applications), optical transport networks [66] (to improve network management flexibility, for the deployment of third-party control systems, and novel services), designing hybrid network architecture [67], and testing newer IoT products and models based on OpenFlow [68, 69].

21.9 Open Challenges and Future Research Directions

SDN is a promising solution for a heterogeneous setting and its advantages can be seen in the near future but not immediately. For the wide-scale adoption of this technology, some other issues related to reliability, security, and scalability must be resolved. In this section, some of these aspects are analyzed.

21.9.1 Standardized Architecture

A comprehensive framework for the complete integration of SDN and IoT has not been established so far. The reason behind this is the difficulty in embodiment of SDN in diverse IoT domains related to topology of IoT networks, management aspects, and security issues. Efforts are still under way, and some of the noticeable frameworks proposed till date include SoftRAN [70], SoftCell [71], SDN-WISE [72], BlackSDN [73], and SDIoT [74]. Selection of the number of controllers and their positioning in the network, desired performance efficiency, traffic encryption, analysis, and classification are some of the determining factors for the development of a full-fledge architecture for SDN-based IoT environment, which in turn affects the network reliability, fault tolerance, flow-setup latencies, and performance latency.

21.9.2 Hardware and Software Development Compatibility

Decoupling of control and data plane enables network programmability and independent development of the associated technologies. The performance of forwarding devices such as routers and switches depends upon the rate at which they process the packets, which in turn depends upon the underlying hardware technology, such as Application-Specific Standard Products, Application-Specific Integrated Circuits, System-on Chip, or Field Programmable Gate Arrays. Similarly, the performance of controller devices depends upon the hardware technology as well as the Network Operating System (NOS), such as Floodlight, NOX, ONOS, ExtremeXOS, or Onix. However, performance degradation at any one of the levels can affect the others as well and the performance of the whole network leading to a number of problems, such as loss of packets, delay in packet transmission, abnormal behavior of the network, and security attacks. Therefore, appropriate balance related to the performance and cost is required in the development of hardware and software components. However, with heterogeneous technologies and diverse application requirements, it is challenging to achieve.

21.9.3 Backward Compatibility or Transition from Legacy to SDN-Based Architectures

Interoperability of the SDN-based architectures with legacy ones is an open issue. Complete transition from the existing network architectures to SDN-based infrastructure is impossible. A number of network devices having OpenFlow compatibility have come to the market. However, coexistence of the protocols, operational mechanisms, and interfaces between the two architectures is required. In the present scenario, a group of Standards Developing Organizations, open development initiatives, and industrial consortiums are involved in this effort for developing standards and guidelines for SDN technology. ONF which is an industrial consortium focusing on the promotion of SDN for its widespread adoption, published the OpenFlow Management and Configuration protocol as the first step to enable configuration of SDN devices [75]. Internet Engineering Task Force (IETF) is also working for developing standards for the interfaces. The Interface to the Routing System project of IETF is focused on allowing conventional routing protocols to run on SDN devices, thereby leveraging the benefits of traditional distributed routing and making the software packages responsive to network events [76]. Similarly, other organizations or projects involved in the standardization effort of SDN are ETSI [77], International Telecommunication Union—Telecommunication Standardization Sector (ITU-T) [78], OpenDaylight, etc.

21.9.4 Security and Privacy Issues

Security is one of the key aspects of SDN-based IoT environment that must be taken into account. Although a number of security solutions related to authentication, authorization, and access privileges have been proposed so far to integrate these two technologies. However, no concrete specifications have been given for multi-controller environment in which exchange of information occurs between multiple controllers and switches. This information exchange is susceptible to a number of security attacks including DoS and MITM. Deployment of intelligent controllers and applications would improve the resilience of the SDN-based networks. But it may also increase the vulnerabilities of the controller toward hacking. Compromised controller may lead to distortion of every aspect of the underlying technologies. Also, control traffic involves consumption of network bandwidth which leads to degradation of spectral efficiency of IoT devices. IoT devices operating on limited battery power are also vulnerable to bulk control traffic due to which conventional security mechanisms cannot be employed in this scenario. In addition, bulk of data generated in the network gives rise to data privacy issues.

21.9.5 Scalability Issues

SDN networks are different from the traditional networks in the sense that they offer decoupled data and control planes, with both the planes evolving independently through API connectivity. This framework is capable of accelerating changes in the control plane. However, this decoupled architecture has its own drawbacks. Scalability issues arise while defining API standards between the two planes. Network scalability in terms of the number of switches or hosts as in case of IoT environment, can lead to SDN controller becoming a bottleneck [79]. With an increasing number of forwarding devices, bandwidth consumption will increase and a more number of requests will be queued at the controller site that cannot be handled at once. This issue will affect the data center networks having high flow rates. In [80], an architecture has been proposed for SDN scalability for multi-domain and multi-vendor networking environment. A coordinator controller is responsible for setting up a cooperative environment among SDN controllers working for different SDN domains.

21.10 Conclusion

IoT being the new era of computing promises to establish a smart ecosystem, which will eventually bring an industrial and social revolution. It is changing the way of interaction between humans and machines. However, with the exponential growth of smart devices and online services exchanging information over the Internet, rigid conventional architectures are inefficient to manage this rapidly growing network of devices and users. SDN is emerging as a new idea in the field of networking which promises to simplify the network management through the concept of network programmability, thereby resolving the existing issues of the conventional networks. It provides flexibility to control the network as per as the need of the organization.

In this chapter, the role of SDN in preserving the security of IoT environment has been described. Starting with the historical background of SDN along with some statistics related to the field, need of analyzing the security needs of IoT has been justified. An integrated architecture for SDN and IoT has been presented along with description of each layer associated with it. It has been divided into five layers—terminal devices or IoT objects, transmission technologies, business services, IoT and SDN applications, and the end users.

An analysis has been done on the security issues in SDN-based IoT environment and existing countermeasures. A taxonomy has been proposed for the same. Security attacks have been classified into component and interface level attacks based on the type of controller-centric architecture of the network. Similarly, countermeasures have been explored for attacks over devices, interfaces, traffic flow, and network policies in detail. Protocols suitable for SDN-based IoT environment have been described along with their security aspects. Some open source tools for simulation and emulation, controller platforms, physical and virtual switches, and Test suite along with the datasets for the development of SDN-based IoT networks have been highlighted.

Application areas of SDN in IoT scenario included smart home networks, real-time streaming, and network virtualization have been covered. Finally, the chapter has been concluded with some of the existing research challenges and open research directions in the field.

References

1. Evans D. The internet of things: How the next evolution of the internet is changing everything. *CISCO White Paper*. 2011 Apr;1(2011):1–1.
2. ITU-T Y. Overview of ubiquitous networking and of its support in NGN. ITU-T Recommendation. 2009.
3. Krco S, Pokric B, Carrez F. Designing IoT architecture (s): A European perspective. In Internet of Things (WF-IoT), 2014 IEEE World Forum on 2014 Mar 6 (pp. 79–84). IEEE.
4. Gartner. www.gartner.com/newsroom/id/3598917.
5. Tayyaba SK, Shah MA, Khan OA, Ahmed AW. Software Defined Network (SDN) based Internet of Things (IoT): A road ahead. In Proceedings of the International Conference on Future Networks and Distributed Systems 2017 Jul 19 (p. 10). ACM.
6. Network World. networkworld.com.
7. Kotronis V, Dimitropoulos X, Klöti R, Ager B, Georgopoulos P, Schmid S. Control exchange points: Providing QoS-enabled end-to-end services via SDN-based inter-domain routing orchestration. *LINX*. 2014;2429(1093):2443.
8. Park SM, Ju S, Kim J, Lee J. Software-defined-networking for M2M services. InICT Convergence (ICTC), 2013 International Conference on 2013 Oct 14 (pp. 50–51). IEEE.
9. Botelho F, Ramos FM, Kreutz D, Bessani A. On the feasibility of a consistent and fault-tolerant data store for SDNs. In Software Defined Networks (EWSDN), 2013 Second European Workshop on 2013 Oct 10 (pp. 38–43). IEEE.
10. Mattos DM, Duarte OC. AuthFlow: Authentication and access control mechanism for software defined networking. *Annals of Telecommunications*. 2016 Dec 1;71(11–12):607–615.
11. An J, Kim K. A study on authentication mechanism in SEaaS for SDN. In Proceedings of the 11th International Conference on Ubiquitous Information Management and Communication 2017 Jan 5 (p. 51). ACM.
12. Klaedtke F, Karame GO, Bifulco R, Cui H. Access control for SDN controllers. In Proceedings of the Third Workshop on Hot Topics in Software Defined Networking 2014 Aug 22 (pp. 219–220). ACM.
13. Shin S, Yegneswaran V, Porras P, Gu G. Avant-guard: Scalable and vigilant switch flow management in software-defined networks. In Proceedings of the 2013 ACM SIGSAC Conference on Computer & Communications Security 2013 Nov 4 (pp. 413–424). ACM.
14. Mousavi SM, St-Hilaire M. Early detection of DDoS attacks against SDN controllers. In Computing, Networking and Communications (ICNC), 2015 International Conference on 2015 Feb 16 (pp. 77–81). IEEE.
15. Neti S, Somayaji A, Locasto ME. Software diversity: Security, entropy and game theory. InHotSec 2012 Aug 7.
16. Jafarian JH, Al-Shaer E, Duan Q. Openflow random host mutation: Transparent moving target defense using software defined networking. In Proceedings of the First Workshop on Hot Topics in Software Defined Networks 2012 Aug 13 (pp. 127–132). ACM.
17. Al-Shaer E, Al-Haj S. FlowChecker: Configuration analysis and verification of federated OpenFlow infrastructures. In Proceedings of the 3rd ACM Workshop on Assurable and Usable Security Configuration 2010 Oct 4 (pp. 37–44). ACM.
18. Kreutz D, Ramos F, Verissimo P. Towards secure and dependable software-defined networks. In Proceedings of the Second ACM SIGCOMM Workshop on Hot Topics in Software Defined Networking 2013 Aug 16 (pp. 55–60). ACM.
19. Ben-Itzhak Y, Barabash K, Cohen R, Levin A, Raichstein E. EnforSDN: Network policies enforcement with SDN. In Integrated Network Management (IM), 2015 IFIP/IEEE International Symposium on 2015 May 11 (pp. 80–88). IEEE.
20. Canini M, Kuznetsov P, Levin D, Schmid S. Software transactional networking: Concurrent and consistent policy composition. In Proceedings of the Second ACM SIGCOMM Workshop on Hot Topics in Software Defined Networking 2013 Aug 16 (pp. 1–6). ACM.
21. Scott-Hayward S, Kane C, Sezer S. Operationcheckpoint: SDN application control. In Network Protocols (ICNP), 2014 IEEE 22nd International Conference on 2014 Oct 21 (pp. 618–623). IEEE.

22. Chandrasekaran B, Tschaen B, Benson T. Isolating and tolerating SDN application failures with LegoSDN. In Proceedings of the Symposium on SDN Research 2016 Mar 14 (p. 7). ACM.

23. Qazi ZA, Lee J, Jin T, Bellala G, Arndt M, Noubir G. Application-awareness in SDN. In ACM SIGCOMM Computer Communication Review 2013 Aug 12 (Vol. 43, No. 4, pp. 487–488). ACM.

24. Stoenescu R, Popovici M, Negreanu L, Raiciu C. Symnet: Scalable symbolic execution for modern networks. In Proceedings of the 2016 ACM SIGCOMM Conference 2016 Aug 22 (pp. 314–327). ACM.

25. Gasparini LA, Gotlieb CE. Inventors; RSA Security LLC, assignee. Method and apparatus for authentication of users and web sites. United States patent US 7,100,049. 2006 Aug 29.

26. Leong CW, Lau CH, Kong YL, Phang TW, Cheong HS. Inventors; E-Lock Corporation Sdn. Bhd., assignee. Method of controlling access to an internet-based application. United States patent US 9,628,460. 2017 Apr 18.

27. Hartung M, Körner M. SOFTmon-traffic monitoring for SDN. *Procedia Computer Science*. 2017 Jan 1;110:516–23.

28. Yu Y, Qian C, Li X. Distributed and collaborative traffic monitoring in software defined networks. In Proceedings of the Third Workshop on Hot Topics in Software Defined Networking 2014 Aug 22 (pp. 85–90). ACM.

29. Phan TV, Bao NK, Park M. Distributed-SOM: A novel performance bottleneck handler for large-sized software-defined networks under flooding attacks. *Journal of Network and Computer Applications*. 2017 Aug 1;91:14–25.

30. Wang M, Liu J, Chen J, Liu X, Mao J. Perm-guard: Authenticating the validity of flow rules in software defined networking. *Journal of Signal Processing Systems*. 2017 Mar 1;86(2–3):157–173.

31. Chen XF, Yu SZ. CIPA: A collaborative intrusion prevention architecture for programmable network and SDN. *Computers & Security*. 2016 May 1;58:1–9.

32. Jia X, Ren D, Yang Y, Li H, Sun G. DFIPS: Toward distributed flexible intrusion prevention system in software defined network. In SEKE 2016 (pp. 124–127).

33. Fayazbakhsh SK, Sekar V, Yu M, Mogul JC. Flowtags: Enforcing network-wide policies in the presence of dynamic middlebox actions. In Proceedings of the Second ACM SIGCOMM Workshop on Hot Topics In Software Defined Networking 2013 Aug 16 (pp. 19–24). ACM.

34. Brandt M, Khondoker R, Marx R, Bayarou K. Security analysis of software defined networking protocols—OpenFlow, OF-Config and OVSDB. In The 2014 IEEE Fifth International Conference on Communications and Electronics (ICCE 2014), DA NANG, Vietnam 2014 Jul.

35. Mininet. http://mininet.org.

36. Xilinx. www.xilinx.com/products/design-tools/software-zone/sdnet.html#overview.

37. NS-3. www.nsnam.org/.

38. Noxrepo/NOX: The NOX Controller. https://github.com/noxrepo/nox.

39. Noxrepo/POX. https://github.com/noxrepo/pox.

40. OpenDaylight. www.opendaylight.org.

41. Software- ONOS. https://onosproject.org/software/.

42. Bigswitch/BeaconMirror. https://github.com/bigswitch/BeaconMirror.

43. Project Floodlight. www.projectfloodlight.org/floodlight/.

44. IRIS: The Recursive SDN Openflow Controller by ETRI. http://openiris.etri.re.kr.

45. Kandoo/Beehive-netctrl. https://github.com/kandoo/beehive-netctrl.

46. Project Floodlight. www.projectfloodlight.org/indigo/.

47. Open vSwitch. http://openvswitch.org.

48. Project Floodlight. www.projectfloodlight.org/oftest/.

49. Mcanini/Nice. https://github.com/mcanini/nice.

50. Statistical Analysis of Network Data. http://math.bu.edu/people/kolaczyk/datasets.html.

51. Knowledge-Defined Networking Training Datasets. http://knowledgedefinednetworking.org.

52. Kim S, Na W. Safe data transmission architecture based on cloud for Internet of Things. *Wireless Personal Communications*. 2016 Jan 1;86(1):287–300.

53. Bull P, Austin R, Popov E, Sharma M, Watson R. Flow based security for IoT devices using an SDN gateway. In Future Internet of Things and Cloud (FiCloud), 2016 IEEE 4th International Conference on 2016 Aug 22 (pp. 157–163). IEEE.

54. Xu K, Wang X, Wei W, Song H, Mao B. Toward software defined smart home. *IEEE Communications Magazine.* 2016 May;54(5):116–122.

55. Kim H, Feamster N. Improving network management with software defined networking. *IEEE Communications Magazine.* 2013 Feb;51(2):114–119.

56. Chen J, Chen J, Ling J, Zhou J, Zhang W. Link failure recovery in SDN: High efficiency, strong scalability and wide applicability. *Journal of Circuits, Systems and Computers.* 2018 Jun 15;27(06):1850087.

57. Cascone C, Sanvito D, Pollini L, Capone A, Sansò B. Fast failure detection and recovery in SDN with stateful data plane. *International Journal of Network Management.* 2017 Mar 1;27(2):e1957.

58. Jeon, S, Guimarães, C, Aguiar, RL. SDN-based mobile networking for cellular operators. In Proceedings of the 9th ACM Workshop on Mobility in the Evolving Internet Architecture (2014, September) (pp. 13–18). ACM.

59. Jeon S, Guimarães C, Aguiar RL. SDN-based mobile networking for cellular operators. In Proceedings of the 9th ACM Workshop on Mobility in the Evolving Internet Architecture 2014 Sep 11 (pp. 13–18). ACM.

60. Jain R, Paul S. Network virtualization and software defined networking for cloud computing: A survey. *IEEE Communications Magazine.* 2013 Nov;51(11):24–31.

61. Hwang J, Ramakrishnan KK, Wood T. NetVM: High performance and flexible networking using virtualization on commodity platforms. *IEEE Transactions on Network and Service Management.* 2015 Mar;12(1):34–47.

62. Hernando AB, Fariña AD, Triana LB, Piñar FJ, Cambronero DF. Virtualization of residential IoT functionality by using NFV and SDN. In Consumer Electronics (ICCE), 2017 IEEE International Conference on 2017 Jan 8 (pp. 86–87). IEEE.

63. Heller B, Seetharaman S, Mahadevan P, Yiakoumis Y, Sharma P, Banerjee S, McKeown N. Elastictree: Saving energy in data center networks. In Nsdi 2010 Apr 28 (Vol. 10, pp. 249–264).

64. Jain S, Kumar A, Mandal S, Ong J, Poutievski L, Singh A, Venkata S, Wanderer J, Zhou J, Zhu M, Zolla J. B4: Experience with a globally-deployed software defined WAN. In ACM SIGCOMM Computer Communication Review 2013 Aug 12 (Vol. 43, No. 4, pp. 3–14). ACM.

65. Omnes N, Bouillon M, Fromentoux G, Le Grand O. A programmable and virtualized network & IT infrastructure for the internet of things: How can NFV & SDN help for facing the upcoming challenges. In Intelligence in Next Generation Networks (ICIN), 2015 18th International Conference on 2015 Feb 17 (pp. 64–69). IEEE.

66. Gringeri, S, Bitar, N, Xia, TJ. Extending software defined network principles to include optical transport. *IEEE Communications Magazine.* 2013;51(3):32–40.

67. Vissicchio S, Vanbever L, Bonaventure O. Opportunities and research challenges of hybrid software defined networks. *ACM SIGCOMM Computer Communication Review.* 2014 Apr 8;44(2):70–75.

68. Vladyko A, Muthanna A, Kirichek R. Comprehensive SDN testing based on model network. In Internet of Things, Smart Spaces, and Next Generation Networks and Systems 2016 Sep 26 (pp. 539–549). Springer, Cham.

69. Yan Z. Design of sensor gateway in IOT open environment. *Microcomputer & Its Applications.* 2015;14:023.

70. Gudipati A, Perry D, Li LE, Katti S. SoftRAN: Software defined radio access network. In Proceedings of the Second ACM SIGCOMM Workshop on Hot Topics in Software Defined Networking 2013 Aug 16 (pp. 25–30). ACM.

71. Jin X, Li LE, Vanbever L, Rexford J. Softcell: Scalable and flexible cellular core network architecture. In Proceedings of the Ninth ACM Conference on Emerging Networking Experiments and Technologies 2013 Dec 9 (pp. 163–174). ACM.

72. Galluccio L, Milardo S, Morabito G, Palazzo S. SDN-WISE: Design, prototyping and experimentation of a stateful SDN solution for WIreless SEnsor networks. In Computer Communications (INFOCOM), 2015 IEEE Conference on 2015 Apr 26 (pp. 513–521). IEEE.

73. Chakrabarty S, Engels DW, Thathapudi S. Black SDN for the Internet of Things. In Mobile Ad Hoc and Sensor Systems (MASS), 2015 IEEE 12th International Conference on 2015 Oct 19 (pp. 190–198). IEEE.

74. Jararweh Y, Al-Ayyoub M, Benkhelifa E, Vouk M, Rindos A. SDIoT: A software defined based internet of things framework. *Journal of Ambient Intelligence and Humanized Computing.* 2015 Aug 1;6(4):453–461.

75. Narisetty R, Dane L, Malishevskiy A, Gurkan D, Bailey S, Narayan S, Mysore S. Openflow configuration protocol: Implementation for the of management plane. In Research and Educational Experiment Workshop (GREE), 2013 Second GENI 2013 Mar 20 (pp. 66–67). IEEE.

76. Hares S, White R. Software-defined networks and the interface to the routing system (I2RS). *IEEE Internet Computing.* 2013 Jul;17(4):84–88.

77. Matias J, Garay J, Toledo N, Unzilla J, Jacob E. Toward an SDN-enabled NFV architecture. *IEEE Communications Magazine.* 2015 Apr;53(4):187–193.

78. Matsubara D, Egawa T, Nishinaga N, Kafle VP, Shin MK, Galis A. Toward future networks: A viewpoint from ITU-T. *IEEE Communications Magazine.* 2013 Mar;51(3):112–118.

79. Voellmy A, Wang J. Scalable software defined network controllers. In Proceedings of the ACM SIGCOMM 2012 Conference on Applications, Technologies, Architectures, and Protocols for Computer Communication 2012 Aug 13 (pp. 289–290). ACM.

80. Wang J, Shou G, Hu Y, Guo ZA. Multi-domain SDN scalability architecture implementation based on the coordinate controller. In Cyber-Enabled Distributed Computing and Knowledge Discovery (CyberC), 2016 International Conference on 2016 Oct 13 (pp. 494–499). IEEE.

Chapter 22

Security Issues and Challenges in Online Social Networks (OSNs) Based on User Perspective

Somya Ranjan Sahoo and Brij B. Gupta

National Institute of Technology Kurukshetra

Contents

22.1 Introduction to Online Social Network

Recently, the Internet use has greatly risen due to the popularity of the social networking sites. The lovechild of the WWW is social media, which comes in many forms like blogs, forums, business networks, photo-sharing platforms, social gaming, micro_blogs, chat apps, and social networks.

According to the Internet world statistics [1], the Internet users are more in Asia in comparison to others, i.e., around 49% of total Internet users in the world. According to world statistics report by Statista [2], there are 3,578 million Internet users in the world. The power of social networking raised in such a way that the number of worldwide users is expected to reach 2.95 billion by 2020, around a third of Earth's entire population. An estimated 650 million of these users are expected to be from China alone and approximately a third of a million from India. Online social networking is a way of virtual communication by which the user can communicate via personal chat, instant messaging, and blog. Users also communicate with other personals for transferring information on user choice. The evolutions of Web 2.0, the Online Social Networks (OSNs) site, gain much popularity with the first social networking sites called Sixdegrees.com in 1997. The OSN is broadly divided into many types based on their user choice and uses that are described in Figure 22.1. Among all social networking sites, Facebook [3], Twitter [4], WhatsApp [5], and Google+ [6] are more popular. Currently, Facebook has 2,061 million users in the world compared with other OSNs according to the statistic reports. Unfortunately, many OSN users are incognizant of the security hazards which survive in these types of communication. The risks include identity theft [7], malware [8], fake profiles [9], spam ware [10], social bots [11], Sybil attacks [12], sexual harassment [13], and others. Every social network sites have its own privacy and security guidelines and methods, but awareness of the people related to that is a main concern in the current scenario and it is a great challenge too. According to the recent studies [14, 16], many OSN users reveal their personal information and intimate details with their friends, relatives, friends of friends, mutual friends by posting photos, videos, and also directly providing information like address, phone number, and bank account details. According to articles by Boshmaf et al. [14] and Elyashar et al. [15, 17] Facebook users have been found to accept friendship requests from unknowns but some mutual friends are in the relation. Mikeyy worm attacked Twitter, and it replaced the user data with some unwanted data. Mikeyy attack did not steal personal information like Sammy attack. Koobface worm attacked Facebook and stole personal information like passwords, and this attack

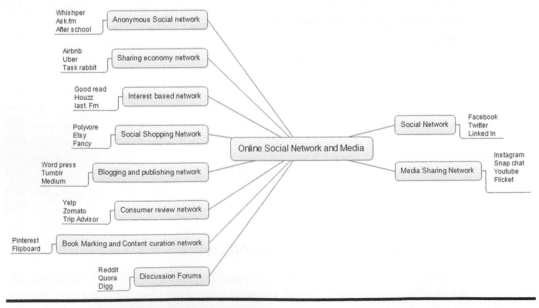

Figure 22.1 Classifications of OSN and media.

spread to other OSNs later. Compared to adults, teenagers and young children are more vulnerable and exposed to OSN. The personal information are exposed and abused due to users' daily lives on the OSN. Some attacker or cyber criminals misuses user's personal information for fun, harassment, steal personal information, company information, information related to bank and other corporate office data for financial benefit. To protect these information in OSN, various tools and framework-based solutions are made by different solution provider. This chapter highlights the potential issues, breaches in OSN, and some pretends also. It also highlights the different threats in the current scenario that affects the personal information of the user and harms the user in different environment.

The remainder of our chapter is structured as follows. In Section 22.2, we introduce the background and scope of OSN security. Next, in Section 22.3, we describe the potential issues and breaches of OSN security. In Section 22.4, we describe taxonomy of the existing security solutions. We describe the guidelines and recommendation for OSN users, in Section 22.5. In Section 22.6, we describe the taxonomy of existing security solutions of OSN. In Section 22.7, we describe future directions, open issues, and challenges related to OSN security. Finally, we conclude our work in Section 22.9.

22.2 Background and Scope of Online Social Network

OSNs have played a significant role in daily life in recent years. Worldwide the users of the OSNs have increased in an exponential emergence rate from 2005 onwards. Different statistics regarding OSNs are described by various statistics report. According to the report by statista.com [2], Facebook is leading with 2,061 million users compared with other social networking sites. Day by day, the use of social networking is becoming a common activity among the human beings for sharing of thoughts and personal information. Due to the popularity of OSNs, the use of the Internet has also increased. The leading OSNs like Facebook for communication and Twitter for comment are major communication platforms among the users. According to the survey by procon.org [19], 76% of American adults use OSN sites such as Facebook, Instagram, Twitter, LinkedIn, and Pinterest. The use of OSNs is higher in United Arab Emirates in comparison to other countries. Among all Internet users around the globe, there are 79% users who use Facebook in their desktop machine and also in mobile platform according to the social plot statistics report [18]. According to the survey by credit donkey [21], the percentage of daily active users of OSNs at different times is shown in Figure 22.2. A large number of users are intensely attacked by adversaries with various cases of attacks such as ransom ware, botnet, phishing, jacking, fake profile, spamming, and much more according to the Sophos security threat report [20]. Different types of threats also affect OSN sites by spreading malicious content through different sources.

Many people use search engines and social media to find information about a particular employee or person's prospects. In some cases, that information, especially social media information from sites like Facebook and Twitter, has been used for malicious purpose. Due to the huge uses of the OSNs, the attackers target this platform for attack.

22.2.1 Scope of Social Networking in Future

In the current scenario, the social networking sites are used not only for the communication purpose but also for marketing and advertising. Due to the widening scope of OSN, today it offers a strong support to the companies in providing much desired touch of concern. Future of OSN

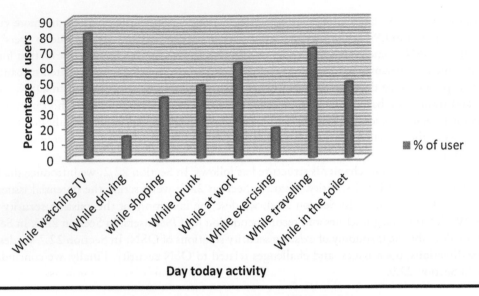

Figure 22.2   Percentage of daily active user of OSN at different time.

brings exciting promises as expected due to the increasing popularity and the easiest ways of communication. People directly communicate with the suppliers or customers and converse without any intervention of third party. OSN is one of the best practicing approaches for dealing with consumers for the betterment of product as well as services. At present, the OSN technology is integrated into the mobile phones and that shows the bright future prospect too. Moreover, in the current scenario, OSN provides solutions to the human being without any hurdles.

22.3 Potential Issues and Breaches in OSN Security

With the increasing usage of OSN in the current scenario, the issues are also rising rapidly. The different issues that are associated with OSN are based on the different premises. In recent trends, the human interventions with the OSN are too risky due to the unawareness of the user. The basic common problems that expose the accounts of OSN users are forgetting to log out the systems, clicking on luring ads, connecting with unknown users, using different third-party services, and surfing different sites with the help of OSN.

Forgetting to logout the system: In most cases, the users after using computer systems and surfing the OSN sites forget to log out. Due to this activity, there is a chance of hijacking the account if someone uses the same system. The person changes the content of your page and may send some unauthorized data to others from that account. It is a better practice to shut down the system after use and also logging out from that site.

Using different third-party services: Third-party application and services use OSN platforms to gain access to user credentials. Before sharing the different applications, the user must know about the genuine applications like games and other services. Some applications contain malicious links. When the user downloads the services, the malicious program gets installed on the user's computer and gets access to user's confidential data. The malicious applications run at the back end of the applications. Some of the applications provide services after downloading the apps.

At that time, the services ask the user to enter their details. Before entering the details, the user must conform about what kind of services are provided by that application.

Clicking on luring ads: In many OSN sites, people spread their contents in the form of link. That link attracts the users by displaying certain content. When the user click on that content it redirects into another page. The concept of redirecting the link into a page is called click jacking. The attacker spread malicious content and viruses in this manner by using different links in OSN platform. So before clicking, the user must verify that the available link is genuine one or not. In the year 2009, Twitter plagued by a "Don't click attack" along with a malicious link. When the Twitter user clicked on that link, the message automatically spread among all users those who are associated with your account [31].

Associate with unknowns: Worldwide, people use OSN sites to communicate with friends and relatives for sharing their information and thoughts virtually. Sometimes people add unknowns as a friend in OSN. When people add the different users, all the information related those users are public to their friend list. Unknown users send malicious content in the form of links, chats, etc. Sharing of information with unknowns is dangerous in OSN platforms. Before exposing personal information with others, you should be aware of strangers' accounts that are now associated with your account.

Surfing different sites by using advertising page: Surfing different sites with the help of advertising is a common practice of OSN users. OSN users are attracted to different advertisements and directly click on those pages to surf the page of their interest. When the user clicks on that page, it redirects the user into a different site and asks to enter personal details of the user to surf that page. Users those who are unaware of the security threats provide their personal information on those sites. Therefore, before visiting any sites, gathering information about that site is a perfect practice for the user.

22.4 Threats in OSN Platform

Due to the popularity of OSN sites among the users, the threats are also increasing day by day from various sites. The attacker tries to infect the user contents/information through OSN by spreading malicious contents. These threats are categorized into different groups based on their activities and behavior. The different threats and their activities are described below.

Infringement of rules by service provider: When the user creates an account in any social networking sites, by the rule of the service provider user must submit personal information like phone number, age, date of birth, etc. for the registration purpose. But service providers disclose the personal information of the users to get financial benefit from different advertising company without prior knowledge of the users [22].

Infringement by the user: In most cases, users share their information in OSN sites publically. Due to the publicly available content the information can be used by any person in the network. The information can be used by the attacker to create new profiles in the same network or in the different networks. These types of attacks are also called as cloning attack or fake profile attack. By this process, the attacker tries to gain the confidential information of the users and their friends, relatives, and colleagues [23].

Vicinity attack [24]: OSN users share their personal information on the different OSNs publicly. Users also communicate with their friends and relatives. When the user communicates, they share personal information like bank account number, mobile number, and many more. Attacker tries to analyze the related content of the user by using some user-related data that are available publicly. The neighborhoods always watch the sensitive information about the user available in different sites. It is a better practice not to share valuable information publicly on any social networking platform.

Risk related to chart [25]: The different social networking service provider provides the facility for online chatting with others. Some of the chat service like IRC (Internet relay chat), Microsoft (MSN), and many more provide the facility for group chatting among users. Teenagers are attracted toward that site for communication with friends and share their personal information. The information provided by the user attracts to a great risk like cyber bullying in OSN. Even if the anonymization techniques are used, the attacker uses graph-based techniques to analyze the related content of the user.

Hacking [26]: Hacking is a vicious activity in OSNs. Hackers are highly skilled professionals and competent to break the security of the users by applying multiple techniques. The focus of the hacker is on the user's related activity. They always try to penetrate into other systems without the permission of the user. If they find any leakage on that system they can easily break the security wall and steal personal information of the user.

Sybil attack [27]: Sybil attack is a type of security threat when a node in a network claims multiple identities. In OSN sites, to gain the popularity of the account a Sybil node shows their presence in multiple instances. By this process, the network computer on identified the distinct account in the network. When one of the profiles in the network is affected and claims multiple identities on the same network, then that account show its presence in the system.

Spammers in the network [28]: In OSN, spammers are the users. The spammer account holder spreads malicious content in the network by creating fake accounts in the same network or may be in the different networks based on their benefit. Spammers are try to send messages in the form of different advertising and comments in OSN platforms. When the malicious content is spread by the spammers account, it automatically spreads to different users in the network due to the sharing and liking feature provided by the service site. In the year 2009, 11% of the Twitter accounts were affected by spamming messages.

Phishing attack: Attacker attempts to gain personal information of the users by using different fraudulent techniques called phishing. By using this technique, user's personal information is stolen by the attackers, and they create some new accounts and send friend requests to others for gaining the credential of different users. This process of creating new accounts by collecting the information regarding the existing users is called fake account attack in OSNs. According to the security intelligence report by Microsoft more than 50% of all phishing attacks targeted social network users [29].

Malware attack [30]: In order to collect the user's information and gain access to the private information, malicious software is processed called malware in OSN sites. In OSN platform, it propagates among users and in the networks too. In many cases, malware sends messages continuously to the user for gaining access to the personal data. The most notorious malware in OSN called Koobface worm according to the report by Thomas et al.

Click_jacking attack [31]: The "clickjacking" attack provides a vicious page to click on a "victim site" *on behalf of the visitor*. It is a process of redirecting a user to a different page to gain access to the user's personal information. When the user clicks on the attracted link or like that page, it automatically visits another page. In many cases, it redirects the page, and the page activates the user camera or microphone to record the user content.

Face recognitions [32]: Most of the OSN sites have the provision to upload their profile photo for better identity. People upload and share their profile photo on those sites. The uploaded photos are publicly available to other users either in the same network or in the different networks. People easily download their photo and use it in many means. Recently, the Facebook provided photo guard feature to save the photo against downloading. But some people can take the snap shot of that photo. By this process, the authenticity of the user lapses. People basically use the same photo to create fake profiles in the same network or in other. Some of the attackers use the same photo in different profiles to create some malicious activities too.

Fake profile or cloned profile: The basic aim of creating fake profiles in OSN is to gain access to the user's credentials and collecting confidential information about the user like bank account no, mobile number, address, and details about the user. After creating fake accounts by the attacker, they initiate a friend request to the friends of original profile to collect the personal information of the user. The main source of Sybil attack is the creation of face profiles [33].

Distributed denial of service (DDos) attack [34]: It attacks the user by the help of spam messages in OSN. It seems to be original sender but it is not actual. It always seeks to make a web resource inaccessible to other applications by delivering huge messages simultaneously.

Online predators and cyber bullying [35]: In present scenario, most of the time the teenagers used OSN sites. Some people get that benefit and spread harassing advertisements and videos continuously to the teenagers. Sometimes, it is very harmful for teenagers due to the harassing messages. The attackers try to send messages in the form of chat, message, and via e-mail too. To avoid the cyber bullying and protect children from these types of attacks, parents should check the systems and monitor their children from time to time.

22.5 Recommendation and Guidelines for OSN Users

In recent trends, people spend much of their time in surfing the Internet. Basically, people are attracted toward social networking sites for communication and entertainment. OSN is a platform for communication among the users having some common interest, friends, and relatives. It avoids the geographical barrier between the users. When people use OSN sites, they must be aware of the different threats and attacks that violate the user identity. Basically, teenagers must know certain guidelines and recommendations provided by the service provider to handle and create accounts. Certain guidelines must be followed by individuals and corporates for protecting their accounts from different attacks.

User account confidentiality and privacy: Some of the service providers have certain rules and guidelines for creating accounts on their platform. At the time of creation, user provides certain data related to him/her in the site. Some of the users provide their details. By collecting information from those sites, attackers do certain malicious activities by using user's personal content. So, it is a better practice when the user creates an account in OSN sites, he/she must follow the guidelines provided by the service provider and also disclose minimum information related to the user. In most cases, service provider provides certain guidelines that users can handle at the time of operation. Strictly follow the security rules provided by the service provider and create a safeguard on that environment. Do not disclose lot of personal information in the web.

Do not harm others: Some of the users in the different social networking sites spread malicious and unethical messages and videos in the network for gaining their reputation in the web. Most of the time people harass teenagers in the social networking sites by sending pornographic materials. According to the IT Act, the act of harassing a user in the web is a criminal activity. Always try to get the positive content in the web by using OSN. Do not spread malicious content that harm other users in the same as well as in the other platforms.

Responsibility of the user: The owner of the accounts should have responsibility of their accounts. When the user shares, likes, posts, or blogs certain contents in the site, they must be aware of the content. Do not share unethical contents in the web that harass the user in the other end. The most important factor to maintain the user privacy is to keep track about the friend requests of friends and also mutual friends.

Verification of account: Before accepting or sending friend request to friends or friends of friends, check the status of the account properly. Some attackers create fake accounts to gather personal information of the users by sending friend request. When the user accepts the friend request, the information shared by the user is public to that account. The fake account holder gathers the personal information of the user and does certain malicious activity.

Maintain transparency: Whenever the user communicates with their friends and mutual friends, they must know the genuineness of the user. Always be transparent in the social networking sites when surfing. Most of the time, the clone profile or Sybil nodes are created and communicated with users to collect the confidential information about the user by chatting and sending messages.

Stay updated about new threats: Day by day, the number of OSN users increases exponentially. Likewise, the threats to different social networking sites are also increasing. Be aware of the recent threats that can affect the user personal content and reputation in the network. To safely operate the account timely verifies the content available in the user site. For better protection, update the operating system and the related softwares timely.

Better protection of your account: To protect your account from unauthorized access use certain softwares and frameworks that will protect the account from unauthorized access. Some of the softwares installed in your browser act as a safeguard for the system and social network accounts. Many service providers provide certain softwares that protect the system from malicious contents like malwares, spammers, and many more.

22.6 Taxonomy of Existing Security Solutions

To provide solutions to the OSN user, different researchers proposed different solutions based on the types of attack and vulnerabilities. In this section, we discuss different existing solutions, which can protect the OSN users from various attacks such as phishing attack, malware attack, and fake profiles attack. The security solution for OSN can be categorized into many groups as shown in Figure 22.3.

22.6.1 Different Solutions from Service Providers

The OSN service provider provides the security-based solutions for its user. Some part of the security solution provided at the time of profile creation, and other solutions are provided directly to the users, i.e., the authoritative power of individual account holders to set their privacy settings in their profiles. The social networking operator provides security services like OTP (one-time password) and CAPTCHA [36], photo identification [37], and multistage authentication principle [38] at the time of creation of profile or at the time of log-in. Every Twitter account goes through two-step authentication principle [39] for registration, i.e., in the first step, the user enters his/her user id with password and after that a verification code can generate and redirect that code to the user's mobile phones and registered email. By using this principle the authentication can be verified by the Twitter account. Many of the social networking services provide user

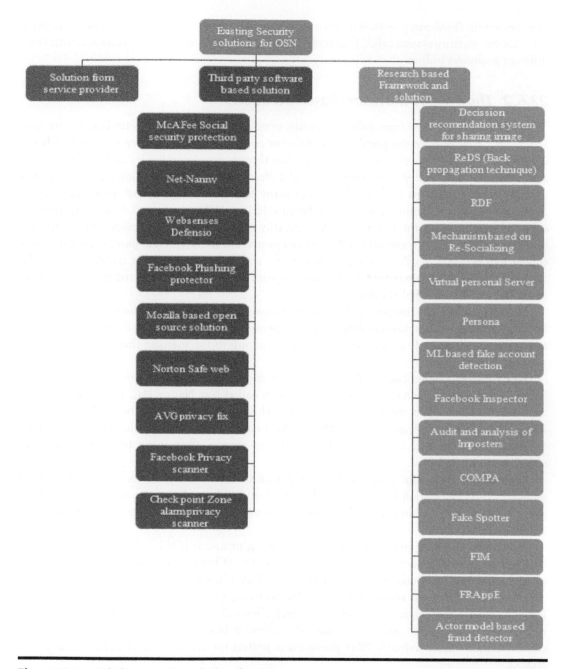

Figure 22.3 Existing security solution for OSN.

authentication setting for protecting their account and valuable information from online predators and attackers. The security setting at user level provides the facility to protect the profile according to the user's choice. One of the social networking sites called Facebook provides the security setting of who will be able to visit and see your account like friends, family member, mutual friends, or all. Similarly, Google+ provides grouping facility in a particular account, i.e., users place every account into different groups according to their choice. Some of the service providers provide certain third-party services for security setting by downloading some softwares. Facebook provides one security system called Facebook immune system to better protect their accounts from different malwares online.

22.6.2 *Third-Party Software-Based Solutions*

To protect the OSN users from different threats, some companies offer software-based protection system to better operate the profiles. The different companies provide different solutions based on the user use and for defensive prospects against threats. Some companies such as checkpoint, semantics, online permission technologies, and different open source solution-based companies provide security solutions to the OSN users in many platforms. The different companies such as Kaspersky security solution, Symantic web-based solution, AVG, panda, and Ariva offer different types of protection to the Internet users, especially OSN users. They provide some software-based firewalls, antivirus, and other OSN-related protection to the Internet users against different threats like malware, phishing attack, ransom ware, and from other Internet fraud. For example, Kaspersky security solutions provide protection against malware, anti-theft, and botnet attacks in many social networking platforms.

McAfee social security protection [40] provides security solution to the Facebook users by better protecting against downloading the profile photo. If someone downloads the profile picture of your account, it sends a message in the form of popup to the user site that who downloaded your picture.

Net Nanny: Parents can monitor and save their children from different threats like cyber bullying and cyber espionage by installing software called Net Nanny [41]. It protects the user from unethical sites and the activity done by the children in many social networking sites like Facebook and Twitter. Parents can also block certain harmful sites by using this software. To keep the family member and relatives safe from different attacks when using Internet is the basic objective of this software.

Websense's Defensio: It is a web-based service for the OSN users for protecting against malwares and information leakage. The software identifies the malwares posted on the Facebook page, and it deletes certain content from the post to protect against malwares by controlling user public information.

Facebook phishing protector: Facebook phishing protector [42] is a Firefox add-on service that protects the Facebook users from phishing attack. Whenever any suspicious activities are carried out in the Facebook platform, it activates and identifies the content in the form of popup.

Mozilla-based open source solution: One software solution called noscript security suite [43] is a Mozilla-based open source solution, which allows the different java script and flash players to be run on the system on user's choice. The software blocks all the java script content that comes from untrusted source in OSN platforms to protect the users against click jacking and XSS attacks.

Norton Safe Web (NSW) [44] is a web-based service developed by Symantec Corporation to help the user in social networking platform to identify malicious websites. Based on the automated analysis and feedback of the user it protects the user from malicious websites. The Norton safe web is a Facebook application with much number of users to safeguard the user privacy.

AVG privacy Fix: AVG provides one web-based security solution on mobile platform called AVG privacy fix [45] to protect the OSN users from different attacks. The security solution is a web browser add on which provide the users to manage their account by privacy setting. The add-on incorporated into different social network platform like Facebook, LinkedIn, and Google+

to provide security to its users. It also tracks the movement of different malicious content and generates a report based on their revenue.

Facebook privacy scanner [46]: Privacy scanner called trend micro is an android application used in Facebook platform to protect the system from unauthorized access of data. The application scans the privacy setting of the user, and if some privacy-related concern is in the profile, it informs the user.

Check-point Zone alarm privacy Scanner [47]: It is a Facebook application that monitors the performance of the system by analyzing different post. The security scanner scans the recent activity of the user and generates a report based on its activity. The checkpoint scanner checks all the recent post or activity in the profile and identify the post that disclose the privacy of user.

22.6.3 Research-Based Framework and Solution

Several researchers proposed several solutions to protect social network users and accounts. The solutions by researchers provide the complete solution to the users like from phishing attack, malware attacks, fake profile identification, and many more. Some of the framework provides the facility to improve the user privacy setting at user level to protect the profile from different attacks.

Decision recommendation system for sharing image [48]: It is a framework for calculating the privacy level of a digital image in the profile based on perceptual hashing and semantic privacy rules. Some of the threats download the profile photo of the user and use the same photo to create different accounts in the same platform or in different platform. By this way, the people can gather personal information of the user including the profile pictures to spread malicious content on the web.

ReDS (a back propagation techniques): It is an approach used to enhance the safety of data in P2P-based network. This framework does not need more user participation for operation. It operates directly on the network based on the principle and features. By using authentication and encryption mechanism, it protects the personal information of the user and confidential data also. This technique does not provide the backup facility to the user as well as the user accounts [49].

RDF (Resource description framework): The RDF framework does not require much participation of the user, it executes at the server end and operates at operator site. The service provider uses this framework to separate the data into different subsets and implement certain encryption techniques to protect the user data and confidential information. The framework uses the principle of encryption and decryption technique to protect the user data from unauthorized access [50].

Mechanism based on re-socializing: This technique based on the principle of coupling and out-of-bound invitation for designing multi-domain OSN [51]. The concept of re-socializing in OSN platform is for communication purpose between different users in the same network. The service provider provides the authentication principles to better protect the user content at their end. The different encryption techniques and methods are also implemented by the service provider to protect the valuable information.

Virtual personal server: Virtual personal server [52] is a virtual machine installed at the user computer to protect the data against the different attacks. The virtual machine installed in the user site and it creates a copy of the entire OSN site. The user can install the third-party applications and services also by using this virtual machine. After creating the copy of the OSN, it can operate the account in any means without getting affected by the attacker. To better protect the account the user can manage the platform and setup their configuration for suitable operations.

Persona [53]: To provide the data access control policy in OSN platform, researchers design an effective way of generating application for the OSN users. To protect the personal data of the user, it uses access control policy called attribute-based encryption techniques. The framework works like an API in Facebook platform to protect the user from unauthorized access. The API is implemented with the help of Firefox extension for compilation of markup languages. The framework or API can be easily installed in the Facebook user computer and also uninstalled easily.

Machine learning-based fake account detector [54]: In this framework, it uses some machine learning pipeline approach for detecting fake accounts in OSN like Facebook, LinkedIn, etc. The actor-based classification of accounts is grouped into different clusters so that the identification of the fake account can be easier by analyzing clusters. The basic objective of the framework is to identify the actor of the individual cluster to know if the account is from the same actor or from different.

Facebook Inspector [55]: The Facebook inspector (FBI) framework used to provide the real-time solution for identifying malicious content in Facebook platform. The framework analyzes the different characteristics of the Facebook profile and categorized the content into two different groups based on their behavior and activities. It processes a pre-trained model on different characteristics to know the exact behavior of the system. It detects the malicious content available in the user profile by analyzing post, blog, message, and chat rooms.

Audit and analysis of Imposters: It is an experimental framework for detecting fake accounts in OSN [56]. The framework is implemented on the individual profiles by analyzing the friends and mutual friends of the account holder. The framework is only applicable to the Facebook profiles. The framework classifies the profile information on the basis of public data available and process through machine learning algorithm with different classification techniques.

COMPA: A behavioral feature-based analysis [60]: COMPA is a tool-based detection technique of fake profiles in different OSN platforms. The tools can be installed at the user's computer, and when the user uses the social networking sites, it is automatically incorporated with the user profile and analyzes the features associated with the account.

Fake Spotter: Fake spotter [57] is a framework for finding fake accounts in OSN platform by sending certain feedback-related question to different users those are in the friend list. All the feedbacks are collected and stored in the database and certain analysis principles on those feedbacks are used to get the information about the user. The framework set an index level based on the feedback question. When all the feedbacks pass that framework, it creates a similarity index for finding genuine or fake profile activities. The framework is only implemented on the LinkedIn platform.

Friend in the middle (FIM) [58]: It is a technique to resilient de-anonymization technique in OSN platform. It provides a gateway to connect two different accounts in the same platform to avoid the attacks from different profiles. The framework creates a path between two users after verifying the content of the user and the activities done by the user on its profile.

FRAppE-based malicious App detector [59]: For detecting malicious content on the Facebook platform, Rahman et al. proposed a solution called FRAppE tool that focused on detecting malicious application in-built with Facebook profiles. The observation of the account can be done by collecting the information from different accounts. The different apps that are found in different profiles are combined in a particular location. Based on certain parameters like activity, the applications are segregated into two different categories called benign and fake applications.

Actor model-based fraud detector: Kelvin et al. proposed a framework for detecting fraud in OSN based on graph-based approach. The framework analyzes the different actor and their characteristics in the network platform for detecting fraudulent content. The frameworks identify the number of links available in the profile and then analyze the content by the help of machine learning principles to detect malicious content attached to that link.

22.7 Future Research Direction, Open Issues and Challenges

Security is the main concern in the field of OSN to protect the user's confidential information and profile for suitable operation of different accounts. Many researchers provide different solutions for protecting confidential information in user account from different attacks and threats. Some softwares are designed to protect the OSN from various prospects. But the solution provided by researchers have not been satisfactory in every scenario due to the recent developed features in different OSN platforms. Some of the framework provides specific applications in specific social network. Due to the above concern, a common framework should be designed that will protect the privacy of the user in any platform. Day-by-day the attackers create new techniques and gateway to penetrate to the user account to collect information about the user.

To provide better protection to the user account, we need certain encryption decryption technique that encrypt the user account and shown to the connected users only. In current scenario, one attack called Fake profile or clone profile attack spread rapidly in any social network to steal confidential information of the user and for many other means too. To detect the fake profiles researchers provide many solutions but the existing solution cannot stop the creation of the fake account or profiles. A framework is required that stop the creation of the fake profile in any platform. Another framework is required whenever any friend request is coming from any user's account, the framework goes through that account properly and sends a message to the receiver account whether the profile is the fake one or legitimate. To analyze the profile activity some researchers use machine-learning approach to analyze and detect the different malicious activity in the profile and generate some performance result. By this process the detection of the fake account is easier as compared to other approaches.

In some cases to improve the performance of the framework some combinational approaches are used to detect and analyze the behavior of the system. To analyze the post and advertise in social networking, data leak prevention (DLP) algorithm is also used to monitor the performance of profiles. Researchers use anomaly detection algorithm for detecting compromised accounts in social networking platform like Facebook and Twitter. Another method for improving privacy and security of the profile in OSN is to implement a combinational model of the existing approach is required to protect the profiles against malware, phishing, fake account detection, and from any other attacks. To update the software at timely basis, researchers are trying to design a proxy-based security solution to the OSN platform. Among all, the performance measure is the main concern in current scenario when researchers incorporate their frameworks and model in different OSNs. For the above concern, a performance evaluator is required for detecting the performance of the different frameworks and security softwares also. The most important factor in the security mechanism scenario is that protection of the image in the profile. Certain image encryption techniques are required to protect the image of user profile in OSN platform.

22.8 Conclusion

The basic objective of using OSN is to alter communication between friends, relative, and others for sharing of thoughts and information without the geological and economical limitations. In the present scenario, OSN has heavy requirements for defensive solutions to avoid recent threats and also works as a barrier between users and attacker. Most of the defensive solutions for OSN security we surveyed are not sufficient to avoid the current threats like fake profile attack, ransom ware, and many more. In this chapter, we have studied the different attacks to the OSN environment and the different security solutions to protect the user account against different threats. Some of the security-related issues are not yet solved that we describe in Section 22.7. Finally, we have concluded that the existing solutions provided by the researchers or corporate are not sufficient to protect the user account in social network sites from different attacks and threats. Hence, to protect the user account researchers should develop certain multi-platform-based security solutions.

References

1. www.internetworldstats.com/.
2. www.statista.com/statistics/272014/global-social-networks-ranked-by-number-of-users.
3. Facebook. Available at: www.facebook.com/.
4. Twitter. Available at: https://twitter.com/.
5. Whatsapp. Avalable at: www.whatsapp.com/.
6. Google+. Available at: https://plus.google.com/.
7. L. Bilge, T. Strufe, D. Balzarotti, and E. Kirda, "All your contacts are belong to us: Automated identity theft attacks on social networks," in Proc. 18th Int. Conf. World Wide Web, 2009, pp. 551–560.
8. J. Baltazar, J. Costoya, and R. Flores, "The real face of koobface: The largest web 2.0 botnet explained," *Trend. Micro. Res.*, vol. 5, no. 9, p. 10, 2009.
9. Q. Cao, M. Sirivianos, X. Yang, and T. Pregueiro, "Aiding the detection of fake accounts in large scale social online services," in Proc. 9th USENIX Conf. NSDI, 2012, p. 15. [Online]. Available: http://dl.acm.org/citation.cfm?id=2228298.2228319.
10. A. Aggarwal, J. Almeida, and P. Kumaraguru, "Detection of spam tipping behaviour on foursquare," in Proc. 22nd Int. Conf. World Wide Web Companion, 2013, pp. 641–648.
11. A. Elyashar, M. Fire, D. Kagan, and Y. Elovici, "Organizational intrusion: Organization mining using socialbots," in Proc. IEEE/ASE Int.Cyber Security Conf., 2012, pp. 7–12.
12. Q. Cao, M. Sirivianos, X. Yang, and T. Pregueiro, "Aiding the detection of fake accounts in large scale social online services," in Proc. 9th USENIX Conf. NSDI, 2012, p. 15. [Online]. Available: http://dl.acm.org/citation.cfm?id=2228298.2228319.
13. J. Wolak, D. Finkelhor, K. Mitchell, and M. Ybarra, "Online "predators" and their victims," *Psychol. Violence*, vol. 1, pp. 13–35, 2010.
14. Y. Boshmaf, I. Muslukhov, K. Beznosov, and M. Ripeanu, "The socialbot network: When bots socialize for fame and money," in Proc. 27th Annu. Comput. Security Appl. Conf., 2011, pp. 93–102.
15. A. Elyashar, M. Fire, D. Kagan, and Y. Elovici, "Organizational intrusion: Organization mining using socialbots," in Proc. IEEE/ASE Int. Cyber Security Conf., 2012, pp. 7–12.
16. A. Acquisti and R. Gross, "Imagined communities: Awareness, information sharing, privacy on the facebook," in *Privacy Enhancing Technologies*. New York, NY, USA: Springer-Verlag, 2006, pp. 36–58.
17. A. Elyashar, M. Fire, D. Kagan, and Y. Elovici, "Homing socialbots: Intrusion on a specific organization's employee using socialbots," in Proc. IEEE/ACM Int. Conf. Adv. Social Netw. Anal. Mining, 2013, pp. 1358–1365.
18. Social media statistics report. Available at: https://socialpilot.co/blog/151-amazing-social-media-statistics-know–2017.
19. https://socialnetworking.procon.org/view.resource.php.
20. Sophos: Two third of business fear that social networking endangers corporate security, Sophos research reveals. Available at: www.sophos.com/en-us/press-office-releasees/2009/04-networking.aspx.

21. Daily active Social network users. Available at www.creditdonkey.com/social-networking-statistics.html.
22. H. Gao, J. Hu, T. Huang, J. Wang, and Y. Chen, "Sucurity issue in online social network," *IEEE Comp. Sec.* 2011, vol. 15, pp. 56–66.
23. L. Bilge et al., "All your contacts are belongs to us: Automate identity theft attack on Social Network," ACM press, 2009, pp. 551–560.
24. P. Joshi and C. Jay Kuo, "Security and privacy in online social network," A survey, IEEE, 2011, pp. 1–6.
25. N. E. Oweis, M. A. Alrababa, W.G. Oweis, S. S. Owais, and M. Alansari, "A Survey of Internet Security Risk Over Social Networks" Published by the IEEE Computer Society, IEEE, 2014, pp. 1–4.
26. M. A. A. Ward, "Internet security," Slideshare, accessed Apr. 28, 2015. [Online]. Availble: www.slideshare.net/mabuward901/internet-security-17705601.
27. J. R. Douceur, "The sybil attack," in Proc. 1st Int. Workshop IPTPS, 2002, pp. 251–260. [Online]. Available: http://dl.acm.org/citation.cfm?id=646334.687813.
28. A. Chowdhury, *State of Twitter Spam*, Mar. 2010, accessed Jan. 14, 2014. [Online]. Available: https://blog.twitter.com/2010/state-twitter-spam.
29. T. Amin, O. Okhiria, J. Lu, and J. An, *Facebook: A Comprehensive Analysis of Phishing on a Social System*, 2010, accessed Feb. 1, 2014. [Online]. Available: https://courses.ece.ubc.ca/412/term_project/reports/ 2010/facebook.pdf.
30. W. Xu, F. Zhang, and S. Zhu, "Toward Worm Detection in Online Social Networks," ACM Press, 2010, pp. 11–20.
31. R. McMillan, "Researchers make wormy twitter attack," PCWorld, San Francisco, CA, USA, March 2009. [Online]. Available: www.pcworld.idg.com.au/article/296382/researchers_make_wormy_twitter_attack/.
32. *The Faces of Facebook.* [Online]. Available: http://app.thefacesoffacebook.com/.
33. J. R. Douceur, "The sybil attack," in Proc. 1st Int. Workshop IPTPS, 2002, pp. 251–260. [Online]. Available: http://dl.acm.org/citation.cfm?id=646334.687813.
34. R. Diebert and J. Stein, "Hacking networks of terror," Dialogue IO, 2002, vol. 1, pp. 1–14.
35. M. Deans, *The Story of Amanda Todd*, The New Yorker, Oct. 2012. [Online]. Available: www.newyorker.com/online/blogs/culture/2012/10/amanda-todd-michael-brutsch-and-free-speechonline.Html.
36. Y. Boshmaf, I. Muslukhov, K. Beznosov, and M. Ripeanu, "The socialbots network: When bots socialize for fame and money," in Proc. 27th Annu. Comput. Security Appl. Conf., 2011, pp. 93–102.
37. A. Jeffries, *Facebook's Security Check Asks Users to Identify Photos of Friends' Dogs, Gummi Bears*, 2010, accessed Feb. 1, 2014.
38. A. Song, *Introducing Login Approvals*, May 2011, accessed Jan. 14, 2014. [Online]. Available: www.facebook.com/note.php?note_id=10150172618258920.
39. J. O'Leary, *Getting Started With Login Verification*, May 2013, accessed Jan. 14, 2014. [Online]. Available: https://blog.twitter.com/2013/getting-started-login-verification.
40. *Mcafee Social Protection.* Available: www.protectmediaonline.com.
41. *Net Nanny.* [Online]. Available: www.netnanny.com/.
42. D. Casorran, *Facebook Phishing Protector.* [Online]. Available: https://addons.mozilla.org/en-US/firefox/addon/facebook-phishingprotector/.
43. NoScript Security Suite. [Online]. Available: http://noscript.net/.
44. Symantec, *Norton SafeWeb.* [Online]. Available: www.facebook.com/appcenter/nortonsafeweb.
45. AVG, *Avg Privacyfix.* [Online]. Available: www.privacyfix.com/.
46. T. Micro, *Privacy Scanner for Facebook.* [Online]. Available: https://play.google.com/store/apps/details?id=com.trendmicro.socialprivacyscanner.
47. CheckPoint, *Zonealarm Privacy Scan.* [Online]. Available: www.facebook.com/appcenter/sgprivacy.
48. D. Hu, F. Chen, X. Wu, and Z. Zhao, "A Framework of Privacy Decision Recommendation for Image Sharing in Online Social Networks," 2016 IEEE First International Conference on Data Science in Cyberspace (DSC), Changsha, 2016, pp. 243–251.

49. M. Wright, A. Kapadia, M. Kumar, and A. Dhadphale, "ReDS: Reputation for directory services in P2P systems," in Proceedings of the Sixth Annual Workshop on Cyber Security and Information Intelligence Research, ACM, 2010, p. 71.

50. B. Carminati, E. Ferrari, R. Heatherly, M. Kantarcioglu, and B. Thuraisingham, "A semantic web based framework for social network access control." in Proceedings of the 14th ACM symposium.

51. M. Dürr, M. Werner, and M. Maier, "Re-socializing online social networks," in Green Computing and Communications (GreenCom), 2010 IEEE/ACM Int'l Conference on & Int'l Conference on Cyber, Physical and Social Computing (CPSCom), IEEE, 2010, pp. 786–791.

52. R. Cáceres, L. Cox, H. Lim, A. Shakimov, and A. Varshavsky, "Virtual individual servers asprivacy-preserving proxies for mobile devices," in Proceedings of the 1st ACM workshop on Networking, systems, and applications for mobile handhelds, ACM, 2009, pp. 37–42.

53. R. Baden, A. Bender, N. Spring, B. Bhattacharjee, and D. Starin, "Persona: an online social network with user-defined privacy," in ACM SIGCOMM Computer Communication Review, *ACM*, 2009, vol. 39, no. 4, pp. 135–146.

54. C. Xiao, D. M. Freeman, and T. Hwa, "Detecting clusters of fake accounts in online social networks," in Proceedings of the 8th ACM Workshop on Artificial Intelligence and Security, ACM, 2015, pp. 91–101.

55. P. Dewan and P. Kumaraguru, Soc. Netw. Anal. Min. "Facebook Inspector (FbI): Towards automatic real-time detection of malicious content on Facebook", 2017. doi:10.1007/s13278-017-0434-5.

56. A. J. Sarode and A. Mishra, "Audit and Analysis of Impostors: An experimental approach to detect fake profile in online social network," ACM Proceeding, 2015, pp. 1–8.

57. D. Freeman. "Can you spot the fakes?: On the limitations of user feedback in online social networks," in WWW, 2017.

58. F. Beato, M. Conti, and B. Preneel, "Friend in the middle (fim): Tackling de-anonymization in social networks," in PERCOM, 2013.

59. S. Rahman, T.-K. Huang, H. V. Madhyastha, and M. Faloutsos, "Detecting Malicious Facebook Applications," 2015.

60. M. Egele, G. Stringhini, C. Kruegel, and G. Vigna, "COMPA: Detecting Compromised Accounts on Social Networks," in Proceedings of Network and Distributed System Security Symposium (NDSS), CA, United States, 2013.

Chapter 23

A Compendium of Security Issues in Wireless Sensor Networks

Jasminder Kaur Sandhu, Anil Kumar Verma, and Prashant Singh Rana

Thapar Institute of Engineering and Technology

Contents

23.1 Introduction

The core consideration for a Wireless Sensor Network (WSN) is its interaction with the environment in which it is deployed. The deployed nodes in this network are known as Motes. The basic tasks of this network are divided into the wireless communication of data, sensing the environment, actuation task (which is an optional component), and processing. The networks with additional actuation component are termed as Wireless Sensor and Actuator Networks [1]. Also, radio signals are used for communicating information in these networks.

The wireless standards used by sensor networks are 802.15.4 and ZigBee. The IEEE 802.15.4 is a Wireless Personal Area Network (WPAN) standard with low-rate transmission capability, which further forms the guiding technology for the wireless communication. ZigBee operates on the specifications of IEEE 802.15.4. Thus, ZigBee is a specification used for networks that requires low data rate and high energy efficiency, and demands secure networking [2].

The IEEE 802.15.4 is a networking standard that specifies the MAC and physical layer functionality for the low-rate WPAN, managed by the IEEE 802.15 working group, since the year 2003. The data rate of up to 250 Kbps is supported by WPAN.

IEEE 802.15.4 also acts as the basis for the ZigBee and has extended the standard up to two upper layers as shown in the Figure 23.1. ZigBee adds to the layers the logical network security and the application software [3]. It supports a large network of the order ≤ 65k nodes.

WSN has attained significant interest from the research community as well as from the application developers in the recent years. This network facilitates the large-scale complex communication in real-time data processing domain. These networks are the building blocks of smart spaces, which include the use of information technology at home and offices. This technology can be compared to pervasive techniques and affects our day-to-day life in numerous ways. A good design of such networks can increase its security and survivability.

WSN comprises multiple nodes, which interact with each other to communicate information wirelessly. These nodes communicate with the environment in which they are deployed by sensing or by physical parameter control. A single node cannot communicate data across the network, so they collaborate with each other. This collaborated data is further filtered using the data agglomeration technique. The Defense Advanced Research Projects Agency's (DARPA) program named SmartDust describes the WSN as follows:

> A sensor network is a deployment of massive numbers (i.e. a number of deployments can range from tens to thousands) of small, inexpensive, self-powered devices that can perform sensing, computation, and communication with other devices for the purpose of gathering local information to make global decisions about a physical environment.

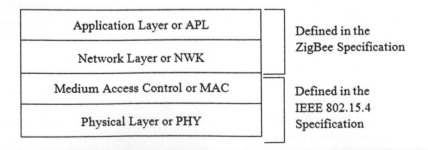

Figure 23.1   IEEE 802.15.4 vs. ZigBee.

In a nutshell, WSN is described as a communicating network which comprises multiple sensors. These sensors are also termed as motes and are deployed densely in the area of interest. The surrounding environment is sensed, and the information is transmitted henceforth. This transmitted information is traversed to the sink node. The sink node performs the filtration, agglomeration task on the data. This also provides a data-centric approach to data communication. One of the simplest WSNs is demonstrated in Figure 23.2. These networks are dynamic as well as static, can change their topology often as demanded by the application, and are much prone to failures. The communication in the network takes place in single or multiple hops. The communicated data reaches the sink node where it can be used on a local basis or can be further used globally with the help of gateways [4].

The WSN can be classified into two ways depending upon its nature:

Proactive WSNs: They collect information on the periodic basis that means they sense the environment at some regular intervals of time. Hence, are best suited for the applications, which require readings at well-defined intervals.

Reactive WSNs: They function on strict time-constraint. They collect information as soon as an event occurs. These nodes can be managed efficiently by using the sleep–wake up cycle for sensor nodes.

23.1.1 Motivation

MEMS (Micro-Electro-Mechanical Systems) technological advances have led to the deployment of multifunctional sensors in a reliable way. These sensors are low power and low price sensors. However, the evolution of networking sensors dates back to the 1970s. At that time, they

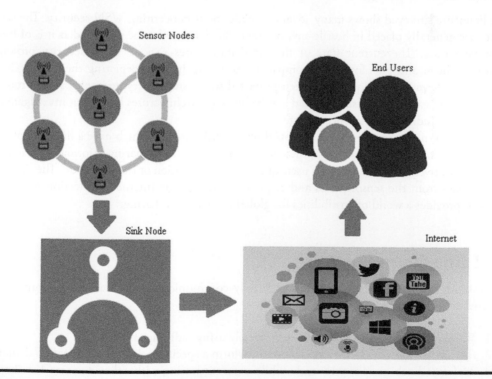

Figure 23.2   Sensor network in its simplest form.

were used for machine monitoring. Current-day research focuses on low-power WSN deployed on a large scale. This research began in the mid-1990s and was further explored in the early 2000s. The primary driver for research on WSN is the DARPA ISAT (Information Science and Technology) in the United States [5]. Environment interaction is the core concept of the WSN. Also, the main application areas encompassing the use of WSN include military, surveillance in war zones, and detection of fire in a forest [6]. Such hostile consideration of WSN causes more security concerns.

Deployed nodes communicate wirelessly. So, certain parameters need to be discussed for evaluating the WSN performance. Some of these parameters are routing overhead, energy efficiency, average delay, packet drop, and packet delivery fraction. Understanding of the existing routing mechanisms, tailoring minimal network delay, minimizing the packet drop, and calculation of optimal packet delivery fraction will lead to reliable results resulting in better performance of the network. Security forms a crucial area of research in WSN. Service availability of the network, its confidentiality, and also taking into account the integrity of data and many more such constraints can be achieved by optimizing the security issues in the network. A holistic view to ensure layered and robust security in WSN is presented. Also, the proposal is laid out for a suitable technique that detects and procures the sensor network from attacks by malicious nodes. The very base of WSN lies in the DARPA, which sponsored a workshop on Distributed Sensor Nets (DSNs, CMU) in the year 1978. Another application was DARPA SensIT in 1998 that focused on ad-hoc and wireless networks and was used for the large distributed military sensor system. NASA Sensor Webs Project in 2001 further paved the way for WSN applications.

23.1.2 State of the Art

The literature surveyed shows many advances made so far concerning WSN security. The sensor nodes are generally placed in hostile environment; the data need to be protected as it is of highly sensitive nature. The current state of the art demonstrates various WSN security protocols, examines them, and puts forward a comparison of the techniques depicting their strength and weaknesses. Several techniques have been proposed so far such as cryptography, secure routing, and data aggregation. Also, security and survivability [7] architectures have been investigated for the WSN, including the resilience aspect.

The sensor nodes in a WSN are equipped with 2 AA batteries which have a life span of three years [8]. In a normal WSN scenario, these nodes communicate by sharing information wirelessly. In a comparatively complex scenario, users queries the base station or the sink node. The sink node gathers data from the sensor nodes and responds to the query. Internet connection to a sensor network provides a world of possibilities for global information sharing.

23.2 The Essence of WSNs

The essence of WSN lies in the way it wirelessly communicates information [9]. Some of the features of WSN are as follows:

1. *Wireless*: These nodes communicate wirelessly using radio signals.
2. *Application Specific*: WSN is designed to perform a specific task as the application demands.
3. *Mobility*: Each node moves freely while communicating with other devices. This implies that the intercommunication pattern among the nodes change continuously.

4. *Multi-hop Routing*: Every node acts as a router and forward packets enabling communication between mobile nodes. Hence, dedicated routers are not necessary.

5. *The Paradigm for Communication*: It has a data-centric paradigm, which means that communication is targeted to nodes placed at a particular location or in accordance with specific data content.

6. *Density and Scale of Network*: The density of nodes can be high. As compared to various other wireless networks, the number of nodes contained in WSNs may be higher.

7. *Node Deployment*: The deployment of nodes in large-scale WSN is in a random fashion. Thus, their replacement and maintenance are impractical. As the requirement and application of deployed WSN may alter, this means that the runtime reprogramming and reconfiguration are required.

8. *Resource Constraints*: The nodes are subject to failure due to depleted batteries or environmental impacts. The limited size and energy means restricted resources in terms of memory, wireless communication, CPU performance, bandwidth, and range.

23.2.1 Design Issues and Constraints

The design issues and constraints differ from one particular application to another. Also, it differs in respect of deployment environment such as terrestrial, underwater deployment [9–11]:

1. *Network Dynamics*: This means that the sensed event can either be dynamic or be static based upon the application. Mostly network architectures assume that the sensor nodes are static or stationary because there are few setups that use the mobile sensors. Hence, sometimes it is necessary to support the mobility of sinks or those of the cluster-head also known as gateway. Some different optimization factors covered in this are route stability, security, energy, bandwidth, etc. Thus, security forms the very basic challenge in such type of networks.

2. *Energy Consumption Issue*: Energy conservation determines the lifetime of a WSN. Sensor nodes use battery power as an energy source. The battery life of sensors is limited. And as the sensors are placed in hostile environment, replacing the battery is impractical. The energy of these nodes is consumed in three operations:
   - Sensing Task,
   - Communicating Information,
   - Processing the data.

   So, the issue is to conserve or minimize the energy consumption in these three operations.

3. *Topology Control*: The topology refers to the deployment of sensor nodes in a particular area or region of interest. The term topology control refers to the deployment of sensor nodes in a fashion covering the entire surrounding environment. The nodes in a sensor network are deployed in the following three phases:
   - *The Pre-deployment and Development Phase*: In this scenario, the nodes are placed by throwing them randomly on the field or by placing them one at a time in the region of interest.
   - *Post-deployment Phase*: There is a change in topology due to limited energy constraints, range, malfunctioning of a particular node, etc.
   - *The Phase for the Redeployment of Additional Nodes*: Redeployment means to rearrange the network dynamically considering factors such as node malfunctioning.

4. *Localization*: Sensor networks have the ad-hoc type of deployment, so knowledge about the position of the sensor node is missing. Thus, this problem of determining the position of

nodes is called Localization. This localization can be computed with the help of the Beacon Nodes, GPS, Moore's Algorithm, etc.

5. *Data Gathering*: It includes the collection of data from various deployed sensors thereby, removing the redundant data. This information is passed on to the sink node without the loss of information. There are various security holes in data gathering which are removed with data compression and data agglomeration techniques.

6. *Coverage*: This optimally covers the entire network to deduce best possible results during communication.

7. *Connectivity*: It ensures the optimal delivery of sensed data to the sink node. This connectivity is achieved using the radio transmission.

8. *Clocks*: The main purpose of a clock is for synchronizing the communication. It is used for tracking and monitoring.

9. *Computation*: It is the amount of data proceeds by each node. Computation must be carried out at each node in sensor network, which forwards data to sink node. This would be beneficial as the sink node would not be overburdened with the task of performing all the computations.

10. *Scheduling*: It tells us for what time period a node will remain in sleep, standby, or active mode. Energy consumption can be reduced by optimal scheduling.

11. *Reliability*: The network should work reliably and produce correct results. If one node fails, the entire system should not be affected. The various forms of reliability are as follows:
    - *Event Reliability*: This determines the successful detection of an event. In this case, not all packets need to be successfully transmitted.
    - *Packet Reliability*: Successful transmission of all packets is required for less sensitive application areas.
    - *Reliability Related to Destination*: Data is to be transmitted to a specific node in a particular area of interest.

12. *Processing the Query*: WSN is a two-tier structure wherein storage sensor node behaves as an intermediate node and sink node is the node that answers queries by collecting the data from various other attached nodes.

13. *Scalability*: The addition and removal of a sensor node in a WSN must be possible. And also, if a new node is added, it must be able to coordinate with the deployed network. This phenomenon is known as scalability and is an important feature of this network.

14. *Production Cost*: It is reasonable to keep into account the application on which the work is going on.

15. *Security*: All the security goals must be achievable such as freshness, confidentiality, non-repudiation, authorization, integrity, availability, and authentication. The next section will elaborate the concept of security attacks in a layered architectonics form.

16. *Hardware Constraints*: The following are hardware components that should operate to support high volumetric densities (Figure 23.3).

23.2.2 Architectonics of a WSN

The sensor nodes can sense and interact with the environment. The ambient conditions which can be sensed include humidity, temperature, vehicular movement, soil composition, noise, etc. [9]. The communication between the nodes takes place wirelessly. The nodes work in collaboration to accomplish a pre-defined task. The data collected from sensor nodes is accumulated at the sink

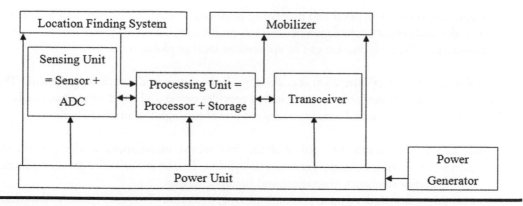

Figure 23.3   The components of a sensor network.

node, where data agglomeration task [12] is performed. This data can be further communicated to the end user with the help of Internet connectivity [13] (Figure 23.4).

Sensor Nodes: The sensor nodes deployed in the area of interest senses the environment. The main functions of a sensor node are to act as a source, destination, sink node, or an actuator in the network. The source is the node that transmits data, the destination is the node that receives data, the sink node performs the main function of agglomeration, and the actuator is basically for acting upon the environment. Hence, the sensor node performs the task of storage, processing, computing, and sending the data.

Gateways: Gateways acts as an interface between the system managers and the sensor nodes, laptops, personal computers, Internet, various other connected networks to enable communication. It also provides a proxy for WSN on Internet. There are three types of gateway: Passive, Active, and Hybrid. The passive gateway sends a request to the sensor nodes. The active gateway forwards the data in an active manner from the sensor nodes to the gateway server. And, the hybrid gateway combines the properties of passive and active gateway.

Task Managers: The gateways are further connected to the task manager with the help of an Internet connection. It comprises data processing, computation facility, and the data service.

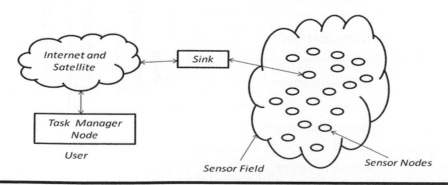

Figure 23.4   The sensor nodes scattered in a sensor field.

It is an information retrieval and processing platform. The sensed information is stored in the task manager for further analysis. This information includes raw, processed, and filtered information. This information can be accessed by local or global users.

The WSN protocol stack (Figure 23.5) is utilized by all the sensor nodes including the sink. This ensures cooperation between various sensor nodes, provides power and route awareness, combines network protocols and data, and communicates the power through the wireless medium.

Physical Layer: It addresses the need of simple but robust modulation. It also governs the transmittal, receiving techniques and data encryption. This layer also addresses the frequency selection, carrier frequency generation, and signal deflection.

Data Link Layer: It includes data stream multiplexing, detection of the data frame, and medium access control (MCA). It also guarantees reliable point-to-point and point-to-multipoint connections. It also provides error control mechanism.

Network Layer: It enables data routing and governs the flow of packets in the network. The address assignment is also specified in this layer.

Transport Layer: The reliable flow of data is maintained at this layer if a particular application demands it.

Application Layer: The interactions with the end users take place at this layer and are responsible for the display of data in the requested format. It takes care of the data presentation format as required by the communicating nodes and the end users.

In addition to the layers, there are three planes: power, mobility, and task management. The power management plane enables communication among nodes in a power-efficient way. The mobility

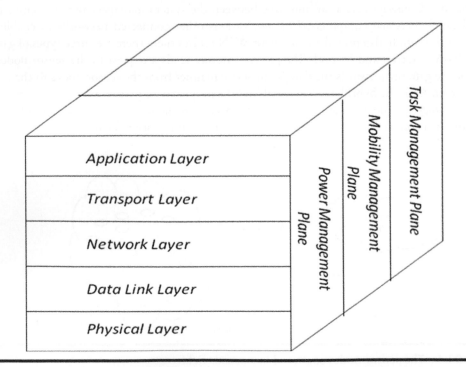

Figure 23.5   The WSN protocol stack.

management takes care of the nodes movement, and the task management ensures the proper distribution of task among the nodes.

Task Management Plane: The sensing task for a particular region of interest can be balanced and scheduled. In an application, some sensors are required to participate simultaneously at the same time for data communication. Hence, the decision as to which sensors are required to work at a particular instance is decided by this plane.

Mobility Management Plane: Each sensor has information about the neighboring node, and also it can track the mobility of sensor node. The route to the user can be backtracked. The power usage is balanced by collecting the knowledge of the neighbor sensors.

Power Management Plane: This plane governs the usage of power by a sensor node. When the sensor power is low, it informs the neighboring nodes. And then, that particular sensor cannot participate in the routing task. This thereby preserves the remaining power for the sensing task.

23.2.3 *Unique Properties of WSN*

The properties of WSN are illustrated below [14,15]:

Tree-Structured Routing: It is the basis of most current sensor networks. In such networks, the sink node or the base station is at the root. This forms a hierarchical arrangement of sensor nodes.

Agglomeration: It is used not only to monitor conditions across the wide area of coverage, but also to compensate for unreliability, miscalibration of sensor devices, and intermittent connectivity.

Tolerable Failures: Sensors are low-cost devices, and the loss or corruption of a sensor can either be mitigated by redundant sensors or be tolerated by the network. The redundancy of sensors and tolerance for a limited quantity of malicious data makes individual sensor nodes less critical and further enhances the ability to cope up with node failure.

In-Network Filtering and Computation: It allows agglomeration and computation to be "pushed" as close as possible to the devices that originate specific sensor readings. This thus enables greater efficiency as fewer data packets must be transmitted.

Sensors as Routers: There is no distinction between the sensing nodes, computing nodes, and the routing nodes. This, combined with the above properties, reduces network traffic significantly.

Phased Transmission Periods: Within a sensor network, each node has a phase in which it senses, a phase in which it receives messages from its subordinate nodes and a phase in which it forwards data to its parent. Thus, the radio link can be kept active for this duration of time.

23.2.4 *Applications of WSN*

Sensors are capable of monitoring the following conditions:

- Humidity,
- Temperature,
- Vehicle mobility,

- Pressure,
- Composition of soil,
- Noise distortion levels,
- Object's presence and absence,
- Attached object (mechanical stress),
- Lightning conditions,
- Object features such as motion, size, and direction.

The applications of WSN are disaster detection, defense, hospital, smart home, flood detection, critical infrastructure issue, etc. [9,15].

- *Defence Applications of WSN*: It involves surveillance of forces, war weapons; battleground monitoring; inspection of opponent area and territory; opponent weapon speculation; after-war damage estimation; and NBC attack (nuclear, biological, and chemical) discovery and investigation.
- *Environmental Application*: It involves detection of firestorm and flood; precision agriculture; population study; tracking environmental circumstances having an effect on agriculture and farm animals; irrigation; and planetary exploration, monitoring marine, soil, and atmospheric contexts.
- *Health Applications*: It includes follow-up of doctors, registered patients; medicine management; diagnostics; integrated patient monitoring; and telemonitoring of human physiological data.
- *Smart Home Applications*: This application has given rise to the smart environment. It includes home automation such as smart usage of vacuum cleaners, microwave ovens, washing machines, and fridge. The sensors inside the home appliances help users to locally and remotely manage home equipment.
- *Various Profit-Making Applications*: These applications assist in monitoring product quality, robot control, interactive toys, constructing smart office spaces, building virtual keyboards, machine diagnosis, environmental control in buildings, monitoring of vehicles, detect and monitor vehicular theft, and interactive museums.

23.3 Security in WSN

WSN are employed in different application areas as discussed above. WSN deployment in crucial environment poses a great threat to security from internal and external sources [7,16]. These attacks are classified as internal and external attacks or insider and outsider attacks.

23.3.1 Security Principles in WSNs

The security principles of WSN are illustrated below [17,18,19]:

1. *Availability*: Availability identifies the node's capability to utilize the resources and the communication network. It provides an insight to whether the network is active or inactive. The breakdown of sink node will ultimately intimidate the whole sensor network. Hence, availability is of vital importance for maintaining an operational network. It also makes sure

that services offered by WSN or by a single node must be available whenever necessary, i.e., even in the presence of denial-of-service (DoS) attacks.

2. *Authorization*: Authorization is the task of providing rights to resources and is related to security. It defines the access control mechanism in particular. During operation, the sensor uses the access control rules to decide whether access requests from (authenticated) users shall be approved (granted) or disapproved (rejected). It thus ensures that only authorized sensors are involved in providing information to network services.

3. *Authentication*: Authentication means identifying the origin, thereby ensuring the reliability of the message. Attacks in sensor networks do not just involve the alteration of packets; adversaries can also inject additional false packets. It makes sure that the data is originated from the exact genuine source, that is, a malicious node should not function as a trusted network node. Data authentication verifies the identity of the senders and receivers.

4. *Confidentiality*: Data packets exchanged between the sender and the recipient is sometimes, being routed through many nodes. This data may also be kept in memory for further processing. This data can be sensitive enough to be known only by the sender and the recipient. Sometimes, the adversary can access this information by eavesdropping between wireless links, gaining admission to the storage, or by other attacks. Data confidentiality means that the data can only be accessed, and thus utilized, by only those entities that are authorized for this purpose. It makes sure that only authorized sensor nodes receive the content of the message, that is, it ensures that only desired recipient gets the intended message.

5. *Integrity*: Data confidentiality ensures the leakage of data, but it is not helpful against insertion of data in the original message by adversary. Integrity of data needs to be assured in sensor networks, which solidifies that the received data has not been altered or tampered with and that new data has not been added to the original contents of the packet. Environmental conditions and channel's quality of service can also change the primitive message. Integrity ensures the correctness of the data, that is, data sent from one node to another should not have been modified by malicious intermediate nodes.

6. *Non-repudiation*: This technique bounds the sender of data, by which it cannot deny that the data received by the recipient is sent by the sender. It provides undeniable proof that a user took a specific action, such as sending a message. Once the message is sent by the sender, he/she cannot deny that in any condition.

7. *Freshness*: It ensures that the data packets are updated. Also, it guarantees that the attacker has not inserted any old data packet in the sent message. It is crucial that recent data packets must be present in the network and no redundant packet must be induced. Data freshness is crucial in case of replay attack in wireless networks. Replay attack occurs when the data packets are manipulated, recurred, or deferred by the attacker. This attack is also known as playback attack. The attacker tries to obtain access to the network and gain vital information or perform redundant transactions. An example of replay attack is when an authenticated user login to a system, and send a message; that message can be recorded and replayed the next day by an attacker. There are two types of data freshness: weak and strong. Weak freshness deals with the incomplete ordering of messages, still providing no delay in information. Whereas, strong freshness deals with the complete ordering of messages and estimate delays. This ordering is based upon the request and reply cycle. Weak freshness is comparative to periodic sensor readings. And, strong freshness is applicable for synchronizing the network.

8. *Forward Secrecy*: This means that future data will not be read by any such sensor that has already been discarded from the network, i.e., the current keys cannot decode the future

messages. After a sensor has been disconnected from the network, then it will not have the access of future messages in the network. The security of data packets transmitted in the network can be enhanced by using the public key cryptographic technique. On the other hand, if the keys used in those transmissions are compromised it can expose the data exchanged in the current session as well as in the previous sessions.

9. *Backward Secrecy*: Any past data cannot be recognized by future joining sensors, i.e., the current keys cannot decode the previous messages. It ensures that a passive adversary who has knowledge about a contiguous subset of keys cannot learn preceding group keys.

23.3.2 Attacker Goals for Sensor Networks

The attacker's goals are illustrated below [20,21]:

1. *Eavesdropping*: The wireless networks are very much prone to eavesdropping. The attacker monitors the traffic flow in the network. The attacker reads, monitors, and can also modify the read packets and hence provide wrong information to the sink node/base station. This attack comes under two main categories: passive and active eavesdropping. In passive eavesdropping attack, the attacker hides his identify and reads the information traversing through the channel without altering it. On the contrary, in active eavesdropping, the attacker queries the sensor nodes, sends multiple messages to the sensors and try to access more information. In this type of attack, the alteration of information takes place while travelling through the channel. The main goal of the attacker is to extract the relevant information about the sensed environment where WSN is deployed.

2. *Disruption*: In this case, the adversary's aim is to disrupt the sensor application. This attack is the amalgamation of two techniques. The first is the semantic disruption, which inserts fake messages, alters the values, or corrupts the messages. This makes the aggregated data useless or incomplete. The second technique is physical disruption, which deviate the original sensor readings by directly manipulating the environment where the network is deployed.

3. *Hijacking*: These attacks come from trusted nodes. These include the eavesdropping and disruption attack from inside the network. This is a type of insider attack in which the readings obtained from sensors are affected as adversary gains control over sensors.

23.3.3 Attacks in Sensor Networks

WSN are quite prone to attacks that are listed below [22–24]:

1. *Secrecy and Authentication Attacks*: These include attacks such as packet modification, eavesdropping, and packets replay. These are type of outsider attacks. The cryptographic techniques can be used to safeguard the authenticity and the secrecy of these communication channels.

2. *Stealthy Attacks against Service Integrity*: The attacker compromises the network and makes it accept false readings from the sensor node.

3. *The Network Availability Attack*: Such attack can occur on any layer of the WSN. The popular attacks in this category are the DoS attack, which further includes attacks such as flooding, sinkhole, and wormhole.

23.3.4 Tree-Structure Analysis of Attacks

i. Active Attacks
   - Routing and DoS Attacks
     • Spoofed, Altered, and Replayed Routing Information
     • Sinkhole
     • Wormhole
     • Sybil
     • Selective Forwarding
     • HELLO Flood
   - Lack of Cooperation
     • Node Outage
   - Fabrication
     • Node Malfunctioning
     • Node Subversion
   - Impersonation
     • Node Replication Attacks
     • False Node
     • Modification
     • Message Corruption
     • Physical Attack
ii. Passive Attacks
   - Attacks against Privacy
     • Traffic Analysis
     • Monitoring and Eavesdropping (Passive Information Gathering)
     • Camouflages Adversaries

23.3.5 Layering-Based Attacks

■ A holistic approach or layering-based technique considers enhancing the efficiency of WSN according to the changing environmental conditions for the terms such as longevity, security, and connectivity [23].

■ This technique of security focuses on each layer of the network and hence ensures the overall security. The overall security is provided for each layer of the protocol stack.

■ The breach of security at any layer will affect the overall security of the network.

■ Therefore, this technique ensures the overall protection of the security layers as described in Table 23.1.

The attacks are illustrated in the following text [25,26]:

Jamming Attack: It is basically a type of DoS attack. In this attack, jammer emits irrelevant data to all the sensor nodes, which obtrudes with the useful signal to be communicated in the network. The physical layer is affected the most by this attack [27]. The crucial parameter in this attack is the signal-to-noise ratio (SNR). It can be formulated as follows:

$$\text{SNR} = \frac{\text{AP}_{\text{Signal}}}{\text{AP}_{\text{Noise}}}$$

Table 23.1 Typical Threats in WSN

Layer	Threat
Physical	Jamming
	Tampering
Data Link	Exhaustion
	Collision
Network	Route Information Manipulation
	Selective Forwarding
	Sybil Attack
	Sinkhole Attack
	Wormhole Attack
	Hello Flood Attack
Transport	Flooding
Application	Clone Attack

where AP is the average power in case of the actual signal and noise in the network. Noise is described as the distortion in the signal. If the value of SNR is less than 1, then the jamming is effective. Jamming is of two types: spot jamming and sweep jamming. Spot jamming is a very powerful technique but with a disadvantage that it jams only a single frequency. Sweep jamming jams multiple frequencies in continuous subsequence. The solution to this attack is blacklisting of the adversary node.

Tampering: It occurs when an attacker gains physical access to the nodes deployed in WSN. The sensor nodes are deployed in a hostile environment where physical access of each and every node is not always feasible. So, the trespassers can knowingly or unknowingly destroy or hamper the sensor node. This destruction leads to the disconnection of such sensors from the network. The professional hacker can cause much harm by accessing the sensor nodes memory and thereby, stealing the important data or keys. Further, this intruder can also add malicious code to the sensor node, thereby making it function inadequately [28]. This attack can be prevented by providing protection using tamper-proof nodes and key changing.

Exhaustion: Exhaustion occurs due to retransmission of data and results in collisions [29]. When a node continuously transmits even after the collision of data packets, then that node will be exhausted. Intruder usually corrupts the longer messages or jams the delivery report from the receiver end. The continuous flow of corrupted messages leads to exhaustion of the network resources. It increases the MAC admission control rate. It increases the number of irrelevant responses. The WSN ID and related information are not safe. This attack can be prevented by using the multiplexing technique based on time division or by optimizing data rates for communication across a WSN. The data rate optimization can be carried out with the help of machine learning techniques.

Collision: When multiple nodes communicate at the same frequency, it leads to the collision of data packets. In case of collision, either a portion or the entire data packet gets disrupted. This scenario causes flawed data transfer across the sensor network [30]. The solution to this problem is the usage of CRC (Cyclic Redundancy Code) for error correction.

Route information manipulation: In this manipulation scheme, the data being transmitted on the communication channel is altered. The solution to this problem can be devised with the help of user authentication as well as the cryptographic techniques. The cryptographic techniques encrypt the data, which is being transferred throughout the network and can be decrypted only by the authenticated end user [31]. The transmittal of data using this technique makes data unreadable by any eavesdropper on the network, hence preventing it from illegal access.

Selective forwarding: This attack takes place in a multi-hop network. The malicious node forms an intermediate node between source and destination; selectively forward certain packets while dropping others. A solution to this attack is to read out the traffic [32].

Sybil attack: In this attack, a node represents itself by multiple identities in the network. To counter this attack, authentication schemes can play an important role [33].

Sinkhole attack: In this attack, an attacker tries to catch the attention of other network nodes to the compromised node by making it more attractive to surrounding nodes. So, in this technique, the adversary is able to degrade the network performance by transmitting the network data through this compromised node [34]. Authentication and monitoring are the techniques by which this attack can be prevented.

Wormhole attack: In a wormhole attack, an attacker chooses data packets at a particular node in the network, tunnels them to some other network node, and resend them into the network. With the help of variant and flexible routing schemes, this attack can be mitigated [35].

Hello Flood attack: The intruder created a fraudulent image for the rest of the nodes in the communication network. The intruder presents high radio transmittal range and better processing power to rest of the sensor network so that they may transmit data through the intruder node. Also, it transmits hello messages and invites them to transmit the packet through it. Hence, during transmittal of data packets to the sink node, the sensor nodes forward data packets using this malicious node as they know that it is their neighbor [36]. They are eventually deceived by the attacker. The solution to this problem is two-way authentication procedure.

Flooding attack: It is one of the kinds of DoS attack. In this, an attacker consumes the network resources by generating bogus information repeatedly. Due to the flood of information, the use of network resources becomes exhausted or reaches a maximum limit [37]. In the cases, genuine requests for using network resource will be ignored. The solution involves limiting connection numbers.

Clone attack: It is also known as node replication attacks. An attacker tries to add a new node to a sensor network by duplicating existing node's unique identity number or popularly known as node ID. It severely degrades the sensor network performance. The solution to this attack is using unique pair-wise keys in the cryptographic measures [38].

DoS Attack: DoS can be defined as the security threat wherein intruder prevents authorized users from accessing the network resources. This attack shut down the server by reporting the network resources as not available. It results in degradation of network efficiency, inability to access network resources [39]. The DoS can be categorized into two techniques: flooding services and crashing services. Flooding services are the flood attacks that flood the traffic on the network, and this ultimately degrades the performance of the network or finally shutdown of the network. The flooding services involve the following:

- *Buffer Overflow Attack*: This occurs when the network is over-flooded with the data packets. Then the network responds very slowly and keeps on buffering. This further leads to the increase in the number of packet drops in the network.
- *ICMP Flood*: The intruders flood the spoofed packets on every node in the network that amplifies the network traffic.
- *SYN Flood*: In this case, multiple requests are sent for connection establishment, but none of the connection is acknowledged, so all the connections become incomplete and are further unavailable for communication of authorized users of the network.

Crashing services lead to network failure and are caused by exploring the vulnerabilities of the communication network. The DoS attacks are described in the text below (refer to Table 23.2):

- *Radio Interference DoS Attack*: The wireless communication is jammed using the radio frequency signals. The SNR is decreased with the help of radio signals thereby leading to disrupt communication between nodes. This further affects the overall Quality-of-Service (QoS) of the network. The radio signals block all the authorized communication devices. The solution to this problem is the use of spread spectrum that establishes a secure communication and reduces the distortion, jamming, etc. [40]. The bandwidth of the spread spectrum is drastically very large as compared to that of the usual communication bandwidth.
- *Physical Tampering*: It is an attack on the node's hardware. The solution to this problem is to use the tamper-resistant nodes for communication in WSN [41]. These nodes have two main components, one being the tamper-vulnerable portion and the other the tamper-resistant portion. The computational core of the sensor node remains protected.
- *Denying Channel*: In this attack, the authenticated user is not allowed to access the communication channel [42]. The solution to this problem is by using the error correction codes.
- *Black Hole*: When the routing table is updated across the network, the Blackhole, i.e., the intruder passes a fake short path and share it with all the neighboring nodes, which result in the wrongly updating of the routing table. Hence, the data packets will not go through the proper channel and will be dump somewhere around in the network which is unwanted [43]. The solution to this problem is multiple routing paths in which the

Table 23.2   DoS Attacks and Their Solutions

DoS Attack	Possible Solutions
Radio Interference	Use Spread Spectrum
Physical Tampering	Mode Node Tamper-Resistant
Denying Channel	Use Error Correction Codes
Black Holes	Multiple Routing Paths
Misdirection	Source Authorization
Flooding	Limit the Connections

transmitter waits for multiple route options from the neighboring nodes. It then chooses the most appropriate path for data transmission by knocking out the irrelevant path.

- *Misdirection*: It moves the messages along an incorrect path due to fabricated intruder node announcements. The target of this attack is either the intermediate node or the transmitter. SMURF is also a kind of misdirection attack. In this attack, multiple nodes pay attention to the intruder node, thereby making rest of the network much more insecure. The solution to this problem is source authorization, wherein the registered nodes can only exchange data packets and information [44].

- *Flooding*: In this attack, random nodes flood the irrelevant information about the routing paths to all the neighboring nodes, which cause DoS among all the neighboring nodes. It also reduces the energy of the network, thereby depleting the network lifetime [45]. The solution to this problem is limiting the number of connections, wherein only the authorized nodes are allowed to join the network and communicate the information wirelessly.

23.4 The WSN Routing Protocols

■ Various routing protocols are proposed for wireless communication in ad-hoc networks, namely, Ad-hoc On-demand Distance Vector (AODV), Dynamic Source Routing (DSR), and Destination Sequenced Distance Vector (DSDV) [45]. The source node recognizes its immediate neighbor and forwards the packet through them. The transmittal of packets to the destination node is performed by the routing strategy. Routing protocol usually optimizes the path for the transfer of packets [12].

■ The traffic overhead and computational load of a node can be minimized by the use of optimal routing protocol.

■ The protocols fall into two categories:

a. *Proactive Protocol*: These protocols are *Table Driven* that regularly modifies the communication routes. These include the protocol DSDV. The benefit of this protocol is that it results in lesser delay for determination of a route.

b. *Reactive Protocol*: These protocols reacts on demand, which means that they create a route dynamically when data transmission requirement arises. And, they are hence known as *On-Demand Protocols*. These include AODV and DSR.

23.4.1 Ad-Hoc On-Demand Distance Vector

AODV is a routing protocol for communicating information wirelessly. It supports multicast and unicast routing between nodes [46]. It constructs the route dynamically, only when requested by the source node. The routes are created on demand, and hence no extra overhead is required for transmission. It generates a sequence number for maintaining route freshness. It is a hop-to-hop routing technique.

23.4.2 Destination Sequenced Distance Vector

DSDV is a distance vector routing protocol where every node broadcast routing updates to its neighboring nodes regularly. Every node preserves a routing table consisting "next router" for every endpoint, number of intermediate paths from source to destination, and the transmission sequence number allotted via endpoints. Information of routing tables is transferred from node to their nearest neighbors in regular intervals. Whenever a routing table is updated, information is passed on to neighboring nodes [47].

23.4.3 Dynamic Source Routing

DSR is an efficient routing protocol specially designed for multi-hops wireless ad-hoc networks. Route discovery and route maintenance are the major two mechanisms where routes are discovered dynamically and self-configured automatically without the need of network administrator. It is an on-demand network protocol, which means that packet overhead is scalable to any extent as per need [48]. This protocol can be implemented in areas with high mobility and can adopt the rapid recovery. DSR provides loop-free routing and efficiently allocates user requests or network load through various servers.

References

1. Biswas, S., Das, R., & Chatterjee, P. (2018). Energy-efficient connected target coverage in multi-hop wireless sensor networks. In Bhattacharyya S., Sen S., Dutta M., Biswas P., Chattopadhyay H. (eds), *Industry Interactive Innovations in Science, Engineering and Technology* (Vol. 11, pp. 411–421). Springer, Singapore.
2. Ahmad, A., & Hanzálek, Z. (2018). An energy efficient schedule for IEEE 802.15.4/zigbee cluster tree WSN with multiple collision domains and period crossing constraint. *IEEE Transactions on Industrial Informatics*, 14(1), 12–23.
3. Godoy, P. D., Cayssials, R. L., & Garino, C. G. G. (2018). Communication channel occupation and congestion in wireless sensor networks. *Computers & Electrical Engineering*. Available at https://doi.org/10.1016/j.compeleceng.2017.12.049
4. Hussien, A. A., & Matloob, S. I. (2018). The comparative study some of reactive and proactive routing protocols in the wireless sensor network. *Journal of University of Babylon*, 26(4), 195–207.
5. Romer, K., & Mattern, F. (2004). The design space of wireless sensor networks. *IEEE Wireless Communications*, 11(6), 54–61.
6. Singh, K., & Verma, A. K. (2018). Flying adhoc networks concept and challenges. In Mehdi Khosrow-Pour, D.B.A. (ed.), *Encyclopedia of Information Science and Technology*, Fourth Edition (pp. 6106–6113). IGI Global, Hershey, PA.
7. Perrig, A., Stankovic, J., & Wagner, D. (2004). Security in wireless sensor networks. *Communications of the ACM*, 47(6), 53–57.
8. Stankovic, J. A. (2008). Wireless sensor networks. *Computer*, 41(10), 92–95.
9. Akyildiz, I. F., Su, W., Sankarasubramaniam, Y., & Cayirci, E. (2002). Wireless sensor networks: A survey. *Computer Networks*, 38(4), 393–422.
10. Goldsmith, A. J., & Wicker, S. B. (2002). Design challenges for energy-constrained ad hoc wireless networks. *IEEE Wireless Communications*, 9(4), 8–27.
11. Chong, C. Y., & Kumar, S. P. (2003). Sensor networks: Evolution, opportunities, and challenges. *Proceedings of the IEEE*, 91(8), 1247–1256.
12. Sandhu, J. K., & Saxena, S. (2014, December). Data agglomeration in wireless sensor networks. In *2014 International Conference on Parallel, Distributed and Grid Computing (PDGC)* (pp. 285–289). IEEE, Solan.
13. Karlof, C., Sastry, N., & Wagner, D. (2004, November). TinySec: A link layer security architecture for wireless sensor networks. In *Proceedings of the 2nd International Conference on Embedded Networked Sensor Systems* (pp. 162–175). ACM, New York, NY.
14. Ye, W., Heidemann, J., & Estrin, D. (2002). An energy-efficient MAC protocol for wireless sensor networks. In *Proceedings. INFOCOM 2002. Twenty-First Annual Joint Conference of the IEEE Computer and Communications Societies* (Vol. 3, pp. 1567–1576). IEEE, New York, NY.

15. Romer, K., & Mattern, F. (2004). The design space of wireless sensor networks. *IEEE Wireless Communications*, 11(6), 54–61.

16. Sivamani, S., Choi, J., Bae, K., Ko, H., & Cho, Y. (2018). A smart service model in greenhouse environment using event-based security based on wireless sensor network. *Concurrency and Computation: Practice and Experience*, 30(2), e4240.

17. Sandhu, J. K., & Saxena, S. (2016). Procuring wireless sensor actuator network security. In *Proceedings of the International Conference on Recent Cognizance in Wireless Communication & Image Processing* (pp. 905–916). Springer, New Delhi.

18 . Shen, J., Gui, Z., Ji, S., Shen, J., Tan, H., & Tang, Y. (2018). Cloud-aided lightweight certificate less authentication protocol with anonymity for wireless body area networks. *Journal of Network and Computer Applications*, 106, 117–123.

19. Gupta, B., Agrawal, D. P., & Yamaguchi, S. (Eds.). (2016). *Handbook of Research on Modern Cryptographic Solutions for Computer and Cyber Security*. IGI Global, Hershey, PA.

20. Karlof, C., & Wagner, D. (2003). Secure routing in wireless sensor networks: Attacks and counter-measures. *Ad Hoc Networks*, 1(2–3), 293–315.

21. Jouini, M., & Rabai, L. B. A. (2016). A security framework for secure cloud computing environments. *International Journal of Cloud Applications and Computing (IJCAC)*, 6(3), 32–44

22. Raymond, D. R., & Midkiff, S. F. (2008). Denial-of-service in wireless sensor networks: Attacks and defenses. *IEEE Pervasive Computing*, 7(1), 74–81.

23. Wood, A. D., & Stankovic, J. A. (2002). Denial of service in sensor networks. *Computer*, 35(10), 54–62.

24. Wood, A. D., & Stankovic, J. A. (2004). A taxonomy for denial-of-service attacks in wireless sensor networks. In Ilas M. & Mahgoub I. (eds), *Handbook of Sensor Networks: Compact Wireless and Wired Sensing Systems* (pp. 739–763).

25. Pelechrinis, K., Iliofotou, M., & Krishnamurthy, S. V. (2011). Denial of service attacks in wireless networks: The case of jammers. *IEEE Communications Surveys & Tutorials*, 13(2), 245–257.

26. Singh, K., & Verma, A. K. (2018). FCTM: A novel fuzzy classification trust model for enhancing reliability in flying ad hoc networks (FANETs). *Adhoc & Sensor Wireless Networks*, 40(1/2), 23–47.

27. Mpitziopoulos, A., Gavalas, D., Konstantopoulos, C., & Pantziou, G. (2009). A survey on jamming attacks and countermeasures in WSNs. *IEEE Communications Surveys & Tutorials*, 11(4), 42–56.

28. Becher, A., Benenson, Z., & Dornseif, M. (2006, April). Tampering with motes: Real-world physical attacks on wireless sensor networks. In *International Conference on Security in Pervasive Computing* (pp. 104–118). Springer, Berlin, Heidelberg.

29. Baig, Z. A., & Khan, S. A. (2010, January). Fuzzy logic-based decision making for detecting distrib-uted node exhaustion attacks in wireless sensor networks. In *2010. ICFN'10. Second International Conference on Future Networks* (pp. 185–189). IEEE, Sanya, Hainan.

30. Basma, F., Tachwali, Y., & Refai, H. H. (2011, October). Intersection collision avoidance system using infrastructure communication. In *2011 14th International IEEE Conference on Intelligent Transportation Systems (ITSC)* (pp. 422–427). IEEE, Washington, DC.

31. Stavrou, E., & Pitsillides, A. (2010). A survey on secure multipath routing protocols in WSNs. *Computer Networks*, 54(13), 2215–2238.

32. Chawla, P., & Sachdeva, M. (2018). Detection of selective forwarding (gray hole) attack on LEACH in wireless sensor networks. In *Next-Generation Networks* (pp. 389–398). Springer, Singapore.

33. Newsome, J., Shi, E., Song, D., & Perrig, A. (2004, April). The sybil attack in sensor networks: analy-sis & defenses. In *Proceedings of the 3rd International Symposium on Information Processing in Sensor Networks* (pp. 259–268). ACM.

34. Krontiris, I., Dimitriou, T., Giannetsos, T., & Mpasoukos, M. (2007, July). Intrusion detection of sinkhole attacks in wireless sensor networks. In *International Symposium on Algorithms and Experiments for Sensor Systems, Wireless Networks and Distributed Robotics* (pp. 150–161). Springer, Berlin, Heidelberg.

35. Yun, J. H., Kim, I. H., Lim, J. H., & Seo, S. W. (2007). Wodem: Wormhole attack defense mechanism in wireless sensor networks. In Stajano F., Kim H. J., Chae J. S., & Kim S.D. (eds), *Ubiquitous Convergence Technology* (Vol. 4412, pp. 200–209). Springer, Berlin, Heidelberg.

36. Singh, V. P., Ukey, A. S. A., & Jain, S. (2013). Signal strength based hello flood attack detection and prevention in wireless sensor networks. *International Journal of Computer Applications*, 62(15), 1–6.

37. Ahmed, A. A., & Fisal, N. F. (2011). Secure real-time routing protocol with load distribution in wireless sensor networks. *Security and Communication Networks*, 4(8), 839–869.

38. Conti, M., Di Pietro, R., Mancini, L., & Mei, A. (2011). Distributed detection of clone attacks in wireless sensor networks. *IEEE Transactions on Dependable and Secure Computing*, 8(5), 685–698.

39. Cao, X., Han, Z. J., & Chen, G. H. (2007). DoS attack detection scheme for sensor networks based on traffic prediction. *Chinese Journal of Computers-Chinese Edition*, 30 (10), 1798.

40. Zhou, G., He, T., Stankovic, J. A., & Abdelzaher, T. (2005, March). RID: Radio interference detection in wireless sensor networks. In *Proceedings. INFOCOM 2005. 24th Annual Joint Conference of the IEEE Computer and Communications Societies* (Vol. 2, pp. 891–901). IEEE, Miami, FL.

41. Becher, A., Benenson, Z., & Dornseif, M. (2006, April). Tampering with motes: Real-world physical attacks on wireless sensor networks. In *International Conference on Security in Pervasive Computing* (pp. 104–118). Springer, Berlin, Heidelberg.

42. Zuba, M., Shi, Z., Peng, Z., & Cui, J. H. (2011, December). Launching denial-of-service jamming attacks in underwater sensor networks. In *Proceedings of the Sixth ACM International Workshop on Underwater Networks* (p. 12). ACM, New York, NY.

43. Tripathi, M., Gaur, M. S., & Laxmi, V. (2013). Comparing the impact of black hole and gray hole attack on LEACH in WSN. *Procedia Computer Science*, 19, 1101–1107.

44. Sachan, R. S., Wazid, M., Singh, D. P., & Goudar, R. H. (2013, April). A cluster based intrusion detection and prevention technique for misdirection attack inside WSN. In *2013 International Conference on Communications and Signal Processing (ICCSP)* (pp. 795–801). IEEE.

45. Arafath, M. S., Khan, K. U. R., & Sunitha, K. V. N. (2018). Pithy review on routing protocols in wireless sensor networks and least routing time opportunistic technique in WSN. *Journal of Physics: Conference Series*, 933 (1), 012016.

46. Singh, K., & Verma, A. K. (2015, March). Experimental analysis of AODV, DSDV and OLSR routing protocol for flying adhoc networks (FANETs). In *2015 IEEE International Conference on Electrical, Computer and Communication Technologies (ICECCT)* (pp. 1–4). IEEE.

47. Chen, Y., & Nasser, N. (2006, August). Energy-balancing multipath routing protocol for wireless sensor networks. In *Proceedings of the 3rd International Conference on Quality of Service in Heterogeneous Wired/wireless Networks* (p. 21). ACM, New York, NY.

48. Barati, M., Atefi, K., Khosravi, F., & Daftari, Y. A. (2012, June). Performance evaluation of energy consumption for AODV and DSR routing protocols in MANET. In *2012 International Conference on Computer & Information Science (ICCIS)* (Vol. 2, pp. 636–642). IEEE.

Chapter 24

Identity Theft, Malware, and Social Engineering in Dealing with Cybercrime

Anupama Mishra

Himalayan University

Brij B. Gupta

National Institute of Technology Kurukshetra

Deepak Gupta

LoginRadius Inc.

Contents

24.1 Key Findings

If we talk about cyber security, consumers are genius and overconfident in their security skills and so making themselves vulnerable and inviting cyber criminals to play with them and their loopholes, which has recorded the crimes in result.

As per research in 2017, approximately 782 million people in 13 countries have been impacted by cybercrime. Figure 24.1 shows the number of people who were affected by the different cyberattacks countrywise, where China, India, and USA are the most affected countries. Also, these three countries have the largest number of people who are netizens and spending more time on the net.

Sometimes there is just a need to follow the fundamental rules for security, and due to avoidance of it, we indirectly invite cybercrimes knowingly or unknowingly such as use of a device on an infected system or use of an infected device on a system, skipping the security checks (antivirus checks), without cross-checking using online web services. Recently, one of my colleagues used a website to send a cake and flowers to her daughter at some place so she paid the required amount and talked to a person associated with that website, but later she found that nothing was delivered and turned into a fraud. Figure 24.2 shows the percentage of common and popular cybercrimes.

Resultant, $172 billion are lost globally in compromising the vulnerabilities of the consumers with an average of $142 per victim, which is a very serious issue in terms of the data loss as well as money loss.

On the cyber space, we have every kind of people such as group of teenagers, group of people who uses Internet only to access social websites for communication. They might not have a proper

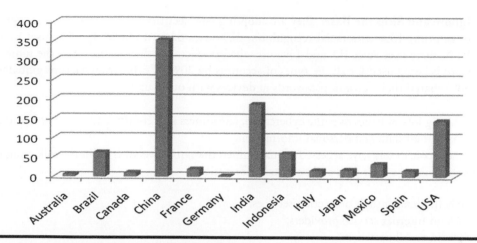

Figure 24.1   Cybercrime numbers country-wise.

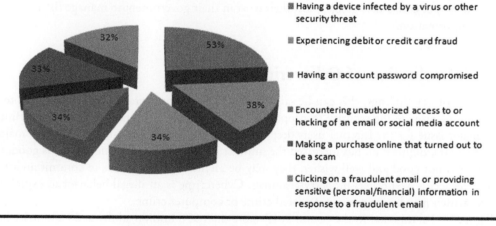

- Having a device infected by a virus or other security threat
- Experiencing debit or credit card fraud
- Having an account password compromised
- Encountering unauthorized access to or hacking of an email or social media account
- Making a purchase online that turned out to be a scam
- Clicking on a fraudulent email or providing sensitive (personal/financial) information in response to a fraudulent email

Figure 24.2   Popular and common cybercrimes.

knowledge of security features of that websites, group of people who wants to show their technical skills on others and exploit others vulnerabilities, and group of professionals who are into e-business and do not want others to grow; therefore, there are some common traits which result in users to fall victim to cybercrimes.

Three common traits are shared by cybercrime victims:

- **Overconfident in Cyber Security Skills:** Customers who talk about the importance of cyber security and fallen prey to cybercrimes are more likely to contradict their own efforts by doing some simple mistakes. While 44% of consumers have personally experienced cybercrime, 39% of cybercrime victims globally report having trust in their ability to hold and protect their personal information and data, and 33% think that they are at minimum risk of becoming a cybercrime victim.
- **Favor Multiple Devices:** Consumers who adopt the newest technologies and own the most devices are also more likely to be victims of cybercrime. More than one-third (37%) own a gaming console and smart device, compared to 28% of non-victims. They are also almost twice as likely to own a connected home device than non-victims.

■ **Ignore and Skip the Base:** They are adopting new security technologies such as 44% uses fingerprint, 13% uses facial recognition, 22% uses pattern matching, 16% uses personal VPN, 10% uses voice ID, and 13% uses the two-factor authentication. Yet, the same password is being used for all the types of accounts by 20% of cybercrime victims globally and 58% shared their account passwords or devices with other users.

Despite facing lots of issues over the cybercrime, consumers still continue to trust the institutions that manage their data and personal information.

Globally consumers have accessed or maintained the same level of trust in the following institutions that manage their data and personal information:

■ 76% in identity theft protection services,
■ 80% in Internet service providers,
■ 80% in email providers,
■ 82% in financial institutions.

However, 41% of consumers globally lost their trust in their government to manage their data and personal information.

24.2 Introduction of Cybercrime

By analysis of key findings, this can be said that there are many factors which are needed to be taken care to provide the security to people and their information. Fraudulent, a cybercrime is still a major issue for the Internet users despite advances in technology and other safety majors. In recent years, digitization has increased the number of users on the Internet which is good, but every user is not good and well-wisher, they may be an attacker and wants to commit an attack to gain the access over others property/resources. Cybercrime is an illegal behavior to exploit the Internet which may be the computer-related crime or computer crime.

Figure 24.3 shows that in the year of 2017, more than 978 million adults in 20 countries have experienced cybercrime, and among all, China, India, and USA gained the highest ranking. Also, every country has an increased number of crimes over cyberspace in comparison to previous years, which shows an interest in making of the cyber war as a conclusion of the growth of the cybercrime, especially in developed countries.

By the statistics of cybercrime, 53% of consumers experienced cybercrime or known someone who has. Table 24.1 depicts the percentage of cybercrimes experienced either personally or by someone else. Among all data we have, 38% fraud is related to debit or credit cards, hacking is 34%, identity theft is 26%, and many more.

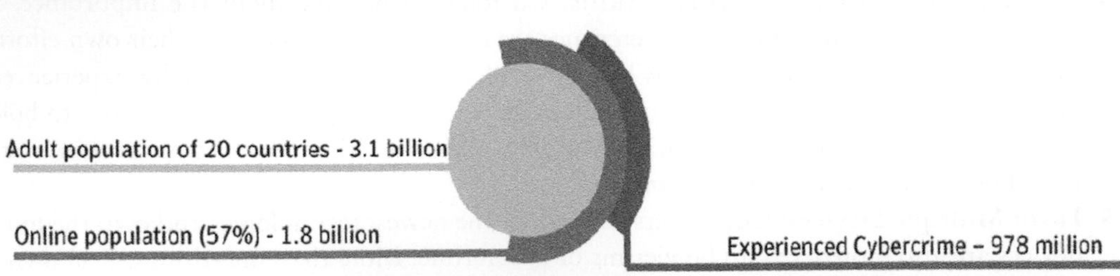

Adult population of 20 countries - 3.1 billion

Online population (57%) - 1.8 billion

Experienced Cybercrime - 978 million

Figure 24.3 Cybercrime population.

Table 24.1   Depicts the Percentage of Cybercrime Experiences

Cybercrime	I Have (%)	Someone I Know Has (%)	Either I or Someone I Know Has (%)
Had a device computer/tablet/phone infected by a virus or other security threat.	36	26	53
Had an account password compromised	18	19	34
Experienced credit or debit card fraud	17	23	38
Been notified that your personal information was involved in a data breach.	16	17	30
Unauthorized access to or hacking of your email or social network profile	16	21	34
Make a purchase online that turn to be a scam	14	20	33
Had others use your home Wi-Fi without permission	14	16	28
Detected unusual activity on your home Wi-Fi network	14	15	27
Clicked on a fraudulent email or provided sensitive (personal/financial) in response to that mail	13	21	32
Received a phone call or text that resulted in malware being downloaded to mobile device	13	17	28
Had a financial information compromised as a result of shopping online	10	16	25
Been a victim of identity theft	10	18	26
Experienced a ransomware attack	8	15	22
Lost a job or a promotion due to a social media posting you did not post	6	12	18

As per 2017 statistics, 64% is the cybercrime victim and 36% are non-victim, which is a very serious issue. There are three important factors that lead to increase in the crime count:

■ Using the same password for all accounts: 20% of the cybercrime victims use the same password across all the accounts over the web.
■ Share the device or online account passwords with others: 58% of the cybercrime victims share at least one device or one account password with each other.
■ Lack of awareness: Time to time, companies send emails and letters to make aware the consumers but people are not reading it carefully.

24.2.1 *Timeline of Cybercrime*

Connectivity among all over the world between citizens, businesses, educational institutes, financial institutions, and governments has crossed the cultural and political boundaries. The world is converting into the digital world by providing digital technology, benefiting the users. But at the same time, it enriches the criminal activity, including stolen identity and theft of classified government information. Here, Table 24.2 shows how the crimes have grown and placed into the world of electric information.

Table 24.2 Timeline of Cyber Crime

Year	Event
1960	Hacking term is originated and used to describe the activity of modifying the product Hacking is a term used to describe the activity of modifying a product or procedure to alter its normal function, or to fix a problem.
1970	In this, 'phreakers" are discovered and they used to modify the information, hardware and software. Also, there were rootkit techniques which are used to obtaining the root-level privilege by compromising the vulnerabilities of a computer. It was discovered that Sony BMG Music Entertainment had used rootkit techniques to disguise digital rights management software that installed itself on consumers' computers when they played a Sony CD.
1978	The first spam email was sent in 1978 over the ARPAnet, the US Defense Department network by a Digital Equipment Corp. marketing executive. Today mass mailings are sent via a vast array of channels—email, newsgroups, instant messaging, and mobile phones—to recipients who have not requested them and cannot remove themselves from the mailing list. Spam has grown more malevolent, as criminals have made it the carrier for a host of scams.
1982	A high school student named Rich Skrenta wrote Elk Cloner for Apple II computers. Hidden on a floppy disk necessary to load the operating system on the computer, it spread when users unknowingly used an infected disk to boot up.
1986	In 1986, computer tempering became a punishable crime by significant time of jail and penalty in terms of money. There was also a forensic technique was evolved to back track the loss data as much as possible which is called "honey pot tactic."
1988	Robert T. Morris, a graduate student at Cornell University, created software that would automatically replicate itself on computers hooked up to the government's ARPAnet (the precursor to the Internet).
1989	1989 was popular for Trojan horse software. In 1989 (or 1987, depending who you speak to), a diskette claiming to be a database of AIDS information was mailed to thousands of AIDS researchers and subscribers to a UK computer magazine. A Trojan is a destructive program that masquerades as a benign application and is named after the Trojan Horse of Greek mythology. The software initially appears to perform a desirable function for the user prior to installation and/or execution, but steals information or harms the system. Unlike viruses or worms, Trojans do not replicate themselves.

(Continued)

Table 24.2 (*Continued*)   Timeline of Cyber Crime

Year	Event
1990	In 1990, during a project dubbed Operation Sundevil, FBI agents confiscated 42 computers and over 20,000 floppy disks that were allegedly being used by criminals for illegal credit card use and telephone services. This 2-year effort involved 150 agents. Despite the low number of indictments, the operation was seen as a successful public relations effort by law enforcement officials. Garry M. Jenkins, the Assistant Director of the U.S. Secret Service, explained at a press conference that this activity sent a message to criminals that, "they were on the watch everywhere, even in those sleazy and secretive dens of cybernetic vice, the underground boards." This evolved from prankware, the kind of software that would install a daft message on your computer screen if you opened an infected email. Demand from organized online criminals has created a supply of easily downloadable malware packages.
1996	The term is coined although activity predates this. Phishing attempts to trick Internet users into divulging their personal information for use or resale by criminals. Also known as social engineering, phishing typically cons users through authentic-looking emails, which link to websites that mimic those of respected financial institutions or retailers. Spear-phishing was coined a decade later and refers to a more sophisticated online con act that targets an individual or an organization.
1998	A man in the middle attack was reported by the National Security Agency in 1998, but more famous attacks occurred in October 2005, when global banks were targeted. Man-in-the-middle depends on interception and has been around since espionage began. However technology has given it a whole new momentum. It can be a as simple as snooping on someone's emails over unencrypted Wi-Fi in an Internet cafe. More malicious attacks use sophisticated Trojans to interrupt banking deals in order to siphon off billions of dollars.
2000	Canadian hacker MafiaBoy launched a distributed denial-of-service attack that took down several high-profile web sites, including Amazon, CNN, and Yahoo! A denial of service attack is identified by its behavior on a computer system or on a network that prevents legitimate use of its resources. A distributed denial of service attack deploys many computers to launch attack to achieve its goal.
2003	The SoBig email worm is thought to be the first organized attempt to create large-scale botnets. A botnet is a collection of infected computers or bots that have been taken over by hackers and are used to perform malicious tasks or functions. A computer becomes a bot when it downloads a file that has bot software embedded in it. A botnet takes action without the hackers having to log in to the client's computer. My Space launches in 2003 and Facebook in 2004, heralding a new era of social networking. The medium is also rapidly colonized by criminals and is now a primary conduit for the proliferation of malware, and also of social engineering attacks.
2005	In 2005, there was a beginning of identity theft, it happens when an attacker steal someone`s identity to access the personal information so that it can be used for making an active attack.

(Continued)

Table 24.2 (*Continued*)   Timeline of Cyber Crime

Year	Event
2010	A Microsoft Windows computer worm was discovered in July 2010 that targets industrial software and equipment. It is the first discovered malware that spies on and subverts industrial systems.
2011	Advanced persistent threat (APT) is the acronym on every cyber security professional's lips. APT usually refers to a group, such as a foreign nation state government, with both the capability and the intent to persistently and effectively target a specific entity.
2012	Through Reveton ransom ware, notifications regarding copyright violations and distribution of pornographic content were sent to victims. That notifications claimed that access was denied to the system until a fine was paid. It was sent to the victims through compromised websites and links. It is also called "Police Ransomeware."
2013	In this year, Through the vulnerable websites and malicious email attachments, a CryptoLocker were distributed, by which the cybercriminal get paid easily and make difficult to track back them. In 2009, the invention of Bitcoin had opened up a method of exploitation to attackers. CryptoLocker used AES-256 to encrypt files, command and control servers spread across the Zeus botnet to distribute decryption keys.
2014	In the flood of ransomware, CryptoWall ransom ware was distributed like anything and collected revenue of $325 million for attackers. It is used to fixed bugs in its predecessor, CryptoDefense, which used 2048-bit RSA encryption but unfortunately, left the decryption key in plain text on the systems.
2015	Have u heard about LockerPin, released to reset the pin on smart phones such as android and demanded money to unlock the devices. At the same time a new type of ransomware was designed and dedicated for web hosting system based on Linux. This ransomware is used to lock files and directories included encrypted files available on system.
2016–2017	In the history of ransomware, WannaCry became the fastest one. More than 270,000 devices were infected from the leaked EternalBlue only in 4 days, which is a hacking tool and a server message block protocol vulnerability. Also there was a series of fake mails intended to corrupt the tax software.

24.2.2 Security Objective

Security means prevent our information or hardware or software from the unauthorized access and fabrication of the data by providing security mechanism such as authorization, digital signature, access control, non-repudiation, authorization, data integrity, and data confidentiality. The objective of security is to maintain confidentiality, integrity, and availability of the data. Figure 24.4 shows that by the help of these three objectives, the secure information can be achieved.

24.2.2.1 Confidentiality

Our aim is to protect our information from unauthorized access. In the confidentiality, the transmission media is important where the information is floating. For example, in the era of e-business, hiding some company information from competitors is crucial to the operation of the company.

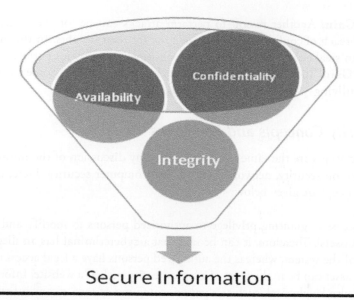

Secure Information

Figure 24.4   Security goals.

Threat to Confidentiality: snooping, traffic analysis, phishing, and social engineering.

24.2.2.2 Integrity

Information keeps changing, and to maintain the integrity, only the authorized entity can modify the information via some authorized mechanism. For example, modification of any employee details can be done through the authorized members such as HR of the company.

Threat to Integrity: modification, replaying, repudiation, data-diddling, man-in-the-middle, and Salami attack.

24.2.2.3 Availability

As per the need of the information, it must be available to the authorized members; it is just garbage if it is unavailable when the information is required by the authenticated entity.

Threat to Availability: DDoS (Distributed Denial of Services), electric power attack, server room environment attack, SYN flood attack, and ICMP flood attack.

24.2.3 Reasons behind the Cybercrimes

There are many reasons behind a cybercriminal; why does a person commit an attack, some of the major reasons are mentioned below:

- **Pleasure:** To show the power and to gain popularity in the hacker community.
  Attacker enjoys that he/she has so much of technical power to control a person. Also getting popularity is one of the major reasons, which gives immense pleasure to the attacker.
- **Revenge:** To let down someone's image or to cut down the e-commerce, i.e.,
  most of the time, the attack is personal which means to block the available resources or degrade the performance of the service which is required by the target (competitor) machine. Therefore, attack is committed for the revenge purpose.

■ **Material Gain:** Another reason to perform attacks can be for the material gain, which means to breach of confidentiality and integrity for their benefits. In the material gain, the attacker can steal either the content or the consumer's identity for performing the crime.

■ **Financial Gain:** The ultimate goal of the attack is to gain money. Sometimes, it will be done by cyber bullying, phishing, or social engineering crimes.

24.2.4 Security Concepts and Key Terms

Some security concepts are the same and essential to any discussion of the information in cyber security, information security, network security, and computer security. Here, the meanings of some security concept are given below:

■ **Access:** Access to granting privilege to authorized persons to modify and manipulate the recourses (assets). Therefore, it can be said that a cybercriminal has an illegal access to the recourses of the system, whereas the authorized persons have a legal access to the system.

■ **Asset:** An asset can be in the form of a logical entity such as a website, information, or data, and it can also be physical, such as a person, computer system, or any other tangible object. Assets especially in the form of information are needed to be protected and secure.

■ **Crime/Attack:** An illegal way to access the assets to exploit or monitor the information. A crime may be intentional or unintentional, direct (attacker uses personal system to gain access into a victim's system, also originated from the threat itself) or indirect (first exploit a vulnerable system and then use it to perform an attack to the victim's system, also originated from a compromised system or resource that is malfunctioning or working under the control of a threat), active (an attack which can alter the information) or passive (an attack which does not modify the information but monitor the traffic information), single or distributed which cause damage to or otherwise compromise information and/or the systems that support it.

■ **Exploit:** A technique used to compromise a system's vulnerabilities. Threat agents are made to make an attempt to compromise a computer or any other information asset by accessing illegally for their personal gain. Or, an exploit can be a documented process to take advantage of a vulnerability or exposure, usually in software, that is either inherent in the software or is created by the attacker. Nowadays, there are many automated existing (customized) software tools which are used by exploits.

■ **Exposure:** In cyber security, when an attacker gets to know the loopholes (vulnerability) of a system and ready to compromise it, this condition is known as exposure.

■ **Loss:** When an instance of an asset suffering from illegal access or damage or unauthorized or unintended modification or disclosure. Stolen of information of an organization is big loss of that organization.

■ **Risk:** The probability or chances of occurring something unwanted. The risk must be minimizing to match their risk appetite that means the nature and quantity of risk will be acceptable by the organization.

■ **Threat:** A class of persons, objects, or other entities that can be a danger to an asset. Threats always exist and can be intentional with a bad idea or undirected such as severe storms incidentally threaten buildings and their contents, while hackers purposefully threaten unprotected information in the cyber world.

■ **Threat agent:** The specific component of a threat. For example, all hackers in the world present a collective threat, while Kevin Mitnick, a threat agent, who was convicted for hacking into phone systems. Same as, hailstorm, a lightning strike, or tornado is a threat agent that is part of the threat for severe storms.

■ **Vulnerability:** A fault, weakness, or loophole in a system or protection mechanism that is exposed to crime or damage. Some examples of vulnerabilities are a defect in a software package, an unprotected system port, and an unlocked door. Some well-known vulnerabilities have been examined, documented, and published.

24.3 Identity Thefts

In the cyber space, identity theft is a major cybercrime, which leads to the financial crime. It happens when an attacker steals the victim's identity in order to achieve the access to credit cards, debit cards, online banking, or other benefits by using this information.

When someone's identity is stolen, it is called identity theft, and when that information is misused, it is called fraud.

24.3.1 Damage Done by Identity Theft

As per the statistics, fraudulent over the Internet has the highest percentage among all the crimes.

Nowadays, stealing the identity is not a big deal, it may happen through phishing or may be by invading the person's computer with some spyware that reads the personal information such as Social Security Number, Credit Card Number, and Online passwords or maybe by stealing your hard copy where you have written all those personal information.

Russian Cyber Hacker Pleads Guilty in Identity Theft Case: A Russian cybercriminal who has been found guilty in Atlanta of selling stolen personal information through an identity theft and credit card fraud ring known as "carder.su."

In 2016, due to fraud $16 billion has been lost and a new chapter for fraudulence has been written for touching its new heights in cyber security.

Figure 24.5 presents a large number of complaints which is increasing day by day.

As per the statistics, fraudulent regarding credit card has its major number and growing like anything.

Also, Figure 24.6 shows the top three identity theft reports, in which it can be seen that credit card fraud and tax-related frauds are gradually increasing and people are suffering from big losses in the form of information and money.

24.3.2 Identity Theft: Breach of Integrity

By pretending to be someone else, an attacker can steal the personal information such as bank card and its PIN and after that he/she will present himself/herself as that customer only to commit a fraud (might transfer the amount to some other account or withdraw some amount from the bank). Here, stealing the information and accessing the amount is breaking the integrity.

24.3.3 Security Mechanism

To reduce the crime of identity theft, some security mechanism has been used such as providing authentication. Through authentication (by some identity proofs), the person can be authorized to access their personal information.

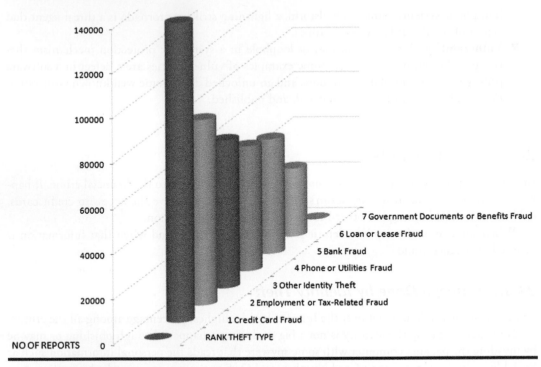

Figure 24.5   Statistics of types of theft complaints in the year of 2017.

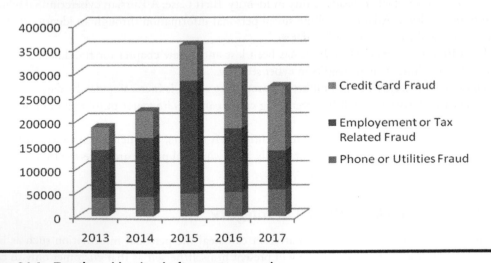

Figure 24.6   Top three identity theft reports year-wise.

24.4 Malware

Many types of "malware," or "malicious software," refer to programs designed to invade and disrupt victims' computers. Malware might be used to delete and destroy valuable information, slow the computer down to a standstill, or spy on and steal valuable personal data from the victim's computer.

Viruses and worms are very popular types of malware, in which the programs are intended to infect computers, replicate, and spread to other computers, Also, they might be spread all over the cyber word via an email communication.

Trojan horse is also a type of malware and majorly attached to all the applications, which will be available free for the netizens (Cyber Users). Many of us always go for the free services, and whenever we download something from the Internet, our enemy friend (Trozen Horse) will be there automatically.

Spyware is a type of malware that collects information without the victim's knowledge. Some forms of spyware gather personal information including login accounts and bank or credit card information. Some may redirect your browser to certain websites, send pop-up ads, and change your computer settings.

Now, malware is not a stereotype, but they are adopting the technology as per the network growth.

The emergence of network-based ransomware cryptoworms does not need the human interference; alone they are launching the ransomware campaign. And the icing on the cake is attackers are not asking money but the destruction of systems and data, as Nyetya—wiper malware masquerading as ransomware. Self-propagating malware is dangerous and has the potential to take down the Internet, according to Cisco threat researchers.

24.4.1 Damage Done by Malware

In May 2017, WannaCry—a ransomware cryptoworm—emerged and spread like wildfire across the Internet.

In the field of medical science, a treatment that is dramatically effective in some patients can be ineffective on others. Our goal is to find out such toxic drugs for the particular disease and specified mutation in the gene. Personalized medicine is based on using an individual's genetic profile to make the best therapeutic choice by facilitating predictions about whether that person will benefit from a particular medicine or not. Figure 24.7 presents that how do the consumers emphasize the importance of online security, whether it is related to password management or about the content seen by children over Internet or about the devices accessing the household directly or indirectly or about the backup—restore plan after being attacked. By the figure, it can be easily said that most of the people want to protect their files and devices from the malicious sites or files.

24.4.2 Malware: Threat to Integrity

In the modern age of information system security, there are many malwares which are being used to steal information. Today, in the era of android and iOs, many malwares are distributed through third-party apps. They have been designed in the way that it can steal the data from the host devices. Sometimes the devices, operating systems, and third-party applications have some vulnerabilities and ready to be either injected by some malware code or ex-filtrations by malicious code. There may be a data loss due to insecure code of third party when we get connected and access it. These threats create a high risk on integrity.

24.4.3 Security Mechanism

To reduce the risk, there is a need to increase the control over access mechanism, also some points that need to be taken care in daily life, such as

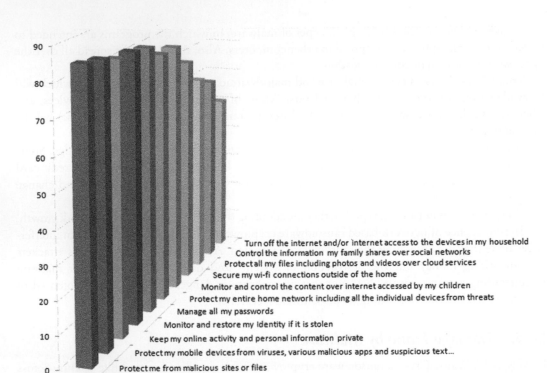

Figure 24.7 Consumers emphasize the importance of online security.

Be at Basics: Craft the complex password: Do not stick a password to publicly available information as it will be easily guessed by the criminal. The password should be sequences of alphanumeric including special symbols so that it would be memorized easily but hard to be cracked. The lengthy a password, the better it is. Also, set a layered security mechanism, so that if a password is compromised, it would be harder to access the account.

Unsecure Wi-Fi Networks: Nothing is free in this beautiful world; therefore, think multiple times before accessing personal information on unprotected public Wi-Fi. Stay away from those unprotected networks that share your personal information such as paying online bill, logging into social media accounts, and paying bills with a credit card. Also, if there is a need to access the information over public Wi-Fi, think about Virtual Private Network (VPN) to make secure connection and provide security to personal information.

Do Not Keep a Default Password: Whenever installing anything related to network devices, such as a router or smart thermostat, do remember to change the default password. Also, when it is not in use, disconnect the connection, it is also recommended that such connections must be strongly encrypted so that the traffic analyzer or other attackers can do nothing with the data travelling in the wireless media. Figure 24.8 presents the percentage of people who understand the value of passwords and play with it accordingly.

24.5 Phishing and Social Engineering

Social Engineering refers to the combination of psychological tricks and technical expert such as a malware programmer, i.e., expert of creating the viruses.

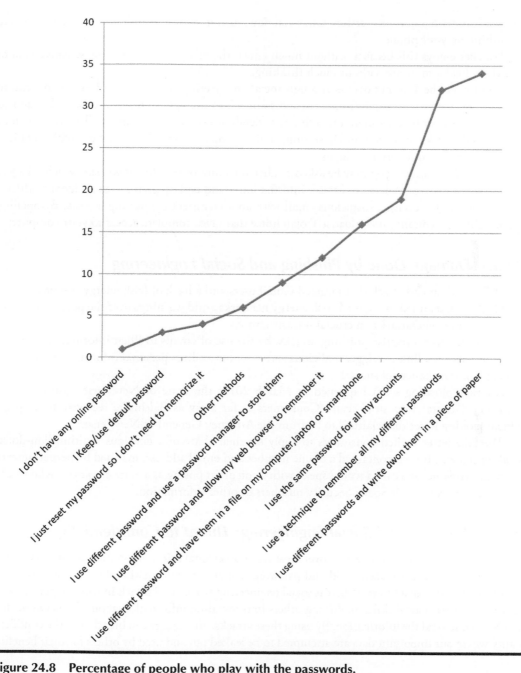

Figure 24.8 **Percentage of people who play with the passwords.**

Social networking is one of the major reasons in the tremendous growth of the Internet. For example, Facebook is the biggest social site where people are connected with each other directly or indirectly. They like, dislike, comment, and share others post, apps, and other things.

Attacker monitors the person's likes and dislikes from their posts on Facebook and easily get to know a user's frequent activities. Suppose an attacker gets to know that you love Temple Run (a popular smartphone game), maybe an attacker would send you an email purporting to be from

Temple Run with a new pro version. Once you download it, he/she would have complete access to everything on your phone.

Attacker enjoys this because without much effort, the victims hand over the sensitive data or may download a malware without much thinking.

Fraud over the Internet occurs through social engineering in the form of emails or instant messages that appear to come from a trusted source. You may get fraudulent emails that appear to come from your bank, a shopping website, a friend, or even the government. The message may even contain links to a counterfeit version of the company's website, complete with genuine-looking graphics, and corporate logos.

In a phishing attack, you may be asked to click on a link or fraudulent website which asks you to submit your personal data or account information—and end up giving it to an identity thief.

Or you might receive a suspicious email with an attachment containing a virus. By opening the attachment, you may download a Trojan horse that gives complete access to your computer.

24.5.1 Damage Done by Phishing and Social Engineering

In 2017, a widespread attack that targeted Gmail users and a hack of Irish energy systems.

Hackers had aimed to targeted Irish energy networks amid warnings over the potential impact of intensifying cyberattacks on crucial infrastructure.

It was just like a regular phishing attacks, by the use of emails to illicit information or make the user click on a link to trigger malicious software, but utilizes personal information on targets to heighten the chances of success.

Another phishing scam happened in March 2012, the State of New Jersey learned of an "Attorney General Impostor" scam. Consumers as far away as Baltimore received an 11-page, official looking letter that claimed to be from the Attorney General of New Jersey.

The fake letter invited consumers to apply for their share of a fictitious multimillion-dollar legal settlement. It even contained a phone number and email address, manned by perpetrators of the scam. Anyone who called would speak with a con artist posing as a State employee, who would ask victims to send their Social Security numbers or other information.

24.5.2 Phishing and Social Engineering: Threat to Confidentiality

Phishing attack is made to get access over sensitive and personal information such as financial information that may include account id and password, credit card information, by sending unwanted emails with false web address. Whereas social engineering is a kind of attack in which a person with very good interpersonal skills modifying others into revealing information about the network that can be used to steal the information. By using these attacks, an attacker can breach into the confidentiality where our important data are attempted to be leaked out and used by others for their benefits.

24.5.3 Security Mechanisms

Do Not Go on a Phishing Expedition: Think twice before opening unsolicited messages or attachments, particularly from people you do not know, or clicking on random links. The message may be from a cybercriminal who has compromised your friend or family member's email or social media accounts.

Be in Control When Online: Protect all your devices with a robust, multi-platform security software solution to help protect against the latest threats.

24.6 Causes behind Cybercrimes and Methods of Committing

There are plenty of ways in which cybercrimes happen. Here, I am mentioning few causes and methods of how cybercrimes can be executed: unauthorized access, theft of data, email bombing, data diddling, Salami attacks, Denial of Service attack, virus/worm attacks, logic bombs, Trojan attacks, Internet time theft, and web jacking.

24.6.1 Unauthorized Access

It is also called hacking, when a person gains access to somebody else's system or network without any permission (unauthorized access). This happens when the system resources have any kind of vulnerabilities such as limited memory, lack in patching, security controls, configuration, or week password construction.

24.6.2 Theft of Data

Theft of data or information happens when the information stored in computer systems are infiltrated and are fabricated or modified or physically being seized via hard disks, removable storage media, or other virtual medium.

24.6.3 Email Bombing

Massive mails to the victim. Here, it is an attempt to make the mailbox overflow. This email box may be referred to an individual or may be a company, who has limited capacity to entertain the mails. After getting lots of mails, the server of the company or an individual's system may get crashed.

24.6.4 Data Diddling

Data diddling is the alteration of data before or during an intrusion into the computer system. This kind of an occurrence involves moving raw data just before a computer can process it and then modifying it back after the processing is completed.

24.6.5 Salami Attacks

This kind of crime is normally consisting of a number of smaller data security attacks together end resulting in one major attack. This method normally takes place in the financial institutions or for the purpose of committing financial crimes. An important feature of this type of offense is that the alteration is so small that it would normally go unnoticed. This form of cybercrime is very common in banks where employees can steal small amount and it is very difficult to detect or trace; an example is the "Ziegler case," wherein a logic bomb penetrated the bank's system, which deducted only 10 cents from every account and deposited it in one particular account which is known as the "penny shaving."

24.6.6 Denial of Service Attack

DDoS (Distributed Denial of Services): This attack is launched in a very coordinated manner in which it uses many compromised computer machines, also known as zombies, to send a useless traffic flow to overload the victim's resources which in turn causes the system to crash.

24.6.7 Logic Bombs

They are basically a set of instructions where it can be secretly be execute into a program where if a particular condition is true, can be carried out and the end result usually is harmful effects. This suggests that these programs are produced to do something only when a specific event (known as a trigger event) occurs, for example, Chernobyl virus.

24.6.8 Trojan Attacks

The term suggests where a program or programs mask themselves as valuable tools but accomplish damaging tasks to the computer. These programs are unlawful which droopily gains control over another's system by assuming the role as an authorized program. The most common form of a Trojan is through email. A Trojan was introduced in the PC of a woman movie chief in the U.S. while visiting. The digital criminal through the web cam introduced in the PC acquired her bare photos. He additionally pestered this woman.

24.6.9 Web Jacking

This is where the hacker obtains access and can control website of another person, where he or she can destroy or alter the information on the site as they see fit to them. This type of method of cybercrime is done for satisfying political agendas or for purely monetary means. As of late the site of MIT (Ministry of Information Technology) was hacked by the Pakistani programmers and some disgusting issue was put in that. Assist the website of Bombay wrongdoing branch was additionally web jacked. Another instance of web jacking is that of the 'gold fish' case. For this situation the site was hacked and the data relating to gold fish was changed. Assist a payment of US $1 million was requested as payment. In this way web jacking is where by power over the website of another is made upheld by some thought for it.

Infrastructure has always been considered a legitimate target. In World War II, we bombed and destroyed the electrical infrastructure of our enemies.

24.7 Solutions: Integrated Cyber Security Framework

Information keeps changing, and there is not a single way to keep it safe over a web where everybody is connected with each other through sharing either the information or the devices. Therefore, there should be a safety measures at every layer. To combat with the attacks we have to put checks at different levels that lead to the creation of a framework of cyber security.

Figure 24.9 presents the Integrated Cyber Security Framework that provides a set of desired cyber security activities and outcomes in a safe manner. The framework intends in managing and reducing their cyber security risks in a way that complements an organization's existing cyber security and risk management processes.

The Integrated Cyber Security Framework consists of six core components: identified, detect, respond, recover, protect, and prevent. These functions are not meant to form a linear path, or lead to a static desired endpoint. Rather, the functions can be performed concurrently and continuously to form an operational culture that addresses the dynamic cyber security risk.

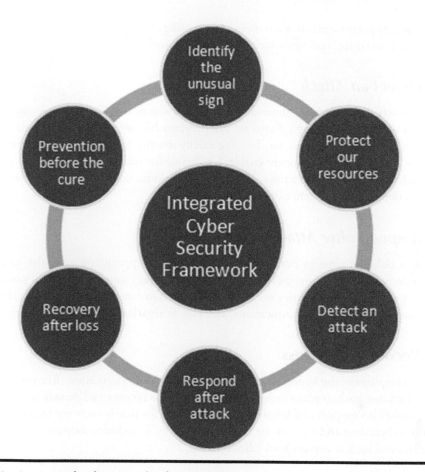

Figure 24.9 Integrated cyber security framework.

24.7.1 *Identify the Unusual Sign*

In view of the organizational understanding to calculate and manage cyber security risks to systems, data, and assets, the objective of the identify component is to understand the business context, the resources that support critical functions, and the related cyber security risks that enable an organization to focus and prioritize its efforts, consistent with its risk management strategy, and business needs. This component includes various categories such as, asset management, business environment, governance, risk assessment, and risk management strategy.

24.7.2 *Protect Our Resources*

The information and other resources must be protected from an unauthorized access; therefore, there is a need to design, develop, and implement the appropriate safety guards to make sure the delivery of critical services. The protect component supports the ability to limit or constrain the impact of a potential cyber security event. This component includes various functions such as access control, awareness and training, data security, information protection processes and procedure, maintenance, and protective technology.

24.7.3 Detect an Attack

It is not necessary always that an unusual activity is an attack that is why this component needs a continuous watch (monitoring). Based on the previous history of attacks or violation of some rules monitoring of such activities may become a daily routine to identify the existence of a cyber security attack. The detect component enables a schedule for such suspicious activities (anomalies detection) which timely discovers the cyberattacks. It includes continuous monitoring and a process that can detect the occurrence of cyberattack.

24.7.4 Respond after Attack

Now what to do! It is time to develop and implement the appropriate activities to take action regarding a detected cyber security event. The respond function supports the ability to contain the impact of a potential cyber security event. Examples of outcome categories within this function include response planning, communications, analysis, mitigation, and improvements.

24.7.5 Recovery after Loss

Develop and implement the appropriate plans to maintain the information. Even after the attack, there must be some backup plans or back track methods to recover and restore the data. Recover function should also support and follow a proper schedule for timely recovery so that it can reduce the effect of cybercrime and back to the normal operation. It includes recovery planning, backup function, and roll back at certain level (checkpoints).

24.7.6 Prevention before the Cure

Precaution is always better than cure! Of course, prevention will take the system and its resources at the reducible and manageable risk level where it also affects the cost, i.e., if the information and data will be monitored properly and checked timely, then there is a less chance of attack. It includes timely watch (monitoring), if any suspicious activity found, then match with the previous record or pattern and use safeguards accordingly, and put a layered security approach to prevent against the cybercrime.

24.8 Conclusions

Crimes are a big deal, and on top of it, a cybercrime will always be a major issue despite the advancements of technology being made by many countries. Many of the countries have designed their own laws to combat cybercrimes, but some do not have any new laws but solely rely on standard terrestrial law to prosecute these crimes. Along with old laws to fight against cybercrime, there are still feeble penalties set in order to punish criminals, therefore doing nothing to prevent the cybercrime, which affects the economy and people's social lives on a large scale by those criminals. Consequently, there is a desperate need for countries on an international level to come together and decide on what constitute a cybercrime, and develop ways in which to prosecute criminals across different countries.

Self-protection remains the first line of safety until there is a proper way to put all the legal way together to handle the cybercrime globally. Therefore, it is always advisable that every individual should be educated enough at least to know and deal with the basic requirements of cyber security. This basic cyber security awareness can help prevent potential cybercrimes against them.

Nothing is secure in this beautiful world. Looking at the past where many different acts passed, history can be eyewitness that no legislation has thrived in total elimination of cybercrime from the world. The only possible solution is to make people aware of their rights and duties and further making more punishable laws, which are more stringent. Further, it is suggested that there is a need to communicate alterations in the Information Technology Act, so it can be more effective to combat against cybercrimes. Precaution, education, and awareness are the fundamental requirements of the cyber laws and if the cyber laws are not prepared so rigorously it may delay the growth of commerce and demonstrate to be counterproductive to many. Remember, cybercriminals are evolving as well in terms of computer knowledge per technological advancement made.

Nevertheless, employee in every field who is connected with the Internet directly or indirectly should be trained with proper safety practices to ensure that integrity and confidentially of stored information is kept at all times to combat cybercrimes. Safety practices are just like warrantee that staying off game sites on company time where viruses can be downloaded, forwarding chain emails, leaving workstation unattended or password sharing over virtual mediums should be prohibited. With all these safety practices implemented, it can be said that the safety of many clients' stored information is optimal.

Bibliography

1. https://www.iii.org/fact-statistic/facts-statistics-identity-theft-and-cybercrime.
2. https://www.cisco.com/c/en/us/products/security/security-reports.html.
3. Player 3 Has Entered the Game: Say Hello to 'WannaCry', *Cisco Talos blog*, May 2017: blog.talosintelligence.com/2017/05/wannacry.html.
4. New Ransomware Variant 'Nyetya' Compromises Systems Worldwide, *Cisco Talos blog*, June 2017: blog.talosintelligence.com/2017/06/worldwide-ransomware-variant.html.
5. Massive Phishing Attack Targets Gmail Users, by Alex Johnson, *NBC News*, May 2017: nbcnews.com/tech/security/massive-phishing-attack-targets-millions-gmail-users-n754501.
6. Hackers Target Irish Energy Networks Amid Fears of Further Cyber Attacks on UK's Crucial Infrastructure, by Lizzie Deardon, *The Independent*, July 2017: independent.co.uk/news/world/europe/cyber-attacks-uk-hackers-target-irish-energy-network-russia-putin-electricity-supply-board-nuclear-a7843086.html.
7. Symantec, Internet Security Threat Report 2017, pp. 69–76.
8. https://www.usnews.com/news/best-states/georgia/articles/2017-09-11/russian-cyber-hacker-pleads-guilty-in-identity-theft-case.
9. https://www.usatoday.com/story/money/personalfinance/2017/02/06/identity-theft-hit-all-time-high-2016/97398548.
10. https://www.cnbc.com/2017/02/01/consumers-lost-more-than-16b-to-fraud-and-identity-theft-last-year.html.
11. https://www.cwjobs.co.uk/careers-advice/it-glossary/cyber-crime-timeline.
12. A. Mishra, B. B. Gupta, R. C. Joshi. A Comparative study of Distributed Denial of Service Attacks, Intrusion Tolerance and mitigation Techniques, *2011 European Intelligence and Security Informatics Conference (EISIC 2011)*, September 12–14, 2011, Athens, Greece.

13. https://www.carbonite.com/blog/article/2017/08/the-evolution-of-a-cybercrime-a-timeline-of-ran-somware-advances.

14. W. G. Kruse, J. G. Heiser (2002). *Computer Forensics: Incident Response Essentials.* Boston, MA: Addison-Wesley. p. 392. ISBN 0-201-70719-5.

15. D. Halder, K. Jaishankar (2011). *Cyber Crime and the Victimization of Women: Laws, Rights, and Regulations.* Hershey, PA: IGI Global. ISBN 978-1-60960-830-9.

16. S. Hower, K. Uradnik (2011). *Cyberterrorism* (1st ed.). Santa Barbara, CA: Greenwood, pp. 140–149. Retrieved 4 December, 2016.

17. J. Matusitz (2005). Cyberterrorism. *American Foreign Policy Interests* 2: 137–147.

18. Latest Viruses Could Mean, End of World as we Know it, "says Man Who Discovered Flame", *The Times of Israel,* 6 June, 2012.

19. J. Harper. There's no such thing as cyber terrorism. RT. Retrieved 5 November, 2012.

20. http://oai.dtic.mil/oai/oai?&verb=getRecord&metadataPrefix=html&identifier=ADA439217 Accessed on 8 April, 2017.

21. *Cyber Terrorism National Conference of State Legislatures.* https://en.wikipedia.org/wiki/Cyberterrorism Accessed on 8 April, 2017.

22. https://en.wikipedia.org/wiki/Cyber-attack Accessed on 8 April, 2017.

23. https://www.tripwire.com/state-of-security/security-data-protection/cyber-security/the-5-most-com-mon-attack-patterns-of-2014/ Accessed on 8 April, 2017.

24. http://ids.nic.in/art_by_offids/CybersecurityinindiabyColSSRaghav.pdf Accessed on 8 April, 2017.

25. http://gadgets.ndtv.com/internet/news/india-must-wake-up-to-cyber-terrorism-349274 Accessed on 8 April, 2017.

26. Cyber defense: How prepared is India for cyber warfare. http://economictimes.indiatimes.com/tech/internet/cyber-defence-howprepared-is-india-for-cyber-warfare/articleshow/19152928.cms Accessed on 8 April, 2017.

27. India must wake up to cyber-terrorism. http://gadgets.ndtv.com/internet/news/india-must-wake-up-to-cyber-terrorism-349274 Accessed on 8 April, 2017.

28. http://www.business-standard.com/article/pti-stories/india-not-prepared-to-handle-cyber-terrorism-threat-ec-council114021900965_1.html Accessed on 8 April, 2017.

29. Cyber terrorism biggest threat: Rajnath Singh. http://www.india.com/news/india/cyber-terrorism-biggest-threat-rajnath-singh-1653594/ Accessed on 8 April, 2017.

30. http://www.newindianexpress.com/nation/2016/dec/19/80000-cyber-attacks-on-december-9-and-12-after-note-ban-1550803.html Accessed on 8 April, 2017.

31. https://www.ftc.gov/policy/reports/policy-reports/commission-staff-reports/consumer-sentinel-network-data-book-2017/main

32. http://www.naavi.org/pati/pati_cybercrimes_dec03.htm.

33. B. B. Gupta, D. P. Agrawal, S. Yamaguchi, N. Asanka, G. Arachchilage, S. Veluru (2017). Editorial security, privacy, and forensics in the critical infrastructure: Advances and future directions. *Annales des Télécommunications* 72(9–10): 513–515.

34. B. B. Gupta, N. Asanka, G. Arachchilage, K. E. Psannis (2018). Defending against phishing attacks: Taxonomy of methods, current issues and future directions. *Telecommunication Systems* 67(2): 247–267.

35. B. B. Gupta, V. Adat (2017). Security in internet of things: Issues, challenges, taxonomy, and archi-tecture. *Telecommunication Systems* 67(3): 423–441.

36. M. Jouini, L. B. Rabai (2016). A security framework for secure cloud computing environments. *International Journal of Cloud Applications and Computing (IJCAC)* 6(3): 32–44. DOI:10.4018/IJCAC.2016070103.

37. P. Ghosh, S. Shakti, S. Phadikar (2016). A cloud intrusion detection system using novel PRFCM clustering and KNN based Dempster-Shafer rule. *International Journal of Cloud Applications and Computing (IJCAC)* 6(4): 18–35. DOI:10.4018/IJCAC.2016100102.

38. Cert coordination center statistics. http://www.cert.org/stats.

Index

Printed and bound by CPI Group (UK) Ltd, Croydon, CR0 4YY

24/10/2024

01778298-0011